Fodor's

ESSENTIAL
ARGENTINA

T0043822

Welcome to Argentina

Argentina's magnificent landscapes create memorable backdrops for amazing experiences. Wine lovers can sample world-class Malbecs at Mendoza's high-altitude vineyards with Andes Mountain views; adventure seekers revel in the colorful canyons of the Northwest; and nature lovers marvel at the thundering torrents of Iguazú Falls. In Patagonia, top-notch outdoor activities beckon, from scaling translucent glaciers to spotting penguins and whales. Urban adventures also await in Buenos Aires, with its thriving food scene, chic shopping districts, and vibrant nightlife.

TOP REASONS TO GO

★ **Stunning Landscapes:** From Iguazú Falls to the Perito Moreno glacier, beauty reigns.

★ **Buenos Aires:** The capital city combines European glamour with Latin American verve.

★ **Food:** Modern Andean cuisine, Patagonian seafood, and some of the world's best beef.

★ **Tango:** On packed dance floors or at ritzy shows, people move to the 2/4 beat.

★ **Mendoza Wineries:** Flavorful vintages flourish in vineyards along the Andean foothills.

★ **Outdoor Adventures:** Riding in the pampas and fly-fishing are just a few top options.

Contents

Fodor's Features

MAPS

Chapter 1

EXPERIENCE ARGENTINA

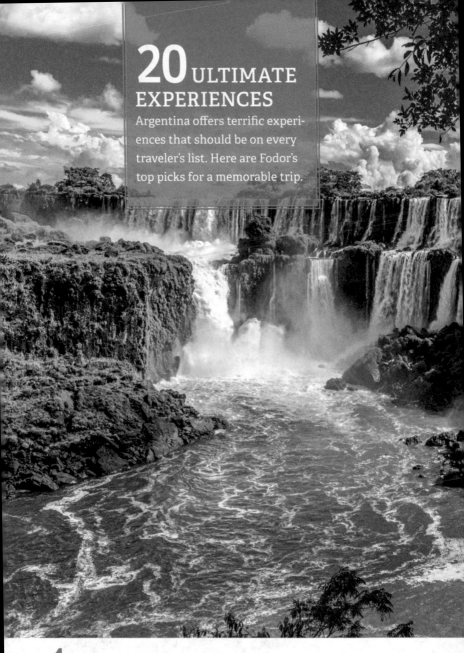

20 ULTIMATE EXPERIENCES

Argentina offers terrific experiences that should be on every traveler's list. Here are Fodor's top picks for a memorable trip.

1 Iguazú Falls just before the crowds

The park opens at 8 am and the first train departs at 8:30, so walk or take a bus or a taxi to the park early and enjoy the falls before the crowds arrive and to avoid the noonday sun in the summer. *(Ch. 4)*

2 Whale-watching in Peninsula Valdés

The majestic southern right whales make their home off the peninsula from early winter through spring, and orcas are present year-round. *(Ch. 9)*

3 Take an architecture tour in Buenos Aires

During wealthier times, Argentine and European architects designed homes, office, and government buildings, along with mansions and museums. *(Ch. 3)*

4 Watch the sunrise from the Andes

Mount your horses in the dark of night and follow your guides up the foothills until you reach the mesa at first light. It's remarkably beautiful. *(Ch. 6)*

5 Ski at Cerro Castor resort

Cold weather isn't limited to winter months at the world's most southerly ski resort, so there's snow on the grounds for months. *(Ch. 9)*

6 Join passionate fans at a soccer match

Being a fútbol fan in Argentina is very frequently a game in itself that's played without referees. Fortunately for more subdued fans, many stadiums have family sections away from the super fanáticos. *(Ch. 3)*

7 Sip wines with the views of the Quebrada

The vast Argentine wine trail has multiple stops, and wine tastings while viewing the Quebrada de Humahuaca is a must while visiting this part of the country. *(Ch. 6)*

8 Visit Jujuy's Salinas Grandes

Wear your sunglasses and sunblock when you visit this stark white salt flat, it's like walking on a sun reflector with only the distant hills to remind you you're on earth. *(Ch. 6)*

9 Opera at Teatro Colón

Along with the house opera, symphony, and dance companies, the theater draws visiting artists from across the globe to one of the finest opera houses in the world. *(Ch. 3)*

10 Explore the diverse Argentine wildlife

Capybara, anteaters, otters, and more create a wildlife experience for the more adventurous, as there are many animals to see that call Argentina home.

11 Dine at the parrilla, Don Julio steakhouse

Each signed, empty wine bottle on the walls signifies a great dining experience at this award-winning parrilla, where the fresh or dry-aged grass-fed beef is always perfectly cooked. *(Ch. 3)*

12 Score tickets to the polo finals in December

Polo is a complete sensory experience, from the thundering rumble of the horses, the thwack of the mallet on the ball, the galloping figures glistening in the summer sun to the smell of the grass. *(Ch. 3)*

13 Stay the night at an estancia

You can pick the level of luxury of an estancia but you'll always be surrounded by pampas used for grazing or crops or just there, and far from the crowds.

14 Hike over the Perito Moreno Glacier

View the glacier from across the lake or by boat to take in its height, but you need to put on your crampons and trek its craggy surface for a true sense of its enormity. *(Ch. 9)*

15 Take a tango class at a milonga (dance hall)

There are plenty of places to take tango lessons in Buenos Aires, but visit a place with at least a touch of grim, like the El Catedral Club, for the most authentic experience. *(Ch. 3)*

16 Visit Jujuy and Salta for painted mountains

The Serranía de Hornocal range, as this part of the Andes is called, is a breathtaking natural wonder of many colors that seems to ebb away from the scrub-carpeted desert. *(Ch. 6)*

17 Check out the thriving Buenos Aires nightlife

Porteños and many visitors to the city live for its nightlife. No matter the scene, it's here. Every barrio has at least a peña, a small live music club, but areas like Palermo are bursting with dance clubs. *(Ch. 3)*

18 Sip Malbecs in Mendoza

Two of the best ways of visiting the wineries and trying their wares is hiring a driver or joining a tour. Both ways allow you to enjoy sipping to your heart's content. *(Ch. 7)*

19 Visit the Buenos Aires Museum of Latin American Art (MALBA)

The collection covers Latin American art from the early 20th century to the region's contemporary artists, from Kahlo and Rivera, to Argentina's treasure, Marta Minujín. (Ch. 3)

20 Hike in Patagonia's Lake District

Whether hiking a short trail or making a trek, you'll meander through a landscape of lush ancient forest and clear lakes. Afterwards, the craft beers of Bariloche await. *(Ch. 9)*

WHAT'S WHERE

1 Buenos Aires.
Elegant boulevards and cobbled streets give the capital a European air, but the chaotic traffic and frequent protest marches are distinctly Latin American. The birthplace of tango is *the* place to take in a show.

2 Side Trips from Buenos Aires. Varied scenery lies a few hours' drive from Buenos Aires. Traditional *estancias* (ranches) dot the Pampas, lush waterways crisscross the Tigre delta, and windswept dunes and resort towns line the Buenos Aires coast.

3 Side Trips to Uruguay. Cobbled lanes and colonial buildings define Colonia del Sacramento. East along the Río de la Plata lies Montevideo, known for its eclectic architecture and down-home dining. Beautiful beaches and people are what the resort town of Punta del Este is all about.

4 The Northwest.
Deep red gorges, verdant valleys, cloud forests, Inca ruins, and the arid landscape of the Puna: the Northwest changes constantly. Rich

FALKLAND ISLANDS
(UK)

Stanley

0   400 mi

0   400 km

SOUTH GEORGIA
(UK)

Andean traditions live on in the region's food and folk music, beautiful Salta city has a colonial feel, and wines from nearby high-altitude vineyards are the latest thing.

5 **Mendoza and the Wine Regions.** Argentina's vintners use desert sun, mountain snow, and extreme altitudes to craft distinctive wines—especially Malbec. Mendoza's wineries enjoy the greatest reputation.

6 **The Lake District.** Alpine scenery on a gigantic scale is one way to describe this region's pine forests and snowcapped peaks. Posh resort towns like San Martín de los Andes and Bariloche are Argentina's best ski spots.

7 **Patagonia.** The monumental natural beauty of the Perito Moreno glacier alone is worth the trip south, but on the Chilean side of the Andes, Parque Nacional Torres del Paine competes in grandeur. Penguins, whales, and sea lions are natural attractions on the wave-battered Atlantic coast.

What to Eat in Argentina

HELADO
Not quite ice cream and not quite gelato, Argentina's favorite frozen dessert is intensely flavored and smooth. Try *samboyán* (zabaglione), bitter chocolate, strawberry, and, naturally, *dulce de leche*.

PIZZA
Not New York– or Neapolitan-style pies, but similar and very much a staple, especially in the capital where a few pizzerias are enormous. Have a slice or two with a *chopp* (draft beer) or, more traditionally, a glass of *moscato*, a fortified white wine.

MEDIALUNAS
Kind of a combination of crescent rolls and croissants, there are two types of these café staples: *de manteca* (butter), which are doughy and brushed with sweet syrup, and *de grasa*, which are savory and more flaky.

MATE
The *yerba* (herb) is added to the *mate* (drinking gourd) and hot water is poured in and the tea sipped through a *bombilla* (metal straw). For generations, a mate would be shared among a groups, each sipping from the same *bombilla*, a tradition that will recover after the pandemic.

DULCE DE LECHE
Very nearly a separate food group in Argentina, this caramelized milk spread is spread on breads and pastries, used as a dessert filling or topping, made into *helado* or eaten straight from the jar. Our favorite is *flan de dulce de leche*.

BEEF
The beef really is more flavorful here. Maybe it's the wood, maybe it's because so many here start learning the art of *asado* from a young age. The provinces and cities in the pampas are abound with good *parrillas*, but try to get an invite to a weekend *asado* by promising to bring good wine.

EMPANADAS
They're ubiquitous, yes, but whether meat or veggie, good *empanadas*—baked or fried pastries—will have a tender, crispy crust and juicy, savory filling, and pair perfectly with beer, wine, or vermouth and soda.

Pizza

MOLLEJAS

In the U.S., we're more accustomed to eating sweetbreads in French restaurants, and they're good, but they're not grilled *mollejas*. Crispy on the outside, firm yet tender on the inside, they're enjoyed with a squeeze of lemon or lightly sweetened sauce to highlight the flavor.

CHORIPÁN

This chorizo sandwich is truly a guilty pleasure; a good one has a slightly charred casing and enough fat to "butter" the fresh bread roll. Slather on some *chimichurri*—an herb dressing—or fresh-chopped salsa and let it dribble down your chin.

MILANESA

This simple breaded fried beef or chicken cutlet is the meal of choice if you're going to hit the bars or do a craft beer pub crawl. Usually served with papas fritas or potato purée, we prefer ours *a la napolitana*, with seasoned tomato sauce and melted mozzarella.

Argentine Wines and Grape Varieties

CRIOLLA
These are actually a group of hybrid varieties descended from Spanish vines brought over in the 16th and 17th centuries and are normally used for blending or lesser quality wines. Now, though, enologists are using the grapes to make some lively wines that are light, fresh, and easy to drink.

BONARDA
This heavily planted red is a transplant of France's Douce Noir and was mostly used for blending, but has exploded in popularity because it has a bit more red fruit flavor than Malbec, and its higher acidity and lower tannins make it fresher and smoother tasting.

TORRONTÉS
No matter how many times you've had this white, the first sip is nearly always a dry, crisp surprise after taking in its tropical fruit and floral bouquet and expecting something sweet. The best is grown in Salta and Jujuy.

MALBEC
Though this variety has a moderate level of tannins, the fruitiness of Argentine Malbec's smooths them out, making it the country's most famous export. Many winemakers are also using concrete eggs for fermentation, creating more vibrant flavor and color.

ESPUMANTES
Argentina makes good quality sparkling wines that are made using methods from the traditional *champenoise* to *Charmat* to *pét-nat*, and grapes from the winning Chardonnay-Pinot Noir combination to Viognier and Malbec.

PINOT NOIR
This varietal does exceptionally well in Mendoza's higher elevations and Patagonia's rugged terrains, and the wines from both present yummy cherry aromas and flavors with varying degrees of other red fruit, herbs and minerality, and refreshing acidity.

Sauvignon blanc

GARNACHA

Famous for its use in blending in Spain and France, where it's called Grenache, as well as Argentina, this grape is being popularized by a handful of creative wineries. It's bright light red in color with plenty of red fruit aromas and flavor, juicy soft tannins and refreshing acidity, and we love it with grilled veggies and salads.

SAUVIGNON BLANC

A favorite wine for exploring regional differences. It can be lightly perfumed, fruity, and austere from San Juan to Chubut, to having more vegetal aroma and flavor from the high elevations of Jujuy.

What to Buy/Souvenirs

ALFAJORES
Dulce de leche, fruit, or chocolate mousse sandwiched between two baked cookies and rolled in grated coconut or covered in chocolate, white chocolate, or powdered sugar, and the favorite sweet treat of every Argentine ever.

PINGÜINOS
These ceramic penguin-shaped wine jugs are great for serving your own wines, cocktails, water or, if you pick up a small one, used as a creamer pitcher. They are classically brown and white, but now come in a variety of colors.

YERBA MATE PARAPHERNALIA
If you've acquired a taste for this infusion, you've probably already picked up a *mate* and *bombilla*. Now find some attractive ones for your friends, yerba is pretty readily available in the United States.

BESPOKE LEATHER JACKET
It will take just a couple of days to have a jacket made—or a skirt or trousers or whatever leather garment or accessory your heart desires.

HANDMADE GAUCHO KNIFE
From hand-tooled silver hilted heirlooms to a hardwood handled steak knife set, these knives make a sharp gift.

GRAFFITI ART
Much of the clever graffiti you've noticed in Buenos Aires is available for sale at artists' collectives and galleries, where you'll find unframed pieces and sometimes t-shirts or caps.

FÚTBOL JERSEY
Get a jersey from your favorite team. Boca, River, or Newell's Old Boys? If you'd rather not commit to a club, you can pick up the sky blue and white striped national team jersey.

FILETEADO SIGN
There are a few shops that will customize a *fileteado* sign for you in the same artistic style of lettering you'll see on newsstands, buses, and many older establishments.

INCA ROSE JEWELRY
Rhodochrosite, or more commonly known as "Inca Rose", is Argentina's national gemstone. Markets in San Telmo and the North-west of the country are the perfect place to browse through jewelry made from the natural stone, making a great gift for the jewelry-lover at home.

ANTIQUE PROMOTIONAL ITEMS
Visit the San Telmo market or the Mercado de las Pulgas for mid-century promotional items for beverages, headache reliever and other products. Something even older, try the antique shops in San Telmo.

Fileteado Sign

Wildlife in Argentina

ANDEAN FLAMINGO, EL CALAFATE
Breeding season, December through February, is the time to enjoy the region's flamboyance of flamingos, and there's no better fitting name to describe the spectacle of this avian colony.

SOUTHERN RIGHT WHALE, PENINSULA VALDÉS
The annual migration of these cetacea, averaging about 50 feet in length, gathers them in the waters off the peninsula from June to December, with peak whale-watching from August to October.

MAGELLANIC PENGUINS, BAHÍA BUSTAMANTE
Just one of the colonies along the rugged Patagonian coast, but 100,000 penguins is a sight to behold. These birds are home in the bay from September through March.

FUR SEALS, BEAGLE CHANNEL
A year-round colony, but best not to visit during winter unless you're a polar explorer. The channel is also home to sea lions, dolphins, porpoise, and dozens of species of wonderful birds.

GIANT ANTEATER, IGUAZÚ
With adults measuring seven feet from snout to the end of their remarkably bushy tails, it's no wonder they're sometimes called ant bears. Other giants to search for at the national park are giant otters and capybaras, those adorable guinea pigs on steroids.

GREAT HORNED FROG, BUENOS AIRES
These nearly-endangered amphibians are more commonly referred to as the "Pac-man Frog," and for good reason: with jaws as wide as their heads, they're known to eat anything they can get their mouth around, including birds and mice. You'd be lucky to see one due to their adept camouflage, but if you do, keep your distance or you might end up with a gnarly bite!

OCELOT, SALTA PROVINCE
Nocturnal by nature, these spotted felines laze and sleep during the day in tree branches of canopied forests. By night, this expert hunter stalks and feeds on most any animal, from iguanas and fish to birds and even monkeys! Their dappled coats make them look like smaller jaguars, but these cats come from a different family and are not known to roar. Instead, it is said ocelots tend to "chuckle" when excited.

BURROWING PARROT, PATAGONIA
As the name would suggest, these charming, conversational birds make their homes in cliffsides. They live in very large flocks, in fact, the largest of any parrot species. Between their numbers and eye-catching plumage, they're hard to miss.

Fur seals

Argentine Liquors

Aperol spritz

FERNET
Fernet y coca (Coca-Cola) remains a favorite among the younger crowd and visitors. Like so many mainstays you'll see on a bar shelf in Argentina, Fernet is originally from Italy. This herbal *digestivo* is kind of like cilantro—you either love it or hate it.

AMARGO OBRERO
This is another bitter herbal beverage, created in Rosario in 1887 by Italian immigrants. It's sipped straight, on the rocks, or mixed with soda water. Mostly because of its lower alcohol content, this one is taken as an apéritif.

HESPERIDINA
Invented in Buenos Aires by an immigrant from Maine in 1864, this triple sec-like apéritif made with bitter orange peels is also the very first product in Argentina to be awarded patent and trademark protection. It's used in a few cocktails, but is quite enjoyable mixed with just tonic water.

Campari

LA FUERZA VERMOUTH
It seems Italian brand vermouths have been available and made in Argentina forever, mostly enjoyed in cafés with a *sifón* of soda water during lunch. Then La Fuerza came along and shook the dust off an old product, using better quality wine and a new, fresh infusion of herbs. Refreshing and delicious on ice with soda water and a slice of orange.

PINERAL
This herbal *aperitivo*, created in 1864 by Italian immigrants, has managed to maintain an aging fan base, but has been given new legs by well-regarded mixologists who are keen to incorporate national drinks into their creations.

CAMPARI
This Italian brand is also made in Argentina and has always been a delicious and popular *aperitivo* when mixed with soda or tonic waters, or for mixing killer Negronis.

APEROL
You know it's spring in Buenos Aires when you see *porteños* enjoying an Aperol spritz at outdoor cafés. Yes, it's an Italian brand but it, too, is made in Argentina. Good stuff, whatever's in it.

Argentina's Natural Wonders

QUEBRADA DE LAS FLECHAS, SALTA
Ruta 40 winds through sandstone rocks that jut from the surface at windblown angles and are so violently eroded they look like petrified whitecaps.

SALINAS GRANDES, JUJUY
Walking around this giant, glaringly white salt flat feels like entering another dimension until the mountains on the horizon bring you back to terra firma.

QUEBRADA DE HUMAHUACA, JUJUY
This UNESCO World Heritage Site has been inhabited by people for millennia and as a trade route was as important to the Inca as it was for the Spanish. This is where the Serranía de Hornocal, the painted mountains, are located.

PERITO MORENO GLACIER, SANTA CRUZ
One of Patagonia's biggest tourist attractions, literally. The glacier is more than three times the size of Manhattan island. You can take in the view of this wonder from across the lake, sailing near its iceface, or trekking its craggy surface.

Siete Lagos Route, Bariloche

ESTEROS DEL IBERÁ WETLANDS, CORRIENTES

Whether you explore on horseback or horse-drawn boat, venturing into this reserve is an adventure not just for the seemingly endless marshland and watercourses, but also for its diversity of wildlife.

IGUAZÚ FALLS, MISIONES

Yet another UNESCO World Heritage Site, and another no-doubter. Watching the upper Iguazú River flow over its ancient basalt base and roaringly leap into the lower river is entirely captivating. The surrounding rainforest is a wonder in itself with countless species of wildlife and flora.

SIETE LAGOS ROUTE, BARILOCHE

With its forests, charming towns, and glacial lakes, this is one of the most beautiful places on earth to hike or just drive around. In the summer, enjoy swimming or snorkeling in the pristine waters.

Argentina Today

The only thing certain in life is change, and no one knows it like Argentineans. Recession and growth, busts and booms, they've seen it all. Though their country's economic star rises, falls, and occasionally sputters out with alarming regularity, the things that really matter in Argentina don't seem to change. The beef and wine-laden table of a family asado; a penalty kick at a fútbol match; the rhythms of tango, cumbia, and chacarera—these are what make locals' hearts beat faster. They might just win yours over, too.

POLITICAL DIVISIONS

Since the country hit rock-bottom in 2001–02, Argentines have taken increasingly vehement positions on their presidents. The political needle swung left during the 12-year Kirchner administration (one term led by the late Néstor Kirchner and two by his wife Cristina Fernández). Critics accused them of corruption, populism, and cutting Argentina off from the global market, while their social spending and renationalization projects earned them many supporters. The scales tipped to the right in 2015, when former Buenos Aires mayor Mauricio Macri's promises to modernize Argentina and reopen the economy to the world brought electoral victory. And with 2019's election, the scales were tipped back to the left with Alberto Fernández assuming the presidency and Cristina Fernández de Kirchner sworn in as the vice president.

For many, soaring inflation and a plummeting peso are causes for concern, as are rising levels of unemployment and violent crime. Argentines feel strongly about politics, and they show it, often by taking to the streets. City avenues and highways are regularly blocked by drum- and banner-toting crowds, and large-scale strikes are becoming common. Sometimes demonstrators are protesting a

law; at others they're celebrating political or sporting victories, or commemorating a historical event.

GOING GLOBAL

Spanish-speakers come to Buenos Aires expecting to hear the sing-song intonation of porteño Spanish. But talk to shop assistants or wait staff in Buenos Aires these days and you might think you're nearer to the Caribbean than the Río de la Plata. Young Colombians and Venezuelans are pouring into Argentina's major cities, where university education is much cheaper than at home. Fast-food joints selling *arepas* and fried plantains are now competing with *empanadas* and *lomitos*. Growing immigrant communities from South Korea, China, Senegal, and Sierra Leone are also changing the cultural and culinary landscape.

Comparatively low property prices and a favorable exchange rate mean that many European and North American visitors are also staying on. Tango enthusiasts are snapping up old apartments in Buenos Aires, wine aficionados are investing in vineyards, outdoors enthusiasts are buying chunks of Patagonia, and early retirees from abroad have opened B&Bs all over the country.

GIRLS JUST WANNA HAVE EQUAL RIGHTS

Before #MeToo there was #NiUna-Menos, a homegrown social movement protesting violence against women and other gender-related issues. The slogan means "Not one woman less," a reference to the wave of femicides that has been sweeping the country. Since 2015, the campaign has grown from smallish protests to hashtag-driven media prominence and massive demonstrations. The largest and most colorful is International Women's Day, March 8, when feminist organizations, the women's branches of labor unions and political parties, celebrities, and thousands of supporters of all genders fill the streets of downtown Buenos Aires and other big cities. Argentinean men think twice now before calling out the *piropos* (catcalls) they once prided themselves on, but real change is still slow in coming: the average gender pay gap is still 20%.

FOODIE CULTURE

Foodie culture has hit Argentina in a big way. Celebrity chefs are enthralling TV audiences, and former table-wine drinkers now debate varietals and name-drop boutique vineyards. Their beer-drinking peers are turning from the ubiquitous bottles of Quilmes lager to local craft beers. Instagram feeds alert locals and visitors to the dishes and cocktails of the day, often found behind the unmarked doors of clandestine restaurants and speakeasies. The food scene is rife with contradiction, however. Argentina is one of the world's largest producers of organic fruits and vegetables, but nearly all of it gets exported. A small slow-food and farm-to-table movement is fighting back at farmers' markets in big cities. Saddest of all, the growth of GM soy farming is pushing Argentina's famed grass-fed cattle from the Pampas and into feedlots—these days only very high-end restaurants can guarantee you a grass-fed and-finished steak.

WHAT'S HOT NOW

Being Out. In 2010, Argentina became the first country in Latin America—and only the ninth in the world—to fully legalize same-sex marriage, sealing Argentina's claim to the title of Latin America's gay capital. The annual Marcha del Orgullo Gay (Gay Pride March) attracts tens of thousands of revelers in Buenos Aires each November.

Green Is the New Black. After years playing second fiddle to other social causes, the *medioambiente* (environment) is suddenly making headlines in Argentina. The local green movement is rallying around issues like fracking and dam construction in Patagonia, open-pit mining in San Juan and Catamarca, and GM crops in the Pampas. In Buenos Aires, two wheels are now cooler than four, thanks to miles of new cycle lanes and a free bike-share program.

Tourism with a Conscience. More visitors to Argentina are stepping off the tourist trail to learn about—or even help change—the country's social and environmental problems. In Buenos Aires, tour worker cooperatives inside one of the city's *villas* (slums) or experience the harrowing history of the 1976–82 dictatorship at the Museo de la Memoria. Choose an ethical homestay when visiting the Andean Northwest or opt for eco-accommodation in Puerto Pirámides. Also, shop for fair-trade crafts made by indigenous communities, textiles from artisan cooperatives, and designer homewares made from recycled materials.

A Victory for Women. It took years of battling, but the women of Argentina have finally won the right to terminate a pregnancy during the first trimester with a new law that went into effect in January 2021.

Best Festivals in Argentina

COSQUÍN FOLK MUSIC FESTIVAL, CÓRDOBA

Argentina's biggest folk music festival gathers performers and styles from across the country during the last week of January.

CARNIVAL, GUALEGUAYCHÚ, ENTRE RÍOS

The country's biggest carnival celebration, replete with dancers, performers, and floats. Festivities start on the weekends in January and February and culminate in a three-day extravaganza at the end of February.

VENDIMIA GRAPE HARVEST, MENDOZA

Not just Mendoza, this wonderful festival includes elaborate floats from all the provinces celebrating the harvests for which they're best known. Produce is tossed to revelers gathered along the parade route and it can get sloppy, especially when melons are in the air. This festival takes place during the first week of March.

BARILOCHE CHOCOLATE FESTIVAL

Giant chocolate eggs, "diplomas" for completing chocolate basic training, Easter bunnies, children's games, and more chocolate. This chocolate-filled festival happens during the third week of April.

TANGO CHAMPIONSHIP AND FESTIVAL, BUENOS AIRES

Two thousand dance competitors from around the world, and many times more visitors, descend on Buenos Aires for two weeks in mid-August for this World Championship of Argentina's famous dance.

DAY OF THE FAITHFUL DEPARTED, JUJUY

The Andean version of the Day of the Dead is celebrated on November 2, and the best known festival is in Humahuaca, a UNESCO World Heritage Site that sits at about 10,000 feet above sea level.

FESTIVAL OF TRADITION, BUENOS AIRES PROVINCE

Otherwise known as the Gaucho Festival, Gauchos from all over Argentina meet in San Antonio de Areco to parade, show off their gaucho finery, and compete in some pretty exciting skills contests. There's also plenty of barbecue.

FERNAND, MAGELLAN,

A PASSIONATE HISTORY by Victoria Patience

If there's one thing Argentinians have learned from their history, it's that there's not a lot you can count on. Fierce—often violent—political, economic, and social instability have been the only constants in the story of a people who seem never to be able to escape that famous Chinese curse, "May you live in interesting times."

Although most accounts of Argentinian history begin 500 years ago with the arrival of the conquistadors, humans have been living in what is now Argentina for around 13,000 years. They created the oldest recorded art in South America—a cave of handprints in Santa Cruz, Patagonia (c. 7500 BC)—and eventually became part of the Inca Empire.

Spanish and Portuguese sailors came in the early 16th century, including Ferdinand Magellan. The Spanish were forced out 300 years later by locals hungry for independence. Though autonomous on paper, in practice the early republic depended heavily on trade with Europe.

Conflict and civil war wracked the United Provinces of the South as the region struggled to define its political identity and the economic model it would follow.

Spanish and Italian immigrants arrived in the 20th century, changing Argentina's population profile forever. Unstable politics characterized the rest of the century, which saw the rise and fall of Juan Perón and a series of increasingly bloody military dictatorships. Nearly 30 years of uninterrupted democracy have passed since the last junta fell, an achievement Argentinians value hugely.

(left) Ferdinand Magellan (c. 1480–1521)
(right) Stamp featuring Evita

	Magellan sails down Argentinian coast	Juan de Garay founds Buenos Aires
PRE-1500s *INCA INVASION*	1500	1600

(top left) Cave paintings, Cueva de las Manos, Santa Cruz; (top right) Río de la Plata aboriginals, pictured by Hendrick Ottsen; (bottom) Relief detail, San Ignacio Miní Mission, Misiones Province.

PRE-CONQUEST/INCA

PRE-1500

Argentina's original inhabitants were a diverse group of indigenous peoples. Their surroundings defined their lifestyles: nomadic hunter-gatherers lived in Patagonia and the Pampas, while the inhabitants of the northeast and northwest were largely farming communities. The first foreign power to invade the region was the Inca Empire, in the 15th century. Its roads and tribute systems extended over the entire northwest, reaching as far south as some parts of modern-day Mendoza.

BIRTH OF THE COLONY

1500—1809

European explorers first began to arrive at the River Plate area in the early 1500s, and in 1520 Ferdinand Magellan sailed right down the coast of what is now Argentina and on into the Pacific. Buenos Aires was founded twice: Pedro de Mendoza's 1536 attempt led to starving colonists turning to cannibalism before running for Asunción; Juan de Garay's attempt in 1580 was successful. Conquistadors of Spanish origin came from what are now Peru, Chile, and Paraguay and founded other cities. The whole area was part of the Viceroyalty of Peru until 1776, when the Spanish king Carlos III decreed present-day Argentina, Uruguay, Paraguay, and most of Bolivia to be the Viceroyalty of the Río de la Plata. Buenos Aires became the main port and the only legal exit point for silver from Potosí. Smuggling grew as fast as the city itself. In 1806–07 English forces tried twice to invade Argentina. Militia from Buenos Aires fought them off with no help from Spain, inciting ideas of independence among criollos (Argentinian-born Spaniards, who had fewer rights than those born in Europe).

Carlos III decrees Buenos Aires the main port
of the Viceroyalty of the Río de la Plata

Independence declared

35

IMMIGRATION DRIVE

1700   1800   1900

In Focus | A PASSIONATE HISTORY

(left) Julio Roca
(right) Monument to
General San Martín;

BIRTH OF THE NATION: INDEPENDENCE AND THE CONSTITUTION

1810—1860s

Early-19th-century proto-Argentinians were getting itchy for independence after the American Revolution. On May 25, 1810, Buenos Aires' leading citizens ousted the last Spanish viceroy. A series of elected juntas and triumvirates followed while military heroes José de San Martín and Manuel Belgrano won battles that allowed the Provincias Unidas de América del Sur to declare independence in Tucumán on July 9, 1816. San Martín went on to liberate Chile and Peru.

Political infighting marked the republic's first 40 years. The conflict centered on control of the port. Inhabitants of Buenos Aires wanted a centralist state run from the city, a position known as unitario, but landowners and leaders in the provinces wanted a federal state with greater Latin American integration. The federal side won when Juan Manuel de Rosas came to power: he made peace with indigenous leaders and gave rights to marginal social sectors like gauchos, although his increasingly iron-fisted rule later killed or outlawed the opposition. The centralist constitution established on his downfall returned power to the land-owning elite.

RISE OF THE MODERN STATE

1860—1942

Argentina staggered back and forth between political extremes on its rocky road to modern statehood. Relatively liberal leaders alternated with corrupt warlord types. The most infamous of these was Julio Roca, whose military campaigns massacred most of Argentina's remaining indigenous populations in order to seize the land needed to expand the cattle ranching and wheat farming. Roca also sold off services and resources to the English and started the immigration drive that brought millions of Europeans to Argentina between 1870 and 1930.

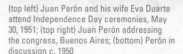

(top left) Juan Perón and his wife Eva Duarte attend Independence Day ceremonies, May 30, 1951; (top right) Juan Perón addressing the congress, Buenos Aires; (bottom) Perón in discussion c. 1950

THE RISE AND FALL OF PERONISM

1942—1973

A 1943 coup ended a decade of privatization that had caused the gap between rich and poor to grow exponentially. One of the soldiers involved was a little-known general named Juan Domingo Perón. He rose through the ranks of the government as quickly as he had through those of the army. Uneasy about Perón's growing popularity, other members of the military government imprisoned him, provoking a wave of uprisings that led to his release and swept him to the presidency as head of the newly formed labor party in 1946. Mid-campaign, he quietly married the young B-movie actress he'd been living with, Eva Duarte, soon to be known universally as "Evita." Their idiosyncratic, his'n'hers politics hinged on a massive personality cult. Together, they rallied the masses with their cries for social justice, political sovereignty, economic independence, and Latin American unity. Then, while he was busy improving worker's rights and trying to industrialize Argentina, she set about press-ganging Argentina's landed elite into funding her social aid program. Their tireless efforts to close the gap between rich and poor earned them the slavish devotion of Argentina's working classes and the passionate hatred of the rich. But everything began to go wrong when Evita died of uterine cancer in 1952. By 1955, the Marshall Plan in Europe reduced Argentina's export advantage, and the dwindling economy was grounds for Perón being ousted by another military coup. For the next 18 years, both he and his party were illegal in Argentina—mentioning his name or even whistling the Peronist anthem could land you in prison.

(top left) Leopoldo Galtieri led the last military dictatorship in Argentina. (top right) Argentina military junta during the Falkland's War; (bottom right) Argentine prisoners of war—Port Stanley;

1973—1983 DICTATORSHIP, STATE TERRORISM & THE FALKLANDS

The two civilian presidencies that followed both ended in fresh military coups until Perón was allowed to return in 1973. Despite falling out with left-wing student and guerrilla groups who had campaigned for him in his absence, he still won another election by a landslide. However, one problematic year later, he died in office. His farcical successor was the vice-president, an ex-cabaret dancer known as Isabelita, who was also Perón's third wife. Her chaotic leadership was brought to an end in 1976 by yet another military

coup widely supported by civil society. The succession of juntas that ruled the country called their bloody dictatorship a "process of national reorganization"; these days it's referred to as state-led terrorism.

Much of the world seemingly ignored the actions of Argentina's government during its six-year reign of terror. Throughout the country, students, activists, and any other undesirable element were kidnapped and tortured in clandestine detention centers. Many victims' children were stolen and given up for adoption by pro-military fami-

lies after their parents' bodies had been dumped in the River Plate. More than 30,000 people "disappeared" and thousands more went into exile. Government ministries were handed over to private businessmen. Massive corruption took external debt from $7 million to $66 million. In 1982, desperate for something to distract people with, the junta started war with Britain over the Islas Malvinas, or Falkland Islands. The disastrous campaign lasted just four months and, together with increasing pressure from local and international human rights activitsts, led to the downfall of the dictatorship.

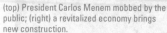

(top) President Carlos Menem mobbed by the public; (right) a revitalized economy brings new construction.

RETURN OF DEMOCRACY

1982—1999

Celebrations marked the return to democracy. The main players in the dictatorship went on trial, but received relatively small sentences and were eventually pardoned. Inflation reached a terrifying 3,000% in 1988 and only stabilized when Carlos Menem became president the following year. Menem pegged the peso to the dollar, privatized services and resources, and even changed the constitution to extend his mandate. But despite an initial illusion of economic well-being, by the time Menem left office in 1999 poverty had skyrocketed, and the economy was in tatters.

CRISIS & THE K YEARS

2000—present

The longer-term results of Menem's policies came in December 2001, when the government tried to prevent a rush on funds by freezing all private savings accounts. Thousands of people took to the streets in protest; on December 20, the violent police response transformed the demonstrations into riots. President Fernando de la Rúa declared a state of emergency, then resigned, and was followed by four temporary presidents in almost as many days. When things finally settled, the peso had devaluated drastically, many people had lost their savings, and the future looked dark.

However, under the center-leftist government of Argentina's following president, Néstor Kirchner, the economy slowly reactivated. Kirchner reopened trials of high-ranking military officials and championed local industry. In a rather bizarre turn of political events, he was succeeded by his wife, Cristina Fernández. Her fiery speeches have inspired both devotion and derision, but her social and economic policies ensured her landslide re-election in 2011. Times may be better than a few years ago, but Argentinians have lived through so many political ups and downs that they never take anything for granted.

MADE IN ARGENTINA

There's no doubt that Argentinians are an inventive lot. And we're not talking about their skill in arguing their way out of parking tickets: several things you might not be able to imagine life without started out in Argentina.

Una *birome* (ballpoint pen)

BALLPOINT PEN

Although László Jósef Bíró was born in Hungary and first patented the ballpoint pen in Paris, it wasn't until he launched his company in Argentina in 1943 that his invention began to attract attention. As such, Argentinians claim the world's most useful writing instrument as their own.

BLOOD TRANSFUSION

Before ER there was Luis Agote, an Argentinian doctor who, in 1914, was one of the first to perform a blood transfusion using stored blood (rather than doing a patient-to-patient transfusion). The innovation that made the process possible was adding sodium citrate, an anticoagulant, to the blood.

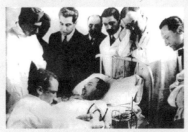

Luis Agote was one of the first to perform a nondirect blood transfusion, in Buenos Aires on November 9, 1914.

FINGERPRINTING

In 1891, Juan Vucetich, a Croatian-born officer of the Buenos Aires police force, came up with a system of classifying fingerprints. He went on to make the first-ever criminal arrest based on fingerprint evidence. Although his method has since been refined, it is still used throughout Latin America.

Huellas digitales (fingerprints)

■ Other useful Argentinian claims to fame include the first working helicopter (1916); the first one-piece floor mop (1953); and the first one-use-only hypodermic syringe (1989).

What to Watch and Read

VOYAGE OF THE BEAGLE, CHARLES DARWIN
Much of this classic takes place in Patagonia, where the young naturalist and geologist marveled at the region's flora and fauna as well as its stark geology.

COLLECTED FICTIONS, JORGE LUIS BORGES
Remarkably imaginative short stories from Argentina's most famous literary son. The collection includes *The Library of Babel*, famous for its mind-numbing permutations.

SANTA EVITA, TOMÁS ELOY MARTÍNEZ
A sometimes bizarre fictional account Eva Perón's life, death, and her corpse's subsequent adventures due to the military dictatorship and, later still, Juan Perón's devotion to her.

IN PATAGONIA, BRUCE CHATWIN
Critically acclaimed lyrical journey many consider among the greatest travel books of all time. The book explores the landscapes and wildlife of the region, and also offers portraits of the people who live and lived there, including Butch Cassidy.

THE SECRET IN THEIR EYES
Juan José Campanella's Academy Award-winning thriller, based on the novel by Eduardo Sacheri, is set in the politically troubled Buenos Aires of the early 1970s.

WILD TALES
Passion and revenge fuel the six shorts in Damián Szifron's dark, often-hilarious, and deliciously twisted look at the Argentinean psyche.

THE SUMMIT
Latin American presidents come to blows in a hotel in the Andes and, as so often happens, the U.S. flashes cash in Santiago Mitre's political drama.

Chapter 2

TRAVEL SMART

Updated by
Allan Kelin

★ **CAPITAL:**
Buenos Aires

💬 **LANGUAGE:**
Spanish

⚡ **ELECTRICITY:**
220 volts/50 cycles; plugs are either have two round prongs or two- or three-angled flat prongs.

👥 **POPULATION:**
43,847,430

☎ **COUNTRY CODE:**
54

💲 **CURRENCY:**
Argentine Peso

⚠ **EMERGENCIES:**
911

🕑 **TIME:**
One hour ahead of New York

💲 **MONEY:**
ATMs common; cash and credit cards common

🚗 **DRIVING:**
On the right

Know Before You Go

SIESTAS
Siestas are a thing here. Large stores, banks, supermarkets, pharmacies, and cafés don't engage in the practice, but small shops are often closed from 1:00 to 3 or 4 o'clock. This might be an inconvenience if you planned on picking up your dry cleaning or some from fruit during those hours.

WHEN TO GO
High Season: City sightseeing in Buenos Aires is most pleasant during September to November (spring) and March to June (fall). For wine regions, it's late spring and summer (October through April). Iguazú Falls is best August through October, when temperatures are lower and the falls are fuller. Late September to February is high season in Patagonia.

Low Season: Buenos Aires is least crowded in January and February, when locals beat the stifling city heat at resorts along the Atlantic and in Córdoba Province. In Atlantic Patagonia, many properties close in April and May; Southern Patagonia shuts down in the winter months of June through August. Between December and February prepare to melt at Iguazú falls.

Value Season: If you're heading to the Lake District or Patagonia, visit during the shoulder seasons of December and March for savings. Late March through April is a good time for value in the wine regions. Prices shoot up everywhere over the long holiday weekends known as *puentes*.

BE MINDFUL OF YOUR CELLPHONE
There's a great deal of poverty in Argentina, for that reason there are also problems with theft. This is especially the case in cities. Keep your phone, purse, or handbag on your lap when at an outdoor café, and be mindful of them when walking around. Even taxi drivers will tell you to roll up your window if you're using your phone. It's also best to not walk around with flashy jewelry or a pricey wristwatch, as they'll attract unwanted attention. If you have a lot of cash, keep it in your hotel room safe and carry only what you think you'll need. Even then, keep a small amount of bills handy should you be robbed, and the greater amount tucked away elsewhere on your person.

TIPPING
Tipping is expected at hotels for handling your bags or hailing you a taxi; 200 pesos will do nicely. For restaurants and cafés, the usual tip is 10% of the bill, and it's nicer if you leave it in cash rather than charge it to your credit card. For tipping a taxi driver, which isn't expected but always appreciated, simply round up the fare; for example, if the fare is 428 pesos, pay 450.

EXCHANGING MONEY
There are two primary rates of exchange for changing dollars in Argentina, the official rate and the blue rate, or *dolar blue*. At the time of this writing the official rate is about 100 pesos to the dollar and the blue rate is about 200 pesos to the dollar. That's right, the blue rate is double the amount. The problem is the official rate is what you'll get at banks, ATMs and most *cambios*, money exchanges. To get the blue rate, you'll need to ask at your hotel for a trusted *cueva*, an unofficial money exchange. Never follow one of the numerous touts you'll

see in *centro* or along the busy avenues as you could end up with counterfeit *plata*. Alternatively, you can get the blue rate by wiring yourself money using Western Union or a service like Xoom.

PLAN FOR LATE, LONG SUPPERS

With very few exceptions, most restaurants open for supper at 8 and serve until 10:30–11 or later. And while wait service is generally good to excellent, diners take their time here as it's a time to chat, drink wine, enjoy one or two *entradas*, a *plato principal*, *postre*, and linger over coffee or more wine. A meal here can easily last two or more hours and waiters won't rush you. In other words, it's dining out as it should be done.

MOUNTAIN TEMPERATURES

One of the factors that contributes to the quality of wine in the regions along the Andean foothills is the wide thermal amplitude, the difference between daytime temperatures and nighttime temperatures. Depending on the season, the differential of day and night temperatures in places like Mendoza, Salta, or Jujuy can range from 20 to 35 degrees Fahrenheit. A lovely 75° spring day can become uncomfortable when you're not prepared for a chilly night.

GET A SUBE TRANSIT CARD

Taxis prices in Buenos Aires are reasonable but two, three, four or more rides a day adds up. At 20 pesos a fare, *colectivo* and *subte*, city, bus, and train respectively, fares are a fraction of the price and service is very regular except for on the lesser traveled bus routes or late at night (there's no *subte* service from 10 pm to 5:30 am). The SUBE card can even be used for trains and buses to Greater Buenos Aires stations. The cards can't be purchased in *subte* stations, but many of the city's thousands of *kioskos* sell and recharge them, and they're rechargeable at *subte* stations.

A LITTLE SPANISH GOES A LONG WAY

You can certainly enjoy yourself in Argentina without speaking *castellano*, but even a few simple words and phrases will make your visit and interactions more enjoyable. It's infinitely better to start even the simplest conversation with a greeting rather than directly with a question or request. It's also more appreciated when you say, *buen día, buenas tardes,* or *buena noche* rather than simply *hola*. And, of course, please and thank you, *por favor* and *gracias*, are magic words around the world. Listening is also important, if a person is addressing

you formally, "¿Quiere la carta de los vinos?", it's not polite to use the informal, "No, ¿tenés cerveza?".

ARGENTINA IS BIG

Argentina is a great country for road trips because of the diversity of its landscapes, from the pampas, mountains, coast, and rainforests to the Patagonian steppe. If you're visiting for just a few days though, it's best to fly. Driving to, say, Mar del Plata from Buenos Aires will take about 5 hours, which is fine if you're spending the night, but not for a day trip. There's also no train service between cities like the capital, Mendoza, Bariloche, or Salta, which means sleeping on an overnight bus, which would save you the cost of a hotel for a night, or, depending on the destination, a two to four hour flight.

Getting Here and Around

Argentina extends approximately 3,650 km (2,268 miles) from tip to tail, and many of its attractions are hundreds of miles apart. So you can save a lot in terms of both time and money by carefully plotting your course. Buenos Aires lies about two-thirds of the way up Argentina's eastern side, on the banks of the Río de la Plata. It's the country's capital and its main transportation hub.

Three of the country's main draws are about 1,000 km (621 miles) from Buenos Aires as the crow flies: Puerto Iguazú, the base for exploring Iguazú Falls, in northeastern Misiones Province; Salta, the gateway to the Andean Northwest; and Mendoza, in the Wine Region, near the Chilean border. Slightly farther, this time southwest of Buenos Aires, is Bariloche, the hub for the Lake District of northern Patagonia. El Calafate, the hub for southern Patagonia and the launch pad for the Glaciar Perito Moreno, is a whopping 2,068 km (1,285 miles) southwest of Buenos Aires.

Flying within the country makes sense given these huge distances. That said, domestic flights are expensive, and flight delays are fairly regular occurrences.

Many visitors opt to take the more reliable overnight sleeper buses for trips of up to 1,000 km (621 miles). A well-developed network of long-distance buses connects Buenos Aires with cities all over Argentina; buses also operate between many urban centers without passing through the capital.

✈ Air

TO ARGENTINA

There are direct daily flights between Buenos Aires and several North American cities, with New York and Miami being primary departure points. Many

Travel Times from Buenos Aires

TO	BY AIR	BY BUS
Montevideo, Uruguay	45 minutes	8 hours
Atlantic Coast	1 hour	5–6 hours
Córdoba	1¼ hours	9–11 hours
Mendoza	1¾ hours	12–14 hours
Puerto Iguazú	1¾ hours	17–20 hours
Salta	2¼ hours	18–20 hours
Bariloche	2¼ hours	21–23 hours
El Calafate	3¼ hours	40 hours

airlines also serve Buenos Aires via Santiago de Chile, Lima, or São Paulo in Brazil, which adds only a little to your trip time.

Aerolíneas Argentinas, the flagship airline, is part of SkyTeam and operates direct flights between Buenos Aires and JFK once a day and Miami twice a day. Aerolíneas' reputation for chronic delays has greatly improved, although strikes do still ground planes.

Chilean airline LATAM is Aerolíneas' biggest local competition. LATAM flies direct from Buenos Aires to Miami, and via Santiago de Chile, São Paulo, or Lima to JFK, Dallas, Washington, D.C., and Los Angeles, often in partnership with Brazilian airline TAM. LATAM also allows you to bypass Buenos Aires by flying into Mendoza and Córdoba from JFK and Miami, both via Santiago de Chile, and into Bariloche via São Paulo.

U.S. carriers serve Buenos Aires, too. There are direct flights from Atlanta on Delta and from Houston and Newark on United; American flies nonstop from JFK, Miami, and Dallas.

Flying times to Buenos Aires are 11–12 hours from New York, 10½ hours from

Atlanta, Dallas, or Houston, and 9 hours from Miami.

WITHIN ARGENTINA

Most domestic flights operate from Buenos Aires, so to fly from the extreme south of the country to the extreme north, you often have to change planes here.

Aerolíneas Argentinas and its partner Austral link Buenos Aires to more Argentinean cities than any other airline, with flights running to Puerto Iguazú, Salta, Mendoza, Córdoba, Bariloche, Ushuaia, and El Calafate at least once a day. Austral also provides direct service between Puerto Iguazú and Salta and Córdoba, bypassing Buenos Aires; LATAM also flies to these cities. Small, Salta-based Andes Líneas Aéreas operates flights between Buenos Aires, Bariloche, Jujuy, Mendoza, Salta, and Puerto Madryn. A new local low-cost airline, FlyBondi, has started operating between Buenos Aires, and Puerto Iguazú, Córdoba, Mendoza, Salta, and Bariloche. It also connects Mendoza and Córdoba direct to Bariloche and Puerto Iguazú, among other routes that bypass Buenos Aires. Chilean budget airline JetSmart is also competing in the national market, in addition to making flights to and from Buenos Aires and Santiago, Chile.

AIRPORTS

Airports in Argentina are mostly small, well maintained, and easy to get around. Security at most isn't as stringent as it is in the States—computers stay in cases, shoes stay on your feet, and there are no random searches.

BUENOS AIRES

Buenos Aires' Aeropuerto Internacional de Ezeiza Ministro Pistarini (EZE)—known as Ezeiza—is 35 km (22 miles) southwest of the city center. Ezeiza is the base for international flights operated by Aerolíneas Argentinas and its partner Austral; these and LATAM run a limited number of domestic flights to Puerto Iguazú, El Calafate, Bariloche, Trelew, Córdoba, Ushuaia, and Rosario from here as well, although most domestic services operate from Aeroparque Jorge Newbery. All international flights arrive at newly renovated Terminal A, and most international services also depart from here. The exceptions are international departures on Aerolíneas Argentinas and SkyTeam-member airlines (including Delta), which go from the newest terminal, C. The small number of domestic Aerolíneas and LATAM flights in and out of Ezeiza also operate from Terminal C. At this writing, Terminal B had recently been demolished ahead of a large-scale overhaul of the entire airport, although no dates have been announced for construction work.

A covered walkway connects terminals A and C. Both have a few small snack bars, a small range of shops—including a pharmacy—a public phone center with Internet services, and a tourist information booth. The ATM, 24-hour luggage storage, and car-rental agencies are in Terminal A. There is free public Wi-Fi throughout the airport.

■ TIP → **Avoid changing money in the baggage claim area. The best exchange rates are at the small Banco de la Nación in the Terminal A arrivals area; it's open round the clock but expect a 15-minute wait.**

Most domestic flights and some flights to or via Chile and Brazil operate out of Aeroparque Jorge Newbery (AEP). It's next to the Río de la Plata in northeast Palermo, about 8 km (5 miles) north of the city center. Low-cost airlines FlyBondi and JetSmart also fly out of Aeroparque, which, along with Ezeiza, is run by the private company Aeropuertos Argentinos 2000.

Getting Here and Around

ELSEWHERE IN ARGENTINA

Several other airports in Argentina are technically international, but only because they have a few flights to neighboring countries; most flights are domestic.

Aeropuerto Internacional de Puerto Iguazú (IGR) is close to Iguazú Falls; it's 20 km (12 miles) from Puerto Iguazú and 10 km (6 miles) from the park entrance. There's another nearby airport just over the border in Brazil, Foz do Iguaçu/Cataratas International Airport (IGU), 10 km (6 miles) from the Brazil–Argentina border. The northwest is served by Salta's Aeropuerto Internacional Martín Miguel de Güemes (SLA), 7 km (5 miles) west of the city of Salta.

The airport for the Wine Region and western Argentina is Aeropuerto Internacional de Mendoza Francisco Gabrieli (MDZ), usually known as El Plumerillo. It's 10 km (6 miles) north of Mendoza. Northern Patagonia's hub is Bariloche, 13 km (8 miles) west of which is the Aeropuerto Internacional San Carlos de Bariloche Teniente Luis Candelaria (BRC), known as the Aeropuerto de Bariloche. The gateway to southern Patagonia is Aeropuerto Internacional de El Calafate Comandante Armando Tola (ECA), 18 km (11 miles) east of El Calafate itself.

🚢 Boat

Ferries run frequently across the Río de la Plata between Buenos Aires and the Uruguayan cities of Colonia and Montevideo. Buquebus operates several high-speed ferries to and from Colonia per day, which take 1¼ hours, and one direct ferry to Montevideo, which takes 2¼ hours. Round-trip tickets cost from 16,000 pesos to Colonia and 20,000

pesos to Montevideo, but there are substantial off-peak and midweek discounts. Colonia Express catamaran, which takes an hour or less to Colonia and connects with a two-hour bus service to Montevideo, offers the best value. Full-price round-trip tickets cost around 15,000 and 17,000 pesos, respectively, but they often drop as low as 14,000 and 16,000 pesos if you book online (midweek same-day return tickets are sometimes even less).

Both companies also sell packages that include bus tickets to other destinations in Uruguay, including Carmelo, La Paloma, La Pedrera, and Punta del Este direct from Colonia's ferry terminal. You can order tickets by phone or online. Both companies leave from Puerto Madero: Buquebus leaves from a terminal at the northern end and Colonia Express from one at the southern end.

Bus

Frequent, comfortable, and dependable long-distance buses connect Buenos Aires with cities all over Argentina and with neighboring countries. Falling airfares and rising bus prices mean that more locals and visitors now opt to fly to far-flung destinations rather than take overnight sleeper buses. All the same, tickets on basic bus services can still be substantially cheaper than last-minute air travel and buses are less prone to delays.

The Plataforma 10 website lets you assess routes, compare prices, and buy tickets for long-distance bus rides throughout Argentina, as well as ones to top international destinations like Montevideo. Most major bus companies have their own online timetables; some allow you to purchase tickets online or by phone. Websites also list alternative *puntos de venta* (sales offices)—in many cases you can buy tickets from booths in shopping malls or subway stations, though outside of peak season you can usually buy them at the terminal right up until departure time. Many now accept credit cards; even so, you should be prepared to pay in cash. In January, February, and July, get your ticket as far in advance as possible (a week or more, at least) and arrive at the terminal extra early.

Most long-distance buses depart Buenos Aires from the Terminal de Omnibus de Retiro, which is often referred to as the Terminal de Retiro or simply Retiro. Ramps and stairs from the street lead you to a huge concourse where buses leave from more than 60 numbered platforms. There are restrooms, restaurants, public phones, lockers, news kiosks, and a tourist office on this floor.

If you didn't buy tickets in advance, you can get them from the *boleterías* (ticket offices) on the upper level; there are also two ATMs here. Each company has its own ticket booth; they're arranged in zones according to the destinations served, which makes price comparisons easy. The terminal's comprehensive Spanish-language website lists bus companies by destination, including their phone number and ticket booth location, as does the more user-friendly website (⊕ *www.retiro.com.ar*).

(See individual chapters for information about local bus stations.)

⚠ **Stay alert in the terminal: pickpockets and bag-snatchers often prey on distracted travelers. Be particularly wary when using the ATMs.**

Long-distance buses have toilets, air-conditioning, videos, and snacks. The most basic service is *semi-cama*, which

has minimally reclining seats and often takes a little longer than more luxurious services. It's worth paying the bit extra for *cama ejecutivo,* which has large, business-class-style seats and, sometimes, pillows and blankets.

On routes between nearby towns you can usually choose between regular buses (*común*) and air-conditioned or heated ones with reclining seats (*diferencial*). The companies that run local services rarely have websites—you buy tickets directly from the bus station.

 Car

Argentina's long highways and fabulous scenery make it a great place for road trips. However, if you're only going to be staying in Buenos Aires and other big cities, parking limitations and downright crazy traffic make renting a car more trouble than it's worth. Stick with public transportation, including taxis or Uber.

TAXIS AND UBER
There are licensed, metered taxi services in all of Argentina's major cities. You can hail cabs on the street or call or, in Buenos Aires, book them via the city government's BA Taxi app. Taxi drivers speak little to no English: the standard way to state your destination is to give the name of the nearest two intersecting streets (*Córdoba y Malabia,* for example). *Remises* are unlicensed taxi services that operate longer routes such as from downtown to airports or for trips to the countryside, usually for a flat, preagreed fare.

Ridesharing apps Uber (⊕ *www.uber. com*) and Cabify (⊕ *www.cabify.com*) are popular in Buenos Aires and other major cities. Both are often substantially cheaper than official metered taxis and

Getting Here and Around

are particularly useful if you don't speak much Spanish. Services are limited beyond downtown areas.

Taxi drivers in big cities are usually honest, but occasionally they decide to take people for a ride, literally. All official cabs have meters, so make sure this is turned on. It helps to have an idea where you're going and how long it will take. Local lore says that if you're hailing taxis on the street, those with lights on top (usually labeled "Radio Taxi") are more trustworthy. Late at night, try to call for a cab—all hotels and restaurants, no matter how cheap, have a number and will usually call for you.

GASOLINE
Gas stations (*estaciones de servicio*) are in and near most towns and along major highways. Most are open 24 hours and include full service, convenience stores, and sometimes ATMs. In rural areas, stations have small shops and toilets; however, they are few and far between and have reduced hours.

On long trips, fill your tank whenever you can, even if you've still got gas left, as the next station could be a long way away (signs at stations often tell you how far). Attendants always pump the gas and don't expect a tip, though most locals add 100 or so pesos for a full tank. Credit cards often aren't accepted even in major cities—look for signs reading *Tarjetas de crédito suspendidas* ("No credit cards") or *Solo efectivo* ("Cash only"). It's safest to check with attendants before filling up: *¿Se puede pagar con tarjeta?* ("Can I pay by credit card?").

The major service stations are YPF, Shell, Petrobras, and Axion. YPF gas tends to be the cheapest. Prices are often higher in the north of Argentina. South of an imaginary line between Bariloche and Puerto Madryn, gas is heavily subsidized

and costs roughly half what it does elsewhere. There are three grades of unleaded fuels, as well as diesel and biodiesel. GNC is compressed natural gas, an alternative fuel. Stations with GNC signs may sell only this, or both this and regular gas.

PARKING
On-street parking is limited in big cities. Some have meter systems or tickets that you buy from kiosks and display on the dashboard, and others use parking apps or SMS-based systems. In meter-free spots, there's often an informal "caretaker" who guides you into your spot and charges 100–200 pesos to watch your car, which you pay when you leave.

Car theft is common, so many agencies insist that you park rental cars in a guarded lot. Many hotels have their own lots, and there are plenty in major cities: look for a circular blue sign with a white "E" for *estacionamiento* (parking). In downtown Buenos Aires, expect to pay 180 pesos per hour, or 900 pesos for 12 hours. Rates are lower elsewhere. Illegally parked cars are towed only from restricted parking areas in city centers, especially in Buenos Aires. Getting your car back is a bureaucratic nightmare and costs around 6,500 pesos if claimed within 12 hours, and much higher if not.

ROAD CONDITIONS
The streets of many Argentinean cities are notorious for potholes, uneven surfaces, and poorly marked intersections. Most major cities have a one-way system whereby parallel streets run in opposite directions: never going the wrong way along a street is one of the few rules that Argentineans abide by. Where there are no traffic lights at an intersection, you give way to drivers coming from the right, but have priority over those coming from the left.

Two kinds of roads connect major cities: *autopistas* (two- or three-lane freeways) and *rutas* (single or dual carriageways) or *rutas nacionales* (main "national routes," usually indicated with an "RN" before the route number). Both types of roads are subject to regular tolls. Autopistas are well maintained, but the state of rutas varies hugely. In more remote locations, even rutas that look like major highways on maps may be narrow roads with no central division. Always travel with a map or GPS, as signposts for turnoffs are scarce and often downright confusing.

Night driving can be hazardous: some highways and routes are poorly lighted, routes sometimes cut through the center of towns, cattle or sheep often get onto the roads, and in rural areas, farm trucks and old cars seldom have all their lights working. Outside of the city of Buenos Aires, be especially watchful at traffic lights, as crossing on red lights at night is common practice.

ROADSIDE EMERGENCIES

All rental-car agencies have an emergency help line in case of breakdowns or accidents—some services take longer than others to arrive. The best roadside assistance is usually that of the Automóvil Club Argentina (ACA), which sends mechanics and tow trucks to members traveling anywhere in the country. The ACA also offers free roadside assistance to members of North American clubs and automobile associations. However, bear in mind when you call for assistance that most operators speak only Spanish.

RULES OF THE ROAD

You drive on the right in Argentina, as in the United States. Seatbelts are required by law for front-seat passengers. You must use your headlights on highways at all times. The use of cell phones while

driving is forbidden, and turning left on two-way avenues is prohibited unless there's a left-turn signal or left-turn traffic light; there are no right turns on red. Traffic lights turn yellow before they turn red, but also before turning green, which is interpreted by drivers as an extra margin to get through the intersection, so take precautions.

The legal blood-alcohol limit is 500 mg of alcohol per liter of blood, but in practice breathalyzing is common only in Buenos Aires and along the highways of the Atlantic coast during January and February. In towns and cities, a 40-kph (25-mph) speed limit applies on streets and a 60-kph (37-mph) limit is in effect on avenues. On autopistas, the limit is 130 kph (80 mph), and on rutas it ranges between 100 kph (62 mph) and 120 kph (75 mph). On smaller roads and highways out of town it's 80 kph (50 mph). Locals take speed-limit signs, the ban on driving with cell phones, and drunk driving lightly, so drive very defensively.

Police tend to be forgiving of foreigners' driving faults and often waive tickets and fines when they see your passport. If you do get a traffic ticket, don't argue. Most tickets aren't payable on the spot, but some police officers offer "reduced" on-the-spot fines in lieu of a ticket: it's bribery, and you'd do best to insist on receiving the proper ticket. During peak local holiday times (January, February, and July), police often check drivers' licenses, registration, and proof of insurance on highways—rental companies should provide the latter two; it's illegal to drive without them.

In Buenos Aires, buses and taxis have exclusive lanes on major avenues. On other streets, they often drive as though they have priority, and it's good to defer to them for your own safety.

Getting Here and Around

If you experience a small accident, jot down the other driver's information (full name, license number, insurance provider, and policy number) and supply your own. In cities, the standard procedure is to call the police and wait for them at the site of the accident. Otherwise, go to the nearest police station in the area to file a report. Contact your rental agency immediately.

Paved highways run from Argentina to the Chilean, Bolivian, Paraguayan, and Brazilian borders. Most rental agencies do not allow you to take their cars out of the country. If you do cross the border by land, you'll be required to present your passport, documentation of car ownership, and insurance paperwork at immigration and customs checkpoints. It's also common for cars and bags to be searched for contraband, such as food, livestock, and drugs.

RENTAL CARS

Daily rates range from around 8,000 to 15,000 pesos, depending on the type of car and the distance you plan to travel. This generally includes tax and at least 200 free km (125 free miles) daily—unlimited mileage deals are common. Note that most cars have manual transmissions; if you need an automatic, request one in advance and be prepared to pay extra—usually only the more expensive vehicle categories have them.

Reputable firms don't rent to drivers under 21, and drivers under 23 often have to pay a daily surcharge. Children's car seats are not compulsory, but are available for about 1,200 pesos per day. Some agencies charge a 10% surcharge for picking up a car from the airport.

A collision damage waiver (CDW) is mandatory and is usually included in standard rental prices. However, you may still be responsible for a deductible fee (known locally as a *franquicia* or *deducible*)—a maximum amount that you'll have to pay if damage occurs. It ranges from 55,000 to 125,000 pesos for a car and can be much higher for a four-wheel-drive vehicle. You can reduce the figure substantially or altogether by paying an insurance premium (anywhere from 300 to 1,000 pesos per day); some companies have lower deductibles than others.

In general, you cannot cross the border in a rental car. Many rental companies don't insure you on unpaved roads and have special insurance clauses that make you responsible for most of the value of the car if it flips over in an accident, which is commonplace on unpaved roads in Patagonia. Discuss your itinerary with the agent to be certain you're always covered.

Essentials

 ## Customs and Duties

Customs uses a random inspection system that requires you to push a button at the inspection bay—if a green light appears, you walk through; if a red light appears, your bags are X-rayed (and very occasionally opened). Officially, foreign tourists are allowed to bring up to 2 liters of alcoholic beverages, 400 cigarettes, and 50 cigars into the country duty-free. You are also allowed another $500 worth of purchases from the duty-free shops, which most of Argentina's international airports have, after you land. In practice, however, most officials wave foreigners through customs controls and are rarely interested in alcohol or tobacco. Fishing gear and skis present no problems.

If you enter the country by bus from Bolivia, Brazil, or Paraguay, you, your bags, and the vehicle may be subject to lengthy searches by officials looking for drugs and smuggled goods.

Argentina has strict regulations designed to prevent the illicit trafficking of antiques, fossils, and other items of cultural and historical importance and a license system for exporting artworks. For more information, contact the Dirección Nacional de Bienes y Sitios Culturales (National Department of Cultural Property and Sites).

 ## Health

COVID-19

COVID-19 has disrupted travel since March 2020, and travelers should expect sporadic ongoing issues. Always travel with a mask in case it's required, and keep up to date on the most recent testing and vaccination guidelines for Argentina.

MEDICAL CONCERNS

No vaccinations are required for travel to Argentina. However, the National Centers for Disease Control & Prevention (CDC) recommend vaccinations against hepatitis A and typhoid for all travelers and against hepatitis B, rabies, and yellow fever for travelers to the northeast of the country, which includes Iguazú. Each year there are cases of cholera in northern Argentina, mostly in the indigenous communities near the Bolivian border; your best protection is to avoid eating raw fish.

The Zika virus is present in Argentina, although relatively few cases have been reported to date. The CDC thus recommends that pregnant women avoid traveling to Argentina and that women planning to get pregnant inform themselves of the risks the virus poses before deciding to travel there. Malaria is a threat only in low-lying rural areas near the borders of Bolivia and Paraguay. There have been periodic outbreaks of dengue fever (another mosquito-borne disease) in northern Argentina, especially in Misiones Province (where Iguazú Falls is), and cases are regularly reported as far south as Buenos Aires. The best preventive measure against both dengue and malaria is to cover your arms and legs, use a good mosquito repellent containing DEET, and stay inside at dusk. American trypanosomiasis, or Chagas disease, is present in remote rural areas.

The CDC recommends chloroquine as a preventive antimalarial for adults and infants in Argentina. To be effective, the weekly doses must start a week before you travel and continue four weeks after your return. There is no preventive medication for Zika, dengue, or Chagas. Children traveling to Argentina should have current inoculations against measles, mumps, rubella, and polio.

Essentials

In most urban areas in Argentina, including Buenos Aires, people drink tap water and eat uncooked fruits and vegetables. However, if you're prone to tummy trouble, stick to bottled water. Take standard flu-avoidance precautions such as hand-washing and cough-covering, and consider contacting your doctor for a flu shot if you're traveling during the austral winter.

OTHER ISSUES

Apunamiento, or altitude sickness, which results in shortness of breath and headaches, may be a problem when you visit high altitudes in the Andes. To remedy any discomfort, walk slowly, eat lightly, and drink plenty of fluids (avoid alcohol). In northwestern Argentina, coca leaves are widely available (don't worry, it's totally legal). Follow the locals' example and chew a wad mixed with a dab of bicarbonate of soda on hiking trips: it does wonders for altitude problems. You can also order tea made from coca leaves (*mate de coca*), which has the same effect. If you experience an extended period of nausea, dehydration, dizziness, or severe headache or weakness while in a high-altitude area, seek medical attention. Dehydration, sunstroke, frostbite, and heatstroke are all dangers of outdoor recreation at high altitudes. Awareness and caution are the best preventive measures.

HEALTH CARE

Argentina has free national health care that also provides foreigners with free outpatient care. Although the medical practitioners working at *hospitales públicos* (public hospitals) are first-rate, the institutions themselves are often chronically underfunded: bed space and basic supplies are at a minimum. Except in emergencies, you should consider leaving these resources for the people who really need them. World-class private clinics and hospitals are plentiful, and consultation and treatment fees are low compared with those in North America. Still, it's good to have some kind of medical insurance.

In nonemergency situations, you'll be seen much quicker at a private clinic or hospital, and overnight stays are more comfortable. Many doctors at private hospitals speak at least some English. Note that only cities have hospitals; smaller towns may have a *sala de primeros auxilios* (first-aid post).

OVER-THE-COUNTER REMEDIES

Towns and cities have a 24-hour pharmacy system: each night there's one *farmacia de turno* (on-duty pharmacy) for prescriptions and emergency supplies.

In Argentina, *farmacias* (pharmacies) carry painkillers, first-aid supplies, contraceptives, diarrhea treatments, and a range of other over-the-counter treatments, including some drugs that would require a prescription in the United States (many antibiotics, for example). Note that acetaminophen—or Tylenol—is known as *paracetamol* in Spanish. If you think you'll need to have prescriptions filled while you're in Argentina, be sure to have your doctor write down the generic name of the drug, not just the brand name.

Farmacity is a supermarket-style drugstore chain with branches all over Buenos Aires and other major cities, including Córdoba, Mendoza, and Salta; many of them are open 24 hours and offer a delivery service.

 Lodging

Argentina has a broad variety of hotels, and the healthy competition between them generally translates into high quality and reasonable rates. Nearly all hotels—even hostels—include breakfast in the room price, but not all include the 21% tax in their quoted rates. Prices are also linked to municipality-run rating systems, which are based on a checklist of amenities (often outdated) rather than detailed evaluation. You can get wildly different things for your money, so do your homework. In destinations popular with locals, room prices soar in high season (usually January, February, and July), and some establishments won't take bookings for less than seven days. In the off-season, the same places can be a steal.

APARTMENT AND HOUSE RENTALS
Airbnb has hundreds of furnished rentals in Buenos Aires and plenty more in other parts of Argentina. International outfit Oasis Collections specializes in luxury rental properties and has 80 Buenos Aires properties on its books. Both process payments through their website.

When choosing your rental, remember that air-conditioning is a must in central and northern Argentina, including Buenos Aires, between December and March. Always check exact street locations on a map, as listings sometimes exaggerate a property's proximity to particular neighborhoods, landmarks, or subway stations.

ESTANCIAS
You get a taste of traditional Argentinean country life—including home-cooked meals and horseback riding or polo— when you stay at an *estancia* (ranch or country estate). Estancias Travel and Estancias Argentinas are two good booking services, but you usually get better rates if you call the estancia directly.

When booking, ask specifically about what activities and drinks are included in

Item	Average Cost
Cup of coffee and three *medialunas* (croissants)	250–350 pesos
Glass of wine	400–700 pesos
Liter bottle of local beer at a bar	600 pesos
Steak and fries in a cheap restaurant	1,300–2,000 pesos
One-mile taxi ride in Buenos Aires	400 pesos
Museum admission	Free–400 pesos

rates, and bear in mind that many establishments accept only cash payments. Be sure to factor in travel times and costs when planning your stay: remote locations may be reachable only by private transport, often at a hefty cost.

💲 Money
Prices go up almost by the day in Argentina: since 2015, annual inflation rates have ranged between 20% and 45%. The number of pesos you get for your dollar has been steadily increasing as well, but even so, Argentina may not seem as good value as it once was at the official exchange rate—eating out and accommodation are on a par with U.S. prices. But read the Currency and Exchange section of this chapter for information about the *Dolar Blue* for the best exchange rate.

Cash remains king for day-to-day dealings in Argentina, although more and more establishments now take debit and credit cards. This change is partly a response to the unpredictability of the banking system: regular strikes in recent years have meant that ATMs often run out of money, especially over weekends or during holiday season. Always withdraw more cash well before your current supply is

Essentials

spent, particularly in small towns. U.S. dollars can be changed at any bank and are often accepted as payment in clothing stores, souvenir shops, and supermarkets.

Note that there's a perennial shortage of change in Argentina. One-thousand-peso bills can be hard to get rid of, so ask for 100s and 500s when you change money.

You can usually pay by debit and credit card in hotels countrywide and in nicer restaurants and stores in big cities. But be advised that even establishments displaying stickers from different card companies may suddenly stop accepting them: look out for signs reading *tarjetas de crédito suspendidas* (credit card pur-chases temporarily unavailable). Outside of urban areas, plastic is less widely accepted. Most establishments use tradi-tional credit card terminals, but TodoPago card readers, which stores insert into a cell phone to swipe your card, are also common.

Prices throughout this guide are given for adults. Substantially reduced fees are almost always available for children.

CURRENCY AND EXCHANGE

Argentina's currency is the peso, which equals 100 centavos. Bills come in denominations of 1,000 (ocher), 500 (green), 100 (violet), 50 (navy blue), 20 (red), 10 (ocher), 5 (green), and 2 (light blue) pesos, although the 2-peso note is being phased out. Check your change when using high-denomination notes: the color of the 1,000-peso note is fairly similar to the 10-peso note, and that of the 500-peso note to the 5-peso note. Coins are in denominations of 2 pesos and 1 peso (both heavy and bimetallic), as well as 50, 25, and 10 centavos. U.S. dollars are widely accepted in big-city stores, supermarkets, and at hotels and top-end restaurants (usually at a slightly

worse exchange rate than you'd get at a bank). You always receive change in pesos, even when you pay with U.S. dollars.

Following a series of devaluations, the official exchange rate at this writing is around 20 pesos to the U.S. dollar. You can change dollars at this rate at most banks (between 10 am and 3 pm), at a *casa de cambio* (money changer), or at your hotel. All currency exchange involves fees, but as a rule banks charge the least and hotels the most. You need to show your passport to complete the transaction.

■ TIP→ **You may not be able to change currency in rural areas at all, so don't leave major cities without adequate amounts of pesos in small denominations.**

Passports

As a U.S. citizen, you need a passport valid for at least six months to enter Argentina as a tourist. Argentina no longer operates its reciprocal entry fee scheme for U.S. citizens, so you don't need a visa for visits of up to 90 days.

If you need to stay longer, you can apply for a 90-day extension (*prórroga*) to your tourist visa at the Dirección Nacional de Migraciones (Department of Immigra-tion). The process takes a morning and costs about 4,000 pesos. Alternatively, you can exit the country (by taking a boat trip to Uruguay from Buenos Aires, or crossing into Brazil near Iguazú, for example); upon reentering Argentina, your passport will be stamped allowing an additional 90 days. Overstaying your tourist visa is illegal and incurs a fine of 9,500 pesos, which you must pay at the Dirección Nacional de Migraciones. Once you have done so, you must leave the country within 10 days. You should carry your passport or other photo ID with you at all times: you need it to make credit-card purchases, change money, and send parcels, as well as in the unlikely event that the police stop you.

Officially, children visiting Argentina with only one parent do not need a signed and notarized permission-to-travel letter from the other parent. However, as Argentinean citizens *are* required to have such documentation, it's worth carrying a letter just in case laws change or border officials get confused.

For information on passport and visa requirements to visit the Brazilian side of Iguazú Falls, see the Planner pages at the start of the Side Trips from Buenos Aires chapter.

☎ Phones

The country code for Argentina is 54. To call landlines in Argentina from the United States, dial the international access code (011) followed by the country code (54), the two- to four-digit area code without the initial 0, then the six- to eight-digit phone number. For example, to call the Buenos Aires number 011/4123–4567, you would dial 011/54–11–4123–4567.

Any number that is prefixed by a 15 is a cell-phone number. To call cell phones from the United States, dial the international access code (011) followed by the country code (54), Argentina's cell-phone code (9), the area code without the initial 0, then the seven- or eight-digit cell-phone number *without* the initial 15. For example, to call the Buenos Aires cell phone (011) 15/5123–4567, you would dial 011/54–9–11–5123–4567.

CALLING WITHIN ARGENTINA

Cell phones are king in Argentina: public phones and phone centers, called *locutorios* or *telecentros,* are quickly becoming a thing of the past. Businesses and hotels still use landlines but many now also list a WhatsApp number, by far the favorite local messaging service. Public Wi-Fi is usually good enough for you to make calls using services like WhatsApp or Skype. You can usually also make local and long-distance calls straight from your hotel room, but hefty surcharges often apply.

MOBILE PHONES

All cell phones in Argentina are GSM 850/1900 Mhz. Cell numbers use a local area code, then the cell-phone prefix (15), then a seven- or eight-digit number. To call a cell in the same area as you from a landline, dial 15 and the number. To call a cell in a different area from a landline, dial the area code, including the initial 0, then 15, then the number. If you're calling from another cell phone, you don't need to include the 15.

There are three main phone companies: Movistar, Claro, and Personal. Although they're similar, Claro has the most users and is said to have the best rates, while Movistar has the best coverage, and Personal the best customer service. All three offer 4G, but service is patchy outside of big cities, so don't be surprised when your signal indicator switches from 4G to H+ and occasionally to E.

There are two ways to use your smartphone in Argentina: activate an international plan or get it unlocked before you travel, then purchase a local pay-as-you-go SIM card (*tarjeta SIM prepagà*) once you land. You can buy one for 230 to 550 pesos from any of the companies' offices and sales stands, which are easy to find countrywide, including at airports. The main three companies offer different

Essentials

pay-as-you-go services that include good-value data packages: expect to pay around 100 pesos per day for 50MB; 7-day and 30-day plans are also available. Most now allow you to use WhatsApp even if you run out of credit. You choose your plan (ask sales staff about the different options) then top up credit as necessary by *carga virtual* (virtual top-ups) at *kioscos* (convenience stores), where sales clerks add credit to your line directly while you wait.

■ TIP→ **Pickpockets often target tourists for their cell phones, so consider leaving your latest-generation model at home and packing an older or cheaper one instead.**

Using data packages for anything other than, say, email eats your pay-as-you-go credit quickly. The wisest strategy is to save your credit for local calls and restrict internet use to times when you have Wi-Fi access. While connected to Wi-Fi take advantage of services like Skype or Google Hangouts that let you touch base with folks back home for free (or a fraction of what roaming would cost).

Local charges for calling a cell phone from a landline depend on factors like the company and time of day, but most around 1.50 pesos per minute. In general, you pay only for outgoing calls from cell phones, which cost around 6 pesos a minute. Calls from pay-as-you-go phones are the most expensive and calls to phones from the same company as yours are usually cheaper. Pay-as-you-go services usually include free calls to at least one other number on the same network and some include a small number of free minutes per day.

 Safety

Argentina is safer than many Latin American countries. However, street crime is still a concern—mainly pickpocketing, bag snatching, and occasionally mugging—especially in Buenos Aires. Taking a few precautions when traveling in the region is usually enough to keep you out of harm's way.

CRIME

As in any major city, walk with purpose; if you don't look like a target, you'll likely be left alone. Avoid wearing flashy jewelry. Keep a grip on your purse or bag, and keep it in your lap if you're sitting (never leave it hanging on the back of a chair or on the floor); many restaurants mount hooks under their tables for you to hang purses on. Try to keep your cash and credit cards in different places about your person (and always leave one card in your hotel safe, if possible), so that if one gets stolen you can fall back on the other.

Other valuables are best left in hotel safes, too. Avoid carrying large sums of money around, but always keep enough to have something to hand over in the unlikely event of a mugging. Another time-honored tactic is to keep a dummy wallet (an old one containing an expired credit card and a small amount of cash) in your pocket, with your real cash in an inside or vest pocket: if your "wallet" gets stolen you have little to lose.

Women can expect pointed looks, the occasional *piropo* (catcalls, usually alluding to some physical aspect), and some advances. These catcalls rarely escalate into actual physical harassment, although a wave of violence against women in recent years means that local women feel more threatened by them than in the past. The best reaction is to follow their example and ignore them and move on; reply only if you're really confident with

Spanish curse words. If you're heading out for the night, it's wise to take a taxi.

There's usually a notable police presence in areas popular with tourists, such as San Telmo and Palermo in Buenos Aires. This deters potential pickpockets and hustlers somewhat. However, Argentineans have little faith in their police forces: officers are often corrupt, and at best, the police are well-meaning but underequipped.

SCAMS

Beware of scams such as a kindly passer-by offering to help you clean a stain that has somehow appeared on your clothes: while your attention is occupied, an accomplice picks your pocket or snatches your bag.

When asking for price quotes while shopping in touristy areas, always confirm whether the amount is given in dollars or pesos. Some salespeople, especially street vendors, have found that they can take advantage of confused tourists by charging dollars for goods that are actually priced in pesos.

 Taxes

Argentina has a $57 departure tax for international flights and an $25 departure tax for domestic flights. These are included in your ticket price when you fly from some airports, including those in Buenos Aires. Otherwise you can pay by credit card or in cash at booths in airports (pesos, dollars, and euros are accepted). Hotel rooms carry a 21% tax. Cheaper hotels and hostels tend to include this in their quoted rates; more expensive hotels add it to your bill. At this writing, Buenos Aires was automatically refunding VAT on accommodation in the city if you pay using your credit card from back home.

Argentina has 21% VAT (known as IVA) on most consumer goods and services. The tax is usually included in the price of goods and noted on your receipt. You can get nearly all the IVA back on locally manufactured goods if you spend more than 70 pesos at stores displaying a Global Blue duty-free sign. You'll be given a Global Blue refund check for the amount you're entitled to; then, after getting it stamped by a customs official at the airport, you can cash it at the clearly signed tax refund booths. Allow an extra hour to complete the process.

 Tipping

Propinas (tips) are a question of rewarding good service rather than an obligation. Restaurant bills—even those that have a *cubierto* (bread and service charge)—don't include gratuities; locals usually add 10% to 15%. Bellhops and maids expect tips only in the very expensive hotels, where a tip in dollars is appreciated. You can also give a small tip (10%) to tour guides. Porteños round off taxi fares (paying, say, 300 pesos for a 280-peso ride), though some cabbies who frequent hotels popular with tourists seem to expect more. Tipping is a nice gesture with beauty and barbershop personnel—5% to 10% is fine.

Visitor Information

All major cities and most smaller tourist destinations have tourist offices that can provide maps as well as information on accommodation and sightseeing. The quality of these offices varies according to local funding, but employees are usually friendly and helpful. The city of Buenos Aires has several tourist information centers and booths around the city

Essentials

Tipping Guidelines for Argentina

Bellhop at high-end hotels	$1–$5 per bag, depending on the level of the hotel
Hotel maid at high-end hotels	$1–$3 a day (either daily or at the end of your stay, in cash)
Hotel room-service waiter	$1 to $2 per delivery, even if a service charge has been added
Taxi driver	5%–10% to round up the fare
Tour guide	10% of the cost of the tour if service was good
Waiter	10%–15%, depending on service
Restroom attendants	10–20 pesos

where you can fill up your water bottle, charge your phone, and buy SUBE travel cards, which you need to use public transport (bring photo ID). Its extensive website includes downloadable maps, an online shop selling tickets for tours and events, a trip planner, and insightful articles on porteño culture, translated into questionable though largely comprehensible English. You can access most of this information on the go via the BA Turismo app; the city's other useful apps include a transportation planner (BA Cómo Llego) and a Wi-Fi hotspot finder (BA WiFi). For more information on these, visit ⊕ turismo.buenosaires.gob.ar/en/article/downloadable-apps.

Each Argentinean province has its own tourism website and also operates a tourist office in Buenos Aires, usually called the "Casa de [Province Name] en Buenos Aires."

Limited tourist information is also available at Argentina's embassy and consulates in the United States.

ONLINE RESOURCES

Argentina's main national newspapers are the conservative La Nación, mainstream Clarín, and progressive Página 12, all of which publish daily print and digital editions in Spanish. For daily national and international news in English, the Buenos Aires Times, run by the editors of the defunct Buenos Aires Herald, is available online (buenosairesherald.com). The Buenos Aires Expat Hub on Facebook is an excellent source of city and province information that draws on the experience of foreign residents and locals. Instagram is a great source of inspiration for trip planning—and shopping, of course. Useful Instagram accounts to follow before you travel include @VisitArgentina, the official Argentinian tourism promotion feed; @TravelBuenosAires, the official B.A. travel feed; @FrancisMallmann, legendary Argentinean chef; and @TripArgentina, gorgeous views from a local travel agency. Like-minded travelers on the Travel Talk Forums at Fodors.com are eager to answer questions and swap travel tales. The crudely translated regional information and itinerary ideas on the government-run Argentina Travel website are a useful planning resource.

Wines of Argentina (⊕ winesofargentina.org) is overflowing with information about Argentina's best beverage. For insight into local cooking, restaurants, and ingredients, head to Saltshaker, the blog of American food writer Dan Perlman. Another food-obsessed American, Allie Lazar, is the sassy voice behind the unflinchingly detailed—and usually hilarious—restaurant and bar reviews at Pick Up the Fork.

Did You Know?

The Perito Moreno Glacier is one of three glaciers in the world that is still growing and not retreating.

Helpful Spanish Phrases

BASICS

Hello	Hola	**oh**-lah
Yes/no	Sí/no	see/no
Please	Por favor	pore fah-**vore**
May I?	¿Me permite?	may pair-**mee**-tay
Thank you	Gracias	**Grah**-see-as
You're welcome	De nada	day **nah**-dah
I'm sorry	Lo siento	lo see-**en**-toh
Good morning!	¡Buenos días!	**bway**-nohs **dee**-ahs
Good evening!	¡Buenas tardes! (after 2pm)	**bway**-nahs-**tar**-dess
	¡Buenas noches! (after 8pm)	**bway**-nahs **no**-chess
Good-bye!	¡Adiós!/¡Hasta luego!	ah-dee-**ohss/ah**-stah **lwe**-go
Mr./Mrs.	Señor/Señora	sen-**yor**/sen-**yohr**-ah
Miss	Señorita	sen-yo-**ree**-tah
Pleased to meet you	Mucho gusto	**moo**-cho **goose**-toh
How are you?	¿Que tal?	keh-tal

NUMBERS

one	un, uno	oon, **oo**-no
two	dos	dos
three	tres	tress
four	cuatro	**kwah**-tro
five	cinco	**sink**-oh
six	seis	saice
seven	siete	see-**et**-eh
eight	ocho	**o**-cho
nine	nueve	new-**eh**-vey
ten	diez	dee-**es**
eleven	once	**ohn**-seh
twelve	doce	**doh**-seh
thirteen	trece	**treh**-seh
fourteen	catorce	ka-**tohr**-seh
fifteen	quince	**keen**-seh
sixteen	dieciséis	dee-**es**-ee-**saice**
seventeen	diecisiete	dee-**es**-ee-see-**et**-eh
eighteen	dieciocho	dee-**es**-ee-**o**-cho
nineteen	diecinueve	dee-**es**-ee-new-**ev**-eh
twenty	veinte	**vain**-teh
twenty-one	veintiuno	**vain**-te-**oo**-noh
thirty	treinta	**train**-tah
forty	cuarenta	kwah-**ren**-tah
fifty	cincuenta	seen-**kwen**-tah
sixty	sesenta	sess-**en**-tah
seventy	setenta	set-**en**-tah
eighty	ochenta	oh-**chen**-tah
ninety	noventa	no-**ven**-tah
one hundred	cien	see-**en**
one thousand	mil	meel
one million	un millón	oon meel-**yohn**

COLORS

black	negro	**neh**-groh
blue	azul	ah-**sool**
brown	marrón	mah-**ron**
green	verde	**ver**-deh
orange	naranja	na-**rahn**-hah
red	rojo	**roh**-hoh
white	blanco	**blahn**-koh
yellow	amarillo	ah-mah-**ree**-yoh

DAYS OF THE WEEK

Sunday	domingo	doe-**meen**-goh
Monday	lunes	**loo**-ness
Tuesday	martes	**mahr**-tess
Wednesday	miércoles	me-**air**-koh-less
Thursday	jueves	hoo-**ev**-ess
Friday	viernes	vee-**air**-ness
Saturday	sábado	**sah**-bah-doh

MONTHS

January	enero	eh-**neh**-roh
February	febrero	feh-**breh**-roh
March	marzo	**mahr**-soh
April	abril	ah-**breel**
May	mayo	**my**-oh
June	junio	**hoo**-nee-oh
July	julio	**hoo**-lee-yoh
August	agosto	ah-**ghost**-toh
September	septiembre	sep-tee-**em**-breh
October	octubre	oak-**too**-breh
November	noviembre	no-vee-**em**-breh
December	diciembre	dee-see-**em**-breh

USEFUL WORDS AND PHRASES

Do you speak English?	¿Habla usted inglés?	ah-blah oos-**ted** in-**glehs**
I don't speak Spanish.	No hablo español	no **ah**-bloh es-pahn-**yol**
I don't understand.	No entiendo	no en-tee-**en**-doh
I understand.	Entiendo	en-tee-**en**-doh
I don't know.	No sé	no **seh**
I'm American.	Soy americano (americana)	soy ah-meh-ree-**kah**-no (ah-meh-ree-**kah**-nah)
What's your name?	¿Cómo se llama?	koh-mo seh **yah**-mah
My name is ...	Me llamo ...	may **yah**-moh
What time is it?	¿Qué hora es?	keh **o**-rah es
How?	¿Cómo?	**koh**-mo
When?	¿Cuándo?	**kwahn**-doh
Yesterday	Ayer	ah-**yehr**
Today	hoy	oy
Tomorrow	mañana	mahn-**yah**-nah
Tonight	Esta noche	es-tah **no**-cheh
What?	¿Qué?	keh
What is it?	¿Qué es esto?	keh es **es**-toh

Why?	¿Por qué?	pore **keh**
Who?	¿Quién?	kee-**yen**
Where is . . .	¿Dónde está . . .	**dohn**-deh es-**tah**
. . . the train station?	la estación del tren?	la es-tah-see-**on** del trehn
. . . the subway station?	estación de metro	la es-ta-see-**on** del **meh**-tro
. . . the bus stop?	la parada del autobus?	la pah-**rah**-dah del ow-toh-**boos**
. . . the terminal? (airport)	el aeropuerto	el air-oh-**pwar**-toh
. . . the post office?	la oficina de correos?	la oh-fee-**see**- nah deh koh-**rreh**-os
. . . the bank?	el banco?	el **bahn**-koh
. . . the hotel?	el hotel?	el oh-**tel**
. . . the museum?	el museo?	el moo-**seh**-oh
. . . the hospital?	el hospital?	el ohss-pee-**tal**
. . . the elevator?	el ascensor?	el ah-sen-**sohr**
Where are the restrooms?	el baño?	el **bahn**-yoh
Here/there	Aquí/allí	ah-**key**/ah-**yee**
Open/closed	Abierto/cerrado	ah-bee-**er**-toh/ ser-**ah**-doh
Left/right	Izquierda/derecha	iss-key-**eh**-dah/ dare-**eh**-chah
Is it near?	¿Está cerca?	es-**tah** sehr-kah
Is it far?	¿Está lejos?	es-**tah** leh-hoss
I'd like . . .	Quisiera . . .	kee-see-**ehr**-ah
. . . a room	un cuarto/una habitación	oon **kwahr**-toh/**oo**-nah ah-bee-tah-see-**on**
. . . the key	la llave	lah **yah**-veh
. . . a newspaper	un periódico	oon pehr-ee-**oh**-dee-koh
. . . a stamp	un sello de correo	oon **seh**-yo deh korr-**eh**-oh
I'd like to buy . . .	Quisiera comprar . . .	kee-see-**ehr**-ah kohm-**prahr**
. . . soap	jabón	hah-**bohn**
. . . suntan lotion	crema solar	**kreh**-mah soh-**lar**
. . . envelopes	sobres	**so**-brehs
. . . writing paper	papel	pah-**pel**
. . . a postcard	una tarjeta postal	**oon**-ah tar-**het**-ah post-**ahl**
. . . a ticket	un billete (travel)	oon bee-**yee**-teh
	una entrada (concert etc.)	**oona** en-**trah**-dah
How much is it?	¿Cuánto cuesta?	**kwahn**-toh **kwes**-tah
It's expensive/ cheap	Es caro/barato	es **kah**-roh/ bah-**rah**-toh
A little/a lot	Un poquito/mucho	oon poh-**kee**-toh/ **moo**-choh
More/less	Más/menos	mahss/**men**-ohss
Enough/too (much)	Suficiente/	soo-fee-see-**en**-teh/
I am ill/sick	Estoy enfermo(a)	es-**toy** en-**fehr**-moh(mah)
Call a doctor	Llame a un medico	**ya**-meh ah oon **med**-ee-koh

Help!	Socorro	soh-**koh**-roh
Stop!	Pare	**pah**-reh

DINING OUT

I'd like to reserve a table . . .	Quisiera reservar una mesa . . .	kee-**syeh**-rah rreh-sehr-**bahr oo**-nah **meh**-sah . . .
. . . for two people.	para dos personas.	**pah**-rah dohs pehr-**soh**-nahs
. . . for this evening.	para esta noche.	**pah**-rah ehs-tah **noh**-cheh
. . . for 8 PM	para las ocho de la noche.	**pah**-rah lahs **oh**-choh deh lah **noh**-cheh
A bottle of . . .	Una botella de . . .	**oo**-nah bo-**teh**-yah deh
A cup of . . .	Una taza de . . .	**oo**-nah **tah**-sah deh
A glass of . . .	Un vaso (water, soda, etc.) de...	oon **vah**-so deh
	Una copa (wine, spirits, etc.) de...	**oona coh**-pah deh
Bill/check	La cuenta	lah **kwen**-tah
Bread	El pan	el pahn
Breakfast	El desayuno	el deh-sah-**yoon**-oh
Butter	La mantequilla	lah man-teh-**kee**-yah
Coffee	Café	kah-**feh**
Dinner	La cena	lah **seh**-nah
Fork	El tenedor	el ten-eh-**dor**
I don't eat meat	No como carne	noh koh-moh **kahr**-neh
I cannot eat . . .	No puedo comer . . .	noh **pweh**-doh koh-**mehr**
I'd like to order . . .	Quiero pedir . . .	**kee**-yehr-oh peh-**deer**
I'd like . . .	Me gustaría . . .	Meh goo-stah-**ee**-ah
I'm hungry/thirsty	Tengo hambre/sed	**Tehn**-goh **hahm**-breh/seth
Is service/the tip included?	¿Está incluida la propina?	es-**tah** in-cloo-**ee**-dah lah pro-**pee**-nah
Knife	El cuchillo	el koo-**chee**-yo
Lunch	La comida	lah koh-**mee**-dah
Menu	La carta, el menú	lah **cart**-ah, el meh-**noo**
Napkin	La servilleta	lah sehr-vee-**yet**-ah
Pepper	La pimienta	lah pee-mee-**en**-tah
Plate	plato	
Please give me . . .	Por favor déme . . .	pore fah-**vor deh**-meh
Salt	La sal	lah sahl
Spoon	Una cuchara	**oo**-nah koo-**chah**-rah
Sugar	El ázucar	el ah-**su**-kar
Tea	té	teh
Water	agua	**ah**-gwah
Wine	vino	**vee**-noh

Great Itineraries

The Big City, Waterfalls, and Wine

Argentina is a very big country. This whistle-stop tour takes in three of its main attractions—Buenos Aires, Iguazú Falls, and wine country—in 10 days. Although it's technically possible to squeeze all these destinations in, a single flight delay could throw all your plans out of step. Consider adding a day or two's padding here and there to be on the safe side.

DAY 1: ARRIVAL

Arrive in Buenos Aires and pick up a city map from the tourist office right before you enter the main airport terminal. Ignore the drivers asking if you need a cab; head straight for the taxi booth, pay up front for your ticket (about 3,500 pesos), and let staffers assign you a driver. Treat your eyes to an afternoon of visual riches in swanky Recoleta. Stroll past Parisian-style mansions as on Avenida Alvear, then visit the equally palatial tombs in Recoleta Cemetery, whose permanent residents include Eva Perón. The world's largest Argentinian art collection is in the nearby Museo de Bellas Artes. Sneak in a power nap to get your body used to the late dinner hours: steak (a bife de chorizo or lomo) is the obvious first-night choice.

DAY 2: PLAZA DE MAYO, SAN TELMO, LA BOCA, AND COSTANERA SUR

Have your morning coffee and croissants at an ultratraditional café like Gran Café Tortoni. Stroll down Avenida de Mayo to take in Plaza de Mayo, including a quick look around the Casa Rosada museum. Hop in a taxi to La Boca, the port neighborhood where tango was born. The main strip is Caminito, which, though colorful and iconic, is too touristy to merit more than an hour. Lunch at El Obrero is a classic.

Tips

1. The Big City, Waterfalls, and Wine itinerary works best if Day 1 (arrival) falls on a Thursday or Friday.

2. A 10-day apartment rental in Buenos Aires could save you money, even if you aren't spending all your time there.

3. Most flights to and from Puerto Iguazú and Mendoza use the Aeroparque Jorge Newbery in Palermo, although some also operate from Ezeiza, the airport for all international flights, which is about 40 minutes from downtown. If you can't avoid same-day arrival and departure, allow at least four hours between landing at one airport and leaving from the other.

Another characteristic old neighborhood, San Telmo, is a short taxi ride back toward downtown. Set aside an hour to get up close to its history with a visit to El Zanjón de Granados, a fascinating house loaded with history. After coffee (or a beer) at one of San Telmo's many cafés, you could spend the rest of the afternoon wandering through the antiques and clothes shops, get a history, or do your walking in greener surroundings at the Costanera Sur Ecological Reserve, a 10-minute taxi ride away.

DAY 3: PALERMO

After a leisurely breakfast, head for a stroll, skate, or cycle through the Parque 3 de Febrero, and linger at the Jardín Japonés or the Rosedal. Walk or take a short taxi ride to MALBA, which opens at noon, and work up an appetite viewing Latin American art.

Take a cab to the perennially trendy Palermo Viejo neighborhood, where you can lunch on gourmet salads and sandwiches or far-out fusion. Afterward, browse the city's coolest clothing, shoe, and homeware stores or stray a few blocks west into Palermo Hollywood for antiques and vintage finds at the Mercado de Pulgas (flea market). When night falls, have coffee or a cocktail near Plaza Serrano, and finish with dinner at a modern restaurant. If you're up for a nightcap, you're already where all the action is.

DAY 4: BUENOS AIRES TO PUERTO IGUAZÚ

Catch an early-morning flight up to Puerto Iguazú. After a quick stop at your hotel, head straight for the Argentine side of Parque Nacional Iguazú. Spend the rest of the day wandering the trails and catwalks, and getting soaked on a Zodiac ride through some of the spectacular waterfalls.

DAY 5: IGUAZÚ FALLS: THE BRAZILIAN SIDE

Spend your second morning at the falls at the Parque Nacional Foz do Iguaçu, Brazil's national park, for amazing views of the Garganta del Diablo (Devil's Throat). (Note that to enter Brazil, U.S. citizens need to present their passport.)

DAYS 6–8: MENDOZA

Catch an early flight to Mendoza via Buenos Aires. Spend your afternoon on the first day wandering through the stately city streets of Mendoza and people-watching in its main square, Plaza Independencia.

Divide your next two days between Mendoza's main wine-producing valleys: Uco and Luján de Cuyo. The wisest way to go is with a wine tour, which will help you make the most of your time, not to mention avoid drinking and driving. Let the wining and dining spill over into the

evening with dinner at some of the city's excellent restaurants. And if raising your glass isn't your idea of exercise, spend the day rafting, hiking, horseback-riding, biking, or kayaking in fabulous natural settings only an hour or two from downtown.

DAYS 9 AND 10: TO BUENOS AIRES AND HOME

Catch a morning flight to Buenos Aires and head to your favorite neighborhood for a late lunch.

You could spend the rest of your last day finding out more about *fútbol* at the Museo de la Pasión Boquense, history at the Museo Evita, or street art on a tour with Graffitimundo. Later, try out your footwork with a tango class and a visit to a milonga, or see the pros in action at an evening show.

If you need to do some last-minute shopping, choose from the clothing outlets on Gurruchaga, high-end mall Paseo Alcorta, and the boutiques in Palermo. On your last day, allow at least an hour to get to Ezeiza for your flight home.

Bariloche to Patagonia

DAY 1: ARRIVAL AND ON TO BARILOCHE

It's a long trip to Patagonia. After you arrive at Buenos Aires' Ezeiza International you need to transfer to the downtown Aeroparque for your flight to Bariloche. Rent a car at the airport, and drive to your hotel (consider a place on the Circuito Chico outside town). If you could use a beer after all that, choose a laid-back downtown pub to enjoy a local craft brew.

DAY 2: BARILOCHE AND CIRCUITO CHICO

Spend the day exploring the Circuito

so you have time for a boat excursion from the dock at Puerto Pañuelo on the peninsula's edge as well as for some late-afternoon shopping for homeware and chocolate back in Bariloche. Spend the evening devouring Patagonian lamb *a la cruz* (spit-roasted over an open fire).

DAY 3: CIRCUITO GRANDE TO VILLA LA ANGOSTURA

Villa La Angostura is a tranquil lakeside retreat that marks the beginning of the legendary Circuito Grande. Driving there is a gorgeous experience, as you hug the shores of Lago Nahuel Huapi on Ruta 237 and Ruta 231. Relax to the full by checking into a hotel in quiet Puerto Manzano, about 10 minutes outside Villa La Angostura.

DAY 4: VILLA LA ANGOSTURA

Spend your second day in Villa La Angostura skiing at Cerro Bayo if it's winter and that's your thing. In warmer weather, explore the Parque Nacional Los Arrayanes, the only forest of these myrtle trees in the world, or simply relax by the lake—if you're staying at Puerto Sur, this might be the most appealing option.

Tips

1. In the dead of winter limit yourself to the ski resorts in the Lake District. That said, Bariloche is teeming with kids on high-school vacation trips July through September.

2. Book your flight to Argentina and your round-trip ticket to Bariloche at the same time. Booking a separate flight with another carrier will mean you won't be able to check your luggage through, and you'll have to time things very carefully to avoid missing your connection.

3. It's difficult to tour the Lake District without a rental car. If you don't want to drive, confine your visit to southern Patagonia, spending more time in El Calafate or extending into Tierra del Fuego.

DAY 5: RUTA DE LOS SIETE LAGOS TO SAN MARTÍN DE LOS ANDES

Head out of Villa La Angostura onto the unbelievable Seven Lakes Route (Ruta 234), which branches right and along the way passes a string of beautiful lakes. The official seven that give the route its name are Correntoso, Espejo, Villarino, Falkner, Hermoso, Machónico, and Lácar. If you leave early, add the hour-long detour to Lago Traful, where you can stop for lunch. Another detour after Lago Machónico takes you to Lago Meliquina. The route brings you to smart San Martín, where you can spend the late afternoon shopping, trying rainbow trout and other delicacies at the smoke shops, then enjoying them all over again for dinner. Note that the Seven Lakes Route is closed during particularly heavy winter snowfall, when you have to go through Junín de los Andes to get to San Martín.

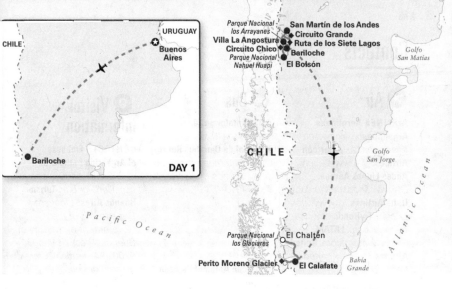

DAY 1

DAY 6: SAN MARTIN DE LOS ANDES

In winter, skiers should plan on at least one full day at Cerro Chapelco, near San Martín. Otherwise, spend the day relaxing on the beach, fishing, horseback riding, rafting, or just strolling the town.

DAY 7: FLIGHT TO EL CALAFATE

Get an early start from San Martín de los Andes for the four-hour drive back to Bariloche and then the two-hour flight to El Calafate, the base for exploring Parque Nacional Los Glaciares. From San Martín, be sure to take the longer but faster route through Junín to Bariloche (Ruta 234 and Ruta 237). If you follow the Ruta de los Siete Lagos, you'll have little chance of making an early afternoon flight.

In El Calafate, grab a taxi to your hotel, have dinner, and get some sleep in preparation for glacier-viewing tomorrow. If money is no object, stay at Hostería Los Notros, the only hotel within the park and in view of the glacier. The sky-high rates include all meals and excursions. Otherwise, stay at a hotel in El Calafate and book your Day 8 glacier visits through El Calafate tour operators (preferably before 7 pm).

DAYS 8–9: EL CALAFATE AND PERITO MORENO GLACIER

Spend two days taking in Perito Moreno from different angles. Devote today either to the Upsala Glacier tour, which traverses the lakes in view of an impressive series of glaciers, or the hour-long Safari Nautico on a boat that sails as close as possible to the front of the glacier. Enjoy a well-deserved dinner back in El Calafate. Make arrangements for a Day 9 ice trek by 7 pm.

Don crampons and trek across Perito Moreno's icy surface. The trip is expensive, but worth every penny. You crawl through ice tunnels and hike across ice ridges that seem to glow bright blue. After all this, dinner—and everything else—will seem insignificant.

DAY 10: DEPARTURE

Board a bus or taxi for the airport and take a flight back through Buenos Aires and home. Note that if you are not connecting to another Aerolíneas flight home, you may have to spend an additional night in Buenos Aires on the way back.

Contacts

Air

AIRLINES Aerolíneas Argentinas. ⊕ *www.aerolineas.com.ar.* **American Airlines.** ⊕ *www.aa.com.* **Andes Líneas Aéreas.** ⊕ *www.andesonline.com.* **Delta Airlines.** ⊕ *www.delta.com.* **FlyBondi.** ⊕ *www.flybondi.com.* **LATAM.** ⊕ *www.latam.com.* **United Airlines.** ⊕ *www.united.com.*

AIRPORT INFORMATION Aeropuerto El Palomar. ☏ *11/4758–7963* ⊕ *www.aa2000.com.ar.* **Aeropuerto Internacional de Ezeiza Ministro Pistarini.** ☏ *11/5480–6111* ⊕ *www.aa2000.com.ar.* **Aeroparque Jorge Newbery.** ☏ *11/5480–6111* ⊕ *www.aa2000.com.ar.*

⊙ Boat

BOAT Buquebus. ✉ *Av. Antártida Argentina 821, Puerto Madero* ☏ *11/4316–6550* ⊕ *www.buquebus.com.* **Colonia Express.** ✉ *Av. Elvira Rawson de Dellepiane 155, Puerto Madero* ☏ *11/4317–4100* ⊕ *www.coloniaexpress.com.*

⊟ Bus

BUS Plataforma 10. ⊕ *www.plataforma10.com.* **Terminal de Ómnibus Retiro.** ✉ *Av. Antártida Argentina at Av. Ramos Mejía, Retiro* ☏ *11/4310–0700* ⊕ *www.retiro.com.ar.*

⊜ Car

American Automobile Association. (*AAA*). ☏ *800/222–4357* ⊕ *www.aaa.com.* **Automóvil Club Argentino.** (*ACA*). ☏ *800/888–9888, 800/777–2894 emergencies* ⊕ *www.aca.org.ar.* **Police.** ☏ *911.*

RENTAL AGENCIES Alamo. ☏ *810/999–2526, 11/4811–9993 in Buenos Aires* ⊕ *www.alamoargentina.com.ar.* **Avis.** ☏ *810/9991–2847,* ⊕ *www.avis.com.ar.* **Budget.** ☏ *810/999–2834,* ⊕ *www.budget.com.ar.* **Hertz.** ☏ *11/3853-2220, 11/7090-4000 in Buenos Aires* ⊕ *www.hertz.com.ar.*

⊙ Visitor Information

CONTACTS Embassy of Argentina in the U.S.. ☏ *202/238–6400* ⊕ *eeeuu.cancilleria.gob.ar.* **Turismo Buenos Aires.** (*Tourism Department of the Government of the City of Buenos Aires*). ☏ *11/5030–9200 in Argentina* ⊕ *www.turismo.buenosaires.gob.ar/en.*

ONLINE RESOURCES Argentina Travel. ⊕ *www.argentina.travel.* **Clarín.** ⊕ *www.clarin.com.* **Embassy of Argentina in the U.S.** ⊕ *eeeuu.cancilleria.gob.ar.* **Fodors.com.** ⊕ *www.fodors.com/community.* **La Nación.** ⊕ *www.lanacion.com.ar.* **Página 12.** ⊕ *www.pagina12.com.ar.*

Chapter 3

BUENOS AIRES

3

Updated by
Sorrel Moseley-Williams

◉ Sights	🍴 Restaurants	🛏 Hotels	🛍 Shopping	🍸 Nightlife
★★★★☆	★★★★★	★★★★★	★★★★☆	★★★★★

WELCOME TO BUENOS AIRES

TOP REASONS TO GO

★ **Dance the Night Away:** This is the capital of tango, that most passionate of dances. But porteños also dance to samba, salsa, and electronic beats until dawn.

★ **Shop 'Til You Drop:** High-quality silver and leather goods, as well as fashionable clothing and accessories are available at world-class boutiques and malls. Open-air markets carry regional and European antiques and provincial handicrafts.

★ **Get Your Culture On:** The architecture, wining-and-dining, and arts activities ensure Buenos Aires is an exciting world-class capital. But the lifestyle, lower prices, and warm locals are more typical of Latin America.

★ **Meat Your Destiny:** Beefy B.A. has more *parrillas* (steak houses) than you'll be able to sample.

★ **The Beautiful Game:** Top fútbol matches play out in Buenos Aires' colorful stadiums, stuffed to bursting with screaming and passionate sports addicts.

1 Centro. The heart of the city is filled with bars, cafés, and bookstores—not to mention crowds.

2 Puerto Madero. An elegant boardwalk and the Museo Fortabat are top draws here. Its high-rise towers are flanked by a sprawling nature reserve.

3 San Telmo. Antiques, shops, and hip clothing stores compete for space along cobbled streets. Relax at cafés and wander world-class museums.

4 La Boca. Come to edgy La Boca for the colorful Caminito area, and for soccer at the Boca Juniors stadium.

5 Recoleta. The elite live, dine, and shop along Paris-inspired streets (and they're buried in its elegant cemetery). Fantastic art galleries and museums are also big draws.

6 Almagro. Peruvian restaurants, fringe theater, a lively tango scene, and sprawling mall distinguish Almagro.

7 Palermo. If it's cool, chances are it's in Palermo Soho: bars, restaurants, boutiques, galleries, and hotels line the streets surrounding Plaza Serrano. Palermo Hollywood also houses its fair share of hot spots.

3

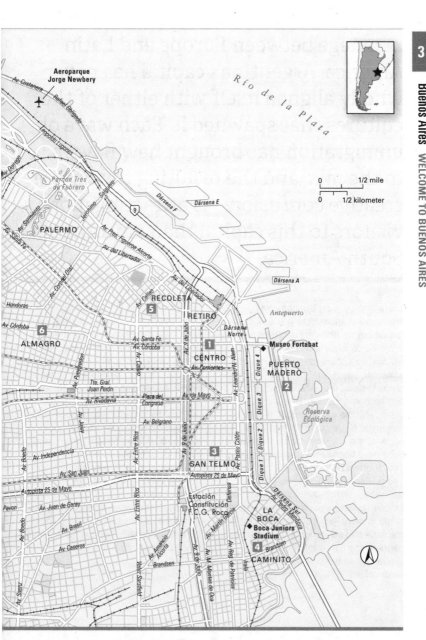

Aeroparque
Jorge Newbery

Av. Costanera

Río de la Plata

Leopoldo Lugones

Av. Dorrego

Parque Tres
de Febrero

Dársena F

Dársena E

Av. Sarmiento

Jerónimo Salguero

9

PALERMO

Av. Pres. Figueroa Alcorta

Av. del Libertador

Av. Santa Fe

Av. Coronel Díaz

Dársena A

Honduras

Av. Callao

RECOLETA

5

RETIRO

Antepuerto

Av. Córdoba

6

ALMAGRO

Av. Santa Fe

Av. Córdoba

Av. Callao

Dársena
Norte

Museo Fortabat

1

CENTRO

Av. Corrientes

Dique 4

PUERTO
MADERO

2

Tte. Gral.
Juan Perón

Av. Rivadavia

Plaza del
Congreso

Av. de Mayo

Av. Leandro N. Alem

Dique 3

Av. Belgrano

Reserva
Ecológica

Dique 2

Av. Independencia

Av. Entre Ríos

3

Av. Boedo

Av. San Juan

SAN TELMO

Av. Paseo Colón

Dique 1

Autopista 25 de Mayo

Dársena Sur

Autopista 25 de Mayo

Pavón

Av. Juan de Garay

Estación
Constitución
F.C.G. Roca

LA
BOCA

Av. Pedro Mendoza

Av. Brasil

Boca Juniors
Stadium

Av. Caseros

4   Brandsen

Av. Amancio
Alcorta

Av. Reg. de Patricios

CAMINITO

Av. Saénz

Brandsen

Av. M. Montes de Oca

Av. 9 de Julio

Tala

0   1/2 mile

0   1/2 kilometer

For 500 years, Buenos Aires has been in the throes of a powerful identity crisis. The unlikely lovechild of a troubled marriage between Europe and Latin America, Argentina's capital has never wholly aligned itself with either of the cultures that spawned it. Each wave of immigration has brought new flavors to the mix, and the resulting fusion—or creative confusion—is attracting more visitors to this capital than any other in South America.

There's no denying Buenos Aires' architectural appeal: the graceful stone facades of its 19th-century town houses and civic constructions speak of Paris or Madrid, so just wandering the streets is a memorable experience. The shopping is world-class, too, whether you covet contemporary couture or quality handicrafts; and the electric nightlife further heightens B.A.'s cosmopolitan ambience. Many of the city's classic cultural institutions have been renovated, while plenty of old-school buildings are being turned into up-and-coming spaces. Traditional dance floors, moreover, have come back to life thanks to a booming tango—and tango tourism—revival. Meanwhile, marriage and equal rights for same-sex partnerships plus a thriving LGBTQ+ scene ensure the city is a popular gay destination.

But grit still offsets the glamour. Crumbling balconies, uneven sidewalks, and fresh layers of photo-worthy street art are reminders of your real coordinates. A very weak peso paired with around 50 percent annual inflation means that Buenos Aires remains very cheap for anyone with hard currency, (though rising prices due to inflation are hard on *porteños,*as the locals are called)—though growing numbers of homeless people and ever-expanding shanty towns within the city limits speak of tough times to come for on-the-edge residents. In the face of so much change, though, some things do remain the same. Food, family, and fútbol are still the holy trinity for most *porteños*, and they approach life with as much dramatic intensity as ever.

Planning

When to Go

Remember that when it's summer in the United States, it's winter in Argentina, and vice versa. Winters (July to September) are chilly. Summer's muggy heat (December to March) can be taxing at midday but makes for pleasantly warm nights. During these months Argentineans crowd resorts along the Atlantic and in Uruguay.

Spring (September to December) and autumn (April to June), with their mild temperatures—and blossoms or changing leaves—are ideal for urban trekking. It's usually warm enough for just a light jacket, and it's right before or after the peak (and expensive) seasons.

The best time for trips to Iguazú Falls is August through October, when temperatures are lower, the falls are fuller, and the spring colors are at their brightest.

Getting Here and Around

Intriguing architecture, an easy-to-navigate grid layout (a few diagonal transverses aside), and ample window-shopping make Buenos Aires a wonderful place to explore on foot. SUBE, a rechargeable swipe card, is used on the subway, all city bus lines, and commuter trains.

SUBWAY
Service on the *subte* (subway) is quick, but trains are often packed and strikes are common. Four of the six underground lines (A, B, D, and E) fan out west from downtown; north–south lines C and H connect them. You can only travel using the magnetic SUBE card (90 pesos, available from most subway stations) and one trip costs 30 pesos. On your 21st journey during a single month, the value goes down to 24 pesos. If you make up to five trips within two hours, the fare

is reduced by 50 percent each time. Monday through Saturday, the subte opens at 5 am and shuts down between 11 and 11:30 pm, depending on the line. On Sunday, trains run between 8 am and 10–10:30 pm. Download the BA Subte app for route information.

BUS
Colectivos (city buses) connect the city center with its barrios and the greater Buenos Aires area. You can only pay by SUBE card, and fares within the city cost 20 to 22 pesos. Bus stops are roughly every other block and the MetroBus rapid transit system has dedicated traffic lanes. You may have to hunt for the small, metal route-number signs on regular routes: they could be stuck on a shelter, lamppost, or even a tree. Download the apps Cuándo Subo or BA Cómo Llego for route information.

TAXI
Black-and-yellow taxis fill the streets and will take you anywhere in town and short distances into greater Buenos Aires. Fares start at 111 pesos, with 11.10 pesos for each click of the meter. You can hail taxis on the street (best to hail a radio taxi with a roof sign) or ask hotel and restaurant staffers to call for them.

BIKE
With 96 miles of cycle lanes (bicisendas) constructed over the past decade, BA has become very bike friendly. The city operates the EcoBici free bicycle-sharing system and after signing up at ⊕ *www.baecobici.com.ar*, you can borrow a bike from one of 200 stations.

HOTELS
From a beautiful Belle Epoque mansion constructed by an enamored fiancé to contemporary high rises with river views and adorable *casa chorizos* converted into cozy accommodation, Buenos Aires houses a wide assortment of hotels and lodging bursting with porteño style and flavor.

Buenos Aires Metro Network

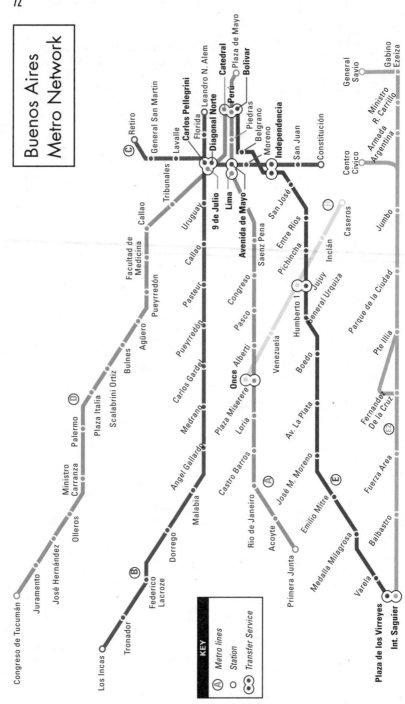

KEY

Ⓐ Metro lines

○ Station

Transfer Service

RESTAURANTS

The area around Centro has something for everyone, from traditional to trendy. At lunchtime, the city's bustling downtown is the place where business deals are negotiated over leisurely lunches of steak, potatoes, salad, and wine; a younger crowd heads for the array of fast food spots that have sprouted up. In the evening, the neighborhood gets quiet except for the pedestrian strip along Avenida Reconquista, which houses bars and restaurants.

A magnet for tourists, Puerto Madero's restaurants charge amounts that would make restaurant owners in other parts of the city blush with shame. Unless you're on an expense account, the food is generally far better and far less expensive elsewhere. The riverside views are always appealing, though.

Restaurant prices are the average cost of a main course at dinner or, if dinner is not served, at lunch. Hotel prices are the lowest cost of a standard double room in high season, including V.A.T. and a service charge (often applied in larger hotels).

What It Costs in Argentine Pesos			
$	$$	$$$	$$$$
RESTAURANTS			
Under 1,500 pesos	1,500– 2,000 pesos	2,001– 2,500 pesos	Over 2500 pesos
HOTELS (IN USD)			
Under $100	$101– 250	$251– $450	US $450

Safety

Although Buenos Aires is safer than most Latin American capitals, petty crime is a concern. Pickpocketing and muggings can happen, so avoid wearing flashy jewelry, be very discreet with money and cameras, and be mindful of bags and wallets. Phone for taxis after dark or download local transport apps such as Cabify or Beat. Police patrol most areas where you're likely to go, but they do have a reputation for corruption.

Protest marches are a part of life in Buenos Aires: most are peaceful, but some end in confrontations with the police. They often take place in the Plaza de Mayo, in the square outside the Congreso, or along Avenida de Mayo.

Tours

Known for superlative customer service, Buenos Aires Tours arranges everything from city walking tours to multiweek Argentine vacations aimed at different budgets. Informed young historians from the University of Buenos Aires lead private tours that highlight the city's art and architecture as well as its intriguing past at Eternautas. Academics also serve as guides at Cultour: the highbrow history- and culture-oriented excursions are complemented by general city tours and boat trips.

For a different take on local life, contact the Cicerones de Buenos Aires. Its resident volunteers take groups of up to six visitors on informal outings, providing a true porteño perspective along the way. The experience is free, but donations are welcome. Meanwhile, BA Cultural Concierge, run by well-connected Maryland transplant Madi Lang, plans trips for families and groups, specializing in off-the-beaten track tours as well as insight into the city's Jewish community.

B.A.'s growing network of bicycle lanes has led to a surge in two-wheel travel. La Bicicleta Naranja has scheduled tours led by bilingual guides; it will also supply do-it-yourselfers with excellent route maps and deliver rental equipment to your hotel. Graffiti and street art are the

This government building is well known as Casa Rosada, or Pink House, for its distinctive color.

focus of one unusual tour run by Biking Buenos Aires; another includes live performances by actors recreating key moments in civic history.

If you would rather rely on public transit and foot power, try Buenos Aires Local Tours, a popular pay-what-you-like service (advance online registration is required).

Also check out the free guided tours offered by Visit Buenos Aires, the city tourist board, where you can follow the footsteps of Pope Francis's beginnings or take an electric tricycle tour.

TOUR COMPANIES BA Cultural Concierge. ☎ 11/15–3876–5937 ⊕ www. baculturalconcierge.com. **Biking Buenos Aires.** ☎ 11/5056–8756 ⊕ www. bikingbuenosaires.com. **Buenos Aires Local Tours.** ☎ 11/5254–1354 ⊕ www. buenosaireslocaltours.com. **Buenos Aires Tours.** ☎ 11/4785–2753 ⊕ www.buenosaires-tours.com.ar. **Cicerones de Buenos Aires.** ☎ 11/4141–9362 ⊕ www.cicerones.org.ar. **Cultour.** ☎ 11/6365–6892.

Eternautas. ☎ 11/5031–9916 ⊕ www. eternautas.tur.ar. **La Bicicleta Naranja.** ☎ 11/4362–1104 ⊕ www.labicicletanaranja.com.ar. **Visit Buenos Aires.** ⊕ www. turismo.buenosaires.gob.ar/en/article/ guided-tours.

Visitor Information

The civic tourism board—Visit Buenos Aires—operates information outlets with English-speaking staff at both airports and seven other locations around the city, including Centro, Recoleta, and Puerto Madero. Hours can be erratic, but the booth at the intersection of Florida and Marcelo T. de Alvear (near Plaza San Martín) is usually open weekdays from 10 to 5 and weekends from 9 to 6.

CONTACT Turismo Buenos Aires. ⊕ www. turismo.buenosaires.gob.ar.

Centro

The quickest way into Centro is by subte. For Microcentro, get off at Florida (Línea B) or Lavalle (C). Retiro and Plaza San Martín have eponymous stations on Línea C. Stations Avenida de Mayo (A), Catedral (D), and Bolívar (E) all serve Plaza de Mayo. Línea A has stops along de Mayo, including at Congreso. Líneas B, C, and D intersect at Carlos Pellegrini/ Diagonal Norte/9 de Julio. Only change lines here if you're going more than one stop. Otherwise, walking is quicker. Puerto Madero is close to L.N. Alem on Línea A and Catalinas (E).

You can take a taxi or bus to the Microcentro, but walking is the best way to move within it. Bus No. 17 connects Centro and Recoleta; so do Bus Nos. 59 and 93. No. 130 connects these areas with Puerto Madero. Bus Nos. 22 and 24 run between San Telmo and Microcentro. The MetroBus system, which opened in 2016, makes moving around a lot faster.

⊙ Sights

The historic heart of Buenos Aires, Centro is still the focus of contemporary civic and commercial life. Plaza de Mayo is the original main square, and civic buildings both past and present are clustered between it and Plaza Congreso. Many of Argentina's most historic events— including revolutions, demonstrations, and terrorist attacks—took place on this square. Bullet-marked facades, sidewalks embedded with plaques, and memorials where buildings once stood are reminders of all this history, and the protesters who fill the streets regularly are history in the making. The city's most highbrow cultural events are hosted a few blocks away in the spectacular Teatro Colón, and high-grossing theatrical productions line Avenida Corrientes. Microcentro is the financial district tucked into Centro.

Calle Florida

PEDESTRIAN MALL | Nothing sums up the chaotic Microcentro better than this pedestrian axis, which has fallen from grace and risen from the ashes at least as many times as Argentina's economy. It's a riotous spot on weekdays, when throngs of office workers eager for a fast-food or high-street retail fix intermingle with buskers and street vendors. You can wander it in less than an hour: start at the intersection with Av. de Mayo, and a bench or patch of grass in shady **Plaza San Martín** will be your reward at the other end.

En route, take in the surrounding buildings. At the ornate **Edificio Bank Boston** (No. 99) attention tends to focus on the battered, paint-splattered 4-ton bronze doors—unhappy customers have been taking out their anger at *corralitos* (banks retaining their savings) since the economic crisis of 2001–02.

The restoration process at **Galería Güemes** has left the soaring marble columns and stained-glass cupola gleaming, and the tacky shops that fill this historic arcade do nothing to lessen the wow factor. Witness Buenos Aires' often cavalier attitude to its architectural heritage at Florida's intersection with Avenida Corrientes, where the neo-Gothic **Palacio Elortondo-Alvear** is now home to Burger King. Go upstairs to check out the plaster molding and stained glass.

Milan's Galleria Vittorio Emanuele served as the model for **Galerías Pacífico**, designed during Buenos Aires' turn-of-the-20th-century golden age. Once the headquarters of the Buenos Aires–Pacific Railway, it's now a posh shopping mall and cultural center. Head to the central stairwell to see the allegorical murals painted by local greats Juan Carlos Castagnino, Antonio Berni, Cirilo Colmenio, Lino Spilimbergo, and Demetrio Urruchúa. The **Centro Cultural**

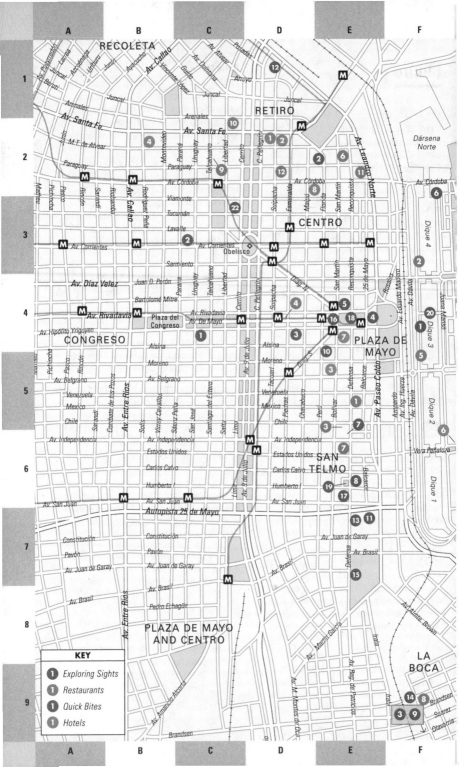

Centro, Puerto Madero, San Telmo, and La Boca

Antepuerto

Rio de La Plata

Reserva Ecológica Norte

Av. Costanera Carlos Noel

PUERTO MADERO

21

5

Reserva Ecológica Sur

Av. Costanera Carlos Noel

0		2,000 ft
0	500 m	

Dársena Sur

Villafañe Wenceslao

Delvalle Aristobulo

Av. Pedro Mendoza

Cabral

G   H   I

Sights ▼

1 Buque Museo Fragata A.R.A. Presidente Sarmiento **F4**
2 Calle Florida **E2**
3 Calle Museo Caminito **F9**
4 Casa Rosada **E4**
5 Catedral Metropolitana **E4**
6 Colección de Arte Amalia Lacroze de Fortabat **F2**
7 El Zanjón de Granados **E6**
8 Feria de San Pedro Telmo **E6**
9 Fundación Proa **F9**
10 La Manzana de las Luces **E4**
11 Museo de Arte Contemporáneo de Buenos Aires **E7**
12 Museo de Arte Hispanoamericano Isaac Fernández Blanco **D1**
13 Museo de Arte Moderno de Buenos Aires (MAMBA) **E7**
14 Museo de la Pasión Boquense **F9**
15 Museo Histórico Nacional **E7**
16 Museo Histórico Nacional del Cabildo y la Revolución de Mayo **E4**
17 Pasaje Defensa **E6**
18 Plaza de Mayo **E4**
19 Plaza Dorrego **E6**
20 Puente de la Mujer **F4**
21 Reserva Ecológica **H4**
22 Teatro Colón **C3**

Restaurants ▼

1 Brasserie Petanque **E5**
2 Cabaña Las Lilas **F3**
3 Café San Juan La Cantina **E6**
4 Café Tortoni **D4**
5 Chila **F5**
6 Dadá **E2**
7 Desnivel **E6**
8 Don Carlos **F9**
9 El Cuartito **C2**
10 Gran Bar Danzón **C2**
11 Mercado de los Carruajes **E2**
12 Mr Ho **D2**

Quick Bites ▼

1 Chan Chan **C4**
2 La Giralda **C3**
3 La Morada **D4**

Hotels ▼

1 Alvear Art Hotel **D2**
2 Casa Calma **D2**
3 Cassa Lepage Art Hotel **E5**
4 Design cE **B2**
5 Faena Hotel **G5**
6 Hotel Madero **F6**
7 Hotel NH City **E4**
8 Libertador **D2**

Borges, which hosts small international exhibitions and musical events, is on the mezzanine level.

Past the slew of leather shops in the blocks north of Avenida Córdoba is **Plaza San Martín**, where you'll see a bronze statue of the namesake saint atop a rearing horse. It's overlooked by several opulent Italianate buildings and South America's tallest art deco structure, the **Edificio Kavanagh**. ⊠ *Microcentro* Ⓜ *A to Plaza de Mayo, D to Catedral, or B to Florida (southern end); C to Plaza San Martín (northern end).*

Casa Rosada

GOVERNMENT BUILDING | The eclectic Casa de Gobierno, better known as the Casa Rosada or Pink House, is at Plaza de Mayo's eastern end. The building houses the government's executive branch—the president works here but lives else-where—and was built in the late 19th century. Its curious hue dates from the presidency of Domingo Sarmiento, who ordered it painted pink as a symbol of unification between two warring political factions: the *federales* (whose color was red) and the *unitarios* (white). Legend has it that the original paint was made by mixing whitewash with bull's blood.

The balcony facing Plaza de Mayo is a presidential podium. From this lofty stage, Evita rallied the *descamisados* (the shirtless—meaning the working class), Maradona sang along with soccer fans after winning one World Cup and coming second in another, and Madonna belted out her movie rendition of "Don't Cry for Me Argentina." Look for a small banner hoisted alongside the nation's flag, indicating "the president is in."

On weekends, hour-long guided tours in English leave at 12:30 and 2:30 (book in advance, take ID), taking in some presidential offices and the newly opened *Galería de los Patriotas Argentinos del Bicentenario* (Bicentennial Gallery

of Patriots), a pictorial who's who of Argentina's national heroes. The country's heroines have a room of their own here, the *Salón Mujeres Argentinas*, where an impassioned Evita presides over black-and-white photographs of Argentina's other great dames. ⊠ *Balcarce 50, Plaza de Mayo* ☎ *11/4344–3804* ⊕ *visitas.casa-rosada.gob.ar* 🎫 *Free, but reservations are essential* Ⓜ *A to Plaza de Mayo, D to Catedral, E to Bolívar.*

Catedral Metropolitana

RELIGIOUS BUILDING | The columned neoclassical facade of the Metropolitan Cathedral makes it seem more like a temple than a church, and its history follows the pattern of many structures in the Plaza de Mayo area. The first of six buildings on this site was a 16th-century adobe ranch house; the current structure dates from 1822, but has been added to several times.

There's been a surge of interest in the building since February 2013, when Cardinal Jorge Bergoglio, then archbish-op of Buenos Aires, was elected Pope Francis. The sanctuary now includes a small commemorative display of the pope's personal objects, watched over by a grinning life-size fiberglass statue of the pontiff in full regalia.

The embalmed remains of another local hero, General José de San Martín—known as the Liberator of Argentina for his role in the War of Independence—rest here in a marble mausoleum lighted by an eternal flame. Soldiers of the Grenadier Regiment, an elite troop created and trained by San Martín in 1811, permanently guard the tomb. Guided tours (in Spanish) of the mausoleum and crypt leave Monday to Saturday at 11:45 am. ⊠ *San Martín 27, at Rivadavia, Plaza de Mayo* ☎ *11/4331–2845* ⊕ *www.catedralbuenosaires.org.ar* 🎫 *Free* Ⓜ *A to Plaza de Mayo, D to Catedral, E to Bolívar.* Metropolitan Cathedral

La Manzana de Las Luces (*The Block of Illumination*)

HISTORIC DISTRICT | A heap of history is packed into this single block of buildings southwest of Plaza de Mayo. Its name, "the Block of Illumination," is a metaphorical nod to the "illuminated" scholars who once worked within. Guided tours are led by excellent historians, and though regular tours are in Spanish, English summaries are offered at each stage.

The site's earliest occupant was the controversial Jesuit order, which began construction in 1661. The only surviving building from then is the galleried **Procuraduría**, the colonial administrative headquarters for the Jesuits' land holdings. Secret tunnels linked it to area churches, the Cabildo, and the port. After the Jesuits' expulsion from Argentina in 1767 (the simple brick-and-mud structure housed the city's first school of medicine and then the University of Buenos Aires). Fully restored, it's now home to a school for stringed instrument makers and a somewhat tacky crafts market.

The Jesuits honored their patron saint at the **Iglesia de San Ignacio de Loyola** (Church of Saint Ignatius of Loyola), at the intersection of Alsina and Bolívar. You can visit without taking a tour.

Argentina's first congress convened in another building on the site, the **Casas Virreinales** (Viceroyal Residences)—ironic, given that it was built to house colonial civil servants. The remaining historic building is the neoclassical **Colegio Nacional**, a high-caliber public school that replaced a Jesuit-built structure. The president often attends graduation ceremonies, and Einstein gave a lecture here in 1925. ⊠ *Entrance at Perú 272, Plaza de Mayo* ☎ *11/4342–9930* ⊕ *www.turismo. buenosaires.gob.ar/en/otros-establecimientos/manzana-de-las-luces* ⌑ *Free* Ⓜ *A to Plaza de Mayo, D to Catedral, E to Bolívar.*

Museo de Arte Hispanoamericano Isaac Fernández Blanco (*Isaac Fernández Blanco Hispanic-American Art Museum*)

ART MUSEUM | The distinctive Peruvian neocolonial-style Palacio Noel is the perfect backdrop for this colonial art and craft museum, which was built in 1920 as the residence of architect Martín Noel. He and museum founder, Fernández Blanco, donated most of the exquisite silver items, religious wood carvings, inlaid furnishings, and paintings from the Spanish colonial period that are on display. Guided tours in English can be arranged by calling ahead. Shaded benches in the lush walled gardens are a welcome respite, and the rustling leaves and birdcalls almost filter out the busy Retiro traffic noise. ⊠ *Suipacha 1422, at Av. Libertador, Retiro* ☎ *11/4327–0228* ⊕ *www.buenosaires.gob.ar/museofernandezblanco* ⌑ *250 pesos, free Wed.* ⊙ *Closed Tues.* Ⓜ *C to San Martín.*

Museo Histórico Nacional del Cabildo y de la Revolución de Mayo (*Cabildo*)

NOTABLE BUILDING | Plaza de Mayo's only remaining colonial edifice was built in 1765 as the meeting place for the city council, now based in the ornate wedge-shaped building on the southwest corner of the square. The epicenter of the May Revolution of 1810, where patriotic citizens gathered to vote against Napoleonic rule, the hall is one of Argentina's national shrines. However, this hasn't stopped successive renovations to its detriment, including the demolition of the whole right end of the structure to make way for the new Avenida de Mayo in 1894 and of the left end for Diagonal Julio Roca in 1931. The small museum of artifacts and documents pertaining to the events of the May Revolution is less of an attraction than the building itself. Thursday and Friday from 11 to 6, a tiny craft market takes place on the patio behind the building. ⊠ *Bolívar 65, Plaza de Mayo* ☎ *11/4334–1782* ⊕ *www.cabildonacional. gob.ar* ⌑ *Free.* ⊙ *Closed Mon. and Tues.*

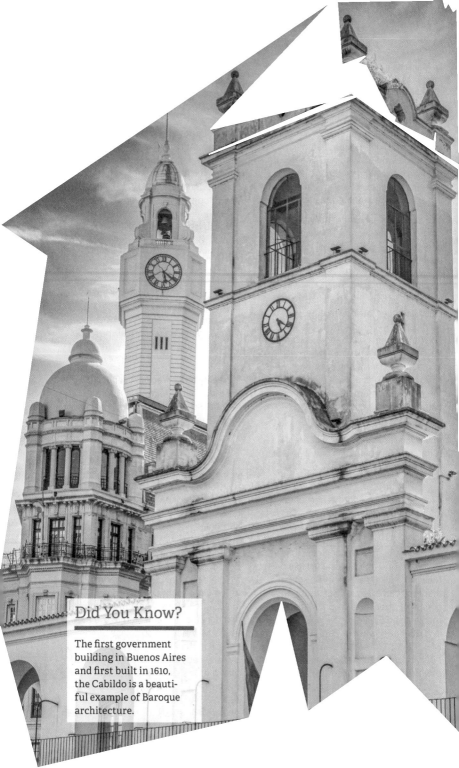

Did You Know?

The first government building in Buenos Aires and first built in 1610, the Cabildo is a beautiful example of Baroque architecture.

Ⓜ *Line A to Plaza de Mayo, Line D to Catedral, Line E to Bolívar.*

★ Plaza de Mayo

PLAZA/SQUARE | Since its construction in 1580, this has been the setting for Argentina's most politically turbulent moments, including the uprising against Spanish colonial rule on May 25, 1810—hence its name. The square was once divided in two by a *recova* (gallery), but this reminder of colonial times was demolished in 1883 and the square's central monument, the Pirámide de Mayo, was later moved to its place. The pyramid you see is a 1911 extension of the original (which is hidden inside), erected in 1811 on the anniversary of the Revolution of May. The bronze equestrian statue of General Manuel Belgrano, the designer of Argentina's flag, dates from 1873.

The plaza remains the traditional site for ceremonies, rallies, and protests. Thousands cheered for Perón and Evita here; anti-Peronist planes bombed the gathered crowds in 1955; there were bloody clashes in December 2001 (hence the heavy police presence and crowd-control barriers); but the mood was jubilant for the nation's bicentenary in 2010. The white head scarves painted around the pyramid represent the Madres de la Plaza de Mayo (Mothers of May Square) who have marched here every Thursday at 3:30 for nearly four decades. Housewives and mothers–turned–militant activists, they demand justice for *los desaparecidos*—the people who were "disappeared" during Argentina's dictatorial military government (1976–83). ✉ *Centro* Ⓜ *A to Plaza de Mayo, D to Catedral, E to Bolívar.*

★ Teatro Colón

PERFORMANCE VENUE | Its magnitude, magnificent acoustics, and opulence earn the Teatro Colón a place among the world's top five opera houses and an ever-changing stream of imported talent bolsters the well-regarded local lyric and ballet companies.

After an eventful 18-year building process involving the death of one architect and the murder of another, the sublime Italianate structure was inaugurated in 1908 with Verdi's *Aïda*. It has hosted the likes of Maria Callas, Richard Strauss, Arturo Toscanini, Igor Stravinsky, Enrico Caruso, and Luciano Pavarotti, who said that the Colón has only one flaw: the acoustics are so good that every mistake can be heard.

The theater's sumptuous building materials—three kinds of Italian marble, French stained glass, and Venetian mosaics—were imported from Europe. The seven-tier main theater is breathtaking, and has a grand central chandelier with 700 lights to illuminate the 3,000 mere mortals in its red-velvet seats.

The opera and ballet seasons run from April through December, and performances include symphonic cycles, chamber music concerts, and avant-garde music, opera, and dramatic performances at the ultraminimal Centro Experimental.

You can get in on the behind-the-scenes action on a guided tour, which takes you up and down innumerable staircases to rehearsal rooms and to the costume, shoe, and scenery workshops, before letting you gaze at the stage from a sought-after box. (Tours are daily 9–5, every hour on the hour and at 11, 1, and 3 in English; arrive at least a half hour before the tour starts, as they fill up quickly.)

Buy performance tickets from the box office on Pasaje Toscanini. If seats are sold out—or beyond your pocket—you can buy 600-peso standing-room tickets on the day of the performance. These are for the lofty upper-tier *paraíso*, from which you can both see and hear perfectly. ✉ *Main entrance: Libertad between*

The Teatro Colón is a world-class opera house and possibly the best in South America.

Tucumán and Viamonte, box office: Pasaje Toscanini 1180, Centro ☎ *11/4378–7100 tickets, 11/4378–7127 tours* 🌐 *www.teatrocolon.org.ar* 🎫 *Guided tours 3,800 pesos* [M] *D to Tribunales.*

🍴 Restaurants

Café Tortoni

$ | **CAFÉ** | Take a seat amid the Tiffany lamps and marble-topped tables, and contemplate the fact that you may be sitting in a chair once occupied by a former president, a renowned tango singer, or a world-famous artist or writer while they nibbled an exquisite pastry. The place and setting are from another age, thankfully well preserved, but you may have to wait for a table at the oldest—and highly popular—café in Buenos Aires. **Known for:** blast from the past; submarino (hot chocolate) and churros; tango. [$] *Average main: pesos900* ✉ *Av. de Mayo 825, at Piedras, Centro* ☎ *11/2393–3108* 🌐 *www.cafetortoni.com.ar* [M] *A to Perú.*

Dadá

$$ | **ECLECTIC** | An intimate and artsy setting are the backdrop for a short but creative menu, which includes house specialties like phyllo-wrapped Morbier cheese salad as a starter and the perfectly cooked *ojo de bife* (rib-eye steak). Relax, enjoy a glass of wine, read the paper, and eat well. **Known for:** intimate setting; buzzy; classy bistro fare. [$] *Average main: pesos1000* ✉ *San Martín 941, Retiro* ☎ *11/4314–4787* 🕒 *Closed Sun. and Mon.* [M] *C to San Martín.*

★ El Cuartito

$ | **PIZZA** | This iconic pizza parlor is frequented by porteños who worship the pies topped with fresh tomato sauce and a mile-high pile of oozing mozzarella. Every square inch of wall space is dedicated to memorabilia of sports legends, musicians, tango dancers, and actors, and every local has their cherished dining spot. **Known for:** pizza; frequented by locals; old-school atmosphere. [$] *Average main: pesos600* ✉ *Talcahuano 937,*

Centro ☎ *11/4816–1758* 💳 *No credit cards* ⏲ *Closed Mon.* [M] *D to Tribunales.*

Gran Bar Danzón

$$ | **WINE BAR** | The city's longest established cocktail and wine bar is a dimly lit lounge that attracts the local wine-geek set as well as hard liquor aficionados. They serve some of the best lounge food in town, including great sushi (don't miss the crispy prawn rolls), appetizers such as ceviche, and a great selection of wines by the glass. **Known for:** great wine list; attracts a cool crowd; loungey ambience. [$] *Average main: pesos2000* ✉ *Libertad 1161, 2nd fl., Retiro* ☎ *11/4811–1108* 🌐 *www.granbardanzon.com.ar* ⏲ *No lunch* [M] *C to San Martín.*

Mercado de los Carruajes

$ | **ARGENTINE** | Opening at the start of 2022, the long-waited Carriages Market is already being touted as Buenos Aires' answer to NYC's Chelsea Market. With more than 40 store fronts housed at this refurbished 19th-century carriage house, this gourmet food and retail marketplace aims to help bring the city center back to life. **Known for:** new in town; upcycled carriage house turned food market; lots of stores under one roof. [$] *Average main: pesos1000* ✉ *Av. Leandro N. Alem 852, Centro* 🌐 *www.mercadodeloscarruajes.com* [M] *E to Catalinas.*

Mr Ho

$ | **KOREAN** | A cheery spot that has lifted Centro's dining options, this family-run spot serves up delicious and authentic Korean dishes. First generation migrant Martín Ho cooks while daughter Abi runs front of house, and together they run an efficient K-food ship, serving up well-priced soups such as Budae Jjigae as well as popular meaty main Bulgogi. **Known for:** well priced; good for veggies too; authentic Korean dishes. [$] *Average main: pesos1200* ✉ *Centro* ✣ *Paraguay 884* ☎ *11/6560–1004* [M] *C to San Martín.*

Hotels

Alvear Art Hotel

$$ | **HOTEL** | The sleek Alvear Art Hotel is set back behind some trees on a pedestrian-only street in the heart of the city's business district. **Pros:** gorgeous views from the sky-high pool; well-appointed gym; quiet location. **Cons:** rooms lack personality; buffet lunch can be hit-and-miss; pool and gym areas open only until 9 pm. [$] *Rooms from: US$210* ✉ *Suipacha 1086, Centro* ☎ *11/4114–3477* 🌐 *www.alvearart.com* 🛏 *141 rooms* 🍴 *No Meals* [M] *C to San Martín.*

★ **Casa Calma**

$$ | **HOTEL** | This "wellness hotel" in the heart of downtown Buenos Aires has taken the concept of in-house spa to a new level, equipping each of its 17 rooms with jetted tubs—six deluxe rooms also have saunas where you can relax after a day of exploring the city. **Pros:** gorgeous design; serene atmosphere; convenient downtown location. **Cons:** sauna is small; some balconies are very tiny; views aren't great on lower floors; on a chaotic city street. [$] *Rooms from: US$116* ✉ *Suipacha 1015, Centro* ☎ *11/4312–5000* 🌐 *www.casacalmahotel.com* 🛏 *17 rooms* 🍴 *No Meals* [M] *C to San Martín.*

Design cE

$$ | **HOTEL** | Kudos go to the architect for this sleek space with spacious, loftlike rooms. **Pros:** supermodern suites; great location; breakfast is served 24 hours a day. **Cons:** limited breakfast; just a few drawers to put your clothes; common areas are on the small side. [$] *Rooms from: US$126* ✉ *Marcelo T. Alvear 1695, Centro* ☎ *11/5237–3100* 🌐 *www.designce.com* 🛏 *20 rooms, 8 suites* 🍴 *Free Breakfast* [M] *D to Callao.*

Hotel NH City

$$ | **HOTEL** | Topped with an eye-catching rooftop pool and patio, this enormous art deco showplace is a reminder of an

earlier era. **Pros:** central location; amazing views from the roof; transports you back to another era. **Cons:** area can be sketchy at night; pool area is cramped with few sun loungers; the gym could do with an upgrade. [$] *Rooms from: US$126* ✉ *Bolívar 160, Centro* ☎ *11/4121–6464* 🌐 *www.nh-hotels.com/hotel/nh-buenos-aires-city* 🛏 *369 rooms* 🍴 *Free Breakfast* [M] *A to Perú, E to Bolívar.*

Libertador

$$ | **HOTEL** | A makeover of this well-placed former Sheraton property on bustling Avenida Córdoba makes for a solid stay for both business travelers and city visitors. **Pros:** great view from some rooms; recently updated premises; central location. **Cons:** area is quiet at night; best to take taxis in and out in the evening; views not great from lower floors. [$] *Rooms from: US$130* ✉ *Córdoba 690, Centro* ☎ *11/4321–0000* 🌐 *www.libertadorhotels.com* 🛏 *200 rooms* [M] *B to Florida.*

🍸 Nightlife

BARS

La Cigale

LIVE MUSIC | Take advantage of happy hour until 10 pm at La Cigale's curvaceously seductive first-floor bar, which leads to the street-side balcony and smokers' corner. Another flight of stairs winds up to the stage, ready and waiting for local indie, jazz, and acoustic bands any night of the week. ✉ *25 de Mayo 597, Centro* ☎ *11/4893–2332* 🌐 *www.lacigalebar.wixsite.com/microcentro* [M] *B to L.N. Alem.*

★ Florería Atlántico

COCKTAIL LOUNGES | A flower shop and wine store combined with a whole lot of bar, this hip basement watering hole opened in 2013, and quickly becoming a fixture on Retiro's growing scene before rising to regular features on the World's 50 Best Bars list. The cocktail menu draws inspiration from Argentina's immigrant history (the Italians, Spaniards, English, and French have all played their part). Join the cool crowd and kick back with a Vinedo Italiano Spritz created by bartender and owner Tato Giovannoni. ✉ *Arroyo 872, Centro* ☎ *11/4313–6093* 🌐 *www.floreriaatlantico.com.ar* [M] *C to Retiro.*

DANCE CLUBS

Bahrein

DANCE CLUBS | This sheik—er, *chic* and stylish—party palace is located in a former bank, and the Funky Room is where beautiful, tightly clothed youth groove to pop, rock, and funk, while the basement Excess Room has electronic beats and dizzying wall visuals. For a more sophisticated dinner-before-dancing vibe, head upstairs to the Yellow Room. This is a great spot to catch local DJs, though there are also big nights with international artists. ✉ *Lavalle 345, Centro* ☎ *11/4315–2403* 🌐 *www.bahreinba.com* [M] *B to Alem.*

Cocoliche

DANCE CLUBS | This happening spot enjoys cult status in both the straight and gay communities. Upstairs is a diverse art gallery big on young locals; downstairs, underground house and techno drives one of the city's darkest dance floors, while DJs with huge followings are frequently on rotation. ✉ *Rivadavia 878, Centro* ☎ *11/6566–3418* [M] *A to Piedras.*

GAY AND LESBIAN

Contramano

BARS | This was a pioneering gay disco when it opened in 1984, but—like its clientele—Contramano has grown up. Today it operates more as a small, laid-back bar with an older, male-only clientele. Occasionally there's live music and male strippers. ✉ *Rodríguez Peña 1082, Centro* ☎ *11/3279–6304* [M] *D to Callao.*

LIVE MUSIC
ND Teatro
LIVE MUSIC | This spacious theater and cultural space mainly showcases midlevel local bands, showmen, and comedians, with a few big Argentine names thrown in for good measure. Get tickets at the box office (open Monday–Saturday, from noon to 8) or through Ticketek (⊕ www.ticketek.com.ar). ⊠ Paraguay 918, Centro ☎ 11/4328–2888 ⊕ www.ndteatro.com.ar Ⓜ C to San Martín.

TANGO
El Beso
DANCE CLUBS | The standard of dancing is usually high at this club, which belongs to La Academia del Tango Milonguero, one of the city's best tango schools. Beginners should consult the online schedule for classes. ⊠ Riobamba 416, Congreso ☎ 11/5833–2338 ⊕ www.elbeso.com.ar Ⓜ B to Callao.

Shopping

JEWELRY AND ACCESSORIES
Plata Nativa
JEWELRY & WATCHES | Tucked into an arcade, this tiny shop is filled with delights for both boho chicks and collectors of singular ethnic jewelry. Complex, chunky necklaces with turquoise, amber, and malachite—all based on original Araucanian (ethnic Argentine) pieces—and Mapuche-style silver earrings and brooches are some of the offerings. Happy customers include Sharon Stone, Pedro Almodóvar, and the Textile Museum in Washington, D.C. ⊠ Galería del Sol, Shop 41, Florida 860, Centro ☎ 11/4312–1398 ⊕ www.platanativa.com Ⓜ C to San Martín.

SHOES, HANDBAGS, AND LEATHER GOODS
Carpincho
LEATHER GOODS | As its name suggests, this spot specializes in supersoft, stippled *carpincho* leather from the capybara—the world's largest rodent, native to Argentina. Gloves (which also come in more conventional kidskin) are the main attraction, and there's a wide variety of lengths and colors to choose from. ⊠ Esmeralda 775, Centro ☎ 11/4322–9919 Ⓜ C to Lavalle.

Casa López
MIXED CLOTHING | Don't let the drab storefront put you off: you're as likely to find a trouser suit in floral-print suede as a staid handbag for grandma at this two-part shopping spot. The right-hand store (No. 658) has totes in chestnut- and chocolate-color leather, as well as classic jackets. More unusual fare—including fur sacks with wool fringe, black cowhide baguettes, and tangerine purses—are sold next door at No. 640. ⊠ Marcelo T. de Alvear 640 and 658, Centro ☎ 11/4311–3044 ⊕ www.casalopez.com.ar Ⓜ C to San Martín.

Puerto Madero

The neighborhood's upswing has even extended to the 865-acre Reserva Ecológica, a nature preserve built on land reclaimed from the river using rubble from major construction projects in the 1970s and '80s.

Sights

Colección de Arte Amalia Lacroze de Fortabat
ART GALLERY | The late Amalia Fortabat was a cement heiress, so it's not surprising that the building containing her private art collection is made mostly of concrete. It was completed in 2003, but after-effects from Argentina's 2001–02 financial crisis delayed its opening until 2008. Amalita (as she was known locally) was closely involved in the design, and her personal touch continues into the collection, which includes several portraits

of her—a prized Warhol among them—and many works by her granddaughter, Amalia Amoedo. In general, more money than taste seems to have gone into the project. The highlights are lesser works by big names both local (Berni, Xul Solar, Pettoruti) and international (Brueghel, Dalí, Picasso), hung with little aplomb or explanation in a huge basement gallery that echoes like a high-school gym. The side gallery given over to Carlos Alonso's and Juan Carlos Castagnino's figurative work is a step in the right direction, however, and so are the luminous paintings by Soldi in the glass-walled upper gallery. They're rivaled by the view over the docks below—time your visit to end at sunset when pinks and oranges light the redbrick buildings opposite. The views from the dockside café are also excellent. ⊠ *Olga Cossettini 141, Puerto Madero* ☎ *11/4310–6600* ⊕ *www.coleccionfort-abat.org.ar* ⊠ *400 pesos* ⊗ *Closed Mon.–Wed.* Ⓜ *B to L.N. Alem (10 blocks away).*

Buque Museo Fragata A.R.A. Presidente Sarmiento (*President Sarmiento Frigate Museum*)
MILITARY SIGHT | The navy commissioned this frigate from England in 1898, and meant for it to be used as an open-sea training vessel. The 280-foot boat used up to 33 sails and carried more than 300 crew members. The beautifully restored cabins include surprisingly luxurious officers' quarters with parquet floors, wood paneling, and leather armchairs; cadets had to make do with hammocks. ⊠ *Dique 3, Alicia M. de Justo 980, Puerto Madero* ☎ *11/4334–9386* ⊕ *www.argen-tina.gob.ar/armada/museos/buque-presi-dente-sarmiento* ⊠ *Free (reserve ahead)* ⊗ *Closed Sun.–Wed.* Ⓜ *B to L.N. Alem (9 blocks away).*

★ **Puente de la Mujer** (*Bridge of the Woman*)
BRIDGE | Tango dancers inspired the sweeping asymmetrical lines of Valencian architect Santiago Calatrava's design for the pedestrian-only Bridge of the Woman. Puerto Madero's street names pay homage to famous Argentine women, hence the bridge's name. (Ironically its most visible part—a soaring 128-foot arm—represents the man of a couple in mid-tango.) The $6-million structure was made in Spain and paid for by local businessmen Alberto L. González, one of the brains behind Puerto Madero's redevelopment; he was also for building the Hilton Hotel here. Twenty engines rotate the bridge to allow ships to pass through. ⊠ *Dique 3, between Pierina Dealessi and Manuela Gorriti, Puerto Madero* Ⓜ *A to Plaza de Mayo, B to L.N. Alem, D to Catedral, E to Bolívar (9 to 13 blocks away).*

Reserva Ecológica
NATURE PRESERVE | Built over a landfill, the 865-acre Ecological Reserve is home to more than 500 species of birds and a variety of flora and fauna. On weekends, thousands of porteños vie for a spot on the grass, so come midweek if you want to bird-watch, sunbathe, or use the jogging and cycling tracks in peace. A monthly guided "Walking under the Full Moon" tour in Spanish begins at 7:30 pm April through October and at 8:30 pm November through March. Even if you don't speak Spanish it's still a great way to get back to nature at night; otherwise avoid the area after sunset. (There are guided daytime visits in Spanish on weekends at 10:30 and 3:30.) The main entrance and visitor center is across from the traffic circle where Avenida Tristán Achával Rodríguez intersects with Avenida Elvira Rawson de Dellepiane, a short walk from the south end of Puerto Madero; you can also enter and leave the reserve at its northern end, across from the intersection of Mariquita Sánchez de Thompson and Avenida Hernán M. Giralt. ⊠ *Av. Tristán Achával Rodríguez 1550, Puerto Madero* ☎ *11/4315–4129, 11/4893–1853 tours* ⊕ *www.buenosaires. gob.ar/ciudadverde/espaciosverdes/res-ervaecologica* ⊠ *Free* ⊗ *Closed Mon.*

The Puente de la Mujer, or the Women's Bridge, is a rotating footbridge that represents the movements of tango.

 Restaurants

Cabaña Las Lilas

$$$ | **STEAKHOUSE** | The beef and pork are sourced from the owner's own ranch at this well-known—and expensive—steak house that attracts a crowd of mostly international travelers to the docklands. Service is impeccable, as are the steaks; of note are the *ojo de bife* and *bife de lomo*, aka the rib eye and the sirloin. **Known for:** impeccable service; fantastic wine list; tender beef. $ *Average main: pesos2200* ✉ *A.M. de Justo 516, at Corrientes, Puerto Madero* ☎ *11/4313–1336* ⊕ *www.restaurantlaslilas.com.ar* Ⓜ *B to L.N. Alem.*

★ Chila

$$$$ | **ARGENTINE** | With a prime harborside location and a carefully curated tasting menu that delves into Argentina's abundant pantry, Chila is worth the splurge. Book a table on the water and allow the exemplary team (helmed by bright young culinary star, Pedro Bargero), to work its magic. **Known for:** great wine list; upscale service; fine-dining tasting menu. $ *Average main: pesos12000* ✉ *Av. Alicia Moreau de Justo 1160, Puerto Madero* ☎ *11/4343–6067* ⊕ *www.chilaweb.com. ar* ☉ *Closed Sun. and Mon.* Ⓜ *B to L.N. Alem (10 blocks).*

Hotels

★ Faena Hotel

$$$$ | **HOTEL** | Argentiné fashion impresario Alan Faena and famed French architect Philippe Starck have created a universe unto itself with this hotel: rooms are feng-shui perfect, with rich reds and crisp whites, sporting velvet curtains and blinds opening electronically to river or city views. **Pros:** quite simply, one of the most dramatic hotels on the planet; luxury abounds; celebrity magnet. **Cons:** extremely pricey to eat in; bar clientele can be tacky; an "are you cool enough?" vibe is ever-present. $ *Rooms from: US$469* ✉ *Martha Salotti 445,*

*Puerto Madero ☎ 11/4010–9000 ⊕ www.
faena.com ⇥ 110 rooms, 16 suites
⦿ Free Breakfast Ⓜ D to Catedral, then a
20-min walk.*

Hotel Madero

$$ | HOTEL | A favorite for visiting British
rock stars, television personalities, and
fashion photographers, this slick hotel
is within walking distance of downtown as well as the riverside ecological
reserve. **Pros:** the lobby bar attracts a
cool after-office crowd; see-and-be-seen
clientele; central location. **Cons:** lack-
ing in-room facilities such as a kettle;
subway far away; the gym and pool are
a bit cramped. **$** *Rooms from: US$160
✉ Rosario Vera Peñaloza 360, Puerto
Madero ☎ 11/5776–7777 ⊕ www.hotel-
madero.com ⇥ 169 rooms, 28 suites
⦿ Free Breakfast Ⓜ C to Independencia,
13 blocks.*

 Nightlife

TANGO

Rojo Tango

DANCE CLUBS | Five-star food, musicians,
choreography, and glamour: you wouldn't
expect anything less from the Faena
Hotel + Universe. Crimson velvet and
gold trim line everything from the walls
to the menu at El Cabaret, and tables
often hold celebs both local and global.
The implausibly good-looking troupe
puts on a tango-through-the-ages show,
which includes jazz-tango, semi-naked
numbers, and even the tango version of
Roxanne from *Moulin Rouge*. It's worth
the splurge. *✉ Martha Salotti 445, Puerto
Madero ☎ 11/4952–4111 ⊕ www.rojotan-
go.com Ⓜ D to Catedral.*

San Telmo

"The south also exists," quip residents
of the bohemian neighborhoods of San
Telmo and La Boca, which historically
played second fiddle to posher northern
barrios. No longer is this the case. Top
designers have boutiques here, there's
a great food scene, an art district is burgeoning, and property prices are soaring.
The south is also a hotbed for the city's
tango revival, appropriate given that the
dance was born in these quarters.

San Telmo, Buenos Aires' first suburb,
was originally inhabited by sailors, and
takes its name from their wandering
patron saint. All the same, the mariners'
main preoccupations were clearly less
than spiritual, and San Telmo became
famous for its brothels.

That didn't stop the area's first experience of gentrification: wealthy local
families built ornate homes here in the
early 19th century, but ran for Recoleta
when a yellow-fever epidemic struck in
1871. Newly arrived immigrants crammed
into their abandoned mansions, known
as *conventillos* (tenement houses). Today
these same houses are fought over by
foreign buyers dying to ride the wave of
urban renewal—the *reciclaje* (recycling),
as porteños call it—that's sweeping the
area and transforming San Telmo into
Buenos Aires' hippest neighborhood.

Although San Telmo does have its share
of sights, the barrio itself is the big attraction. Simply watching the world go by as
you linger over coffee is one quintessen-
tial experience. Soaking up some history
by wandering down cobbled streets
edged with Italianate townhouses is
another. You can get closer to the past at
two small museums, or even take a piece
of it home from the shops and stands
selling antiques and curios. However,
there's plenty of contemporary culture on
offer in the neighborhood's art museums,
cutting-edge galleries, and bars.

Sights

★ El Zanjón de Granados
HISTORIC HOME | All of Buenos Aires' history is packed into this unusual house. The street it's on was once a small river—the *zanjón*, or gorge, of the property's name—where the first, unsuccessful attempt to found Buenos Aires took place in 1536. When the property's current owner decided to develop it, he discovered all sorts of things below: pottery and cutlery, the foundations of past constructions, and a 500-foot network of tunnels that has taken over 25 years to excavate. With the help of historians and architects, they've now been restored, and the entire site has been transformed into a private museum that's valuable urban archeology. Excellent 50-minute-long guided tours in English Monday through Friday and Sunday at 12 pm and 4 pm take you through low-lighted sections of the tunnels. Expect few visitors and plenty of atmosphere on weekdays; you can also visit next-door property Casa Mínima. ⊠ *Defensa 755, San Telmo* 🕾 *11/4361–3002* ⊕ *www.elzanjon.com.ar* 🖃 *Guided tours 2,600 pesos (1 hr, weekdays only); 200 pesos (30 min, Sun. only)* 🕙 *Closed Sat.* Ⓜ *C or E to Independencia.*

★ Feria de San Pedro Telmo
MARKET | Plaza Dorrego is the heart of the Feria de San Pedro Telmo—an open-air market that stretches for more than a kilometer (0.6 mile) along Calle Defensa each Sunday. Thrust your way through the crowds to pick through antiques and curios of varying vintages as well as tango memorabilia, or watch professional tango dancers perform on the surrounding cobbled streets. The unofficial "stalls" (often just a cloth on the ground) of young craftspeople stretch several blocks up Defensa, away from the market proper. As it gets dark, the square turns into a milonga, where quick-stepping locals show you how it's done. ⊠ *Plaza Dorrego, Humberto I and Defensa, San Telmo* 🕙 *Closed Mon.–Sat.* Ⓜ *C to San Juan.*

Museo de Arte Contemporáneo de Buenos Aires
ART MUSEUM | Geometric abstraction is the guiding principle for both the collection and the construction of Buenos Aires' contemporary arts museum. Sharply sloped walkways connect four floors of concrete-walled galleries, creating an austere backdrop for the bright lines and shapes of local financier Aldo Rubin's private collection. Regularly changing exhibitions may include pieces by contemporary local stars like Pablo Siquier and Guillermo Kuitca. ⊠ *Av. San Juan 328, San Telmo* 🕾 *11/5263–9988* ⊕ *www.museomacba.org* 🖃 *400 pesos, Wed. half price* 🕙 *Closed Tues.* Ⓜ *C to San Juan.*

Museo de Arte Moderno de Buenos Aires (MAMBA) (*Museum of Modern Art of Buenos Aires*)
ART MUSEUM | Some 7,000 contemporary artworks make up the permanent collection at this block-long museum. Formerly the site of a tobacco company, the MAMBA retains its original exposed-brick facade and fabulous wooden doors with wrought-iron fixtures. Inside, galleries showcasing a carefully curated selection of paintings, sculptures, and new media are complemented by large temporary exhibitions of local or Latin American works as well as smaller installations. Highlights include the unusual portraits of superstar collective Grupo Mondongo, who eschew paint in favor of materials like crackers, sliced ham, and chewing gum. ⊠ *Av. San Juan 350, San Telmo* 🕾 *11/4361–6919* ⊕ *www.buenosaires. gob.ar/museoartemoderno* 🖃 *50 pesos, Wed. free* 🕙 *Closed Tues.* Ⓜ *C to San Juan.*

Museo Histórico Nacional
HISTORY MUSEUM | What better place for the National History Museum than overlooking the spot where the city was supposedly founded? Once owned by entrepreneur and horticulturalist Gregorio Lezama, the beautiful chestnut-and-white

The San Telmo flea market in Plaza Dorrego is the perfect Sunday outing.

Italianate mansion that houses it also did duty as a quarantine station during the San Telmo cholera and yellow-fever epidemics before it became a museum in 1922. Personal possessions and thoughtful explanations (in Spanish) chronicle the rise and fall of Argentina's liberator José de San Martín. Other galleries celebrate the heroes of independence and foreign forces' unsuccessful attempts to invade Argentina. ⊠ *Calle Defensa 1600, San Telmo* ☎ *11/4300–7540* ⊕ *museohis-toriconacional.cultura.gob.ar* ✉ *Free* ⊙ *Closed Mon.–Tues.* Ⓜ *C to Constitución (10 blocks).*

Pasaje Defensa

STORE/MALL | Wandering through this well-preserved house affords a glimpse of life in San Telmo's golden era. Behind an elegant but narrow stone facade, the building extends deep into the block, around a series of internal courtyards. This type of elongated construction—known as a *casa chorizo* or "sausage house"—is typical of San Telmo. Once the private residence of the well-to-do

Ezeiza family, it became a *conventillo* (tenement), but is now a picturesque spot for antiques and curio shopping. ⊠ *Defensa 1179, San Telmo* Ⓜ *C to San Juan.*

Plaza Dorrego

PLAZA/SQUARE | During the week a handful of craftspeople and a few scruffy pigeons are the only ones enjoying the shade from the stately trees in the city's second-oldest square. Sunday couldn't be more different: scores of stalls selling antiques and collectibles move in to form the Feria de San Pedro Telmo (San Pedro Telmo Fair). Tango dancers take to the cobbles come late afternoon, as do hundreds of shoppers (mostly tourists) browsing the tango memorabilia, antique silver, brass, crystal, and Argentine curios. Note that prices are high at stalls on the square and astronomical in the shops surrounding it.

More affordable offerings—mostly handicrafts and local artists' work—are on the ever-growing web of stalls along Calle Defensa.

Be sure to look up as you wander Plaza Dorrego, as the surrounding architecture provides an overview of the influences—Spanish colonial, French classical, and ornate Italian masonry—that shaped the city in the 19th and early 20th centuries.

⚠ **Pickpockets work as hard as stall owners on Sundays, so keep a firm hold on bags and purses or—wiser still—leave them at home.** ✉ *Defensa and Humberto I, San Telmo* [M] *C to San Juan.*

🍴 Restaurants

Brasserie Petanque

$$ | **BRASSERIE** | One of the few classic French brasseries in Buenos Aires, Petanque is a place to enjoy hearty French fare accompanied by local wines. The ambience is lively, with marble-topped tables so close to each other that you may find yourself participating in neighboring conversations, though service can be snooty. **Known for:** quality wine list; lunchtime specials; bistro fare. [$] *Average main: pesos1500* ✉ *Defensa 596, at Mexico, San Telmo* ☎ *11/4342–7930* 🌐 *www.brasseriepetanque.com* ⏲ *Closed Mon.–Wed.* [M] *E to Bolivar.*

Café San Juan La Cantina

$$ | **ARGENTINE** | Its façade leads into tiny vermouth bar but the back is a huge dining room, where tattooed celebrity chef Lele Cristobal prepares tasty dishes with Spanish and Italian flavors such as lamb meatballs with chickpea mash and ossobuco stew. Start an evening with a glass of the house aperitivo—vermouth comes on tap—with soda at the bar with just eight stools, then move onto the main event for a buzzy evening. **Known for:** hearty fare; buzzy ambience; celebrity chef. [$] *Average main: pesos1600* ✉ *Chile 474, San Telmo* ☎ *11/4300–9344* ⏲ *Closed Mon.*

Desnivel

$ | **STEAKHOUSE** | **FAMILY** | Don't expect any frills here, just great steaks, and side dishes such as the *papas fritas provenzal,* golden french fries tossed in fresh parsley and garlic. Take a table in the cavernous dining room, or grab something to go—steak sandwiches and empanadas fly out the door as fast as they can make them. **Known for:** large portions; cheap and cheerful; casual ambience. [$] *Average main: pesos900* ✉ *Defensa 855, at Giuffra, San Telmo* ☎ *11/4300–9081* 💳 *No credit cards* ⏲ *No lunch Mon.* [M] *E to Independencia.*

🛏 Hotels

Cassa Lepage Art Hotel

$$ | **HOTEL** | A cozy boutique hotel with 22 rooms located on the historical cusp of San Telmo, Cassa Lepage uniquely brings together art and history under its roof, given that it houses its own archeology museum and art gallery featuring contemporary Argentine artists. **Pros:** in the city's historical heart; unique in-house archeology museum; walking distance to San Telmo's sights. **Cons:** street-facing rooms can be noisy; parking isn't free; busy area weekdays, very quiet on weekends. [$] *Rooms from: US$120* ✉ *Bolívar 373, Montserrat* ☎ *11/5352–6999* 🌐 *www.cassalepage.com* 🛏 *22 rooms* 🍴 *Free Breakfast* [M] *E to Belgrano.*

🍸 Nightlife

BARS

★ **Bar Británico**

BARS | Opened in 1928, this traditional corner bar opposite Parque Lezama is an iconic spot. Day and night it's full of characters who engage in passionate discussions or simply watch the world unfold through the oversized windows. Imbued with nostalgia, Bar Británico has a cinematic appeal—which may explain why it has appeared in movies like *The*

Motorcycle Diaries and Francis Ford Coppola's *Tetro*. ✉ *Brasil 399, at Defensa, San Telmo* ☎ *11/4361–2107* Ⓜ *C to San Juan.*

Doppelgänger
COCKTAIL LOUNGES | With a list of 100 cocktails and an excellent menu to match, this corner bar on the edge of San Telmo is a hidden gem. The fancy glassware and quotations in the menu show that the "double" concept has been thought through down to the finest details. Happy hour runs from 7 to 9. ✉ *Av. Juan de Garay 500, San Telmo* ☎ *11/4300–0201* ⊕ *www.doppelganger.com.ar* Ⓜ *C to San Juan.*

LIVE MUSIC
Centro Cultural Torquato Tasso
DANCE CLUBS | Classic trios and quartets share the stage with young musicians performing hip tango and folk sets here. There are also milongas on weekends. ✉ *Defensa 1575, Montserrat* ☎ *11/4307–6506* Ⓜ *C to San Juan.*

La Trastienda
LIVE MUSIC | A San Telmo institution, this cabaret-style club is one of Buenos Aires' most popular venues, so grab a table and enjoy an intimate performance for 900. La Trastienda is the place to catch electrotango or new tango groups, although it takes pains to promote other genres as well. Check out national pop and rock legends, as well as local rock, reggae, and funk. ✉ *Balcarce 460, Montserrat* ☎ *11/4342–5162* ⊕ *www.latrastienda. com* Ⓜ *A to Bolivar.*

TANGO
Buenos Ayres Club
DANCE CLUBS | Rousing live orchestras keep even nondancers entertained at the nontraditional *milongas* that are this club's hallmark. La Orquesta Típica el Afronte provides the music for Maldita Milonga (☎ *11/2189–7747*) on Sunday, Monday, and Wednesday, while El Toque Cimarron Salsa (☎ *11–15/5891–4421*)

takes charge on Thursday. Tuesday's Tango Queer (☎ *11–15/3252–6894* *www. tangoqueer.com*) draws both gay and straight dancers looking to escape the confines of more conservative dance floors; and Friday takes a different turn with Latin American music. ✉ *Perú 571, San Telmo* ☎ *11/4331–1518* Ⓜ *E to Belgrano.*

El Viejo Almacén
DANCE CLUBS | This place was founded by legendary tango singer Edmundo Rivero, though he wouldn't recognize the slick outfit his bar has become. Inside the colonial building a tireless troupe of dancers and musicians perform showy tango and folk numbers. ✉ *Independencia 299, at Balcarce, San Telmo* ☎ *11/4307–7388* ⊕ *www.viejoalmacen.com.ar* Ⓜ *C to Independencia.*

Shopping

ANTIQUES AND COLLECTIBLES
Gabriel del Campo Anticuario
ANTIQUES & COLLECTIBLES | Gabriel's good taste means 50-year-old Louis Vuitton trunks don't look out of place beside wooden church statues or scale-model ships with canvas sails. Ceramic rubber-glove molds, one of his specialties, are some of the more accessible conversation pieces. The flagship store takes up a sizable patch of the Plaza Dorrego shop front; there's a second shop at Libertad 1214 in Recoleta. ✉ *Bethlem 427, on Plaza Dorrego, San Telmo* ☎ *11/3319–4686* Ⓜ *C to San Juan (walk 6 blocks along Humberto I).*

Gil Antigüedades
ANTIQUES & COLLECTIBLES | Sequined flapper dresses, dashing white-linen suits, and creamy lace wedding veils are some of the items you might stumble across in this *casa chorizo*, a typical multiroom property that stretches back to the next block. Period accessories include Castilian hair combs and lacy fans that

beg you to bat your lashes from behind them. ✉ *Humberto I 412, San Telmo* ☎ *11/4361–5019* ⊕ *www.gilantiguedades. com.ar* ✿ *Closed Mon.* Ⓜ *C to San Juan (walk 6 blocks along Av. San Juan).*

GIFTS AND SOUVENIRS
Artepampa

CRAFTS | An artist-and-architect duo is behind these singular works, which are inspired by native Argentine art. They use an unusual papier-mâché technique to create boxes, frames, tapestries, and freestanding sculptures. The primitive-looking pieces, a vision of rich rusts and earthy browns, make highly original gifts. ✉ *Defensa 917, on Plaza Dorrego, San Telmo* ☎ *11/4362–6406* Ⓜ *C to San Juan.*

Juan Carlos Pallarols Orfebre

CRAFTS | Argentina's legendary *orefebre* (silversmith) has made pieces for a mile-long list of celebrities including Frank Sinatra, Sharon Stone, Antonio Banderas, Bill Clinton, Nelson Mandela, and the king and queen of Spain. A set of ornate silver-handled steak knives is the perfect memento of cow country, although it will set you back several grand. ✉ *Defensa 1039, San Telmo* ☎ *11/4300–6555* ⊕ *www.pallarols.com.ar* Ⓜ *C or E to Independencia (walk 6 blocks along Estados Unidos).*

★ Marcelo Toledo

CRAFTS | Sunlight and the smell of solder fill the rooms of this old San Telmo house, which doubles as a store and open workshop for celebrity silversmith Marcelo Toledo. A huge silver mosaic of Evita gives away who Toledo's main muse is: he has created replicas of her own jewelry (he is the only silversmith authorized by her estate to do so) as well as pieces inspired by her. Eva Duarte Perón isn't the only crowd-pleasing politician Toledo's been associated with: a local magnate commissioned cuff links as an inauguration gift for President Obama. He also designed a *mate* gourd especially for Prince William and his bride, the Duchess of Cambridge. ✉ *Humberto I 458, San Telmo* ☎ *11/4362–0841* ⊕ *www. marcelotoledo.net* ✿ *Closed Sat.* Ⓜ *C to San Juan (6 blocks away).*

JEWELRY AND ACCESSORIES
Abraxas

JEWELRY & WATCHES |"Yes" is pretty much guaranteed if you propose with one of the period engagement rings that dazzle in the window of this antique jeweler. If you're not planning on popping the question any time soon, surely you can find a home for a pair of art deco earrings with the tiniest of diamonds or a gossamer-fine bracelet? ✉ *Defensa 1092, San Telmo* ☎ *11/4362–7512* ⊕ *www. abraxasantiques.com* Ⓜ *C to San Juan (walk 6 blocks along Humberto I).*

La Boca

The waterfront near the iconic Caminito area may be the most unashamedly touristy part of town, but the neighborhood surrounding it is the most fiercely traditional. Cafés, pubs, and general stores that once catered to passing sailors (and now reel in vacationers) dot the partially renovated area. For high-brow hipsters, the gallery of the Fundación Proa is the main draw.

Two quite different colors have made La Boca famous internationally: the blue and gold of the Boca Juniors soccer team, whose massive home stadium is the barrio's unofficial hub. For many local soccer devotees, the towering Boca Juniors stadium makes La Boca the center of the known world.

Sights

Calle Museo Caminito

MARKET | Cobblestones, tango dancers, and haphazardly constructed, colorful *conventillos* have made Calle Museo

Caminito the darling of Buenos Aires' postcard manufacturers since this pedestrian street was created in 1959. Artists fill the block-long street with works depicting port life and the tango, said to have been born in La Boca. These days it's commercial, but it can make a fun outing if you embrace it. The name "Caminito" comes from a 1926 tango by Juan de Dios Filiberto. It was chosen by local artist Benito Quinquela Martín, who helped establish the street as an open-air museum.

Painters peddle their creations from stalls along Caminito. Quality varies considerably; focus on the mosaics set into the walls, such as Luis Perlotti's *Santos Vega*. Brightly colored scrollwork known as *fileteado* adorns many store fronts; another highlight here are the tango dancers. Expect to be canvassed aggressively by rival restaurant owners touting overpriced menus near the start of Caminito. ⊠ *Caminito between Av. Pedro de Mendoza (La Vuelta de Rocha promenade) and Gregorio Aráoz de Lamadrid, La Boca* 🎫 *Free*.

Fundación Proa

ART MUSEUM | This thoroughly modern art museum continues to nudge traditional La Boca into the present. Its facade alone reads like a manifesto of local urban renewal: part of the original 19th-century Italianate house-front has been cut away and huge plate-glass windows accented by unfinished steel stand alongside it. The space behind them now includes three adjacent properties. The luminous main gallery retains the building's original Corinthian-style steel columns, artfully rusted, but has sparkling white walls and polished concrete floors. With every flight of stairs you climb, views out over the harbor and cast-iron bridges get better. On the roof, an airy café serves salads, sandwiches, and cocktails. Grab one of the outdoor sofas around sunset and your photos will rival the work below. English

versions of all exhibition information are available. The museum also runs guided tours in English, with two days' notice. ⊠ *Av. Pedro de Mendoza 1929, La Boca* 🕾 *11/4104-1000* ⊕ *www.proa.org* 🎫 *150 pesos* 🕑 *Closed Mon.–Wed.*

Museo de la Pasión Boquense

SPORTS VENUE | **FAMILY** | Inside Estadio Boca Juniors (aka La Bombonera or "the candy box"), this modern, two-floor museum is heaven for *fútbol* fans. It chronicles Boca's rise from a neighborhood club in 1905 to its current position as one of the best teams in the world. Among the innovative exhibits is a giant soccer ball that plays 360-degree footage of an adrenaline-fueled match, recreating all the excitement (and the screaming) for those too faint-hearted to attend the real thing. A huge mural of the late Maradona (the club's most revered player), a hall of fame, jerseys, and trophies complete the circuit. For the full-blown experience, buy a combo ticket that includes museum entry plus an extensive tour of the beloved stadium. Lighthearted exhibits take you all over the stands as well as to press boxes, locker rooms, underground tunnels, and the emerald grass of the field itself. Everything you need to Boca up your life—from official team shirts to school folders—is available in the on-site gift store (shops outside La Bombonera sell cheaper copies). ⊠ *Brandsen 805, La Boca* 🕾 *11/4362-1100* ⊕ *www.museoboquense.com* 🎫 *800 pesos*.

🍴 Restaurants

Don Carlos

$$ | **ARGENTINE** | With a prime location right in front of the Boca Juniors stadium, this bodegón is an institution not only for soccer fans but for the likes of movie director Francis Ford Coppola and chef Francis Mallmann. Owner Carlitos Zinola basically chooses your Italo-Argentine menu for you, which could be steak, pasta, tortilla, pascualina tart, or a

Did You Know?

Graffiti here can be political, whimsical, inspirational, or controversial, but it's technically always illegal. Popular targets like the Congreso building now sport graffiti-resistant paint for quick cleanup.

La Boca is well known as a colorful and lively neighborhood in Buenos Aires.

combination of them all. **Known for:** daily menu; located opposite Boca Juniors stadium; traditional dining spot. $ *Average main: pesos1700* ✉ *Brandsen 699, La Boca* ☎ *11/4362–2433* ⊘ *Closed Sun. and Mon.*

Recoleta

Recoleta wasn't always synonymous with elegance. Colonists, including city founder Juan de Garay, farmed here. So did the Franciscan Recoleto friars, whose 1700s settlement inspired the district's name. Their church, the Basílica del Pilar, was almost on the riverbank then: tanneries grew up around it, and Recoleta became famous for its *pulperías* (taverns) and brothels. Everything changed, though, with the 1871 outbreak of yellow fever in the south of the city.

The elite swarmed to Recoleta, building the *palacios* and stately Parisian-style apartment buildings that are now the neighborhood's trademark. They also laid the foundations for Recoleta's concentration of intellectual and cultural activity: the Biblioteca Nacional (National Library), a plethora of top-notch galleries, and three publicly run art museums are based here. Combine all of that with Recoleta's exclusive boutiques and its beautiful parks and squares—many filled with posh pooches and their walkers—and sightseeing becomes a visual feast. An unofficial subdistrict, Barrio Norte, is one step north of Recoleta proper and one small step down the social ladder. Shopping is the draw in Barrio Norte: local chains, sportswear flagships, and mini-malls of vintage clothing and clubwear line Avenida Santa Fe between 9 de Julio and Puerreydón.

Sights

Basílica de Nuestra Señora del Pilar
RELIGIOUS BUILDING | This basilica beside the famous Cementerio de la Recoleta is where Buenos Aires' elite families hold

weddings and other ceremonies. Built by the Recoleto friars in 1732, it is a national treasure for its six German baroque–style altars. The central one is overlaid with Peruvian engraved silver; another, sent by Spain's King Carlos III, contains relics. The basilica's cloisters house the **Museo de los Claustros del Pilar**, a small museum that displays religious artifacts as well as pictures and photographs documenting Recoleta's evolution. There are excellent views of the cemetery from upstairs windows. ⊠ *Junín 1898, Recoleta* ☎ *11/4806–2209* ⊕ *www.basilicadelpilar. org.ar* ◷ *Museum closed Sun.* Ⓜ *H to Las Heras, 6 blocks.*

★ Cementerio de la Recoleta

CEMETERY | The ominous gates and labyrinthine paths of the city's oldest cemetery, founded in 1822, is the final resting place for the nation's most illustrious figures. Covering 13½ acres and said to be the most expensive real estate in town, the cemetery has more than 6,400 elaborate vaulted tombs and majestic mausoleums, 70 of which have been declared historic monuments. Architectural styles run the gamut from chapels to Greek temples to pyramids to art deco and miniature mansions. The biggest name is Eva Duarte de Perón, after 17 years of posthumous wandering, found in the Duarte family vault. Other highlights include the tombs of landowner Dorrego Ortíz Basualdo, who resides in Recoleta's most monumental sepulcher, complete with chandelier, and Rufina Cambaceres, the girl who died twice. Entombed on her 19th birthday in 1902, she awoke inside her casket and clawed the top open, dying of a heart attack before she could be rescued. The names of many key players in Argentina's history are chiseled over other sumptuous mausoleums: Alvear, Quintana, Sáenz Peña, Lavalle, Sarmiento. There are guides for hire at the entrance or the administrative office can provide a free photocopied map if you wish to wander at your own pace.

On weekends catch the open-air market known as La Feria de Artesanos de Plaza Francia outside the cemetery. It's usually teeming with shoppers eager to stock up on quality crafts. ⊠ *Junín 1760, Recoleta* ☎ *11/4803–1594* ⊕ *turismo.buenosaires. gob.ar/en/otros-establecimientos/recoleta-cemetery* Ⓜ *H to Las Heras, 6 blocks.*

Centro Cultural Recoleta

ARTS CENTER | FAMILY | Art exhibitions, concerts, fringe theater performances, and workshops are some of the offerings at this cultural center; one must-visit is Fuerza Bruta, a fantastic water and acrobatics collective that pops up in summer and for one-off shows. The rambling building it occupies was converted from the cloister patios of the Franciscan monks. ⊠ *Junín 1930, Recoleta* ☎ *11/4803–1040* ⊕ *www.centroculturalrecoleta.org* ◷ *Closed Mon.* Ⓜ *H to Las Heras, 8 blocks.*

Floralis Genérica

PUBLIC ART | The gleaming steel and aluminum petals of this giant flower look very space age, perhaps because they were commissioned from the Lockheed airplane factory by architect Eduardo Catalano, who designed and paid for the monument. The 66-foot-high structure opens at dawn and closes at dusk, when the setting sun turns its mirrored surfaces a glowing pink. The flower stands in the Plaza Naciones Unidas (behind El Museo Nacional de Bellas Artes over Avenida Figueroa Alcorta). ⊠ *Plaza Naciones Unidas at Av. Figueroa Alcorta and J.A. Biblioni, Recoleta* ⊕ *www. turismo.buenosaires.gob.ar/en/otros-establecimientos/floralis-genérica* Ⓜ *H to Facultad de Derecho.*

Museo Nacional de Arte Decorativo

(*National Museum of Decorative Art*)
ART MUSEUM | The harmonious, French neoclassical mansion that houses the National Museum of Decorative Art is as much a reason to visit as the period furnishings, porcelain, and silver

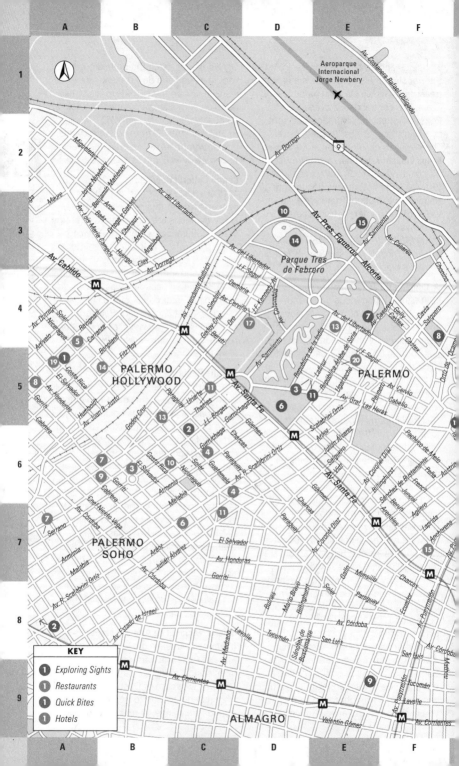

Recoleta, Almagro, and Palermo

Río de La Plata

Dársena F

0   2,000 ft
0   500 m

RECOLETA

RETIRO

Av. Santa Fe

Av. Corrientes   Obelisco

Sights ▼

1 Basilica de Nuestra Señora del Pilar......... **H6**
2 Cementerio de la Chacarita **A8**
3 Cementerio de la Recoleta **H6**
4 Centro Cultural Recoleta **H6**
5 Floralis Genérica........ **H5**
6 Jardín Botánico Carlos Thays **D5**
7 Jardín Japonés **E4**
8 MALBA **F4**
9 Museo Casa Carlos Gardel............. **E9**
10 Museo de Artes Plásticas Eduardo Sívori **D3**
11 Museo Evita **D5**
12 Museo Nacional de Arte Decorativo........ **G5**
13 Museo Nacional de Bellas Artes **H6**
14 Parque Tres de Febrero **D3**
15 Planetario Galileo Galilei............. **E3**

Restaurants ▼

1 Aramburu................ **H7**
2 Buller Brewing Company................. **H7**
3 Chori...................... **B6**
4 Don Julio................. **C6**
5 El Sanjuanino.............. **I6**
6 Gran Dabbang............ **C7**
7 Julia **A7**
8 La Biela **H6**
9 La Cabrera............... **B6**
10 La Parolaccia **G8**
11 Las Pizarras **C5**
12 Marti **I7**
13 Mishiguene.............. **E4**
14 Osaka **B5**
15 Oviedo.................... **F7**
16 Restó S.C.A. **H8**
17 Río Alba.................. **D4**
18 Roux...................... **G7**
19 Siamo nel Forno........ **A5**
20 Trattoria Olivetti.......... **E5**

Quick Bites ▼

1 Cuervo Café **A5**
2 El Preferido de Palermo................... **C6**
3 Museo Evita Restaurante **D5**

Hotels ▼

1 A Hotel **G7**
2 Algodon Mansion......... **I7**
3 Alvear Palace Hotel......**I6**
4 Duque Hotel Boutique & Spa **C6**
5 Fierro Hotel.............. **A4**
6 Four Seasons Hotel Buenos Aires..............**I7**
7 The Glu Hotel............ **B6**
8 Home Hotel Buenos Aires............ **A5**
9 Hotel Bel Air..............**I8**
10 Legado Mítico............**C6**
11 Magnolia Hotel Boutique **C7**
12 Mio Buenos Aires **H7**
13 Miravida Soho Hotel & Wine Bar....... **B5**
14 Palacio Duhau Park Hyatt Buenos Aires..............**I7**

The Cementerio de Recoleta is the final home for many of Argentina's important historical figures.

within it. Ornate wooden paneling in the Regency ballroom, the imposing Louis XIV red-and-black-marble dining room, and a lofty Renaissance-style great hall are some of the highlights in the only home of its kind open to the public here. There are excellent English descriptions of each room, and they include gossipy details about the original inhabitants, the well-to-do Errázuriz-Alvear family. The museum also contains some Chinese art. Guided tours include the Zubov Collection of miniatures from Imperial Russia. ✉ *Av. del Libertador 1902, Recoleta* ☎ *11/4801–8248* ⊕ *museoartedecorativo. cultura.gob.ar* 🖼 *100 pesos (suggested donation)* ⊘ *Closed Mon.* Ⓜ *H to Las Heras, 5 blocks.*

★ Museo Nacional de Bellas Artes

ART MUSEUM | The world's largest collection of Argentine art is contained in this neoclassical wine-color building, which once housed the city's waterworks. Here, you can see many lesser works by big-name European artists from the 12th through 20th centuries, and the MNBA also hosts high-profile temporary exhibitions on its refurbished second floor. The European collection and 19th-century Argentine works are on display in the 24 ground-floor galleries; highlights include Cándido López's panoramic battle scenes, which he painted with his left hand after losing his right arm in the 1870s during the War of the Triple Alliance. His work spearheaded contemporary primitive painting and is showcased in Gallery 23. A whole room (Gallery 8) is given over to European master Goya's dark, disturbing works. The room behind the entrance hall (Gallery 10) contains Rodin sculptures. The right wing includes paintings by Manet, Degas, Monet, Pissarro, Gaugin, and Toulouse-Lautrec. The large modern pavilion behind the museum also hosts excellent temporary exhibitions, often showcasing top local artists little known outside Argentina. Free one-hour guided visits in English are offered on Tuesday, Thursday, and Friday at 12:30, and Saturday at 2. ✉ *Av. del*

Libertador 1473, Recoleta ☏ 11/5288–9900 ⊕ www.bellasartes.gob.ar 🔲 Free. ⊗ Closed Mon. Ⓜ H to Las Heras, 7 blocks.

🍴 Restaurants

Aramburu

$$$$ | **ECLECTIC** | Tucked away down a cobbled alley is one of the most beautiful and romantic restaurants in the city. Night after night chef Gonzalo Aramburu turns out an exquisite 18-course tasting menu of seasonal dishes, each reinterpreted through the lens of what is here called *cocina vanguardia* , or cutting-edge cooking. **Known for:** fantastic wine list; intimate; fine dining. 💲*Average main: pesos12000*✉ Vicente López 1661, Recoleta ☏ 11/4811–1414 ⊕ www.arambururesto.com.ar ⊗ Closed Sun. and Mon. No lunch.

Buller Brewing Company

$ | **AMERICAN** | The city's first microbrewery is in a prime position opposite Recoleta Cemetery, and it's a prince among frogs in a saturated craft beer market. There are seven different styles of beer (the Porter is highly recommended), and you can have a sampler of the whole range. **Known for:** pub grub; happy hour; craft beer. 💲*Average main: pesos800*✉ Junín 1747, Recoleta ☏ 11/4806–0556 ⊕ www.bullerbrewingco.com Ⓜ H to Las Heras.

★ El Sanjuanino

$ | **ARGENTINE** | It may be cramped, crowded, and kitschy—and very warm in hot weather due to the roaring wood-fired ovens—but the empanadas are delicious and they serve the city's best *locro* (corn, squash, and meat stew) as well as delicious and iconic game dishes. Ignore the wine list and opt for the house *vino* served in pitchers, which is just as good and half the price. **Known for:** solid fare from the north; cheap and cheerful; laid-back ambience. 💲*Average main:*

pesos500 ✉ Posadas 1515, at Callao, Recoleta ☏ 11/4804–2909 ⊗ Closed Mon. Ⓜ C to Retiro.

La Biela

$ | **ARGENTINE** | A blast from the past, this traditional café is one of the best spots in Recoleta for people-watching and celebrity-spotting. For the most part, it's a place to linger over coffee and a pastry, or perhaps a savory sandwich at midday, but there's also a full menu of local specialties, and it's open until 2 am. **Known for:** teatime crowd; outdoor dining; old-school vibe. 💲*Average main: pesos1200* ✉ Quintana 600, at Junín, Recoleta ☏ 11/4804–0449 ⊕ www.labiela.com Ⓜ H to Las Heras.

La Parolaccia

$$ | **ITALIAN** | **FAMILY** | A family-run and family-friendly Italian *trattoria* of the sort you might find in any big city, La Parolaccia stands out for its excellent home-made pastas—particularly good are the hand-rolled fusilli. And don't overlook the three-course lunch specials, which can be a great deal. **Known for:** homemade pastas; friendly service; kids welcome. 💲*Average main: pesos1500* ✉ Riobamba 1046, Recoleta ☏ 11/4812–1053 ⊕ www.laparolaccia.com Ⓜ C to Congreso, B to Callao.

★ Marti

$$ | **VEGETARIAN** | Having made a name with award-winning fine dining establishment Tegui, which closed in 2021, chef-patron Germán Martitegui has taken a fresh approach with Marti. The discreetly signed entrance leads you to a stylish greenhouse complete with open-plan kitchen, where the team creates a delicious seasonal plant-led menu that's leading the veggie pack. **Known for:** veggie spot; excellent service; celebrity chef. 💲*Average main: pesos2000* ✉ Rodríguez Peña 1973, Recoleta ☏ 11/5848–7663 ⊕ www.marti.meitre.com ⊗ Closed Sun. Ⓜ C to Retiro.

The Museo des Bellas Artes holds the largest collection of Argentine art.

★ Oviedo

$$ | SEAFOOD | In a meat-centric city like Buenos Aires, excellently cooked seafood is a welcome change, and Oviedo turns out beautifully plated fillets of fish—don't miss the daily catch with pickled baby vegetables or the pristine shellfish. Top it all off with wine from one of the city's finest cellars–the pride and joy of owner Emilio Garip–and you're in for a memorable lunch or dinner. **Known for:** knowledgeable service; sophisticated ambience; great wine list. $ Average main: pesos2000 ⊠ Beruti 2602, at Ecuador, Recoleta ☎ 11/4821–3741 ⊕ www.oviedoresto.com.ar ⊘ No dinner Sun. Ⓜ D to Pueyrredón.

★ Restó SCA

$$ | ARGENTINE | A haunt for foodies who adore the creative, contemporary Argentine cuisine and beautiful presentation, there's nowhere better in the neighborhood for lunch or an atmospheric dinner. The star of the lineup is the roasted, stuffed whole quail with squash. **Known for:** low key; great wine list; romantic.

$ Average main: pesos1800 ⊠ Sociedad Central de Arquitectos, Montevideo 938, between M.T. Alvear and Paraguay, Recoleta ☎ 11/4816–6711 ⊘ Closed weekends. No dinner Mon.–Wed. Ⓜ D to Callao.

Roux

$$ | ARGENTINE | A cozy corner bistro, Roux is a fantastic spot for relaxed business lunches or special occasions. Try the Patagonian king crab ravioli or perfectly cooked venison steak, paired with recommendations from the sommelier. **Known for:** intimate setting; great wine list; great seafood. $ Average main: pesos1900 ⊠ Peña 2300, Recoleta ☎ 11/4805–6794 ⊕ www.rouxresto.com ⊘ Closed Sun. Ⓜ H to Las Heras.

Hotels

A Hotel

$ | B&B/INN | This lodging has an impressive ground-floor gallery where exhibits of paintings, photographs, and sculptures by acclaimed Argentine artists change monthly—you may run into art aficionados sipping wine and admiring the creations. **Pros:** its bohemian vibe will make you feel like you've joined an artists' colony; great location without the price tag; on-site gallery is fun. **Cons:** breakfast could be more exciting; some rooms need a makeover; hotel is a bit antiquated. $ *Rooms from: US$50* ⊠ *Azcuénaga 1268, Recoleta* ☎ *11/4821–4744* ⊕ *www.ahotel.com.ar* ⮂ *34 rooms* ⬩○⬩ *Free Breakfast* Ⓜ *D to Pueyrredón.*

Algodon Mansion

$$$$ | **HOTEL** | Every detail of this hotel, one of the ritziest properties in the city, makes it clear that your comfort is of the utmost importance. **Pros:** unparalleled service; luxe location; rooms come with a complimentary bottle of wine. **Cons:** pricey; terrace is small; not much buzz to the place. $ *Rooms from: US$486* ⊠ *Montevideo 1647, Recoleta* ☎ *11/3530–7777* ⊕ *www.algodonhotels.com/mansion* ⮂ *10 suites* ⬩○⬩ *Free Breakfast* Ⓜ *D to Callao.*

Alvear Palace Hotel

$$$$ | **HOTEL** | The standard-bearer for upscale sophistication since 1932, the Alvear Palace is undoubtedly the shining star of the city's hotel scene: scores of dignitaries, celebrities, and VIPs have passed through its doors over the years, and they keep coming back for the world-class service and refined atmosphere. **Pros:** in-house Alvear Grill serves fantastic steak; top-notch service; beautiful spa features a sauna and steam rooms. **Cons:** one of Argentina's most expensive hotels; some rooms could use a makeover; bathrooms are on the small side. $ *Rooms from: US$500* ⊠ *Av. Alvear 1891, Recoleta* ☎ *11/4804–7777, 800/448–8355 in U.S.* ⊕ *www.alvearpalace.com* ⮂ *191 rooms* ⬩○⬩ *No Meals* Ⓜ *H to Las Heras.*

★ Four Seasons Hotel Buenos Aires

$$$$ | **HOTEL** | One of the city's swankiest lodgings, the Four Seasons is a magnet for famous folk. **Pros:** all the class

you'd expect from this brand; wonderful eateries in Elena and Nuestro Secreto; swanky bar. **Cons:** room aesthetics can seem impersonal; the bar can seem too cool to hang out at; the pool is outdoors, so unusable in winter. $ *Rooms from: US$565* ⊠ *Posadas 1086, Recoleta* ☎ *11/4321–1200* ⊕ *www.fourseasons.com/buenosaires* ⮂ *165 rooms* ⬩○⬩ *No Meals* Ⓜ *C to Retiro.*

Hotel Bel Air

$$ | **HOTEL** | Given the frilly French-style facade, you could mistake the Bel Air for a neighborhood hotel somewhere in Paris. **Pros:** great location on one of the city's swankiest streets; attractive rooms; a legit "Paris of the South" hotel. **Cons:** hallways and common areas are cramped; basic aesthetics; the staff is easily distracted. $ *Rooms from: US$180* ⊠ *Arenales 1462, Recoleta* ☎ *11/4021–4000* ⊕ *www.hotelbelair.com.ar* ⮂ *77 rooms* ⬩○⬩ *Free Breakfast* Ⓜ *D to Tribunales.*

Mio Buenos Aires

$$ | **HOTEL** | The winemaking Catena family owns this luxurious boutique hotel, and all the rooms come stocked with wines straight from their own Mendoza vineyards. **Pros:** located on a picturesque Recoleta street; mixes rustic and contemporary design elements; open and airy feel. **Cons:** the pool is good for swimming lengths but shallow; dining in the basement is a bit glum; the ground-floor common areas feel elegant but somewhat somber. $ *Rooms from: US$218* ⊠ *Av. Pres. Manuel Quintana 465, Recoleta* ☎ *11/5295–8500* ⊕ *www.miobuenosaires.com* ⮂ *30 rooms* ⬩○⬩ *Free Breakfast* Ⓜ *Linea D to Callao.*

★ Palacio Duhau Park Hyatt Buenos Aires

$$$$ | **HOTEL** | This landmark hotel ups the ante for elegance in Buenos Aires—its two buildings, a restored 1930s-era mansion and a 17-story tower, are connected by an underground art gallery and an expansive, leafy garden that's among the city's most attractive outdoor

Buenos Aires RECOLETA

3

areas. **Pros:** understated splendor; two great restaurants; has the city's largest indoor pool. **Cons:** far from the subway; elevators are small; a long walk from one side of the hotel to the other. $ *Rooms from: US$620* ✉ *Av. Alvear 1661, Recoleta* ☎ *11/5171–1234* 🌐 *www.hyatt.com/en-US/hotel/argentina/palacio-duhau-park-hyatt-buenos-aires/bueph* 🛏 *165 rooms* 🍴 *No Meals* [M] *C to San Martín or H to Las Heras.*

Nightlife

BARS

Milión

COCKTAIL LOUNGES | One of the city's most stunning bars is spread across three floors of a perfectly restored French-style mansion. A cool vibe and cooler drinks (try the frozen basil daiquiri) keep this place packed on weekends. When the back garden fills on balmy summer nights, squeeze onto the marble steps with the beautiful people. ✉ *Paraná 1048, Recoleta* ☎ *11/4815–9925* 🌐 *www.milion.com.ar* [M] *D to Callao.*

★ Pony Line

COCKTAIL LOUNGES | No expense has been spared at the polo-themed Pony Line, a cool watering hole in the Four Seasons hotel. Creative cocktails, its own line of craft beer, luxury bar snacks, and great tunes have made this a go-to spot for sassy ladies, suave gentlemen, and models. ✉ *Posadas 1086/88, Recoleta* ☎ *11/4321–1728* 🌐 *www.fourseasons.com/buenosaires/dining/lounges/pony_line* [M] *C to San Martín.*

Shoeless Joe's El Alamo

BARS | From the outside, the signs asking patrons–a mix of expats and fun-loving porteños–to leave quietly are the only hint that this isn't the demure bar it appears to be. The generous drinks promotions (ladies drink free until midnight on Friday) add substantial rowdiness, and it turns into a raucous party zone on weekends. A sports bar at heart, El Alamo also hosts bikini competitions—just so you know. ✉ *Córdoba 5267, Palermo Soho* ☎ *11/4813–7324* [M] *D to Tribunales.*

Winemakers Vinoteca Bar de Vinos

WINE BARS | This intimate wine store and bar stocks an array of vintages carefully curated by sommelier and owner Juan Casarsa. Drop in for a bottle of Criolla, a light red, to take home or let Juan and his team serve you a glass of what's open, and stay for some tasty snacks that go beyond charcuterie. There's also a second branch in Mercado de Belgrano indoor food market on calle Juramento. ✉ *Montevideo 1444, Recoleta* ☎ *11/3576–2288* [M] *D to Callao.*

GAY AND LESBIAN

Zoom

BARS | Half a block from the very cruisey section of Santa Fe, between avenidas Callao and Coronel Díaz, Zoom offers a lounge bar, a maze, video cabins, and plenty of dark corners. It can get pretty intense, but there's good security. ✉ *Uriburu 1018, Recoleta* ☎ *11/4827–4828* 🌐 *www.zoombuenosaires.com* [M] *D to Pueyrredón.*

Shopping

JEWELRY AND ACCESSORIES

★ Celedonio

JEWELRY & WATCHES | Local design hero Celedonio Lohidoy has created pieces—often with frothy bunches of natural pearls—for Kenzo and Emanuel Ungaro and his work has even been slung around Sarah Jessica Parker's neck on *Sex in the City*. He favors irregular semiprecious stones, set in asymmetrical, organic-looking designs such as butterflies and daisies. ✉ *Av. del Libertador 1774, Recoleta* ☎ *11/4803–7598* 🌐 *www.celedonio.com.ar* 🕒 *Open by appointment only* [M] *H to Las Heras.*

Fahoma

JEWELRY & WATCHES | This small boutique has enough accessories to make the rest of your outfit a mere formality. Berry-size beads go into chunky but affordable necklaces, which take flora and fauna as their inspiration, while all manner of handbags line the back wall. Need a royal seal of approval? Argentina-born Queen Máxima of the Netherlands has been photographed wearing their fun, oversize earrings. ✉ *Libertad 1169, Recoleta* ☎ *11/4813–5103* ⊕ *www.fahoma.es* Ⓜ *D to Tribunales (5 blocks away)*.

MARKETS

Feria de Artesanos de Plaza Francia (*Feria Plaza Francia*)

MARKET | Each weekend, artisans sell handmade clothes, jewelry, and housewares as well as traditional crafts at this sprawling open-air market that winds through several linked squares outside the Recoleta Cemetery. ✉ *Avs. Libertador and Pueyrredón, Recoleta* ⊕ *www.feriaplazafrancia.com* Ⓜ *H to Las Heras.*

SHOES, HANDBAGS, AND LEATHER GOODS

Guido

LEATHER GOODS | In Argentina loafers mean Guido, whose retro-looking logo has been the hallmark of quality footwear since 1952. Try on timeless handmade Oxfords and wing tips; there are also fun items like a tomato-red handbag or a cow-skin tote. Accessories include simple belts and suede wallets. ✉ *Av. Quintana 333, Recoleta* ☎ *11/4811–4567* ⊕ *www.zapateriaguido.com* Ⓜ *H to Facultad de Derecho (10 blocks away)*.

WINE

Grand Cru

WINE/SPIRITS | Savvy staff, some trained as sommeliers, will guide you through Grand Cru's peerless selection; the vast range is dominated by high-end wines from small wineries. ✉ *Rodríguez Peña 1886, Recoleta* ☎ *11/4816–2223* ⊕ *www.grandcru.com.ar* ⊙ *Closed Sun.* Ⓜ *D to Callao.*

Almagro

Almagro lies southwest of Recoleta but feels like a different world. Traditionally a gritty, working-class neighborhood, it spawned many tango greats, including the legendary Carlos Gardel. The Abasto subdistrict has long been the heart of the barrio: it centers on the massive art deco building (at Corrientes and Agüero) that was once the city's central market. The abandoned structure was completely overhauled and reopened in 1998 as a major mall, spearheading the redevelopment of the area, which now has several top hotels and an increasing number of restaurants and tango venues. More urban renewal is taking place a few blocks away at Sarmiento and Jean Jaurés, where the Konex Foundation has transformed an old factory into a cutting-edge cultural venue.

👁 Sights

Almagro lies southwest of Recoleta but feels like a different world. Traditionally a gritty, working-class neighborhood, it spawned many tango greats, including the legendary Carlos Gardel. The Abasto subdistrict has long been the heart of the barrio: it centers on the massive art deco building (at Corrientes and Agüero) that was once the city's central market. The abandoned structure was completely overhauled and reopened in 1998 as a major mall, spearheading the redevelopment of the area, which now has several top hotels and an increasing number of restaurants and tango venues. More urban renewal is taking place a few blocks away at Sarmiento and Jean Jaurés, where the Konex Foundation has transformed an old factory into a cutting-edge cultural venue.

Museo Casa Carlos Gardel

HISTORIC HOME | Hard-core tango fans must visit the home of tango's greatest hero, Carlos Gardel. The front rooms

3

Buenos Aires ALMAGRO

of this once-crumbling *casa chorizo* (sausage house—that is, a long, narrow house) contain extensive displays of Gardel paraphernalia—LPs, photos, and old posters. The maestro's greatest hits play in the background. The back of the house has been restored with the aim of re-creating as closely as possible the way the house would have looked when Gardel and his mother lived here, right down to the placement of birdcages on the patio. Concise but informative texts in Spanish and English talk you through the rooms and the history of tango in general. Guided visits are available in Spanish Wednesdays and Fridays at 12 and 4, and on weekends at 12, 2, 4 and 6. English tours are usually available on request on weekdays. ⊠ *Jean Jaurés 735, Almagro* ☎ *11/4964–2015* ⊕ *www.buenosaires. gob.ar/museocasacarlosgardel* ⊠ *250 pesos; free Wed.* ☉ *Closed Tues.* Ⓜ *B to Carlos Gardel.*

Cementerio de la Chacarita

CEMETERY | This cemetery is home to Carlos Gardel's tomb, which features a dapper, Brylcreemed statue and dozens of tribute plaques. It's treated like a shrine by hordes of faithful followers who honor their idol by inserting lighted cigarettes in the statue's hand. On June 24, the anniversary of his death, aging *tangueros* in suits and fedoras gather here to weep and sing. Fellow tango legends Aníbal Troilo and Osvaldo Pugliese are also buried in this cemetery, which is about equidistant from Palermo and Almagro. If you're heading from Almagro, hop on subte Line B at the Carlos Gardel Station for a 10- to 15-minute ride north to Federico Lacroze. Depending on where you are in Palermo, a cab here will cost 300–400 pesos. ⊠ *Guzmán 680, at Corrientes, Chacarita* ☎ *0800/444-2363* Ⓜ *B to Federico Lacroze.*

 Nightlife

LIVE MUSIC
★ Ciudad Cultural Konex
LIVE MUSIC | FAMILY | A well-curated line-up of live music, film screenings, fun parties, and interactive theater ensures this huge converted factory is one of the best cultural centers in the city. The outdoor space morphs into an inner-city beach complete with hammocks in summer; the winter months see DJs and bands hash it out indoors. The Konex is also home to percussion band Bomba de tiempo, which plays every Monday evening. ⊠ *Sarmiento 3131, Abasto* ☎ *11/4864–3200* ⊕ *www.cckonex.org* Ⓜ *B line to Carlos Gardel.*

TANGO
La Catedral
DANCE CLUBS | This former grain factory has been converted into a hip club where the tango is somehow very rock. There are classes and milongas every evening, although Tuesdays are the most popular. It's a cool night out even if you're not planning to dance, as you can watch aficionados in action over a beer or a bottle of wine. Note that the real pros tend not to come here because of the uneven floorboards. ⊠ *Sarmiento 4006, Almagro* ☎ *15/5325–1630* ⊕ *www.lacatedralclub.com* Ⓜ *B to Carlos Gardel.*

 Shopping

MALLS
Abasto Shopping
SHOPPING CENTER | FAMILY | The soaring art deco architecture of what was once the city's central market is as much a reason to come here as the 250 shops spread over its three levels. Abasto has many top local chains, so it isn't as exclusive as other malls, so bargains await at retailers like Ver, Yagmour, and Markova. Women can dress up at Paula Cahen d'Anvers, Akiabara, and Rapsodia, while men can hit trendy shops such as Bensimon,

MALBA holds a large range of art collections from almost every time period of Argentine history.

Prototype, and Old Bridge, or go for the *estanciero* look with smart La Martina polo wear. There's a food court on the top floor. The mall is also home to Museo de los Niños (a hands-on children's museum) and a 12-screen movie theater, and many Bafici festival films are shown here; you can pick up tickets for entertainment elsewhere in town at the Ticketek booth near the food court, too. ⊠ *Av. Corrientes 3247, Almagro* ☎ *11/4959–3400* ⊕ *www.abasto-shopping.com.ar* Ⓜ *B to Carlos Gardel.*

Palermo

Some say Palermo takes its name from a 16th-century Italian immigrant who bought land here, others from the abbey honoring Saint Benedict of Palermo. Either way, the area was largely rural until the 1830s, when national governor Juan Manuel de Rosas built an estate in Palermo. After the dictatorial Rosas was overthrown, his property north of Avenida del Libertador was turned into a huge patchwork of parks and dubbed Parque Tres de Febrero—a reference to February 3, 1852, the day he was defeated in battle. More commonly known as Los Bosques de Palermo (the Palermo Woods), the green space provides a peaceful escape from the rush of downtown. The botanical gardens are at its southern end. High-brow culture is provided by the gleaming Museo de Arte de Latinoamericano (Museum of Latin American Art) on Avenida Figueroa Alcorta. The streets around the intersection of avenidas Santa Fe and Coronel Díaz are home to mainstream clothing stores and the mid-range Alto Palermo mall. More upscale alternatives, meanwhile, abound in Palermo Viejo. Top boutiques—along with minimalist lofts, endless bars, and the most daring restaurants in town—have made Palermo Viejo (and its unofficial subdistrict, Palermo Soho) the epicenter of Buenos Aires' design revolution.

Sights

Campo Argentino del Polo

SPORTS VENUE | The Campo Argentino del Campo (Argentine Polo Ground), is commonly known as the Cathedral of Polo. The venue opened in 1928 and hosts polo, field hockey, and pato matches throughout the year. The grounds are most popularly known for the Argentine polo finals in December. ☒ *Av. del Libertador 4096, Palermo* ⊕ *aapolo.com.*

★ Jardín Botánico Carlos Thays

GARDEN | **FAMILY** | Wedged between three busy Palermo streets, this unexpected haven has 18 acres of gardens filled with 5,500 varieties of exotic and indigenous flora. Different sections re-create the environments of Asia, Africa, Oceania, Europe, and the Americas. An organic vegetable garden aims to teach children healthy eating habits, and winding paths lead to hidden statues and a brook. The central area contains an exposed-brick botanical school and library, plus a beautiful greenhouse brought from France in 1900 but unfortunately not open to the public. ☒ *Av. Santa Fe 3951, Palermo* ☏ *11/4831–4527* ⊕ *www.buenosaires. gob.ar/ambienteyespaciopublico/mantenimiento/espaciosverdes/jardinbotanico* ☎ *Free.* ⊗ *Closed Mon.* Ⓜ *D to Plaza Italia.*

Jardín Japonés *(Japanese Garden)*

CITY PARK | **FAMILY** | Like the bonsais in the nursery within it, this park is small but perfectly formed, and maintained by the Argentine-Japanese Cultural Foundation. A slow wander along the arched wooden bridges and walkways is guaranteed to calm frazzled sightseeing nerves. A variety of shrubs and flowers frame ornamental ponds that are filled with friendly koi carp—you can actually pet them if you feel so inclined (kids often do). The restaurant, where you can enjoy sushi, adzuki-bean sweets, and tea, overlooks the zen garden. ☒ *Av. Casares at Av. Figueroa Alcorta, Palermo* ☏ *11/4804–9141* ⊕ *www.jardinjapones. org.ar* ☎ *416 pesos.*

★ MALBA

ART MUSEUM | Comprising works of 19th- and 20th-century Latin American art collected by founder Eduardo Constantini, the fabulous Museum of Latin American Art of Buenos Aires (MALBA) is one of the cornerstones of the city's cultural life. Early works in the permanent collection reflect the European avant-garde experiences of artists such as Diego Rivera, Xul Solar, Roberto Matta, and Joaquín Torres García. These, in turn, gave rise to paintings like *Abaporu* (1928) by Tarsila do Amaral, a Brazilian involved in the "cannibalistic" Movimento Antropofágico. Geometric paintings and sculptures from the 1940s represent movements such as Arte Concreto, Constructivism, and Arte Madí. Argentina's undisputed modern master, Antonio Berni, is represented by a poptastic collage called *The Great Temptation* (1962) and the bizarre sculpture *Voracity or Ramona's Nightmare* (1964). Pieces by local greats Liliana Porter, Marta Minujín, Guillermo Kuitca, and Alejandro Kuropatwa form the end of the permanent collection. The MALBA also hosts world-class temporary exhibitions—recent examples include Yoko Ono and Jeff Koons—and two small basement galleries show art by cutting-edge Argentines. ☒ *Av. Presidente Figueroa Alcorta 3415, Palermo* ☏ *11/4808–6500* ⊕ *www.malba.org.ar* ☎ *600 pesos, Wed. half price* ⊗ *Closed Tues.* Ⓜ *H to Facultad de Derecho.*

Museo de Artes Plásticas Eduardo Sívori

(Eduardo Sívori Art Museum)
ART MUSEUM | If you're looking for a respite from the sun or sports in Parque Tres de Febrero, check out this sedate museum. Focused on 19th- and 20th-century Argentine art, the collection includes paintings by local masters like Emilio Petorutti, Lino Eneo Spilimbergo, Antonio Berni, and the museum's namesake Sívori. The shaded sculpture garden

The Japanese Gardens are a peaceful escape from city life.

is the perfect combination of art and park. ✉ *Av. Infanta Isabel 555, Palermo* ☎ *11/4774–9452* ⊕ *www.buenosaires. gob.ar/museos/museo-sivori* ✉ *250 pesos, free Wed.* ⊙ *Closed Tues.* Ⓜ *D to Plaza Italia.*

Museo Evita

HISTORY MUSEUM | Eva Duarte de Perón, known as Evita, was the wife of populist president Juan Domingo Perón. Revered by working-class followers and despised by the Anglophile oligarchy, the Museo Evita shies from pop culture clichés and conveys facts about Evita's life and works. Exhibits include family photos that document Evita's humble origins, and mannequins wearing some of her fabulous designer outfits. The Evita myth can be baffling to the uninitiated but excellent guided visits shed light on the phenomenon and are available in English for groups of six or more, but must be arranged by phone in advance. Exhibits include 1952 film footage showing hundreds of thousands of mourners lined up to view their idol's body, family photos

that document Evita's humble origins and time as a B-list actress, and a set of mannequins wearing some of her fabulous designer outfits. A video chronicles the fate of Evita's cadaver after dying of cancer at age 33: embalmed by Perón, stolen by political opponents, and moved and hidden for 17 years before being returned to Argentina, where it now rests in Recoleta Cemetery. Knowledgeable staffers are on hand to answer questions. Book a table at the on-site restaurant, whose checkered floors and glossy black tables are as stylish as the great lady herself. ✉ *Lafinur 2988, 1 block north of Av. Las Heras, Palermo* ☎ *11/4807–9433* ⊕ *web.museoevita.org.ar* ✉ *Free* ⊙ *Closed Mon.* Ⓜ *D to Plaza Italia.*

Parque Tres de Febrero

CITY PARK | **FAMILY** | Known locally as Los Bosques de Palermo (Palermo Woods), this 400-acre green space is actually a crazy quilt of smaller parks. A stroll along the paths takes you through the Jardín de los Poetas (Poets' Garden), dotted with statues of literary figures, and to the enchanting Patio Andaluz (Andalusian Patio), where majolica tiles and Spanish mosaics sit under a vine-covered pergola. Near the lakes in the northwestern part, some 12,000 rosebushes (more than 1,000 different species) bloom seasonally in the Paseo El Rosedal.

You can jog or rent bikes, in-line skates, and pedal boats. The park gets crowded on sunny weekends, as this is where families come to play and have picnics. If you like the idea of the latter, take advantage of the street vendors who sell refreshments and *choripán* (chorizo sausage in a bread roll) within the park. There are also several posh cafés lining the Paseo de la Infanta (running from Libertador toward Sarmiento in the park). ✉ *Bounded by Avs. del Libertador, Sarmiento, Leopoldo Lugones, and Dorrego, Palermo* [M] *D to Plaza Italia.*

Planetario Galileo Galilei (*Galileo Galilei Planetarium*)
OBSERVATORY | **FAMILY** | One of the city's most iconic buildings, the Planetario Galileo Galilei is a great orb positioned on a massive concrete tripod in the middle of Palermo's Parque Tres de Febrero. Built in the early 1960s, it looks like something out of *Close Encounters of the Third Kind*—especially at night, when the dome glows with eerie blue and red lighting. Tickets for the twice-daily sky shows (five times on weekends), narrated in Spanish, go on sale at 9:30 am Tuesday through Friday and at noon on weekends; note that they usually sell out fast. Three meteorites that landed in northern Argentina 4,000 years ago guard the entrance. The nearby pond with swans, geese, and ducks (also lit up at night) is always a hit with kids. ✉ *Avs. Sarmiento and Figueroa Alcorta, Palermo* ☎ *11/4771–6629* 🌐 *www.planetario.gob.ar* 🎫 *300 pesos* 🕒 *Closed Mon.* [M] *D to Plaza Italia.*

🍴 Restaurants

The city's largest neighborhood, Palermo offers something for every taste, style, and budget. It's the city's undisputed culinary hot spot, with enclaves that have their own distinct styles and vibes. If you want the tastiest, most cutting-edge, most traditional, most ethnic, most daring, and most fashionable food in Buenos Aires, then head to Palermo. It's that simple.

★ Chori
$ | **ARGENTINE** | This bright yellow corner storefront has given the humble sausage sandwich called choripán a radical and much-needed makeover, turning it from basic street food to a sleek fast-food meal. All the chorizos that are the base of the sandwich—from lamb to mushroom and even fish—are produced in house, and there are side dishes such as sweet potato fries as well as beer, wine, and cocktails. **Known for:** sausage specialist; budget-friendly; upmarket street food. [$] *Average main: pesos600* ✉ *Thames 1653, Palermo Soho* ☎ *11/3966–9857* 🌐 *www.chori.com.ar* [M] *D to Plaza Italia.*

★ Don Julio
$$ | **STEAKHOUSE** | One of the finest steak houses in the planet that ranks in the World's 50 Best Restaurants, Don Julio features cowhide tablecloths, wag-on-wheel lighting fixtures, a vast indoor grill, and rows of empty wine bottles signed by satisfied customers. A mix of locals and expats packs the place at lunch and dinner to feast on the fantastic *ojo de bife* (rib eye) and *entraña* (skirt steak). **Known for:** excellent attention and service; fantastic wine cellar; tender rib eye. [$] *Average main: pesos1800* ✉ *Guatemala 4691, at Gurruchaga, Palermo Soho* ☎ *11/4831–9564* 🌐 *www.parrilladonjulio.com* [M] *D to Plaza Italia.*

★ Gran Dabbang

$ | **SOUTH AMERICAN** | A small and deconstructed spot on busy Scalabrini Ortiz, the focus is firmly on raw ingredients in the kitchen, where chef Mariano Ramón brings together Asian and Latin American flavors using locally sourced products. The result is a taste explosion that has caught the attention of many die-hard Dabbang followers keen for spice and spices who return for lamb curry, oven-roasted carrots with garbanzo miso, and squash seed mole, and don't mind the fast table turnaround. **Known for:** dishes for sharing; award-winning spot; Asian flavor. $ *Average main: pesos1400* ✉ *Raúl Scalabrini Ortiz 1543, Palermo Viejo* ☎ *11/3501–0481* ⊘ *Closed Sun.* Ⓜ *D to Scalabrini Ortiz.*

★ Julia

$ | **ARGENTINE** | An intimate space for just 22 diners led by talented young chef Julio Martín, enjoy a plant-led (but not exclusive) menu at this adorable bistro named after his daughter. Low lighting makes for an intimate ambience, ideal for a date, while you can also take a table on the sidewalk. **Known for:** highly creative menu; great for a date; intimate spot. $ *Average main: pesos1400* ✉ *Loyola 807, Villa Crespo* ☎ *11/7519–0514* ⊕ *www.juliarestaurante.com.ar* ⊘ *Closed weekends* Ⓜ *B to Malabia.*

La Cabrera

$$ | **STEAKHOUSE** | Huge slabs of Hereford and Aberdeen Angus steaks for sharing are cooked to perfection at this classic parrilla, and they're always accompanied by a variety of small side dishes, so there's little need to order anything other than french fries, though *provoletas* (gooey, slightly crispy grilled cheese slabs) are a must to start. The same menu is served down the block at La Cabrera Norte, at 5127 Cabrera, which handles the overflow. **Known for:** friendly service; happy hour 6:30 to 8; casual ambience. $ *Average main: pesos1600* ✉ *Cabrera 5099, at Thames, Palermo Soho* ☎ *11/4831–7002* ⊕ *www.lacabrera.com.ar* Ⓜ *D to Plaza Italia, 10 blocks.*

Las Pizarras

$$ | **BISTRO** | The chalkboard-covered walls *(las pizarras)* at this appealing spot list the market-driven menu of a dozen or so creative dishes. The wine list is equally intriguing. **Known for:** classy bistro fare; great wine list; relaxed ambience. $ *Average main: pesos1600* ✉ *Thames 2296, at Charcas, Palermo* ☎ *11/4775–0625* ⊘ *Closed Mon. No lunch* Ⓜ *D to Plaza Italia.*

★ Mishiguene

$$ | **ISRAELI** | The first purveyor of contemporary Jewish cuisine in the city, Mishiguene brings classic Middle Eastern, Polish, and Russian dishes such as baba ghanoush, varenikes, pastrami, and borscht up-to-date. Vibrant Klezmer music, efficient service, and a party atmosphere add to the reason why these are some of the hottest tables around. **Known for:** classic dishes brought up-to-date; fun ambience; innovative concept. $ *Average main: pesos2000* ✉ *Lafinur 3368, Palermo Botánico* ☎ *11/5029–1979* ⊕ *www.mishiguene.com* ⊘ *No dinner Sun.* Ⓜ *D to Plaza Italia.*

Osaka

$$$ | **JAPANESE** | A bamboo facade gives way to a slick setting with plenty of black lacquer, creating a sleek ambience for Buenos Aires' leading Japanese-Peruvian (known as Nikkei cuisine) restaurant. The sushi is excellent, though pricey, and the service is spot-on, particularly at the gleaming counter. **Known for:** great cocktails; smart clientele; fusion cuisine. $ *Average main: pesos2100* ✉ *Soler 5608, at Fitz Roy, Palermo* ☎ *11/4775–6964* ⊕ *www.osaka.com.pe* Ⓜ *D to Palermo.*

Río Alba

$$ | STEAKHOUSE | This venerable steak house has waiters in bow ties and vests who maneuver around the farmhouse-style dining room, serving flavorful, tender cuts of meat including *entraña* (hanger steak) and *matambrito* (pork flank). Although the menu appears pricey, portions are massive, and they know it: the steaks are set atop small hibachis to keep them hot. **Known for:** friendly service; abundant portions; casual ambience. $ *Average main: pesos1800* ⊠ *Cerviño 4499, at Fray J.S. de Oro, Palermo* ☎ *11/4773–9508* Ⓜ *D to Plaza Italia.*

Siamo nel Forno

$ | PIZZA | After spending a year studying traditional techniques in Naples, *pizzero* Néstor Gattorna imported a wood-burning oven, specially milled flour, and extra-virgin olive oil to reproduce the best Neapolitan-style pizza. Italophiles looking for an alternative to cheesy pizza *porteña* jam into the place for his smoky, perfectly charred pies and equally good calzones. **Known for:** fast turnaround; traditional Neopolitan pies; casual ambience. $ *Average main: pesos1,400* ⊠ *Costa Rica 5886, Palermo Hollywood* ☎ *11/4775–0337* ⊙ *Closed Mon. No lunch* Ⓜ *D to Ministro Carranza.*

Trattoria Olivetti

$ | ITALIAN | FAMILY | Casual style, fantastic service and atmosphere, and a prime location in Palermo Chico make this one of the city's top Italian restaurants. For the more adventurous, don't miss the "surf and turf" of *gamberi e animelle* (perfectly grilled prawns and sweetbreads), or *guanciale* (braised pork cheeks). **Known for:** excellent wine list; genuine Italian fare; casual ambience. $ *Average main: pesos1450* ⊠ *Cerviño 3800, República Arabe Siria, Palermo Botánico* ☎ *11/4802–4075* ⊕ *www.trattoriaolivetti.com* Ⓜ *D to Plaza Italia.*

 Coffee and Quick Bites

Cuervo Café

$ | CAFÉ | This specialty coffee shop, which roasts its own beans, located on a buzzy Hollywood corner is the ideal spot for a flat white or iced coffee, and a little people watching. **Known for:** hipster vibe; great caffeine; in-house coffee roaster. $ *Average main: pesos400* ⊠ *Costa Rica 5801, Palermo Hollywood* ⊕ *www.cuervocafe.com* ⊙ *Closed Mon.*

El Preferido de Palermo

$$ | ARGENTINE | Though it was recently overhauled by the Parrilla Don Julio team, much care has been taken to retain El Preferido de Palermo's authentic and traditional character. Order a plate of cold cuts—the charcuterie cellar is on display—and savor them at the kitchen counter. **Known for:** updated blast from the past; award-winning restaurant; delicious classic Argentine dishes for sharing. $ *Average main: pesos1800* ⊠ *Jorge L. Borges 2108, Palermo Viejo* ☎ *11/4774–6585* Ⓜ *D to Plaza Italia.*

Museo Evita Restaurante

$$ | ARGENTINE | The checkered floors and glossy black tables of Museo Evita Restaurante are as stylish as the great lady herself. Sticky and flaky, the *medialunas* here are some of the best in town. **Known for:** open from lunch thru dinner; historical and elegant spot; good wine list. $ *Average main: pesos1700* ⊠ *J.M. Gutiérrez 3926, Palermo Botánico* ☎ *11/4800–1599* ⊕ *www.museoevitaresto.com.ar* ⊙ *No dinner Sun.* Ⓜ *D to Plaza Italia.*

Hotels

Duque Hotel Boutique & Spa

$$ | B&B/INN | As the name suggests, this 1920s French-style hotel is fit for a duke—or even a president, as the mansion once served as an Argentine president's private residence. **Pros:** gorgeous entrance; spacious and inviting common areas; an enclosed patio means many guests use rooms only for sleeping. **Cons:** swimming-pool and deck area are small; far from central Soho fun; some rooms are small. $ *Rooms from: US$105* ✉ *Guatemala 4364, Palermo Soho* ☎ *11/4832–0312* ⊕ *www.duquehotel.com* ↻ *14 rooms* ❐ *Free Breakfast* Ⓜ *D to Scalabrini Ortiz.*

★ Fierro Hotel

$$ | **HOTEL** | A choice lodging for travelers looking for a five-star stay in a boutique package, all rooms boast top-of-the-line beds, spacious living areas with chaise lounges, and flat-screen TVs. **Pros:** among the city's best dining and drinking; rooftop pool with skyline views; helpful staff. **Cons:** pool is not large; the back patio is a bit sterile; common areas are small. $ *Rooms from: US$160* ✉ *Soler 5862, Palermo* ☎ *11/3220–6800* ⊕ *www.fierrohotel.com* ↻ *22 rooms, 5 suites* ❐ *Free Breakfast* Ⓜ *D to Carranza.*

★ The Glu Hotel

$$ | **HOTEL** | Attention to detail is key at this small boutique hotel where all of the spacious rooms are stylishly modern and minimalist and equipped with low-slung furnishings, bright wooden floors, and small bar areas. **Pros:** sought-after location; sleek interior decor; excellent concierges provide highly personalized and attentive service. **Cons:** roof terrace has a Jacuzzi rather than a pool; the breakfast room is cramped; its location on a happening street means constant traffic, though rooms are soundproofed. $ *Rooms from: US$130* ✉ *Godoy Cruz 1733, Palermo* ☎ *11/4831–4646* ⊕ *www.thegluhotel.com* ↻ *11 rooms* ❐ *Free Breakfast* Ⓜ *D to Plaza Italia, 10 blocks.*

Home Hotel Buenos Aires

$$ | **B&B/INN** | Run by an Anglo-Argentinean couple, the Home Hotel oozes coolness, style, and class. **Pros:** hip and fun; eclectic mix of people stay here; great pool area. **Cons:** breakfast is good, lunch is less exciting; some guests might not feel cool enough; lots of nonguests come here to hang out. $ *Rooms from: US$160* ✉ *Honduras 5860, Palermo Hollywood* ☎ *11/4779–1006* ⊕ *www.homebuenosaires.com* ↻ *14 rooms, 4 suites, 2 apartments* ❐ *Free Breakfast* Ⓜ *D to Ministro Carranza.*

Legado Mítico

$$ | **B&B/INN** | Blessed with the city's most gorgeous sitting room, the Legado Mítico also has an enormous library with plush leather couches, antique furnishings, a fireplace, and bookshelves stocked with English- and Spanish-language classics. **Pros:** exquisitely decorated rooms; welcoming; an authentic and unique Argentine experience. **Cons:** the upstairs terrace disappoints for a property of this quality; not much ambience; common areas and hallways are very dark. $ *Rooms from: US$250* ✉ *Gurruchaga 1848, Palermo* ☎ *11/4833–1300* ⊕ *www.legadomitico.com* ↻ *11 rooms* ❐ *Free Breakfast* Ⓜ *D to Plaza Italia.*

★ Magnolia Hotel Boutique

$$ | **B&B/INN** | This boutique lodging feels like home—if home were a high-ceilinged, lavishly decorated Palermo town house dating from the 1890s. **Pros:** top-floor terrace is the perfect urban escape; lots of cozy common areas; homemade baked goods at breakfast. **Cons:** rooms could use a minibar; quite far from Palermo's Soho buzz; some rooms require walking outdoors. $ *Rooms from: US$160* ✉ *Julián Alvarez 1746, Palermo* ☎ *11/4867–4900* ⊕ *www.magnoliahotelboutique.com* ↻ *8 rooms* ❐ *Free Breakfast* Ⓜ *D to Scalabrini Ortiz.*

★ Miravida Soho Hotel & Wine Bar

$$ | **B&B/INN** | This enchanting boutique hotel offers thoughtful and personalized service starting the minute you walk in the door. **Pros:** charm to spare; breakfast includes options like homemade granola; very helpful staff. **Cons:** this road is a bit dark and quiet at night; some rooms are small; if street noise is a concern, request a room in the back.

$ *Rooms from: US$180* ✉ *Darregueyra 2050, Palermo* ☎ *11/4774–6433* 🌐 *www.miravidasoho.com* 🛏 *7 rooms* 🍴 *Free Breakfast* [M] *D to Palermo.*

Nightlife

BARS

Antares

BREWPUBS | Founded in the city of Mar del Plata in 1999, this is now a successful national brewer making dozens of brews. The spacious bar attracts a cosmopolitan group of drinkers who keep it packed from after-office until the wee hours. Service is friendly and efficient, the music is feel-good, and the bar snacks are tasty. Also check out other outposts in Las Cañitas at Arévalo 2876 and San Telmo at Bolivar 491. ✉ *Armenia 1447, Palermo Soho* ☎ *11/4833–9611* 🌐 *www.cervezaantares.com* [M] *B to Malabia.*

★ CoChinChina

COCKTAIL LOUNGES | Decadence meets southeast Asia at this theatrical cocktail bar helmed by Buenos Aires' mixology queen Inés de los Santos. Enjoy one of her signature Umami Martinis streetside, in a cozy booth or at the bar itself (made from egg shells). Watching the slick team slinging drinks makes for the best seats in the house. The food menu is equally tempting; try the lacquered pork bao. Still thirsty? Snap up one of Ines' ready-to-drink cocktails from the boutique for the walk home. ✉ *Armenia 1540, Palermo Soho* ☎ *11/2247–6452* 🌐 *www.inesdelossantos.com.ar* [M] *B to Malabia.*

Congo Club Cultural

BARS | Beautiful people—in faded fitted jeans, hipster sneakers, and leather jackets—frequent this hangout post-dinner and pre-club. Browse the great cocktail list at Congo's lengthy bar, or head for the large back patio: either way, you'll easily be able to convince new friends to stick around for another drink or three. ✉ *Honduras 5329, Palermo Soho* ☎ *11/6185–9368* 🌐 *www.congoclubcultural.com.ar* [M] *D to Plaza Italia.*

★ 878

COCKTAIL LOUNGES | B.A.'s original speakeasy has spawned a spate of followers over the past few years, but it remains a classic for cocktail lovers: 878 has an extensive drinks list, many made with its own line of spirits, armchairs to sink into, plus a supercool clientele. Be sure to stick your head around the more private back bar. ✉ *Thames 878, Villa Crespo* ☎ *11/4773–1098* 🌐 *www.878bar.com.ar* [M] *B to Malabia.*

The Harrison Speakeasy

COCKTAIL LOUNGES | One of the classiest speakeasies around, the Harrison is inspired by the Prohibition-era and the time-warped cocktails have earned a cluster of awards, so you're in expert hands. Membership is required; alternatively, you can dine at the shop-front sushi restaurant, then ask "to see the bodega" to gain access. ✉ *Malabia 1764 and Costa Rica, Palermo Soho* 🌐 *www.nicky-harrison.com* [M] *D to Scalabrini Ortiz.*

★ Naranjo

WINE BARS | Champions of low-intervention wines and those made by small producers, Naranjo has captured the attention of Buenos Aires' young wine lovers. While 180 labels sourced from all over the country are always available, in a bid to demystify wine, there's just one single crystal glass for all grapes and styles. Drinkers keen to try something new take a seat under the orange tree after which it was named, and stay for delicious gluten-free, often vegan, small plates to share. ✉ *Ángel Justiniano Carranza 1059, Chacarita* [M] *B to Dorrego.*

★ Verne Club

COCKTAIL LOUNGES | Themed around Jules Verne's *Twenty Thousand Leagues Under the Sea*, Verne Club runs a tight ship

Continued on page 122

The Dance
of Buenos
Aires

by Victoria Patience

"THE TANGO IS MACHO, THE TANGO IS STRONG. IT SMELLS OF WINE AND TASTES LIKE DEATH."

So goes the famous tango "Why I Sing Like This," whose mix of nostalgia, violence, and sensuality sum up what is truly the dance of Buenos Aires. From its beginnings, tango and its two-four beat marked and reflected the character of Buenos Aires. You may hear strains of tango on the radio while sipping coffee in a café, see high-kicking sequined dancers in a glitzy dinner show, or listen to musicians in a darkened cabaret. But one of the most memorable ways to experience the best of this broody, melancholic, impassioned art form is through dancing it yourself.

DANCING THE TANGO

Many milongas now kick off with group dance classes which usually last an hour or two and cost 15–20 pesos; some lessons are free, though chaotic. These classes are great for getting over nerves and getting you in the mood. However, most *milongueros* (people who dance at milongas, or tango dance halls) take tango very seriously and don't look kindly on left-footed beginners crowding the floor. We recommend you take a few private classes first—they can make a huge difference to your technique.

English-speaking private teachers abound in Buenos Aires; classes generally last 1½ hours and prices can range from $20 to $80 a class. Complete beginners should plan on at least three or four classes before hitting a milonga. Many private instructors organize milonga outings with groups of their students (usually for a separate fee). Others even offer a so-called "taxi dance service": you pay for them to dance with you all night. See the end of this feature for a rundown of some of the best options for lessons and milongas.

DANCE STYLES

Tango milonguero, the style danced at milongas and taught in most classes in Buenos Aires, is quite different from the so-called salon or ballroom tango danced in Hollywood movies and in competitions outside Argentina. Ballroom tango is all fixed steps and staccato movements, and dancers' backs arch away from each other in a stiff embrace. Tango milonguero is a highly improvised style built around a variety of typical movements, not fixed steps Dancers embrace closely, their chests touching. There are other, historical tango styles, but it's less common to see them on milonga floors. (Confusingly, "milonga" refers both to traditional tango dance halls and to a style of music and dance that predates the tango; though similar to tango, it has a more syncopated beat and faster, simpler steps.)

AT THE MILONGA

Dancers of all ages sit at tables that edge the floor, and men invite women to dance through *cabeceo* (subtle eye contact and head-nodding), a hard art to master. Note that women sitting with male partners won't be asked to the floor by other men.

Dances come in sets of three, four, or five, broken by a *cortina* (obvious divider of non-tango music), and it's common to stay with the same partner for a set. Being discarded in the middle is a sign that your dancing's not up to scratch, but staying for more than two sets with the same partner could be interpreted as a come-on.

To fit in seamlessly, move around the floor counterclockwise without zigzagging, sticking to the inside layers of dancers if you're a beginner. Respect other dancers' space by avoiding collisions and keeping your movements small on crowded floors. Don't spend a long time doing showy moves on the spot: it holds up traffic. Finally, take time to sit some out, catch your breath, and watch the experts.

TANGO TALK

Abrazo: the embrace or stance dancers use; in tango, this varies from hip-touching and loose shoulders to close chests and more fluid hips, depending on style.

Abrazo

Barrida: literally, "a sweep"; one partner sweeps the other's foot into a position.

Caminada: a walking step that is the basis of the tango.

Barrida

Caminada

Canyengue: style of tango dancing with short and restricted steps; from the 1910s and '20s when tight hobble skirts were popular.

Ocho: eight; a criss-crossing walk.

Parada: literally a "stop"; the lead dancer stops the other's foot with his own.

Petitero: measured style of tango developed after the 1955 military coup, when large tango gatherings were banned and the dance relegated to small cafés.

MILONGA STYLE

Wearing a fedora hat or fishnet stockings is as good as a neon sign reading "beginner." Forget what on-stage tango dancers wear and follow a few basic rules.

Go for comfortable clothes that allow you to move freely; a sure bet are breathable, natural fabrics with a bit of stretch. Be sure it's something that makes you feel sexy. If in doubt, wear black. Avoid showy outfits: it's your footwork that should stand out. It's also smart to steer clear

of big buckles, studs, stones, or anything that might catch on your partner. Try not to wear skirts that are too long or too tight. Also a bad idea are jeans or gymwear.

A good example of what to wear for men would be black dress pants and a black shirt; for women, two of many options are a simple halter-neck dress with a loose, calf-length skirt or palazzo pants with a fitted top.

As for your feet: look for dance shoes with flexible

leather or suede soles that allow you to glide and pivot. The fit should be snug but comfortable. Note that rubber-soled street shoes or sneakers mark the dance floor and are often forbidden. High heels are a must for women; the most popular style is an open-toed sandal with an ankle strap (which stops them coming off). Black lace-ups are the favorite among men, so leave your two-tone spats at home.

TANGO THROUGH TIME

The tango and modern Buenos Aires were born in the same place: the *conventillos* (tenement houses) of the port neighborhood of La Boca in the late 19th century, where River Plate culture collided with that of European immigrants. The dance eventually swept from the immigrant-quarter brothels and cabarets to the rest of the city; rich playboys took the tango to Paris on their grand tours, and by the 1920s the dance had become respectable

Carlos Gardel

enough to fill the salons and drawing rooms of the upper class in Argentina and abroad. In the 1930s, with the advent of singers like Carlos Gardel, tango music became popular in its own right. Accordingly, musical accompaniment started to come from larger bands known as *orquestas típicas*.

By the '40s and '50s, porteños (people from Buenos Aires) celebrated tango as the national music of the people, and tango artists lent Evita and Perón their support. The military coup that ousted Perón in 1955 forbade large tango dances, which it saw as potential political gatherings, and (bizarrely) encour-

aged rock 'n' roll instead. Young people listened, and tango fell out of popular favor.

The '90s saw a huge revival in both traditional *milongas* (dance halls) and a more improvised dance style. Musical offerings now include modern takes on classic tangos and electrotango or *tangofusión*. Even local rock stars are starting to include a tango or two in their repertory. And since 1998, thousands of people from around the world have attended the annual fortnight-long Festival de Tango in Buenos Aires (⊕ *www.tangobuenosaires.gob.ar*), held late winter or spring.

Whether you decide to take in a show or take up dancing yourself, sit down for a classic concert or groove at an electrotango night, there are more ways to experience tango in Buenos Aires than anywhere else on earth.

DID YOU KNOW?

■ Tango so horrified Kaiser Wilhelm and Pope Pius X that they banned the dance.

■ In 1915, before he was famous, Carlos Gardel was injured in a barroom brawl with Ernesto Guevara Lynch, Che's father.

■ One of Gardel's most famous numbers, "Por Una Cabeza," is the tango featured in *Schindler's List*, *Scent of a Woman*, and *True Lies*.

■ The coup of 1930 prompted composers like Enrique Santos Discépolo to write protest tangos.

■ Finnish tango has been a distinct musical genre since at least mid-century and is still one of the most popular in Finland; there's even an annual *Tangomarkkinat* (tango festival) in Seinäjoki, complete with the crowning of a Tango King and Queen.

thanks to it's top-notch mixologists. This old-school cocktail bar serves innovative offerings that are often inspired by the eponymous author's characters, including a Phileas Fogg Martini. ⊠ *Medrano 1475, Palermo* ☎ *11/4822–0980* ⊕ *www.verne-cocktailclub.com* Ⓜ *D to Scalabrini Ortiz.*

DANCE CLUBS
Club Aráoz
DANCE CLUBS | A serious party crowd is found at Club Aráoz. Bump and grind it at Thursday's block-rocking hip-hop night; Friday and Saturday see DJs spinning rock and electronic dance music for a relatively laid-back bunch of Buenos Aires youth. ⊠ *Aráoz 2424, Palermo* ☎ *11/5977–9922* Ⓜ *D to Bulnes.*

Kika
DANCE CLUBS | Right in the heart of Palermo and next door to Congo Club Cultural, Kika is much bigger than you'd guess from the outside. Thanks to its funky musical orientation, its two dance floors fill up quickly. The back room sometimes hosts live bands while Tuesdays are all about Hype, an all-in-one electro, hip-hop, indie, and dubstep night that gets the student-heavy crowd moving till dawn. ⊠ *Honduras 5339, Palermo Soho* ☎ *11/4833–9171* ⊕ *www.kikaclub.com.ar* Ⓜ *D to Palermo.*

La Uat
DANCE CLUBS | As if the drinks team behind award-winning cocktail bar 3 Monos didn't have enough on their plate, they also opened La Uat, a small and hidden dance floor whose street face is Cacho Rotisería canteen. Push through the curtain to unveil DJs playing a range of music from 80s to hip hop, while a hipster crowd pulls moves fluorescent cocktails in hand. For more space, head upstairs to the terrace bar. La Uat's late hours attracts the young gastronomic crowd, keen to wind down. ⊠ *Thames 1627, Palermo Soho* Ⓜ *D to Plaza Italia.*

★ Niceto
DANCE CLUBS | One of the city's best venues for two decades features everything from demure indie rock to the outrageous and legendary Club 69 on Thursday (think underdressed cross-dressers). Check out live bands and dancing on the A Side, while something contrasting and chill simultaneously takes place in the back B Side room. ⊠ *Cnel. Niceto Vega 5510, Palermo Hollywood* ☎ *11/4779–9396* ⊕ *www.nicetoclub.com* Ⓜ *B to Dorrego.*

GAY AND LESBIAN
Amerika
DANCE CLUBS | This immense gay disco has three floors of high-energy action and shows. Friday and Saturday are fun and frivolous verging on hectic thanks to its one-fee, all-you-can-drink-entry. Thursday and Sunday are quieter, with greater emphasis on the music. Amerika remains the city's gay club to check out—and be checked out in. ⊠ *Gascon 1040, Palermo* ☎ *11/5427–2577* Ⓜ *B to Medrano.*

LIVE MUSIC
Thelonious Club
LIVE MUSIC | The best *porteño* jazz bands (and occasional foreign imports) play at this upscale spot. Arrive early for a good seat, as it's a long, narrow bar and not all tables have good views; on weekends there are usually two shows per night. ⊠ *Nicaragua 5549, Palermo* ⊕ *www.thelonious.com.ar* Ⓜ *D to Palermo.*

Virasoro Bar
LIVE MUSIC | This is an intimate art deco venue for local jazz maestros and appreciative audiences. It's a great space and you can get up close and personal with the musicians, who draw from a deep well of talent and cover a lot of ground, from improv to standards and experimental. ⊠ *Guatemala 4328, Palermo* ☎ *11/4831–8918* ⊕ *www.virasorobar.com.ar* Ⓜ *D to Scalabrini Ortiz.*

Nightclub Tips

Don't be afraid to stand in line outside. Lines are generally quick and painless—and if there isn't one, the place might not be worth visiting.

Buy a ticket or make a reservation. For concerts, festivals, shows, and club events, people buy tickets in advance, as many fill up or sell out, especially international offerings.

Go late—really. The night starts late in Buenos Aires, so go early and you'll miss out on the atmosphere. If necessary, help smooth the adjustment with a *merienda* (a snack of coffee and *tostados* at around 6 pm) and a "disco siesta."

Find out what's on and where. Scour flyers, websites, ticket agencies, and magazine listings for up-to-date information. There's a lot more going on than you can find out from any single source.

Dress to impress. *Porteños* like to dress up, though their style tends to be on the conservative side. Skip the shorts and flip-flops (both social no-nos) in favor of something trendy. With the exception of one or two scruffy bars in San Telmo, you'll never feel overdressed.

Never imagine you've seen it all. Private parties, pop-ups, and last-minute underground events are where it's at. Keep an ear out and tell people you're looking, and you might strike it lucky.

TANGO
★ Salón Canning
DANCE CLUBS | Several milongas call this large dance hall home. The coolest is Parakultural, which takes place late on Monday, Tuesday, and Friday. Reservations are essential for the last of these—the dance floor is totally packed by midnight, so get here early. Originally an alternative, "underground" milonga, it now attracts large numbers of porteños, as well as longtime expats. ⊠ *Av. Scalabrini Ortíz 1331, Palermo* ☎ *11/4833–3224* ⊕ *www.parakultural.com.ar* Ⓜ *B to Malabia.*

Shopping

CLOTHING: MEN
La Dolfina
MIXED CLOTHING | Being a number-one polo player wasn't enough for Adolfo Cambiaso—he founded his own team in 1995, then started a clothing line that he also models for. If you think polo is all about knee-high boots and preppy chinos, think again: Cambiaso sells some of the best urban menswear in town and this store includes a café. The Italian-cotton shirts, sharp leather jackets, and to-die-for totes are perfect for any occasion. ⊠ *Av. Figueroa Alcorta 3301, Palermo Botánico* ☎ *11/4806–3233* ⊕ *www.ladolfina.shop/tiendas.*

GIFTS AND SOUVENIRS
★ Elementos Argentinos
CRAFTS | A fair-trade agreement links this luminous Palermo town house to a team of craftswomen in northwest Argentina who spin, dye, and weave the exquisite woolen goods sold here. Some of the handmade rugs, blankets, and throws follow traditional patterns and use only natural pigments (such as *yerba mate* or beetroot juice); others are contemporary designs using brighter colors. Packable souvenirs include sheep-wool table runners, alpaca scarves, and knitted cacti. Ask about designing your own

rug. ⊠ *Gurruchaga 1881, Palermo Viejo* 📞 *11/4832–6299* ⊕ *elementosargentinos. com.ar* Ⓜ *D to Plaza Italia.*

JEWELRY AND ACCESSORIES
María Medici
JEWELRY & WATCHES | Industrial-looking brushed silver rings and necklaces knit from fine stainless-steel cables are some of the attractions at this tiny shop. Architect and sculpturist María Medici also combines silver with primary-color resin to make unusual-looking rings. ⊠ *Niceto Vega 4619, Palermo Viejo* 📞 *11/4773– 2283* ⊕ *mariamedici.blogspot.com.ar* Ⓜ *B to Malabia.*

SHOES, HANDBAGS, AND LEATHER GOODS
★ 28Sport
SHOES | These Argentine leather bowling sneakers and boxing-style boots are the heart and "sole" of retro. All the models are variations on a classic round-toed lace-up, but come with different-length legs. Plain black or chestnut uppers go with everything, but equally tempting are the two-tone numbers—in chocolate and orange, or black with white panels, for example. Even the store is a nod to the past, kitted out like a 1950s living room. ⊠ *Gurruchaga 1481, Palermo Viejo* 📞 *11/4833–4287* ⊕ *www.28sport.com* Ⓜ *D to Plaza Italia (10 blocks away).*

Uma
LEATHER GOODS | Light, butter-soft leather takes very modern forms here, with geometric stitching the only adornment on jackets and asymmetrical bags that might come in rich violet in winter and aqua-blue in summer. The top-quality footwear includes teetering heels and ultrasimple boots and sandals. Ultratight jeans, leather boots, and tops are also on offer. ⊠ *Alto Palermo, Av. Santa Fe 3253, Palermo* 📞 *11/5777–8521* ⊕ *www.uma. com.ar* Ⓜ *D to Bulnes.*

WINE
Pain & Vin
WINE/SPIRITS | Wine lovers' dreams come true at this independent store and bar. English-speaking sommeliers are on hand to help you make sense of the wide selection of Argentine wine sourced from many unexpected corners of the country. They also host arrange wine-tastings with guest oenologists to get you up to speed on local vintages. ⊠ *Gorriti 5132, Palermo Soho* ⊕ *www.painetvin. mitiendanube.com* Ⓜ *B to Malabia.*

Chapter 4

SIDE TRIPS FROM BUENOS AIRES

4

Updated by
Allan Kelin

Sights	Restaurants	Hotels	Shopping	Nightlife
★★★★★	★★★★☆	★★★★☆	★★★☆☆	★★☆☆☆

WELCOME TO
SIDE TRIPS FROM BUENOS AIRES

TOP REASONS TO GO

★ **Wall of Water:** Nothing can prepare you for the roaring, thunderous Cataratas del Iguazú (Iguazú Falls). We think you'll agree.

★ **Cowboy Culture:** No visit to the pampas (grasslands) is complete without a stay at an *estancia*, a stately ranch house, like those around San Antonio de Areco. Sleep in an old-fashioned bedroom and share meals with the owners for a true taste of the lifestyle.

★ **Delta Dreaming:** Speeding through the Paraná River Delta's thousands of kilometers of rivers and streams, we'll forgive you for humming "Ride of the Valkyries"—it does feel very Mekong.

Argentina's famous pampas begin in Buenos Aires Province—an unending sea of crops and cattle-studded grass that occupies nearly one-quarter of the country's landscapes. Here are the region's most traditional towns, including San Antonio de Areco.

Suburban trains connect Buenos Aires to Tigre, close to the labyrinthine waterways of the Paraná Delta, explorable only by boat. On Argentina's northeastern tip, readily accessible by plane, are the jaw-dropping Cataratas del Iguazú.

1 San Antonio de Areco. Just 90 minutes from the city (2 hours by bus), this picturesque town is devoted to all things *guacho*, with museums, world-class silversmiths, and deeply relaxing *estancias*.

2 Tigre. This small city on the Paraná River is inviting in itself with its very beautiful art museum and numerous rowing clubs and water taxis, but the real attraction is the lush, labyrinthine delta, dotted with weekend homes and secluded hotels.

3 Iguazú Falls (Cataratas del Iguazú). The grandeur of this vast sheet of white water cascading in constant cymbal-banging cacophony makes Niagara Falls and Victoria Falls seem sedate. Allow at least two full days to take in this magnificent sight.

To hear *porteños* (inhabitants of Buenos Aires) talk of their city, you'd think Argentina stops where Buenos Aires ends. Not far beyond it, however, the skies open up and the *pampas*—Argentina's huge flat grasslands—begin. Pampean traditions are alive and well in farming communities that still dot the plains that make up Buenos Aires Province.

The best known is San Antonio de Areco, a well-preserved provincial town that's making a name for itself as gaucho central. You can ride across the pampas and get a taste of country life (and lots of grass-fed beef) by visiting—or staying at—a traditional *estancia* (ranch).

Ranchland gives way to watery wonders. The quiet suburban town of Tigre is the gateway to the network of rivers and tributaries that form the delta of the Paraná River, lined with luscious tropical vegetation. Low wooden launches speed along its waterways to the houses, restaurants, and lodges built on stilts along the riverbanks.

If you like your natural wonders supersized, take a short flight or a long bus ride to Iguazú Falls, northeast of Buenos Aires in semitropical Misiones Province. Here, straddling the border between Argentina and Brazil, two natural parks contain and protect hundreds of roaring falls and a delicate jungle ecosystem. The spectacle caused Eleanor Roosevelt to exclaim "Poor Niagara!" but most people are simply left speechless by the sheer size and force of the Garganta del Diablo, the grandest falls of them all.

MAJOR REGIONS

Buenos Aires Province. With an area of nearly 120,000 square miles, much of it cultivated *pampas*, 758 miles of Atlantic coastline, and the world's widest river at its northern boundary, Buenos Aires Province offers visitors cities, beaches and resorts, rustic or luxurious getaways, and plenty of history to explore. And as the country's powerhouse agricultural and livestock producer, there's plenty to eat.

Iguazu Falls. After snaking through Brazil and endless miles of jungle, the wide Iguazú river spreads out lazily over a basalt bed before much of its volume crashes down the mouth and sides of the chasm that's called Garganta del Diablo, the Devil's Throat, especially aptly named because of the roar of the water and the force of the rising mist.

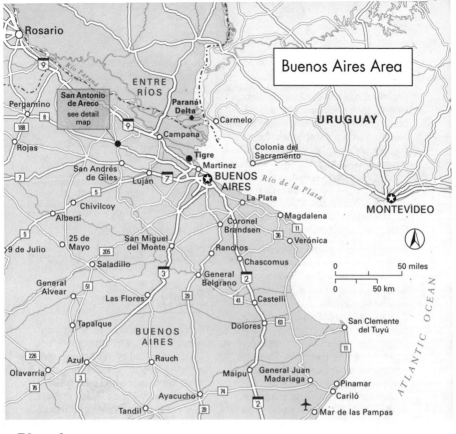

Planning

When to Go

Temperatures in Buenos Aires Province rarely reach extremes. Note that some hotels and restaurants in areas popular with local tourists open *only* on weekends outside of peak season—this coincides with school holidays in summer (January and February), winter (July), and the Easter weekend. You'll get great discounts at those that open midweek in winter.

Early November's a good time to visit San Antonio de Areco, which holds its annual gaucho festival then. Like Buenos Aires, it feels curiously empty in January, when everyone decamps to the coast.

Though Iguazú Falls is thrilling year-round, seasonal rainfall and upstream Brazilian *barrages* (minidams) can affect the amount of water. If you visit between November and March, booking a hotel with air-conditioning and a swimming pool is as essential as taking mosquito repellent.

Border Crossings

Crossing into Brazil from Argentina used to be a thorny issue, but now U.S. citizens no longer need a visa to enter Brazil. So, by all means, make the extra excursion for another view of the falls and lunch.

Car

Argentina has one of the world's worst records for traffic accidents, and the busy highways of Buenos Aires Province are often where they happen. January and February are the worst times, when drivers anxious to get to and from their holiday destination speed, tailgate, and exercise illegal maneuvers even more alarmingly than usual. If you're driving, do so very defensively and avoid traveling on Friday and Sunday, when traffic is worst.

Expressways and interprovincial routes tend to be atrociously signposted, so take a map. Getting a GPS-equipped rental car costs an extra 700 pesos or so per day: devices usually work well in cities, but the calibration is often a couple of hundred yards off in rural areas. Major routes are usually privately owned, which means frequent tolls. There are sometimes alternative roads to use, but they're generally smaller, slower, and in poor condition. On main roads the speed limit is 80 kph (50 mph), while on highways it's 130 kph (80 mph), though Argentinean drivers rarely pay heed to this.

Dining

Fantastic waterfront views accompany a variety of meat and fish dishes in these regions, creating varied experiences from a rural *comida del campo* to a peaceful waterfront dinner.

Hotels

Luxury hotels and other lodgings hide within the varying terrain of areas that are a mere day trip from the capital city. Thundering you hear in the distance lets you know how close some hotels are to Iguazú Falls. These peaceful stays make a perfect getaway from the commotion of Buenos Aires.

Restaurant prices are per person for a main course at dinner. Hotel prices are for a standard double room in high season.

What It Costs in Argentine Pesos

	$	$$	$$$	$$$$
RESTAURANTS				
	under 600 pesos	600–1,500 pesos	1,501–2,500 pesos	over 2,500 pesos
HOTELS				
	under $50	$50–$155	$156–$310 pesos	over $315

Safety

Provincial towns like San Antonio de Areco are usually extremely safe, and the areas visited by tourists are well patrolled. Puerto Iguazú is fairly quiet in itself, but mugging and theft are common in nearby Foz do Iguaçu in Brazil, especially at night, when its streets are deserted.

Tigre and the Paraná Delta

30 km (19 miles) northwest of Buenos Aires on the Ruta Panamericana, 35 km (22 miles) northwest of Buenos Aires on Avenida Libertador.

A coastal train ride or a drive through the shady riverside suburbs of Buenos Aires takes you to the riverport town of Tigre, the embarkation point for boats that ply the Delta del Paraná. A couple of hours is plenty of time to visit the town itself from Buenos Aires; allow a whole day if you also plan to explore the delta—a vast maze of canals, tributaries, and river expanding out like the veins of a leaf. Heavy vegetation and rich birdlife (as well as clouds of mosquitoes) make the network of rivers feel tropical. The delta's many islands hide peaceful luxury getaways and cozy riverside restaurants accessible only by boat.

The waterways and close-packed islands that stretch northwest of Tigre are the most accessible part of the 14,000 square km (5,400 square miles) that make up the delta, where roads are replaced by rivers. Churning brown waters and heavy vegetation are vaguely reminiscent of Southeast Asia, though the chic houses and manicured gardens that line the rivers of the Primera Sección (closest to Tigre) are a far cry from Mekong River settlements.

If you want to take in more of the delta than a short boat trip allows, do as porteños do and combine it with a day's wining and dining at an island restaurant or a weekend at one of the hotels or luxury lodges a little farther afield. Many offer private transportation. The delta gets very hot and humid in summer, and the mosquitoes are ferocious, so bring insect repellent.

GETTING HERE AND AROUND
The cheapest way to get to Tigre by train is on the suburban commuter train from Estación Retiro to the central Estación Tigre. There are about four departures an hour on the Ramal Tigre (Tigre Branch) of the Línea Mitre; round-trip tickets cost 15.50 pesos with a SUBE card, 37 pesos without. Alternatively, take the slick, tourist-oriented Tren de la Costa. It meanders through some of Buenos Aires' most fashionable northern suburbs and along the riverbank, stopping at nine stations before arriving at Estación Delta, near the Río Luján and Puerto de Frutos market. It starts halfway between Buenos Aires and Tigre, so you'll have to first take Línea Mitre, Ramal Mitre from Retiro to Estación Bartolomé Mitre, where you can change to the Tren de la Costa's Maipú Station. Round-trip fare is 24 pesos with a SUBE card, 48 pesos without. The center of Tigre is small enough to walk

around easily, but there are also taxis outside both train stations.

The most comfortable—and the most touristy—way to travel the delta's waterways is aboard the two-story catamarans that leave from docks on the Luján River, inside the Puerto de Frutos market. Rio Tur catamarans meander through 14 miles of waterways in about 90 minutes. They're a great way to glimpse delta life, and you'll see houses on stilts and boats piled high with provisions for towns upriver.

■TIP→ The last boat of the day usually catches the sunset.

The low-slung wooden *lanchas colectivas* (boat buses) are the cheaper and more authentic way to explore the waterways; locals use them to get around the delta. These leave from the Estación Fluvial (Boat Station), on the other side of the roundabout from Estación Tigre, the main train station. The main transport company for the delta is Interisleña, which serves all of the closest islands to the Tigre. Round-trip tickets are about 300 pesos. Líneas Delta Argentino uses similar boats but also runs one-hour tourism-oriented trips every couple of hours on weekends and holidays, which cost 2,000 pesos. Buy tickets from Booth 6, opposite the jetty. Touts offering private boat trips loiter outside the Tigre tourist board offices at the train and boat stations, but it's best to stick with recognized companies. As the boats leave the delta, they pass the magnificent turn-of-the-20th-century buildings of Tigre's heyday and colorfully painted houses built on stilts to protect them from floods.

ESSENTIALS
TOURS Río Tur. ⊠ *Sarmiento and Buenos Aires, on the Río Luján, Tigre* ☎ *11/4731–0280* ⊕ *www.rioturcatamaranes.com.ar.*

VISITOR INFORMATION Tigre Tourist Board. ⊠ *Estación Fluvial, Bartolome Mitre 305, Tigre* ☎ *11/4512–4480* ⊕ *www.vivitigre.gob.ar.*

The exterior of the Museo de Arte de Tigre alone makes this museum worth the visit.

Sights

★ Museo de Arte de Tigre

ART MUSEUM | An ornate colonnade leads from the Luján River to this Beaux Arts building, built in 1909 to house a social club and casino. It contains a modest collection of Argentine paintings by artists like Quirós, Castagnino, Soldi, and Quinquela Martín, as well as works portraying life in the delta. The real showstopper, however, is the beautifully restored architecture: a sweeping marble staircase, stained-glass windows, gilt-inlaid columns, and soaring ceilings conspire to form a microcosm of the *fin de siècle* European style adored by the porteño elite. A trim sculpture garden and flower-filled park surround the museum, which is best reached by walking along Paseo Victorica. ⊠ *Paseo Victorica 972, Tigre* 🕾 *11/4512–4528* ⊕ *www.mat. gov.ar* 🖃 *50 pesos* ⊘ *Closed Mon.–Tues.*

Museo Naval de la Nación

OTHER MUSEUM | Although most visitors are into naval, military, or nautical history, this museum's collection will fascinate even those whose interests point elsewhere. The interior of the building, which looks like a hangar-size barn, is filled with paintings, statues, uniforms, and beautifully crafted model ships. On the grounds are long-retired planes from Argentina's aviation history, including a great example of a North American AT-6 "Texan" from 1939. ⊠ *Av. Victorica 602, Tigre* 🕾 *11/4506–9332* ⊕ *museonavaldelanacion.wordpress.com/* 🖃 *40 pesos* ⊘ *Closed Sun.–Wed.*

Paseo Victorica

PROMENADE | Italianate mansions, museums, restaurants, and several rowing clubs dot this pictureseque paved walkway and waterside park that curves alongside the Río Luján for about 10 blocks. To reach it, cross the bridge next to the roundabout immediately north of Estación Tigre, then turn right and walk five blocks along Avenida Lavalle, which runs along the Río Tigre. ⊠ *Along Río Luján between Río Tigre and Río Reconquista, Tigre.*

Puerto de Frutos

MARKET | The center of the action at Tigre is its picturesque market. Hundreds of stalls selling furniture, handicrafts, and reasonably priced souvenirs fill the area around the docks along the Río Luján. It's particularly busy on weekends (indeed, many stalls are closed midweek). Grab a quick lunch from stands selling steak and chorizo sandwiches. ⊠ *Sarmiento at Buenos Aires, Tigre* ⊕ *www.puertodefrutos-arg.com.ar.*

 Restaurants

Almacén de Tigre

$$ | ARGENTINE | About 100 yards west of the Estación Fluvial, this cozy eatery is seemingly miles away from the automobile and boat traffic. In a quiet quarter among a scattering of shops and cafés with bohemian flair, it's a great place to get away from the weekend crowds and enjoy a freshly made salad or sandwich. **Known for:** peaceful setting; trendy spot; good salads. $ *Average main: pesos1500* ⊠ *Bul. Saenz Peña 1336, Tigre* ☎ *11/5197–4009.*

Danilo Restaurante

$$$ | ITALIAN | An enchanting Italian/Spanish lunch spot at the confluence of two waterways. Take a water taxi for freshly made pastas, seafood and, of course, beef, and later, enjoy a glass of wine on the lawn surrounded by nature. **Known for:** inviting antipasti; perfect freshly made pasta; waterfront dining. $ *Average main: pesos2500* ⊠ *Canal Arias and Arroyo Guayraca, Tigre* ☎ *11/3919–4194* ⊗ *Closed weekdays* ☞ *Water taxi required for access.*

María Luján Ristorante

$$$ | ARGENTINE | An expansive terrace overlooking the river is the appropriate backdrop for Tigre's best fish dishes. The kitchen favors elaborate preparations: some are so packed with unlikely ingredients that the fish gets lost; others, such as the sole in lemon-infused cream,

are spot-on. **Known for:** seafood; lively atmosphere; outdoor dining. $ *Average main: pesos2200* ⊠ *Paseo Victorica 511, Tigre* ☎ *11/4731–9613* ⊕ *www.ilnovomariadellujan.com.*

Hotels

The city of Tigre is so close to Buenos Aires that there's little reason to stay overnight there. However, a night or two in the Paraná Delta is a rewarding experience.

Bonanza

$$ | B&B/INN | Thick vegetation surrounds the tomato-red 19th-century country house that's the center of the eco-action at Bonanza. **Pros:** very back-to-nature; great home cooking; river swimming. **Cons:** no pool; minimal luxury; remote. $ *Rooms from: US$80* ⊠ *Río Carapachay km 13, Tigre* ☎ *11/4409–6967* ⊗ *Closed mid-Apr.–Jul.* ⇨ *4 rooms* ¶○ℓ *All-Inclusive* ☞ *Round trip water taxi 370.*

Itaca Delta Cabañas

$$$ | HOUSE | Six spacious, individually themed cabañas that allow you to unwind at your own pace. **Pros:** many nature activities; river fun; spacious cabins. **Cons:** no restaurant; Wi-Fi can be spotty; far from any amenities. $ *Rooms from: US$179* ⊠ *Río Capitán 222, Tigre* ☎ *11/3052–7964* ⊕ *itacadelta.wixsite.com/itacadelta* ⇨ *Six cabañas (cabins)* ¶○ℓ *Free Breakfast* ☞ *Couples only.*

La Becasina Delta Lodge

$$$ | RESORT | Wooden walkways connect the luxurious bungalows—each with a private riverside deck. **Pros:** peace and quiet; lots of creature comforts; wild delta surroundings. **Cons:** nothing else nearby; no kids under 14; expensive. $ *Rooms from: US$264* ⊠ *Arroyo las Cañas, San Fernando* ☎ *11/3621–5810* ⊕ *www.labecasina.com* ⇨ *15 bungalows* ¶○ℓ *All-Inclusive* ☞ *Price is per person and includes activities but guides and instructors are extra.*

San Antonio de Areco

110 km (68 miles) west of Buenos Aires.

There's no better place to experience traditional provincial life in the pampas than this well-to-do farming town. Grand estancias dot the land in and around San Antonio. Many of the families that own them, which form a sort of local aristocracy, mix lucrative soy farming with estancia tourism. The gauchos who were once ranch hands now cook up huge *asados* (barbecues) and lead horseback expeditions for the ever-growing numbers of foreign tourists. You can visit one for a day—*un día de campo*—or immerse yourself with an overnight visit.

Porteño visitors tend to base themselves in the town itself, which is becoming known for its B&Bs. The fiercely conservative inhabitants have done a good job of preserving the turn-of-the-20th-century Italianate buildings that fill the sleepy *casco histórico* (historic center). Many contain bars and general stores, which maintain their original fittings; others are the workshops of some of the best craftspeople in the country.

In summer, the banks of the Río Areco (Areco River), which runs through town, are teeming with picnickers—especially near the center of town, at the Puente Viejo (Old Bridge), which is overlooked by the open-air tables of various riverside parrillas. Nearby is the Museo Gauchesco y Parque Criollo Ricardo Güiraldes, which celebrates historical gaucho life. During the week surrounding November 10, the Día de la Tradición (Day of Tradition) celebrates the gaucho with shows, community barbecues, riding competitions, and a huge crafts fair. It's more fun to visit San Antonio on weekends, as many restaurants are closed Monday to Thursday.

GETTING HERE AND AROUND

To drive to San Antonio de Areco, leave Buenos Aires on RN9, crossing to RN8 when it intersects at Km 35 (total tolls of 100 pesos). There are more than 20 buses daily from Buenos Aires' Retiro Station to San Antonio; most are run by Nueva Chevallier, and some by Pullman General Belgrano. Each company operates from its own bus stop in San Antonio. Once you've arrived, the best way to get around is on foot, but you'll need a *remis* (radio taxi) to get to most estancias, though some have their own shuttle service.

ESSENTIALS

VISITOR INFO San Antonio de Areco Tourist Board. ⊠ *Bul. Zerboni, at Arellano, San Antonio de Areco* ☏ *2326/453–165* ⊕ *www.sanantoniodeareco.com.*

 Sights

Museo Draghi Plateros Orfebres

OTHER MUSEUM | San Antonio is famed for its silversmiths, and the late Juan José Draghi was the best in town. This small museum adjoining his workshop showcases the evolution of the Argentine silver-work style known as *platería criolla.* Pieces are ornate takes on gaucho-related items: spurs, belt buckles, knives, stirrups, and the ubiquitous *mate* gourds, some dating from the 18th century. Also on display is the incredibly ornate work of Juan José Draghi himself; you can buy original pieces in the shop. His son keeps the family business alive—he's often at work shaping new pieces at the back of the museum. ⊠ *Lavalle 387, San Antonio de Areco* ☏ *2325/15–650–600* ⊕ *www. marianodraghi.com* ⊠ *500 pesos.*

Museo Gauchesco y Parque Criollo Ricardo Güiraldes

OTHER MUSEUM | Gaucho life of the past is celebrated—and idealized—at this quiet museum just outside town. Start at the 150-year-old *pulpería* (the gaucho version

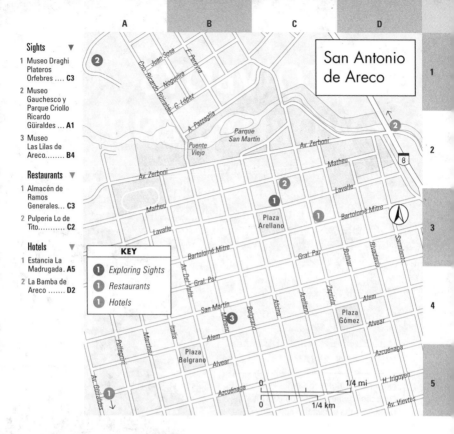

San Antonio de Areco

Sights ▼

1 Museo Draghi Plateros Orfebres **C3**

2 Museo Gauchesco y Parque Criollo Ricardo Güiraldes ... **A1**

3 Museo Las Lilas de Areco........ **B4**

Restaurants ▼

1 Almacén de Ramos Generales... **C3**

2 Pulpería Lo de Tito........... **C2**

Hotels ▼

1 Estancia La Madrugada. **A5**

2 La Bamba de Areco **D2**

KEY

1 *Exploring Sights*

1 *Restaurants*

1 *Hotels*

of the saloon), complete with dressed-up wax figures ready for a drink. Then head for the museum, an early-20th-century replica of a stately 18th-century *casco de estancia* (estancia house). Polished wooden cases contain a collection of traditional gaucho gear: decorated knives, colorful ponchos, and elaborate saddlery and bridlery. The museum is named for local writer Ricardo Güiraldes (1886–1927), whose romantic gaucho novels captured the imagination of Argentinean readers. Several rooms document his life in San Antonio de Areco and the real-life gauchos who inspired his work. ⊠ *Camino Ricardo Güiraldes, San Antonio de Areco* ☎ *2326/455–839* ⊕ *museoguiraldes.areco.gob.ar* ☞ *Free.*

Museo Las Lilas de Areco

ART MUSEUM | Although iconic Argentinean painter Florencio Molina Campos was not from San Antonio de Areco, his humorous paintings depict traditional pampas life. The works usually show red-nosed, pigeon-toed gauchos astride comical steeds, staggering drunkenly outside taverns, engaged in cockfighting or folk dancing, and taming bucking broncos. The collection is fun and beautifully arranged, and your ticket includes coffee and croissants in the jarringly modern café, which also does great empanadas and sandwiches. Behind its curtained walls lie huge theme park–style re-creations of three paintings. The lively and insightful voice-over explaining them is in Spanish only. ⊠ *Moreno 279, San Antonio de Areco* ☎ *2326/456–425* ⊕ *www.museolaslilas.org* ☞ *600 pesos* ☉ *Closed Mon.–Wed.*

Continued on page 143

THE COWBOYS at WORLD'S END

by Victoria Patience

Along a country road, you may come across riders herding cattle. Dressed in baggy pants and shirts, a knife stuck in the back of their belts, these are the descendants of the gauchos, Argentina's cowboys. These men of few words symbolize honor, honesty, and courage—so much so that a favor or good deed is known locally as a *gauchada*.

WHAT'S IN A NAME?

No one can agree on where the word "gaucho" comes from. Some say it's derived from the native Quechua-language word *guachu*, meaning "orphan" or "outcast"; others attribute similar meanings to the French word *gauche*, another suggested source. Yet another theory traces it (via Andalusian Spanish) to the Arabic word *chaouche*, a kind of whip for herding cattle.

Gauchos were the cattle-herding settlers of the pampas (grasslands), renowned for their prowess as horsemen. Most were criollos (Argentina-born descendants of Spanish immigrants) or mestizos (of mixed Spanish and native Argentine descent). They lived in villages but spent much of their time riding the plains, much like North American cowboys.

With the establishment of big estancias (ranches) in the early- and mid-19th century, landowners began taking on gauchos as hired hands. The sheer size of these ranches meant that the gaucho's nomadic lifestyle remained largely unchanged, however.

In the 1860s Argentina's president Domingo Faustino Sarmiento encouraged massive settlement of the pampas, and branded gauchos as barbaric, potentially criminal elements. (Despite being of humble origins, Sarmiento as a snob about anything he saw as uncivilized.) Laws requiring travelers to carry passes ended the gaucho's right to roam. Many more than ever signed on as permanent ranch hands; others were drafted into military service, at times becoming deserters and outlaws.

Vindication came in the late-19th and early-20th century, when a wave of literary works like José Hernández's Martín Fierro and Ricardo Güiraldes's Don Segundo Sombra captured the national imagination with their dramatic, romantic descriptions of gauchos and their nomadic lifestyle. The gaucho—proud, brave, and melancholy—has been a national icon ever since.

Gaucho on an estancia near
El Calafate, Patagonia, Argentina

GAUCHO GEAR

SOMBRERO
Although a sombrero (flat-crowned, wide-brimmed hat) is the most typical style, conical felt hats (shown), berets, flat caps, and even top hats are also worn.

CAMISA
Traditionally smocked shirt with baggy sleeves. Modern gauchos wear regular long-sleeved cotton shirts.

BOMBACHA
Baggy pants cinched at the ankle; the story goes that after the Crimean War, surplus Turkish-style army pants were sold to Argentina by Britain and France. The fashion caught on: no gaucho is seen without these.

BOTAS
Early gauchos wore rough, rawhide boots with open toes or a flip-flop-style thong. Today, gauchos in colder parts of Argentina wear flat-soled, tapered boots, usually with a baggy pirate-style leg.

PAÑUELO
Large, brightly colored kerchief, worn knotted around the neck; some gauchos drape them under their hats to protect their necks from the sun or cold.

CHAQUETA
Jacket; often kept for special occasions, and usually worn short and unbuttoned, to better display the shirt and waistcoat underneath.

CHIRIPÁ
Before bombachas arrived, gauchos used to wind a large swathe of woven fabric (like an oversize loincloth) over thin, long underpants.

FAJA
A long strip of colorful woven fabric once worn to hold the pants up, now mainly decorative and often replaced by a leather belt. Either way, gauchos stick their knives in the back.

ESPUELAS
Spurs; most gauchos favor those with spiked wheel-like designs.

Gaucho traditionally dressed

SUPER GAUCHOS

REBENQUE
A short rawhide crop, often with a decorative metal handle.

PONCHO
Woven from sheep's or llama's wool, usually long and often vertically striped. Some colors denote certain provinces.

ALPARGATAS
Spanish immigrants in the 18th century popularized flat, rope-soled espadrilles in warmer parts of Argentina. Today, rubber-soled versions are more common.

BOLEADORAS
Gauchos adopted this native Argentinian device for catching animals. It's made of two or three stones wrapped in cowhide and mounted at the end of a cowhide cord. You whirl the boleadora then release it at the animal's legs.

LAZO
A braided rawhide lasso used for roping cattle.

CUCHILLO OR FACÓN
No gaucho leaves home without his knife. Indeed, most Argentine men have one to use at barbecues (early gauchos used theirs for fighting, too). Handles are made of wood or horn, blades are triangular.

Unsigned mural of Gauchito Gil, a saint-like character in popular Argentine belief (supposedly a Robin Hood-type outlaw called Antonio Mamerto Gil Núñez).

EL GAUCHITO GIL: legend has it that this gaucho from Corrientes Province was hunted down by a sheriff over a woman. He was hung by his feet from a tree but, just before his throat was cut, he predicted that the sheriff would find his son at home mortally ill and only able to recover if the sheriff prayed to Gil. The prediction came true, and the repentant sheriff spread the word. Today, roadsides all over Argentina are dotted with red-painted shrines to this folk saint. Superstitious locals leave offerings, hoping for help with their problems.

MARTÍN FIERRO: the fictional hero of an eponymous 19th-century epic poem written by José Hernández. Fierro is a poor but noble gaucho who's drafted into the army. He deserts and becomes an outlaw. His pride, independence, and love of the land embody the national ideal of what a man should be. Writer Jorge Luis Borges so loved the poem that he started a literary magazine with the same name.

JUAN MOREIRA: a real-life gaucho who married the daughter of a wealthy landowner, provoking the wrath of a jealous local judge. Wrongly accused of various crimes, Moreira became a fugitive and a famed knife-fighter, killing 16 men before eventually dying in a police ambush in 1874 in the town of Lobos in Buenos Aires Province. A 1973 biographical film by arty local director Leonardo Favio was a box-office smash.

UN DÍA DE CAMPO

In the late 19th century, well-to-do European families bought huge blocks of pampas land on which to build estancias, often with luxurious houses reminiscent of the old country. The advent of industrial agriculture has led many estancias to turn to tourism for income; others combine tourism with small-scale farming.

The gauchos who once herded cows now have a new sideline shepherding visitors, putting on riding shows or preparing large-scale *asados* (barbecues). You can visit an estancia for a *día de campo* (day in the country) or to stay overnight or for a weekend. There are estancias for most budgets: some are ultraluxurious bed-and-breakfasts, others are homey, family-run farms.

A day at an estancia typically involves a late breakfast; horseback riding or a long walk; a full-blown asado accompanied by Argentine red wine; and afternoon tea. Longer stays at upscale establishments might also include golf or other sports; at working farms you can

Gaucho on an estancia near El Calafate, Patagonia, Argentina

feed animals or help with the milking. Estancia accommodation generally includes all meals, and although some estancias are close to towns, it's rare to leave the grounds during a stay.

HORSEMANSHIP

During a visit to an estancia, you may see gauchos demonstrating traditional skills and games such as:

Zapateo Criollo: a complicated, rhythmic, foot-stomping dance.

Jineteada or Doma: rodeo, gaucho-style.

La Carrera de Sortija: riders gallop under a bar from which metal rings are hung, trying to spear a ring on a stick as they pass.

Carrera Cuadrera: a short horseback sprint that riders start from a standstill.

Boleadas and Pialadas: catching an animal using boleadoras or a lasso, respectively.

La Maroma: participants hang from a bar or rope and jump onto a horse that gallops beneath them.

GAUCHO GRUB

When gauchos were out on the pampas for weeks, even months, at a time, their diet revolved around one food—beef—and one drink—mate (a type of tea). Times may have changed, but most Argentinians still consume a lot of both.

MAKING THE MOST OF AN ASADO

Whether you're just at someone's home or out on an estancia, a traditional Argentinian asado is a drawn-out affair. All sorts of meats go on the grill initially, including chorizo sausage, black pudding, and sweetbreads. These are grilled and served before the larger cuts. You'll probably also be served a picada (cheese, salami, and other snacks). Follow the local example and go easy on these starters: there's lots more to come.

The main event is, of course, the beef. Huge, grass-fed chunks of it, roasted for at least two hours over hot coals and flavored with little more than salt. While the asador (barbecuer) does his stuff, it's traditional to admire his or her skills; interfering (criticism, touching the meat, or the like) is not part of this tradition. The first meat to be served is often thick-cut ribs, accompanied simply by a mixed salad and bread. Then there will be a pause for digestion, and the asador will serve the choicest cuts: flank or tenderloin, usually. All this is washed down with a robust red wine and, not surprisingly, followed by a siesta.

Gaucho asado (barbecue), Argentina

MATE FOR BEGINNERS

Gauchos drinking mate

Mate (mah-tay) is a strong tea made from the dried leaves of *Ilex paraguariensis*, known as yerba. It's drunk from a gourd (also called a mate) through a metal straw with a filter on the end (the *bombilla*).

Mate has long been a traditional drink for the Guaraní people native to Argentina's northeast. They introduced it to Jesuit missionaries, who learned to cultivate it, and today, most yerba mate is still grown in Misiones and Corrientes provinces. The drink eventually became popular throughout Argentina, Uruguay, and southern Brazil.

Much like tea in England, mate serves as the basis of social interaction: people drink it at any hour of the day. Several drinkers share the same gourd, which is refilled and passed round the group. It's often extended to strangers as a welcoming gesture. If you're shown this hospitality be sure to wait your turn, drink all the mate in the gourd fairly quickly, and hand the gourd directly back to the *cebador* (server). Don't pour yourself a mate if someone else is the cebador, and avoid wiping or wiggling the straw around. Also, you don't say "gracias" until you've had your fill.

WHAT'S IN A MATE?

Caffeine: 30 mg per 8-oz serving (versus 47 mg in tea and 100 mg in coffee)

Vitamins:
A, C, E, B1, B2, B3, B5, B complex

Minerals:
Calcium, manganese, iron, selenium, potassium, magnesium, phosphorus, zinc

Antioxidant properties:
similar to green tea

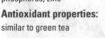

SERVING MATE

1) Heat a kettle of water to just before boiling (176°F/80°C)—boiling water ruins yerba.

2) Fill 2/3 of the gourd with yerba.

3) Without the bombilla in place, cover the gourd with your hand, and turn it quickly upside down (to get rid of any fine yerba dust that can block the bombilla).

4) For some reason, yerba never sits flat in the gourd; pour some hot water in the empty space left by the slightly slanting yerba leaves. Let the yerba swell a little, cover the top of the bombilla with your thumb, and drive it firmly into the leaves.

5) Finish filling the gourd with water, pouring it in slowly near the bombilla's base. (Some people also add sugar at this point.)

6) Drink all the mate in the gourd (the cebador traditionally drinks first, so the mate isn't so bitter when brewed for others) and repeat Step 5, passing the gourd to the next drinker—and so on—until the yerba mate loses its flavor.

🍴 Restaurants

★ Almacén de Ramos Generales

$$ | **ARGENTINE** | Airy and charming, this traditional eatery's classic Argentine fare is consistently delicious. You can snack on cheeses, olives, prosciutto, salami, and eggplant *en escabeche* (pickled). **Known for:** generous portions; genuine rural ambience; timewarp tavern. Ⓢ *Average main: pesos1200* ⊠ *Zapiola 143, between Lavalle and Sdo. Sombra, San Antonio de Areco* ☎ *2326/456–376* ⊕ *www.ramosgeneralesareco.com.ar.*

Pulpería Lo de Tito

$$ | **ARGENTINE** | Looking very much an old saloon/general store, this restaurant is part of what makes visiting the town like going to a museum. A solid choice for lunch where the fare doesn't try to be anything other than honest and abundant. **Known for:** gaucho spirit; lively ambience; authentic watering-hole. Ⓢ *Average main: pesos1400* ⊠ *Matheu 411, San Antonio de Areco* ☎ *2326/409–384* ⊙ *Closed Mon.–Tues.* 🍴 *Casual.*

🛏 Hotels

★ Estancia La Madrugada

$$$$ | **ALL-INCLUSIVE** | Just a few minutes from San Antonio de Areco takes you from town to the vastness of the Pampas... **Pros:** genuinely hospitable staff; great food and drink; peace and quiet. **Cons:** isolated, transport to or from town is extra (about 600 pesos each way); horses are perhaps, too tame; no televisions. Ⓢ *Rooms from: US$700* ⊠ *Off Camino de Yameo, San Antonio de Areco* ☎ *923/2643–4222* ⊕ *www.estancialamadrugada.com* ☎ *3 rooms* 🍴 *All-Inclusive.*

La Bamba de Areco

$$$$ | **B&B/INN** | Dating from the 1830s, the venerable La Bamba de Areco was once an important stop along the road from Buenos Aires to the northern reaches of Argentina. **Pros:** peace and quiet; gorgeous decor; great for outdoors

lovers. **Cons:** staff can seem harried; pricey; might be too isolated for some. Ⓢ *Rooms from: US$735* ⊠ *Ruta 31, San Antonio de Areco* ☎ *2326/454–895, 11/4519–4996* ⊕ *www.labambadeareco.com* ☎ *11 rooms* 🍴 *Free Breakfast.*

🍸 Nightlife

"Pulpería," "*almacén*" (general store), and "*despacho de bebidas*" (drinks counter) are some of the labels you might find on San Antonio's many traditional bars. Some genuinely haven't changed in 50 years (neither have their clientele), and others are well-intentioned re-creations; all provide truly atmospheric surroundings for a coffee or a drink.

Boliche de Bessonart

BARS | The ancient two-story brick building looks like it's right out of old western movie, and the interior also fits the part. Nothing fancy here, this is a place for vermouth and soda, beer, and platter of good cured meats and cheese. If you're around at night, you'll find it's a regular watering hole for the local gauchos. ⊠ *Corner, Zapiola and Segundo Sombra, San Antonio de Areco* ☎ *2325/655–600.*

La Cuadra

BARS | Silver and leather aren't the only hand-crafted products in San Antonio. A few varieties of artisanal beer, have been brewed locally for La Cuadra. The amber-colored Scottish ale packs a punch in winter; the paler pilsner's ideal for cooling off in summer. Pizzas, sandwiches, and other snacks accompany them. Just don't sit too closely to the speakers. ⊠ *Zapiola 76, San Antonio de Areco* ☎ *11/3901–0244* ⊙ *Closed Mon.–Wed.*

🛍 Shopping

San Antonio de Areco is an excellent place to pick up high-quality handicrafts and gifts, especially traditional silverware and leather goods. Workshops that double as stores fill the old houses lining

Calle Alsina and other streets leading off Plaza Arellano, the main square.

Gustavo Stagnaro

CRAFTS | Gustavo Stagnaro is a big name in San Antonio silversmithing. His majestic corner store sells gaucho knives, no-nonsense silver jewelry, and mate paraphernalia. ✉ Arellano at Matheu, San Antonio de Areco ☎ 2326/454–801, 2325/657–165 ⊕ www.stagnaro.com.ar.

La Olla de Cobre

CHOCOLATE | All the mouthwatering chocolates and alfajores (dulce de leche sandwich cookies) at La Olla de Cobre are handmade on the premises. Best of all, you can sample before you buy. ✉ Matheu 433, San Antonio de Areco ☎ 2326/453–105 ⊕ www.laolladecobre. com.ar ⊗ Closed Tues.

Lo de Arnaldi

GENERAL STORE | Housed in beautiful old Italianate building, this shop carries all you need for country life, from clothing and hand-loomed ponchos to cutlery sets and home decorations. The products aren't just lovely to look at, they're meant to be used. It's a great for souvenirs beyond fridge magnets and alfajores. ✉ Arellano 45, San Antonio de Areco ☎ 11/6002–9998.

Patricio Draghi Platería & Joyería

JEWELRY & WATCHES | Much like his brother Mariano, Juan Patricio Draghi is a master artisan, and his shop is itself a jewelry box from another time where one wouldn't be surprised bumping into Henry James or Edith Wharton. The exquisite craftsmanship of his silver works and jewelry is breathtaking. Much of his heirloom-quality work is custom made, so you'll need to order well in advance of your visit, but all his items are of the finest quality. ✉ Arellano 45, San Antonio de Areco ☎ 2325/1565–3196 ⊕ patricio-draghi-plateria-joyeria.negocio. site.

Iguazú Falls

1,358 km (843 miles) north of Buenos Aires; 637 km (396 miles) west of Curitiba; 544 (338 miles) west of Vila Velha.

Iguazú consists of some 275 separate waterfalls—in the rainy season there are as many as 350—that plunge more than 200 feet onto the rocks below. They cascade in a deafening roar at a bend in the Iguazú River (Río Iguazú in Spanish, Rio Iguaçu in Portuguese) where the borders of Argentina, Brazil, and Paraguay meet. Dense, lush jungle surrounds the falls: here the tropical sun and the omnipresent moisture produce a towering pine tree in two decades instead of the seven it takes in, say, Scandinavia. By the falls and along the roadside, rainbows and butterflies are set off against vast walls of red earth, which is so ubiquitous that eventually even paper currency in the area turns red from exposure to the stuff.

The falls and the lands around them are protected by Argentina's Parque Nacional Iguazú (where the falls are referred to by their Spanish name, the Cataratas de Iguazú) and by Brazil's Parque Nacional do Iguaçu (where the falls go by the Portuguese name of Cataratas do Iguaçu).

To visit the falls, you can base yourself in the Argentine town of Puerto Iguazú, or its sprawling Brazilian counterpart, the city of Foz do Iguaçu. The two cities are 18 km (11 miles) and 25 km (15 miles) northwest of the falls, respectively, and are connected by an international bridge, the Puente Presidente Tancredo Neves.

Puerto Iguazú, Argentina

Originally a port for shipping wood from the region, Puerto Iguazú now revolves around tourism. This was made possible in the early 20th century when Victoria Aguirre, a wealthy visitor from Buenos Aires, funded the building of a road to the falls. Despite the constant stream of visitors from Argentina and abroad, Puerto Iguazú remains small and sleepy. Many of its secondary roads still aren't paved.

Many travelers to the falls—including those from Brazil—opt to stay on the Argentine side of the border because it's less expensive than the Brazilian side. The town is also a good place to wind down after a day or two of high-energy adventure before heading back to Buenos Aires. So spare some time to experience being surrounded by hummingbirds in a garden, or just grab some *helado* (ice cream) and meander to el Hito Tres Fronteras.

GETTING HERE AND AROUND

Aerolíneas Argentinas flies four to five times daily between Aeroparque Jorge Newbery in Buenos Aires and the Aeropuerto Internacional de Puerto Iguazú, which is about 20 km (12 miles) southeast of Puerto Iguazú; the trip takes 1¾ hours. JetSMART does the same trip two or three times daily and Flybondi once a day. Normal rates start at about 17,000 pesos roundtrip. Four Tourist Travel runs shuttle buses from the airport to hotels in Puerto Iguazú. They leave after every flight lands and cost 400 pesos. Taxis to Puerto Iguazú cost 1,100 pesos.

Vía Bariloche operates several daily buses between the Retiro bus station in Buenos Aires and the Puerto Iguazú Terminal de Omnibus in the center of town. The trip takes 17–19 hours, so it's worth paying the little extra for *coche cama* (sleeper) or *cama ejecutivo* (deluxe sleeper) services, which cost about 10,500 pesos one-way (regular semi-cama services cost around 9,500 pesos) but you save about 20 percent by ordering 30 days in advance. You can travel direct to Rio de Janeiro (26 hours) and São Paolo (18 hours) with Crucero del Norte; the trips cost from 9,000 and 4,000 pesos, respectively.

From Puerto Iguazú to the falls or the hotels along RN12, take El Práctico from the terminal or along Avenida Victoria Aguirre. Buses leave every 15 minutes from 7 to 7 and cost 300 pesos round-trip for tourists (100 pesos for residents).

There's little point in renting a car around Puerto Iguazú: daily rentals start at 7,300 to 11,000 pesos, many times what you pay for a taxi between the town and the falls.

Crucero del Norte runs an hourly cross-border public bus service (400 pesos) between the bus stations of Puerto Iguazú and Foz do Iguaçu. Locals don't have to get on and off for immigration, but be sure you do so. To reach the Argentine falls, change to local minibus service El Práctico at the intersection with RN12 on the Argentine side. For the Brazilian park, change to a local bus at the Avenida Cataratas roundabout.

Argentinean travel agency Sol Iguazú Turismo organizes door-to-door transport to both sides of the falls, and can reserve places on the Iguazú Jungle Explorer trips.

VISITOR INFORMATION Cataratas del Iguazú Visitors Center. ✉ *Off Ruta Nacional 101, Puerto Iguazú* ⊕ *www.iguazuargentina.com.* **Puerto Iguazú Tourist Office.** ✉ *Av. Victoria Aguirre 337, Puerto Iguazú* ☎ *3757/423–951* ⊕ *www.iguazuturismo. gob.ar.* **Sol Iguazú Turismo.** ✉ *Av. Victoria Aguirre 237, Puerto Iguazú* ☎ *3757/421–409, 3757/421–147* ⊕ *www.soliguazu. com.ar.*

Sights

The falls are not the only sights to see in these parts, though few people actually have time (or make time) to go see others.

Güirá Oga

WILDLIFE REFUGE | Although Iguazú Falls is home to around 450 bird species, the parks are so busy these days that you'd be lucky to see so much as a feather. It's

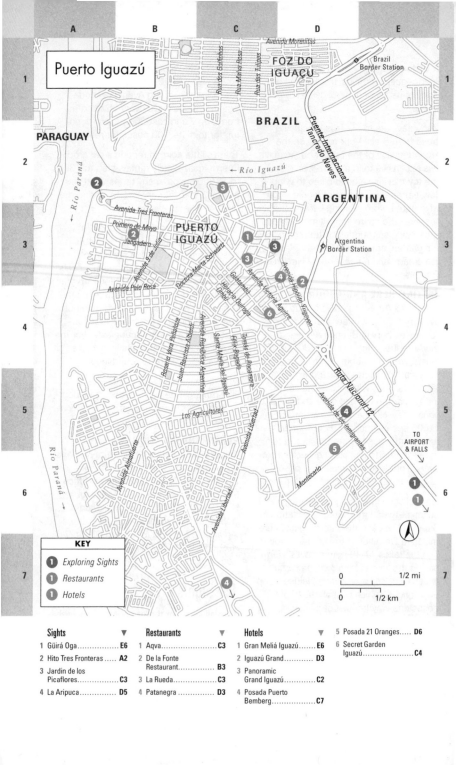

Puerto Iguazú

FOZ DO
IGUAÇU

Brazil
Border Station

PARAGUAY

BRAZIL

Río Paraná

Puente Internacional
Tancredo Neves

← Río Iguazú

ARGENTINA

Avenida Tres Fronteras

2

Primero de Mayo

Jangadero

PUERTO
IGUAZÚ

Argentina
Border Station

Avenida Palo Rosá

Avenida Victoria Aguirre

Ruta Nacional 12

TO
AIRPORT
& FALLS

Río Paraná

Montecarlo

KEY

1 Exploring Sights
1 Restaurants
1 Hotels

0   1/2 mi
0   1/2 km

another story at Güirá Oga, which means "House of the Birds" in Guaraní. Birds that were injured, displaced by deforestation, or confiscated from traffickers are brought here for treatment. The large cages also house species you rarely see in the area, including the gorgeous red macaw. The sanctuary is in a forested plot halfway between Puerto Iguazú and the falls. Entrance includes a 90-minute guided visit (in English and Spanish). ✉ *RN12, Km 1638, Puerto Iguazú* ☎ *3757/423–980* 🌐 *www.guiraoga.com.ar* 🎟 *1,200 pesos.*

Hito Tres Fronteras

VIEWPOINT | This viewing point west of the town center stands high above the turbulent reddish-brown confluence of the Iguazú and Paraná rivers, which also form the Triple Frontera, or Triple Border Landmark. A mini pale-blue-and-white obelisk reminds you you're in Argentina. Take binoculars to see Brazil's green-and-yellow equivalent across the Iguazú River; across the Paraná is Paraguay's, painted red, white, and blue. A row of overpriced souvenir stalls stands alongside the Argentine obelisk. ✉ *Av. Tres Fronteras, Puerto Iguazú.*

Jardín de los Picaflores

GARDEN | With more than 400 species of birds in the national parks surrounding Iguazú Falls, bird-watchers will be kept happily busy. This tiny garden north of Puerto Iguazú serves as more of a feeding station than a refuge, but it's busy with the little powerhouses zipping about. ✉ *Fray Luis Beltran 150, Puerto Iguazú* ☎ *3757/547–026* 🎟 *80 pesos.*

La Aripuca

NOTABLE BUILDING | It looks like a cross between a log cabin and the Pentagon, but this massive wooden structure—which weighs 551 tons—is a large-scale replica of a Guaraní bird trap. La Aripuca officially showcases different local woods, supposedly for conservation purposes—ironic, given the huge trunks used to build it and the overpriced wooden furniture that fills the gift shop. ✉ *RN12, Km 4.5, Puerto Iguazú* ☎ *3757/423–488* 🌐 *www.aripuca.com.ar* 🎟 *400 pesos.*

🍴 Restaurants

Aqva

$$$ | **MODERN ARGENTINE** | Locals are thrilled: finally, a date-night restaurant in Puerto Iguazú. Although the high-ceilinged split-level cabin seats too many to be truly intimate, the owners make up for it with well-spaced tables, discreet service, and low lighting. **Known for:** great service; excellent fish dishes; local ingredients. [$] *Average main: pesos2300* ✉ *Av. Córdoba at Carlos Thays, Puerto Iguazú* ☎ *3757/422–064* 🌐 *www.aqvarestaurant.com.*

De la Fonte Restaurant

$$$ | **ARGENTINE** | **FAMILY** | A single large restaurant with a large patio that's perfect for outdoor dining with lively folk music. The primary menu includes well-prepared pastas, local fish and meats, but there are separate menu pages for pizza, East Asian, and burgers, all of which they take seriously. **Known for:** lovely patio dining; live music; eclectic menu. [$] *Average main: pesos1950* ✉ *1° de Mayo 611, Puerto Iguazú* ☎ *3757/512–802* 🌐 *boutiquehoteldelafonte.com.ar/index.php/menu-del-restaurante/* 🕓 *Closed Sun.* 👔 *Casual.*

La Rueda

$$$ | **ARGENTINE** | This parrilla is so popular that it starts serving dinner at 6 pm—teatime by Argentine custom. The local beef isn't quite up to Buenos Aires standards, but La Rueda's perfectly cooked *bife de chorizo* is one of the best in town. **Known for:** efficient service gets diners in and out quickly; well priced; good grilled fish and steak. [$] *Average main: pesos1900* ✉ *Av. Córdoba 28, Puerto Iguazú* ☎ *3757/422–531* 🌐 *www.larueda1975.com.ar* 🕓 *No lunch Mon.*

Patanegra

$$$ | ARGENTINE | A chic new open-air restaurant with a sleek, sexy bar that turns out great cocktails. The restaurant is most proud of their aged steaks but everything from the *picadas* (cured meats and cheeses), fish and salads is perfectly turned out. **Known for:** aged beef; craft-beer oasis; best bar in town. $ *Average main: pesos2300* ✉ *Tareferos 155, Puerto Iguazú* ☎ *3757/451–072* ⊕ *patanegragourmet.com.*

Hotels

Gran Meliá Iguazú

$$$$ | HOTEL | That thundering you hear in the distance lets you know how close this hotel is to the falls—the lobby opens right onto the park trails, and half the rooms have big balconies with a fabulous view of the falls. **Pros:** the falls are on your doorstep; great buffet breakfast; well-designed spa. **Cons:** not much else other than the falls; restaurants and shops are an expensive taxi ride away; expensive. $ *Rooms from: US$520* ✉ *Within Parque Nacional Iguazú, Off Ruta Nacional 101, Puerto Iguazú* ☎ *3757/49–1800, 3757/49–1848* ⊕ *www. melia.com/en/hotels/argentina/iguazu-national-park/melia-iguazu/index.html* ⟿ *176 rooms, 8 suites* ¶ *Free Breakfast.*

Iguazú Grand

$$$ | RESORT | FAMILY | A full-on resort designed with families in mind, Iguazú Grand is bursting with facilities to keep every family member satisfied. **Pros:** spacious rooms and comfy beds; indoor and outdoor pools; courteous and helpful staff. **Cons:** slow elevators; passageways reverberate noise; downtown is a 20-minute walk or pricey cab ride away. $ *Rooms from: US$239* ✉ *Ruta 12, Km 1640, Puerto Iguazú* ☎ *3757/498–050* ⊕ *www.iguazugrand.com* ⟿ *134 rooms* ¶ *Free Breakfast.*

Panoramic Grand Iguazú

$$$ | HOTEL | The falls aren't the only good views in Iguazú: half the rooms at this chic hotel look onto the churning, jungle-framed waters of the Iguazú and Paraná rivers. **Pros:** river views; great attention to detail; gorgeous pool. **Cons:** staff can seem indifferent; airport transfers are overpriced; the in-house casino makes the lobby noisy. $ *Rooms from: US$200* ✉ *Cordoba y Felix de Azara, Puerto Iguazú* ☎ *3757/498–100, 3757/498–050* ⊕ *www.panoramicgrand. com* ⟿ *91 rooms* ¶ *Free Breakfast.*

Posada Puerto Bemberg

$$ | B&B/INN | Less than an hour south of Puerto Iguazú (35 minutes from the falls), the posada (inn) was built in 1943 to lodge guests to the yerba mate plantation and the new owners, a lovely and helpful couple, reopened it in 2007. **Pros:** not far from Iguazú falls; relaxing atmosphere; knowledgeable staff. **Cons:** limited dining menu; limited activities; far from the city. $ *Rooms from: US$116* ✉ *Fundadores Bemberg s/n, Puerto Iguazú* ☎ *3757/496–500* ⊕ *www.posadapuertobemberg.com* ⟿ *14 rooms, 1 five-room house* ¶ *Free Breakfast.*

Posada 21 Oranges

$$ | B&B/INN | You'll get a warm welcome at this rootsy B&B, which is surrounded by a lush garden. **Pros:** helpful and attentive owners; peaceful surroundings; abundant homemade breakfasts served on the garden terrace. **Cons:** low on luxury; some rooms are cramped; too far to walk to town center. $ *Rooms from: US$180* ✉ *Montecarlo s/n, near RN12, Km 5, Puerto Iguazú* ☎ *3757/558–848* ⊕ *www.21oranges.com* ▭ *No credit cards* ⟿ *10 rooms* ¶ *Free Breakfast.*

Continued on page 156

By Victoria Patience

IGUAZÚ FALLS

Big water. That's what y-guasu—the name given to the falls by the indigenous Guaraní people—means. As you approach, a thundering fills the air and steam rises above the trees. Then the jungle parts. Spray-soaked and speechless, you face the Devil's Throat, and it's clear that "big" doesn't come close to describing this wall of water.

Taller than Niagara, wider than Victoria, Iguazú's raging, monumental beauty is one of nature's most awe-inspiring sights. The Iguazú River, on the border between Argentina and Brazil, plummets 200 feet to form the Cataratas de Iguazú (as the falls are known in Spanish) or Foz do Iguaçu (their Portuguese name). Considered to be one waterfall, Iguazú is actually made up of around 275 individual drops, that stretch along 2.7 km (1.7 mi) of cliff-face. Ranging from picturesque cascades to immense cataracts, this incredible variety is what makes Iguazú so special. National parks in Brazil and Argentina protect the falls and the flora and fauna that surround them. Exploring their jungle-fringed trails can take two or three days: you get right alongside some falls, gaze down dizzily into others, and can take in the whole spectacle from afar. You're sure to come across lizards, emerald- and sapphire-colored hummingbirds, clouds of butterflies, and scavenging raccoonlike coatis. You'll also glimpse monkeys and toucans, if you're lucky.

GEOLOGY 101

Over 100 million years ago, lava surged up through cracks in the earth's crust near Iguazú. It spread out over the surrounding area, forming three layers of basalt (a dark, fine-grained rock) tens of meters high. The Iguazú River, which starts 1,200 km (745 mi) east, flowed over this. Later, the movement of tectonic plates raised parts of the surface, which became stepped. As the river flowed over these steps it eroded the rock surface it fell on even more, and over the next few million years, the waters carved out what are now the falls.

WHEN TO GO

Time of year	Advantages	Disadvantages
Nov.—Feb.	High rainfall in December and January, so expect lots of water.	Hot and sticky. December and January are popular with local visitors. High water levels stop Zodiac rides.
Mar.—Jun.	Increasingly cooler weather. Fewer local tourists. Water levels are usually good.	Too cold for some people, especially when you get wet. Occasional freak water shortages.
Jul.—Oct.	Cool weather.	Low rainfall in July and August—water levels can be low. July is peak season for local visitors.

WHERE TO GO: ARGENTINA VS. BRAZIL

Argentines and Brazilians can fight all day about who has the best angle on the falls. But the two sides are so different that comparisons are academic. To really say you've done Iguazú (or Iguaçu), you need to visit both. If you twist our arm, we'll say the Argentine side is a better experience with lots more to do, but (and this is a big "but") the Brazilian side gives you a tick in the box and the best been-there-done-that photos. It's also got more non-falls-related activities (but you have to pay extra for them).

	ARGENTINA	BRAZIL
Park Name	Parque Nacional Iguazú	Parque Nacional do Iguaçu
The experience	Up close and personal (you're going to get wet).	What a view!
The falls	Two-thirds are in Argentina including Garganta del Diablo, the star attraction.	The fabulous panoramic perspective of the Garganta do Diablo is what people really come for.
Timing	One day to blitz the main attractions. Two days to explore fully.	Half a day to see the falls; all day if you do other activities.
Other activities	Extensive self-guided hiking and Zodiac rides.	Organized hikes, Zodiac rides, boat rides, helicopter rides, rafting, abseiling.
Park size	67,620 hectares (167,092 acres)	182,262 hectares (450,379 acres)
Animal species	80 mammals/450 birds	50 mammals/200 birds

VITAL STATISTICS

Number of falls: 160—275*	Total length: 2.7 km (1.7 mi)	Average Flow: 396,258 gallons per second Peak Flow: 1,717,118 gallons per second
Major falls: 19	Height of Garganta del Diablo: 82 m (270 feet)	Age: 120—150 million years

*Depending on water levels

IGUAZÚ ITINERARIES

LIGHTNING VISIT. If you only have one day, limit your visit to the Argentine park. Arrive when it opens, and get your first look at the falls aboard one of Iguazú Jungle Explorer's Zodiacs. The rides finish at the Circuito Inferior: take a couple of hours to explore this. (Longer summer opening hours give you time to squeeze in the **Isla San Martín**.) Grab a quick lunch at the Dos Hermanas snack bar, then blitz the shorter Circuito Superior.

Tren Ecologico de la Selva

You've kept the best for last: catch the train from **Estación Cataratas** to **Estación Garganta del Diablo,** where the trail to the viewing platform starts (allow at least two hours for this).

BEST OF BOTH SIDES. Two days gives you enough time to see both sides of the falls. Visit the Brazilian park on your second day to get the panoramic take on what you've experienced up-close in Argentina. If you arrive at 9 AM, you've got time to walk the entire trail, take photos, have lunch in the Porto Canoas service area, and be back at the park entrance by 1 PM. You could spend the afternoon doing excursions and activities from Macuco Safari and

KEY

♿	Wheelchair Accessible
🍴	Restaurants
⬧	Scenic Viewpoint
- - -	Walking/Hiking Trails
◯	Ferry Lines
====	Rail Lines

Estación Garganta del Diablo

Garganta del Diablo

Garganta del Diablo

ARGENTINA

Parque Nacional do Iguaço

Isla San Martin

BRAZIL

Rio Iguaz

Garganta del Diablo

Macuco EcoAventura, or visiting the Itaipú dam. Alternatively, you could keep the visit to Brazil for the afternoon of the second day, and start off with a lightning return visit to the Argentine park and see the **Garganta del Diablo** (left) with the sun rising behind it.

SEE IT ALL. With three days you can explore both parks at a leisurely pace. Follow the one-day itinerary, then return to the Argentine park on your second day. Make a beeline for the Garganta del Diablo, which looks different in the mornings, then spend the afternoon exploring the **Sendero Macuco** (and Isla San Martín, if you didn't have time on the first day). You'll also have time to visit Güira Oga bird sanctuary or La Aripuca (both on RN 12) afterwards. You could spend all of your third day in the Brazilian park, or just the morning, giving you time to catch an afternoon flight or bus.

Estación Central

Estación Cataratas

Circuito Superior

Parque Nacional Iguazú

Circuito Inferior

Dos Hermanas

VISITING THE PARKS

Garganta del Diablow

Argentina's side of the falls is in the **Parque Nacional Iguazú,** which was founded in 1934 and declared a World Heritage Site in 1984. The park is divided into two areas, each of which is organized around a train station: Estación Cataratas or the Estación Garganta del Diablo. (A third, Estación Central, is near the park entrance.)

Paved walkways lead from the main entrance past the **Visitor Center,** called *Yvyrá Retá*—"country of the trees" in Guaraní (☎ 3757/49-1469 ⊕ www.iguazuargentina.com ✉ 60 pesos ⊘ Mar.–Aug. 8–6; Sept.–Feb. 8–8). Colorful visual displays provide a good explanation of the region's ecology and human history. To reach the park proper, you cross through a small plaza containing a food court, gift shops, and ATM. From the nearby Estación Central, the gas-propelled Tren de la Selva (Jungle Train) departs every 20 minutes.

In Brazil, the falls can be seen from the **Parque Nacional Foz do Iguaçu** (☎ 45/3521–4400 ⊕ www.cataratasdoiguacu.com.br ✉ R$21.15 ⊘ Apr.–Sep 9–5; Oct.–Mar. 9–6). Much of the park is protected rain forest—off-limits to visitors and home to the last

viable populations of panthers as well as rare flora. Buses and taxis drop you off at a vast, plaza alongside the park entrance building. As well as ticket booths, there's an ATM, a snack bar, gift shop, and information and currency exchange. Next to the entrance turnstiles is the small **Visitor Center,** where helpful geological models explain how the falls were formed. Double-decker buses run every 15 minutes between the entrance and the trailhead to the falls, 11 km (7 mi) away; the buses stop at the entrances to excursions run by private operators Macuco Safari and Macuco Ecoaventura (these aren't included in your ticket). The trail ends in the **Porto Canoas** service area. There's a posh linen-service restaurant with river views, and two fast-food counters the with tables overlooking the rapids leading to the falls.

VISAS

U.S. citizens don't need a visa to visit Argentina as tourists, but the situation is more complicated in Brazil. ⇨ See the planning section at the beginning of the chapter.

EXCURSIONS IN AND AROUND THE PARKS

Parque Nacional Foz do Iguaçu, Brazil

Iguazú Jungle (☎ 3757/42–1696 ⊕ www.iguazujungle.com) runs trips within the Argentine park. Their standard trip, the Gran Aventura, costs 150 pesos and includes a truck ride through the forest and a Zodiac ride to San Martín, Bossetti, and the Salto Tres Mosqueteros (be ready to get soaked). The truck carries so many people that most animals are scared away: you're better off buying the 75-peso boat trip—Aventura Nautica—separately.

You can take to the water on the Brazilian side with **Macuco Safari** (☎ 045/3574–4244 ⊕ www.macucosafari.com.br). Their signature trip is a Zodiac ride around (and under) the Salto Tres Mosqueteros. You get a more sedate ride on the Iguaçu Explorer, a 3½ hour trip up the river.

In Brazil, **Cânion Iguaçu** (☎ 045/3529–6040 ⊕ www.campodedesafios.com.br) offers rafting and canopying, as well as abseiling over the river from the Salto San Martín. They also offer wheelchair-compatible equipment.

Macuco Ecoaventura (☎ 045/3529–6927) is one of the official tour operators within the Brazilian park. Their Trilha do Pozo Negro combines a 9-km guided hike or bike ride with a scary boat trip along the upper river (the bit before the falls). The aptly-named Floating trip is more leisurely; shorter jungle hikes are also offered.

ON THE CATWALK

You spend most of your visit to the falls walking the many trails and catwalks, so be sure to wear comfortable shoes.

Secret Garden Iguazú

$$ | **B&B/INN** | Dense tropical vegetation overhangs the wooden walkway that leads to this tiny guesthouse's three rooms, tucked away in a pale-blue clapboard house. **Pros:** wood deck overlooking the back-to-nature garden; owner's charm and expert mixology; home-away-from-home vibe. **Cons:** no pool; comfortable but not luxurious; the three rooms book up fast. [$] *Rooms from: US$108* ✉ *Los Lapachos 623, Puerto Iguazú* ☎ *3757/423–099* 🌐 *www.secretgardeniguazu.com* 💳 *No credit cards* 🛏 *3 rooms* 🍴 *Free Breakfast.*

Foz do Iguaçu, Brazil

The construction of the Itaipú Dam (now the world's second largest) in 1975 transformed Foz do Iguaçu into a bustling city with seven times more people than nearby Puerto Iguazú. It's precisely because of the city's size that many visitors to the falls arrange accommodations in or near Foz do Iguaçu. After daytime adventures in the national park, the city's nightlife extends the fun. Aside from pubs, clubs, and all kinds of live music, there's even a samba show.

GETTING HERE AND AROUND

There are direct flights between Foz do Iguaçu and São Paulo (1½ hours; $230), Rio de Janeiro (2 hours; $260), and Curitiba (1 hour; $280) on LATAM, which also has connecting flights to Salvador, Recife, Brasilia, other Brazilian cities, and Buenos Aires. Low-cost airline GOL operates slightly cheaper direct flights on the same three routes.

The Aeroporto Internacional Foz do Iguaçu is 13 km (8 miles) southeast of downtown Foz. The 20-minute taxi ride should cost R$50 to R$60; the 45-minute regular bus ride about R$4. Note that several major hotels are on the highway to downtown, so a cab ride from the airport to these may be less than R$40. A cab ride from downtown hotels directly to the Parque Nacional in Brazil costs about R$80.

Via bus, the trip between São Paolo and Foz do Iguaçu takes 17 hours (R$153). The Terminal Rodoviário in Foz do Iguaçu is 5 km (3 miles) northeast of downtown. There are regular buses into town; they stop at the Terminal de Transportes Urbano (local bus station, often shortened to TTU) at Avenida Juscelino Kubitschek and Rua Mem de Sá. From platform 2, Bus No. 120 (labeled "Parque Nacional") also departs every 15 minutes (from 7 to 7) to the visitor center at the park entrance; the fare is R$4. The buses run along Avenida Juscelino Kubitschek and Avenida Jorge Schimmelpfeng, where you can also flag them down.

There's no real reason to rent a car in Foz do Iguaçu, as you can't cross the border in a rental car. There are *pontos de taxi* (taxi stands) at intersections all over town. Hotels and restaurants can call you a cab, but you can also hail them on the street.

VISITOR INFORMATION Foz do Iguaçu Tourism Office. ✉ *Av. das Cataratas, 166-205, Vila Yolanda, Foz do Iguaçu* ☎ *800/045–1516* 🌐 *www.destino.foz.br.*

👁 Sights

Ecomuseu de Itaipú (*Itaipú Eco-Museum*)
OTHER MUSEUM | At the Ecomuseu de Itaipú, you can learn about the geology, archaeology, and efforts to preserve the flora and fauna of the area since the Itaipú Dam was built. This museum is funded by the dam's operator, Itaipú Binacional, so the information isn't necessarily objective. ✉ *Av. Presidente Tancredo Neves 6731, Foz do Iguaçu* ☎ *045/3576–7000* 🌐 *www.turismoitaipu.com.br* 🎟 *R$35, tours from R$46.*

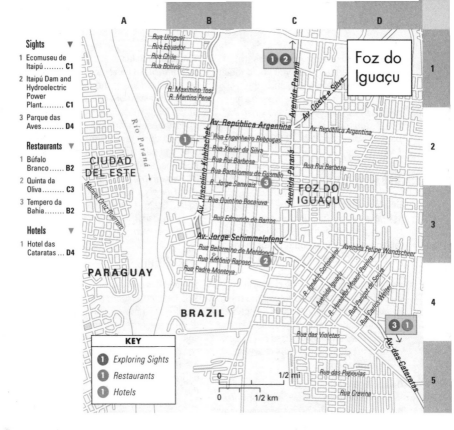

Foz do Iguaçu

CIUDAD DEL ESTE

PARAGUAY

BRAZIL

FOZ DO IGUAÇU

KEY

1 Exploring Sights

1 Restaurants

1 Hotels

0   1/2 mi

0   1/2 km

Itaipú Dam and Hydroelectric Power Plant

DAM | It took more than 30,000 workers eight years to build this 8-km (5-mile) dam, voted one of the Seven Wonders of the Modern World by the American Society of Civil Engineers. The monumental structure, which produces roughly 17% of Brazil's electricity and 75% of Paraguay's, was the largest hydroelectric power plant in the world until China's Three Gorges Dam was completed.

You get plenty of insight into how proud this makes the Brazilian government— and some idea of how the dam was built—during the 30-minute video that precedes the hour-long guided panoramic bus tours of the complex. Although commentaries are humdrum, the sheer size of the dam is an impressive sight. To see more than a view over the spillways,

consider the special tours, which take you inside the cavernous structure and into the control room. Night tours—which include a light-and-sound show—begin at 8 on Friday and Saturday, 9 during the summer months (reserve ahead). ⊠ Av. Tancredo Neves 6702, Foz do Iguaçu ☎ 0800/645–4645 ⊕ www.turismoitaipu.com.br ☒ Panoramic tour R$46, special tour R$130.

Parque das Aves (Bird Park)

ZOO | Flamingos, parrots, and macaws are some of the more colorful inhabitants of this privately run park. Right outside the Parque Nacional Foz do Iguaçu, it's an interesting complement to a visit to the falls. A winding path leads you through untouched tropical forest and walk-through aviaries containing hundreds of species of birds. One of the amazing experiences is the toucan enclosure, where they are so close you could touch them. Iguanas, alligators, and other nonfeathered friends have their own pens. ✉ *Rodovia das Cataratas, Km 17.1, Foz do Iguaçu* ☎ *045/3529–8282* 🌐 *www.parquedasaves.com.br* 🎫 *R$70* 🕒 *Closed Mon.*

🍴 Restaurants

Búfalo Branco

$$$ | **BRAZILIAN** | The city's finest and largest churrascaria does a killer *rodizio* (all-you-can-eat meat buffet). The *picanha* (beef rump cap) stands out among the dozens of meat choices, but pork, lamb, and chicken find their way onto the metal skewers they use to grill the meat. **Known for:** meat palace; salad selection; Brazilian churrasco (skewers). [$] *Average main: R$120* ✉ *Av. Rebouças 530, Foz do Iguaçu* ☎ *045/3523–9744* 🌐 *www.bufalobranco.com.br.*

Quinta da Oliva

$$$ | **ITALIAN** | Open, sleek, and comfortable space for terrific pizzas, freshly-made pastas, and grilled meats. The brick ovens are impressive, and the dishes are fresh and tasty. **Known for:** extensive wine list; fresh pasta; wood-oven pizza. [$] *Average main: R$100* ✉ *R. Estanislau Zambrzycki, 197, Centro* ☎ *45/99157–0719, 45/33572–3131* 🌐 *www.quintadaoliva.com.br* 🕒 *No lunch.*

Tempero da Bahia

$$$ | **BRAZILIAN** | If you're not traveling as far as Salvador and the state of Bahia, you can at least check out its flavors at this busy restaurant. It specializes in northeastern fare like *moquecas* (a rich seafood stew made with coconut milk and palm oil). **Known for:** abundant portions; seafood; Moqueca stew. [$] *Average main: R$120* ✉ *Rua Marechal Deodoro 1228, Foz do Iguaçu* ☎ *045/3025–1144* 🌐 *www.restaurantetemperodabahia.com* 🕒 *No lunch Tues. No dinner Sun.*

🛏 Hotels

★ Hotel das Cataratas

$$$$ | **RESORT** | Not only is this stately hotel *in* the national park, with views of the smaller falls from the front-side suites, but it also provides the traditional comforts of a colonial-style establishment: large rooms, terraces, vintage furniture, and hammocks. **Pros:** right inside the park, a short walk from the falls; serious colonial-style charm; friendly, helpful staff. **Cons:** far from Foz do Iguaçu so you're limited to the on-site restaurants; only the most expensive suites have views of the falls; rooms aren't as luxurious as the price promises. [$] *Rooms from: R$2,000* ✉ *Rodovia das Cataratas, Km 32, Foz do Iguaçu* ☎ *045/2102–7000, 0800/726–4545* 🌐 *www.belmond.com/hotels/south-america/brazil/iguassu-falls/belmond-hotel-das-cataratas* 🛏 *197 rooms, 5 suites* 🍴 *Free Breakfast.*

SIDE TRIPS TO URUGUAY

Updated by
Allan Kelin

⊙ Sights	🍴 Restaurants	🛏 Hotels	⬤ Shopping	🍸 Nightlife
★★★★★	★★★★★	★★★★★	★★★★★	★★★★★

WELCOME TO SIDE TRIPS TO URUGUAY

TOP REASONS TO GO

★ **Bask in Colonial Splendor:** There's little that could be called old in this modern, progressive country—except for the once-walled 1680 Portuguese settlement of Colonia del Sacramento. Flowers spill over balconies, balladeers serenade their sweethearts, and lanterns illuminate the streets of this well-preserved colonial city.

★ **Frolic with the Rich and Famous:** One visit to Uruguay's tony Punta del Este, and Brazil's beaches will forever seem a tad too déclassé. From December through February, fun-in-the-sun crowds flock here.

★ **Ride 'Em, Cowboy:** The *gaucho* embodies the country's spirit, and these rugged cowboys still mount their trusty horses to round up livestock on vast ranges. If your time is limited, you don't even need to leave urban Montevideo to see the spectacle: the capital's El Prado district is the site of the best rodeos.

Uruguay is one of South America's smallest countries, both in area (it's roughly the size of England) and population. Montevideo anchors the coast, and most of the population and action hugs the water line. Vast ranches and farms fill the hilly, sparsely developed interior. Uruguay's elite beach destination Punta del Este attracts beachgoers from across South America and beyond while historic Colonia del Sacramento offers a quiet getaway for many Buenos Aires residents who take a quick ferry ride across the Río de la Plata. Ferries also reach Montevideo from Buenos Aires in a couple hours, making Uruguay a favorite and easy trip from Argentina's capital.

1 Montevideo. True to developing-country patterns, all roads, literal and figurative, lead to Montevideo. Uruguay's friendly capital strings for miles along the southern coast with an odd positioning that means you can walk south, north, or west from the center city to reach the water.

2 Colonia del Sacramento. It's hard not to fall in love with Colonia. The picturesque town has a six-by-six-block old city with wonderfully preserved architecture, rough cobblestone streets, and a sleepy grace. Tranquility reigns here—bicycles and golf carts outnumber cars.

3 Punta del Este. One of the world's trendiest beach communities, Punta del Este is a glitzy destination that doesn't sleep in peak season. Every summer, families and the occasional celebrity jet-set flock to its shore for sun, good food, and luxury.

It used to be that Uruguay missed out on the touristic attention it deserved, dwarfed by its larger neighbors Argentina and Brazil. That has changed dramatically in recent years, though, as many around the world have turned their attention to this serene, welcoming country. The government has mounted concerted efforts to advertise Uruguay and its offerings to international travelers, and there is plenty to show: Colonia del Sacramento, one of South America's most historic cities; beach-side resort town Punta del Este; and the coastal capital city Montevideo. Many travelers come away impressed and inspired with Uruguay's tranquil beauty and laid-back vibe.

On a continent with a turbulent past, Uruguayans have parlayed their human and natural resources into a history of success. A strong middle class, a high standard of living, relative prosperity, and a long tradition of peace, good government, and democracy have defined Uruguay (although that last feature did disappear for a dozen years in the last century). The country has enacted landmark legislation that made it the first in South America to sever relations between church and state, to grant women the right to vote, to permit same-sex civil unions, to legalize cannabis, and to enact a generous social-welfare system. The *Economist* even named Uruguay its "country of the year in 2013" for its landmark legislation.

Today about half the country's population lives in Uruguay's capital city. The country takes pride in the number of famous artists it produces, and Uruguayans like to claim their country as the birthplace of the internationally renowned tango singer Carlos Gardel, although the Argentineans and French also vie for this honor. As in Argentina, the legendary *gaucho* is Uruguay's most potent cultural fixture, and it's difficult to pass a day without some reference to these cowboys who once roamed the country singing their melancholy ballads or, of course, to drive without seeing grazing cows or horses. You can still see remnants of the gaucho lifestyle on active ranches throughout the country.

Planning

When to Go

Between October and March the temperatures are pleasant—it's warm and the country is in bloom. Unless you're prepared to tangle with the multitude of tourists that overwhelm Punta del Este in January and February, late spring (November–December) and late winter (March) are the most appealing months to lounge on the beach.

Uruguay's climate has four distinct seasons. Summer (January–March) can be hot and humid, with temperatures as high as 90°F. Fall (April–June) is marked by warm days and evenings cool enough for a light sweater. Winter (July–September) is cold and rainy, with average temperatures generally below 50°F. Although it seldom reaches freezing, the wind off the water can give you quite a chill. Spring (October–December) is much like the fall, except that the trees will be sprouting, rather than dropping, their leaves.

Getting Here and Around

AIR

Most international flights land at Montevideo's Aeropuerto Internacional de Carrasco, about 24 km (15 miles) east of downtown. Nearly all Montevideo-bound flights are routed through Buenos Aires. Aerolíneas Argentinas, LATAM, GOL, and Avianca run regular flights to Latin American metropolises like Buenos Aires and São Paulo, and there also is a nonstop American Airlines flight from Miami as well as direct flights to Paris and Madrid.

If you fly a strictly Argentina–Uruguay itinerary, you'll likely depart from Buenos Aires' domestic airport, the Aeroparque Jorge Newbery. Through flights on American Airlines use the capital's international airport at Ezeiza.

Service to the Aeropuerto Internacional de Punta del Este is frequent from many South American cities during the resort's December–March high season, but less so the rest of the year.

BOAT

Ferries cross the Río de la Plata between Argentina and Uruguay several times daily. Both Buquebus and Colonia Express travel to Colonia, where they have buses to Montevideo and Punta del Este, and Buquebus also offers direct service to Montevideo.

BUS

You can go almost anywhere in Uruguay by bus. Some are quite luxurious, with air-conditioning, movies, and snack service. Departures are frequent and fares low. Most companies are based in Montevideo and depart from its state-of-the-art Terminal Tres Cruces. The station's website (⊕ *www.trescruces.com. uy*) lists all bus schedules to and from Montevideo.

CAR

From Argentina, you can transport your car across the Río de la Plata by ferry. Alternatively, you can cross the Argentina–Uruguay border in three places: Puerto Unzue-Fray Bentos, Colón-Paysandu, or Concordia-Salto.

Roads between Montevideo and Punta del Este or Colonia del Sacramento are quite good, as are the handful of major highways. In the countryside, roads are usually surfaced with gravel. If you want to leave the main roads, it's best to speak with locals about current conditions before setting off. Trips will often take longer than expected, so budget extra time. On the upside, country roads often have little traffic and spectacular scenery.

Car-rental rates are often higher in Uruguay than in the United States because of the value-added tax. For an economy-size car, expect to pay around US$55 per day. Uruguayans tend to drive carefully, but visitors from Argentina have the reputation of driving with wild abandon. Since almost all roads have only two lanes, keep an eye out for passing vehicles.

Health and Safety

It's a good idea to avoid tap water, as pipes in many older buildings are made of lead. Almost everyone drinks locally bottled *agua mineral* (mineral water), which is available *con gas* or *sin gas* (with or without carbonation).

Uruguay would win most "Safest South American Country" competitions, but standard travel precautions apply. Keep an eye on your purse or wallet, avoid unnecessary displays of wealth, and avoid wandering back streets of Montevideo at night.

Restaurants

Argentina may leap to mind when discussing South American beef, but some 12 million cattle, primarily Hereford and Angus, graze Uruguay's open, vast grasslands—this in a nation of roughly 3.5 million people. Beef is the staple of the Uruguayan diet. It's quality, cheap, abundant, and often grilled in a style borrowed from the gauchos, and known as *parrillada*. A meal in an Uruguayan steak house should be on your agenda. Beef is also made into sausages, such as *chorizo* and *salchicha*, or is combined with ham, cheese, bacon, and peppers to make *matambre*.

Seafood is also popular here—and it's fresh and delicious, especially the *lenguado* (flounder), *merluza* (hake), and *calamar* (squid). Try the *raya a la manteca negra* (ray in blackened butter). If you are not up to a full meal, order what is often considered the national sandwich, *chivito*, a steak sandwich with thin strips of beef.

Uruguayan wines under the Bouza, Santa Rosa, and Calvinor labels are available in most restaurants. As Uruguayan wines also have raised their profile in the past decade, a vineyard visit or wine tasting is highly recommended. *Clericó* is a mixture of white wine and fruit juice, while *medio y medio* is part sparkling wine, part white wine.

Lunch is served between noon and 3; restaurants begin to fill around 12:30 and are packed by 1:30. Many restaurants do not open for dinner until 8 pm, and often don't start to get crowded until 9:30. Most pubs and *confiterías* (cafés) are open all day. Formal dress is rarely required. Smart sportswear is acceptable at even the fanciest establishments.

Hotels

Hotels here are generally comfortable and good value for your money. Most include breakfast in their rates. All but the most basic hotels have air-conditioning—you'll appreciate it during the hot summers. *Hosterías* are country inns that not only offer modest rooms, but are open for dinner as well. Menus tend to be limited, though the food served is unfailingly hearty.

Lodging at the beach requires reservations no matter what the time of year. Rooms fill up quickly (and prices increase dramatically) during the December–February high season. Rates go down during the shoulder months of November and March, but you can still count on good weather. Many hotels close for a few weeks between Easter and late May and/or in September.

Hotel reviews have been shortened. For full information, visit Fodors.com. Restaurant prices are the average cost of a main course at dinner or, if dinner is not served, at lunch. Hotel prices are the lowest cost of a standard double room in high season.

What It Costs in Uruguayan Pesos

	$	$$	$$$	$$$$
RESTAURANTS				
	Under 300	300–550	551–900	over 900
HOTELS				
	Under 2,500	2,500–7,000	7,001–15,000	over 15,000

Montevideo

Uruguay's capital city hugs the eastern bank of the Río de la Plata. A massive coastal promenade (*malecón*) that passes fine beaches, restaurants, and numerous parks recalls the sunny sophistications of the Mediterranean and is always dotted with Montevideans strolling, exercising, and lounging along the water. Montevideo has its share of glitzy shopping avenues and modern office buildings, balanced with its historic old city and sumptuous colonial architecture, as well as numerous leafy plazas and parks. It is hard not to draw comparisons to its sister city Buenos Aires across the river, and indeed Montevideo strikes many as a calmer, more manageable incarnation of Argentina's capital.

When the weather's good, La Rambla, a 22-km (14-mile) waterfront avenue that links the Old City with the eastern suburbs and changes names about a dozen times, gets packed with fishermen, ice-cream vendors, and joggers. Around sunset, volleyball and soccer games wind down as couples begin to appear for evening strolls. Polls consistently rate Montevideo as having the highest quality of life of any city in Latin America. After one visit here, especially on a lovely summer evening, you probably will agree.

GETTING HERE AND AROUND

Uruguay's principal airport, Aeropuerto Internacional de Carrasco (MVD), is 24 km (15 miles) east of Montevideo. A taxi to downtown costs about 1,600 pesos; plan on 1,800 pesos to reach the Ciudad Vieja. A city bus (marked Ciudadela) is cheap—about 32 pesos—but the drawback is that it takes an hour to get downtown.

AIR CONTACTS Aerolíneas Argentinas.
✉ *Plaza Independencia 818, Montevideo* ☎ *0810/222–86527* ⊕ *www.aerolineas. com.ar.* **Aeropuerto Internacional de**

Carrasco. ✉ *Ruta 101, km 19.950, Ciudad de la Costa* ☎ *598/2604–0329* ⊕ *www. aeropuertodecarrasco.com.uy.* **American Airlines.** ✉ *Carrasco International Airport, Montevideo* ☎ *1802/618–6115 In Uruguay* ⊕ *www.aa.com.*

Buquebus operates ferry service between Buenos Aires and the ports at Montevideo and Colonia. The trip takes less than three hours to Montevideo and about an hour to Colonia. A direct round-trip ticket between Buenos Aires and Montevideo costs about 26,300 pesos. A package that includes a round-trip ticket between Buenos Aires and Colonia and a shuttle bus to or from Montevideo costs about 19,000 pesos.

BOAT CONTACTS Buquebus. ✉ *Dársena Norte, Puerto Madero, Puerto Madero* ☎ *11/4316–6500* ⊕ *www.buquebus.com.*

Montevideo's public buses are a great alternative to taxis, which can be difficult to find during peak hours. Buses criss-cross the entire city 24 hours a day. You don't need exact change, and the price for any trip within Montevideo is only 32 pesos.

Colonia is serviced by several regional bus lines, including COT and Turil. The three-hour ride costs 500 pesos.

BUS CONTACTS COT. ☎ *2409–4949 in Montevideo* ⊕ *www.cot.com.uy.* **Terminal Tres Cruces.** ✉ *Bulevar General Artigas 1825, Centro* ☎ *598/2408–8601* ⊕ *www. trescruces.com.uy.* **Turil.** ☎ *1990 in Montevideo* ⊕ *www.turil.com.uy.*

Because La Rambla, Montevideo's riverside thoroughfare, extends for dozens of miles, driving is a good way to see the city. Roads are well maintained and drivers obey the traffic laws—a rarity in South America. It's easy to rent a car, both downtown and at the airport. In Montevideo, you can rent from several major international companies, including Avis, Budget, and Dollar, and from

What's In a Name?

Stories abound about the origin of Montevideo's unusual name. The generally accepted account holds that Magellan, traveling along the coast from Brazil in 1520, counted off six hills from the Brazilian border and thus named the city Monte (mountain) vi (roman numeral six) de (from) eo (este a oeste, or east to west).

smaller companies such as Inter Car and Multicar.

CAR-RENTAL CONTACTS Avis. ☎ *21700* ⊕ *www.avis.com.uy.* **Dollar.** ☎ *2682–8350 at Aeropuerto de Carrasco* ⊕ *www.dollar. com.uy.*

All cabs have meters that count *fichas,* or pulses, each 1/10 km (1/20 mile). When you arrive at your destination, the driver will take out an official chart that calculates the fare from the number of fichas elapsed. You can hail taxis on the street with ease, or call one to pick you up at your hotel. A ride to the airport from the Old City costs about 1,800 pesos, and 1,600 pesos from downtown.

TAXI CONTACTS Taxi Aeropuerto Internacional de Carrasco. ✉ *Montevideo* ⊹ *Aeropuerto Internacional de Carrasco* ☎ *2604–0323* ⊕ *www.taxisaeropuerto. com.*

SAFETY AND PRECAUTIONS

Although Montevideo doesn't have the problems with crime that larger cities in South America do, it's best to watch your wallet in crowded markets and to avoid walking down deserted streets at night. Most of Montevideo's residents stay up late, so the streets are usually full of people until 1 am. The city bus authority discourages boarding empty buses at

The Plaza Independencia is the heart of Montevideo, a great place for history lovers and people-watchers.

night. Look for the helpful tourist police decked out in blue berets and yellow vests that say *policía turística*. They patrol Avenida 18 de Julio, Ciudad Vieja, and the Mercado del Puerto.

ESSENTIALS

VISITOR INFORMATION Ministry of Tourism and Sport. ⊠ *Rambla 25 de Agosto 1825, Ciudad Vieja* ☎ *2/1885* ⊕ *www. uruguaynatural.com.*

Ciudad Vieja

Ciudad Vieja is fairly compact, and you could walk from one end to the other in about 15 minutes. Take care at night, when the area is fairly deserted.

 Sights

Cabildo de Montevideo

GOVERNMENT BUILDING | The original City Hall is where the Uruguayan constitution was signed in 1830. This two-story colonial edifice houses an impressive collection of paintings, antiques, costumes, and rotating history exhibits. Fountains and statuary line the interior patios. English-speaking guides are available. ⊠ *Calle Juan Carlos Gómez 1362, Ciudad Vieja* ☎ *2915–9685* ⊕ *cabildo.montevideo.gub. uy* 🎫 *Free* 🕐 *Closed Sun.*

Casa de Fructuoso Rivera

HISTORIC HOME | Once the home of General Fructuso Rivera, Uruguay's first president, this neoclassical Rivera House from the early 1800s was acquired by the government in 1942 and opened as a national history museum. Exhibits inside this pale yellow colonial house with an octagonal cupola document the development of Uruguay and showcase daily life in Montevideo of the 1900s. ⊠ *Calle Rincón 437, Ciudad Vieja* ☎ *2915–3316* ⊕ *www.museohistorico.gub.uy* 🎫 *Free* 🕐 *Closed Mon.–Tues.*

Casa de Lavalleja Museum

HISTORIC HOME | This Spanish neoclassical home was built in 1783 and later became the home of General Juan A. Lavalleja, who distinguished himself in Uruguay's war for independence. This pristine

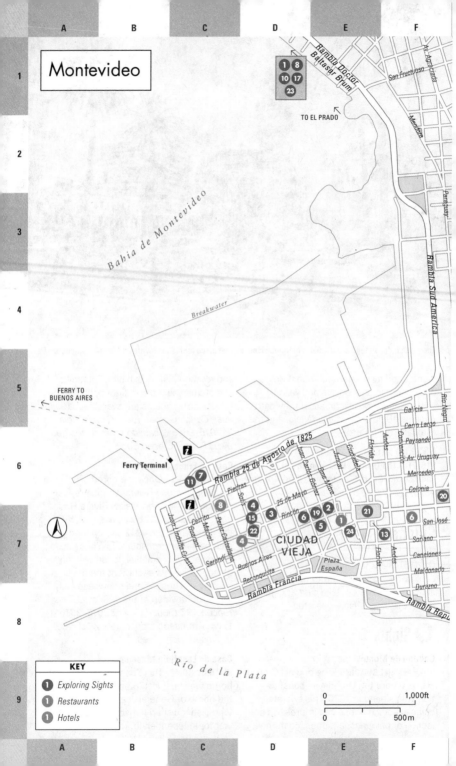

Montevideo

KEY
- ① Exploring Sights
- ① Restaurants
- ① Hotels

Bahía de Montevideo

Breakwater

FERRY TO
BUENOS AIRES

Ferry Terminal

Rambla 25 de Agosto de 1825

Rambla Francia

Plaza
España

CIUDAD
VIEJA

Río de la Plata

TO EL PRADO

Rambla Doctor
Baltasar Brum

Rambla Sud America

Rambla Repu

0   1,000ft
0   500m

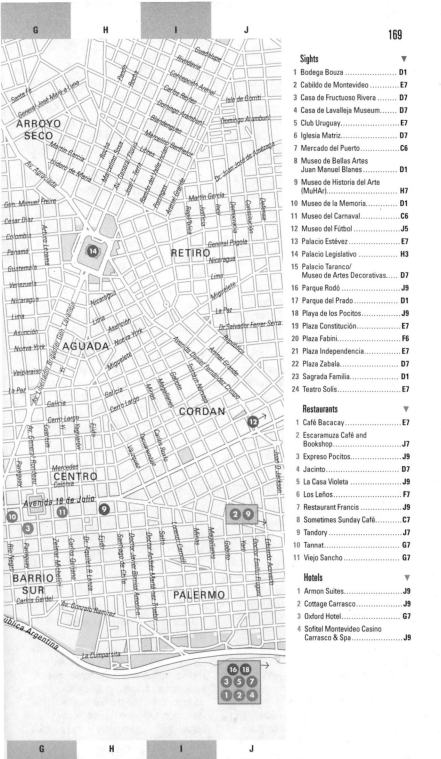

Sights ▼

Restaurants ▼

Hotels ▼

colonial home with lovely wrought-iron balconies displays manuscripts and historical memorabilia. ⊠ *Calle Zabala 1469, Ciudad Vieja* ☏ *2915–3316* 🖃 *Free* 🕓 *Closed Mon.–Tues.*

Club Uruguay

HISTORIC HOME | Uruguay's most prestigious private social club, founded in 1888, is headquartered in this eclectic, three-story neoclassical national monument on the south side of Plaza Matriz. Formed for high society of European descent, today it opens to the public. Friendly, English-speaking guides bring visitors up the marble staircases so they can marvel at the elegant salons. The club also hosts cultural events, including music performances and art shows, throughout the year. Nonmembers are welcome at the on-site bar and restaurant, but full access to the club's luxe facilities, including a library and billiards room, is reserved for its exclusive members. ⊠ *Calle Sarandí 584 CP, Ciudad Vieja* ☏ *2915–7820* ⊕ *www.cluburuguay.com. uy* 🖃 *Free.*

Iglesia Matriz (*Matriz Church*)

RELIGIOUS BUILDING | It's officially the Cathedral of the Immaculate Conception and St. Phillip and St. James, but it is known to Montevideans as the Matriz ("head") Church, as well as the Catedral Metropolitana de Montevideo. The cathedral is the oldest public building in Montevideo, with a distinctive pair of dome-cap bell towers that stand guard over the plaza below. Besides its rich marble interior, colorful floor tiling, stained glass, and dome, the Matriz Church is notable as the final resting place of many of Uruguay's most important political and military figures. ⊠ *Calle Ituzaingó 1373, at Calle Sarandí, Ciudad Vieja* ☏ *2915–7018* ⊕ *www.icm.org.uy.*

★ Mercado del Puerto

MARKET | For Montevideo's quintessential lunch experience, head to the old port market, a restored 1868 building of vaulted iron beams and colored glass, and a terrific example of urban renewal at its best. The market shields 14 stalls and eateries where, over large fires, the best *asado* (barbecue) in the city is cooked. It's a mix of casual lunch-counter places and sit-down restaurants. The traditional drink here is *medio y medio* (champagne mixed with white wine). Other eateries congregate outside around the perimeter of the building and are open for dinner as well as lunch. ⊠ *Rambla 25 de Agosto, between Av. Maciel and Av. Pérez Castellano, across from port, Piedras 237, Ciudad Vieja* ☏ *27/116–801* ⊕ *www. mercadodelpuerto.com.*

Museo del Carnaval

OTHER MUSEUM | Move over, Rio. Montevideo's annual Carnaval celebration may be more low-key than that of its northern neighbor, but it lasts for a full 40 days. This museum next to the Mercado del Puerto celebrates and honors the pre-Lenten festivities year-round with displays featuring the elaborate costumes and photos of processions. Guided tours are available. ⊠ *Rambla 25 de Agosto 1825 No. 218, Ciudad Vieja* ☏ *2916–5493* ⊕ *www.museodelcarnaval.org* 🖃 *150 pesos.*

Palacio Estévez

CASTLE/PALACE | On the south side of Plaza Independencia, Estévez Palace, one of the most beautiful old buildings in the city, was the seat of government until 1985, when the president's offices were moved to a more modern building. This building, unfortunately closed to the public, is used on occasion for ceremonial purposes. ⊠ *Plaza Independencia, Ciudad Vieja.*

Palacio Taranco/Museo de Artes Decorativas

CASTLE/PALACE | Built in 1907, the ornate Taranco Palace in the Ciudad Vieja is representative of the French-inspired architecture favored in fin-de-siècle Montevideo. Even the marble for the floors was imported from France. Today you can survey that bygone glory in the palace's new incarnation as the Museo de Artes Decorativas (Museum of Decorative Arts). Its rooms are filled with period furniture, statuary, draperies, clocks, and portrait paintings. A cultural center within has a calendar of performances and live music. ✉ *Museo de Artes Decorativas, Calle 25 de Mayo 376, Ciudad Vieja* ☎ *2915–6060* 🌐 *www.museos.gub.uy* 🎟 *Free* 🕒 *Closed Sat.–Sun.*

Plaza Constitución

PLAZA/SQUARE | This plaza, also known as Plaza Matriz, is the heart of Montevideo's Ciudad Vieja. An ornate cantilever fountain in the center of this tree-filled square was installed in 1871 to commemorate the construction of the city's first water system. ✉ *Ciudad Vieja* ☎ *1950–7052.*

★ **Plaza Independencia**

PLAZA/SQUARE | Connecting Cuidad Vieja and the Centro, Independence Square is the heart of Montevideo. All that remains of the original walls of the Spanish fort is the Puerta de la Ciudadela, the triumphal gate to the Old City. In the center stands a 30-ton statue of General José Gervasio Artigas, the father of Uruguay and founder of its 19th-century independence movement. At the base of the monument, polished granite stairs lead to an underground mausoleum that holds Artigas's remains, open Tuesday through Sunday, 10–6. The mausoleum is a moving memorial: bold graphics chiseled in the walls of this giant space detail the feats of Artigas's life. There's a changing of the guard every Friday at noon. ✉ *Plaza Independencia, Montevideo.*

Plaza Zabala

PLAZA/SQUARE | At this charmed spot in the heart of the Ciudad Vieja, it's easy to image the splendor of the old Montevideo. Around the fountain and flowers of the park are the turn-of-the-century Palacio Taranco and a bank headquarters in a renovated older building—a refreshing sight in the Old City. ✉ *Circunvalacion Durango, Montevideo.*

Criollas

Also known as *jineteadas*, the Uruguayan-style rodeos called *criollas* are held all over the country, but the most spectacular one takes place in Montevideo's El Prado neighborhood every Easter. Gauchos from all over the country come to display their skill in riding wild horses.

★ **Teatro Solís**

PERFORMANCE VENUE | Named in honor of the discoverer of the Río de la Plata, Juan Díaz de Solís, the 1856 Solís Theater is famed for its fine acoustics. Informative guided tours of the building are offered in Spanish Tuesday through Sunday at 4; call ahead to arrange one in English. (The afternoon tours are occasionally canceled if the theater is in use for rehearsals.) The theater maintains an active calendar of concerts, dance, and plays, all in Spanish, and all for prices much lower than you'd pay for a comparable evening back home. ✉ *Reconquista at Bartolomé Mitre, Ciudad Vieja* ☎ *1950–3323* 🌐 *www.teatrosolis.org.uy* 🎟 *90 pesos.*

🍴 Restaurants

Café Bacacay

$ | **SOUTH AMERICAN** | This small and smartly designed restaurant facing Teatro Solís inhabits a building that dates to 1844 and attracts a young, hip crowd. The owner takes special care in preparing the excellent salads, such as the Bacacay (spinach, raisins, carrots, nuts, grilled eggplant) or the Sarandí (celery, chicken, apples, carrots). **Known for:** great wine list; streetside tables; unique and historic space. [$] *Average main: pesos250* ✉ *Bacacay 1306, at Calle Buenos Aires, Ciudad Vieja* ☎ *2916–6074* 🕒 *Closed Sun.*

172

Escaramuza Café and Bookshop

$$ | CAFÉ | The bookshop is classic, with floor to ceiling books, and a nifty rolling platform to browse the upper shelves. The café, though, is airy and serves innovative dishes such as beet and goat cheese pie, and grilled polenta and veggie gratin, along with fresh baked breads and sinfully delicious desserts. **Known for:** good coffee; delicious vegetarian food; sinful pastries. $ Average main: pesos540 ⊠ Dr. Pablo de María 1185, Montevideo ☎ 2401–3475 ⊕ escaramuza. com.uy ⊗ Closed Sun.

★ Jacinto

$$$ | SOUTH AMERICAN | The smell of fresh-baked bread wafts through this pleasant, sunny spot off Plaza Zabala. Plates are fresh, inspired, and expertly prepared, from the soup of the day to desserts like panna cotta with red grapes and a sweet orange sauce. Jacinto is a favorite among the city's foodie crowd and stylish set. **Known for:** efficient service; trendy space; seasonal menu. $ Average main: pesos650 ⊠ Sarandí 349, Ciudad Vieja ☎ 2915–2731 ⊕ www.jacinto.com.uy ⊗ Closed Sun.

Sometimes Sunday Café

$$ | SANDWICHES | The painted white brick helps make the café bigger than it is, but the food and vibe are so good that size hardly matters. Open for lunch on Thursday through Sunday, and breakfast on the weekend, Sometimes serves up super sandwiches, such as brisket, pulled pork or avocado, salads and other dishes with international influences, along with freshly baked breads and great coffee. **Known for:** best coffee; wholesome breakfast; great sandwiches. $ Average main: pesos550 ⊠ Calle Perez Castellano 1518, Ciudad Vieja ☎ 2916–4058 ⊗ Closed Mon.–Wed.

Nightlife

Baar Fun Fun

CABARET | An institution in Ciudad Vieja, Baar Fun Fun is a cabaret that serves up plenty wine, beer, and cocktails to go with their live shows. The crowd age is usually pretty mixed, but tends to be younger if the night's music is contemporary rock. Shows, which run the gamut from folk, tango, neotango to rock, start between 9 and 9:30. The food is okay, but don't go with an empty stomach as the dinner service can be spotty. ⊠ Ciudadela 1229, Ciudad Vieja ☎ 2915–8005 ⊕ barfunfun.com ⊗ Closed Sun.–Mon.

Cerveceria Malafama

BREWPUBS | Set inside the cavernous space of the brewhouse, this brewpub still manages to fill up inside and outside. And for good reason, too. The dizzying selection of beers, whether on tap, canned, or bottled, are expertly and creatively crafted, with a variety that's sure to satisfy the most serious brewhounds. The food is imaginative and well-prepared, and their brick-oven pizza alone is a great reason to visit. ⊠ Maldonado 1970, Montevideo ☎ 097/313–349 ⊕ cervezamalafama.com ⊗ Closed Sun.–Mon.

Inmigrantes

PUBS | This pub attracts all ages for its tapas (and sushi, too), a decent selection of bottled beer, wine, and the serious cocktails mixed by the pro bartenders behind the well-stocked bar. Later in the evening, though, the younger crowd is there for the drinks and live music or DJs. The food is surprisingly good, with the fried empanadas and milangas (as they call their milanesas) going particularly well with a beer or wine. ⊠ Juan Paullier 1252, Montevideo ☎ 097/959–652 ⊕ inmigrantes.com.uy ⊗ Closed Sun.–Mon.

Street food markets are filled with Uruguayan goods.

La Pasiva

PUBS | For an ice-cold beer, this popular pub is a late-night favorite. Specialties are frankfurters, chivitos, and other bar food. In good weather, you can socialize at the outdoor tables in Plaza Matriz. This Montevideo staple has an array of franchises throughout the city, including a prominent location on Plaza Fabini. ⊠ *Calle Sarandí at Calle J.C. Gómez, Ciudad Vieja* ☎ *2915–7988* ⊕ *www.lapasiva.com.uy* ☽ *Closed Sun.*

Montevideo Wine Experience

WINE BARS | This funky corner space is the perfect place to sample some of Uruguay's terrific wines, from refreshing Albariños to their surprisingly smooth Tannats. With a 200-strong wine list, it's ideal for a glass or two after dinner, or perhaps a cocktail from the well-stocked bar, and nibble their really good *picadas* and *tapas*. There's also a separate room for guided wine tastings; check their social media for availability and prices. ⊠ *Piedras 300, Ciudad Vieja* ☎ *9293–9992* ☽ *Closed Sun.*

🛍 Shopping

Louvre

ANTIQUES & COLLECTIBLES | This antiques store is the only source for handmade and painted trinket boxes—the perfect *recuerdos* (souvenirs). It also offers an impressive selection of jewelry and silver. ⊠ *Sarandí 652, Ciudad Vieja* ☎ *2916–2686* ⊕ *www.louvreantiguedades.com.uy.*

Centro

Montevideo's main street, the Avenida 18 de Julio, runs through the heart of the city's center. You'll find everything here—shops and museums, cafés and plazas, bustling traditional markets, chrome-and-steel office towers, and places to change money. The avenue runs east from Plaza Independencia, away from the Ciudad Vieja, passing through bustling Plaza Fabini and tree-lined Plaza Cagancha.

It's a 20-minute walk from Plaza Independencia to the Palacio Municipal. If shopping is your main interest, you may want to devote an entire afternoon to browsing and buying along the avenida.

Sights

Museo de Historia del Arte (MuHAr)
ART MUSEUM | In the Palacio Municipal (an ambitious name for this unremarkable brick city hall) you'll find the Museum of Art History, which has the country's best collection of pre-Columbian and colonial artifacts. You'll also find Greek, Roman, and Middle Eastern art, including ceramics and other antiquities. On the street level is the **Biblioteca de Historia del Arte** (Art History Library), worth a stop if you're a student of the subject matter. ✉ *Calle Ejido 1326, Centro* ☎ *19/502–191* 🌐 *muhar.montevideo.gub.uy* 🎟 *Free* 🕒 *Closed Sun.*

Plaza Fabini
PLAZA/SQUARE | In the center of this lovely, manicured square is the Monumento del Entrevero, a large sculpture depicting a whirlwind of gauchos, *criollos* (mixed-blood settlers who are half native, half European), and native Uruguayans in battle. It's one of the last works by sculptor José Belloni (1882–1965). An open-air market takes place here every morning. ✉ *Surrounded by Av. 18 de Julio and Calles Río Negro, Colonia, and Julio Herrera y Obes, Centro.*

Restaurants

Los Leños
$$$ | **SOUTH AMERICAN** | While the polished wood and wicker interior is attractive, it's the food that draws diners here. The meat, seafood, pasta, and risotto dishes are all carefully prepared, so everyone at your table will be happy. **Known for:** perfect risottos; extensive wine list; excellent steaks. $ *Average main: pesos800* ✉ *San José 909, Centro* ☎ *2900–2285* 🕒 *Closed Mon. No dinner Sun.*

Smoke-Free Uruguay

Lighting up is prohibited in enclosed public places, including stores, offices, transportation terminals, restaurants, bars, and casinos. Ubiquitous black-red-and-white signs in Spanish, English, and Portuguese remind patrons of the law. Heavy fines both to noncomplying smokers and to the locale where they're caught mean nearly perfect compliance.

Tannat
$$$ | **BARBECUE** | There are several good seafood dishes here, and the pastas are done right, but Tannat is really the place for meat lovers; even nose-to-tail carnivores will leave satisfied. The service is courteous and quick, as the embers are always burning. **Known for:** efficient service; fresh pasta; grilled meats. $ *Average main: pesos700* ✉ *San Jose 1065, Centro* ☎ *2903–2120* 🕒 *Closed Mon.*

Viejo Sancho
$$ | **STEAKHOUSE** | What draws the post-theater crowds to this friendly, but plain restaurant near Plaza Cagancha are gargantuan portions of smoked pork chops and fried potatoes. **Known for:** bustling ambience; friendly staff; cheap and cheerful. $ *Average main: pesos400* ✉ *Calle San José 1229, Centro* ☎ *2900–4063* 💳 *No credit cards* 🕒 *Closed Sun.*

Hotels

Oxford Hotel
$ | **HOTEL** | Glass walls, broad windows, and mirrors give the small lobby an open but intimate feel, much like that of the hotel itself. **Pros:** central location; attentive staff; fast Wi-Fi. **Cons:** small bathrooms; basic breakfast; some oddly configured rooms. $ *Rooms from:*

pesos2260 ✉ *Paraguay 1286, Centro* ☎ *2902–0046* ⊕ *www.hoteloxford.com. uy* ⮌ *125 rooms* ⑩ *Free Breakfast.*

Nightlife

El Mingus

LIVE MUSIC | A happening jazz club with a lively cocktail and wine scene that's also well known for their tasty, imaginative tapas. It's a great place to meet and chat with some *Montevideanos* or just enjoy the music and cocktails. ✉ *San Salvador 1952, Centro* ☎ *2410–9342* 🕙 *Closed Mon.* ☞ *Call to reserve a table for jazz shows.*

Joventango

FOLK/TRADITIONAL DANCE | If you're itching to try out your dance steps, Joventango is the best place in the city to learn tango. Shows and classes are frequent; call or check the website for times. ✉ *Aquiles Lanza 1235 esq. Soriano, Centro* ☎ *2901–15561, 2908–6813* ⊕ *joventango. com.uy* ⮌ *300 pesos.*

Shopping

★ Feria Tristán Narvaja

MARKET | Started in the early 1900s by Italian immigrants, Feria Tristán Narvaja is Montevideo's top attraction on Sunday and one of the city's largest and most popular fairs. (It operates only on Sunday, a day when all other markets, and much of the city, are closed. Hours run about 9–3.) The fair, a 5- to 10-minute walk from the Old City and in the Centro district, is plentifully stocked with secondhand goods and antiques. ✉ *Dr. Tristán Narvaja 1545, Centro.*

Mercado de los Artesanos

SOUVENIRS | Don't let the kitsch turn you away, this shop also sells well-crafted jewelry and other objects by local designers that are elegant and eye-catching. You can also pick up the typical souvenir for your relative who loves that stuff. Given the Centro location, the prices are quite fair. ✉ *Plaza Cagancha 1365, Centro* ☎ *2901–0887* ⊕ *www.mercadodelosartesanos.com.uy.*

Plaza Cagancha

MARKET | Between Avenida 18 de Julio and Calle Rondeau in Centro, Plaza Cagancha regularly has vendors set up in the area at all hours selling trinkets and crafts. ✉ *Av. 18 de Julio between Av. Gral Rondeau and Pasaje de los Derechos Humanos, Punta Carretas.*

Portones Shopping

MALL | Adjacent to the Portones terminal, Portones Shopping is an indoor mall with more than 130 stores and a movie theater. ✉ *Av. Italia 5775, Carrasco* ☎ *2601–7733, 0800–1807* ⊕ *www. portones.com.uy.*

El Prado

The district known as El Prado lies roughly 6 km (4 miles) north of Plaza Independencia. You could make the long uphill walk along the busy Avenida Agraciada, but it's a lot easier in a taxi. It is pleasant to walk along Avenida Buschental in fall and spring when the trees are in full color. The Jardín Botánico (Botanical Garden) inside the Parque del Prado is a worthwhile stop, where you can admire thousands of plant species, many of which were brought to Uruguay in the 19th century by Charles Racine.

Sights

Museo de Bellas Artes Juan Manuel Blanes (*Museum of Fine Arts*)

ART MUSEUM | Known locally as the Blanes Museum, the Museum of Fine Arts is housed in an elegant colonial mansion that once belonged to Uruguay's foremost 19th-century painter, Juan Manuel Blanes. He was entirely self-taught, and did not begin painting until he was in his fifties. His realistic portrayals of gauchos and the Uruguayan countryside compose the core of the museum's collection.

✉ *Av. Millán 4015, Prado* ☎ *2336–7134*
⊕ *blanes.montevideo.gub.uy* 🖂 *Free*
🕐 *Closed Mon.*

Museo del Fútbol

OTHER MUSEUM | "Other countries have
their history," Helenio Herrera, Uruguay's
most famous soccer coach once said.
"We have our fútbol." Indeed, *fútbol*—
that's "soccer" to U.S. readers—is played
anywhere there's space, by kids of all
ages. Uruguay both hosted and won the
first World Cup competition in 1930 here
at the Estadio Centenario. In the pits of
the stadium is this museum (the AUF)
dedicated to the country's soccer heritage. It's worth a detour if you're a big fan
of the sport. ✉ *Av. Dr. Americo Ricaldoni,
Prado* ☎ *2480–1259* ⊕ *www.auf.org.uy*
🖂 *150 pesos* 🕐 *Closed weekends.*

Museo de la Memoria

HISTORY MUSEUM | The question still
pains Uruguayans who remember the
era: How did South America's strongest
democracy dissolve into 12 years of
brutal military dictatorship? This museum
documents the history of the 1973–85
period that people here call simply the
dictadura, during which an astounding
2% of the population experienced arrest
for "political crimes" at some time or
other. (The government did not begin
investigating abuses by the military government until 2011.) The museum won't
be a stop on most visitors' Montevideo
itineraries, but if you're a student of Latin
American history and politics, it's worth a
look. ✉ *Av. Las Instrucciones 1057, Prado*
⊹ *Esq. Bvar. José Batlle and Ordoñez.*
☎ *2355–5891* ⊕ *mume.montevideo.gub.
uy* 🖂 *Free* 🕐 *Closed Sun.*

Palacio Legislativo

GOVERNMENT BUILDING | Almost 50 differ-
ent types of native marble were used
in the construction of the Legislative
Palace, the seat of Uruguay's bicameral
legislature. Free Spanish- and English-lan-
guage tours are available when the congress is in session; passes are available
inside at the information desk. ✉ *Av.*

De las Leyes s/n, Prado ☎ *2400–9111*
⊕ *www.parlamento.gub.uy* 🖂 *140 pesos*
🕐 *Closed Mon.*

Parque del Prado

CITY PARK | The oldest of the city's parks
is also one of the most popular. Locals
come to see El Rosedal, the rose garden
with more than 800 different varieties,
and the fine botanical garden. Also in
the 262-acre park, you'll find the statue
called *La Diligencia*, by sculptor José
Belloni. ✉ *Av. Delmira Agustini, Prado*
☎ *1950–3660.*

Sagrada Familia

RELIGIOUS BUILDING | Too tiny to require
flying buttresses, the ornately Gothic
Holy Family Church, also known as
Capilla Jackson, is complete in all other
respects. A troop of gargoyles peers
down at you from this Jesuit house of
worship, and the finely wrought stained-
glass windows become radiant when
backlit by the sun. ✉ *Calle Luis Alberto
de Herrera 4246, Prado* ☎ *2203–3686.*

Greater Montevideo

 Sights

★ Bodega Bouza

WINERY | Argentina and Chile grab all the
attention in discussions of South American wines, but Uruguay has a number
of impressive wineries of its own. It's
worth stopping by the Bodega Bouza
outside of Montevideo for a tour and
sampling; it's one of the few wineries
open for daily visits. For a real treat
(4,500 pesos), reserve the works: a tour,
tasting, and extravagant lunch with, of
course, wines to accompany each course
and that all-important transfer to and
from Montevideo. It's worth visiting the
winery for its standout restaurant alone.
✉ *Camino la Redención 7658, Montevideo* ☎ *2323–7491* ⊕ *www.bodegabouza.
com* 🖂 *Winery tour free; tasting and tour
1,500 pesos* 🕐 *Closed Tues.*

Parque Rodó

CITY PARK | FAMILY | This park has a little something for everyone, with two amusement parks, a number of decent eateries, and the National Museum of Visual Arts. The park also has an outdoor theater and hosts an open-air *feria* (fair) on Sunday. ✉ *Julio Maria Sosa, Punta Carretas.*

★ Playa de los Pocitos

BEACH | FAMILY | This stretch of sand is the city's most attractive beach, and surprisingly tranquil. Throughout the day you'll see locals running, biking, strolling, and rollerblading along the *rambla* (boardwalk) here. Snap a picture with the sculpture spelling out "Montevideo" for a classic tourist shot. **Amenities:** food and drink; lifeguards; showers; toilets. **Best for:** solitude; sunrise; sunset; swimming; walking. ✉ *Rambla Perú at Gabriel A. Pereira, Pocitos* ☎ *4141–9285.*

 Restaurants

★ Expreso Pocitos

$$ | ITALIAN | This classic and beloved diner-style establishment has been around for more than a century, and it is clear that some of the customers have been frequenting it for almost as long. Many congregate here for a coffee or beer, and the *chivito,* which is made with fresh, fluffy bread, is considered one of the best in town. **Known for:** traditional decor; chivito bread; local institution. $ *Average main: pesos350* ✉ *Juan Benito Blanco 956 at Av. Brasil, Pocitos* ☎ *2708–0496.*

La Casa Violeta

$$$ | STEAKHOUSE | Meats are the specialty at this beautiful restaurant set in a restored 1920s house and facing the Carrasco Beach. You can opt for the meat-tasting option with sausage, sweetbreads and three cuts of beef, or try the grilled fish or seafood paella. **Known for:** salad bar; marina views; steak-tasting menu. $ *Average main:*

pesos750 ✉ *Avda. Bolivia 1271, Carrasco* ☎ *099/828–716* ⊘ *Closed Mon.*

★ Restaurant Francis

$$$ | SEAFOOD | This bright, upscale restaurant is a local favorite and always filled, yet the efficient, friendly staff manages to keep up. The menu is gourmet and extensive, ranging from sushi to paella to cuts of meat on the grill. **Known for:** chipirones (baby cuttlefish); extensive menu; excellent wine list. $ *Average main: pesos800* ✉ *Luis de la Torre 502, Punta Carretas* ☎ *2711–8603* ⊕ *francis. com.uy* ⊘ *Closed Mon.*

★ Tandory

$$$ | ASIAN FUSION | With Tandory, French-Uruguayan chef and owner Gabriel Coquel has created an intimate yet convivial restaurant with top-level service. Fusion dishes harmoniously blend Asian, Latin American, and European flavors, and the eclectic decor includes heirlooms and souvenirs from his travels around the world. **Known for:** seasonal, local ingredients; great wine list; eclectic menu. $ *Average main: pesos800* ✉ *Libertad 2851 at Ramon Masini, Pocitos* ☎ *2709–6616* ⊕ *www.tandory.com.uy* ⊘ *Closed Mon. No dinner Sun.*

🛏 Hotels

Armon Suites

$$ | HOTEL | This hotel in a quiet neighborhood east of downtown is an all-suites hotel, and the spaces are huge. **Pros:** good value; ample-size suites; courteous staff. **Cons:** slow Internet access; uninteresting breakfast; far from sights. $ *Rooms from: pesos3700* ✉ *21 de Setiembre 2885, Pocitos* ☎ *2712–4120* ⊕ *www.armonsuites.com.uy* 🛏 *40 rooms* ‖◎‖ *Free Breakfast.*

Cottage Carrasco

$$ | HOTEL | Overlooking the sea, the hotel's sleek design translates directly to the stylish rooms where nary a line is wasted. **Pros:** oceanfront; outside the city; good breakfast. **Cons:** spotty

service; maybe too far from the city; somewhat sterile rooms. $ *Rooms from: pesos6000* ⊠ *Miraflores 1360 at Rambla, Carrasco* ☎ *2600–1111* ⊕ *hotelcottage. com.uy* ⇆ *64 rooms* ⧖ *No Meals* ⚲ *Breakfast is an additional US$10.*

Sofitel Montevideo Casino Carrasco & Spa

$$$ | HOTEL | Originally opened in 1921 as a summer escape for the Uruguayan elite, this stunning Belle Epoque waterfront building, known as the "palace on the sand," underwent an intensive restoration process. **Pros:** attractive casino, restaurant, and bar on-site; inspired spa treatments; open river views from many rooms. **Cons:** showing wear and tear in places; service could be sharper; a lengthy taxi ride to the sights of Montevideo. $ *Rooms from: pesos9400* ⊠ *Rambla República de México 6451, Montevideo* ☎ *2604–6060* ⊕ *www.sofitel.com* ⇆ *116 rooms* ⧖ *No Meals.*

Nightlife

★ Lotus Club

DANCE CLUBS | Located in Montevideo's World Trade Center, this club for years has been considered one of Montevideo's best. The red-and-black color scheme gives the place an upscale feel, and Montevideans dance until the wee hours under shimmering disco balls. ⊠ *Lecuender at Bonavita, Pocitos* ☎ *2628–1379* ⊕ *www.lotus.com.uy.*

Volvé Mi Negra

BARS | Lines form frequently outside this nightlife spot on weekends, where locals come for generous-size drinks. While it's technically a pub complete with wood paneling, bar stools, and pool tables, live DJs get people dancing and give it a club vibe. ⊠ *Francisco Muñoz 3177, Pocitos* ☎ *097/087–922.*

🛍 Shopping

El Mercado de la Abundancia

MARKET | Dating back to 1836, El Mercado de la Abundancia is a fun indoor market in Centro, a few blocks from the Palacio Municipal. Inside are a tango dance center, a handful of good choices for a lunchtime *parrillada*, and a crafts fair. ⊠ *San José 1312, and Aquiles Lanza, Centro* ☎ *2901–5902.*

★ Manos del Uruguay

CRAFTS | With six locations total in Montevideo and Punta del Este, Manos del Uruguay stock a wide selection of woolen wear and locally produced ceramics crafted by women's artisan cooperatives around the country. ⊠ *Punta Carretas Shopping, José Ellauri 350, Centro* ☎ *2710–6108* ⊕ *www.manos.com.uy.*

Montevideo Shopping

MALL | There are three major shopping centers in Montevideo, offering everything from designer clothing to gourmet foods to art supplies. Montevideo Shopping is the oldest along the Rio de la Plata and has more than 175 stores and entertainment options including a movie theater. ⊠ *Luis Alberto de Herrera 1290, Punta Carretas* ☎ *2622–1005* ⊕ *www.montevideoshopping.com.uy.*

Parque Villa Biarritz

MARKET | The Saturday morning market at Parque Villa Biarritz in the neighborhood of Pocitos sells crafts, clothes, and some antiques. You can find some vendors set up other days of the week, as well. The small park also has a recreational center, Club Biguá, with tennis courts and other sports facilities. ⊠ *José Vazquéz de Ledesma, Punta Carretas.*

Pecarí

WOMEN'S CLOTHING | Contemporary women's clothing store specializing in knitwear, shoes, and the place to buy your leather pants. ⊠ *Juan C. Gómez 1412, Ciudad Vieja* ☎ *2915–0016, 2915–6696* ⊕ *www.pecari.com.uy.*

★ **Punta Carretas Shopping**

MALL | Housed in a former prison, Punta Carretas Shopping is the city's largest and most upscale mall, measuring in at around 200 stores mixing local and international brands. It's in a pleasant residential area near the Sheraton Montevideo, a 10-minute cab ride from the Old City. ⊠ *José Ellauri 350, Punta Carretas* ☎ *2711–6940* ⊕ *www.puntacarretas. com.uy.*

Colonia del Sacramento

The peaceful cobbled streets of Colonia are just over the Río de la Plata from Buenos Aires, but they seem a world away. Charm might be an overused descriptor, but Colonia, with its old-world architecture, serenity, and water lapping at sandy shores is a place that redefines it.

The best activity in Colonia is walking through its peaceful Barrio Histórico (Old Town), a UNESCO World Heritage Site. Porteños come to Colonia for romantic getaways or for a break from the city. If you like to keep busy on your travels, a late-morning arrival and early-evening departure give you plenty of time to see the sights and wander at will. To really see the city at its own pace, spend the night in one of its many colonial-style bed-and-breakfasts: This offsets travel costs and time and makes a visit here far more rewarding.

GETTING HERE AND AROUND

Hydrofoils and ferries cross the Río de la Plata between Buenos Aires and Uruguay several times a day. Boats often sell out, particularly on summer weekends, so book tickets at least a few days ahead. The two competing companies that operate services—Buquebus and Colonia Express—often wage a reduced-rates war in the low season.

Buquebus provides two kinds of service for passengers and cars: the quickest crossing takes an hour by hydrofoil and the slower ferry takes around three hours. The Buquebus terminal in Buenos Aires is at the northern end of Puerto Madero at the intersection of Avenida Alicia M. de Justo and Avenida Córdoba (which changes its name here to Bulevar Cecilia Grierson). It's accessible by taxi or by walking seven blocks from L.N. Alem subte station along Trinidad Guevara.

Colonia Express operates the cheapest and fastest services to Colonia but has only four daily services in each direction. There often are huge discounts on the 50-minute catamaran trip if you buy tickets in advance. The Colonia Express terminal in Buenos Aires is south of Puerto Madero on Avenida Pedro de Mendoza, the extension of Avenida Huergo. It's best reached by taxi, but Bus No. 130 from Avenidas Libertador and L.N. Alem also stops outside it.

The shortest way to the Barrio Histórico is to turn left out of the port parking lot onto Florida—it's a six-block walk. Walking is the perfect way to get around this part of town; equally practical—and lots of fun—are golf carts and sand buggies that you can rent from Thrifty.

FERRY CONTACTS Buquebus. ⊠ *Av. Antartida Argentina 821, Puerto Madero* ☎ *11/4316–6530* ⊕ *www.buquebus.com.* **Colonia Express.** ⊠ *Ticket office at Av. Córdoba 753, Microcentro, Av. Pedro de Mendoza 330, La Boca* ☎ *11/5167–7700 in Buenos Aires* ⊕ *www.coloniaexpress. com.*

RENTAL CARS Thrifty. ⊠ *Av. Gral. Flores 172, Colonia del Sacramento* ☎ *18488 In Uruguay* ⊕ *www.thrifty.com.uy.*

TAXI CONTACT Taxis Colonia.
☎ *598/4522–2920.*

ESSENTIALS

VISITOR INFORMATION Colonia del Sacramento Tourism Office. ⊠ *At ferry terminal, Also at Manuel Lobo, between Ituzaingó and Paseo San Antonio, Colonia del Sacramento* ☎ *4523–7707* ⊕ *turismo.gub.uy.*

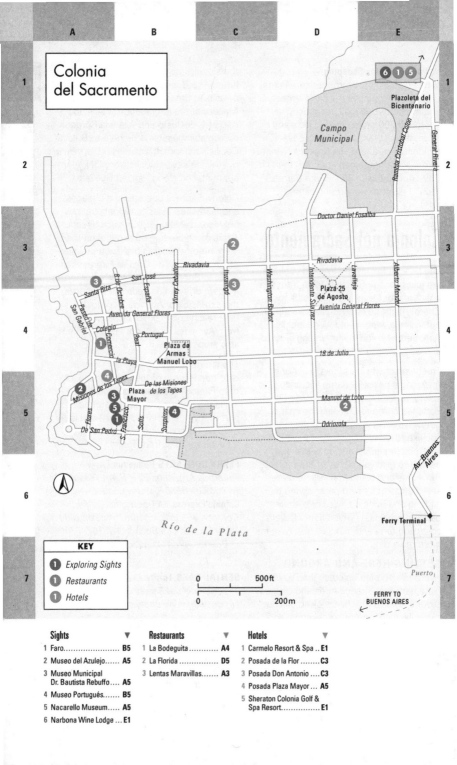

Colonia del Sacramento

◉ Sights

Begin your tour at the reconstructed Portón de Campo or city gate, where remnants of the old bastion walls lead to the river. A block farther is Calle de los Suspiros, the aptly named Street of Sighs, a cobblestone stretch of one-story colonials that can rival any street in Latin America for sheer romantic effect. It runs between a lookout point on the river, called the Bastión de San Miguel, and the Plaza Mayor, a lovely square filled with Spanish moss, palms, and spiky, flowering *palo borracho* trees. The many cafés around the square are ideal places to take it all in. Clusters of bougainvillea flow over the walls here and in the other quiet streets of the Barrio Histórico, many of which are lined with art galleries and antiques shops.

Another great place to watch daily life is the Plaza de Armas Manoel Lobo, where you can find the Iglesia Matriz, the oldest church in Uruguay. The square itself is crisscrossed with wooden catwalks over the ruins of a house dating to the founding of the town. The tables from the square's small eateries spill from the sidewalk right onto the cobblestones: they're all rather touristy, but give you an excellent view of the drum-toting *candombe* (a style of music from Uruguay) squads that beat their way around the Old Town each afternoon.

You can visit all of Colonia's museums with the same ticket, which you buy from the Museo Portugués or the Museo Municipal for 150 pesos. Most take only a few minutes to visit, but you can use the ticket on two consecutive days.

Faro (*Lighthouse*)
LIGHTHOUSE | Towering above the Plaza Mayor is the lighthouse, which was built in 1857 on top of a tower that was part of the ruined San Xavier convent. The whole structure was engulfed in flames in 1873 after a lighthouse keeper had an accident with the oil used in the lamp at the time. Your reward for climbing it are great views over the Barrio Histórico and the River Plate. ✉ *Plaza Mayor, Colonia del Sacramento* 🕾 *80 pesos.*

Museo del Azulejo
OTHER MUSEUM | A small collection of the beautiful handmade French majolica tiles that adorn fountains all over Colonia are on display at the tile museum, housed in a small 18th-century building near the river. The 50-peso entry fee is good for all Colonia's museums. ✉ *Misiones de los Tapies 104, at Paseo San Gabriel, Colonia del Sacramento* 🕾 *4522–1065* ⊕ *www.museoscolonia.com.uy* 🕾 *50 pesos* 🕙 *Closed Thurs.*

Museo Municipal Dr. Bautista Rebuffo
OTHER MUSEUM | A sundry collection of objects related to the city's history is housed here. ✉ *Plaza Mayor at Misiones de los Tapies, Colonia del Sacramento* 🕾 *50 pesos* 🕙 *Closed Tues.*

Museo Portugués
HISTORY MUSEUM | The museum that's most worth a visit is this one, which documents the city's ties to Portugal. It's most notable for its collection of old map reproductions based on Portuguese naval expeditions. A small selection of period furnishings, clothes, and jewelry from Colonia's days as a Portuguese colony complete the offerings. Exhibits are well labeled, but in Spanish only. ✉ *Plaza Mayor between Calle de los Suspiros and De Solís, Colonia del Sacramento* 🕾 *80 pesos* 🕙 *Closed Sun.*

Nacarello Museum
OTHER MUSEUM | A colonial Portuguese residence has been lovingly re-created inside this 17th-century structure. The simple bedroom and kitchen furnishings are period pieces, but the real attraction is the house itself, with its thick whitewashed walls and low ceilings. For 50 Uruguayan pesos, you gain access to all Colonia's museums, including this

one. ✉ *Plaza Mayor at Henríquez de la Peña, Colonia del Sacramento* 🌐 *www.museoscolonia.com.uy* 🎟 *80 pesos* 🕑 *Closed Fri.*

Narbona Wine Lodge
WINERY | For an upscale, indulgent Uruguayan wine experience, Narbona Wine Lodge in Carmelo, an hour's drive from Colonia, is worth a visit. The peaceful property includes a vineyard, a restaurant with exposed brick walls that serves Italian-influenced dishes featuring the wines and products like cheeses made on-site, and a luxurious tasting room. If you find yourself unable to leave at the end of the day, book a stay at one of property's five sophisticated, bright, yet rustic rooms named after grape varietals. Your stay includes a vineyard tour, mountain bikes for borrowing, and access to Narbona's private beach. ✉ *Ruta 21, Km 268, Carmelo* ☎ *4544–6831* 🌐 *www.narbona.com.uy.*

🍴 Restaurants

In Colonia, both dollars and Uruguayan pesos are accepted. Uruguayan food is as beef-based as Argentine fare, and also has a notable Italian influence. Here, enticing cafés and restaurants with plaza and riverfront views are numerous.

La Bodeguita
$$ | **SOUTH AMERICAN** | This hip restaurant serves delicious, crispy pizza, sliced into bite-size rectangles. The backyard tables overlook the river, and inside is cozy, with warm walls. **Known for:** casual spot; well priced; lovely views. [$] *Average main: pesos325* ✉ *Calle del Comercio 167, Colonia del Sacramento* ☎ *598/4522–5329* 🌐 *www.labodeguita.net* 💳 *No credit cards* 🕑 *No lunch.*

★ **La Florida**
$$$$ | **LATIN AMERICAN** | The black-and-white photos, lace tablecloths, and quaint knickknacks that clutter this long, low house belie the fact that it was once a brothel. It still has private rooms, but the politicians and occasional celebs rent them for dining these days. **Known for:** dishes for sharing; kingfish, sole, and salmon; plenty of ambience. [$] *Average main: pesos1100* ✉ *Manuel Lobo 384, Colonia del Sacramento* ☎ *097/293–036* 💳 *No credit cards* 🕑 *Closed Apr.–Nov.*

★ **Lentas Maravillas**
$$ | **CAFÉ** | There's no spot more perfect in Colonia to while away an afternoon with a leisurely salad for lunch or tea than this café nestled along the water. Don't miss the baked goods—the *redondos* (rich, round cheesecakes) are particularly heavenly. **Known for:** great lunch spot; lovely views; adorable setting. [$] *Average main: pesos380* ✉ *Santa Rita 61, Colonia del Sacramento* ☎ *098/592–884* 💳 *No credit cards* 🕑 *Closed Tues. No dinner Mon. and Wed.*

🛏 Hotels

Since Colonia is the consummate day trip from Montevideo or Buenos Aires, few visitors actually spend the night here. Consider breaking that mold; there's no shortage of homey lodgings to choose from, and an overnight stay really gives you the opportunity to unwind and adopt the relaxed Colonia pace.

Carmelo Resort & Spa
$$$ | **RESORT** | Serenity pervades this harmoniously decorated resort an hour west of Colonia del Sacramento, reachable by car, boat, or a 25-minute flight from Buenos Aires and a destination in and of itself. **Pros:** all rooms are spacious bungalows; personalized service; on-site activities compensate for distance to sights and restaurants. **Cons:** food quality is erratic; popular with groups and families; despite copious netting and bug spray, the mosquitoes can get out of hand. [$] *Rooms from: pesos14000* ✉ *Ruta 21, Km 262, Carmelo* ☎ *4542–9000* 🌐 *www.*

Cobblestones abound in the Old Town section of Colonia del Sacramento, Uruguay.

carmeloresort.com 🛏 *20 bungalows, 24 duplex suites* 🍴 *Free Breakfast.*

Posada de la Flor

$ | **B&B/INN** | This colonial-style hotel is on a quiet street leading to the river and is arranged around a sunny courtyard. **Pros:** peaceful location near river and the Barrio Histórico; gorgeous breakfast area and roof terrace; great value. **Cons:** standard rooms are cramped; ground-floor rooms open onto the courtyard and can be noisy. [$] *Rooms from: pesos1725* ✉ *Calle Ituzaingó 268, Colonia del Sacramento* ☎ *098/4523–0794* 🌐 *www.posada-delaflor.com* 💳 *No credit cards* 🛏 *14 rooms* 🍴 *Free Breakfast.*

Posada Don Antonio

$$ | **HOTEL** | Long galleries of rooms overlook an enormous split-level courtyard at Posada Don Antonio, the latest incarnation of a large, elegant building that has housed one hotel or another for close to a century. **Pros:** sparkling turquoise pool, surrounded by loungers; two blocks from the Barrio Histórico; rates are low, but there are proper hotel perks like poolside snacks. **Cons:** ill-fitting doors let in courtyard noise; some rooms open onto the street. [$] *Rooms from: pesos3900* ✉ *Ituzaingó 232, Colonia del Sacramento* ☎ *098/4522–5344* 🌐 *www.posadadonantonio.com* 🛏 *38 rooms* 🍴 *Free Breakfast.*

Posada Plaza Mayor

$$ | **B&B/INN** | A faint scent of jasmine fills the air at this lovely old hotel, where all the rooms open onto a large, plant-filled courtyard complete with a bubbling fountain. **Pros:** cheerful, accommodating staff; beautiful green spaces; on a quiet street of the Barrio Histórico. **Cons:** the three cheapest rooms are small; cramped bathrooms. [$] *Rooms from: pesos4000* ✉ *Calle del Comercio 111, Colonia del Sacramento* ☎ *598/4522–3193* 🌐 *www.posadaplazamayor.com* 🛏 *17 rooms* 🍴 *Free Breakfast.*

Sheraton Colonia Golf & Spa Resort
$$$ | **RESORT** | Materials like copper, terra-cotta, and golden-color stone add warm touches to the airy, light-filled atrium as does the massive wood-fronted fireplace, which is always lit in winter. **Pros:** peaceful location with river views from many rooms; great spa; rooms are often discounted midweek. **Cons:** some rooms need better maintenance; can be noisy on weekends; it's a 10-minute drive or taxi ride north of the Barrio Histórico. $ *Rooms from: pesos7800* ✉ *Cont. Rambla de las Américas s/n, Colonia del Sacramento* ☎ *4522–9000* 🌐 *www.sheraton.com* 🛏 *96 rooms, 8 suites* 🍴 *Free Breakfast.*

🍸 Nightlife

Much of Colonia's nightlife centers on its restaurants, which become default drinking and bar-snacking spots after 11 or midnight. In summer, outdoor tables on the Plaza Mayor, which is often lighted with torches, are particularly atmospheric.

Bardot Brew Pub
BREWPUBS | With their own on-premise brewhouse, this popular brew pub boasts 20 varieties of suds to please any taste. Offering standard Uruguayan fare, including some crazy pizza variations, there's also live music on weekends (Thursday, Friday, and Saturday), when they're open until 3 am. ✉ *Washington Bardot 160, Colonia del Sacramento* ☎ *098/459–732.*

Chopería Mastra
BREWPUBS | Happily, Mastra, a craft brewer with a few locations in the country, has opened a pub in Colonia. With several beers on tap, many seasonal, it's a perfect place to unwind and sample a couple, or a few, styles. The ancient brick and masonry makes it feel like drinking in a museum. Best to eat before you go. ✉ *Del Comercio 158, Colonia del Sacramento* ☎ *092/818–496* 🌐 *mastra.com.uy.*

Punta del Este

134 km (83 miles) east of Montevideo.

Often likened to the Hamptons or St-Tropez, Punta del Este is a flashy destination where parties run nonstop in peak season. But it is also a destination that draws a range of beachgoers to its shores, from summering families to the celebrity jet-set. There's a bustling city on the beach downtown, as well as quiet countryside populated solely with upscale ranches called *chacras* or *estancias,* and creative, buzzing hamlets like La Barra and José Ignacio. Though it's pricey and at times a logistical challenge to get around, everyone finds something about Punta to love.

The resort takes its name from the "east point" marking the division of the Río de la Plata on the west from the Atlantic Ocean to the east. It also lends its name to the broader region encompassing the nearby communities of Punta Ballena and La Barra de Maldonado. These days even José Ignacio, some 20 miles away, is grouped in. It's usually a given that Argentina's upper class spends at least part of the summer in Punta, soaking in the ample rays.

GETTING HERE AND AROUND

Most visitors headed to the beach fly into Montevideo's Aeropuerto Internacional de Carrasco (MVD). Flights arrive from many South American cities, in high season only, directly to the Aeropuerto Internacional de Punta del Este (PDP), about 24 km (15 miles) east of town.

Many bus lines travel daily between Montevideo's Terminal Tres Cruces and Punta del Este's Terminal Playa Brava. Two companies that serve the entire region are Copsa and Cot. Buquebus also offers flights, and ferries with a bus connection to Punta.

To get to Punta del Este from Montevideo, follow Ruta 1 east to the Ruta 93 turnoff. The road is well maintained and marked, and the trip takes about 1½ hours. Rental agencies, such as Avis, Budget, and Dollar, are in downtown Punta del Este.

AIRPORT CONTACT Aeropuerto Internacional de Punta del Este. ✉ *Ruta 93, Km 113* ☎ *4255–9777* ⊕ *www.puntadeleste.aero.*

BUS CONTACTS COT. ☎ *2409–4949 in Montevideo* ⊕ *www.cot.com.uy.* **Copsa.** ☎ *2408–6668* ⊕ *www.copsa.com.uy.* **Terminal de Omnibus.** ✉ *Rambla Artigas and Calle 32, Punta del Este.*

SAFETY AND PRECAUTIONS

For such a touristy locale, Punta maintains a reassuring level of security. Nevertheless, it pays to watch your things. Swimming is not safe at several of the beaches, especially those on the Atlantic side of the point. Never swim alone, and gauge your abilities carefully.

ESSENTIALS

VISITOR INFORMATION Maldonado Tourist Office. ✉ *Parada 1, Calles 31 and 18, Punta del Este* ☎ *4222–1921* ⊕ *www. maldonadoturismo.com.uy.* **Punta del Este Tourist Office.** ✉ *Av. Gorlero 942, Punta del Este* ☎ *4244–1218* ⊕ *www.turismo. gub.uy.*

Sights

Arboretum Lussich

CITY PARK | Naturally perfumed with the scent of eucalyptus, this huge arboretum is one of the most important botanical gardens in the world. Its creation was the labor of love of Croatian-Uruguayan botanist Antonio Lussich (1848–1928). The approximate 474 acres contain more than 350 species of trees from outside Uruguay as well as 70 domestic species. Guided tours are in Spanish only. ✉ *Av. Antonio Lussich* ☎ *2713–5915* ⊕ *arboretumlussich.uy* 🆓 *Free.*

Avenida Gorlero

BUSINESS DISTRICT | Punta del Este is circled by the Rambla Artigas, the main coastal road that leads past residential neighborhoods and pristine stretches of beach. You can find everything on Avenida Gorlero, Punta's main commercial strip. The thoroughfare runs northeast–southwest through the heart of the peninsula and is fronted with cafés, restaurants, boutiques, and casinos. ✉ *Av. Gorlero, Punta del Este.*

Casapueblo

HOTEL | A hotel and museum at the tip of a rocky point with tremendous views of the Río de la Plata is the main draw in Punta Ballena. Uruguayan abstract artist Carlos Páez Vilaró created his work as a "habitable sculpture" and it defies architectural categorization. With allusions to Arab minarets and domes, cathedral vaulting, Grecian whitewash, and continuous sculptural flourishes that recall the traceries of a Miró canvas, this curvaceous 13-floor surrealist complex climbs a hill and is highly unique.

The spaces include an excellent series of galleries dedicated to the artist's work and peruse copies of his books: one book tells the true story of his son Carlos Miguel, who survived a plane crash in the Andes, which was made into the 1993 film *Alive*. ✉ *Punta Ballena, Punta del Este* ☎ *4257–8041* ⊕ *casapueblo.com.uy* 🔖 *350 pesos.*

Isla de Lobos

ISLAND | This island is a government-protected natural reserve and national park home to one of the world's largest colonies of sea lions. You can view them from tour boats that leave regularly from the marina. Its 1907 lighthouse stands nearly 190 feet tall. ✉ *Punta del Este* ☎.

Isla Gorriti

ISLAND | Once the site of a prison, Isla Gorriti now attracts a different type of exclusive crowd. High-end residents

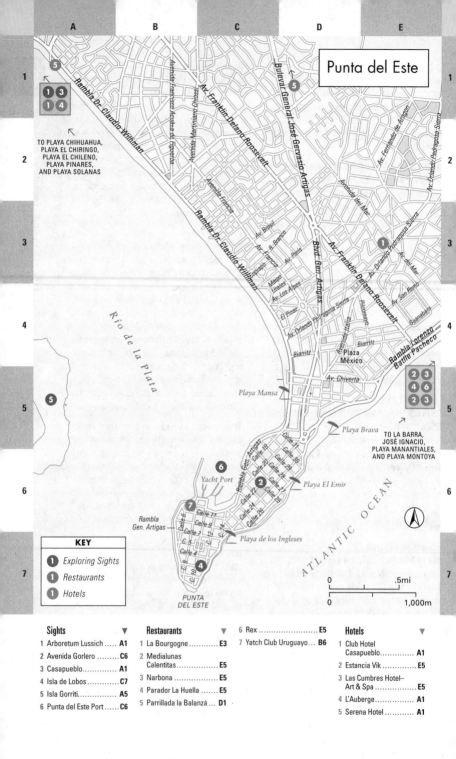

Punta del Este

KEY

- ① Exploring Sights
- ① Restaurants
- ① Hotels

TO PLAYA CHIHUAHUA,
PLAYA EL CHIRINGO,
PLAYA EL CHILENO,
PLAYA PINARES,
AND PLAYA SOLANAS

TO LA BARRA,
JOSÉ IGNACIO,
PLAYA MANANTIALES,
AND PLAYA MONTOYA

Río de la Plata

ATLANTIC OCEAN

Playa Mansa

Playa Brava

Playa El Emir

Playa de los Ingleses

Yacht Port

Rambla Gen. Artigas

PUNTA
DEL ESTE

Rambla Dr. Claudio Williman

Av. Franklin Delano Roosevelt

Bulevar General José Gervasio Artigas

Avenida Francisco Acuña de Figueroa

Avenida Martiniano Chiossi

Avenida Francia

Blvd. Gen. Artigas

Av. Franklin Delano Roosevelt

Av. Fernando de Aragón

Av. Orlando Pedragosa Sierra

Av. del Mar

Avenida del Mar

Av. Brasil

R. Branco

Av. Francia

Copacab.

Av. París

Maldo

Urales

Av. Los Alpes

El Pinar

Av. Orlando Pedragosa Sierra

Biarritz

Biarritz

Av. Italia

Pitágoras

Av. San Remo

Guanabará

Rambla Lorenzo Batlle Pacheco

Plaza
México

Av. Chiverta

Rambla Gen. Artigas

Calle 31

Calle 18

Calle 20

Calle 30

Calle 28

Calle 22

Calle 27

Calle 26

Calle 29

Calle 25

Calle 24

Calle 26

Calle 11

Calle 9

Calle 7

Calle 5

Calle 4

| 0 | | .5mi |
| 0 | | 1,000m |

Sights ▼	**Restaurants** ▼	6 Rex **E5**	**Hotels** ▼
1 Arboretum Lussich **A1**	1 La Bourgogne............ **E3**	7 Yatch Club Uruguayo... **B6**	1 Club Hotel Casapueblo.............. **A1**
2 Avenida Gorlero **C6**	2 Medialunas Calentitas................. **E5**		2 Estancia Vik **E5**
3 Casapueblo.............. **A1**	3 Narbona **E5**		3 Las Cumbres Hotel– Art & Spa **E5**
4 Isla de Lobos **C7**	4 Parador La Huella **E5**		4 L'Auberge................. **A1**
5 Isla Gorriti................ **A5**	5 Parrillada la Balanzà ... **D1**		5 Serena Hotel **A1**
6 Punta del Este Port **C6**			

with their own boats often set Gorriti as their destination to play and party for the day. You can catch a ferry ride from the marina, though, and make a day trip of it. Note that the island is reachable only by boat. (The *parador,* or beach club, has a good restaurant.) ⊠ *Punta del Este.*

Punta del Este Port

PROMENADE | Punta's sunsets seem even more spectacular when witnessed over its port, with sails and boats dotting the bay. Stop for a drink at any one of the many restaurants lining the street, or make it your destination for a leisurely walk or scenic run. ⊠ *2 de Febrero at Mareantes, Punta del Este.*

 Beaches

This stretch of coast has a dozen or so beaches, each with its own high-season personality. All bets are off on activity levels the rest of the year, and remember: what's hot one season may be so "last year" the next. Punta is that kind of place. Locals frequently shorthand things to the *mansa* (calm) side fronting the Río de la Plata—many sections are fine for swimming—and the *brava* (rough) side lining the Atlantic Ocean—its waves draw surfers but should make you think twice about going into the water. By law, all beaches in Uruguay are public.

RÍO DE LA PLATA SIDE
Playa Chihuahua

BEACH | One of Uruguay's only two sanctioned nude beaches (the other being in Rocha, well up the coast)—look for the *playa naturista* ("naturalist beach") sign—sits out near the airport west of Punta Ballena and divides into a straight and a gay section. Be cool about it if you go: no cameras, no binoculars, no gawking. **Amenities**: none. **Best for**: nudists. ⊠ *Punta del Este.*

Playa El Chiringo

BEACH | This beach, just east of Punta Ballena, can be a bit rough, with gritty sand and deep water. Chiringo catches full sun

A Cavalcade of Stars

Visitors to Punta del Este during its first heyday in the '50s and '60s rubbed shoulders with the likes of Ingmar Bergman and Yul Brynner. Even Brigitte Bardot, that then-icon of similarly themed St-Tropez, appeared here periodically. Recently celebrities such as Shakira, Madonna, Enrique Iglesias, Antonio Banderas, Ralph Lauren, Bob Dylan, Eric Clapton, and Leonardo DiCaprio have done the Punta circuit. You never know who you might see—in season, that is.

at midmorning, but shadows descend as the afternoon progresses, and the sun sets behind Punta Ballena. The wind and waves make swimming risky here. **Amenities**: lifeguards. **Best for**: solitude; sunrise. ⊠ *Punta del Este.*

Playa El Chileno

BEACH | The wind gusts dramatically at Playa El Chileno, making this beach a favorite among windsurfers. **Amenities**: toilets; showers. **Best for**: surfing; windsurfing. ⊠ *Punta del Este.*

Playa Pinares

BEACH | A continuation of Playa Mansa, Playa Pinares has deep water and rocky sand that make this a beach you'll likely have to yourself. Expect little in the way of facilities. **Amenities**: none. **Best for:** sunrise; sunset; walking. ⊠ *Punta del Este.*

★ **Playa Mansa**

BEACH | **FAMILY** | The waters are calm at Punta's longest beach and one of its most popular. Good sand, shallow water, many food stands, and proximity to the center of town make it the area's most family-oriented stretch of coast. Catch good sunset views here, and take in one of the late-afternoon beach aerobics

Famous lighthouse near Punta Del Este.

classes, too. **Amenities**: food and drink; lifeguards; parking; showers; toilets; water sports. **Best for**: sunset; swimming; walking. ✉ *Punta del Este.*

Playa Solanas

BEACH | The famous Casapueblo museum and hotel sit above this calm beach, also called Portezuelo, at Punta Ballena. Its shallow water shielded from the wind makes it a favorite of families with small children. Great sunset views are a plus here, too. **Amenities**: lifeguards; showers; toilets. **Best for**: sunrise; sunset; swimming; walking. ✉ *Punta del Este.*

ATLANTIC SIDE

★ La Barra

BEACH | The La Barra hamlet is both artistic and trendy, with a number of popular boutiques, restaurants, and nightlife spots that spring into life in January. A mostly locally patronized beach sits here, too, where the Río Maldonado spills into the ocean. Keep in mind that swimming is risky. **Amenities**: food and drink; lifeguards; parking; toilets. **Best for**: partiers; sunrise; sunset; surfing; walking. ✉ *Punta del Este.*

★ José Ignacio

BEACH | This hamlet with a vibrant art community and some of the most jaw-dropping properties for miles is the choice beach for Punta's most well-heeled and stylish visitors. José Ignacio sits on a miniature peninsula and has beaches with both calm and rough waters. Because it's just enough outside the downtown Punta orbit, visiting is a day trip for most, but if you're an art lover, make time to visit artist James Turrell's new Ta Khut Skyspace (US$40). **Amenities**: food and drink; lifeguards; toilets. **Best for**: partiers in the know; sunrise; sunset; surfing; swimming; walking; windsurfing. ✉ *Punta del Este.*

Playa Brava

BEACH | The golden sand and numerous food stands here draw a young crowd that mostly stays on the beach rather than braving the rough water (*brava* means "rough"). Brava is one of the most frequented beaches—largely thanks to *La Mano de Punta del Este*, a giant sculpture with the fingers of an enormous hand appearing to reach out of the sand—where many visitors will surely be snapping photos. This work by Chilean artist Mario Irarrázabal gives the beach its colloquial name, Playa de los Dedos (Beach of the Fingers). **Amenities**: food and drink; lifeguards; showers; toilets. **Best for**: sunrise; sunset; walking. ⊠ *Punta del Este.*

Playa de los Ingleses

BEACH | While this beach has fine sand, the wind and waves are strong here. Venture into the water at your own risk. You're still close to the center of Punta, meaning this beach sees many non-swimming visitors. Restaurants lining this so-called Englishmen's Beach were the spots for afternoon tea in a bygone era. **Amenities**: none. **Best for**: walking. ⊠ *Punta del Este.*

Playa El Emir

BEACH | This beach is named for an eccentric Middle Eastern emir who vacationed here and built a house near this stretch of sand. High waves make this beach popular with surfers, but somewhat dangerous for swimmers. **Amenities**: food and drink; lifeguards; showers; toilets. **Best for**: surfing; walking. ⊠ *Punta del Este.*

★ Playa Manantiales

BEACH | Locals have dubbed this trendy stretch of sand Bikini Beach. The swimwear skews a tad more daring here, where people come to see and be seen, as well as swim or play volleyball. During peak season DJs often spin through sunset. If you're looking for a party beach, this is where you want to be. **Amenities**: food and drinks; lifeguards; parking; showers; toilets. **Best for**: partiers; sunrise; sunset; surfing; swimming; windsurfing. ⊠ *Punta del Este.*

Sunrise, Sunset

How many beach resorts let you enjoy spectacular sunrises *and* sunsets over the water? Punta's orientation on a narrow north–south peninsula allows you to take in both.

Playa Montoya

BEACH | Just east of La Barra beach (but still belonging to La Barra) is this stretch of sand, where a young, attractive crowd mostly stays dry but always seems to have volleyball or soccer games going. Montoya also is the site of a number of surf competitions. **Amenities:** lifeguards; showers; toilets. **Best for:** partiers; sunset; surfing; swimming; walking. ⊠ *Punta del Este.*

Restaurants

★ La Bourgogne

$$$$ | FRENCH | A shaded terra-cotta terrace gives way to a breezeway with arched windows at this restaurant, considered one of Latin America's finest, and opens onto a large split-level dining room with antique sideboards. French chef Jean Paul Bondoux is at the helm, and the food, served by impeccably clad waiters, is prepared with only the finest and freshest ingredients. **Known for:** French family at the helm; excellent service and wine list; fine dining. $ *Average main: pesos4100* ⊠ *Av. del Mar at Calle Pedragosa Sierra, Punta del Este* 🕾 *4248–2007* ⊕ *www.labourgognepde.com* ⊗ *Closed Mon.–Wed. mid-April–Nov.*

★ Medialunas Calentitas

$ | CAFÉ | People flock to this classic Punta spot at all hours for their piping-hot *medialunas,* which are crescent moon–shape pastries that taste like fluffy croissants and come brushed with a sweet syrup. Many patrons profess they're the best medialunas to be found anywhere. **Known for:** takeaway; popular bakery; pastries and teatime treats. $ *Average main: pesos280* ✉ *Ruta 10 at Camino del Cerro Eguzquiza, Punta del Este* ☎ *4277–2347* ⊕ *www.medialunascalentitas.com.*

Narbona

$$$$ | **ITALIAN** | Set inland from Barra's center on an expansive, rolling property is the upscale, rustic Narbona restaurant. The property is so tranquil and removed from the Punta frenzy that the restaurant provides GPS coordinates as their address. **Known for:** Italian fare; uses own products such as olive oil; beautiful setting. $ *Average main: pesos1500* ✉ *R21, km. 268, Punta del Este* ☎ *9103–4100* ⊕ *www.narbona.com.uy.*

★ Parador La Huella

$$$ | **SOUTH AMERICAN** | *Huella* means footprint, and this now-legendary restaurant certainly has left its mark. Built right on the sand, La Huella takes beach dining to an unrivaled level with exquisite grilled seafood and meats—the octopus is not to be missed—as well as fresh sushi, pastas, and pizzas. **Known for:** very trendy; cool and relaxed vibe; delectable seafood. $ *Average main: pesos850* ✉ *Calle de los Cisnes, Brava Beach, Punta del Este* ☎ *4486–2279* ⊕ *www. paradorlahuella.com* ⊘ *Closed Mon.– Thurs. and Apr.–Nov. No dinner Sun.*

Parrilla la Balanza

$$$ | **STEAKHOUSE** | It's a bit hard to believe a place as low-key and affordable as this traditional Uruguayan steak house exists in chic Punta del Este, but it does—and that's precisely why locals love it. Your best bet is to stick to steak and sides to share, including the platter of mini *provoleta* (grilled cheese) with a bottle of wine to wash it all down. **Known for:** open all year round; great beef; cheap and cheerful. $ *Average main: pesos620* ✉ *25 de Mayo y Santa Teresa, Punta del Este* ☎ *4225–3909* ⊕ *www.parrillala-balanza.com.*

Rex

$$ | **SOUTH AMERICAN** | In peak season this laid-back, Americana-style diner serving up classic Uruguayan fare in La Barra is open 24 hours a day to accommodate everyone's beach and partying hours. The atmosphere is lively no matter when you come, and the fried calamari and chivito—they claim to have the best in town—are popular menu items. **Known for:** diner-style ambience; abundant sandwiches; fast and fun food. $ *Average main: pesos400* ✉ *Ruta 10, Km 161, Punta del Este* ☎ *4277–1504* ⊕ *www. rexbestchivitointown.com* ▭ *No credit cards.*

Yacht Club Uruguayo

$$$ | **SEAFOOD** | Loved by locals, this small eatery has a great view of Isla Gorriti. The menu includes a bit of everything, but the specialty is seafood. **Known for:** outdoor tables; great waitstaff; fish and seafood. $ *Average main: pesos630* ✉ *Rambla Artigas between Calles 6 and 8, Punta del Este* ☎ *4244–1056* ⊕ *www. ycu.org.uy.*

Hotels

Punta hotels operate on a multi-tier rate system. Prices go through the roof during Christmas and Easter weeks. Standard high-season rates apply in January and go slightly lower in February. March and December see prices a bit lower still, and then November creeps down a bit more, with some real bargains to be found the rest of the year. On the "rest of the year" topic, lodgings may close for a few weeks in the off-season. Always check ahead. Renting also is popular for long-term stays.

Club Hotel Casapueblo

$$$ | **HOTEL** | It would be hard not to feel like an artist in this whitewashed marvel. **Pros:** secluded location; conversation-starting architecture; interesting adjoining museum. **Cons:** difficult to procure space in summer; pricey; far

from the Punta action. $ *Rooms from: pesos9600* ⊠ *Punta Ballena, Punta del Este* ☎ *4257–8611* ⊕ *www.clubhotelcasapueblo.com* ⟿ *72 rooms* ⦿ *Free Breakfast.*

Estancia Vik

$$$$ | **HOTEL** | This luxe yet bohemian 12-suite ranch property set on 4,000 acres in José Ignacio offers guests the best of both a countryside and beach retreat. **Pros:** tranquil; impressive amenities; stylish and bespoke rooms. **Cons:** quite remote; expensive; 4-mile walk to the beach. $ *Rooms from: pesos19600* ⊠ *Camino Eugenio Saiz Martínez, Km 8, Punta del Este* ☎ *598/9460–5212, 598/9460–5314* ⊕ *www.estanciavik.com* ⟿ *12 suites* ⦿ *Free Breakfast.*

Las Cumbres Hotel–Art & Spa

$$ | **HOTEL** | At this alluring, un-Punta-like lodging up a 160-meter (520-foot) hill north of Punta Ballena, you can expect great views and a wooded, away-from-it-all vibe. **Pros:** quiet location; attentive staff; cooler temperatures than in town. **Cons:** need car to stay here; open weekends only during off-season; far from Punta. $ *Rooms from: pesos5400* ⊠ *Ruta 12, Km 3.5, Laguna del Sauce, Punta del Este* ☎ *4257–8689* ⊕ *www.cumbres.com.uy* ⊗ *Closed Mon.–Thurs., Apr.–Nov.* ⟿ *18 rooms, 10 suites* ⦿ *Free Breakfast.*

L'Auberge

$$$ | **HOTEL** | At this hotel in the heart of Parque del Golf, one of Punta's chicest neighborhoods, a stone water tower, which now contains guest rooms, rises from a double-wing chalet and affords spectacular Punta panoramas. **Pros:** secluded neighborhood; great restaurant; friendly staff. **Cons:** not close to downtown; some rooms are poky; not on beach. $ *Rooms from: pesos9100* ⊠ *Pda. 19 Brava. Carnoustie y Av. del Agua, Punta del Este* ☎ *4888–8888* ⊕ *www.laubergehotel.com* ⟿ *34 rooms, 2 suites* ⦿ *Free Breakfast.*

Serena Hotel

$$$ | **HOTEL** | While few Punta hotels actually sit on the beach, this is the rare exception: a stay here puts you steps from tranquil Playa Mansa and all its amenities. **Pros:** right on beach; attended by owner; lovely pool area with double sunbeds. **Cons:** some rooms are cramped; service could be friendlier; not an option for families with young children. $ *Rooms from: pesos8300* ⊠ *Rambla Williman Parada 24, Punta del Este* ☎ *4223–3441* ⊕ *www.serenahotel.com.uy* ⟿ *32 rooms* ⦿ *Free Breakfast.*

❿ Nightlife

Nightlife and tastes change capriciously from season to season. Expect fast-paced evenings in bars and nightclubs that might open as late as 1 am and reach a fever pitch around sunrise. Many places are open only in high season and have steep covers.

BARS AND PUBS
Moby Dick

PUBS | Punta del Este's most classic and popular pub sits right across from the city's port. While most other establishments close or slow in low season, Moby Dick keeps whistles wet year-round until 6 am every day of the week. ⊠ *Rambla de Artigas 650, Punta del Este* ☎ *4244–1240* ⊕ *www.mobydick.com.uy.*

Negroni

DANCE CLUBS | During peak season the sunset party at nearby Bikini Beach invariably migrates to Negroni, anchoring the Manantiales strip along Punta's main artery, Ruta 10. Bartenders serve up top-notch cocktails while DJs spin. ⊠ *Ruta 10, Km 164.5, Punta del Este* ☎ *9436–3400* ⊕ *www.negronibistrobar.com* ⊗ *Closed March–Nov.*

LIVE ENTERTAINMENT
Enjoy Punta del Este Casino

THEMED ENTERTAINMENT | For many visitors, Enjoy PDE—formerly known as the Conrad—defines nightlife in Punta with its casino and a year-round slate of Las Vegas–style shows by some of the biggest stars in Latin entertainment. Even if you don't recognize the names, taking in a performance at the area's largest hotel is *de rigueur.* ✉ *Rambla Claudio Williman at Parada 4, Punta del Este* ☎ *4249–1111* ⊕ *www.enjoy.cl/#/punta-del-este/casino.*

Shopping

Feria Artesanal
MARKET | An essential part of visiting Punta is exploring the colorful Feria Artesanal on the town's central Plaza Artigas. It's open weekend evenings all year; between Christmas and Easter it's open weekday evenings as well. Popular items include gourds for sipping *mate* (local green tea) and leather and silver crafts. ✉ *Plaza Artigas, Punta del Este.*

Activities

Not everyone is in Punta for beach bumming—many spend their time in the water. Surfing is popular on the Brava side, as is swimming on the Mansa side.

GOLF
Cantegril Country Club
GOLF | This country club has welcomed visitors to its golf course since 1947. At its main location on Salt Lake and Avenida Mauricio Litman, it offers tennis, and at Honorato de Balzac y Calderón de la Barca, it has rugby and soccer fields and tennis courts. ✉ *Av. San Pablo s/n, Punta del Este* ☎ *4222–3211* ⊕ *www.can-tegrilcountryclub.com.uy* ✉ *US$150 in high season; US$50 in low season* ⵊ *18 holes, 6412 yards, par 71.*

Club del Lago Golf
GOLF | You can play a round of golf at the challenging Club del Lago Golf, the only green in Punta del Este with 20 holes. As the course is popular in peak season, reservations are recommended, as well as confirming hours during off-season. ✉ *Ruta Interbalnearia, Km. 116.5, Punta del Este* ☎ *4257–8423* ⊕ *www.clubdellagogolf.com* ✉ *US$100* ⵊ *20 holes, 6823 yards, par 82.*

HORSEBACK RIDING
Haras Godiva
HORSEBACK RIDING | There's something sublime in horseback riding along natural surroundings, and something other-worldly when riding across a wide expanse of barren sandy beach. The Haras Godiva riding tour starts inland, a couple of miles north of José Ignacio, works it way towards the town along the countryside, on to the beach, and wends its way back in the direction of Laguna Garzón. The tour takes 90 minutes and covers just under 9 miles. ✉ *Ruta 10 Km 183.5, Camino de la Escuela Nr. 41, Punta del Este* ☎ *99/100–057* ⊕ *www.harasgodiva.com* ✉ *US$130.*

Chapter 6

THE NORTHWEST

Updated by
Sorrel Moseley-Williams

⦿ Sights	🍴 Restaurants	🛏 Hotels	🛍 Shopping	🍸 Nightlife
★★★★★	★★★★☆	★★★☆☆	★★☆☆☆	★★☆☆☆

WELCOME TO THE NORTHWEST

TOP REASONS TO GO

★ **The Quebrada:** In this vast, mountainous, color-splashed landscape, gaze up at an eternity of stars or the otherworldly carved walls of the gorge.

★ **Sports and the Outdoors:** Rivers deep, mountains high, valleys, lakes, and plains all play their part in tempting the adventurous to hike, ride, raft, fish, and rock climb. Take a spin in a kite buggy on the Salinas Grandes or try trekking with a llama.

★ **Folk Music:** Dive into the fabled Argentine folk scene by spending a night out at one of Salta's *peñas* (halls of food, music, and dancing). Wind instruments, diverse percussion, and soaring harmonies define the evocative high-Andean soundtrack.

★ **Wine:** Vintners from the Northwest—especially the Cafayate region of Salta and Quebrada de Humahuaca in Jujuy—continue to gain worldwide recognition for their cépages grown at great heights. The area is part of Argentina's Wine Trail and offers ample touring opportunities for oenophiles.

The landscape in Argentina's northwestern reaches is incredibly varied—from 22,000-foot Andean peaks to the high, barren plateau known as La Puna, from subtropical jungles to narrow sandstone canyons. Much of the area is desert, cut and eroded by raging brown rivers that wash away everything in sight during the rainy season in summer. The region's inhabitants have a tough, resilient quality. Here you'll find some of the country's most vibrant cities—but even they grind to a halt each afternoon for a siesta.

1 Jujuy. A province of varied histories and geographies, Jujuy (pronounced "hoo-hoo-wee") combines a respect for ancestral customs with stunning high-altitude landscapes—its most famous, the Quebrada de Humahuaca, is a UNESCO World Heritage Site.

2 Salta. The colonial city of Salta is a perfect base for exploring the wonders of the eponymous province. Chief among them is the Calchaquíes Valley, which follows the Inca Trail and Ruta 40 through improbably charming towns in a dusty, cactus-studded wilderness. And in the midst of this are some of the world's highest vineyards.

3 Tucumán. Argentina's smallest province is also the most varied—deserts are just a short drive from jungle, and rich agricultural lands that have earned the region its title Garden of the Republic. Retreat from the capital city to the cooler Tafí del Valle or the ruins of Quilmes.

4 La Rioja. La Rioja has lots of off-the-beaten-track territory. It's not for tourists, but rather for travelers who require very little logistical support. Its draws include vineyards, paleontological parks, a flamingo-flocked lake, and some very special places to stay.

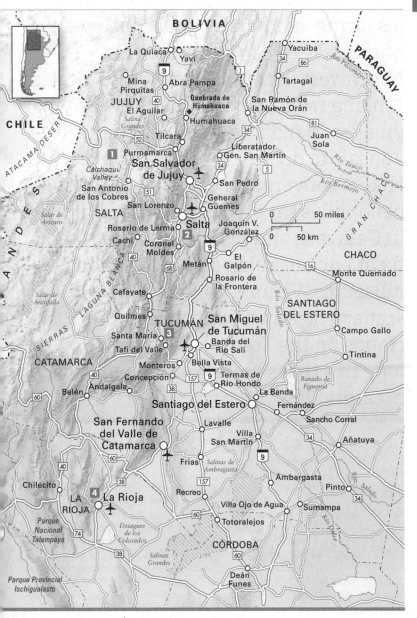

BOLIVIA

PARAGUAY

CHILE

La Quiaca
Yavi
Yacuiba
9
34
86
Río Pilcomayo
Mina Pirquitas
Abra Pampa
Tartagal
JUJUY
El Aguilar
Quebrada de Humahuaca
San Ramón de la Nueva Orán
40
81
Salina Grandes
Humahuaca
Juan Sola
Tilcara
34
52
Río Teuco
Liberatador Gen. San Martín
1
Purmamarca
34
5
Río Bermejo
San Salvador de Jujuy
Calchaquí Valley
San Pedro
GRAN CHACO
San Antonio de los Cobres
General Güemes
51
SALTA
San Lorenzo
Salar de Arizaro
Rosario de Lerma
Salta
Joaquín V. González
0   50 miles
0   50 km
2
Cachi
CHACO
Coronel Moldes
9
ANDES
40
El Galpón
16
Metán
68
Monte Quemado
LAGUNA BLANCA
Rosario de la Frontera
Salar de Antofalla
Cafayate
SANTIAGO DEL ESTERO
Río Salado
SIERRAS
Quilmes
Campo Gallo
Santa María
TUCUMÁN
San Miguel de Tucumán
3
Tintina
Tafí del Valle
Banda del Río Salí
CATAMARCA
Monteros
Bella Vista
40
Concepción
157
9
Termas de Río Hondo
Banado de Figueroa
38
60
Belén
Andalgalá
Santiago del Estero
La Banda
Fernández
San Fernando del Valle de Catamarca
Lavalle
Sancho Corral
Villa San Martín
34
Añatuya
Frias
Salinas de Ambragasta
9
40
Chilecito
38
157
Ambargasta
Pinto
LA RIOJA
4
La Rioja
Recreo
34
Río Salado
Parque Nacional Talampaya
74
Villa Ojo de Agua
Sumampa
60
Desagües de los Colorados
Totoralejos
Río Dulce
Salinas Grandes
CÓRDOBA
Parque Provincial Ischigualasto
60
Deán Funes

ATACAMA DESERT

This region flourished under the Inca, then attracted treasure-seeking Spaniards during colonial times; now it's luring an international contingent of tourists—and rightly so. The Northwest is notable for diverse locales, ranging from colonial towns to thriving vineyards and arid Andean deserts. It appeals to diverse types of travelers, too. Hikers converge on colorful canyons; oenophiles satisfy their wine cravings in Cafayate; and history buffs get their fix at ancient ruins and archaeology museums. Visitors who swoon over scenery, meanwhile, ascend to the clouds on the Tren a las Nubes: a day-long trip that's literally and figuratively breathtaking.

Despite their proximity, the provinces of Jujuy and Salta are at opposing ends of the cultural and geographical spectrum. The capital of the former is San Salvador de Jujuy. A quiet business-oriented city with a historic center, it serves as the provincial gateway. To the north is the Quebrada de Humahuaca, a stunning UNESCO-designated valley poised 2,300 meters (7,545 feet) soaring to 3,000 meters (9,843 feet) above sea level; colorful mineral deposits make its sandstone walls particularly photogenic, and small towns like Purmamarca, Tilcara, and Humahuaca that are rich in indigenous culture as well as natural beauty give it added appeal. Llama-trekking through the foothills and a visit to a well-preserved pre-Inca settlement are among the highlights here. The Quebrada is also a great base for exploring the vast elevated salt flats known as Salinas Grandes.

Salta Province, to the south, is anchored by its capital city—also called Salta. The jewel in Argentina's colonial crown is blessed with bright, beautiful religious architecture, interesting museums, and atmospheric streets. More sophisticated than San Salvador de Jujuy but still a world away from Buenos Aires, the city has an array of restaurants specializing in local dishes, plus a lively nightlife scene led by folk-music peñas. Continuing south to the vineyard-studded Calchaquí Valley, you can sample wares at the bodegas in and around Cafayate, where wine tourism opportunities abound. This region is proud of its own spectacular canyon, dubbed Quebrada de Las Conchas. Looping back from it to Salta on fabled Ruta 40, you'll encounter the picturesque Andean villages of Cachi and Molinos, as well the cactus-capped hills of Parque Nacional Los Cardones.

Planning

When to Go

January and February are Argentina's summer vacation months, meaning hotels get booked up and prices rise. Ironically, these two months coincide with rainy season, when flooding and/or landslides can block mountain roads. (The Salta–Cachi route is notorious for this.) Other busy times are winter break (July), Easter week, and moveable feasts such as Carnaval in the Quebrada de Humahuaca. Most facilities remain open year-round.

Getting Here and Around

AIR

Aerolíneas Argentinas/Austral has direct flights from Buenos Aires to Jujuy and Salta, as well as connecting flights between Salta and Iguazú. Flybondi and JetSmart fly from Buenos Aires to Salta

and Jujuy, the latter also connecting with Iguazú. All flights between Buenos Aires and the Northwest use the capital's Aeroparque Jorge Newbery, about 20 minutes north of downtown.

CONTACTS Aerolíneas Argentinas. ☎ 0810/222–86527 ⊕ www.aerolineas. com.ar. **Flybondi.** ⊕ www.flybondi.com. **JetSmart.** ⊕ www.jetsmart.com.

BUS

Buses are reliable, affordable, and well used, though certain routes require a little advance planning. Some companies offer roadside pickup; others have luxury double-decker vehicles offering overnight services and maybe even a glass of sparkling wine and a game of bingo. Tourist offices can advise which companies go where. In peak season, buy tickets a few days in advance.

CAR

Traveling outside of urban centers is often easiest by car. However, picking up a rental vehicle in one city and dropping it off in another incurs significant extra costs, so plan to drive for only parts of your journey or commit to a round trip. Roads are generally good and not very crowded, but be prepared for paved roads turning *ripio* (unpaved) and bumpy for long stretches. Very few routes require a 4X4 (apart from in wet weather).

Two main roads cross the area: the legendary Ruta 40, winding its unpaved way through small towns nearly 3,000 miles to the country's southern tip, and Ruta 9, the ancient road of the Inca, which takes you from Bolivia through San Salvador de Jujuy, Salta, and on toward Córdoba. Before you set out, visit an Automóvil Club Argentino office for maps and information, especially during the January–March rainy season.

REMIS

For short trips (e.g., Salta to Cafayate), consider taking a *remis* (a hired car with driver). Some routes have shared services, where you split the cost with others making the same journey; usually you have to wait for the car to reach capacity. You can find a remis at airports, bus stations, and on main plazas—or your hotel can call one for you. Be sure to agree on the price before setting off.

Health and Safety

Visitors unaccustomed to traveling at great heights may be susceptible to *soroche,* or altitude sickness, resulting in shortness of breath and headaches. Walk slowly, eat light meals, and drink plenty of fluids (but avoid alcohol). Locals swear by the *coqueando* remedy: sucking on coca leaves (bags sold at corner groceries and street vendors for around 300 pesos). Tear off the stems and stuff several leaves into the space between your teeth and cheek; leave them in for around 20 minutes or so then add a few more, neither chewing nor spitting, but swallowing when you salivate.

Aside from being sold an overpriced tour (recommended rates are listed in Salta's tourism office), you're unlikely to encounter crime, and local people are happy to receive visitors. Many hotels pride themselves on not needing safety deposit boxes.

The many roadside shrines marking car accidents, especially on winding mountain routes, are a reminder to check your speed. Also take care on the many bumpy, unpaved roads. And wear your seatbelt, as it is the law.

Restaurants

The Northwest's indigenous heritage still influences its cuisine: corn, grains, beans, and potatoes are common ingredients stemming back to the days of the Inca empire. Dishes worth trying include *locro,* a spicy soup with corn,

beans, and red peppers that becomes a rich stew when meat is added; *tamales,* ground corn baked with potatoes and meat and tied up in a corn husk; and *humita,* grated corn with melted cheese cooked in a corn husk. Grilled *cabrito* (goat) is also a regional specialty. For dessert, you may come across *cayote,* an interesting concoction of green-squash marmalade served with walnuts and local goat cheese.

Hotels

Hotels in the Northwest's major cities tend to be modern and comfortable. Most accept credit cards; if you are paying in cash, however, do ask whether a discount is offered. Many *estancias* (ranches) in the foothills welcome guests and are listed with local tourist offices. Although the whole region has really started to open up to local and foreign tourism, chain hotels are few and far between. Instead, take advantage of a dazzling array of boutique hotels and estancias built—or remodeled—to reflect history and ever mindful of their location.

Hotel reviews have been shortened. For full information, visit Fodors.com. Restaurant prices are the average cost of a main course at dinner or, if dinner is not served, at lunch. Hotel prices are the lowest cost of a standard double room in high season.

What It Costs in Argentine Pesos

	$	$$	$$$	$$$$
RESTAURANTS				
	Under 600 pesos	600 pesos–1,000 pesos	1,001 pesos–1,500 pesos	Over 1,500 pesos
HOTELS (IN $USD)				
	Under $80	$80–$200	$201–$300	Over $300

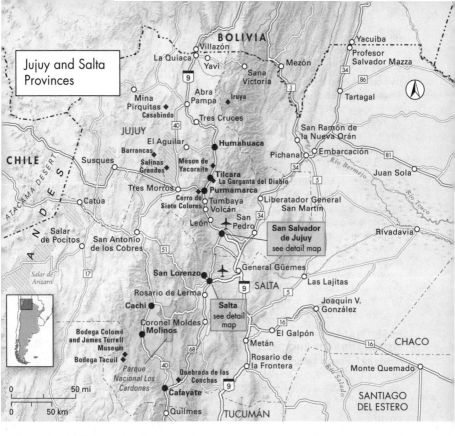

Jujuy and Salta Provinces

San Salvador de Jujuy

1,643 km (1,020 miles) northwest of Buenos Aires; 92 km (57 miles) north of Salta on RN9.

Founded by Spaniards in 1593, San Salvador de Jujuy (known as Jujuy to most Argentineans and as "S.S. de Jujuy" on signs) is a compact city. Its focal point is Plaza General Belgrano, in the city center between the Río Grande and Río Xibi Xibi. The square is home to a number of key sights, the 18th-century cathedral and grand Casa de Gobierno among them.

The city's quarter-million inhabitants—including a large indigenous population—busy themselves with administering the province's main sources of income (tobacco, mining, and sugarcane),

although more are now dealing with tourism. Jujuy may lack nearby Salta's colonial dreaminess and ample hotel selection, but it has a laid-back, unadulterated local culture plus a touch of frontier-town charm. It also makes a great stop-off point and touring base (although staying in the Quebrada's small towns is infinitely more pleasing on the eye). Just outside town you can ride horses along mountain paths in the jungle or go boating in valley waterways.

GETTING HERE AND AROUND

Aerolíneas Argentinas (⊕ www.aerolineas.com.ar) flies six times a day from Buenos Aires, as does Flybondi (⊕ www.flybondi.com) and JetSmart, making the trip in two hours and 15 minutes. Jujuy's Aeropuerto Dr. Horacio Guzmán is 30 km (19 miles) southeast of town. La Veloz del Norte, Balut, and Panamericano buses travel between Salta and Jujuy; the latter two continue north to Purmamarca, Tilcara, Humahuaca, and La Quiaca at the Bolivian border. La Quiaqueño buses also depart for La Quiaca nine times a day. Other bus companies serving Jujuy include Andesmar, Crucero del Norte, and El Quiaqueño.

The city's one-way grid system is easy to navigate in a rental car or cheap red cab, although traffic builds up a bit around the beginning and end of the siesta. Proceeding on foot is an alternative because Jujuy is flat despite the altitude. Most attractions, restaurants, and hotels are within easy walking distance of Plaza Belgrano; the exception is the Alto de la Viña district, which is worth the 400-peso taxi fare to reach.

ESSENTIALS

VISITOR AND TOUR INFORMATION Sec-retaría de Turismo y Cultura de la Provincia de Jujuy. ⊠ *Gorriti 295, San Salvador de Jujuy* 🕾 *388/422–1325* ⊕ *www.turismo. jujuy.gob.ar.*

TOURS

Paisajes del Noroeste
GUIDED TOURS | This Jujuy specialist runs a range of tours and day trips, including minibus outings to the remote village of Iruya and excursions to Hornocal (an impressive 21-colored hill near Humahua-ca). ⊠ *San Martín 134, San Salvador de Jujuy* 🕾 *388/423–7565* ⊕ *www.paisajes-delnoroeste.tur.ar* 🕮 *From 5,000 pesos.*

Equipa Tu Aventura
ADVENTURE TOURS | This northwest Argen-tina specialist knows the Altiplano or Puna like the back of its hand, leading tai-lor-made adventure and mountaineering expeditions. Expeditions range between four and 15 days. 🕾 *387/589–8143* ⊕ *www.equipatuaventura.com.ar.*

 Sights

★ **Casa de Gobierno**
GOVERNMENT BUILDING | The 1907 Casa de Gobierno (Government House) fronts the plaza on San Martín and contains the pro-vincial government offices. A first-floor hall, the Salón de la Bandera, displays the original Argentine flag donated by Gener-al Belgrano in 1813, a gift to the city after it cooperated with the Belgrano-headed Exodus of Jujuy during the War of Inde-pendence. Entry is on Sarmiento street. The flag was replaced a few years later by the current white and sky-blue stripe version, and the one here is now used as the national coat of arms. ⊠ *San Martín 450, San Salvador de Jujuy* 🕾 *388/423–9400* ⊕ *www.jujuy.gob.ar* 🕮 *Free.*

Catedral de Jujuy
RELIGIOUS BUILDING | The cathedral dates from 1765 and was the first building con-structed in the city; however, it has been augmented and remodeled so many times that it's now a hodgepodge of architectural styles. The interior contains an ornately carved, gold-plated pulpit, said to be the finest in South America. A close look reveals an intricate population of carved figures, biblical and otherwise. It was inspired by the Cusqueña school of art from Cuzco, Peru, as were the building's ornate doors and confession-als. The cathedral museum next door houses a wealth of religious art. ⊠ *West side of Plaza General Belgrano, San Sal-vador de Jujuy* 🕾 *388/423–5333* ⊕ *www. catedraldejujuy.blogspot.com.ar* 🕮 *Free; museum 100 pesos* ⊙ *Closed Sun.*

Iglesia de San Francisco
RELIGIOUS BUILDING | An ornate 18th-centu-ry wooden pulpit with dozens of figures of monks is the centerpiece of the Church of St. Francis, two blocks west of Plaza General Belgrano. There's some debate about who carved the pulpit: it may have been local artisans, or the pulpit may have been transported from Bolivia. Although the church and bell

tower look colonial, they date from 1930. Also stop by the bijou Museo de arte sacro museum (entrance on Belgrano) to see religious art dating back to the 17th century. ⊠ *Lavalle 325, San Salvador de Jujuy* ⊕ *www.turismo.jujuy.gob.ar/item/ iglesia-san-francisco/* ☞ *Free; museum 100 pesos* ☉ *Closed weekends.*

Museo Histórico Provincial Juan Galo Lavalle (*Juan Lavalle Provincial History Museum*)

HISTORY MUSEUM | Arms, trophies, and military memorabilia collected from the 25 years of fighting for independence are on display at the Juan Lavalle Provincial History Museum. In this adobe building, General Juan Lavalle, a hero of the War of Independence and an enemy of the dictator Juan Manuel de Rosas, was assassinated. A replica of the door through which Lavalle was shot in 1746 is part of the exhibit. ⊠ *Lavalle 256, San Salvador de Jujuy* ☎ *388/422–1355* ⊕ *www.turismo.jujuy.gob.ar/item/museo-historico-provincial* ☞ *80 pesos* ☉ *Closed Sun.*

Museo y Centro Cultural Culturarte

ARTS CENTER | Drop into Culturarte to get a quick hit of contemporary art and photography. After seeing the exhibits, you can order a coffee and pull up a breezy balcony seat for a different side-on view of Government House. ⊠ *Sarmiento and San Martín, San Salvador de Jujuy* ☎ *388/431–4657* ☞ *Free.*

★ **Plaza General Belgrano**

PLAZA/SQUARE | Orange trees and vendors populate the central square, which is surrounded by colonial buildings—including the imposing government palace. It's empty by day, but starts to fill with gossiping *jujeños*, old and young, by late afternoon. ■TIP➡ **The plaza benefits from free Wi-Fi.** ⊠ *San Salvador de Jujuy.*

★ **Quebrada de Humahuaca**

NATURE SIGHT | About 60 km (37 miles) north of San Salvador de Jujuy, the inimitable Ruta 9 runs into the Quebrada de Humahuaca—a riotously colorful gorge that ranks among Argentina's most distinctive landscapes. Running alongside the Río Grande, variegated tones of pink, red, and gray brighten canyon walls.

As the gorge deepens approaching Humahuaca on its northern tip, the colors become more vibrant. Brilliant-green alamo and willow trees surround villages, contrasting with the red hues in the background. In summer and fall, torrential rains mixed with mud and snowmelt from the mountains rush down, carving ravines before pouring into the chalky gray river.

🍴 Restaurants

Finca

$$$$ | ARGENTINE | Managing various restaurants around NW Argentina, including overseeing the Quebrada's Hotel Huacalera, chef Walter Leal raises the bar in terms of Andean cuisine. Working with ingredients from across Jujuy including the highly elevated Puna plateau, his creations look to recuperate, then plate, these remote ecosystems. **Known for:** local celebrity chef; fresh, local ingredients; excellent wine pairings. $ *Average main: pesos2000* ⊠ *General Belgrano 575, at Patio Gamez, San Salvador de Jujuy* ☎ *388/522–3070* ☉ *Closed Sat. No lunch Sun.*

Manos Jujeñas

$$ | ARGENTINE | Ponchos on the walls, old paintings, native artifacts, stucco archways, and Andean background music are clues that this might be one of the best places to sample authentic Northwestern cuisine. Try the *locro*: a stew of maize, white beans, beef, chorizo, pancetta, and a wonderful red pepper–oil glaze, all of which come together in a mélange of savory, starchy flavors. ■TIP➡ **Ask for a table at the back for a more authentic and less hurried dining experience. Known for:** busy atmosphere drawing locals; great place to try locro; traditional dishes. $ *Average main: pesos900* ⊠ *Senador Pérez*

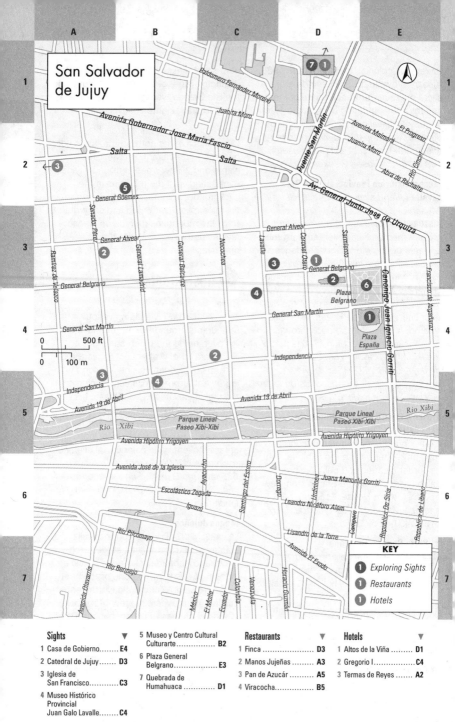

San Salvador de Jujuy

KEY
- Exploring Sights
- Restaurants
- Hotels

Sights ▼
1. Casa de Gobierno........ **E4**
2. Catedral de Jujuy....... **D3**
3. Iglesia de
   San Francisco............ **C3**
4. Museo Histórico
   Provincial
   Juan Galo Lavalle........ **C4**
5. Museo y Centro Cultural
   Culturarte................ **B2**
6. Plaza General
   Belgrano................. **E3**
7. Quebrada de
   Humahuaca **D1**

Restaurants ▼
1. Finca **D3**
2. Manos Jujeñas **A3**
3. Pan de Azucar **A5**
4. Viracocha................ **B5**

Hotels ▼
1. Altos de la Viña **D1**
2. Gregorio I **C4**
3. Termas de Reyes **A2**

379, San Salvador de Jujuy ☎ *388/424–3270* 🖃 *No credit cards* ⊗ *Closed Mon.*

Pan de Azucár

$$ | ARGENTINE | For *jujeña* classics with an eclectic twist, head to Pan de Azucár, where an ample menu offers original concoctions of the local staple, llama—think curry, carpaccio, grilled fillet, or stuffed in ravioli. House specialties also include quinoa, pork, and pasta. **Known for:** relaxed ambience; llama dishes; regional ingredients. $ *Average main: pesos850* 🖂 *Senador Perez 110, San Salvador de Jujuy* ☎ *388/423–2392* 🖃 *No credit cards* ⊗ *Closed Sun.*

★ Viracocha

$$ | ARGENTINE | The menu at this unassuming *picanteria* (restaurant specializing in spicy foods) has everything from trout to rabbit, but llama or quinoa are the dishes to try: give them a go as an *empanada* starter. Less adventurous eaters can sample one of the pasta dishes. **Known for:** Northwestern cuisine; buzzy atmosphere; spicy food. $ *Average main: pesos900* 🖂 *Independencia 994, corner of Lamadrid, San Salvador de Jujuy* ☎ *388/423–3554* 🖃 *No credit cards* ⊗ *Closed Mon. No dinner Sun.*

 Hotels

★ Altos de la Viña

$$ | HOTEL | FAMILY | This former state-owned hotel, a short ride out of town, has comfortable rooms and recreational facilities that invite you to linger; the view from the swimming pool takes in most of the city and the mountains beyond. **Pros:** great pool; good for families; helipad. **Cons:** own transport is useful; some rooms could do with an update; very little within walking distance. $ *Rooms from: US$114* 🖂 *Pasquini López 50, Alto La Viña, San Salvador de Jujuy* ☎ *388/426–2626* ⊕ *hotelaltosdelavina.com.ar* ⇌ *60 rooms* ⦿ *Free Breakfast.*

Gregorio 1

$$ | HOTEL | This downtown boutique hotel has sober rooms with parquet floors and all the modern conveniences. **Pros:** close to everything; attentive service; comfy rooms. **Cons:** isn't quite "boutique"; breakfast isn't very imaginative; few in-hotel services. $ *Rooms from: US$85* 🖂 *Independencia 829, San Salvador de Jujuy* ☎ *388/424–4747* ⊕ *www.gregoriohotel.com* ⇌ *19 rooms* ⦿ *Free Breakfast.*

Termas de Reyes

$ | HOTEL | Built on the edge of a spectacular river valley, this countryside complex has natural thermal baths—both indoor and out—that bubble up from underground hot springs. **Pros:** the chance to take the cure and find inner peace; fantastic views; good in-house restaurant. **Cons:** thermal baths are popular and crowded; rooms could do with an update; located 19 km (12 miles) outside of Jujuy on a partially paved road. $ *Rooms from: US$62* 🖂 *R4, Km 19, San Salvador de Jujuy* ☎ *388/492–2522* ⇌ *60 rooms* ⦿ *Free Breakfast.*

 Nightlife

El Bodegón

LIVE MUSIC | This popular *peña* with hundreds of vinyl records on the walls calls itself "the cathedral of Jujuy folklore." It's predominantly filled with a young crowd of locals who have no qualms about taking to the small stage, and is a great space to see up-and-coming musicians. 🖂 *Sarverri, at José Peres, Alto La Viña, San Salvador de Jujuy* ☎ *388/504–3215.*

La Peña de Carlitos

LIVE MUSIC | This restaurant on the main plaza doubles up as a spot for live regional music and local bands. 🖂 *Lavalle 397, at Rivadavia, Tilcara* ☎ *11/5483–7278.*

🛍 Shopping

Paseo de los Artesanos

SOUVENIRS | The modest Paseo de los Artesanos on Plaza General Belgrano has reasonable prices on all kinds of woven and handcrafted souvenirs. And those *coca* tea bags, imported from Bolivia, are a curiosity that's hard to resist. The small café at the back is ideal for a quick *empanada* pitstop. ⊠ *Sarmiento 524, San Salvador de Jujuy* 📷.

🏃 Activities

With its jungles, lakes, waterfalls, and wild rivers, the area around San Salvador de Jujuy is great for hiking and horseback riding. There are a number of companies offering excursions, but only a handful have an online presence, which makes things hard, as most trips must be booked a few days in advance. Check the Jujuy tourism board's website (⊕ *www. turismo.jujuy.gob.ar*) for a complete list of operators.

Calilegua National Park

WILDLIFE-WATCHING | Besides craggy canyons and mountain ranges, Jujuy is also home to the Yungas, a lush cloud forest and semi-tropical jungle that will transport you straight into *Jurassic Park*. A 90-minute drive from SS de Jujuy, protected species who reside within the Calilegua National Park include jaguars, South Andean deer, and neotropical otters. ⊠ *San Lorenzo, Calilegua, San Salvador de Jujuy* 📷 *388/642-2046* ⊕ *www. argentina.gob.ar/parquesnacionales/ calilegua.*

Purmamarca

65 km (40 miles) north of San Salvador de Jujuy.

Nestled in the shadow of craggy rocks and multicolor, cactus-studded hills— with the occasional low-flying cloud

Hiking and Other Activities 🏃

Hikers with the lungs to take on Jujuy's elevations will love the challenge of scaling Nevado del Chañi (5,896 masl), the province's highest peak that's found in the Cordillera Oriental. For a less intensive hike that's teeming with wildlife, visit Potrero de Yala provincial park located 27 km (16.77 miles) from SS de Jujuy, known for its abundance of avian wild life. Equine lovers will love trekking the pre-Hispanic trails in the Quebrada a las Yungas by horseback.

floating by—the colonial village of Purmamarca is one of the best bases from which to explore the Quebrada. Its 2,195-meter (7,200-foot) altitude, dry air, and dearth of artificial light also make it a great spot for stargazing.

Here blazing red adobe replaces the white stucco used in architecture elsewhere, and the simple, square buildings play off the matching red rock. While there are a few more stores and restaurants open for business, and a heap of artisans selling their wares in the pleasant, tree-shaded plaza, do visit before it's completely transformed from a two-horse town into a more exclusive destination.

GETTING HERE AND AROUND

Located on Ruta 52, Purmamarca is just a 3-km (2-mile) detour from Ruta 9. Balut buses traveling between Jujuy and Humahuaca run through about 10 times a day. Almost no place here has its own street number (they're marked *s/n* or *sin número* ["no number"] in addresses), but the town is so small that everything is either on or within two blocks of the main square, Plaza 9 de Julio. There's

The Hill of Seven Colors is a breathtaking sight from many viewpoints.

no bank or hospital, but there is a cash machine next to the tourist information office.

ESSENTIALS
VISITOR AND TOUR INFORMATION
Tourist Office. ⊠ *Florida casi Rivadavia, Purmamarca* ☎ *388/490–8443* ⊕ *www. turismo.jujuy.gob.ar/item/purmamarca/.*

 Sights

★ Bodega Fernando Dupont
WINERY | On the lovely grounds of this bodega, cardon cacti mingle with Malbec, Cabernet Sauvignon, and Syrah vines, which thrive at 2,500 meters (8,202 feet) thanks to hot days and very cool nights. The Paleta del Pintor hill provides a stunning and vibrant backdrop. You can call ahead for a brief yet interesting tour; take home the Rosa de Maimará Rosé or the Sikuri Syrah. Although there is a bridge, reaching the winery remains impossible when the river floods in the rainy season (summer). ⊠ *RN9, Km 1776, 19 km (12 miles) north of Purmamarca,* *Maimará* ☎ *388/15–473–1918* ⊕ *www. bodegafernandodupont.com* ✉ *Free tour; 3-wine tasting 600 pesos* ☽ *Closed Sun.*

Bodega Kindgard
WINERY | A new bodega that opened its doors in 2022 while marking its third grape harvest, Kindgard was set up by two Jujuy cousins who come from winemaking and agricultural backgrounds. Offering one of the Quebrada's more complete wine experiences, buoyed by a unique view of the Siete Colores mountains, visitors can enjoy a three-vintage tasting and vineyard visit with charcuterie plate (3,500 pesos) or a paired three-course lunch in the restaurant (12,000 pesos). ⊠ *RN9 km 1739, Purmamarca* ☎ *388/409–6930.*

★ Cerro de Siete Colores (*Hill of Seven Colors*)
MOUNTAIN | Looming above Purmamarca is the brightly tinted Cerro de Siete Colores (Hill of Seven Colors). Look closely and see if you can find all seven—most people can pick out only four. The best way to see the hill is by walking a

The Salinas Grandes are a blinding sight that's worth it with sunglasses.

3-km (2-mile) loop called the **Paseo de Siete Colores,** which starts to the left of the church on the main square. This one-lane gravel road winds through bizarre, humanlike formations of bright, craggy, red rock, before passing a series of stark, sweeping, Mars-like vistas with stands of trees in the river valley. The road then passes a few family farms and ends with a striking view of the Cerro itself before bringing you back to the center of Purmamarca.

■ TIP→ **The colors are most clearly visible in the morning. The tourist office on Florida Street has a map showing the best points for photos.** ⊠ *Purmamarca.*

Iglesia de Santa Rosa de Lima
RELIGIOUS BUILDING | The most notable landmark downtown on the central plaza is Iglesia de Santa Rosa de Lima. Dating from 1778, it was constructed from adobe and thistle wood. On calle Belgrano, to the left of the church, is a 620-year-old carob tree. ⊠ *Plaza 9 de Julio, Purmamarca.*

★ Salinas Grandes
NATURE SIGHT | West of Purmamarca you can ogle one of the area's most eye-popping sights: the Salinas Grandes, more than 200 square km (80 square miles) of dazzling salt flats at the top of a mountain. Take the sinuous Ruta 52 for 64 km (40 miles) over the majestic Cuesta de Lipan (Lipan Rise)—which tops out at 4,170 meters (13,700 feet) above sea level—and cross Ruta 40. The salty landscape is surreal, and it's made even more so by a building constructed entirely out of slabs of salt turned a brownish color and salt furniture set up like church pews, complete with lectern. A series of small pools have been cut out of the salt flats' surface, revealing a layer of water and freshly forming crystals underneath. For 1,000 pesos, you can contract a guide from the kiosk at the entrance to lead you in your vehicle through the flats.

■ TIP→ **Remember to carry a camera, a hat, some water, and sunblock.** ⊠ *Purmamarca.*

Restaurants

La Posta

$$ | **ARGENTINE** | Empanadas, llama dishes, and other hearty regional specialties dominate the menu at this eatery on the main square. Take a seat by the window and watch the scene at the market stalls outside while enjoying *jujeño* staples such as *picante de pollo* (spicy chicken) or regional stews, or avoid the bustle on the airy back patio. **Known for:** attracting families; lively atmosphere; traditional dishes. [$] *Average main: pesos1000* ✉ *Rivadavia s/n, on Plaza 9 de Julio, Purmamarca* ☎ *388/490–8040* 💳 *No credit cards.*

★ **Los Morteros**

$$$ | **ARGENTINE** | For a contemporary spin on regional delicacies, head to Los Morteros. The llama in Malbec, fresh grilled trout, and succulent lamb stew are all noteworthy picks; this busy spot also cooks up a sizzling barbecue worth ordering for its smell alone. **Known for:** good wine list; barbecue; regional cuisine. [$] *Average main: pesos1200* ✉ *Salta s/n, Purmamarca* ☎ *388/490–8063* 💳 *No credit cards* 🕒 *Closed Wed.*

Hotels

El Cardon

$ | **B&B/INN** | It's small and no-frills, but if you're just looking for a place to sleep in between excursions, this friendly lodging a short walk from the main square is a good bet. **Pros:** a reliable, in-town option; budget-friendly; great terrace. **Cons:** often full in high season; staff can be cross; few, basic facilities. [$] *Rooms from: US$34* ✉ *Belgrano s/n, Purmamarca* ☎ *388/490–8672* 💳 *No credit cards* 🛏 *7 rooms* 🍴 *Free Breakfast.*

★ **El Manantial del Silencio**

$$$ | **HOTEL** | At this tranquil retreat, weeping willows, red rocks, and gardens filled with birdsong are hemmed in by the craggy Quebrada and its utter calm; inside the colonial-style stucco mansion, local artifacts and earth tones make things warm and harmonious throughout. **Pros:** one of the grandest lodgings in the Quebrada; great gardens, restaurant, spa, and pool; welcoming shared areas. **Cons:** noise reverberates down hallways; friendly staff aren't necessarily on the ball; one of the most expensive lodgings in the area. [$] *Rooms from: US$200* ✉ *RN52, Km 3.5, Purmamarca* ☎ *388/490–8080* 🌐 *www.hotelmanantialdelsilencio.com* 🛏 *20 rooms* 🍴 *Free Breakfast.*

La Comarca

$$ | **HOTEL** | The various rooms, cabins, and houses here surround a garden of flowers and cacti; all accommodations are built with traditional local materials—adobe, cane, wood—and are decorated with a contemporary eye. **Pros:** heated pool has a view of the Siete Colores; good restaurant; houses can sleep up to six guests. **Cons:** a little way out of town; hallways are noisy in high season; showers not designed for tall people. [$] *Rooms from: US$115* ✉ *RN52, Km 3.8, Purmamarca* ☎ *388/490–8098* 🌐 *www.lacomarcahotel.com.ar* 🛏 *18 rooms* 🍴 *Free Breakfast.*

Los Colorados

$$ | **B&B/INN** | All the reddish adobe walls of the cabins at Los Colorados, on the Cerro de Siete Colores, have rounded corners, giving the whole place a look of having been sculpted straight from the earth; it's a perfect spot for kicking back, whether you're curled up by the fireplace in your room or stargazing on the communal terrace. **Pros:** quiet and peaceful environment; cozy; six-person Jacuzzi. **Cons:** slow Wi-Fi; staff can be inattentive; small bathrooms. [$] *Rooms from: US$115* ✉ *El Chapacal 511, Purmamarca* ☎ *388/407–2532* 🌐 *www.loscoloradosjujuy.com.ar* 🛏 *7 rooms/cabins* 🍴 *Free Breakfast.*

★ **Pristine Camps**

$$$$ | ALL-INCLUSIVE | An ambitious glamping project tucked away in a salt mine south of the Salinas Grandes, this debut lodging from Pristine Camps comprises four luxurious domes, two including Jacuzzis, and a restaurant located 3,600 meters (11,811 feet) above sea level. **Pros:** friendly staff come from the local indigenous community; all-inclusive experience means seeing the Salinas from a different perspective; the night skies balance out the high cost. **Cons:** more salt-related activities should be welcomed; the high elevation is hard for some to deal with; it can be extremely hot in the day then cold at night. [$] *Rooms from: US$900* ✉ *Salinas Grandes, Purmamarca* 🌐 *www.pristine-camps.com* 🛏 *4* 🍴 *All-Inclusive.*

🍸 Nightlife

Don Heriberto

LIVE MUSIC | You'll meet a mix of locals and visitors at the town's only late-night bar, which also doubles up as a *peña*, where folk musicians and singers gather to perform. In high season, it opens at 10 pm and closes at 5 am or when the last customer leaves—whichever comes first. ✉ *Sarmiento s/n, close to corner of Libertad, Purmamarca* ☎ *388/604–1688.*

Tilcara

85 km (53 miles) north of San Salvador de Jujuy; 18 km (11 miles) northeast of Purmamarca via RN9.

Founded in 1600 and witness to many battles during the War of Independence, Tilcara is on the eastern side of the Río Grande at its confluence with the Río Huasamayo. Purveyors of local crafts crowd the main plaza, and artists and musicians escaping the big cities fill the cafés and bars. There are several reasons to stop off in this 2,469-meter-high (8,100-foot-high) Quebrada town: an interesting museum; nearby Inca ruins, caves, and waterfalls; and a good selection of accommodations and restaurants.

GETTING HERE AND AROUND

Tilcara is well served by buses running between Jujuy and Humahuaca or La Quiaca. Taking a shared taxi from San Salvador de Jujuy's old bus station is another option; the cost is about the same. Arriving from the south, look out for the surprisingly large cemetery of Maimará, which sprawls on either side of the road outside town.

👁 Sights

La Garganta del Diablo

NATURE SIGHT | Seven km (4 miles) west of town is La Garganta del Diablo (The Devil's Throat), a red-rock gorge with waterfalls (the number depends on the season). The tourist office in Tilcara can point you in the right direction; ask about the path that knocks about half the distance off the journey. Ask, too, for directions to the wind-eroded caves that are a similar distance east of town. ✉ *Tilcara.*

Museo Arqueológico y Antropológico Dr. Eduardo Casanova

HISTORY MUSEUM | Exhibits at the Museo Arqueológico, run by the University of Buenos Aires, can be a little confusing due to a lack of explanatory labels. The two mummies here are considerably less well cared for than those in Salta's MAAM (Museum of High Altitude Archaeology), but no less fascinating. The clothes, hair, and skin of the first, which was found in San Pedro de Atacama in Chile, are well preserved. Other rooms display Nazca, Inca, Moche, and other remains from the past 2,000 years. ✉ *Belgrano 445, Tilcara* ☎ *388/495–5006* 🌐 *tilcara.filo.uba.ar* 🎟 *Free* 🕒 *Closed Mon.*

The unique architecture of indigenous homes in Tilcara.

★ Museo en los Cerros

ART MUSEUM | You'll find this surprising photography gallery by following a stony road that runs alongside the River Huichaira up into the mountains. The brainchild of photographer Lucio Boschi, the "museum in the hills" has two spaces displaying permanent collections as well as a temporary exhibit room. For the ultimate in artsy tranquility, kick back in the library while browsing coffee table books with a coca leaf tea. ☒ *Quebrada de Huichaira, 4 km (3 miles) off R9, Tilcara* ☎ *388/332-2229* ⊕ *www.museoen-loscerros.com.ar* ☒ *Free.*

★ Pucará de Tilcara

RUINS | Set on a hill above the left bank of the Río Grande, this fortified, pre-Inca *pucará* (settlement) is the best-preserved of several in the Quebrada de Humahuaca and the only one that can be visited. Its different areas (some of which have been rebuilt) can be clearly discerned. Allow at least 90 minutes to walk around the site, where an estimated 2,000 Omaguaca once lived, worshipped, and kept their animals. On your way out, turn right at the entrance to the fort for the Jardín Botánico (Botanical Garden): inside you can admire a large array of cacti and other plants. Don't miss the chance to strike the Piedra Campana with a mallet disguised as a stick—true to its name (Bell Stone) it rings like a bell. ☒ *About 1½ km (1 mile) south of Tilcara, Tilcara* ☒ *500 pesos* ⊘ *Closed Mon.*

Huichaira Vineyard

WINERY | One of the more notable additions to Jujuy's elevated winemaking landscape, Huichaira Vineyard offers two tasting experiences in the gorge of the same name..Located on the opposite of the mountain to the Museo en los Cerros, enjoy a picnic accompanied by the delicious Cielo Arriba Malbec/Syrah/Cabernet Franc blend (US$50) or work up an appetite on a bicycle expedition from Tilcara to the vineyard (US$70). ☒ *Quebrada de Huichaira, Tilcara.*

🍴 Restaurants

★ El Nuevo Progreso

$$$ | **ARGENTINE** | The food, from steak to quinoa salad, is superb; the wine list is fairly priced; and the wooden floors, whimsical lights, and artwork make the space appealing. What's more, some evenings around 9:30 there's live music, generally performed by friends of the owners. **Known for:** friendly, on-the-ball service; abundant portions; traditional dishes with a modern twist. [$] *Average main: pesos1500* ✉ *Lavalle 351, Tilcara* ☎ *388/495-5237.*

El Patio

$$ | **ARGENTINE** | With three dining rooms, a patio out back, a location just yards from the central plaza, and well-priced regional cuisine, El Patio is one of Tilcara's most popular restaurants. Anita Ponce's menu is an unpretentious yet delectable mix of regional specialties and standard Argentinian fare, and service is friendly. **Known for:** good wine list; an easygoing atmosphere that attracts locals and visitors; local dishes. [$] *Average main: pesos900* ✉ *Lavalle 352, Tilcara* ☎ *388/495–5044* ⏲ *Closed Tues.*

Los Puestos

$$$ | **ARGENTINE** | A poetic narrative in the menu describes this place as "a haven for parched travelers," along the lines of the watering holes used for centuries by local shepherds. Top picks include empanadas baked in the oven right by the entrance and a llama fillet served with orange sauce and colorful Andean potatoes. **Known for:** asado; buzzy vibe; empanadas. [$] *Average main: pesos1200* ✉ *Belgrano, corner of Padilla, Tilcara* ☎ *388/495–5100* ⏲ *Closed Tues.*

La Picantería

$$ | **ARGENTINE** | Slotted neatly into the tiny Plaza Peloc, La Picanteria's street-side setting makes for a great lunch spot to watch people come and go about their business. You can, of course, also dine inside, and enjoy the simple yet cozy aesthetic. [$] *Average main: pesos800* ✉ *Paraje Pucará 4, Tilcara* ☎ *388/495–5269.*

🛏 Hotels

El Refugio del Pintor

$ | **HOTEL** | The building that houses this hotel was formerly used by the painter Medardo Pantoja from Jujuy, hence the name (Refuge of the Painter) and the artwork adorning the walls. **Pros:** great views; plenty of common spaces; good breakfast with homemade bread. **Cons:** stairs can be difficult with luggage; staff could be more attentive; small rooms. [$] *Rooms from: US$60* ✉ *Alverro 660, between Jujuy and Ambroseti, Tilcara* ☎ *388/427–1432* 🌐 *www.elrefugiodelpintor.com* 🛏 *13 rooms* 🍴 *Free Breakfast.*

★ Hotel Huacalera

$$ | **HOTEL** | This hotel, on the main road in the heart of the Quebrada de Humahuaca, is a stunning colonial-style property, complete with a spa, an outdoor swimming pool, and spacious, well-appointed guest rooms. **Pros:** courteous staff; good restaurant; large breakfast. **Cons:** the restaurant lacks atmosphere; echoing in hallways; trucks on the main drag can be noisy. [$] *Rooms from: US$180* ✉ *R9, Km 1790, Huacalera, Tilcara* ☎ *388/581–3417* 🌐 *www.hotelhuacalera.com* 🛏 *32* 🍴 *Free Breakfast.*

Las Terrazas

$$ | **B&B/INN** | A few blocks from the square in a quieter area, Las Terrazas has nine spacious rooms, each with its own balcony. **Pros:** good-size rooms and bathrooms; great views; swimming pool and bar on-site. **Cons:** some rooms are dated; lots of stairs; not very central. [$] *Rooms from: US$112* ✉ *Calle de la Sorpresa s/n, at San Martín, Tilcara* ☎ *388/495–5589* 🌐 *www.lasterrazastilcara.com.ar* 🛏 *9 rooms* 🍴 *Free Breakfast.*

Viento Norte

$$ | **HOTEL** | This long, thin, adobe boutique hotel overlooks a decent-size swimming pool; inside, rooms have simple decorations and low lighting. **Pros:** great bathrooms; central yet quiet; a good breakfast. **Cons:** dust can gather at the pool area; pool is visible from the street. [$] *Rooms from: US$145* ✉ *Jujuy 536, Tilcara* ☎ *388/495–5605* 🌐 *www.hotelvientonorte.com.ar* 🛏 *11 rooms* 🍴 *Free Breakfast.*

★ **Villa del Cielo**

$$ | **HOTEL** | Tucked away in one of the more elevated parts of Tilcara, thereby offering priceless panoramas, cosy rooms and cabins sporting traditional style and plenty of comfort for up to four guests await at Villa del Cielo. Given that the hotel's owner is also behind Huichaira Vineyard near Tilcara, there's also a small vineyard. Shared spaces include a relaxing zone and a restaurant with local wine list. **Pros:** close to the center of Tilcara; friendly service; knowledgeable staff to help with planning. **Cons:** no on-site restaurant; not the best WiFi; walking back up the mountain can be hard work. [$] *Rooms from: US$120* ✉ *Prospero Nieva s/n, Barrio La Falda, Tilcara* ☎ *388/495–5537* 🌐 *www.villadelcielotilcara.com.*

Activities

★ **Caravana de Llamas**

WILDLIFE-WATCHING | For an unforgettable trekking experience, sign on with Caravana de Llamas. You'll lead a team of llamas along trails that have been used for thousands of years. Trips run the gamut from half-day picnics to 10-day adventures: on overnight excursions, you're hosted by the inhabitants of remote mountain huts. ✉ *Calle Corte and Viltipoco, Tilcara* ☎ *388/495–5326* 🌐 *www.caravanadellamas.com.ar* 🎟 *From 6,750 pesos.*

Shopping

The shops just east of the plaza are full of the same ponchos, bags, hats, and shirts sold elsewhere in the Quebrada. Though things are reasonably priced, they're more expensive than they would be in Bolivia, which is where much of the stock originates. There are also some interesting souvenirs on sale in the main plaza. Also check out the central market, a small yet busy hub packed with stands selling ingredients such as chuño freeze-dried potato cultivated in the Puna.

Tejedores Andinos

KNITTING | A skill that's taught from generation to generation, Celeste Valero Jujuy learned to weave, embroider, sew, and two-needle knit from her parents. Today the young weaver runs a collective with other jujeños from around the Quebrada and the Puna, whose llama and vicuña wool ponchos, scarves, and rugs express landscapes and emotions. Make an appointment to visit the showroom and pick up a unique piece. ✉ *Ruta 9 in Huacalera, Humahuaca* ☎ *388/504–9817* 🌐 *www.tejedoresandinos.com.ar.*

Humahuaca

126 km (78 miles) north of San Salvador de Jujuy; 42 km (26 miles) north of Tilcara on RN9.

Humahuaca—at an altitude of 2,957 meters (9,700 feet)—is the gateway to the Puna. Its narrow stone streets hark back to pre-Hispanic civilizations, when indigenous people fought Incan marauders from the north. The struggle for survival continued into the 16th century, when the Spanish arrived.

Given its location, the village feels a bit touristy today—especially at midday, when an automated carving of Saint Francisco Solano emerges like a cuckoo from a clock to bless the folks gathered in the main plaza with his mechanized arm. More visitor amenities are slowly becoming available, too: however, the tourist board is less than organized (if you find it open) and lodgings are predominantly hostels. That said, if you're near Humahuaca around the time of Carnaval (40 days before Easter), it's worth putting up with whatever accommodations you can find to participate in the wonderful festivities that are a complicated mix of Catholicism and paganism.

GETTING HERE AND AROUND

Most people visit Humahuaca either on a day trip from Tilcara, Purmamarca, Jujuy, or Salta; or as a stopover en route to Iruya. If you're not coming by car or with a tour group, you can catch a bus. Balut, La Veloz del Norte, Panamericano, and other lines serving the San Salvador de Jujuy-to-La Quiaca route have buses running through almost every hour during the day.

ESSENTIALS

VISITOR INFORMATION Tourist Office.
✉ *Cabildo, central plaza, Humahuaca*
☎ *388/421–375.*

 Sights

Barrancas and Casabindo

RUINS | From Purmamarca, it's a two-hour drive up into the high-altitude Puna past the Salinas Grandes on RN 9 to visit the rural Andean community of Barrancas (also known as Abdón Castro Tolay) to see cave paintings and petroglyphs. Also stop by the new (2020) Centro de Interpretación Arqueológica de interpretation center and base for archeologists for a glimpse of an 8,870-year-old mummy. The center also houses a fascinating replica of a stone map.

Continue getting to know the Puna driving north for another hour to Casabindo, a 17th-century Spanish founded village found at 3,606 masl known for the

Nuestra Señora de la Asunción church and Toreo de la Vincha, an annual bull fighting contest that takes palace every August 15th in honor of the said virgin in the main square (no bulls are harmed). ✉ *Purmamarca* ⊕ *www.turismo.jujuy.gob. ar/item/barrancas.*

Cabildo

GOVERNMENT BUILDING | Humahuaca's *cabildo* (town hall), the most striking building in the village, has a beautifully colored and richly detailed clock tower. Each day at noon crowds fill the small main square outside to watch a life-size mechanized statue of San Francisco Solano pop out of the tower—it's kitschy fun and one of the world's few clock performances. You can't enter the cabildo, but you can peer into the courtyard. ✉ *Central plaza, Humahuaca.*

Iglesia de la Candelaria

RELIGIOUS BUILDING | The 1631 Iglesia de la Candelaria contains fine examples of Cusqueño art, most notably paintings depicting elongated figures of Old Testament prophets by 18th-century artist Marcos Zapaca. ✉ *Calle Buenos Aires, west side of central plaza, Humahuaca.*

Iruya

SCENIC DRIVE | If you can endure a harrowing five-hour, 50-km (31-mile) ride east from Humahuaca on an unpaved cliffside road, you'll be rewarded with one of Argentina's most stunning settings. (Take the bus from Humahuaca rather than driving yourself; you really have to know the road, as the bus drivers do, to negotiate it safely.) This cobblestoned town, which clings to sheer rock, has become an increasingly popular stop despite its small size. It has just a couple of accommodations, the **Hotel Iruya** (☎ *3887/442–3536*) and **Hostal Milmahuasi** (☎), but many villagers offer rooms for rent. The busiest times to visit are at Easter and during the first and second weekends in October, when the village celebrates its festival. There are some

Iruya, a tiny town tucked in a valley northeast of the Quebrada de Humahuaca, is the end of the road. To explore beyond, you'll need to leave your vehicle behind.

good hikes from Iruya to even more remote towns like San Isidro, three hours away through the mountains. For more information and guide recommendations, call Adelina López at the **Tourist Office** (☎ *3887/155–094–799*) or visit 🌐 *www.iruyaonline.com.* ✉ *Humahuaca.*

Mesón de Yacoraite

HIKING & WALKING | A rocky yet rewarding three-hour trek from Ruta 9 leads you to this vibrant two-tone cantle known as the coya's skirt, for its thin top that flares out. On route, look out for the Los Amarillos, a pre-Hispanic settlement and archeological site. ✉ *Humahuaca* ✣ *20 km (12 miles) south of Humahuaca.*

Museo Arqueológico Torres Aparicio

HISTORY MUSEUM | The former home of its founder, divided into two parts, visitors to this small museum can first enjoy a musical instrument collection that belonged to Justiniano Torres Aparicio, before stepping into the second room for a more archeological and paleontological experience. Exhibits include a pre-Hispanic mummy, everyday implements such as axes, pipes, and ceramics from the San Francisco culture, as well as pieces from Bolivia's Tiawanaco culture and hunter-gatherers who inhabited the Quebrada de Humahuaca. ✉ *Córdoba 249, Humahuaca* 🎫 *50 pesos donation.*

🍴 Restaurants

K'allapurca

$ | **ARGENTINE** | At lunch, the best tables are taken by groups of tourists being serenaded by a band of minstrels, but don't let that put you off. The food is simple, well-presented Andean fare, and the prices are very reasonable. **Known for:** lamb stew; fixed menu; welcoming groups. [$] *Average main: pesos600* ✉ *Belgrano 210, Humahuaca* ☎ *388/410–5139.*

Continued on page 225

TOURING THE
QUEBRADA DE HUMAHUACA

by Andy Footner, updated by Sorrel Moseley-Williams

This rugged, windswept canyon connects Argentina's desert-like Puna near Bolivia with the city of San Salvador de Jujuy 150 km (93 mi) further south. It's a natural passage through the surrounding mountains, so it's no surprise that thousands of years of history have played out between its sandstone walls. For many, those very walls are the main attraction: colorful minerals, seismic activity, and a powerful river continue to shape one of Argentina's most fascinating geological formations.

Cardones, or cacti, and sandstone formations are a major part of the landscape in Argentina's northwest

HISTORY OF THE QUEBRADA

Jujuy Province, Quebrada de Humahuaca landscape behind Purmamarca village

The Quebrada de Humahuaca continues to be carved into existence by the ever-changing Rio Grande. A roaring, splashing force in summer, the river in winter reduces to barely a trickle in its wide, dry riverbed. You'll have a good view wherever you are in the main canyon of the Quebrada; Route 9, the main north-south road through here, runs parallel to it. Like the river, people have come through this canyon in both trickles and torrents over the centuries—but unlike the river, the sense of history is strong whenever you visit.

PRE-INCAN TO THE CAMINO INCA

Ten thousand years ago, the first humans to inhabit the Southern Cone came from the north through this very canyon. Some stayed, becoming this area's original indigenous peoples. In the 15th and 16th centuries, the Incan Empire left its mark on the valley and the culture; the single road through this protected canyon became part of the hugely important Camino Inca—the Inca Trail, a system of

PEÑAS

Clubs, restaurants, and *peñas* attract both locals and tourists, who come to hear regional folk bands give it their all on small, cramped stages. Adding to the rowdy, dinner-theater atmosphere are the local dancers who entice (and often entrap) foreigners into strutting their stuff on stage; it's always a good laugh, no matter what language you speak.

roads used to travel through the empire which eventually spanned much of the Andes. Because of this unique Andean history, the culture here can seem to share more with those of Bolivia and Peru than with other parts of Argentina; keep your ears open in town squares: in this part of Argentina you can still hear people speaking Quechua and Aymara, two of the main languages of the Incas.

Tilcara, Children's carnival, Quebrada de Humauaca

JESUITS AND VICEROYALTIES

The Incans weren't the only conquering force that found the protected valley appealing: in the 17th century, Jesuit priests used Aymara and Quechua to convert the locals to Catholocism, which helped the Spanish eventually use the Quebrada to connect the Viceroyalties (administration center) of Peru in Lima and La Plata in what would later become Buenos Aires. Today, the local mix of pre-Incan, Incan, and Christian traditions and symbols are reflected in everything from dress to architecture to the kinds of items you'll find for sale.

WORLD HERITAGE

Traditions and festivals celebrated along the Quebrada include a unique combination of ancient Andean rites and European religious celebrations. In 2003, UNESCO added the Quebrada to its World Heritage list for its continued legacy of pre-Hispanic and pre-Incan settlements in the area.

SHOPPING CULTURE

The best shopping is in Humahuaca. Numerous small shops sell tourist trinkets, and there's a daily handicrafts market on the steps leading up the hill to the monument. Most of the items for sale will be familiar to anyone who has traveled in the central Andean region, and there are a few artisans making jewelery and other items in more modern Argentine styles.

white composed
of limestone

purple/violet colored
by lead and calcium

yellow composed
of iron hydroxides

400 MILLION YEARS | 80–90 MILLION YEARS

The hills in the Quebrada de Humahuaca are famous for their colors—caused by mineral deposits formed from 1 to 400 million years ago. The two best places to see the colors are the Paleta del Pintur (Painter's Palette, pictured) and the Cerro de los Siete Colores (Hill of Seven Colors).

red composed of clay and iron oxide	light orange composed of red clay, mud, and sand	green colored by copper oxides	brown colored by manganese oxides and hydroxides

3–4 MILLION YEARS ———————————— 1–2 MILLION YEARS

ITINERARY

Salinas Grandes

DAY ONE

MORNING: Purmamarca

The smallest and most picturesque town in the Quebrada, Purmamarca is about two hours north of Salta or over an hour north of San Salvador de Jujuy on R9. The turnoff (left side) onto RA52 is well marked. Arrive as early as possible for the morning light. Get your bearings with a view of the Cerro de Los Siete Colores (Hill of Seven Colors) from a popular viewpoint on the north side of RA52; the trailhead is on your right as you approach town. You can also walk along Paseo de los Colorados, a dirt road (watch for vehicles) that winds around the base of hill itself; to get to it from Plaza 9 de Julio, head west on Florida for 3 blocks.

AFTERNOON: Siesta or Salinas Grandes

Purmamarca goes from quiet to dead during the afternoon siesta; take a siesta yourself, or head out on a half-day side trip. Drive farther west on RA52 as it winds its way up the **Cuesta de Lipan** (the Lipan Slope, the Quebrada's mountainous western barrier) and on to the **Salinas Grandes** (Big Salt Flats). If you're without your own transport, there are plenty of taxis, remises, or guides to take you. Technically, the Salinas Grandes themselves are outside of the Quebrada, but the drive there takes you through a dramatic mountain pass—and the highest driveable point in the Quebrada; look for a sign marking your altitude of 4170 m (13,681 ft). After an hour or two (depending on your vehicle's horsepower and photo stops), you'll take unpaved EX-RN40 south to the turnoff (right side) for the Salinas Grandes. Drive until you're on the salt flats themselves—this is the parking lot. This is a working salt flat; don't miss gazing into the clear blue harvesting pools.

NIGHT: Purmamarca

Once back in Purmamarca, explore some nouveau Andean cuisine in town. After dinner, head to a peña where musicians offer renditions of folk songs about the Quebrada.

DAY TWO

MORNING: Tilcara

Set out early and take R9 north to Tilcara; head straight to the **Pucará de Tilcara**. This partially reconstructed pre-Columbian fort shows one of the most complex ruins in Argentina. Make time to visit the botanical garden next door.

Wander through the central square's market, one of the best in the region. Leave to arrive in Humahuaca before noon.

AFTERNOON: Humahuaca to Maimara

Every day at noon at San Francisco Solano church, a statue of the church's namesake pops out of the clock tower and, as the story goes, delivers a blessing. Catch this if you can, then have lunch and explore the market near the monument steps. Stop in at the small yet atmospheric folklore museum. On your way back to Salta or Jujuy, make brief photo stops at the **Tropic of Capricorn** at Huacalera, the church at Uquia (known for its Cuzco School angel paintings), and the photogenic cemetery of the town of Maimara. If sunset is approaching, however, simply head straight for Maimara—visible behind the cemetary is the Painter's Palette. This flat segment of the east canyon wall contains colored layers of mineral deposits that attain stunningly rich hues as the light shines in from the west.

Pucará de Tilcara

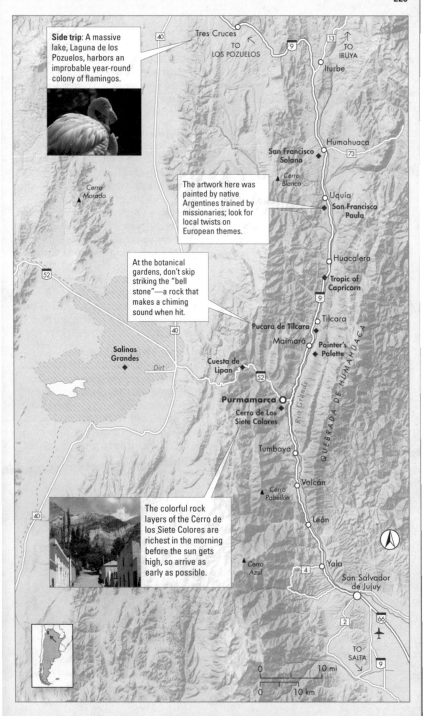

Side trip: A massive lake, Laguna de los Pozuelos, harbors an improbable year-round colony of flamingos.

The artwork here was painted by native Argentines trained by missionaries; look for local twists on European themes.

At the botanical gardens, don't skip striking the "bell stone"—a rock that makes a chiming sound when hit.

The colorful rock layers of the Cerro de los Siete Colores are richest in the morning before the sun gets high, so arrive as early as possible.

Tres Cruces
TO LOS POZUELOS
TO IRUYA
Iturbe
Humahuaca
San Francisco Solano
Cerro Blanco
Cerro Morado
Uquía
San Francisco Paula
Huacalera
Tropic of Capricorn
Tilcara
Pucará de Tilcara
Maimará
Painter's Palette
Salinas Grandes
Cuesta de Lipán
Purmamarca
Cerro de Los Siete Colores
Tumbaya
Cerro Pabellón
Volcán
León
Cerro Azul
Yala
San Salvador de Jujuy
TO SALTA
QUEBRADA DE HUMAHUACA
Río Grande

0   10 mi
0   10 km

PLANNING YOUR VISIT

PUBLIC TRANSIT

A good and frequent bus system and shared taxis between the main towns mean hitchhiking isn't common or necessary. However, although buses reach all destinations described, renting a car or going with a guide mean you can stop at any point to explore, take pictures, and admire the views.

SELF-DRIVE LOGISTICS

Cars can be rented in Salta and Jujuy. Check the conditions for off-road driving and the options for crossing a pass into Chile—these are not automatically included in the rental.

Good to Know:

■ Car hire agencies like to calculate the price on the spot and there's little transparency in their calculations. Many destinations from Salta and San Salvador de Jujuy involve unpaved roads that are punishing on cars, so it might help to let them know your itinerary if you're only visiting the Quebrada (where all the roads are paved). Pricing systems favor round trips (i.e. there's a big surcharge for dropping off a car in another city).

■ Gas stations can be found in most of the towns, but they don't all take credit cards. Except for in Humahuaca (ACA—the Automovil Club Argentino) and San Salvador de Jujuy, plan for cash only. As well as providing gas and good maps, ACA is the Argentine equivalent of the AAA and can help you out if your car breaks down somewhere.

■ The roads in the Quebrada are better than most in the area—they're well marked and have clear passing lanes—but during the rainy season (between October and February), falling rocks or mudslides can block the roads.

GUIDED TOURS

Personal guides, with their own cars or ones owned by their companies, can be found through the tourism offices of Salta and Jujuy.

For Indigenous Culture:

When you pull into the town of Humahuaca, you'll see a group of locals waiting under the main sign. These are tour guides; if you know a little Spanish, they're a wealth of information on how Wichí and other indigenous peoples live and work in Humahuaca today. Even if you're here with a tour guide of your own, he or she might hire one of these guides—they're part of an initiative to provide career alternatives in a place where drug smuggling (Bolivia is just a few clicks north, after all) has in the past been one of the only decent-paying jobs available.

For Getting Out Into the Landscape:

Caravana de Llamas (☎ *0388/408–8000* ⊕ *www.caravanadellamas.com.ar*), out of Tilcara, offers an experience you won't get at home: llama treks along trails that have been used for thousands of years. You lead the llamas along; they carry everything you need for trips that can last from 1 to 10 days. On overnight excursions, you're hosted by the inhabitants of remote mountain huts.

Llama in Purmamarca, Jujuy Province

Salta and San Lorenzo

92 km (57 miles) south of San Salvador de Jujuy on RN9 or 311 km (193 miles) south of San Salvador de Jujuy on R34 (La Cornisa Road).

It's not just "Salta" to most Argentineans, but "Salta la Linda" ("Salta the Beautiful"). That nickname is actually redundant: "Salta" already comes from an indigenous Aymara word meaning "beautiful." But for the country's finest colonial city, it's worth stating twice. Walking among its well-preserved 18th- and 19th-century buildings, single-story houses, and narrow streets, you could easily forget that this is a city of more than half a million people. But the ever-increasing traffic, the youthful population, and the growing number of international itinerants also give Salta a cosmopolitan edge. All in all, it's a hard place to leave. For its friendliness, its facilities, its connections, and its central location, Salta is also the best base for a thorough exploration of the Northwest. Do make good use of the tourist office, which has a helpful staff armed with a wealth of maps and information.

GETTING HERE AND AROUND

Salta is two hours by air from Buenos Aires. Aerolíneas Argentinas flies the route six times a day, as does Flybondi and JetSmart a couple of times day. From Aeropuerto Martín Miguel de Güemes, it's a 10-km (6-mile) drive southeast into Salta; the trip costs 600 pesos by taxi or 20 pesos by bus. Balut buses connect Salta to Jujuy (15 trips daily) and Humahuaca (six trips daily). El Indio has two daily buses to Cafayate, while Marco Rueda has at least one to Cachi. Buy tickets the day before, as most buses leave early in the morning.

Most city sights are within walking distance of one another, and taxis are cheap and easy to find. Note that some visitors opt to stay in the quieter hillside suburb of San Lorenzo, 10 km (6 miles) northwest and a cooler 299 meters (980 feet) higher. It's a great place if you have a car or are prepared to rely on the half-hourly bus to and from Salta.

ESSENTIALS
VISITOR AND TOUR INFORMATION
Tourist Office. ⊠ *Buenos Aires 93, Salta* ☎ *0800/222–3752* ⊕ *www.turismosalta. gov.ar.*

TOURS
MoviTrack
This Northwest specialist offers excursions around Salta but is best known for its Safari to the Clouds, an oxygen-equipped vehicle that follows the same route that the Tren a las Nubes used to take. Trips last 16 hours; they depart daily in winter and nearly every day in summer. Check the website for schedules and prices. ⊠ *Caseros 468, Salta* ☎ *387/431–6749* ⊕ *www.movitrack. com.ar.*

Uma Travel
Knowledgeable, English-speaking guides at Uma lead day trips to Cafayate or through the Quebrada de Humahuaca. Rafting, riding, and biking tours are also available; if you're more into local culture, there's a folklore circuit as well. ⊠ *Avenida Los Incas 3106, Salta* ☎ *387/459-2768* ⊕ *www.umatravel.com.ar.*

 Sights

★ Basílica Menor y Convento San Francisco
NOTABLE BUILDING | Every *salteño*'s soul belongs to the landmark St. Francis Church and Convent, with its white pillars and bright terra-cotta-and-gold facade. The first sanctuary was built in 1625; the second, erected in 1674, was destroyed by fire; the present version was completed in 1882. A 53-meter (173-foot) belfry houses the Campaña de la Patria. This bell, made from the bronze cannons used in the War of Independence, sounds once a day at 7:30 pm. In

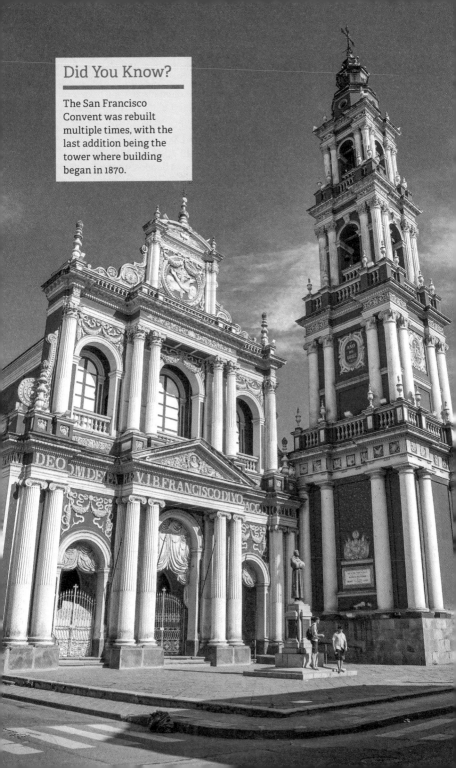

Did You Know?

The San Francisco Convent was rebuilt multiple times, with the last addition being the tower where building began in 1870.

the sacristy, the Museo Convento San Francisco displays religious art. Guided visits are at 11, 12, 4, 5 and 6, Mondays, Wednesdays, Thursdays, and Fridays, and at 5 and 6 pm on Saturday. ⊠ *Córdoba 33, Salta* 🕾 *387/431–0830* 🖳 *Church free; museum 400 pesos* ⊗ *Closed weekends.*

Cabildo

GOVERNMENT BUILDING | The whitewashed town hall, first constructed in 1582 and rebuilt many times since, used to house Salta's municipal government. Not only a colonial gem in itself, the Cabildo—the most well-preserved council building in Argentina—is home to the Museo Histórico del Norte, which includes a relevant collection of pre-Hispanic stone sculptures, as well as religious artifacts and a rather obscure assortment of vintage cars in the back garden. ⊠ *Caseros 549, Salta* 🕾 *387/421–5340* ⊕ *museodelnorte.cultura.gob.ar/noticia/la-historia-del-cabildo-de-salta/* 🖳 *Free* ⊗ *Closed Mon.*

Catedral Basílica de Salta

RELIGIOUS BUILDING | The city's 1882 neoclassical cathedral fronts the central plaza. It's notable for the enormous frescoes portraying the four gospel writers on the portico around the altar and its impressive stained glass windows. Inside the entrance is the Panteón de las Glorias del Norte, enclosing the tombs of General Martín Miguel de Güemes and other heroes from the War of Independence. Wander to the back of the rose-colored cathedral for a peek at the beautiful, jasmine-infused garden. ⊠ *España 558, Salta* 🕾 *387/431–8206* ⊕ *www.arzobispadodesalta.org.ar/category/catedral-basilica-de-salta/* 🖳 *Free.*

Convento de San Bernardo

NOTABLE BUILDING | Salta's oldest religious building served as a chapel first, then a hospital. Today it is home to a cloistered order of Carmelite nuns. The wooden rococo-style door, carved by indigenous craftsmen in 1762, contrasts markedly with the otherwise stark exterior of this 1625 structure. ⊠ *Caseros 73, Salta* 🕾 *387/431–0092* 🖳 *Free.*

★ Museo de Árqueología de Alta Montaña

HISTORY MUSEUM | The fascinating Museum of High Mountain Archaeology (MAAM) holds the mummified remains of three children born into Incan nobility—aged 6, 7, and 15—and the 146 objects buried with them in sacrificial services some 600 years ago. They were discovered at the summit of the 22,058-foot Volcán Llullaillaco, on the Argentine–Chilean border, in 1999. The high altitude and freezing temperatures kept their skin, hair, and clothes in impeccable condition, although the face of one was damaged by lightning. The museum also contains an exhibition about the Qhapaq Ñan Inca trading route from southern Colombia to Mendoza and another mummy, the Reina del Cerro (Queen of the Mountain), which for decades was illegally in the hands of private collectors. ⊠ *Mitre 77, Salta* 🕾 *387/437–0592* ⊕ *www.maam.gob.ar* 🖳 *400 pesos* ⊗ *Closed Mon.*

Museo de Bellas Artes

ART MUSEUM | The Fine Arts Museum's collection of colonial-era religious works includes figures from Argentina's Jesuit missions as well as Cuzco-style paintings from Peru and Bolivia. Another part of the museum highlights 20th-century pieces by Salta artists. ⊠ *Belgrano 992, Salta* 🕾 *387/422–1745* 🖳 *Free* ⊗ *Closed Mon.*

Museo de la Ciudad Casa de Hernández

HISTORIC HOME | The City Museum is in Casa de Hernández, an 1879-constructed neocolonial house. The ground floor displays an exceptional collection of musical instruments. Rooms upstairs document the history of Salta through paintings and photographs. ⊠ *Florida 97, Salta* 🕾 *387/437–3352* ⊕ *www.facebook.com/MuseodelaCiudadCasadeHernandezSalta* 🖳 *Voluntary donation.*

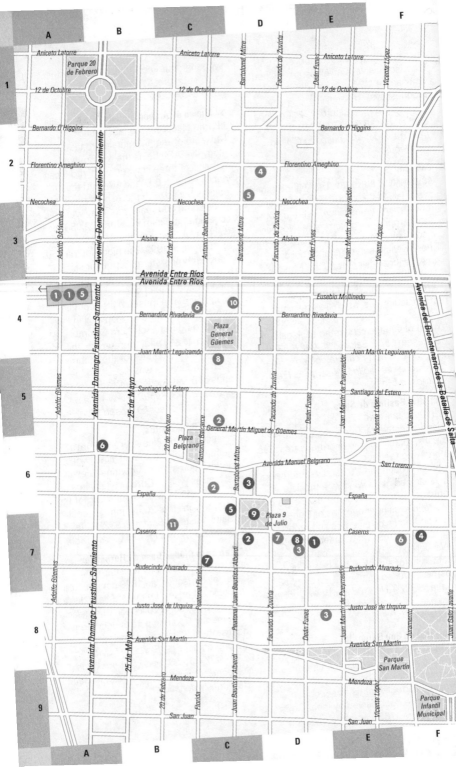

Salta

Sights ▼

1 Basílica Menor y Convento
San Francisco.................... **D7**

2 Cabildo............................... **C7**

3 Catedral Basilica de Salta **C6**

4 Convento de San Bernardo........ **F7**

5 Museo de Árqueologia de
Alta Montaña..................... **C7**

6 Museo de Bellas Artes........... **A6**

7 Museo de la Cuidad
Casa de Hernández................. **C7**

8 Museo Presidente
José Evaristo Uriburu **D7**

9 Plaza 9 de Julio **D7**

10 Teleférico a Cerro
San Bernardo **G8**

Restaurants ▼

1 Andrés **A4**

2 Casa Moderna **C6**

3 Doña Salta......................... **D7**

4 El Baqueano........................ **J7**

5 José Balcarce **D3**

6 Jovi Dos............................. **C4**

Hotels ▼

1 Amalinas............................ **A4**

2 Ayres de Salta **C5**

3 Carpe Diem........................ **D8**

4 Delvino Boutique Hotel **D2**

5 Eaton Place........................ **A5**

6 Hotel del Antiguo Convento **F7**

7 Hotel Salta......................... **D7**

8 Hotel Solar de la Plaza **C5**

9 Kkala **H1**

10 Legado Mítico...................... **C4**

11 Provincial Plaza................... **B7**

KEY

① Exploring Sights

① Restaurants

① Hotels

0   1,000 ft

0   200 m

Museo Presidente José Evaristo Uriburu

HISTORIC HOME | Fine examples of late-colonial architecture—an interior courtyard, thick adobe walls, a reed-and-tile roof—abound in this simple building, the 19th- and 20th-century home of the Uriburu family, which gave Argentina two presidents. Furniture, costumes, paintings, and family documents are on display across six rooms. ✉ *Caseros 417, Salta* ☎ *387/421–8174* 🌐 *museodelnorte.cultura.gob.ar/noticia/museo-casa-de-uriburu* 🎫 *Free* ⏲ *Closed Mon.*

Plaza 9 de Julio

PLAZA/SQUARE | The heart of Salta is quintessential Latin America: a leafy central plaza named after Argentina's date of independence. Arcaded buildings line the streets surrounding it, and some have been converted into cafés, providing perfect spots to while away a warm afternoon. Popular with families who take shade under the palm and jacaranda trees, the square is dotted with craftsmen selling their wares and teens canoodling by the bandstand. ✉ *Salta.*

Teleférico a Cerro San Bernardo

VIEWPOINT | The Cerro San Bernardo rises east of downtown Salta, a cool 268 meters (880 feet) higher than the city center. This cable car takes you up the hill from a station across from Parque San Martín in 10 minutes. Views of the entire Lerma Valley await at the top; you can also wander the breezy garden and browse around a small crafts market.

■ TIP→ If you're in the mood for a little light exercise, take the winding road back down. ✉ *San Martín and H. Yrigoyen, Salta* ☎ *387/431–0641* 🌐 *www.telefericosanbernardo.com* 🎫 *1,000 pesos.*

🍴 Restaurants

Andrés

$$ | **ARGENTINE** | Folks from Salta and San Lorenzo favor this bright, semi-enclosed brick-and-glass building with a vaulted ceiling for weekend dining. Lo de Andrés prepares a lightly spiced Argentine-style *parrillada*, but if you're not up for a full-on feast, there are *empanadas* and *milanesas* (breaded steak), as well as regional dishes like *humita*. **Known for:** quick service; cheap and cheerful; steak and barbecue. [$] *Average main: pesos1000* ✉ *Juan Carlos Dávalos 1401 and Gorriti, San Lorenzo* ☎ *387/492–1600.*

Casa Moderna

$$ | **SANDWICHES** | *Picadas*—assorted cured meats and local cheeses, accompanied by home-baked breads—are the star attractions here (be sure to try the smoked boar and trout). Although this deli and wine bar does get busy, the staff is generally friendly, and you can escape the bustle by retreating to the back terrace. **■ TIP→ Wash down your meal with one of the hearty Los Morros-brand reds, produced by Casa Moderna's own small winery.** **Known for:** picnic food; wine store; excellent charcuterie. [$] *Average main: pesos900* ✉ *España 674, Salta* ☎ *387/422–0066* 💳 *No credit cards.*

Doña Salta

$ | **ARGENTINE** | This warm, festive, family-friendly locale serves dishes quite typical of Salta and the Northwest such as classics like *humita* (steamed corn husks filled with cheese) or the local *locro* stew, with beans and hunks of beef. You'll dine in a room steeped in local tradition, amid wine jugs and old wooden implements. *Empanadas* and meats are also reliable; the pastas are unremarkable, though. **Known for:** its popularity, especially with tourists; classic fare from the Northwest; beef empanadas. [$] *Average main: pesos500* ✉ *Córdoba 46, Salta* ☎ *387/432–1921* 💳 *No credit cards.*

El Baqueano

$$$$ | **ARGENTINE** | When one of Buenos Aires' top restaurants upped sticks for the northwest, salteños couldn't believe their luck. Taking their concept of cooking exclusively with Argentine ingredients, chef Fernando Rivarola and sommelier Gabriela Lafuente now focus on giving a strong contemporary identity to the northwest's abundant pantry with a focus on alternative proteins on the tasting menu. **Known for:** award-winning team; fine dining; top chef and sommelier on hand. $ *Average main: pesos10000* ✉ *Cerro San Bernardo, Salta* ⊕ *www.restoelbaqueano.com.*

★ José Balcarce
$$$ | ARGENTINE | A group of chefs launched a restaurant and catering service with high Andean cuisine as its goal—"high" referring to both the altitude and the gourmet techniques. The result is José Balcarce, in a brick-and-wood building with large windows just two blocks from bustling Balcarce Street. **Known for:** sophisticated setting; the most haute cuisine in Salta; creativity with traditional ingredients. $ *Average main: pesos1500* ✉ *Necochea 590, Salta* ☎ *387/421–1628* ⊕ *www.josebalcarcebistro.com.ar* ▭ *No credit cards* ♥ *Closed Sun. No lunch.*

Jovi Dos
$$ | ARGENTINE | A great-value restaurant on a bustling downtown corner, Jovi Dos has several airy, high-ceilinged rooms with wood beams and plate-glass windows. Noteworthy starters include marinated eggplant and baked beef *empanadas* while grilled meats, seafood, pizza, and pasta have equal billing on the ridiculously long menu. **Known for:** abundant portions; lunch spot for local businesspeople; fast service. $ *Average main: pesos1000* ✉ *Balcarce 601, Salta* ☎ *387/432–9438* ♥ *Closed Sun. No dinner.*

Hotels

Amalinas
$ | HOTEL | A more contemporary option than Salta's often more traditional hotels, Amalinas' design features poured cement and soothing natural hues adorned with splashes of primary colors, plus airy rooms offering views across

leafy San Lorenzo. **Pros:** rooms with a view of rolling hills; quiet and peaceful; restaurant puts fresh spin on local classics. **Cons:** check-out time is early at 10 am; pool isn't heated; you need a car to get around. $ *Rooms from: US$75* ✉ *Ruta Provincial 28, Km 11.5, San Lorenzo* ☎ *0387/492–1738* ⊕ *www.amalinashotel.com* ⌨ *10 rooms* ⦿| *Free Breakfast.*

Ayres de Salta
$$ | HOTEL | Conveniently located between the main plaza and Balcarce Street, Ayres de Salta has a small pool and fitness center on the roof and a good little restaurant on the ground floor; rooms are large and well equipped. **Pros:** efficient, professional staff can arrange excursions; good location; buffet breakfast. **Cons:** street-facing rooms are noisy; could do with new paint; some rooms look into the windows of other rooms. $ *Rooms from: US$165* ✉ *General Güemes 650, Salta* ☎ *387/422–1616* ⊕ *www.ayresdesalta.com.ar* ⌨ *40 rooms* ⦿| *Free Breakfast.*

★ Carpe Diem
$ | B&B/INN | Run by a German-Italian couple, this B&B in a heritage home surrounded by a beautiful garden has an eclectic mix of singles and doubles; rooms fuse antiques sourced from Buenos Aires with ethnic art, and period details with modern amenities. **Pros:** homemade bread and cakes at breakfast; greenhouse, back garden, and library on-site; convenient location. **Cons:** guests with cat allergies will need to ask the owners to relocate their pets to the garden, which they'll happily do; eerily quiet at times; no children under 14. $ *Rooms from: US$50* ✉ *Urquiza 329, Salta* ☎ *387/421–8736* ⊕ *www.carpediemsalta.com.ar* ⌨ *8 rooms* ⦿| *Free Breakfast.*

Delvino Boutique Hotel
$ | HOTEL | Oenophiles will appreciate the decor at Delvino—a remodeled, Spanish-style villa where the airy guest rooms are painted in grape tones (Malbec red among them) and decorated with

Tren a las Nubes

With a bird's-eye view of its passage over the 64-meter-high (210-foot-high) Viaducto La Polvorilla, the Tren a las Nubes (Train to the Clouds) is one of the Northwest's most famous attractions, though, given that it no longer traverses the complete 217-km (135-mile) circuit, it has had its heyday. A lack of investment in the single railroad means the incredible 16-hour return journey it once made is now a thing of the past.

These days, you can take a snippet of a train ride on a one-hour journey to the high, desolate Puna from the small mining town of San Antonio de los Cobres, the only town of any size in the Puna. Take the bus from Salta or make your own way to San Antonio de los Cobres; you can bargain with locals selling textiles and ceramics next to the railway line, and buy coca leaves to ease the effects of the 4,197-meter (13,770-foot) altitude.

What's Out the Window

An ethereal landscape offers view after spectacular view as the train twists and turns along the route. In San Antonio de los Cobres and on the lookout point at Viaducto La Polvorilla, locals gather round the train for a chat—and to sell handicrafts and trinkets.

San Antonio de los Cobres

San Antonio, the highest town in Argentina, is as slow-moving as many of the country's small rural communities; it's also heavily battered by sun and wind, and there is little oxygen in the air. Essential accessories for visitors are sunscreen, extra clothes for warmth, and coca leaves—they're chewed as an aide to digestion (which helps with altitude sickness). All that saliva production promotes swallowing, too, which will pop your ears.

Only in the past decade have there been any lodging options: the sweet **Sumaq Sumay** (✉ *Las Vicuñas and Yrigoyen* ☎ *387/516–2271*) and the smarter **Hosteria de las Nubes** (✉ *RN51, Km 160 s/n* ☎ *387/490–9059*) are the best. Renting a room in someone's house is an option, too. A small ethnographic and archaeological museum, ANTAPU, fills in some detail on the town's background, but it needs more work. The main business is making *artesanías*—handmade goods that can be sold to tourists.

Reservations

Reservations can be made at many agencies in Salta and cost 10,400 pesos (train only) or 15,600 pesos (bus and train). ✉ *Salta Station, Ameghino 666 and Balcarce 387/510–4822.*

Extending Your Trip

Though you can only buy return tickets, you can stay in San Antonio and continue north to the *salinas* (salt flats) and on to Purmamarca in Jujuy. There's no public transport; for the right price, however, drivers will take you in their own cars. Going south to Cachi isn't as easy; the road is narrow and dangerous. Make sure to tell the *gendarmería* (border guards) in San Antonio if you're going to attempt this route.

The views on the Tren a las Nubes will keep you glued to the windows.

wine-themed artworks. **Pros:** two blocks from Train to the Clouds railway station; glass of wine on arrival; swimming pool. **Cons:** no elevators; some rooms are poky; exposed stairway can be chilly. $ *Rooms from: US$73* ✉ *Ameghino 555, Salta* ☎ *387/432–0092* ⊕ *www.delvinosalta. com.ar* ⇆ *18 rooms* ❖ *Free Breakfast*.

Eaton Place
$ | **B&B/INN** | Despite appearances, this striking Georgian-style mansion only dates from the 1980s, when it was built as a private home; it still feels like one, with bright and airy rooms in the main house and in a guesthouse with huge windows, hardwood floors, and period furniture. **Pros:** well appointed; large breakfast; lovely property with pool and gardens. **Cons:** no on-site restaurant; a vehicle is necessary; a long way from the center of Salta. $ *Rooms from: US$70* ✉ *San Martín 2457, San Lorenzo* ☎ *387/492–1347* ⊕ *www.eatonplacesal-ta.com.ar* ⇆ *9 rooms* ❖ *Free Breakfast*.

Hotel del Antiguo Convento
$$ | **HOTEL** | This charming property in a former convent is run by a cheerful, attentive young staff; rooms are clean, bright, and well-priced. **Pros:** staffers go out of their way to be helpful; convenient location; private, apartment-style suites available. **Cons:** some rooms are cramped; rooms next to the courtyard are noisy; courtyard and pool are small. $ *Rooms from: US$102* ✉ *Caseros 113, Salta* ☎ *387/422–7267* ⊕ *www.hoteldel-convento.com.ar* ⇆ *15 rooms* ❖ *Free Breakfast*.

Hotel Salta
$$ | **HOTEL** | Designated as a National Historic Monument, the Salta occupies a handsome neocolonial building in the heart of the city; antique furniture and views of either the plaza or the surrounding mountains make every room attractive. **Pros:** ideal location; access to Salta Polo Club; decent spa. **Cons:** corridors can echo; bathrooms are dated; rooms facing the plaza can be noisy. $ *Rooms from: US$136* ✉ *Buenos Aires 1, Salta*

☎ *387/431–0740* 🌐 *www.hotelsalta.com* 🛏 *99 rooms* 🍴 *Free Breakfast.*

Hotel Solar de la Plaza

$$$ | B&B/INN | The exterior of this beautiful old house belies the modern comforts within; an elegant lobby leads to a tastefully appointed sitting room, an airy courtyard, and a good (though expensive) restaurant. **Pros:** rooftop pool with city views; some rooms have balconies; buffet breakfast. **Cons:** doors slam loudly; rooms facing the square can be noisy; costly in-house dining. [$] *Rooms from: US$185* ✉ *Leguizamón 669, Salta* ☎ *387/431–5111* 🌐 *www.solardelaplaza.com.ar* 🛏 *30 rooms* 🍴 *Free Breakfast.*

★ Kkala

$$$ | B&B/INN | This elegant 10-room abode represents Salta, right down to the cardon cactus door panels and hand-stitched headboards depicting Andean landscapes. **Pros:** delightful bilingual staff; stylish en suite rooms; honesty bar. **Cons:** not that close to main attractions; some rooms are compact; some areas could use paint. [$] *Rooms from: US$184* ✉ *Las Higueras 104, Salta* ☎ *387/439–6590* 🌐 *www.hotelkkala.com.ar* 🛏 *10 rooms* 🍴 *Free Breakfast.*

★ Legado Mítico

$$$ | B&B/INN | Sister to the Buenos Aires hotel of the same name, the family-run Legado Mítico attends to every detail—from the gorgeous guest rooms named after notable figures from the city's past and individually decorated to suit the titular person right down to the welcome glass of wine. **Pros:** warm and pleasing spaces; the living room and terrace are comfy spots for a moment of relaxation; attractive decor. **Cons:** street-facing rooms can be noisy; noisy doors; located on a rather busy main drag. [$] *Rooms from: US$180* ✉ *Bartolomé Mitre 647, Salta* ☎ *387/422–8786* 🌐 *www.legadomitico.com* 🛏 *11 rooms* 🍴 *Free Breakfast.*

Provincial Plaza

$ | HOTEL | This hotel is on a corner, just blocks from Plaza 9 de Julio; standard rooms have had recent renovations—superior and executive floors are spruced up and have good facilities. **Pros:** central location; views from the top floor; rooftop swimming pool. **Cons:** decor in some rooms needs updating; maintenance needs attention; lower floors get street noise. [$] *Rooms from: US$80* ✉ *Caseros 786, Salta* ☎ *387/432–2000* 🌐 *www.provincialplaza.com.ar* 🛏 *88 rooms* 🍴 *Free Breakfast.*

🍸 Nightlife

Salta is a young and lively city, with a bar district along a few blocks of calle Balcarce that can get quite busy. Clubs, restaurants, and peñas attract both locals and tourists, who come to hear regional folk bands perform on small, cramped stages. Adding to the rowdy, dinner-theater atmosphere are the local gaucho dancers who entice (and often entrap) foreigners into strutting their stuff on stage; it's always a good laugh, no matter what language you speak. For a more authentic musical experience, head to La Casona del Molino.

La Casona del Molino

GATHERING PLACES | Twenty-odd blocks down Caseros Street from the main plaza, La Casona del Molino is an authentic gem renowned for nightly folk performances; join in by clapping or dancing. It also serves great regional food at extremely decent prices. ✉ *Luis Burela 1, Salta* ☎ *387/434–2835.*

La Vieja Estación

LIVE MUSIC | The self-proclaimed "home of folklore" stages nightly shows; it's a top spot for regional music and gaucho dancing. ✉ *Balcarce 875, Salta* ☎ *387/523–4888* 🌐 *www.laviejaestacion.com.ar.*

Macondo

LIVE MUSIC | Live music and beer are always on tap at this raucous pub, where you're as likely to meet backpacking Aussies as you are local law students. ⊠ *Balcarce 980, Salta* ☎ *387/431–7191.*

🔴 Shopping

Feria de la Balcarce

CRAFTS | Every Sunday, on Balcarce street between Entre Ríos and Ameghino, around 200 local artisans get together for this weekly handicrafts market. It's considered to be the most important in the north. Pick up ceramics, knitwear, rugs, shawls, and even furry llama toys. On Saturdays, there are similar if smaller markets, Feria de la Plaza Güemes and the Paseo de Arte y Diseño located at Paseo de los poetas. ⊠ *Balcarce 700 between Entre Ríos and Ameghino, Salta.*

Mercado Artesanal

CRAFTS | Although Salta has all the usual high-street shops where you can stock up on sundries, provincial villages are a better bet for souvenirs and regional products. There are, however, a few proud exceptions to that rule—including the huge 1882 Jesuit monastery that holds the Mercado Artesanal and the open stalls across the street. Look for emblematic red-and-black *salteño* ponchos, alpaca knitwear and weavings, leather goods, wooden masks, carved animals, and fine silver from around the province. Everything is open daily 9–9. ⊠ *Av. San Martín 2555, Salta* ☎ *387/434–2808.*

🏃 Activities

Salta has just a handful of outfitters, but the options they offer feel fresh and exciting. Horseback riding is popular, as is rafting.

HORSEBACK RIDING

MacDermott's Argentina

HORSEBACK RIDING | Despite being told by local gauchos that he and his horse Pancho wouldn't make it across the Andes, Hugh MacDermott proved the cynics wrong. Now he shares his expertise by leading horse-riding holidays across the Northwest, with options ranging from short breaks to two-week treks. ⊠ *Salta* ☎ *11/7507–3785* ⊕ *www.macdermottsargentina.com* 🛏 *From $100.*

Sayta

HORSEBACK RIDING | Rural tourism specialist Sayta offers stays out at a ranch in Chicoana, 40 km (24 miles) south of Salta, and horseback treks lasting from one to five days for riders of all levels. ⊠ *Chicoana, Salta* ☎ *387/683–6565* ⊕ *www.saltacabalgatas.com.ar* 🛏 *From 5,000 pesos.*

RAFTING

Salta Rafting

WHITE-WATER RAFTING | This company specializes in whitewater rafting, operating from a base 35 km (21 miles) south of Salta by the Cabra Corral dam. Kayaking excursions, 4X4 adventures, and tandem paragliding are also available. For a breathtaking canopy surfing experience, try its "death slide"—a network of zip-line cables that crosses high above the Río Juramento. ⊠ *Caseros 117, Salta* ☎ *387/421–3216* ⊕ *www.saltarafting.com* 🛏 *From 5900 pesos.*

Cachi

157 km (97 miles) southwest of Salta.

This small colonial village on Ruta 40 is fast becoming a base for exploring the north of Calchaqui Valley. Cachi itself has a charming church, a small archaeological museum, and a couple of decent hotels and restaurants, although there is nothing in the way of nightlife. Watching over it all is the 6,340-meter (20,800-foot) Nevado de Cachi, a few miles away.

Drying chilies near Cachi, Calchaquí Valley

The surrounding area is loaded with archaeological sites that have scarcely been explored. El Tero contains the remains of pre-Inca dwellings, and within 15 km (10 miles) are two more important sites: Puerta La Paya to the southwest and Las Pailas to the north (at the foot of the Nevado de Cachi). A little farther north, en route to La Poma, are the Graneros Incaicos, stunning cave-carved granaries from the Inca era.

GETTING HERE AND AROUND

Just one bus company, Ale Hermanos, serves Cachi from Salta, leaving at 7 am and 1:30 pm daily, returning at 4 am and 4 pm. You're advised to buy tickets for the journey (which takes just over four hours) a day in advance. For more flexibility, Remis Marcelo runs a taxi service; the cost is about 12,000 pesos, also offering sightseeing en route, as well as transfers to Cafayate and the villages in between.

ESSENTIALS

VISITOR INFORMATION Tourist office. ✉ *General Güemes s/n, Cachi* ☎ *3868/491–902.*

TOURS

Aventura Calchaquí
From two-hour walking trips around Cachi to day-long treks and quad bike excursions deep into Salta's elevated countryside, this tour company covers most areas from its Cachi base. ✉ *Cachi* ☎ *387/15–511–8396* ⊕ *www.aventura-calchaqui.wix.com/cachi* 🖼 *From 2,300 pesos.*

 Hotels

ACA Hosteria

$$ | HOTEL | Once the only decent place to stay in Cachi, the Argentine Automobile Club hosteria is gaining some stiff competition, but is still a practical option thanks to its swimming pool, children's facilities, attractive garden, and reliable restaurant. **Pros:** lovely pool views; buffet breakfast; large play area. **Cons:** rooms can echo; lacks character of other local hotels; compact rooms. $ *Rooms from: US$93* ⊠ *Av. Automóvil Club Argentino s/n, Cachi* ☎ *3868/491–904* ⊕ *www.hosteriacachi.com.ar* ⇆ *33 rooms* ⦿❘ *Free Breakfast.*

El Cortijo

$$ | B&B/INN | Converted from a vintage villa, this boutique hotel stands out for its chic and traditional style and friendly service; the 12 guest rooms are tastefully decorated with traditional antiques and art. **Pros:** artistic decor; charming courtyard and wine cellar; free Wi-Fi. **Cons:** breakfast is basic; passageways echo; rooms vary in terms of size and views. $ *Rooms from: US$145* ⊠ *Av. Automóvil Club Argentino s/n, Cachi* ☎ *3868/587–8513* ⊕ *www.elcortijohotel.com* ⇆ *12 rooms* ⦿❘ *Free Breakfast.*

★ La Merced del Alto

$$$ | HOTEL | Although this stately white-adobe building looks like it's been here forever, it was in fact built in 2006; inside, rooms are huge and comfortable with tasteful wood and iron furniture. **Pros:** expansive grounds with great views; spa, wine cellar, bar, and restaurant on-site; accessible for people with disabilities. **Cons:** echoing corridors; Wi-Fi is flaky; 3 km (2 miles) from Cachi. $ *Rooms from: US$161* ⊠ *Fuerte Alto s/n, Cachi* ☎ *3868/490–020* ⊕ *www.lamerceddelalto.com* ⇆ *13 rooms* ⦿❘ *Free Breakfast.*

Molinos

206 km (128 miles) southwest of Salta (via Cachi); 50 km (31 miles) south of Cachi.

Molinos, a village with about 2,000 inhabitants, has a photogenic 17th-century church and a small vicuña-breeding farm (*vicuñas* are similar to llamas but their fur makes a much finer, more expensive wool). The main draw, however, is its location on the way to Argentina's oldest

winery, Bodega Colomé, as well as Bodega Tacuil and to many more in Cafayate.

Molinos is also just a few miles from Seclantás' Camino de Artesanos (Road of the Artisans), where weavers make ponchos and scarves by the roadside on contraptions improvised from wood and old bicycle parts. The Laguna de Brealito, 10 km (6 miles) due west of Seclantás, is a picturesque and remote lake. Eight km (5 miles) east of Molinos are the pre-Columbian ruins of Chicoana.

 ## Sights

★ Bodega Colomé and James Turrell Museum

WINERY | Remote wineries and museums are one thing; Bodega Colomé is something else altogether. Yet finally arriving at this world-class spot puts the miles of driving along bumpy, unpaved roads firmly into perspective. Established in 1831, Colomé is Argentina's oldest winery. A visitor center runs daily tours and offers tastings, while a terrace restaurant serves delectable lunches with views of one of the world's highest vineyards. Colomé is also home to the breathtaking and unexpected James Turrell Museum, which showcases five decades of the artist's works with light and space, and includes a fun tunnel of color (book in advance). ■ TIP➔ **Turrell's contemporary light installations are at their most striking at sunset.** ⊠ *RP53, Km 20, 20 km (13 miles) west of Molinos, Molinos* ☎ *3868/494–000* ⊕ *www.bodegacolome. com* ⛴ *Tastings with lunch and guided visit, 8,800 pesos; museum free.*

Bodega Tacuil

WINERY | A 20-minute drive on from Colomé is Tacuil, a tiny community crowned by this lovely winery, whose simplicity is notable in comparison with its neighbor. Run by the sixth generation of the Dávalos family, Alvaro Dávalos uses little oak in his world-class vintages, allowing the elevated terroir to

The Northwest Shopping Experience

Throughout the Northwest, almost every town has an area where vendors sell *artesenías*—emblematic crafts using local materials and incorporating the culture. Spending time at these markets, which may simply be set up around the main plaza, isn't just a great way to find the perfect souvenir; it's also a real opportunity to interact with locals.

Andean artesanías come in two forms: mass-produced products (generally imported from Bolivia) and locally produced handmade items. Often, stall owners will sell a mix of the two; ask which fall into the latter category and opt for them, as they do more to support the local community. Bolivian goods get cheaper the farther north you go. Some towns such as Humahuaca and Tilcara have shops that are exclusively fair trade, so look out for the signs reading, *comercio justo*.

Also, you'll see lots of dimpled *cardon* (cactus) wood carved into all manner of souvenirs, but there's no system right now for verifying the origin of the wood (only souvenirs carved from already-dead cardones are legal). We encourage you to ask your guide or another local for vendor recommendations.

Alpaca knits. Alpacas look like a cross between a llama and a sheep with a glossy, silky fleece. Textiles from them feel lovely and are unmistakably Andean, with the traditional designs.

Coca leaves. Freely available, coca here is a medicine rather than a narcotic. Coca tea is neatly packaged and tastes better than green tea. Don't try taking it home without checking customs regulations first.

Leather. Unless there's an item that particularly catches your eye, save your leather purchases for the pampas. They do use leather in the Quebrada, but not in the decorative ways of elsewhere in the country.

Masks. If you don't experience Humahuaca at carnival time, you might be surprised by the number of masks—of humans and animals, made of wood or pottery—among the stalls. If you do go during *carnaval*, it'll make more sense.

Musical instruments. Panpipes are easy to play (though harder to play well) and instantly evocative of the windswept Quebrada. There are more intricate instruments available for musicians or the curious. For some tips on how to play, take it to a peña—a musical gathering at a bar—one evening and corner one of the performers.

Ponchos. Made from sheep or llama wool, ponchos go with everything, are useful against the cool cloudless nights in the Quebrada, and make great souvenirs (just resist the temptation to wear one out in Buenos Aires if you want to blend in). You can also pick up hats and gloves in matching patterns. The most renowned are made in—and can be bought in—the Salta village of Seclantás, which forms part of the **Camino del Artesano**.

Silver. It was its position on the road to the Potosí silver mines that made the Quebrada so important in colonial days, but don't count on the silver on sale now being locally sourced. Look for traditional motifs and symbols cast into silver as jewelry and, borrowing traditions from elsewhere, tableware.

shine through. Book ahead for a tasting with cheese platter. ✉ *Tacuil, Molinos* 🌐 *www.tacuil.com.ar* 🎟 *Tastings from 1,000 pesos.*

🍴 Restaurants

Casa Díaz

$$$$ | ARGENTINE | >At this adorable spot in Seclantás, Pío Díaz and his family cultivate ingredients in their organic garden then harvest them to create delicious regional dishes revered by top Argentine chefs. Many recipes, such as *charquisillo* made from jerky, have been passed down through the generations and are served in this gorgeous 18th-century farmhouse. [$] *Average main: pesos1800* ✉ *Seclantás* ☎ *387/442–3415* 🌐 *www.casadiaz.ar* 💳 *No credit cards.*

🛏 Hotels

Estancia Colomé

$$$$ | HOTEL | An ideal stopover between Salta capital and Cafayate on the Ruta 40, this stunning lodge is located on the Colomé wine estate 20 km (13 miles) from Molinos. **Pros:** spacious and well-designed rooms; restaurant uses ingredients from its organic garden; authentic experience at a working vineyard. **Cons:** very remote; not all staff speak English well; Wi-Fi is spotty. [$] *Rooms from: US$400* ✉ *RP53, Km 20, 20 km (13 miles) west of Molinos, Molinos* ☎ *3868/494–200* 🌐 *www.bodegacolome.com* 🛏 *9 rooms* 🍴 *Free Breakfast.*

★ Hacienda de Molinos

$$ | B&B/INN | This lovely 18th-century hacienda belonged to the last Spanish governor, its fantastic open courtyard, white adobe walls, and racing green doorways denoting the colonial era. **Pros:** spacious rooms; good restaurant with local wine list; swimming pool. **Cons:** service can be slow at peak times; noisy doors. [$] *Rooms from: US$160* ✉ *Molinos s/n, Molinos* ☎ *387/684–8090* 🌐 *www.haciendademolinos.com.ar* 🛏 *18 rooms* 🍴 *Free Breakfast.*

Cafayate

185 km (115 miles) southwest of Salta via RN68; 340 km (211 miles) southwest of Salta via R40.

Thanks to a microclimate and fertile soil, Cafayate and the surrounding area is one of Argentina's small yet booming wine regions, and there's a delightful Ruta del Vino to be enjoyed (🌐 *www.visitcafayate.travel*). The town itself is civilized and orderly, with various bodegas offering tours and tastings, lots of decent restaurants, and some delightful hotels. But wander a couple of blocks from the central plaza and you're back on unpaved roads. Take a bit of a hike, and you're in the mountains—probably enjoying a wine-tasting session at a *finca* and trying hard to get your camera to do justice to the view.

GETTING HERE AND AROUND

Chevallier and Flechabus both run about six buses a day from Salta. It's best to buy your ticket for the four-hour trip a day or two in advance, especially in summer. In Cafayate, many agencies and hotels rent bikes, which can come in handy when visiting bodegas and sights within a few miles of town.

ESSENTIALS

VISITOR INFORMATION Tourist Office. ✉ *Nuestra Senora del Rosario, at Plaza 20 de Febrero, Cafayate* ☎ *3868/422–224* 🌐 *www.turismosalta.gov.ar.*

👁 Sights

Although Salta makes only 1.5% of Argentina's wine, the province accounts for 8% of the country's exports. Most of the production is in or around Cafayate, which has around 20 bodegas, ranging from boutique family businesses to small

branches of multinational concerns. Book ahead for tastings and paired lunches.

Bodega Nanni

WINERY | Nanni has been in the same family and in the same building—just a block from the main square—since 1897. Thanks to its organic certification, much of its small production of Torrontés, Malbec, Cabernet Sauvignon, and Tannat is exported to the United States. Book lunch or dinner at Retoño, the rustic little restaurant in the back garden, for hearty stews and regional cuisine. ⊠ *Silverio Chavarria 151, Cafayate* ☎ *3868/421–527* ⊕ *www.bodegananni.com* 🍷 *400 pesos for tour and 3-wine tasting.*

★ Domingo Molina

WINERY | About 2 km (1 mile) north of Cafayate, Domingo Molina has been making Torrontés, a 90-point Malbec, and various blends since 2000. Tastings are available, and you can book in advance for a *picada* or *asado*. A drive leads you high up into the hills, offering stunning views of the wine lands to the east.
■ **TIP➜ Take a look at Domingo Molina's oldest vine—a 130-year-old Malbec, still providing excellent grapes. Domingo Hermanos, a sister winery in town, is one of Cafayate's biggest operations, producing 3 million liters a year.** ⊠ *RN40, Km 6, Yacochuya Norte, Cafayate* ☎ *3868/1545–2887* ⊕ *www.domingomolina.com.ar* 🍷 *500 pesos* 🕒 *Closed Mon. and Tues.*

★ El Porvenir de Cafayate

WINERY | Old blends with new at Bodega El Porvenir. Founded at the turn of the 20th century by Italian immigrants, the winery was bought by the Romero Marcuzzi family in 2000 and brought up-to-date. The result is a small yet sleek facility surrounded by old carob casks and presses. Drop by the tasting room to sample the Laborum-label Malbec and Torrontés, as well as the top-end Amauta three-grape red blend; ask to see the small olive oil factory. If you have time, book a private asado or picnic at Finca El Retiro, the family's downtown vineyard,

for lunch among the vines. ⊠ *Córdoba 32, Cafayate* ☎ *3868/422–007* ⊕ *www. elporvenirdecafayate.com* 🍷 *250 pesos for 3 wines.*

El Transito

WINERY | A contemporary building in the center of town houses El Transito's bodega and visitor center, a business run by a family that shares common ancestors with the folks at Bodega Nanni across the street. Pop in for a short tour and the chance to sample Malbec, Cabernet Sauvignon, and Torrontés. ⊠ *Belgrano 102, Cafayate* ☎ *3868/422–385* ⊕ *www. bodegaeltransito.com* 🍷 *300 pesos for 4 wines.*

★ Estancia Los Cardones

WINERY | Head south out of Cafayate toward Tolombón, then drive 7 km up the eastern mountain to this remote vineyard and winery. One of the valley's newer projects, Mendoza winemaker Alejandro Sejanovich teamed up with the Salta Saavedra Azcona family to create this project, named for the towering cacti. The mica-speckled rock ensures terroir characteristic wines; try the Tigerstone line that includes Garnacha and Malbec. ⊠ *Road to Hualinchay Km 7, Tolombon, Cafayate* ⊕ *www.estancialoscardones. com* 🍷 *Guided visit and tasting from 1,000 pesos* 🕒 *Closed Mon. and Tues.*

Finca Las Nubes

WINERY | In 1996, nothing was cultivated on José L. Mounier's land in El Divisadero, 4 km (2 miles) outside of town. Now Finca Las Nubes is one of Salta's best boutique wineries with fabulous views down into the valley. Almost half its small line of reds, whites, rosés, and sparkling wine is sold in the bodega itself. The tour includes sampling three wines, and lunch on the veranda is available if you book ahead. ⊠ *El Divisadero, Km 4, Cafayate* ☎ *3868/461–472* ⊕ *www.fincalasnubes. com.ar* 🍷 *800 pesos.*

Museo de la Vid y del Vino

OTHER MUSEUM | This museum, located in a warehouse dating from 1881, has undergone an extensive refurbishment to include more flash and 3D exhibitions. You can learn about wine-making in the Calchaquí Valley. Machinery, agricultural implements, and old photographs also tell the history of wine-making in this area. ⊠ *Guemes Sur and Fermín Perdiguero, Cafayate* ☎ *3868/422–322* ⊕ *www.museodelavidyelvino.gov.ar* 🖃 *250 pesos* ⊗ *Closed Mon.*

Museo Regional y Arqueológico Rodolfo Bravo

HISTORY MUSEUM | For 66 years, Rodolfo Bravo collected and cataloged funerary and religious objects from local excavations. These objects, made of clay, ceramic, metal, and textiles, are on display at the private Museo Regional y Arqueológico Rodolfo Bravo (Rudolfo Bravo Regional and Archaeological Museum). Artifacts from the Incas and Diaguitas of the Calchaqui Valley also form part of the collection. ⊠ *Colón 191, Cafayate* ☎ *3868/421–054* 🖃 *Voluntary contribution.*

Piattelli Vineyards

WINERY | The first winery in Cafayate to be constructed with tourism in mind, Piattelli caused a bit of a flurry with locals when it opened in 2013 thanks to the modern aesthetic conceived by its American owners. The state-of-the-art bodega, halfway up the foothills towards Yacochuya, offers tastings, tours, and fabulous valley views. Kick back on one of the two terraces with a refreshing Torrontés before tucking into slow-roasted lamb for lunch at the winery's restaurant. In 2022, the winery opened the Piattelli Wine Resort. ⊠ *R2, on way to Yacochuya, Cafayate* ☎ *3868/1540–5881* ⊕ *www.piattellivineyards.com* 🖃 *1,000 pesos for tour and three-wine tasting, 1,800 pesos for premium six-wine tasting with cheese platter.*

Quebrada de las Conchas

SCENIC DRIVE | The first 50 km (30 miles) of the direct road to Salta (or the last stretch if you don't come via Cachi and Molinos) is known as the Gorge of the Shells, and breathtaking scenery makes it an attraction in its own right. Various rock formations have been eroded into wildly different shapes that have been nicknamed the Windows, the Castles, the Frog, the Friar—each name seems fanciful, that is until the road winds around the corner and you're actually confronted by the formation itself. The climax is the Amphitheater, sometimes used as a venue for proper orchestras thanks to its outstanding natural acoustics; wandering minstrels offer impromptu performances. ■TIP➔ **If you've rented a car, keep valuables out of view as thieves have become more prevalent at the Amphitheater.** ⊠ *RN68, Km 6–Km 46, Cafayate.*

★ San Pedro de Yacochuya

WINERY | Head 8 km (5 miles) northwest of town toward the hills to find the Etchart family's boutique winery. Born into the local winemaking dynasty, Arnaldo Etchart established it in 1988, collaborating with flying winemaker Michel Rolland to create a trio of award-winning wines; today it's run by his sons Marcos and Arnaldo. Book in for a tasting to sample the Coquena or San Pedro de Yacochuya lines while enjoying stunning views over the valley. ⊠ *Cafayate* ☎ *3868/421–233* ⊕ *www.yacochuya.com. ar* 🖃 *3-wine tasting 1,050 pesos, 5-wine tasting 2,400 pesos* ⊗ *Closed Sun.*

Vasija Secreta

WINERY | Occupying a grand 1850s building on the northern edge of town, Vasija Secreta's museum displays imported oak barrels and machinery for pumping and bottling wine. Short tours give a historical overview and show how production methods have changed. Tasty local dishes are served at the rustic on-site restaurant. ⊠ *RN40 s/n, Cafayate* ☎ *3868/615–146* ⊕ *www.vasijasecreta.*

Did You Know?

The winding roads and overwhelming landscapes of the Salta region are a great road trip option.

246

com ✉ *Tastings from 1600 pesos to 3000 pesos.*

 Restaurants

El Rancho

$ | **ARGENTINE** | Facing the main plaza, this big barn of a restaurant serves regional specialties (like baked rabbit and *cabrito al horno*), as well as pastas and classic Argentine steaks. Expect generous portions, a bustling atmosphere, live folk music, and wines from the owner's Bodega Río Colorado, just a block away. **Known for:** traditional fare; efficient service; bustling atmosphere. $ *Average main: pesos600* ✉ *Vicario Toscano 4, Cafayate* ☎ *3868/421–256* 💳 *No credit cards* ☉ *Closed Mon.*

Macacha Gourmet

$$ | **ARGENTINE** | A 100-year-old converted school building houses one of Cafayate's more ambitious restaurants. Overseen by the friendly owner Matías, it has three dining rooms themed after the Nanni, Domingo Hermanos, and Etchart bodegas, with wine displays and special cutlery. **Known for:** wine list; jolly ambience; traditional fare such as llama steaks. $ *Average main: pesos900* ✉ *Av. Güemes Norte 28, Cafayate* ☎ *3868/422–319* 💳 *No credit cards* ☉ *Closed Sun.*

★ Doña Argentina Espacio Cultural

$$ | **ARGENTINE** | Good food and great music roll together at this peña, located in a traditional 19th-century casona which brings in both locals and visitors. Start with tiny empanadas and lashings of spicy llajua tomato sauce then follow up with pizza. **Known for:** historical venue; live music; busy ambience. $ *Average main: pesos800* ✉ *Colón 124, Cafayate* ☎ *3868/422–083.*

☕ Coffee and Quick Bites

Heladería Miranda

$ | **ARGENTINE** | For wine-tasting with a difference, stop at Heladería Miranda in Cafayate. In 1994, at the age of 60, Ricardo Miranda decided that he wasn't going to succeed as a painter. **Known for:** quirky ice cream flavors; Torrontés and Cabernet sorbet; popular tourist spot. $ *Average main: pesos200* ✉ *Av. Güemes Norte 170, Cafayate* ☎ *3868/421–106* 💳 *No credit cards.*

Hotels

Altalaluna Boutique Hotel & Spa

$$ | **HOTEL** | This gorgeous boutique hotel in the village of Tolombón, 14 km (9 miles) south of Cafayate, occupies an 1892 colonial mansion; there's a wine bar and cellar, an excellent restaurant, a reading room complete with fireplace, and a peaceful spa overlooking endless vines. **Pros:** great facilities; perfect for star-spotting; spacious rooms. **Cons:** a bit far from the town center; passageways can echo; the pool isn't heated. $ *Rooms from: US$156* ✉ *RN40, Km 4326, Cafayate* ☎ *387/582–4501* 🌐 *www.altalaluna.com* 🛏 *20 rooms* 🍴 *Free Breakfast.*

Cafayate Wine Resort

$$ | **RESORT** | Three km (2 miles) from the plaza on a straight dusty road lined with vineyards and in the shadow of San Isidro is a large white adobe building with 22 rooms built around a wide courtyard. **Pros:** spacious shared areas and access to veranda from all rooms; swimming pool with great views; lovely garden surrounded by vines. **Cons:** a little isolated from the town; some furniture may feel dated; some noise from hallways. $ *Rooms from: US$182* ✉ *25 de Mayo s/n, Camino al Divisadero, Cafayate* ☎ *3868/154–528–883* 🌐 *www.cafayatewineresort.com* 🛏 *22 rooms* 🍴 *Free Breakfast.*

El Hospedaje

$ | **B&B/INN** | This century-old building used to be a youth hostel until the owner got tired of the noise and chaos; rooms are basic, but they're set around a pleasant courtyard or around the inviting swimming pool. **Pros:** quiet and close to center; continental breakfast in a large dining room; friendly staff. **Cons:** rooms are basic; rooms next to street are noisy; few facilities. $ *Rooms from: US$50* ✉ *Salta 13, and Camila Quintana de Niño, Cafayate* ☎ *3868/421–680* ⊕ *www. saltaweb.com.ar/elhospedaje* ⊟ *No credit cards* ⇲ *12 rooms* ℗ *Free Breakfast.*

Fancy Rancho

$$ | **B&B/INN** | An adorable one-room B&B located on the vineyard slopes that form part of the San Pedro de Yacochuya wine estate, Fancy Rancho makes for a very private stay. **Pros:** stunning valley vista; close to wineries; peaceful setting. **Cons:** few kitchen facilities; best reached by car; cash only. $ *Rooms from: US$155* ✉ *Ruta Prov. N° 2 km 6, Cafayate* ☎ *3868/639–027* ⊟ *No credit cards* ⇲ *1 suite* ℗ *Free Breakfast.*

★ Finca El Retiro

$$ | **B&B/INN** | For a taste at playing vineyard owner, book a room at this charming, colonial-style B&B located on the vineyards that forms part El Porvenir de Cafayate's estate. **Pros:** peaceful despite being three blocks from the main square; great shared spaces including outdoor barbecue area; mountain views. **Cons:** not the most attentive service; you can't use the kitchen facilities to cook; breakfast isn't very exciting. $ *Rooms from: US$155* ✉ *Belgrano, at Jujuy, Cafayate* ☎ *387/218–3071* ⊕ *www. elporvenircasadebodega.com* ⇲ *5 rooms* ℗ *Free Breakfast.*

★ Grace Cafayate

$$ | **HOTEL** | A contemporary offering in the area, Grace Cafayate isn't just a step away from the local style—it's a whole world away; located within the well-heeled La Estancia de Cafayate residential and recreational complex, its lodging options include suites overlooking vineyards in the main building, as well as stand-alone villas and apartments across the way. **Pros:** infinity pool and spa on-site; supercomfy king beds; spacious communal areas. **Cons:** it can seem overly quiet; not all staff speak English; breakfast is on the small side. $ *Rooms from: US$200* ✉ *RN40, Km 4340, Cafayate* ☎ *3868/427–000* ⊕ *www.graceargentina. com.ar* ⇲ *52 rooms* ℗ *Free Breakfast.*

Hotel Asturias

$$ | **HOTEL** | The swimming pool is terrific, the garden is ample, and this—the biggest and oldest hotel in town—is quite comfortable. **Pros:** great garden and pool; central; walking distance to wineries. **Cons:** many staff don't speak English; breakfast is standard. $ *Rooms from: US$95* ✉ *Av. Güemes Sur 154, Cafayate* ☎ *3868/421–328* ⊕ *www.cafayateasturias.com* ⇲ *57 rooms* ℗ *Free Breakfast.*

La Casa de la Bodega

$$ | **HOTEL** | Carob wood and local boulders from the Quebrada de las Conchas were used to construct the little Casa de la Bodega, a rustic space with most mod cons that feels like peace personified. **Pros:** total peace and quiet in a beautiful setting; winery attached to the hotel; restaurant and pool on-site. **Cons:** the piped '80s music gets a bit much; you need a vehicle as it's isolated; if it's windy, you'll feel it here. $ *Rooms from: US$86* ✉ *RN 68, Km 18.5, 18 km (11 miles) from Cafayate center, Cafayate* ☎ *3868/492–056* ⊕ *www.lacasadelabodega.com.ar* ⇲ *8 rooms* ℗ *Free Breakfast.*

★ Patios de Cafayate Wine Hotel

$$ | **HOTEL** | Creature comforts, a fine restaurant, and rustic-chic rooms overlooking the vineyards make this luxury property a top choice. **Pros:** exclusive; wonderful pool surrounded by vines; fabulous facilities including wine spa, restaurant, and bodega. **Cons:** you'll need a car to get around; large tours can spoil the ambience; pricey. $ *Rooms from: US$170* ✉ *R40 at RN68, 3 km (2 miles) from Cafayate center, Cafayate* ☎ *3868/422–229* ⊕ *www.patiosde-cafayate.com* ⇲ *31 rooms* ℗ *Free Breakfast.*

Portal del Santo

$$ | **B&B/INN** | Just two blocks from the plaza but already on the edge of town, this place feels like a hideaway; behind the large colonial-style building, with its big guest rooms and its fireplace-warmed common area, is a garden with a blue-and-white swimming pool and great views. **Pros:** both central and quiet; good bathrooms; big breakfast. **Cons:** small communal spaces; rooms look dated; many guests are families, which tends to disturb the peace. $ *Rooms from: US$112* ✉ *Silvero Chavarria 250, Cafayate* ☎ *3868/422-500* ⊕ *www.portaldelsanto.com* ↻ *13 rooms* ¶ *Free Breakfast.*

Shopping

Cesteria (weaving with cane), *tejidos* (weaving with fabric), and *cerámica* (pottery) are the local specialties. Find these goods in the Paseo de Artesanos on the main plaza or in individual workshops. The tourist office opposite the Paseo de Artesanos has details. Cafayate has also seen a boom in wine stores selling products from local bodegas.

Calchaquitos

FOOD | Just next to the plaza, Calchaquitos sells cookies and chocolates, local jams, wine, and clothes. ✉ *Güemes Sur 118, Cafayate* ☎ *3868/421-799.*

Destilería Etchart & Argerich

WINE/SPIRITS | When you fancy trying something other than wine, head to this Tolombón distillery to sample an array of grappas—one even made from coca leaves. The former warehouse is covered in vintage signs and distilling memorabilia; snap up local produce from nuts to olive oil and preserves that make for great gifts. ✉ *Ruta 40 Km 4323, Tolombón, Cafayate* ☎ *3868/464-456* ⊕ *www.instagram.com/ladestileria2017.*

La Ultima Pulpería

FOOD | For a time-warp trip, just step into this store. La Ultima Pulpería, which has barely changed since opening in 1923, is an Aladdin's Cave selling loose herbs and spices, animal hides, and fresh produce. If you can pry owner Miguel Dioli away from his regular Salta-brand beer-drinking customers at the makeshift bar, he's good for a chat in Spanish. ✉ *Mitre 20, Cafayate* ☎ *3868/421-629.*

Vinoteca La Escalera

WINE/SPIRITS | Plenty of wine stores have popped up of late in Cafayate but Vinoteca La Escalera is one of the more established ones. It carries a solid selection from around the valley. ✉ *San Martín 71, Cafayate* ☎ *3868/421-142* ⊙ *Closed afternoons.*

Activities

Getting active in Cafayate involves the gentler end of adventure tourism: there are lots of opportunities for hikes, horseback rides, and bike excursions, but nothing too extreme. The waterfalls in the Río Colorado make a good excursion on a bike or on foot.

HORSEBACK RIDING

Tolombón Aventuras y Experiencias

HORSEBACK RIDING | By morning he's a registrar in Tolombón, but Baltasar Puló prefers to spend his time trekking by horseback with visitors over Sierras del Cajón foothills. Excursions are complemented with a bottle of refreshing Tukma Torrontés and local cheese. ✉ *Cafayate* ☎ *387/588-5434* ⊕ *www.tolombonaventurasyexperiencias.com.*

Chapter 7

MENDOZA AND THE WINE REGIONS

Updated by
Sorrel Moseley-Williams

7

⊙ Sights	🍴 Restaurants	🛏 Hotels	🛍 Shopping	🍸 Nightlife
★★★★★	★★★★★	★★★★☆	★★★☆☆	★★☆☆☆

WELCOME TO
MENDOZA AND THE WINE REGIONS

TOP REASONS TO GO

★ **Majestic Mountains:** Wherever you are in Mendoza, the sight of those towering Andean peaks never ceases to amaze.

★ **Fun in the Sun:** With more than 320 days of sunshine a year, Mendoza is the ultimate sunseekers' destination, whether you pedal a bike along flat vineyard roads, ride a horse along Andean trails, or ski down challenging slopes.

★ **Bed and Bodega:** Country inns with gourmet restaurants, vineyard visits and tastings, cooking classes, and discussions with oenologists make wine touring a pure pleasure.

★ **Food and Wine:** Some of Argentina's premier chefs have chosen to relocate to wine-country lodges and bodegas.

★ **Unique Terroir:** Known worldwide for its Malbec—and increasingly for its Cabernet Franc, Chardonnay, and other grapes—Mendoza's wine region is one of the most sought-after in the New World with big international investment and an impressive wine heritage.

The provinces of Mendoza and San Juan, in the central-west portion of Argentina, lie at the foot of the highest Andean ranges along the border with Chile. The city of Mendoza and its surrounding departments are in Mendoza Province's northern portion, 1,040 km (646 miles) from Buenos Aires but only 360 km (224 miles) from Santiago, Chile. The east–west Ruta Nacional 7 (RN7, part of the Ruta Panamericana or Pan-American Highway) crosses the Andes from Mendoza to Chile and links Argentina and neighboring countries (Brazil, Uruguay, Paraguay) with Pacific ports. Ruta Nacional 40 runs north–south the length of the country, passing through San Juan and down to Mendoza, the Valle de Uco, and San Rafael.

1 Gran Mendoza. Gran, or greater, Mendoza refers to the city and the surrounding *departments* (urban areas) of Godoy Cruz, Guaymallén, Maipú, Junín, Luján de Cuyo, and Las Heras—most of which house vineyards, bodegas, small hotels, and restaurants.

2 Valle de Uco. At the foot of the Cordón del Plata, between the towns of Ugarteche and Pareditas, the valley spreads its green mantle of vineyards and fruit orchards for 125 km (78 miles). The Río Tunuyán and its many *arroyos* (streams) create an oasis in this otherwise dry desert region.

3 San Rafael Region. The vineyards and olive groves that ring this burgeoning agricultural town in the southern portion of Mendoza Province are irrigated by the Ríos Atuel and Diamante, which flow from the nearby Andes.

4 San Juan Region. From this historic town surrounded by three important wine-producing valleys—Tulum, Ullum, and Zonda—you can travel west up the Río San Juan into a landscape of mountains, valleys, and desert.

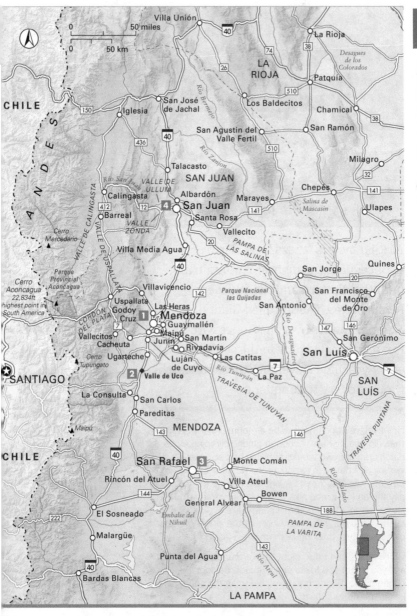

CERRO ACONCAGUA VIA THE USPALLATA PASS

At 6,957 meters (22,825 feet), Cerro Aconcagua is the highest mountain in both the Western and the Southern hemispheres. The so-called Giant of America towers over the Andes with its five glaciers gleaming in the sun; and every year, late November through March, thousands try to conquer it.

However, you don't have to be a mountaineer to enjoy the wild beauty here. Although guided climbing expeditions require two weeks of hiking and acclimating, a worthy alternative is to park at the rangers' cabin right off Ruta Nacional 7 just beyond the Puente del Inca, pay the park fee, and hike three hours from the Río Horcones to a lagoon. If this seems like a short hike for such a drive out, relax knowing that the journey to this place is as breathtaking as Aconcagua itself.

While fauna isn't thick, sight lines are unobstructed, and you might see foxes or shy guanacos; look up for condors, too. Alpine meadows bloom in the spring, and lichen are up to 500 years old.

DRIVE SAFELY

Ruta Nacional 7 is the only road that connects the Pacific ports of Chile with Argentina, Brazil, and Uruguay. Be prepared for heavy truck traffic.

In winter, icy roads can close for days; mudslides can cause closures in all seasons. The altitude jumps from 762 meters (2,500 feet) in Mendoza to 3,184 meters (10,446 feet) at the top of the pass; winds can sometimes be brutal.

ALONG THE USPALLATA PASS
(RN7, THE PANAMERICAN HIGHWAY)

Leaving Mendoza, green vineyards give way to barren hills and scrub brush as you follow the river for 30 km (19 miles). If you find yourself engulfed in fog and drizzle, don't despair: you'll likely encounter brilliant sunshine when you reach the Potrerillos Valley 39 km (24 miles) away. The road passes a long dam and then follows the Río Mendoza for 105 km (65 miles) to Uspallata, the last town before the Chilean frontier.

Along the way, the ríos Blanco and Tambillos rush down from the mountains into the Río Mendoza, and remnants of Inca *tambos* (resting places) marked by signs en route remind you that this was once an Inca trail; if you're traveling with a guide, she or he will stop for you to check them out. At Punta de Vacas, corrals that held cattle on their way to Chile lie abandoned alongside defunct railway tracks. Two km (1 mile) beyond the army barracks and customs office three valleys converge. Looking south, the region's third-highest mountain—Cerro Tupungato, an inactive volcano (6,800 meters/22,310 feet)—reigns above the Valle de Uco.

After passing the ski area at Los Penitentes, you arrive at Puente del Inca (2,950 meters/9,680 feet). Legend has it that long before the Spaniards arrived, an Inca chief traveled here to cure his paralysis in the thermal waters. Today, in addition to the thermal springs, you'll see a natural bridge of red rocks encrusted with yellow sulfur that spans the Río Cuevas; what's left of a spa hotel, built in the 1920s and destroyed in a 1965 flood, is covered in copper and gold sediment below the bridge.

Condor sightings are common in this area.

Poplar trees en route to the pass.

HIKING GUIDES AND LOGISTICS

November through March, you can sign on for two- or three-day guided treks to the Plaza de Mulas base camp at 4,260 meters (13,976 feet), where there's a *refugio* (cabin with bunk beds).

Guides will often take care of the necessary paperwork (Hiking and Mountaineering in Uspallata); otherwise, you have to purchase a permit online at ⊕ *www. entradasanp.mendoza. gov.ar.*

Trekking permits to Laguna de los Horcones cost upward of 3,400 pesos, for a day pass; ascent permits cost between US$120 and US$800 depending on the season, level, and number of days. Day permits must be purchased online and start at around 235 pesos depending on the activity.

INTO CHILE

Some tour groups and independent travelers continue on through to Chile to explore the vintages there. Visas, required of U.S. citizens, can be obtained at the border.

Exceptional wine, top-quality cuisine, exhilarating outdoor activities, and the skyscraping Andes framing almost every view: it's easy to see why people come here, and why many stay longer than they'd planned. In the center of Argentina, this region is often referred to as the Cuyo; and the name—passed down from the early indigenous Huarpe people, who called it Cuyum Mapu (Land of Sand)—is a reminder that the terrain is naturally semi-arid.

It is only because of carefully managed snowmelt from the mountains that the provinces are so green and, through irrigation, able to produce more than 90% of the country's wine. *Acéquias* (canals) built by the Huarpes and improved on by the conquering Incas and Spaniards, as well as by modern engineers, continue to capture the flow of the region's great rivers and channel it along the shady streets of the major cities: Mendoza, San Juan, and San Rafael.

Jesuit missionaries crossed the Andes from Chile to plant the first grape vines in 1556. Today more than 180,975 hectares (447,200 acres) of vineyards bask in the sun from the hills of San Juan down to the suburbs of Mendoza City and farther south through the Valle de Uco to San Rafael. The grapes are protected from the humid winds of the Pacific by the Andes, and grow at altitudes between 609 and 2,000 meters (2,000 to 6,500

feet), where they ripen slowly during long, hot summer days, while cool nights maintain acidity for long-lasting taste. Indeed, many vineyards could be classified as organic, as chemicals are seldom used or needed, and vintages are consistent.

Many bodegas offer tours and tastings; some also have atmospheric restaurants that pair fine wine with inspired food. But beyond the wineries, active adventures await. With more than 320 days of annual sunshine, this region is a four-season destination for outdoor enthusiasts. Ski resorts like Las Leñas attract snow bunnies in winter, and Aconcagua, the highest peak outside of the Himalayas and one of the world's Seven Summits, lures ambitious hikers and climbers in summer. At lower altitudes, there are less dizzying activities for all ages year-round, including horseback riding, whitewater rafting, and soaking in thermal baths.

Planning

When to Go

The wine harvest ends in autumn and is celebrated with festivities that culminate in the *vendimia* (wine festival). In Mendoza, this usually takes place during the last days of February and first week of March. A parade circles the Plaza Independencia and ends in San Martín Park with a grand finale of music, dancing, and religious ceremonies to ensure a good harvest. People shop and graze at food stands in the parks and plazas.

Winter is time for pruning and tying vines. Ski season begins in mid-June (depending on the year). July, the month with the best weather, is most favored by Argentineans and Brazilians. August usually has plenty of snow, and September offers spring conditions. Weather in the Andes is unpredictable, though; pack clothes for all conditions, and get up-to-date reports from ski areas. Springtime in the Valle de Uco brings fruit trees covered in pink and white blossoms, and new life in the vineyards. The snow-capped Andes form a spectacular backdrop, so bring your wide-angle lens.

Getting Here and Around

There are direct flights from Buenos Aires to Mendoza (about 90 minutes) and Santiago in Chile (45 minutes). Flights to nearby cities San Juan and San Rafael are routed through Buenos Aires, making them easier to reach by road. Comfortable buses between the three major cities are cheap, and bus stations are centrally located. On arrival, you'll find that all three cities have car-rental agencies and *remises* (hired cars with drivers), as well as wine-oriented tour companies that will take care of local transportation for you.

Hiring a *remis* for a full- or half day is a good use of money, as frequent detours, road construction or washed-out roads, and misleading (or nonexistent) signs can make driving yourself frustrating. Further, finding wineries on your own sometimes needs a GPS grid but also a working knowledge of Spanish. That said, if you have the time and the temperament for it, exploring on your own—stopping to snap photos and chat with locals—has its rewards. Driving to Andean villages and the border with Chile is a particularly remarkable experience.

If you are using Mendoza City as a base for independent winery visits, just bear in mind that Maipú is about a 30-minute drive away; reaching Luján de Cuyo by car also takes around 30 minutes and the Valle de Uco can take upward of an hour and a half. In San Rafael, you can reach many wineries by bike. In San Juan, some are within cycling distance, while others are on quiet, pretty roads that are best accessed by car; driving onward from San Rafael is also a practical solution if you're combining wine tours with a ski vacation in Las Leñas.

Restaurants

Most of the region follows national culinary trends—think beef, lamb, chicken, and pork *a la parrilla* (grilled). Malargüe, southwest of San Rafael, famously adds *chivito* (goat) to the mix—whether cooked *a la parrilla* or *al asador* (skewered on a metal cross stuck in the ground aslant a bed of hot coals). But you don't have to be a carnivore to eat well; after all, more than grapes grow in this part of Argentina. The vineyards are matched by olive groves, vegetable fields, and fruit orchards, which provide local chefs with an abundance of fresh ingredients. You'll taste them in the side dishes served at *asados* (barbecues); in the hearty Spanish-style stews and casseroles that are an edible connection to the region's past; and in the innovative gourmet fare prepared at next-generation winery restaurants.

Hotels

Like the altitude, the types of accommodations available here vary widely, so tourist offices can recommend all kinds of lodgings. Mendoza City has a wide selection to meet all budgets, with options including basic hostels, practical "apart-hotels" (furnished units with kitchen facilities), stylish boutique hotels, plus a healthy handful of luxury properties. In the countryside, you'll find everything from traditional *estancias* (ranches) that offer horseback riding and other outdoors activities to rustic *cabañas* (cabins), homey *residenciales* (bed-and-breakfasts), and modern ski lodges—all of which are generally well maintained and well priced. Vacationing hedonists can also choose between several posh resorts and *posadas* (country inns) around Valle de Uco, where the on-site amenities include top-notch restaurants, extensive wine cellars, and soothing spas.

Hotel reviews have been shortened. For full information, visit Fodors.com. Restaurant prices are the average cost of a main course at dinner or, if dinner is not served, at lunch. Hotel prices are the lowest cost of a standard double room in high season.

What It Costs in Argentine Pesos

	$	$$	$$$	$$$$
RESTAURANTS				
	Under 800 pesos	800–1,400 pesos	1,400–2,500 pesos	Over 2,500 pesos
HOTELS (IN $USD)				
	Under $100	$100–$200	$201–$300	Over $300

Wine Tours

Wineries require reservations, so arrange visits through your hotel, a local tour operator or book online yourself. Organized tours are particularly good if there isn't a specific bodega you wish to see or if you're traveling alone and/or during busy periods like the harvest. Most last a full day and include transportation from city hotels. If you do head out yourself, remember that many wineries charge for tastings (often redeemable against wine purchases); be sure to ask about fees when making your reservation.

ORGANIZED TOURS
Ampora
FOOD AND DRINK TOURS | This well-established outfit runs full-day group tours (maximum eight people) to Luján de Cuyo and the Valle de Uco. Ampora also has a private wine bar for tastings. ⊠ *Sarmiento 647, Mendoza* ☎ *261/429–2931* ⊕ *www.mendozawinetours.com* ✉ *From $155.*

Aventura and Wine (Bacchus Tours)
GUIDED TOURS | Over the last 10 years this company has been creating private tours for individuals and groups. ⊠ *Mendoza* ☎ *261/420–4230 in Mendoza* ⊕ *www.aventurawine.com* ✉ *From $25.*

Aymará Turismo
FOOD AND DRINK TOURS | In business for more than 20 years, Aymará offers a variety of tours—the most popular of which includes two Maipú wineries and an olive oil producer. Prices are cheap but groups are large. ☎ *261/420–2064 in Mendoza* ⊕ *www.aymaramendoza.com.ar* ✉ *From US$20.*

Mendoza Viajes
FOOD AND DRINK TOURS | This big agency offers a diverse selection of excursions (usually in large groups and in Spanish); wine-themed options include half- or full-day tours. Prices are reasonable, but

the service is less personal. ✉ *Sarmiento 129, Mendoza* ☎ *261/682–1751* ⊕ *www.mendozaviajes.com* ✈ *From US$21.*

Mendoza Wine Camp
FOOD AND DRINK TOURS | This company has full- or multiday tours to Luján de Cuyo and Valle de Uco in small private groups. ✉ *Garibaldi 7, 4th Floor, Mendoza* ☎ *261/526–0368* ⊕ *www.mendozawine-camp.com* ✈ *From US$130.*

Trout & Wine Tours
FOOD AND DRINK TOURS | Owned by a cheery Irish expat, one of the longest-running, high-end operators in Mendoza offers full-day group tours (eight people maximum) to Luján de Cuyo and the Valle de Uco. Fly-fishing tours are available, too. ✉ *Mendoza* ☎ *261/425–5613, 261/15–541–3892 cell phone* ⊕ *www.troutandwine.com* ✈ *From US$180.*

Uncorking Argentina
FOOD AND DRINK TOURS | This custom-package creator will book the wineries and driver for you. Most clients opt to visit the Valle de Uco or Luján de Cuyo, but the choice is yours. ✉ *Mendoza* ☎ *261/15–601–3298 in Mendoza* ⊕ *www.uncorkingargentina.com.*

Vintura
FOOD AND DRINK TOURS | From cooking classes with a top chef suitable for all the family, atelier visits, horseback riding, trekking in the Andean foot hills, and private winery tours, the Vintura team can organize many made-to-measure activities all over Mendoza. Serious wine lovers should ask about vertical tastings. ✉ *Mendoza* ☎ *261/535–9360* ⊕ *www.vintura.com.ar* ✈ *From US$200.*

SELF-GUIDED TOURS
Each area has its own unique *caminos del vino* (wine routes), and the Caminos del Vino de Argentina's Spanish-language website is a valuable trip planning tool. Wineries in San Juan Province have

pooled their resources to print a booklet, *Ruta del Vino,* with maps, photos, and information in Spanish. In Mendoza Province, you can pick up the free WINEMAP at bookstores and wineries; it consists of four maps and a guidebook in Spanish. DIY types based in Mendoza City can also take advantage of the convenient, cost-effective Vitivinicola bus service.

Bus Vitivinicola
SELF-GUIDED TOURS | Mendoza's hop on, hop off Vitivinicola bus is an affordable way to reach area wineries without your own transportation. Tuesday through Saturday, the comfy, air-conditioned vehicle picks up passengers at various points in the city and then starts its run to select venues. You then pay for the tasting at the winery. ■TIP➔ **Because you'll be going without a guide, you'll need to make your own advance reservations for the wineries you wish to visit and pay your own way at each once you arrive.** Bus tickets can be purchased online or on-board; they're also sold at visitor information centers and participating hotels. ✉ *Av. Las Heras 601, Mendoza* ⊕ *www.busviti-vinicola.com* ✈ *From 3,200 pesos.*

Mendoza City

1,060 km (659 miles) southwest of Buenos Aires; 250 km (155 miles) east of Santiago, Chile.

Mendoza's streets are shaded from the summer sun by a canopy of poplars, elms, and sycamores. Water runs along its sidewalks in *acéquias*, disappears at intersections, then bursts from fountains in the city's 74 parks and squares. Many *acéquias* were built by the Huarpe Indians and improved upon by the Incas long before the city was founded in 1561 by Pedro del Castillo.

Thanks to the booming wine and tourism industries, Mendoza bustles with innovative restaurants and lodgings that range from slick high-rises with conference rooms for serious wine tasting to low-key inns and B&Bs for serious relaxing. Low-rise colonial buildings with their lofty ceilings, narrow doorways, and tile floors house restaurants and shops. In the afternoon shops close, streets empty, and siesta-time rules—until around 5, when the city comes back to life and goes back to work. Don't expect much to be open on a Sunday, either.

GETTING HERE AND AROUND

Mendoza's El Plumerillo Aeropuerto Internacional is 6 km (4 miles) north of town on Ruta Nacional 40. Flights from Buenos Aires operated by Aerolíneas Argentinas (⊕ *www.aerolineas.com. ar*), Flybondi (⊕ *www.flybondi.com*) and Jetsmart (⊕ *www.jetsmart.com*) take about 90 minutes; flights from Santiago, Chile, operated by Aerolíneas, LATAM (⊕ *www.latam.com*) and Sky Airline (⊕ *www.skyairline.com*) take 45 minutes. Bus Terminal del Sol is on the outskirts of the city, about a 10-minute drive from downtown. From here buses provide daily service to San Juan (3 hours), Buenos Aires (14 hours), Santiago (8 hours), and other destinations. Never cut it close on timing when it comes to bus

connections. If the bus company says a trip will take 10 hours, it may, more likely, take 12 or 13. Leave a decent amount of time for extenuating circumstances— especially if you're crossing the Chilean border and have to account for customs queues.

Driving from Buenos Aires (on lonely but paved Ruta Nacional 7, aka the Pan-American Highway) or Santiago (again, on Ruta Nacional 7, which is sometimes closed along this stretch in winter) is an option, provided you have plenty of time and speak some Spanish. There's little need for a car in town, and it can be hard to find wineries in outlying areas on your own—even when you *do* speak Spanish. Furthermore, *mendocinos* are known for their cavalier attitude toward traffic rules. Pay attention to weather and road information. If you fear getting lost or breaking down in remote areas, hire a *remis* or arrange a tour.

■ TIP→ **Downtown streets have ankle-breaking holes, steps, and unexpected obstacles, including (irrigation canals) so watch where you're going.**

ESSENTIALS

VISITOR INFORMATION Mendoza Tourist Board. ⊠ *Av. San Martín 1143, at Garibaldi, Mendoza* ☎ *261/420–1333* ⊕ *www. turismo.mendoza.gov.ar.*

 Sights

After a devastating earthquake in 1861, Mendoza was reconstructed on a grid, making it easy to explore on foot. Four small squares (Chile, San Martín, Italia, and España) radiate from the four corners of Plaza Independencia, the main square. Their Spanish tiles, exuberant fountains, shaded walkways, and myriad trees and flowers lend peace and beauty. Avenida San Martín, the town's major thoroughfare, runs north–south out into the southern departments and wine districts. Calle Sarmiento intersects San Martín at the tourist office and becomes a *peatonal*

Water runs along Mendoza City's sidewalks in acéquias, disappears at intersections, then bursts from fountains in the city's 74 parks and squares.

(pedestrian road) with cafés, shops, offices, and bars. It crosses the Plaza Independencia, stops in front of the Park Hyatt, then continues on the other side of the hotel to a busy restaurant strip.

Bodegas CARO

WINERY | A small joint enterprise between the Catena family from Mendoza and the Rothschild family who own Chateau Lafite Rothschild in Bordeaux, CARO crafts Argentine blends with French accents. Visit includes ducking down into the historic cellar before sampling three vintages. Come in the evening and you might catch some tango. Tastings take place Monday to Friday. ✉ *Presidente Alvear 151, Godoy Cruz* ☎ *261/4530–963* 🌐 *www.lafite.com/fr/les-domaines/bodegas-caro/.*

Bodega Los Toneles

WINERY | This 19th-century winery close to downtown Mendoza was brought into the 21st century by the local Millán family. Besides producing a great selection of wine, visitors can enjoy the art gallery (curator Paula Dreidemie is available for private tours), guided visits, and tastings (from 1800 pesos). Book in for lunch or dinner at Abrasado restaurant, which specializes in dry-aged beef. The winery also produces award-winning olive oil. ✉ *Avenida Acceso Este 1360, Guaymallén* ☎ *261/661–8624* 🌐 *www.bodegalostoneles.com* ⏲ *Closed Mon.*

Bonafide

RESTAURANT | Caffeine fans can get their espresso fix at Bonafide. The Bonafide brand was the first to bring a coffee roasting machine to Argentina in 1917, and it now has locations city-wide. On the corner of Sarmiento and 9 de Julio near the central plaza, enjoy a steaming cup of joe with *medialunas* (sweet croissants) and *alfajores* (cookies with *dulce de leche*, sweet caramelized milk jam). ✉ *Peatonal Sarmiento 102, Mendoza* ☎ *261/591–5012* 🌐 *www.bonafide.com.ar.*

Heladerías

RESTAURANT | Mendoza has no shortage of *heladerías* (ice cream shops) ranging from artisan producers to national chains.

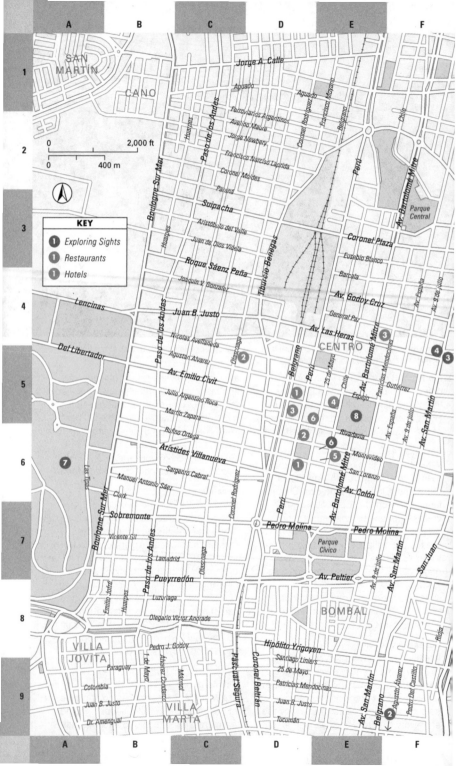

Mendoza City

Sights ▼

Restaurants ▼

Hotels ▼

It's a favorite pastime of locals to sit down to a few scoops, at any time of the day or night. Try local flavors, including wine ice creams, at Soppelsa (on Belgrano and Civit), Perin (on Sarmiento and Belgrano), Michel (on Belgrano and Montevideo), and Bianco & Nero (on Aristides and Belgrano). ✉ *Mendoza.*

Museo del Área Fundacional (*Foundation Museum*)
HISTORY MUSEUM | On the site of the original *cabildo* (town hall), the Foundation Museum explains the region's social and historical development. Of note is the display of a mummified child found on Aconcagua, with photos of his burial treasures. Excavations, made visible by a glass-covered viewing area, reveal layers of pre-Hispanic and Spanish remains. ✉ *Beltrán and Videla Castillo, Mendoza* ☎ *261/425–6927* 🎫 *160 pesos* 🕒 *Closed Mon.*

Museo del Pasado Cuyano
HISTORY MUSEUM | Home of former governor and senator Emilio Civit, this 26-bedroom 1873 mansion was the gathering place of the Belle Epoque elite. Today it's the Museum of the Cuyo's Past with paintings, antiques, history books, and artifacts from Argentina's War of Independence on display. ✉ *Montevideo 544, Mendoza* ☎ *261/423–6031* 🎫 *Donations accepted* 🕒 *Closed Mon.*

Parque General San Martín
CITY PARK | Dating back to 1896, this 971-acre park has more than 50,000 trees from all over the world. Fifteen km (9 miles) of paths meander through it. You can stop and smell the roses (a dedicated garden contains hundreds of varieties), observe aquatic competitions from the rowing club's balcony restaurant, or set the kids free on the numerous playgrounds. Scenes of the 1817 Andes crossing by José de San Martín and his army during the campaign to liberate Argentina are depicted on a monument atop Cerro de la Gloria (Glory Hill), a steep 20-minute walk up from the park's center. The stadium here (built for the 1978 World Cup, which Argentina won) hosts popular soccer matches; the amphitheater (capacity 22,500) fills to the brim during Vendimia, the annual wine-harvest festival; and there are markets and open aerobics classes on the weekend. ✉ *Avenida Emilio Civit 701, Mendoza.*

Plaza Independencia
PLAZA/SQUARE | In Mendoza's main square you can sit on a bench in the shade of a sycamore tree and watch children playing in the fountains, browse the stands at the daily artisan fair, or stroll past the historic Plaza Hotel (now the Park Hyatt) on your way to the shops and outdoor cafés on pedestrian-only Calle Sarmiento, which bisects the square. ✉ *Mendoza.*

🍴 Restaurants

Azafrán
$$$$ | **ARGENTINE** | This character-filled spot is more than just a restaurant: grocery shelves are stocked with local olive oils, smoked meats, and homemade jams, and more than 80 wineries are represented in the wine shop, where an old press has been converted into a tasting table. Offering a welcome break from *parrilla* fare, the two short tasting menus give traditional Argentine ingredients a creative twist. **Known for:** colorful decor; charcuterie; creative Argentine cuisine. [$] *Average main: pesos5400* ✉ *Sarmiento 765, Mendoza* ☎ *261/429–4200* 🌐 *www.azafranresto.com.*

Fuente y Fonda
$$$ | **ARGENTINE** | **FAMILY** | Priding itself on cooking dishes like your Italian *nonna* would make, Fuente y Fonda offers hearty Argentine fare in family size portions that are designed to be shared by big groups. Expect deep dishes filled with stuffed cannelloni, cheese and ham-topped milanesas, or roast meats. **Known for:** great milanesas; lively family atmosphere; big portions. [$] *Average main:*

pesos1600 ⊠ Montevideo 675, Mendoza ☏ 261/429–8833 ⊕ fuenteyfonda.com.

La Marchigiana

$$$ | ITALIAN | FAMILY | They've been serving homemade pasta at La Marchigiana since 1950, and many of the recipes were passed down from founder Nonna Fernanda; today her descendants carry on the tradition in the kitchen. The original premises burned down in 2006, but a modern version with underground parking is just as popular with Mendocinos looking for a reasonably priced meal (and a great lasagna). **Known for:** homemade pasta; suited and booted waiters; Italian cuisine. $ *Average main: pesos1500* ⊠ *Patricias Mendocinas 1550, Mendoza* ☏ *261/423–0751* ⊕ *www.marchigiana. com.ar.*

Parrilla y Restaurant Don Mario

$$$ | ARGENTINE | FAMILY | Mendocinos have been coming here for years to get their basic beef fix—*lomo* and *bife de chorizo* are grilled to perfection at this comfortable country-style restaurant. Pastas, grilled vegetables, and salads are also on the menu. **Known for:** old-school service; a Mendoza institution; carnivore's menu. $ *Average main: pesos1,500* ⊠ *25 de Mayo 1324, Guaymallén* ☏ *261/4310–810* ⊕ *donmario. com.ar.*

 ## Hotels

Amérian Executive Hotel

$$ | HOTEL | The tall, elegant tower of this downtown hotel looks out on the Plaza Italia, and the rooftop pool gives you a view over the city center. **Pros:** good value in city center; rooftop pool; helpful concierge. **Cons:** rooms need a refurb; breakfast buffet disappointing; windowless bar-restaurant. $ *Rooms from: US$115* ⊠ *San Lorenzo 660, Mendoza* ☏ *261/524–5000* ⊕ *www.amerian.com* ⊅ *74 rooms* ⊙⊙ *Free Breakfast.*

Casa Lila Bed and Breakfast

$$ | B&B/INN | With only four rooms, this handsome bed-and-breakfast guarantees personalized service within walking distance of the city center, lots of restaurants, and Parque General San Martín. **Pros:** charming, quiet home base; spacious en suite bathrooms; complimentary bikes. **Cons:** not for pet shy (friendly dogs live here); close quarters; meals on request, but no on-site restaurant. $ *Rooms from: US$124* ⊠ *Nicolás Avellaneda 262, Mendoza* ☏ *261/429– 6349* ⊕ *www.casalila.com.ar* ⊅ *4 rooms* ⊙⊙ *Free Breakfast.*

Diplomatic

$$ | HOTEL | One of the city center's larger top-end hotels, the Diplomatic often hosts conferences and football teams that each take advantage of the central location, modern facilities, and various event spaces. **Pros:** excellent central location with parking; good amenities; large rooms. **Cons:** small swimming pool gets crowded; needs some TLC; not the five stars it claims to be. $ *Rooms from: US$190* ⊠ *Belgrano 1041, Mendoza* ☏ *261/405–1900, 0810/122–5000 reservations* ⊕ *www.diplomatichotel.com.ar* ⊅ *156 rooms* ⊙⊙ *Free Breakfast.*

Park Hyatt Mendoza

$$$ | HOTEL | The Hyatt has preserved the landmark Plaza Hotel's 19th-century Spanish colonial façade: a grand pillared entrance and a wide veranda that extends to either side of the street. **Pros:** ideal location; staff accustomed to accommodating foreign guests; comfortable rooms. **Cons:** rooms look onto public areas; impersonal service; small pool with street noise. $ *Rooms from: US$335* ⊠ *Calle Chile 1124, Mendoza* ☏ *261/441–1234* ⊕ *www.hyatt.com/ en-US/hotel/argentina/park-hyatt-mendoza-hotel-casino-and-spa/menph* ⊅ *186 rooms* ⊙⊙ *Free Breakfast.*

Raíces Aconcagua Hotel

$$$ | HOTEL | Classic gray granite creates a businesslike atmosphere in the lobby of this popular city center hotel. **Pros:** central location; nice suites on top floor; cheap option. **Cons:** rooms could do with an update; basic breakfast; public areas are often crowded. $ *Rooms from: US$211* ✉ *San Lorenzo 545, Mendoza* ☎ *261/520–0500* ⊕ *www.raicesaconcagua.com* ↪ *150 rooms* †○† *Free Breakfast.*

Villaggio Hotel Boutique

$$ | HOTEL | If you want to stay right in the city, but prefer to sidestep the big hotel chains, Villaggio is just one block from the main plaza with attractive guest rooms and two self-catering apartments. **Pros:** central location; free Wi-Fi; spa with sauna and Jacuzzi. **Cons:** some rooms have views of air shaft; street noise in some rooms; needs some TLC. $ *Rooms from: US$140* ✉ *25 de Mayo 1010, Mendoza* ☎ *261/256–2892* ⊕ *www.hotelvillaggio.com* ↪ *26 rooms, 2 apartments* †○† *Free Breakfast.*

Nightlife

BARS AND PUBS

Avenida Arístedes Villanueva

BARS | Full of bars, cafés, microbreweries, and restaurants, this avenida begins to wake up around 9 pm (don't even bother going any earlier). As the evening progresses, crowds get bigger, and the music—rock, tango, salsa—gets louder. Action peaks at midnight. ✉ *Avenida Arístedes Villanueva, Mendoza.*

Chachingo Craft Beer

PUBS | Brewing has turned into a successful side project for winemaker Alejandro Vigil and at this pub, one of several around the province, you can freshen up like grape pickers do, with a cooling lager or IPA. ✉ *Av. Arístides Villanueva 383, Mendoza* ☎ *261/685–3946* ⊕ *www.universovigil.com/aristides-clubgin.html.*

Tip

A change in regulation pushed the nightclubs out of Mendoza's city center. If you want to dance, you'll find the nightclub strip just beyond Chacras on the Panamericana between Guardia Vieja and Gobernador Ortiz crossroads. Doors don't usually open until after midnight.

El Mercadito

BARS | A pretty bar with a nice patio on busy Arístides Street, El Mercadito plays good music and even serves a decent salad. ✉ *Arístides Villanueva 521, Mendoza* ☎ *261/463–8847.*

Juan B Justo

GATHERING PLACES | Locals call Juan B Justo street the "new Aristides" and, only six streets up, it shares a similar vibe. While Aristides is busier, Juan B Justo street has a growing number of (more affordable) pubs, bars, and its own handful of microbreweries. ✉ *Juan B Justo, Mendoza.*

Vico Wine Bar

WINE BARS | Wine dispensers that serve an array of by-the-glass options means you can try around 80 styles and regions under one roof. It's also a great spot for dinner too, with a delicious array of tapas and small plates designed for sharing on the menu. ✉ *Rivadavia 789, Mendoza* ☎ *261/333–8660* ⊕ *www.vicowinebar.com.ar/mendoza.*

CASINOS

Regency Casino

GATHERING PLACES | Inside the Park Hyatt, this casino has blackjack, stud poker, roulette tables, slot machines, and a bar. ✉ *25 de Mayo 1115 and Sarmiento, Mendoza* ☎ *261/441–2843.*

🛍 Shopping

Pick up leather goods, shoes, and clothing along Sarmiento and its cross streets, or on Avenida Las Heras, where you'll find regional products to eat, drink, wear, or decorate your house with. On summer evenings and weekends, Plaza Independencia becomes an artisan market, with stands selling jewelry, handmade sweaters, ponchos, mate gourds, olive oil, and other regional wares.

CLOTHES AND ACCESSORIES

La Matera

LEATHER GOODS | Mendocinos shop at La Matera for boots, vests, belts, scarves, and riding gear. ⊠ *Villanueva 314, Mendoza* 🕾 *261/563–5608* 🕙 *Closed Sun.*

FOOD AND WINE

Juan Cedrón

WINE/SPIRITS | Before your picnic, grab a bottle of Malbec at Juan Cedrón. The store also stocks many older vintages of wine worth collecting (or drinking!). ⊠ *Sarmiento 282, Mendoza* 🕾 *261/563–5608.*

Sol y Vino

WINE/SPIRITS | This spot has a great stock of wines and gourmet food. Handicrafts and other local items are sold as well. ⊠ *Sarmiento 664, Mendoza* 🕾 *261/425–6005* ⊕ *www.solyvinomendoza.com.*

MALLS

La Barraca Mall

MALL | A 10-minute drive from Mendoza City, La Barraca has lots of local brands, a children's playground, restaurants, and a pharmacy. ⊠ *Las Cañas 1833, Dorrego, Guaymallén* 🕾 *261/459–8019* ⊕ *www.labarracamall.com.*

Mendoza Plaza Shopping Center

MALL | This mall in Guaymallén, 10 minutes from Mendoza, has more than 160 stores, including an American-style department store, cafés and restaurants, a movie theater, bowling, and an indoor amusement park. ⊠ *Lateral Accesso Este 3280, Guaymallén* 🕾 *261/449–0100* ⊕ *www.mendozaplazashopping.com.*

Palmares Open Mall

MALL | A 15-minute drive south of Mendoza, the Palmares Open Mall has 120 stores, lots of good restaurant options, and 10 movie theaters (including one in 3-D). ⊠ *Panamericano 2650, Godoy Cruz* 🕾 *261/413–9100* ⊕ *www.palmares.com. ar.*

MARKET

Mercado Central

MARKET | For more than 120 years, the Mercado Central has been selling local foods from stalls including butchers, cheese shops, grocers, and a couple of restaurants for a quick bite on the go. ⊠ *Av. Las Heras 279 and Patricias Mendocinas, Mendoza.*

Activities

The high peaks of the Andes provide a natural playground, with miles of trails to hike, bike, or ride on horseback. Rivers invite rafters and kayakers to test the water in the spring. Some of the wildest and most remote mountain areas are made accessible by the Ruta Nacional 7, which crosses the Andes right by Parque Provincial Aconcagua.

HORSEBACK RIDING

Cabalgata (horseback riding) is an enjoyable and natural way to explore the mountains west of Mendoza. You can ride to the foot of Aconcagua or Tupungato, or follow the hoofprints of General San Martín on a multiday trip over the Andes.

Trekking Travel

HORSEBACK RIDING | Offering everything from one-day excursions to eight-day trips that take you across the Andes, this outfitter can accommodate beginner and expert riders alike. ⊠ *Adolfo Calle 4171, Villa Nueva, Mendoza* 🕾 *261/421–0450* ⊕ *www.trekking-travel.com.ar.*

MULTISPORT TOUR OPERATOR
Argentina Rafting
WHITE-WATER RAFTING | Whether you want to go rafting, kayaking, climbing, or zip-lining, this company can set you up. Let the adrenaline ease off by sinking a pint at their pool bar by the river. ☎ 261/657–2582 ⊕ www.argentinarafting.com.

Maipú

16 km (10 miles) southeast of Mendoza City.

Lying south and slightly east of Mendoza City, Maipú—the province's oldest wine region—is spread over the districts of General Gutiérrez, Coquimbito, and Cruz de Piedra. While not as glamorous as neighboring Luján de Cuyo, on the other side of the Acceso Sur, Maipú does have its virtues. Thirty-odd bodegas are open to tourism.

GETTING HERE AND AROUND
Acceso Sur (Ruta Nacional 40), the main highway south, is the fastest way to get to the area. Driving yourself here can be a bit of a headache, though, given Maipú's notorious road works and diversions. If you're on a tight budget, you can catch a public bus or the Metrotranvía (tram) from Mendoza City, and then rent a bike to visit wineries (one of the last stops is at Bodegas López); alternately, you come by cab (most wineries are only a 20-minute taxi ride from Mendoza City). If you want to drink, the best options are to hire a remis for a day or sign on for a wine tour.

 Sights

Bodega La Rural
WINERY | In 1855, Felipe Rutini left the hills of Italy to found a winery in the raw land of Coquimbito, Argentina. His descendants planted the first grapes (Chardonnay and Merlot) in the now-popular Tupungato District of the Valle de Uco. Today, Bodega la Rural is still family-owned and -operated. The winery's well-known San Felipe label was created by Alejandro Sirio, a famous Spanish artist. Inside the original adobe barns the Museo del Vino (Wine Museum) displays leather hoppers, antique pressing machines, vintage carriages, 105-year-old tools, and even an amazing mousetrap. ⊠ Montecaseros 2625, Coquimbito, Maipu ☎ 261/497–2013 ⊕ www.bodegalarural.com.ar ⊗ Closed Sun.

Bodegas López
WINERY | Wines up to 60 years old are stored in the main cellar of this traditional winery, established in 1898 and still owned by the same family. Easily accessible by tram from Mendoza, this is a great budget option with free tours and a range of tastings. The restaurant, upstairs from the wine store, serves à la carte and fixed-menu lunches, and there's also an on-site museum documenting Mendoza's winemaking history. ⊠ Ozamis Norte 375, Maipu ☎ 261/497–2406 ⊕ www.bodegaslopez.com.ar.

Carinae
WINERY | FAMILY | Founded by a charming French couple, Philippe and Brigitte, who came to Mendoza to start a new life in wine-making, you can book in for a free short tour at this boutique winery. The garden is available should you wish to bring your own picnic. ⊠ Videla Aranda, 2899, Cruz de Piedra ☎ 261/336–4324 ⊕ www.carinaevinos.com.

★ Casa del Visitante
WINERY | FAMILY | The Zuccardi family set up here in 1950 and has since expanded to the Valle de Uco, but their location in Maipú remains an important base for producing their popular, fully organic, Santa Julia range. The extensive tourist offerings here include harvest experiences and olive oil-making sessions in season, as well as tastings, cooking classes, and dining at one of two restaurants

for lunch, including Pan y Oliva, where every dish uses the house olive oil. Be sure to appreciate the exhibitions, which support local artists' work. ✉ *RP33, Km 7.5, Maipu* ☎ *261/441–0000* 🌐 *www.santajulia.com.ar.*

Casa Vigil

WINERY | Getting to this boutique winery requires a car, but the drive to reach the home winery of one of Argentina's top winemakers, Alejandro Vigil, is worth it. Enjoy a short tour ahead of the lunch and dinner tasting menus before sampling his renowned El Enemigo wines. Guided visits and tastings are also available. One of the few winery restaurants that opens for dinner. ✉ *Videal Aranda 7008, Mendoza* ☎ *261/341–1729* 🌐 *www.universovigil.com.*

Restaurants

★ La Cayetana 1865

$ | ARGENTINE | Hidden between the vineyards of Maipú is this historic manor, lovingly restored as an intimate restaurant, which serves a five-course tasting menu of farm-to-table Argentine cuisine (including recipes from a 19th-century cookbook found on the property) paired exclusively with Ver Sacrum wines. Tastings, cooking classes, and live art shows are all on offer, and the limited lunchtime reservations fill up fast. **Known for:** authentic Argentine cooking; delicious wines; ingredients picked from the garden. [$] *Average main: pesos400* ✉ *Manuel Cruz Videla 2605, Mendoza* ☎ *261/639–2757* 🌐 *www.lacayetana1865.blogspot.com.ar* 🕒 *Closed Sun. Jun.–Aug.*

Hotels

Club Tapiz

$$ | HOTEL | Set in a 19th-century mansion surrounded by vineyards and tall trees, Club Tapiz feels like a private villa; guests can lounge in the olive-tree lined garden and gaze at the Andes from the outdoor pool or indoor Jacuzzi before sampling the estate's wines at the informal evening tasting. **Pros:** great restaurant; complimentary perks include daily wine tasting, and a visit to Bodega Tapiz (20 minutes away); charming and peaceful setting. **Cons:** spa is a little outdated; noise travels between rooms; close to vineyards but far from shops or town. [$] *Rooms from: US$190* ✉ *Pedro Molina (RP60) s/n, Maipu* ☎ *261/496–3433, 261/596–6853 WhatApp* 🌐 *www.club-tapiz.com.ar* 🛏 *11 rooms* 🍴 *Free Breakfast.*

Nightlife

CASINOS

Arena Maipú Casino Resort

GATHERING PLACES | The huge Arena Maipú Casino Resort features more than 480 slots, 40 electronic roulette tables, five traditional roulette tables, and six card tables. An on-site stadium, cinema, and hotel—plus several bars and restaurants—make this complex popular with nongamblers, too. ✉ *Emilio Civit y Maza, Maipu* ☎ *261/481–9800* 🌐 *www.arena-maipu.com.ar.*

DANCE CLUBS

Black Jagger

DANCE CLUBS | Late-night dancing and a fun crowd make for good times at the Black Jagger. It's part of the Arena Maipú Casino complex. ✉ *Emilio Civit y Maza, Maipu* ☎ *261/701–7030* 🌐 *www.facebook.com/blackjaggermendoza.*

Activities

BIKING

Many of Mendoza's back roads lead through the suburbs and vineyards into the Andean foothills and upward to mountain villages—or all the way to Chile.

Maipú Bikes

BIKING | Bikers are provided with helmets, water, and a free glass of wine on your return at this popular bike rental in Maipú. ✉ *Urquiza 5175, Maipu* ☎ *261/467–0761* ⊕ *www.maipubikes. com.*

Mr. Hugo Wineries and Bikes
BIKING | Genial Mr. Hugo owns one of the longest-running bike rental spots on the Maipú wine route. He'll provide water and maps before you head out and lemonade when you return. ✉ *Urquiza 2288, Maipu* ☎ *261/497–4067.*

Luján de Cuyo

20 km (12 miles) south of Mendoza City.

Bordering both banks of the Mendoza River, Luján de Cuyo is known as the home of Malbec because it was here that the variety first started showing great potential. With more than 50 bodegas, ranging from the traditional to the ultramodern, this is one of the largest Wine Regions in Mendoza—and one of the province's best pastimes is hopping between them (you can expect to visit three or four a day), enjoying tours and tasting great vino along the way. Luján also has a smattering of luxury lodges and boutique hotels should you wish to extend your stay.

GETTING HERE AND AROUND
Some wineries are accessible by public transport (you can catch a bus to ones in Chacras de Coria or on the main San Martín road); however, the large majority—and often the cream of the crop—are best visited by car. A self-driving tour is doable, provided you carry a good map (and remember alcohol tolerance levels are 0.5), but hiring a *remis* or joining a tour group is more convenient, and means you can enjoy the tipples.

 Sights

Achaval Ferrer
WINERY | This winery made its name on single variety Malbec, but today it has expanded to a handful of other varieties

as well. Today it's owned by a renowned vodka distiller, and you can learn about the evolution of the company and its different single-site Malbecs in Mendoza. ✉ *Calle Cobos 2601, Perdriel, Luján de Cuyo* ☎ *261/481–9205* ⊕ *www.acha-val-ferrer.com.*

Bodega Catena Zapata
WINERY | A contemporary Mayan pyramid rising from the vineyards fronts the towering Andes at this landmark winery owned by the fourth generation of the Catena family. Descend from a crystal cupola through concentric spaces to the tasting room, which is surrounded by 400 oak barrels. The winery is due to open its first restaurant and cellar in 2022. ✉ *Calle J. Cobos s/n, Alto Agrelo* ☎ *261/490–0214* ⊕ *www.catenawines. com.*

★ Bodega Lagarde
WINERY | Built in 1897, Lagarde is one of the oldest wineries in Mendoza, and it's led by Sofía and Lucila Pescarmona, third-generation sisters who now cultivate grapes and make wine. Tour the 19th-century property before enjoying lunch or dinner alongside the centenary vines at Fogón, a delicious tasting and à la carte menu with many ingredients sourced from the organic garden; you can also enjoy a picnic on the grounds. Those after a fully immersive eno-gastro experience can sign up to the cooking school. ■TIP→ **Lagarde rents an adorable two-bedroom cottage on its Perdriel estate.** ✉ *San Martín 1745, Mayor Drummond, Luján de Cuyo* ☎ *261/15–6815–961* ⊕ *www.lagarde.com.ar* ۞ *Closed Wed. for lunch; closed Mon. for tastings.*

Bodega Norton
WINERY | In 1895, English engineer Sir Edmund Norton, built the first winery in the valley south of the Mendoza River and much of the historical building is still intact. Today production is much larger and there's a wide portfolio. Tours with tastings and other vineyard experiences are available with advance reservations,

and the stylish on-site restaurant, La Vid ($$$$), welcomes lunch guests for a five-course tasting menu or à la carte dishes. ✉ RP15, Km 23.5, Perdriel, Luján de Cuyo ☎ 261/490–9700 ⊕ www.norton.com.ar ⌂ Reservations essential.

Carmelo Patti

WINERY | Carmelo—a legendary garage winemaker—is the passionate owner of this operation. He answers the phone, greets you at the door, and personally conducts tours (in Spanish only), drawing wine from the barrel and entertaining guests with anecdotes and fascinating facts about everything from growing grapes to preserving corks. The winery may be nothing fancy, but Carmelo has a cult-like following and he exports his red blends around the world. ✉ San Martín 2614, Luján de Cuyo ☎ 261/207–0789 ⌚ Closed Sun.

Chandon

WINERY | The president of Moët & Chandon was so impressed by Agrelo's *terroir* (the soil, climate, and topography that contribute to making each wine unique) that he decided to build the first foreign outpost of his family's company here in 1959. Today the winery is producing *vino espumante* (sparkling wine) in great quantities. Chandon is popular, so book ahead for private tours. The pretty bistro serves a tasting menu paired exclusively with sparkling wine. ✉ RN40, Km 29, Agrelo, Luján de Cuyo ☎ 261/490–9968 ⊕ www.chandon.com.ar.

Club Tapíz

WINERY | When the Ortiz family bought this 1890-constructed bodega from Kendall Jackson in 2003, CEO Patricia Ortiz and oenologist Fabián Valenzuela decided to make more food-friendly wines. Tours begin in the vineyard, followed by tank, barrel, and bottle tastings. In summer, a two-horse carriage driven by a local gaucho takes you on a fun yet educational tour of the vineyard and to visit the resident llamas. Stay on for a farm-to-table lunch created by executive chef Soledad Nardelli. ✉ RP15, Km 32, Agrelo, Luján de Cuyo ☎ 261/596–6853 ⊕ www.bodega-tapiz.com.ar ⌚ Closed Sun. for tastings.

Durigutti Family Winemakers

WINERY | Brothers Hector and Pablo Durigutti worked for various bodegas for many years before finally setting roots in Las Compuertas. Take a guided visit, with a strong focus on terroir, at this new complex located on Finca Victoria, which includes a winery, visitors' center, and 5 Suelos restaurant, led by renowned chef Patricia Courtois. ■ **TIP→ There are two vineyard cottages available to rent on the estate.** ✉ Pasaje La Reta s/n, Las Compuertas, Luján de Cuyo ⊕ www.durigutti.com ⌚ Closed Sun. ⌂ Reservations essential.

★ Matervini

WINERY | This modern winery in the heart of Lujan is Santiago Achaval (co-founder of Achaval Ferrer) and Roberto Cipresso's personal project. They make a series of exciting, exclusive Malbecs, producing just 40,000 bottles from different wine regions in Argentina. The dollar price tag (tours start at $30) reflects the exclusive pours and attentive experience. There's also Mater House, a small lodge, worth staying at. ✉ Cobos 2142, Luján de Cuyo ⌖ Perdriel ☎ 261/561–6691 ⊕ www.matervini.com ⌚ Closed Sun.

Mendel Wines

WINERY | This modest winery is home to one of Argentina's best-known winemakers, Roberto de la Mota, and quality, not quantity, is the mantra. Informal tours of the unassuming 85-year-old adobe building highlight the loving care grapes receive—from handpicking to hand-crushing to storage. ✉ Terrada 1863, Luján de Cuyo ☎ 261/524–1621 ⊕ www.mendel.com.ar.

Nieto Senetiner

WINERY | White adobe walls, tile roofs, flower-bed-lined walkways, and huge shade trees welcome you to this historic

Did You Know?

There are two main pruning methods for grape vines. Spur (or head) pruning involves allowing only two shoots per branch to bear grapes; this is most common in older vineyards or in the warmest growing climates. Cane pruning trains up to 4 shoots per branch along a trellis so that up to 16 new shoots will bear fruit along the trellis the next season.

bodega. Visits typically include a winery tour and either a wine tasting or a chocolate-and-wine pairing. You can also opt for a 2-km (1-mile) horseback ride to a hilltop for a view of the mountains and vineyards. Most activities finish with an *asado* lunch at the bodega. ⊠ *Guardia Vieja, between RN7 and Rosque Sáenz Peña s/n, Vistalba, Luján de Cuyo* ☏ *261/496–9099* ⊕ *www.nietosenetiner. com.ar* ⌲ *Reservations essential.*

Pulenta Estate

WINERY | Two brothers from one of the most iconic wine families in Mendoza— the Pulentas—started their own premium winery in 2002. The attractive, modern facility runs excellent tours and tastings (including a fantastic Cabernet Franc) and also offers a sensory aroma class. ⊠ *RP 86, Km 6.5, Alto Agrelo* ☏ *261/15–507–6426* ⊕ *www.pulentaestate.com* ⊙ *Closed Sun.*

★ Riccitelli Wines

WINERY | Trendy young winemaker Matías Riccitelli made his name with innovative and eye-catching labels and fortunately what's in his bottles live up to all expectations. At his Las Compuertas–based winery, enjoy a short guided visit of the premises before sampling some vintages on the balcony overlooking the vineyards. Book in for lunch at Riccitelli Bistró, helmed by chef Juan Ventureyra, for a delightful, plant-based six-course menu, many of whose ingredients are cultivated by Juan. ⊠ *Roque Saénz Peña, Luján de Cuyo* ☏ *261/316–7775* ⊕ *www.matiasriccitelli.com* ⊙ *Closed Sun.*

Ruca Malén

WINERY | This winery is known not just for its stylish wines, but its plentiful lunch— six courses of a delectable seasonal tasting menu created by chef Lucas Bustos are paired with predominantly red wines. Vertical tastings of different vintages and wine blending sessions are also on offer in the modern winery. ⊠ *RN7, Km 1059, Agrelo, Luján de Cuyo* ☏ *261/454–1236* ⊕ *www.bodegarucamalen.com.*

Séptima

WINERY | Spanish wine group Codorniú constructed their Argentine winery in the *pirca* style of the Huarpe natives, by piling stones one atop the other. The end result is both practical (it helps keep the winery naturally cool) and visually arresting. A highlight is the panoramic view from the terrace over the vineyards and mountains, where you can have lunch at their restaurant. In summer, enjoy sunsets over the mountains with a glass of something special. ⊠ *RN7, Km 6.5, Agrelo, Luján de Cuyo* ☏ *261/498–9558* ⊕ *www.bodegaseptima.com* ⊙ *Closed Sun.* ⌲ *Reservations essential.*

★ Susana Balbo Wines

WINERY | Susana Balbo—Argentina's first licensed female winemaker—has been making a name for herself since 2001, when she pioneered the making of a high-quality Torrontés. Today, she and her family make reds, whites, and rosés, which you can enjoy in the tasting room or over lunch at one of the two restaurants on-site, Osadía de Crear for tasting menus, and Espacio Crios for picnics and light snacks. ⊠ *Cochabamba 7801, Agrelo, Luján de Cuyo* ☏ *261/498–9231* ⊕ *www.susanabalbowines.com.ar* ⌲ *Reservations essential.*

Terrazas de Los Andes

WINERY | Bare brick walls, high ceilings, and a labyrinth of soaring arches shelter premium wines in stainless-steel tanks and oak barrels in this restored 1898 winery. Everything in the tasting room— from the bar to the tables to the leather chairs—is made with recycled barrels. The restaurant serves a well-paired tasting menu. You can also take a cooking class with the chef, and, if you're too full to drive anywhere, stay at Terrazas' guest house. ⊠ *Thames and Cochabamba, Perdriel, Luján de Cuyo* ☏ *261/490–9862* ⊕ *www.terrazasdelosandes.com.*

🍴 Restaurants

Most of the top restaurants in Luján de Cuyo are, in fact, in the wineries. Few open for dinner—exceptions include Fogón at Lagarde—but if you have just had a large winery lunch you'll likely only want a light bite in the evening. Chacras de Coria, a small town outside of Mendoza City, is the perfect spot for a drink and bite in the evening with several casual bars, beer gardens, and restaurants around the main square.

★ Brindillas
$$$ | INTERNATIONAL | Partners in life and in the kitchen, Mariano and Florencia traveled the world working in restaurants; they've brought that experience to their own intimate eatery, which offers a sophisticated tasting menu. The space may be small (it sits only 18 people), but you can expect delightful culinary creations with consistently appealing flavors and presentation. **Known for:** quiet setting; professional service; five- and seven-course tasting menus. *[$] Average main: pesos2000 ✉ Guardia Vieja 2898, Luján de Cuyo ☎ 261/496–3650 🌐 www.brindillas.com ⏲ Closed Sun., Mon., and Jun.*

🛏 Hotels

★ Cavas Wine Lodge
$$$$ | HOTEL | Secluded adobe guesthouses have their own plunge pool, star-gazing roof terrace (with a fireplace), living room, and walk-in shower—a romantic setting that's made this one of the top honeymoon destinations in Mendoza. **Pros:** luxurious and private; wine tastings held in the private cellar every evening; surrounded by vineyards and wineries. **Cons:** advance reservations needed for most activities; far from other restaurants; expensive. *[$] Rooms from: US$750 ✉ Luján de Cuyo ✣ RN40 south, west on RN7, turn off onto Costa Flores just before Ruca Malen Winery. Follow signs for 2.2 km (1.4 miles) ☎ 261/456–1748 🌐 www.cavas-winelodge.com 🛏 17 cottages 🍴 Free Breakfast.*

Entre Cielos
$$$$ | HOTEL | Set in the middle of vineyards, this stunning resort has big, beautiful guest rooms with vibrant design, and suites come with private terraces looking out onto the pool, garden, and vineyards. **Pros:** the Swiss founders have impeccable taste; terrific spa; good sunset view. **Cons:** expensive; pool can get crowded; noise travels through hallways. *[$] Rooms from: US$610 ✉ Guardia Vieja 1998, Vistalba ☎ 261/498–3377 🌐 www.entrecielos.com 🛏 16 rooms 🍴 Free Breakfast.*

★ Finca Adalgisa
$$$$ | HOTEL | Behind tall terra-cotta walls hides one of the best-kept secrets in Chacras: a large, yet intimate estate with regal bedrooms and suites, almost 5 acres of well-kept century-old Malbec vines, a pool set in gardens, and a cozy winery restaurant reserved exclusively for guests to enjoy evening wine tastings and tapas. **Pros:** modern amenities; homemade wine and farm-to-table kitchen; close to everything in Chacras. **Cons:** closed in winter; 11 am check-out; some rooms are darker than others. *[$] Rooms from: US$355 ✉ Pueyrredon 2222, Chacras de Coria ☎ 261/496–0713 🌐 www.fincaadalgisa.com ⏲ Closed Jun.–Sept. 🍴 Free Breakfast.*

Lares de Chacras
$$ | HOTEL | This long-running boutique hotel in the heart of little Chacras de Coria has comfortable rooms with stone fireplaces, wood floors, and exposed beams that are at once handsome and homey. **Pros:** good value; pleasant, small-town location with wineries nearby; pool and garden on-site. **Cons:** slow restaurant service; bathrooms are a bit dark; some street noise. *[$] Rooms from: US$200 ✉ Larrea 1266, Chacras de Coria ☎ 261/496–1061 🌐 www.laresdechacras.com 🛏 10 rooms 🍴 Free Breakfast.*

★SB Winemaker's House and Spa Suites
$$$$ | **HOTEL** | Tucked away in the heart of Chacras de Coria, this luxurious lodge is the passion project of top winemaker Susana Balbo and her daughter Ana Lovaglio. **Pros:** great restaurant open all day; fantastic art collection; excellent wellness program. **Cons:** some noise from neighbors; lots of controls to manage the room's blinds. $ Rooms from: US$800 ⊠ Viamonte 5022, Chacras de Coria ☎ 261/417–1144 ⊕ www.susanabalbohotels.com.

 Activities

Parque de Agua
WATER SPORTS | FAMILY | Like its sister property, Termas Cacheuta, Parque de Agua takes advantage of the area's hot springs; this spot, though, is focused on family fun rather than adult-only activities. It's a popular water park for its naturally heated water (65–102°F), wave pool, and 270-meter (886-foot) canal through a tunnel and waterfall. In addition to an on-site restaurant, the park has covered eating areas with picnic tables, and you can grill your own *bife* on the many *parrillas* provided. ⊠ RP82, Km 38, 24 km (15 miles) west of Luján de Cuyo, Cacheuta ☎ 261/519–1676 ⊕ www.termascacheuta.com ⛉ Day pass 1,200 pesos.

★ Termas Cacheuta
WATER SPORTS | Locals have been soaking in the natural hot springs here for centuries; these days they're joined by day-tripping tourists, who come to enjoy both the thermal waters and an attractive spa. The latter features hot and cool indoor and outdoor pools, a steamy grotto sauna, a thermal mud bath, and high-powered showers. Day passes include a huge lunch buffet, with countless salads and all the cuts of a traditional Argentine asado. Dedicated spa-goers can spend the night in one of the 16 all-inclusive rooms at Hotel Termas Cacheuta; doubles from 30,000 pesos ($$$). ■TIP→ **Unlike the Parque de Agua next door, this is a child-free zone.** ⊠ RP82, Km 38, 24 km (15 miles) west of Luján de Cuyo, Cacheuta ☎ 261/490–153 ⊕ www.termascacheuta.com ⛉ From 1,200 pesos.

Uspallata

125 km (78 miles) west of Mendoza City.

At the crossroads of three important routes—Ruta Nacional 7 from Mendoza across the Andes, Ruta 57 from Mendoza via Villavicencio, and Ruta 39 from San Juan via Barreal—this small town lies in the Calingasta Valley between the foothills and the front range of the Andes. Although most people will use Uspallata only as a food- and gas-refill point, it's also a good base for memorable excursions into the mountains by 4X4 or on horseback. Metals have been forged at **Las Bóvedas,** the pointed adobe cupolas a few miles north of town, since pre-Columbian times. Weapons for San Martín's army were made here, and some of them were melted down to create the Cristo Redentor monument on the Chilean border; other big Andean attractions in the vicinity include Parque Provincial Aconcagua and Puenta del Inca.

GETTING HERE AND AROUND
From Mendoza City, head south on Avenida San Martín to the Ruta Nacional 7 and turn west. You can make this 125-km (78-mile) journey in two to three hours by bus or rental car; the easiest option, though, is to visit Uspallata and nearby attractions on a guided day trip from Gran Mendoza.

SAFETY
An adventurous way to explore the dramatic landscape around Uspallata is by driving yourself. There are things to keep in mind, though, if you want to have a safe, stress-free time. Always leave town with a full tank of gas, as there are few

Hikers traverse a low portion of the south face of Cerro Aconcagua.

services available, and traffic is minimal. Carry a flashlight if you leave late in the day, be mindful of weather conditions (the drive is not recommended in winter snowstorms), and always keep your lights on while driving.

Sights

Camino del Año

SCENIC DRIVE | From Mendoza traveling 47 km (29 miles) north on Ruta Provincial 52, passing through Canota, you arrive at Villavicencio, the source of mineral water sold throughout Argentina. The nearby Hosteria Villavicencio offers a simple lunch menu.

Farther up the road, the Camino del Año begins its ascent around 365 turns to El Balcón atop the pass at Cruz de Paramillo (3,000 meters/9,840 feet). Look for the ruins of a Jesuit mine, the Arucarias de Darwin (petrified trees found by Darwin in 1835), and the 1,000-year-old petroglyphs on Tunderqueral Hill. From the top

of the pass you can see three of the highest mountains outside of Asia, all over 6,000 meters (20,000 feet): Aconcagua to the west, Tupungato to the south, and Mercedario to the north.

At Km 67, the road straightens and descends into Uspallata, where you can continue west on Ruta Nacional 7 to Chile or take the lonely road north on Ruta 39 (which turns into Ruta 412) onward to Barreal in San Juan Province, 108 km (67 miles) away. The road to Barreal crosses a high desert valley, where the only sign of life is an occasional ranch obscured by a grove of alamo trees.

At Los Tambillos, about 40 km (25 miles) north of Uspallata, the route is intersected by the Inca road that ran from Cusco, Peru, through Bolivia and into northern Argentina. The site is surrounded by a fence that protects traces of the original road and remains of an Inca *tambo* (resting place). A map shows the route of the Incas.

The mountains to the west get higher and more spectacular as you approach Barreal. At the San Juan Province border, the road becomes Ruta 412, and is paved the remaining 50 km (31 miles) to Barreal. ⊠ *Uspallata, Uspallata.*

Cristo Redentor de los Andes

PUBLIC ART | A steep, bumpy ascent off of Ruta 7 leads to a stunning view of the Andes and a large statue of Christ that was erected to mark the end of the war between Chile and Argentina. Made from melted weaponry when peace was declared in 1902, it's poised right on the border at an altitude of 4,206 meters (13,800 feet). At the top there's a food truck serving coffee and local sweet bites. The gravel path is not for the faint-hearted, but can just about be done in a hired car; the drive up from the road takes half an hour. ■ TIP→ **Bring a jacket!** ⊠ *RN7, Puente del Inca.*

★ Parque Provincial Aconcagua

NATIONAL PARK | Extending 66,733 hectares (164,900 acres) over wild, high country, this provincial park has few trails other than those used by expeditions ascending the impressive Cerro Aconcagua (Aconcagua Mountain). You can get multiday permits for climbing it either through your tour operator or on your own at the Mendoza Tourist Board Visitor's Center in Parque San Martín; it's open weekdays 8–6 and weekends 9–1. Day permits (to visit as a tourist, not trekker) are only available online. ⊠ *San Martín Park Office, Las Tipas at Los Robles, Mendoza* ⊕ *www.entradasanp. mendoza.gov.ar* 🖅 *Day permits 2 pesos; trekking permits 110–280 pesos, depending on season, permit level, and number of hiking days.*

Puente del Inca

NATURE SIGHT | Spanning the Río Cuevas, Puente del Inca is a natural rock bridge that was formed over thousands of years. The abandoned hotel below is a more recent addition, built in the 1920s to accommodate guests who came to

soak in the therapeutic hot springs here. Both are now covered in bright yellow sulfur deposits, giving the surreal site an eerie appeal. An artisan market sells unusual souvenirs like healing stones and sulfur-coated bottles or shoes. ⊠ *RN7, 3 km (2 miles) east of Parque Provincial Aconcagua, Puente del Inca.*

Uspallata Pass on Ruta Nacional 7 (*Panamerican Highway*)

SCENIC DRIVE | This route heads west on R13 and then RN7 (also known as the Panamerican Highway) and takes you straight into the mountains. You'll go from vineyards to barren hills until you reach the Potrerillos Valley, then head farther west on R7 into the heart of the Andes. This was a major Inca route, so keep your eyes peeled for Inca tambos. You'll pass the Puente del Inca ancient thermal springs and the ruins of a spa from the 1920s. This is the only route between Chile and Argentina for miles and miles, so if you're self-driving, be ready to share the road with cargo trucks. ⊠ *Uspallata.*

Restaurants

La Juanita

$$ | **ARGENTINE** | **FAMILY** | This colorful spot is known for its large dishes of warming pasta, succulent local trout, and king-size milanesas. Decor is minimal but service is warm, and there are splendid mountain views. **Known for:** homemade pasta; empanadas; mountain views. $ *Average main: pesos 1400* ⊠ *Ruta 52 Uspallata, Uspallata* 🖀 *261/15–653–4699* ⊕ *www. lajuanitaresto.com* 🚫 *No credit cards.*

El Rancho

$ | **ARGENTINE** | This spit-and-sawdust-style eatery has monster-size steaks, irresistible BBQ smells, and cheap wine by the jug. If you've had a long day in the mountains and need a place to refuel, old-school El Rancho is open daily for lunch and dinner, it also serves coffee and snacks outside of mealtimes. **Known**

for: comfort food; reliable choice in the mountains; big portions. $ *Average main: pesos1000* ✉ *RN7, Km 1147, Uspallata* ☎ *2624/420–134.*

 Hotels

Hotel Uspallata
$ | **HOTEL** | In spite of the cavernous hallways, minimal decor, barren walls, and dim lighting (legacies of the Perón era, when the government built hotels for its employees), this grand old hotel offers comfortable refuge en route to Aconcagua, Chile, or Barreal in the opposite direction. **Pros:** big rooms; proximity to outdoor activities including skiing; pool and gardens. **Cons:** mediocre service; past its heyday; impersonal decor. $ *Rooms from: US$90* ✉ *RN7, Km 1149, Uspallata* ☎ *2624/420–003* ⊕ *www.granhoteluspallata.com.ar* ⤴ *74 rooms* ❍ *Free Breakfast.*

Hotel Valle Andino
$$ | **HOTEL** | Approaching Uspallata on Ruta Nacional 7, you'll see this wood-trimmed brick building with a pitched tile roof by the roadside. **Pros:** family-friendly; practical base; scenic vistas in all directions. **Cons:** facilities are spread out; basic services; rooms could use updating. $ *Rooms from: pesos3600* ✉ *RN7, Uspallata* ☎ *2624/420–095, 261/597–7858* ⤴ *25 rooms* ❍ *Free Breakfast.*

 Activities

HORSEBACK RIDING
El Rincón de los Oscuros
HORSEBACK RIDING | **FAMILY** | Gentle horses and experienced guides make riding at this ranch near Potrerillos a pleasure. Two-hour and full-day outings take you to high-altitude sites where condors and guanacos are often seen. ✉ *Av. Los Cóndores s/n, 50 km (30 miles) southeast of Upsallata, Potrerillos* ☎ *261/653–8839* ⊕ *www.rincondelososcuros.com.ar.*

HIKING AND MOUNTAINEERING
November through March is the best time for hiking and climbing. You can arrange day hikes with area tour operators. Of the longer treks, the most popular lasts four to seven days and begins at Puente del Inca (2,950 meters/9,680 feet), where you spend a night to get acclimated, and then set out for Aconcagua's base camp. On the first day, a steady climb takes you to Confluencia, where most people spend two nights and enjoy a day hike to the south wall and its incredible glacier. The hike continues to the Plaza de Mulas (4,260 meters/13,976 feet) and ends at the base camp for climbers making a final ascent on Cerro Aconcagua.

Fernando Grajales Expeditions
HIKING & WALKING | Guiding since 1976, Fernando Grajales is a veteran of many Aconcagua ascents. His company leads 18-day excursions to the summit in season. ✉ *Los Penitentes, Mendoza* ☎ *261/658–8855* ⊕ *www.grajales.net.*

Inka Expeditions
HIKING & WALKING | This outfit has more than 20 years' experience leading tours both to the base camp and to Aconcagua's summit. Other treks in the area can also be organized. ✉ *Juan B Justo 345, Mendoza* ☎ *261/4250–871* ⊕ *www.inka.com.ar.*

SKIING
Los Puquios
SKIING & SNOWBOARDING | **FAMILY** | Each winter, Los Puquios opens its slopes for family snow activities including skiing, sledding, and tubing. There's a host of evening activities in peak winter when flood lights, bonfires, and live music bring more action to the slopes. ✉ *Ruta 7, Puente del Inca, Puente del Inca* ☎ *261/588–7830* ⊕ *www.puquios.com.*

Continued on page 286

Wines *of* Chile & Argentina

The wine regions of both Chile and Argentina are set against the backdrop of the Andes. And while these mountains do play an important role in the making of wine in both countries, Chile and Argentina have very different traditions and strengths.

Although wine-loving Spaniards settled both countries in the 16th century, only Chile's wine industry developed quickly, largely because the land around Santiago was particularly good for growing grapes. Buenos Aires, on the warm and humid Atlantic coast, however, was hardly an ideal place for viticulture. Mendoza, Argentina's present-day wine wonderland, was impossibly far away to be a reliable supplier of wine to the capital until the railroad united it with the coast in the mid-19th century.

Chile also experienced a boom in the 19th century as new, French-inspired wineries sprang up. Both countries continued without significant change for more than 100 years, until the 1990s international wine boom sparked new interest in South American wines. Big investments from France, Spain, Italy, the United States, and elsewhere—plus some extraordinary winemakers—have made this an exciting place for oenophiles to visit.

(left) Bottle of Maradona red wine;
(above) Mendoza, Argentina

NEIGHBORS ACROSS THE ANDES

CHILE

In the early days, the emphasis was on growing cheap wine to consume domestically. Then, in the middle of the 20th century, Chile's political turmoil caused the business to stagnate. It wasn't until the 1980s that wine exports became a major business, and today Chile exports more than it imports.

Chile's appellation system names its valleys from north to south, but today's winegrowers stress that the climatic and geological differences between east and west are more significant. The easternmost valleys closest to the Andes tend to have less fog, more hours of sunlight, and greater daily temperature variations, which help red grapes develop deep color and rich tannins while maintaining bright acidity and fresh fruit characteristics. On the other hand, if you're after crisp whites and bright Pinots, head to the coast, where cool fog creeps inland from the sea each morning and Pacific breezes keep the vines cool all day.

Elqui valley, Chile

Interior areas in the Central Valley are less prone to extremes and favor varieties that require more balanced conditions, such as Merlot, and Chile's own rich and spicy Carmenère. Syrah, a relatively new grape in Chile, does well in both cold and warm climates.

Colchagua Valley, Chile

BE SURE TO TASTE:

Sauvignon Blanc: Cool-climate vineyards from Elqui to Bío Bío are producing very exciting Sauvignon with fresh green fruit, crisp acidity, and often an enticing mineral edge.

Carmenère: Chile's signature grape arrived in Chile during the mid-19th century from France, where it was usually a blending grape in Bordeaux. Over time Chileans forgot about it, mistaking it for Merlot, but during the Chilean boom times of the 1990s they realized that they had a very unique grape hidden among the other vines in their vineyards.

Harvesting Grapes in Chile

Cabernet Sauvignon: The king of reds grows well almost anywhere it's planted, but Cabernets from the Alto Maipo are particularly well balanced, displaying elegance and structure.

Syrah: Chile produces two distinct styles of this grape. Be sure to try both: luscious and juicy from Colchagua or enticingly spicy from coastal areas, such as Elqui or San Antonio.

Malbec: True, this is Argentina's grape, but Chile produces award-winning bottlings that have appealing elegance and balance.

Syrah vineyards, Chile

ARGENTINA

Unlike Chile, Argentina exports far less wine than it consumes, and much of its wine is produced in accordance with local tastes and wallets. The 1990s wine boom sparked a greater emphasis on export, and following new investments, the country is now widely recognized for the quality of its red wines, particularly its signature Malbec.

Monteviejo Winery, Clos de los Siete, Mendoza

Broad-shouldered Argentina looks west to the Andes for a life-giving force. Its wine regions receive no cooling maritime influence, as Chile's do, and its vineyards rely on the mountain altitudes not only to irrigate its lands, but also to attenuate the effects of the blazing sun. The climate here is capricious, so producers must be ever-prepared for untimely downpours, devastating hailstorms, and scorching, dehydrating Zonda winds.

Estancia San Pablo Tupungato

BE SURE TO TASTE:

Malbec: Just one sip of Argentina's most widely known wine evokes gauchos and tangos. Deep, dark, and handsomely concentrated, this is a must-try on its home turf.

Cabernet Sauvignon: Argentine Cabs are big, bold, and brawny, as is typical of warmer climates. They're perfect with one of those legendary Argentine grilled steaks.

Red Blends: The red blends here may be mixtures of classic Bordeaux varietals with decidedly Argentine results, or audacious combinations that are only possible in the New World.

Torrontés: Argentina's favorite white has floral overtones, grown most often in Cafayate, in the northwestern province of Salta.

Colome Winery, Molinos, Salta

TASTING TIPS ON BOTH SIDES OF THE BORDER

1. Make reservations! Unlike wineries in the U.S., most wineries are not equipped to receive drop-in visitors.

2. Don't expect wineries to be open on Sunday. Winery workers need a day off too.

3. The distances between wineries can be much longer than they look on the map. Be sure to allot plenty of travel time, and plan on no more than three or four wineries per day.

4. Do contact the wine route offices in the region you're visiting. They can be extremely helpful in coordinating visits to wineries and other local attractions.

5. Hire a driver, or choose a designated driver.

6. Know what you are walking into. Some wineries offer free tours and tastings, others can charge upwards of 150 pesos per person.

GREAT WINE ITINERARIES

Chile and Argentina are wine paradises in terms of the climate they usually enjoy. On the Argentine side, Mendoza is blessed with over 330 days of sunshine, a dry climate, and a low risk of mold or disease. On the other side of the Andes, Chile enjoys great light and air purity, and a cooling Humboldt current. Its natural fortunes are balanced with natural disasters, though. Chile has been ravaged by some of the world's worst earthquakes; the devastating 2010 quake and tsunami wiped out more than 130 million liters of wine. The greatest frustration for winemakers in Mendoza is the infamous zonda (a burning and dusty foehn wind that burns grapes and tears vines down) and occasional hail storms. Even paradise has its share of difficulties!

Crossing the Andes will be one of the highlights of your trip, especially the series of switchbacks that wind into the mountains just before the border crossing.

Haras de Pirque. Horses are the owners' first love. You'll pass the breeding farm and the race track on the way to this horseshoe-shaped winery tucked up into the Andean hills.

COLCHAGUA ITINERARY

If it's Saturday, book a ride on the Wine Train, which travels from San Fernando to the heart of the Colchagua Valley in Santa Cruz.

Viña Bisquertt. This family-run winery houses several 15-foot-tall wooden casks from the 1940s.

Lapostolle. Viña Casa Lapostolle built this gravity-flow wonder exclusively for their red blend, Clos Apalta.

Viña Santa Cruz. More than just a winery, this is an entire wine complex. Take the cable car to the "indigenous village."

ALTO MAIPO ITINERARY

Plenty of wineries are a day trip from Santiago. You can go solo and hire a taxi ($70 for a half day), but for around US$160 (full day) a guide provides better access.

Concha y Toro. Start the day at one of Chile's oldest and best known wineries, located just outside of the capital in Pirque.

Antiyal. One of Chile's first boutique-garage wineries, Antiyal only makes two red blends, both of which are organic and biodynamic.

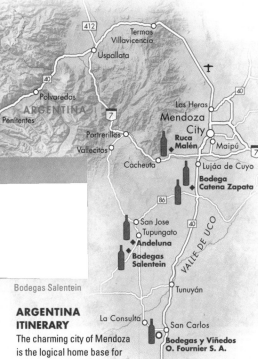

Bodegas Salentein

ARGENTINA ITINERARY

The charming city of Mendoza is the logical home base for exploring Argentine wine country, and the country's finest wineries surround the city.

Ruca Malén. The fame of Ruca Malen's award-winning restaurant has overtaken that of the winery. However, no great meal in Mendoza works without good wines, so it's best to walk off the five-course lunch here with a tour afterward.

Pulenta Estate. Owned by the renowned Pulenta wine dynasty, this modern winery makes a fabulous Cabernet Franc and has a great boutique feel to it. Tours can include a sensory aroma game.

Bodega Catena Zapata. Rising like a Mayan temple from the fertile soil, this winery produces some of Argentina's most memorable blended wines.

Familia Zuccardi, Mendoza

Harvest time at Andeluna

WINERY-ARCHITECTURE ITINERARY

Fans of spectacular architecture will enjoy visiting Argentina's wineries. Big, modern, sometimes whimsical, and often surprising, many of these enormous high-tech facilities have restaurants and even lodgings to make the long distances between them bearable. Plan for a long day in the beautiful Valle de Uco visiting some striking examples.

Salentein. A perfect example of the "winery-plus" experience in South American wine tourism, this property is a work of art set against a natural backdrop of the Andes, complete with an art gallery, restaurant, chapel, and award-winning wines.

Andeluna. With a stellar view of Tupungato and the Cordon del Plata, this stellar winery draws your eyes to the mountains and your nose to the open-plan kitchen serving great food to pair with their full-bodied wines.

O. Fournier. End your day at this highly unusual building that looks, from a distance, like a city of Oz for the new millennium. An enormous, flat roof seems to hover over the building, and the large U-shaped ramp accommodates gravity-flow winemaking.

CROSSING THE ANDES

Vineyard in Mendoza, Argentina.

■ If you're coming all the way to South America to taste wine, be sure to visit both sides of the Andes. There are frequent hour-long jet flights between Santiago and Mendoza for US$200–$300 that provide a spectacular condor's-eye view of the craggily snow-covered peaks below.

■ If you are visiting in the summer months and have time for the day-long 250 km (155 miles) overland route, by all means take it. Know that you will most likely have to get a roundtrip car rental. Most companies will not allow one-way international crossings. Better to rent a car in Santiago or Mendoza to see the wineries in each country, then fly or catch a bus to cross the border. On the Argentina side, a flight from Buenos Aires to Mendoza can save time.

■ Roads are well-maintained and reasonably marked. Take Ruta 57 north from Santiago to the small city of Los Andes, then head east on Ruta 60 toward the mountains and the Argentine border, where the highway's name changes to Ruta 7, to Mendoza.

■ Crossing the Andes will be one of the highlights of your trip, especially the series of switchbacks that wind into the mountains just before the border crossing some 8,200 feet above sea level. Be aware that the Libertadores Pass is often closed for days at a time during the winter months, so don't risk it unless you're willing to spend several days sleeping in your car while you wait for things to clear up. Be sure to bring a jacket any time of year, as it can be very chilly at that altitude.

■ Plan a couple of stops along the way; make the Portillo Ski Resort your last stop on the Chilean side, where you can visit the Laguna del Inca at nearly 10,000 feet. The ski resort is a great place to stop for lunch. On the Argentine side, stop for gas and a bite to eat in Upsallata, about 100 km (65 miles) before reaching Mendoza.

WINE-TASTING PRIMER

Ordering and tasting wine—whether at a winery, bar, or restaurant—is easy once you master a few simple steps.

LOOK AND NOTE

Hold your glass by the stem and look at the wine in the glass. Note its color, depth, and clarity.

For whites, is it greenish, yellow, or gold? For reds, is it purplish, ruby, or garnet? Is the wine's color pale or deep? Is the liquid clear or cloudy?

SWIRL AND SNIFF

Swirl the wine gently in the glass to intensify the scents, then sniff over the rim of the glass. What do you smell? Try to identify aromas like:

Are there any unpleasant notes, like mildew or wet dog that might indicate that the wine is "off?"

- **Fruits**—citrus, peaches, berries, figs, melon

- **Flowers**—orange blossoms, honey, perfume

- **Spices**—baking spices, pungent, herbal notes

- **Vegetables**—fresh or cooked, herbal notes

- **Minerals**—earth, steely notes, wet stones

- **Dairy**—butter, cream, cheese, yogurt

- **Oak**—toast, vanilla, coconut, tobacco

- **Animal**—leathery, meaty notes

SIP AND SAVOR

Prime your palate with a sip, swishing the wine in your mouth. Then spit in a bucket or swallow.

Take another sip and think about the wine's attributes. Sweetness is detected on the tip of the tongue, acidity on the sides of the tongue, and tannins (a mouth-drying sensation) on the gums. Consider the body—does the wine feel light in the mouth, or is there a rich sensation? Are the flavors consistent with the aromas? If you like the wine, try to pinpoint what you like about it, and vice versa if you don't like it.

Take time to savor the wine as you're sipping it—the tasting experience may seem a bit scientific, but the end goal is your enjoyment.

Tupungato

78 km (48 miles) south of Mendoza.

Tupungato is a sleepy agricultural town most of the year. During harvest (February and March), though, the roads in and around it overflow with carts and tractors loaded with grapes from many surrounding vineyards. The population rises by half from its official number of 52,000 as pickers arrive.

GETTING HERE AND AROUND

The most direct route from Mendoza to the Valle de Uco is south on Ruta Nacional 40 for 37 km (23 miles) to Ugarteche, where you turn west onto Ruta 86 for another 37 km (23 miles), passing through the village of San José just before arriving in Tupungato. Although buses arrive several times a day from Mendoza, the best way to get around the area is to join a tour or rent a car. If you're driving north, turn off Ruta Nacional 40 onto Ruta Provincial 88 at Zapata.

If you have some time and aren't put off by driving on a dirt road, a scenic way here is south on Ruta Nacional 40 from Mendoza and west on Ruta Nacional 7 to the dam at Potrerillos; exiting at the dam, take the unpaved Ruta Provincial 89 south through the villages of Las Vegas and El Salto, where clusters of vacation cottages brim with flowers in summer and are covered with snow in winter. The road climbs steeply out of the canyon and over a pass, then crosses a high valley with a magnificent view of the Andes. Soon the great expanse of the Valle de Uco lies before you, with its miles of vineyards and orchards of peaches, almonds, and chestnuts, adding wide swaths of pink and white blossoms in spring (late September–October). This drive is equally impressive in reverse.

ESSENTIALS

VISITOR INFORMATION Oficina de Turismo de Tupungato. ⊠ *Av. Belgrano 348, Tupungato* ☎ *2622/520–788* ⊕ *www.tupungato. gov.ar.*

Sights

Andeluna

WINERY | Surrounded by miles of vineyards, with the majestic Andes as a backdrop, this red-brick bodega blends beautifully into the scenery. Inside, the large reception and tasting room—with leather furnishings and high ceiling of reeds and open beams—evokes an old Mendocino mansion. The open kitchen at one end serves two- and six-course tasting menus; you can also participate in a cooking class with two days' notice. ⊠ *R89, Km 11, Tupungato* ☎ *261/508–9525* ⊕ *www. andeluna.com.ar* ☉ *Closed Sun.*

★ Bodega Atamisque

WINERY | The gray adobe building with its uneven slate roof almost disappears against the background of bushes and mountains. This enormous estancia property (whose boundaries date back to 1658, when the Jesuits owned it) is owned by a French family who named it after a native tree. In addition to the winery, where you can undertake three tastings, Atamisque includes a trout farm, a 9-hole golf course, a restaurant, and lodge. ⊠ *RP86, Km 30, Tupungato* ☎ *261/518–1786* ⊕ *www.atamisque.com* ☉ *Closed Mon.*

Bodega Salentein

WINERY | On a knoll with an Andean backdrop, this ultramodern winery has breathtaking architecture that draws the eye to cavernous winery halls and into the circular barrel room where a grand piano sits center stage. This complex also contains Galería Killka art museum featuring Argentine and Dutch artists' works, a wine bar, a sculpture garden, a pretty chapel, and a restaurant serving four-course tasting menus, making it easy to spend a leisurely afternoon here. ✉ R89 at Elias Videla, Los Árboles, 15 km (9 miles) south of Tupungato, Tupungato ☎ 2622/429–500 ⊕ www.bodega-salentein.com.

Sitio La Estocada

WINERY | This organic and biodynamic vineyard and winery is a new and hip addition to this elevated corner of Tupungato, given that the winemaker in charge is one of Argentina's best, Matías Michelini of Passionate Wine. The family leads the bodega's exclusive, twice-monthly, full-moon and new-moon communal dinners that focus on local ingredients paired with his wines. ✉ Av. Correa 1221, Tupungato ☎ 2615/937–876 ⊕ www.instagram.com/sitiolaestocada ⌕ Reservations essential.

🍽 Restaurants

If you are in Tupungato, you really ought to be eating at the local wineries for lunch. Andeluna, La Azul, Domaine Bousquet, Sitio La Estocada, and Atamisque are top options in the Tupungato Wine Region.

★ La Azul

$$$ | ARGENTINE | While this family-run winery also cultivates peaches, plums, cherries, and apples, La Azul's boho restaurant is a go-to in this corner of Uco Valley, and especially busy on weekends. Sink into a cozy armchair or pitch up under the trellis vines to enjoy tasty empanadas, stews, and barbecue prepared and served by local chefs with lovely views of the Andes. **Known for:** views of the Andes; traditional Argentine staples; locally grown fruits. $ Average main: pesos1700 ✉ R89, Tupungato ☎ 2622/603–443 ⊕ www.bodegalaazul.com ⊗ Closed Mon.

Restaurante Valle de Tupungato

$$$ | ARGENTINE | Traditional grilled meats, homemade pastas, and appetizers featuring locally made cold cuts comprise the hearty fare at this friendly family-style

restaurant. On Sunday, you can help yourself to steak, lamb, chicken, and goat at the open grill. **Known for:** weekend buffet; good value; family-sized portions. $ Average main: pesos1600 ✉ Belgrano 540, Tupungato ☎ 2622/304–165 ⊟ No credit cards ⊗ No dinner Sun.–Fri.

★ Tupungato Divino

$$$ | ARGENTINE | Overlooking Tupungato volcano and the family vineyards, this small restaurant is the perfect spot for a lazy lunch in wine country. The colorful tasting menu is served with flair, from the assortment of starters to the juicy steak and hearty pasta dishes, and the final tasting platter of puddings. **Known for:** excellent Valle de Uco cellar; great valley views; sampler of starters and desserts. $ Average main: pesos1500 ✉ Los Europeos, Ruta 89, Tupungato ☎ 2622/15–448–948 ⊕ www.tupungato-divino.com.ar.

Hotels

Posada Salentein

$$$$ | B&B/INN | Tucked into the foothills behind Bodega Salentein, this posada is delightfully off the beaten track, and you can choose between modern en suite rooms or one of the homey 100-year-old cottages, all of which look onto the vineyards, large lawn, and swimming pool. **Pros:** peaceful vineyard setting; best value in the Valle de Uco; intimate, exclusive restaurant. **Cons:** pool isn't heated; horse-riding costs extra; far from it all. $ Rooms from: US$330 ✉ RN89 at Elias Videla, Los Árboles, 15 km (9 miles) south of Tupungato, Tupungato ☎ 2622/429–500 ⊕ www.bodegasalentein.com ⇨ 16 rooms (8 in cottages) ⊙ Free Breakfast.

Rural Guesthouses

$$$$ | B&B/INN | Rural guesthouses make for relaxing and unique stays in Mendoza, and several are located within elevated vineyard and farm estates. $ Rooms from: US$450 ✉ La Carrera, Tupungato.

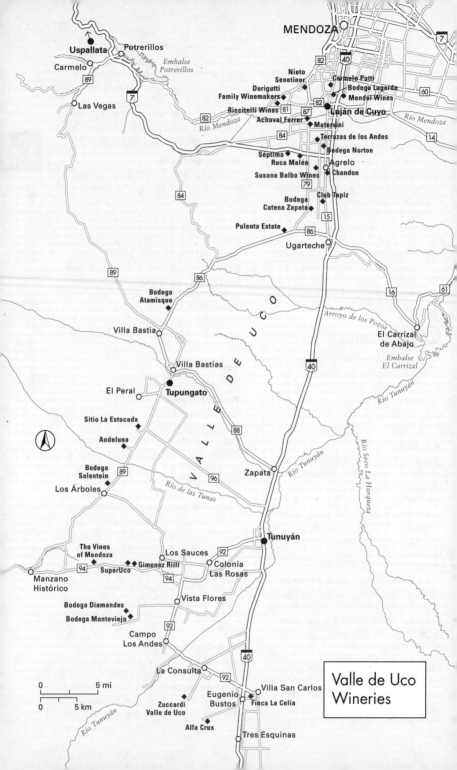

Valle de Uco
Wineries

Tupungato Divino

$$ | B&B/INN | This popular posada in the heart of Uco wine country has rustic chalets with sweeping views of the Andes, offering top value lodging near Tupungato's wineries; each is equipped with a woodstove for the winter, plus a private patio looking out onto the property's own biodynamic vineyards. **Pros:** gorgeous mountain views; quality restaurant; good value. **Cons:** own transport required; in-room decor lacking; the pool isn't very private when the restaurant fills up at lunchtime. $ *Rooms from: US$160* ✉ *RP89 and Calle Los Europeos s/n, Tupungato* ☎ *2622/1544–8948* ⊕ *www. tupungatodivino.com.ar* ▭ *No credit cards* ⇨ *4 rooms* ❧ *Free Breakfast.*

Shopping

KDS Hecho a Mano

HOUSEWARES | Five members of the da Silva family have been designing and selling handmade knives and leather cases at KDS Hecho a Mano since the 1970s. You can watch the process and choose the right knife for your next *asado* from many designs in their showroom. ✉ *Ruta 92, Km 5, Tupungato* ☎ *2622/488–852* ⊕ *www.kdscuchillos.com.ar.*

Activities

HORSEBACK RIDING

You can ride in the foothills of the Andes for a day or conquer the Andes on a six-day crossing to Chile that takes you through a treeless landscape of rocky trails, roaring rivers, tiny green meadows, and lofty peaks. Argentine horses aren't allowed in Chile, so you'll have to either change horses at the border or return.

Estancia El Puesto

HORSEBACK RIDING | This five-bedroom ranch offers accommodations, meals, and assorted excursions—most notably horseback riding. The owner, Raúl Labat, has made more than 30 crossings to Chile and still finds each trip rewarding.

He leads riders there on six-day journeys each summer. ✉ *Los Árboles, off R89, Tupungato* ☎ *261/610–5876* ⊕ *www. estanciaelpuesto.com.ar* ✈ *From 6,000 pesos* ⇨ *Reservations essential.*

★ La Quebrada del Cóndor

HORSEBACK RIDING | While horseback expeditions up and over Condor Valley in the are the main attraction here, trekkers can also enjoy the hike past a cattle ranch, across streams and up in the Andean foothills. Refuel with the excellent asado lunch. ✉ *RN 89, La Carrera, Tupungato* ☎ *2622/666–708* ⊕ *www.facebook.com/ laquebradadelcondor.*

Parque Provincial Volcán Tupungato

HIKING & WALKING | Tupungato Volcano rises 6,800 meters (22,310 feet) in snowbound splendor, looming above the high peaks that march along the border between Chile and Mendoza Province. The park that's named for it covers 110,000 hectares (272,000 acres) in the western portion of the departments of Luján de Cuyo, Tupungato, and Tunuyán. There are no roads into the park, but local tour companies lead horseback rides and hikes into the area. Some offer six-day horseback rides to the Chilean border. Mules can be hired to climb to South Glacier at 2,000 meters (6,562 feet). ✉ *Tupungato* ⊕ *www.mendoza.gov.ar/areasnaturales/ parque-provincial-tupungato.*

Tunuyán

81 km (50 miles) south of Mendoza.

Twice the size of Tupungato, Tunuyán makes a good base for touring the Valle de Uco wineries. Downtown consists of two traffic circles on either side of two blocks, where most of the shops are geared to local agricultural pursuits. Along with grape cultivation, said pursuits include growing cherries, pears, and apples and making apple cider.

GETTING HERE AND AROUND

There's bus service here from Mendoza, but you'll have a hard time getting around without a car unless you're on a tour. From Mendoza City, you can take Ruta Nacional 40 directly to Tunuyán. Wineries are spread out toward the west (in the direction of the Andes) and Ruta 94 and 92 are where you'll find access to the majority. In Vista Flores, you'll find Clos de los Siete (a complex of wineries owned by well-known Bordeaux wine families) and the Winemakers Village at The Vines (a handful of boutique wineries and passion projects owned by some of Argentina's best-known winemakers).

ESSENTIALS

TOURIST INFORMATION Oficina de Turísmo. ⊠ *San Martín, Dalmau, Tunuyán* ☎ *2622/422–193* ⊕ *www.tunuyan.gov.ar.*

Sights

Alfa Crux

WINERY | Approaching this ultramodern winery on a lonely dirt road, you could be forgiven for thinking you'd discovered a flying saucer instead. But, as your tour guide will tell you, every part of the futuristic building has a function—whether it's to make the best use of gravity or to direct the sometimes brutal winds that whip through. The wines come from the local estate, which sits at an altitude of 1,200 meters (3,940 feet), which you enjoy at Crux Cocina restaurant. ⊠ *Calle Los Indios s/n, La Consulta* ☎ *2622/303–2822* ⊕ *www.agostinowinegroup.com/vinos-alfa-crux.*

Bodega Diamandes

WINERY | The newest winery in the Clos de los Siete complex, Diamandes has some of the most striking architecture in the valley with a steel diamond in the center of the showpiece winery. Most visits focus on the four-course pairing menu from which you'll taste the Bordeaux-inspired wine portfolio with local cuisine. ⊠ *Clodomiro Silva, Tunuyán*

☎ *261/657–5472* ⊕ *www.diamandes.com* ⚲ *Reservations essential.*

Bodega Monteviejo

WINERY | The first winery to be constructed in the Clos de los Siete complex in Vista Flores, Bodega Monteviejo is not only an icon in the local wine scene, but also in the cultural scene, boasting rotating art exhibitions, regular concerts, and Mendoza's top rock festival each April. A visit to this winery includes an informative tasting, a tour of the wine-making facilities, and a walk up to the stunning rooftop with jaw-dropping views over the valley. There is a great restaurant on site, too. ⊠ *Clodomiro Silva s/n, Vistaflores* ☎ *261/532–8126* ⊕ *www.monteviejo.com.ar.*

Finca La Celia

WINERY | Built by Eugenio Bustos in 1890, this winery flourished under his daughter Celia's leadership, producing an excellent Malbec. Today it's owned by a Chilean company that has invested in the latest technology. Tastings, traditional lunches, and tours of the winery and experimental garden are available with advance booking. In season, pruning and harvesting programs are offered in the vineyard as well. ■TIP➔ **There is a rustic posada on-site for anyone interested in spending the night.** ⊠ *Circunvalación Celia Bustos de Quiroga 374, San Carlos* ☎ *2622/451–193* ⊕ *www.lacelia.com.ar.*

Gimenez Riili

WINERY | FAMILY | Federico Gimenez-Riili or his father are often available to show you around this family-owned boutique operation and offer you a taste of their wines straight from the barrel. If you want to stay for lunch, enjoy the paired tasting menu accompanied by fantastic Andean vistas. There's also a seven-room guesthouse for overnight stays. ⊠ *Ruta 94, Vistaflores* ☎ *261/498–7863* ⊕ *www.gimenezriili.com.*

SuperUco

WINERY | Off-beat and contemporary describes not only the wine style of the Michelini brothers, but also SuperUco, their boutique winery in The Vines' renowned Winemakers Village. In between the biodynamic vines, the winery rises up like a cement crown. Enjoy a pour of the family's different wine labels that range from steely Sauvignon Blanc and juicy Bonarda to skin-contact wines and hand-riddled sparkling wine; alternatively book in for a paired lunch. ■ TIP→ **Reserve ahead for a BBQ lunch.** ✉ *Ruta 94 Km 11, Los Chacayes, Tunuyán* 🌐 *www.superuco.com.*

The Vines of Mendoza

WINERY | Making hundreds of small labels for different private estate owners, The Vines of Mendoza offers an educative tasting in Tunuyán where you'll learn about the art of blending and working in microlots. ✉ *Ruta 94, Tunuyán* ☎ *261/461–3900* 🌐 *www.vinesofmendoza.com.*

★ Zuccardi Valle de Uco

WINERY | This showstopping winery was built by the Zuccardi family to celebrate their newfound passion for the Valle de Uco, following the success of their other family winery in Maipú. In the heart of Paraje Altamira, this winery's impressive architecture is made of local natural materials that reflect the wild, rocky landscape while incorporating artistic touches, such as a colorful cupola and twisted metalwork door. The efforts have paid off; it's thrice been crowned the world's best vineyard. You can tour the estate, taste the family's top wines in the wine bar, or have a paired lunch at the excellent Piedra Infinita restaurant ($$$$). ✉ *Calle Costa Canal Uco, La Consulta* ☎ *261/441–0090* 🌐 *www.zuccardiwines.com* 🕑 *Closed Mon.*

🍴 Restaurants

★ Cundo Cocina

$$$$ | **ARGENTINE** | Warm up with a tasting of Uco region wines at Cundo's cellar door before taking your seat at the table. Adhering to local terroir philosophy, chef Seba Juez prepares three- and six-course paired tasting menus using only regionally sourced ingredients in his al fresco kitchen (even in winter), which sits neatly in front of Malbec vines. **Known for:** paired tasting menus; vineyard and mountain views; knowledgeable staff. [$] *Average main: pesos3900* ✉ *Ghilardi Km 3, La Consulta, La Consulta* ☎ *261/707–3214* 🌐 *www.cundoaltamira.com.ar* 🕑 *Closed Mon.–Wed. No dinner* ☞ *Tasting menu only.*

La Juntada Pulpería

$$ | **BARBECUE** | **FAMILY** | Serving a buffet of salads and starters followed by a main course straight from the grill, La Juntada updates the classic *pulperia* (tavern) atmosphere with a good wine list and a fresh lick of paint. Expect typical Argentine fare such as grilled goat kid that's well prepared. **Known for:** BBQ aromas; traditional folk music; big buffet. [$] *Average main: pesos1300* ✉ *R92, Vista Flores, Tunuyán* ☎ *262/266–6355* 🌐 *www.lajuntadapulperia.negocio.site* 🕑 *Closed Mon.–Wed.*

Posada del Jamón

$$ | **ARGENTINE** | This casual, family-run restaurant has been a staple in the valley for 30 years, serving up pork cooked in every way imaginable. There are also a surprising number of vegetarian options available, and all of the wines offered are from the neighborhood wineries. **Known for:** roadside dining; friendly welcome; ham, ham, and more ham. [$] *Average main: pesos1400* ✉ *Ruta 92, Km 13, Tunuyán* ☎ *2622/545–314* 🌐 *www.laposadadeljamon.com.ar* 🕑 *No dinner.*

Hotels

Casa de Uco
$$$$ | **HOTEL** | You can tell the owner of this luxury hotel is an architect as soon as you enter: majestic views of vineyards and mountains are expertly placed through a series of shapely windows, skylights, and sloping walls, and there's a handsome infinity pool that drops off into the vineyards below. **Pros:** stunning Valle de Uco location; great on-site restaurant; relaxing spa and pool. **Cons:** bar stocks run low; lakeside rooms have less impressive views; extras add up. [$] *Rooms from: US$675* ✉ *Ruta 94, Km 14.5, Tunuyán* ☎ *261/476–9831* 🌐 *www.casadeuco.com* 🛏 *18 rooms* 🍴 *Free Breakfast.*

La Morada de los Andes
$$$ | **B&B/INN** | This lovely vineyard guesthouse offers plenty of peace and quiet thanks to its rural location in a Los Chacayes estate. **Pros:** attentive service; great and filling breakfast; quiet and ideal for relaxing. **Cons:** rural location far from sights; need a car to get around; not all meals included. [$] *Rooms from: US$209* ✉ *Calle La Siesta, Los Chacayes, Tunuyán* ☎ *261/330–6000* 🌐 *lamoradahouse.com* 🍴 *Free Breakfast.*

Postales
$$ | **B&B/INN** | Tucked away on a quiet country road, this casona-style wine lodge has simple, but comfortable rooms that each look out onto old vines, distant mountains, and the peaceful garden and pool area. **Pros:** quiet, countryside setting; nice restaurant option; nearby wineries. **Cons:** poor Wi-Fi; pool can get crowded; little to do without a car. [$] *Rooms from: US$175* ✉ *Calle Ezequiel Tabanera, Colonia Las Rosas, Tunuyán* ☎ *2622/490–024* 🌐 *www.postalesarg.com* 🛏 *9 rooms* 🍴 *Free Breakfast.*

The Vines Resort & Spa
$$$$ | **RESORT** | Stunning sunsets, luxury villas, and seven-course flame-grilled dinners are the norm at The Vines Resort & Spa, which has a superb on-site restaurant, pool, gym, and boutique winery. **Pros:** great restaurant and bar; luxury offerings in the remote Valle de Uco; beautiful location. **Cons:** limited spa (only a pool); hit and miss service; expensive. [$] *Rooms from: pesos19500* ✉ *Ruta 94, Tunuyán* ☎ *261/461–3900* 🌐 *www.vinesresortandspa.com* 🛏 *21 rooms* 🍴 *Free Breakfast.*

San Rafael

240 km (150 miles) south of Mendoza.

San Rafael (population 130,000) is the second largest city in Mendoza. Wide avenues lined with leafy sycamores and tall poplars fed by streetside canals give it a bucolic charm, but the bodegas are reason enough for many visitors to make the trip. Wine-making took off here in the late 19th century when immigrants from Italy, Switzerland, and France came with advanced viticulture skills and new grape varieties. When the railroad arrived in 1903, the fledgling industry was connected to Buenos Aires and the rest of the world. Today the city has about 100 wineries. Although most are small, family-owned operations, a number do have tourist-friendly facilities within walking or cycling distance of the center. If you're looking for more active alternatives, local tour operators can arrange rafting, riding, and hiking excursions in the surrounding mountains and lakes. About 75 km (47 miles) west of San Rafael, the Cañón del Atuel (aka the "other" Grand Canyon) can also be explored.

GETTING HERE AND AROUND

A daily flight makes the 90-minute trip from Buenos Aires to San Rafael's airport, located about 15 minutes west of downtown on Ruta 150, but if you want to arrive by air from Mendoza, you'll (frustratingly) have to fly via Buenos Aires. By road, take Ruta Nacional 40 south from Mendoza to Pareditas, where you pick up

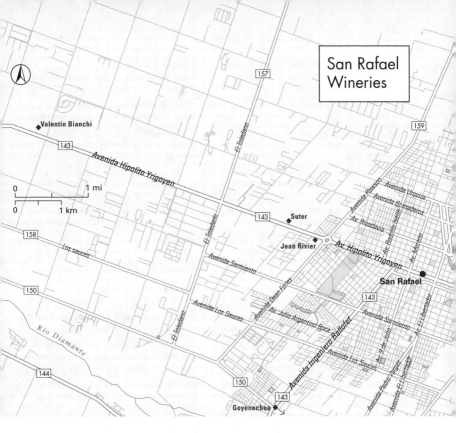

Ruta Nacional 143 to San Rafael. Coming on a bus (overnight from Buenos Aires) is another option, as it's less expensive than flying.

San Rafael is flat and laid out on a grid, which makes it easy to tour on foot. At Km 0, Avenida Yrigoyen crosses the downtown area (north–south) and becomes Bartolomé Mitre. At this same intersection (east–west), Avenida El Libertador becomes San Martín—the main shopping street. Hotels are scattered on the edge of residential areas, but you can still walk (or take a short cab ride) to downtown.

■TIP→ Beware of the acéquias—canals between the sidewalks and streets. At night people riding bicycles with no lights or reflectors on narrow dirt roads can also be a hazard.

San Rafael's wineries are mainly within cycling distance (or a taxi ride) of the city center; if you're driving, use a GPS because note road signs can be scarce in the region. Before heading for the wineries, make an appointment as owners are often busy in the vineyard, working in the bodega, testing wine with the oenologist, or tending to customers.

BUS CONTACTS Andesmar. ✉ San Rafael ☎ 2627/427–720 ⊕ www.andesmar.com. Iselin. ☎ 260/444–6463 ⊕ www.iselin. com.ar. Terminal de Ómnibus. ✉ General Paz 980, San Rafael ☎ 260/444–5495.

ESSENTIALS

MEDICAL ASSISTANCE Farmacia 16 Horas. ✉ Libertador 206, San Rafael ☎ 260/443–0214. Hospital Schestakow. ✉ Cte. Torres 150, San Rafael ☎ 260/442–4290.

VISITOR AND TOUR INFORMATION San Rafael Tourist Board. ✉ *Av. H. Yrigoyen 1530, San Rafael* ☎ *260/442–4217* ⊕ *www.sanrafaelturismo.gov.ar.*

 Sights

Goyenechea
WINERY | One of the country's oldest wineries, Goyenechea was founded in 1868 by a Basque immigrant family that had the foresight to build not only a solid brick winery, but also 60 houses for the working families, a school for their children, a repair shop, and a chapel. As you pass through the arched caves where wine ages in bottles, you can see the *piletas*, huge concrete vats that held 8,976 gallons of wine when the industry was focused on quantity, not quality. Family members often lead tours, which are free in Spanish; ask ahead for prices in English. ✉ *Sotero Arizú s/n, Villa Atuel, San Rafael* ☎ *260/461–7294* ⊕ *www. goyenechea.com* ✉ *Free* ⊗ *Closed Sun.*

Jean Rivier
WINERY | The Swiss-French brothers who own this winery produce a limited quantity of quality wines from their own grapes. Guided tours of the spotless facility include crushing, fermentation, and tasting areas. ✉ *Hipólito Yrigoyen 2385, Rama Caída, San Rafael* ☎ *260/443–2676* ⊕ *www.jeanrivier.com.*

Suter
WINERY | In 1897, the Suter family journeyed to Argentina from Switzerland and planted the first Pinot Blanco variety in the country. Today, the fourth generation of the family continues to produce good value white wines, Malbec, Cabernet Sauvignon, and sparkling wine. A winery tour leads you through a labyrinth of underground caves filled with huge oak casks—used more to evoke atmosphere than to store wine. ✉ *Hipólito Yrigoyen 2850, near airport, El Toledano, San Rafael* ☎ *260/442–1076* ⊕ *www.bodegasuter.com.ar.*

Valentín Bianchi
WINERY | Bianchi is the largest of San Rafael's wineries, receiving more than 100,000 visitors per year to its lush, garden setting, which is just a little over 5 km (3 miles) from the center of San Rafael. Book in for horseback riding or cycling through the vineyards to work up thirst for a tasting in the family cellar, which includes their renowned sparkling wine. ✉ *R143 at Valentin Bianchi, Las Paredes, San Rafael* ☎ *260/481–6963* ⊕ *www.bodegasbianchi.com.ar* ⊗ *Closed Sun. and Mon.*

 Restaurants

Al Antojo del Cocinero
$$$ | **ARGENTINE** | This intimate eatery serves up comforting Argentine cuisine each evening for a maximum of 10 tables in a romantic, candlelit garden. The menu changes regularly, but some favorites include homemade gnocchi and shrimp gratin. **Known for:** intimate setting; Argentine tasting menu; comforting food. $ *Average main: pesos2000* ✉ *Av. Ballofet 173, San Rafael* ☎ *261/333–7364* ⊗ *Closed Sun. and Mon.*

Bonafide
$ | **CAFÉ** | A popular gathering place for both locals and visitors just one block from Km 0 (the very center of town), Bonafide serves up fresh coffee, sandwiches, cakes, and other goodies for the road. Grab one of the window seats with leather couches and take advantage of the Wi-Fi. **Known for:** decent Wi-Fi; cheap bites; coffee. $ *Average main: pesos700* ✉ *San Martín 102, San Rafael* ☎ *260/442–0420* ⊕ *www.bonafide.com.ar.*

★ Chez Gastón at Algodón
$$$$ | **ARGENTINE** | Nestled between a golf green and tennis courts, Chez Gastón serves up unpretentious and fresh local cuisine in the smart Algodón Wine Resort. Surrounded by ancient olive groves and vineyards, you can sit outside on the brick patio where pine-log

tables are surrounded by comfy couches with puffy white cushions. **Known for:** Algodon wine pairings; meat straight from the grill; farm fresh ingredients. ⓢ *Average main: pesos5200* ✉ *RN144, Km 674, Cuadro Benegas, San Rafael* ☎ *260/442–9020* ⊕ *www.algodonhotels. com* ☾ *Closed Mon.–Wed.*

★ L'Obrador

$$ | ARGENTINE | Daniel Ancina, his wife Graciela, and a team of cooks will greet you at this typical ranch house, about 20 minutes from town; then they'll fill your wine glass, introduce you to the other guests, and seat you family-style at a long table. Regional cuisine rules; little pots of sauces for spreading on *pan casero* (homemade bread) line the center of the table and out out of the mud-brick oven comes a platter of crisp baked empanadas followed by a protein—goat, lamb, beef, chicken, or chorizo. **Known for:** a warm intro to the local cuisine; hard to find, but worth the effort; everything cooked on the spot. ⓢ *Average main: pesos1200* ✉ *Camino Bentos 50, San Rafael* ☎ *260/460–1347* ▤ *No credit cards* ☾ *Closed Mon. and Tues.*

 ## Hotels

★ Algodón Wine Resort

$$$ | RESORT | Country casual meets luxury at the Algodón Wine Resort, which combines a remodeled 1920s farmhouse and a modern lodge offering rooms with their own patio and woodstove. **Pros:** relaxing countryside setting; great option for golfers; great restaurant. **Cons:** closed in winter; expensive for what it is; 20 minutes from downtown San Rafael. ⓢ *Rooms from: US$280* ✉ *RN144, Km 674, Cuadro Benegas, San Rafael* ☎ *260/4429–020* ⊕ *www.algodonhotels. com* ☾ *Closed in winter* ⇱ *8 rooms* ⦿ *Free Breakfast.*

Hotel Tower Inn and Suites

$$ | HOTEL | Across the street from the tourist office, this modern hotel has spacious accommodations with big picture windows that fill the rooms with natural light and have views of the main street and the mountains in the distance. **Pros:** large rooms; poolside dining in summer; central. **Cons:** unimpressive breakfast; small pool for quantity of guests; street noise can carry. ⓢ *Rooms from: US$168* ✉ *H. Irigoyen 774, San Rafael* ☎ *260/442–7190* ⊕ *www.towersanrafael.com* ⇱ *111 rooms* ⦿ *Free Breakfast.*

Tierra Mora

$$ | APARTMENT | This apart-hotel is a compact three-story building overlooking a large park; it's about 14 blocks from downtown, but within walking distance of an up-and-coming area with restaurants and shops. **Pros:** large rooms; in a nice part of town with park; free parking. **Cons:** small breakfast; basic services; not a lot of amenities. ⓢ *Rooms from: US$107* ✉ *Ameghino 350, San Rafael* ☎ *260/444–7222* ⊕ *www.tierramora. com* ⇱ *19 apartments, 17 rooms* ⦿ *Free Breakfast.*

 ## Shopping

FOOD
Ketobac

FOOD | Wines, jams, and homemade goodies (such as chocolate-covered figs, raisins, and dried apricots from the region) are all sold at Ketobac. ✉ *San Martín 175, San Rafael* ☎ *260/442–2082.*

Yancanelo

FOOD | An olive oil factory that offers tastings, Yancanelo also sells local olive oil, balsamic vinegar, and other regional foods. ✉ *Hipólito Yrigoyen 4030, San Rafael* ☎ *260/15–402–2907* ⊕ *www. yancanelo.com.*

A Recreational Drive

Cañón del Atuel (Atuel Canyon). This has been called the world's second Grand Canyon, as they were both formed at the same time, and their coloring is similar. To traverse the photogenic, 160-km (99-mile) route with its four hydroelectric stations along the Atuel River, start at the top of the canyon in the village of El Nihuel, 75 km (47 miles) west of San Rafael. Take Ruta Provincial 144 from San Rafael in the direction of Malargüe, turning south at El Desvío onto 180. At the dam, Ruta 173 descends into a labyrinth of red, brown, and gray sandstone rock formations. Unfortunately, the river disappears into underground pipes—supplying energy for the growing population and the vineyards of Mendoza Province. At Valle Grande, the water is collected behind a large dam, after which the river runs freely between sandstone cliffs, beneath shady willows and poplar trees. Swimming holes, sheltered picnic spots, and rafting adventures offer escape from the city on hot summer days. Small hotels, cottages, campsites, and shops that rent rafting and kayaking equipment line the road before it returns across the desert to San Rafael.

Las Leñas

200 km (124 miles) south of San Rafael.

Las Leñas is the largest ski area served by lifts in the Western Hemisphere—bigger than Whistler/Blackcomb in British Columbia, and larger than Vail and Snowbird combined. Although it should be thriving, the area has suffered bankruptcies, absentee owners, and several management teams. You must go through tour operators and travel agents to book into area hotels, all of which have minimum-stay requirements. Accommodations range from dorm-style houses and apart-hotels—some in disrepair—to hotels with indoor/outdoor pools, decent restaurants, bars, and a ski concierge. Travel offices in Buenos Aires, Mendoza, and San Rafael sell ski packages with lift tickets, equipment, and, in some cases, transportation—which may involve a combination of bus rides and charter flights.

The ski season runs June through October, depending on the year's snow. Most South Americans take their winter vacation in July, the month to avoid if you don't like crowds and high prices, although the weather is more benign. August has the most reliable snow conditions, September the most varied. Prices for lifts and lodging are lowest in June and from September to closing; rates are highest in July.

GETTING HERE AND AROUND

In high season (July and August) there are two charter flights a day from Buenos Aires to Malargüe, a town 80 km (50 miles) from the resort. A more reliable alternative is to take a 90-minute flight from Buenos Aires to San Rafael, then a three-hour drive onward to Las Leñas. From San Rafael, follow Ruta Provincial 144 for 141 km (88 miles) to El Sosneado, then pick up Ruta Nacional 40 to the turnoff onto Ruta Provincial 222 that passes through Los Molles, 20 km (12 miles) from Las Leñas. This is a dramatically beautiful drive, but carry chains and be aware of weather conditions.

If you want to save your pesos for lift tickets and good lodgings, consider

Atuel Canyon has been called the world's second Grand Canyon, as they were both formed at the same time, and their coloring is similar.

taking the Las Leñas "Coche-cama" from Buenos Aires. This sleeper bus departs on Friday and Sunday evening, making the trip in 14 hours; return tickets (bookable directly through the resort) cost about 20,000 pesos.

ESSENTIALS

VISITOR INFORMATION Malargüe Tourism Office. ✉ *Hipólito Yrigoyen 774, San Rafael* ☎ *260/447–1659* 🌐 *www.malargue.tur.ar.*

Hotels

Aries

$ | **HOTEL** | This slope-side luxury hotel has plenty of diversions for stormy days—including a space for children's games and activities, a piano bar in the lobby, a wine bar serving cheese and regional smoked meats, a movie theater, a heated pool, and a sauna. **Pros:** proximity to slopes; good facilities; post-ski entertainment. **Cons:** two-night minimum stay; outdated interiors; no direct reservation service. [$] *Rooms from: US$40* ✉ *Las Leñas Ski Resort, Las Leñas* ☎ *11/4819–6060 in Buenos Aires off-season, 260/447–0683 ski season* 🌐 *www.laslenas.com* 🛏 *100 rooms* 🍴 *Free Breakfast.*

Escorpio

$ | **HOTEL** | **FAMILY** | This small, intimate ski lodge is right on the slopes; you can watch the action from the terrace while having lunch, or hit the cozy piano bar for après-ski board games with tea or cocktails. **Pros:** ski in, ski out; mountain views; terrace bar. **Cons:** few facilities; two-night minimum; difficult to make reservations directly at times. [$] *Rooms from: US$50* ✉ *Las Leñas Ski Resort, Las Leñas* ☎ *11/4819–6060 in Buenos Aires off-season, 260/447–0683 in Mendoza ski season* 🌐 *www.laslenas.com* 🛏 *47 rooms* 🍴 *Free Breakfast.*

Piscis

$ | **HOTEL** | This deluxe hotel pampers its guests with spa services, ski-equipment delivery, and an indoor-outdoor pool. **Pros:** lots of post-ski activity; indoor-outdoor pool; slope-side location. **Cons:** two-night minimum stay; outdated interiors; difficult to make direct reservations.

Did You Know?

The first incarnation of Las Leñas ski resort was built in a mere four months; construction began January 20, 1983, and by June 16 there were 400 beds ready for guests. Now with more than 3,000 beds, Las Leñas has become one of the most popular resort complexes in Latin America.

Ⓢ *Rooms from: US$50* ✉ *Las Leñas Ski Resort, Las Leñas* ☎ *11/4819–6060 in Buenos Aires off-season, 260/447–0683 in Mendoza ski season* ⊕ *www.laslenas. com* ⮐ *98 rooms* ⑂ *Free Breakfast.*

 Activities

SKIING
Las Leñas Ski Resort
SKIING & SNOWBOARDING | From the top (3,429 meters/11,250 feet), a treeless lunar landscape of white peaks extends in every direction. There are steep, scary, 610-meter (2,000-foot) vertical chutes for experts; machine-packed routes for beginners; and plenty of intermediate terrain. A terrain park for snowboarders has jumps and a half pipe. There's also a free-style slope. Off-piste skiing can be arranged through the ski school.

Facilities: 3,300 hectares (8,154 acres) skiable terrain; 1,230-meter (4,035-foot) vertical drop; 64 km (40 miles) of groomed runs, the longest of the 29 runs is 8 km (5 miles); 15% beginner, 40% intermediate, 45% expert; 1 quad, 6 double chairs, 5 surface lifts. There are no detachable quad chairs or high-speed lifts.

Seasonal Rate Information: Low: September. Medium: June and August. High: July.

Lessons and Programs: Multilingual ski and snowboard instructors give 2½-hour classes or two-hour private lessons for all levels. Good intermediate skiers to experts can experience untracked slopes with heli-ski and off-piste skiing accompanied by trained guides and avalanche experts.

One-Day Adult Lift Tickets: Low: 1,000 pesos, Medium: 1,400 pesos, High: 1,600 pesos

Rentals: Rentals of boots, skis, snowboards, and poles are readily available. ✉ *Las Leñas, Las Leñas* ☎ *11/4819–6060 in Buenos Aires* ⊕ *www.laslenas.com.*

San Juan

167 km (104 miles) northwest of Mendoza.

Easygoing San Juan makes a good base if you want to combine active pursuits (a good selection of which can be found in and around the Ullum Valley Dam Reservoir) with visits to local bodegas. This small city was founded in 1562 as part of the Chilean viceroyalty, and *sanjuaninos* began making wine almost immediately; however, it wasn't until the 1890s, when Graffigna and other major operations put down roots here, that production increased. At that point wineries began offering varieties other than the sweet white table wines, sherries, and ports that the area had been known for. Today, although the city remains steeped in history and awash in wine, it is surprisingly modern. San Juan was devastated by earthquakes in 1944 and 1977 (the first of these helped establish Juan Perón, who led the relief effort, as a national figure): all of the low-rise buildings, tree-lined plazas, and pedestrian walkways you see are the results of reconstruction.

GETTING HERE AND AROUND
San Juan is a 1½-hour drive from Mendoza on Ruta Nacional 40. The trip from Buenos Aires takes 10 hours by car, slightly longer by bus, but daily flights on Aerolíneas Argentinas take just 1¾ hours. The Domingo Faustino Sarmiento Airport is 11 km (7 miles) southeast of San Juan; a taxi in takes about 15 minutes and costs about 1,100 pesos. The city is easy to navigate: there's one main shopping area in a three-block radius around the Plaza 25 de Mayo, and most hotels are within walking distance of it. Some wineries are within cycling distance, whereas others are drive-to destinations. Always try to reserve visits ahead of time.

BUS CONTACTS Andesmar. ☎ *264/422–2871* ⊕ *www.andesmar.com.* **Autotransportes.** ☎ *264/427–6864* ⊕ *www.atsj.*

com.ar. **CATA Internacional.** ☎ 264/427–
7600, 800/122–2282 ⊕ www.catainter-
nacional.com. **Chevallier.** ☎ 264/422–1388
⊕ www.nuevachevallier.com. **Terminal
de Ómnibus.** ⊠ Estados Unidos 530,
between Santa Fe and España 985, San
Juan ☎ 264/422–1604.

CAR RENTALS Avis. ⊠ Domingo Sarmiento Sur 164, San Juan ☎ 264/420–0571,
264/15–499–1472 ⊕ www.avis.com.ar.

TAXIS Argentina Remise. ⊠ Gral.
Mariano Acha Norte 989, San Juan
☎ 264/422–5522. **Radio Taxi.** ⊠ San Juan
☎ 264/427–2705.

ESSENTIALS
**MEDICAL ASSISTANCE Farmacia
Echague.** ⊠ Pedro Echague Este, Esq.
Sarmiento, San Juan. **Hospital Dr. G.
Rawson.** ⊠ Av. Rawson Sur 494, San Juan
☎ 264/422–4005.

**VISITOR INFORMATION San Juan Secre-
taria de Turismo.** ⊠ Sarmiento 24 Sur, San
Juan ☎ 264/421–0004 ⊕ www.sanjuan.
tur.ar.

TOURS
Dante Montes Turismo
GUIDED TOURS | Anna Maria de Montes
and her partners at Dante Montes
Turismo are experienced local agents
with a full-service agency for lodging and
transportation. They offer guided tours
to bodegas, Valle Fertí (where they own
their own cabins), Ischigualasto Park,
and beyond. ⊠ Santa Fe 58 Este, Galeria
Estornell, Loc 31, San Juan ☎ 264/422–
9019, 264/421–5198 ⊕ www.agencia-
montes.com.

Moneytur
GUIDED TOURS | This outfit conducts
tours of local bodegas; outings to
Ischigualasto, Talampaya, Las Quijades,
and Jachal; plus rafting trips on the Río
San Juan and horseback trips in the
Calingasta Valley. ⊠ Local 6, Laprida
190 Oeste, San Juan ☎ 264/420–1010
⊕ www.moneytur.com.ar.

Sights

Antigua Bodega 1929
WINERY | At this landmark bodega and
museum, great concrete wine-storage
tubs are exposed in a cavernous old
building that survived three earthquakes
and now functions as part of the museum. Wine and espumante are served in
the lovely garden or at a wine bar in the
front room. ⊠ Salta 782 Norte, Capital,
San Juan ☎ 261/459–7777 ⊕ www.
antiguabodega.com.

Callia
WINERY | In a hot, dry, wide open valley
35 km (22 miles) from town and with
vineyards planted in every direction, Cal-
lia produces fantastic Syrah. The winery
looks modern, but inside its superstruc-
ture is the old bodega (albeit with all new
equipment). Take a guided visit that ends
with a tasting. It's owned by Salentein,
the formidable Dutch-owned company
that also makes wine in the Valle de Uco.
⊠ Calle de los Ríos s/n, Caucete, San
Juan ☎ 264/496–0000 ⊕ www.bodegas-
callia.com ☉ Closed Sun.

Champañera Miguel Más
WINERY | There's a lot going on at this
unassuming little winery. It doesn't run
fancy tours, but workers will stop to
show you how they make sparkling wine,
turning the bottles slowly on the many
racks. Everything is certified organic—
from the wine to the garlic and tomatoes
that grow out back. Book in for a three-
wine tasting (500 pesos). ⊠ Calle 11 s/n,
300 meters (984 feet) east of RN40, San
Juan ☎ 264/660–4901 ⊕ www.miguel-
mas.com.ar ☉ Closed weekends.

Fabril Alto Verde
WINERY | Grapes from this spotless win-
ery are grown organically, and the wine
and espumosos are stabilized without
preservatives or additives. They are made
in small quantities, and a great deal of
care and control go into the production.
Take a short 40-minute guided tour

before sampling some of their wares (350 pesos) or upgrade to a paired tasting (1,600 pesos). ✉ *RN40, between Calles 13 and 14, San Juan* ☎ *264/438–5862* 🌐 *www.fabrilaltoverde.com.ar.*

Merced del Estero

WINERY | The same family has been cultivating vines at this *finca* (estate) since 1897, but it wasn't until the 1990s they started producing varietals, including Cabernet Franc, Cabernet Sauvignon, Malbec, and Syrah. A visit offers three experiences, including a tour of the winery and a taste of its modern portfolio to a picnic in the lovely garden. ✉ *Av. Moron 432, San Juan* ☎ *264/15–4400–388* 🌐 *www.merceddelestero.com.ar* ⏲ *Closed Mon.–Thurs.*

Museo Casa Natal de Sarmiento (*Sarmiento's Birthplace*)

HISTORIC HOME | This modest house was the birthplace of Domingo Faustino Sarmiento (1811–88), known to Argentines as the Father of Education. Sarmiento was a prolific writer, a skilled diplomat, and a successful politician who served as president from 1869 to 1874. Casa Natal de Sarmiento—Argentina's first designated National Historic Landmark—pays tribute to his achievements and gives an overview of Argentine history during his era. ✉ *Sarmiento 21 Sur, San Juan* ☎ *264/422–4603* 🌐 *casanatalsarmiento.cultura.gob.ar* 🎟 *Free* ⏲ *Closed Mon.*

Ullum Dam (*Ullum Valley Dam Reservoir*)

DAM | Fifteen km (9 miles) west of San Juan, this huge hydroelectric complex—also known as the Ullum Valley Dam Reservoir—offers grand views of the Río San Juan. Windsurfing, sailing, swimming, rowing, fishing, and diving keep San Juaninos cool on hot summer days. You can rent boating equipment just beyond the dam, where you'll also find a café and change cabins. There's a public beach at the Embarcadero turnoff. You can go white-water rafting and kayaking on the San Juan, Los Patos, and Jachal rivers. Fly fishing, mostly for trout, in Las Hornillas River can be arranged through local tour companies. ✉ *Dique de Ullum, San Juan.*

Viñas de Segisa

WINERY | Segisa claims to be the first boutique winery in San Juan after Don Vicente Perez Ganga settled here in 1925. Several earthquakes have left nothing of the original building, but it's still worth a visit to taste new wines on their daily tours. ✉ *Aberastain at Calle 15, La Rinconada, Pocito, San Juan* ☎ *264/492–2000* 🌐 *www.saxsegisa.com.ar.*

🍴 Restaurants

★ La Madeleine

$$ | FRENCH FUSION | There's a friendly atmosphere in this small bistro, which started out as a teahouse until the French owners expanded into Argentine-Franco breakfasts, lunch, dinner, and a wine bar. **Known for:** eclectic wine list; European menu; delicious cakes. [$] *Average main: pesos1100* ✉ *Mitre Oeste 202, San Juan* ☎ *264/427–7825* 🌐 *www.lamadeleinebistrot.com.ar* ⏲ *Closed Sun.*

Pa' Pueblo

$$$$ | ARGENTINE | Inspired by local ingredients, dynamic young chef Alfredo Morales creates a delicious seasonal menu, cooking out of an upcycled San Juan casona. Order the six- or three-course tasting menus; dishes might include pork empanadas, artichoke ceviche, and flame-grilled pears with ricotta and pak choi. [$] *Average main: pesos3300* ✉ *Maipú Este s/n, Santa Lucia, San Juan* ☎ *264/541–6201* ⏲ *Closed Mon.–Wed.*

Restaurante Palito—Club Sirio Libanés

$$ | MEDITERRANEAN | FAMILY | Tiled walls that look straight out of the Middle East mark the entrance to this eatery, which offers top value Lebanese food. Don't be dismayed by the bright lights; just

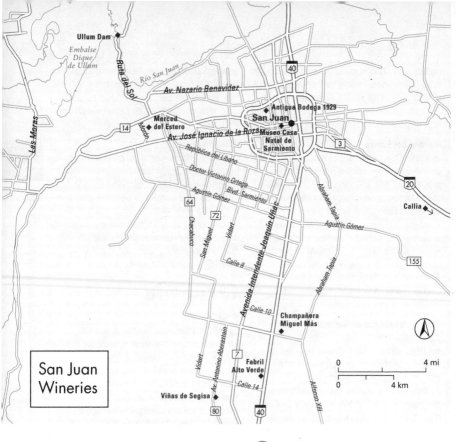

San Juan
Wineries

order a bottle of Malbec, head for the table of appetizers, and fill your plate with crab brochettes, pickled eggplant, fresh tomatoes, and sliced tongue. **Known for:** Middle Eastern flavors; eccentric design; good value buffet. Ⓢ *Average main: pesos1000* ✉ *Entre Ríos 33 Sur, San Juan* ☎ *264/422–3841* ⊕ *www.hostalde-palito.com.ar* ⊙ *No dinner Sun.*

Soychu
$ | VEGETARIAN | Dedicated to natural foods, this buffet-style restaurant has lots of vegetarian and even vegan options. The atmosphere is laid-back, and your meal—which is priced by weight—can be eaten in or taken out. ■**TIP→ Be sure to try the fresh-squeezed fruit and vegetable juices.** Ⓢ *Average main: pesos660* ✉ *Av. José de la Roza 223, San Juan* ☎ *264/422–1939* ⊙ *No dinner Sun.*

Hotels

Albertina
$$ | HOTEL | Bright white walls with colorful art and slick modern furniture decorate this central four-story hotel, which offers good value, if simple, lodgings in San Juan. **Pros:** convenient location; affordable rates; on-site eatery. **Cons:** basic amenities; lots of stairs; tiny windows. Ⓢ *Rooms from: US$120* ✉ *Mitre 202 oeste, San Juan* ☎ *264/421–4222* ⊕ *www.hotelalbertina.com* ⤴ *36 rooms* ⦿ *Free Breakfast.*

Del Bono Park
$$ | HOTEL | Light shines from a skylight four stories above the registration area, lobby, bar, and gathering spaces, and a third-floor glass bridge connects rooms by spanning the atrium, with a circular

staircase winding around a glass cylinder down into the basement bar, restaurant, and casino. **Pros:** San Juan's sleekest hotel; lots of light; varied amenities. **Cons:** breakfast can get busy; room size varies; just off the Circunvalación (Ring Road). [$] *Rooms from: US$120* ✉ *Av. J.I. de La Roza 1946, San Juan* ☎ *264/426–2300* 🌐 *www.delbonohotels.com* 🛏 *100 rooms* 🍴 *Free Breakfast.*

Villa Don Tomás

$ | HOTEL | FAMILY | This resort-like hotel on the outskirts of town has a spacious lawn, pool with swim-up bar, and casual restaurant, giving children plenty of space to play and offering respite from a busy day sightseeing. **Pros:** huge lawn; pool; low rates. **Cons:** no nearby shops or restaurants; basic accommodation; 15-minute drive from town. [$] *Rooms from: US$50* ✉ *Comandante Cabot 568 Oeste, 5400, San Juan* ☎ *264/428–3842* 🌐 *www.villadontomas.com.ar* 🛏 *32 rooms, 11 cottages, 8 apartments* 🍴 *Free Breakfast.*

Barreal

136 km (85 miles) northwest of San Juan.

Beyond the streets of Barreal, hiding in the shade of *sauce llorones* (weeping willows) and alamos, lie apple orchards, vineyards, and fields of mint, lavender, and anise. Using this tranquil village as your headquarters, you can mountain bike, horseback ride, hike, climb, or drive a 4X4 east into the Sierra Tontal, where at 3,999 meters (13,120 feet) you can see the highest peaks in the Andes, including Aconcagua (6,957 meters/22,825 feet) and Mercedario (6,770 meters/22,211 feet).

GETTING HERE AND AROUND

You can reach Barreal by bus or car in about three hours. Leave San Juan on Ruta Nacional 40 driving north, then head west on 436 to Talacasto, which becomes 149 to the Calingasta Valley and then continues south to Barreal. Another option is the long, lonely but scenic drive from Uspallata on north–south Ruta 39 (which turns into Ruta 412) all the way to Barreal. The optimal way to explore the surrounding area is by car, using a 4X4 for forays into the mountains, or by joining a tour.

ESSENTIALS

VISITOR INFORMATION Tourist Office. ✉ *Municipalidad, Presidente Roca, Barreal* ☎ *264/844–1066.*

Sights

Reserva Natural El Leoncito

NATURE PRESERVE | Twenty-two km (14 miles) south of Barreal on Ruta 412 toward Uspallata, a dirt road turns off into Reserva Natural El Leoncito (Little Lion Natural Reserve), a vast, rocky area with little vegetation. You can continue on this road for 17 km (11 miles) to the CASLEO observatory (🌐 *www.casleo.conicet.gov.ar*), known for its exceptional stargazing.

Near the turnoff, on the western side of Ruta 412 at Pampa Leoncito, the sport of *carrovelismo* (land-sailing) is practiced during summer months in wheeled sand cars called wind yachts that can travel up to 150 kph (93 mph) across a cracked-clay lake bed.

An all-day drive (160 km/100 miles round-trip) in a 4X4 to Las Hornillas at 3,300 meters (9,500 feet) takes you along the Río Los Patos into a red rock–walled canyon. The road narrows, clinging to the canyon walls, as it winds around closed curves, eventually opening into a small valley where, in 1817, General San Martín's troops gathered before crossing the Andes over Los Patos Pass on one of his historic liberation campaigns.

A brief glimpse of Aconcagua looming in solitary splendor about 160 km (100 miles) south is a preview of coming attractions: four peaks over 6,000 meters (20,000 feet) tall are visible in the Ramada Range to the northwest: Polaco, Alma Negra, La Ramada, and Mercaderio. The last of these—rising to 6,770 meters (22,211 feet)—is the fourth highest peak in the Americas. As the road winds ever higher, herds of guanacos graze on the steep slopes, pumas prowl in the bush, and condors soar above. ⊠ *Cordillera de Ansilta, Barreal.*

🛏 Hotels

El Mercedario
$$ | B&B/INN | This 1928 adobe farmhouse on the main street is a gathering place for like-minded lovers of all that Barreal has to offer: good books and music are noticeable in the living room, comfort food comes from the kitchen, and the quaint rooms lead out onto an ample garden. **Pros:** local flavor and friendly owners; good value; bike and 4X4 excursions can be arranged. **Cons:** must preorder dinner; simple breakfast; basic amenities. Ⓢ *Rooms from: US$120* ⊠ *Av. Presidente Roca and Calle Los Enamorados, Barreal* ☎ *264/509–0907* ⊕ *www.elmercedario. com.ar* ⤶ *7 rooms* ⦿ *Free Breakfast.*

Posada Paso de los Patos
$$ | B&B/INN | A charming property run by a porteño couple who left the big city for Barreal, Andean views from this posada are second to none. **Pros:** delightful hands-on owners; beautiful and stylish lodges. **Cons:** meals are a little basic; hot water doesn't always run hot. Ⓢ *Rooms from: US$170* ⊠ *Patricias Mendocinas y Gualino, Barreal* ⊕ *www.posadapasolospatos.com.ar.*

🏃 Activities

Tour offices in Barreal, San Juan, and as far away as Mendoza City offer assorted activities—including hikes or horseback rides of varying lengths—in the Reserva Natural El Leoncito and the high mountain ranges of the Cordillera Ansilta.

Fortuna Viajes
HIKING & WALKING | In business for more than 30 years, this outfit arranges horseback trips lasting from one to nine days—including ones to Valle Colorado, where you'll see six peaks over 6,000 meters (20,000 feet). Hiking, mountaineering, fishing, and 4X4 excursions are also offered. ⊠ *Presidente Roca s/n, Barreal* ☎ *264/404–0913, 264/404–0914* ⊕ *www.fortunaviajes.com.ar.*

Chapter 8

THE LAKE
DISTRICT

8

Updated by
Melissa Kitson

 Sights
★★★★★

 Restaurants
★★★★☆

 Hotels
★★★★★

 Shopping
★★☆☆☆

 Nightlife
★★☆☆☆

WELCOME TO THE LAKE DISTRICT

TOP REASONS TO GO

★ **The Great Outdoors:** Hikers following well-marked trails in the national parks will encounter atmospheric forests, camera-ready cascades, and magnificent vistas. Waterways can carry rafters and kayakers all the way to Chile.

★ **Water, Water Everywhere:** Forty different lakes, seven major rivers flowing into two oceans, and you can spend days just staring at Nahuel Huapi Lake with its shoreline disappearing under distant peaks and volcanoes.

★ **Summer Skiing:** In the northern Lake District of Patagonia, June through September is ski season on the slopes of Cerro Catedral, near Bariloche, and Cerro Chapelco, near San Martín de los Andes.

★ **Savage Beauty:** One day a lake is silent, a mirror of the surrounding mountains. Another day waves are crashing on its shores, with wind tearing limbs from trees.

The Lake District lies in the folds of the Andes along the Chilean border in the provinces of Neuquén, Río Negro, and Chubut, where myriad glacial lakes lap at the forest's edge beneath snowcapped peaks.

The area includes three national parks, with towns in each. Bariloche is the base for exploring Parque Nacional Nahuel Huapi, and the departure point for the lake crossing to Chile. North of Bariloche is Parque Nacional Lanín, which contains the town of San Martín de los Andes. South of Bariloche and El Bolsón is Parque Nacional Lago Puelo in the Pacific watershed.

1 Bariloche. Full of sightseers, shoppers, and skiers in winter, this unashamedly touristy city on the southeastern shore of Nahuel Huapi Lake welcomes the world with all levels of lodgings, restaurants, and tour offices. The best part of Bariloche is beyond the city limits.

2 San Martín de los Andes and Nearby. Tourist amenities, combined with the alpine setting and distinctive architecture, make San Martín both a pretty and practical base for exploring Parque Nacional Lanín. The town's location also makes it a logical stopover on the Seven Lakes Route.

3 Ruta de los Siete Lagos (Route of the Seven Lakes). The highlight of this 105-km (65-mile) drive is the scenic leg between Villa La Angostura and San Martín de los Andes, where the road winds up and around lake after lake—all of them different in shape, size, and setting.

4 Parque Nacional Nahuel Huapi. Founded in 1934, Argentina's oldest national park covers more than 7,050 square km (2,720 square miles): 800,000-plus visitors per year come to explore its high mountain glaciers, endless lakes, and enticing trails in buses, boats, and private vehicles.

5 El Bolsón and Nearby. Known as a refuge for hippies and ex-urbanites, amiable little El Bolsón is a valley town that straddles Ruta Nacional 40 just north of Parque Nacional Lago Puelo on the Chilean border. Hops and berry farms thrive in the microclimate along the Río Azul.

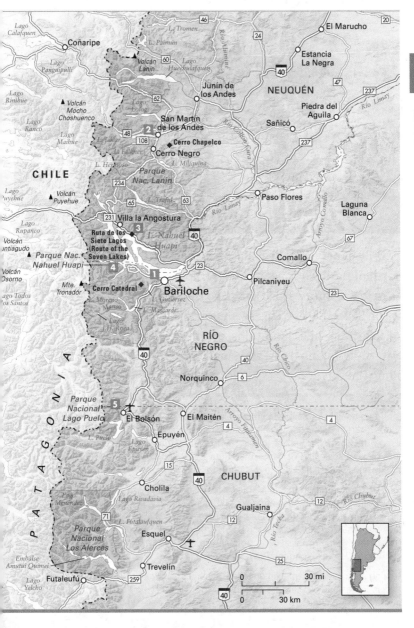

RUTA DE LOS SIETE LAGOS

Route of the Seven Lakes

To fully experience the Lake District, head north of Bariloche past Nahuel Huapi Lake to the Ruta de los Siete Lagos (Route of the Seven Lakes). This excursion has it all: lake after lake, mountains, wildflowers, waterfalls, hiking trails, and small towns along the way.

The route itself links Bariloche and San Martín de los Andes. Start in Bariloche and follow the Circuito Grande along Ruta 237 and Ruta 231 to Villa La Angostura, then pass Lagos Espejo and Correntoso on Ruta 231 to get to mostly unpaved Ruta 234; take this north to San Martín.

For a day trip, return from San Martín de los Andes through Junín de Los Andes and Alicura (rutas 234, 40, and 237) on 260 km (161 miles) of paved road. If you have the time, though, overnight in San Martín de los Andes, take Ruta Provincial 63 to Confluencia, and then join Ruta 237 south along the Río Limay to Bariloche.

Renting a car is best, but even on a group tour it's spectacular. Buses and bicycles are available from Bariloche or Villa La Angostura.

TIPS

Ask about road conditions before you leave Villa La Angostura; the route's unpaved portion north of there is often closed during heavy rains, winter storms, or construction. Best bets for picnic spots or campsites are the beaches of lakes Villarino, Falkner, and Hermoso. For maps, pick up *Guía Busch* and *Viajar Hoy* (tour pamphlets in English and Spanish). There are no gas stations on the Ruta de los Siete Lagos.

HIGHLIGHTS OF THE DRIVE

Rivers. Just past Villa La Angostura, the Río Correntoso—one of the world's shortest rivers at 300 meters (984 feet)—flows from the lake of the same name into Nahuel Huapi. This is a classic mouth-of-the-river fishing spot; you can watch the action from the glassed-in deck at the Hotel Correntoso or from the old fishing lodge on the shore of Nahuel Huapi Lake.

Rainbow trout

Lakes. Traveling north from Villa Angostura to San Martín de los Andes is the most scenic part of the drive, and it's no coincidence that this is where you'll find the region's most scenic namesake natural features—lakes. Lago Correntoso (Rapid Water Lake) is the first one you'll pass, and you'll do so immediately after you cross over the Río Correntoso. Drive along its northern shore to arrive at an abandoned hotel site; from here you'll see a road that leads to Lago Espejo Chico (Little Mirror Lake), with a beach, a campground, and trails. Return to the main road and you'll come to Lago Espejo (Mirror Lake)—head to the viewpoint for a good lunch spot, or use the camping area's tables. Lago Falkner (east side of the road) has sandy beaches and a popular campground. It is linked by a stream and an isthmus, which you will cross to Lago Villarino (west side of the road). Finally, before you reach San Martín de los Andes, enjoy Lago Machónico's dry landscape via the scenic overlook, or take the short walk to the shore.

Waterfalls. Between Lakes Villarino and Falkner, Cascada Vulignanco, a 20-meter (66-foot) waterfall, is visible on the left-hand side of the road, where you can pull off at the *mirador* (overlook).

DETOURS

Four km (3 miles) south of Lago Villarino, jade-green **Lago Escondido** (Hidden Lake) lies veiled in a thick forest. You'll need to park and walk in.

At Pichi Traful, turn east onto a bumpy road for 2 km (1 mile) and walk to the sandy beach at **Pichi Traful Lake** (aka Brazo Norte of Lago Traful). Fishermen, bikers, and hikers enjoy camping or picnicking here.

About 30 km (18 miles) north of the junction of Ruta Provincial 234 and Ruta Provincial 65, look on your left for a sign indicating the trail to **Casacada Ñivinenco** (Whispering Falls). The 2-km (1-mile) trail crosses a river (in November and December the river is high; check conditions ahead of time), then follows the river into a silent forest.

If you pass through **Confluencia**, take Ruta Provincial 65 along the Traful River west a few km to **Cuyín Manzano**, a dirt road that continues along the river into a world of strange caves and limestone rock formations.

8

The Lake District RUTA DE LOS SIETE LAGOS

One of many stunning views along the way.

CIRCUITO CHICO Y CIRCUITO GRANDE

"We drove the Circuito Chico and stopped at this overlook." —HappyTrvlr

If you're in Bariloche, get out of town to take in some of the spectacular scenery and old-school resort feel of the area on either the Circuito Chico (Small Circuit) or Circuito Grande (Large Circuit) by rental car, hired driver, or tour group.

The Circuito Chico is a 70-km (44-mile) half-day round-trip from Bariloche along the southern shore of Lago Nahuel Huapi. Visitors head out to the Llao Llao Peninsula to ski or take in the lake views and waterfalls without ever being too far from a cup of tea.

The Circuito Grande covers 250 km (155 miles) and is an all-day excursion across the lake from Bariloche. This drive is more about wooded hikes and hidden lakes, and includes two towns where you could spend a night.

You can do the Circuito Chico on one tank of gas. Circuit Grande, however, has longer unpopulated spans. Leave Bariloche with a full tank and refuel at Confluencia or Villa La Angostura.

WEATHER TIPS

The Circuito Chico has lots of traffic but is otherwise an easy drive whatever the weather. The Circuito Grande is another story. The roads to Villa La Angostura and Confluencia are good, but Ruta Provincial 65 past Lago Traful is unpaved and can be treacherous in bad weather. Always check road conditions with the Automóvil Club Argentino, the park office, or your hotel.

CIRCUITO CHICO

From Bariloche's Centro Cívico (Km 0), follow the shore of Lago Nahuel Huapi west on Ruta 237. At Km 7, stop at Playa Bonita's sandy beach. At Km 10, take the chairlift or climb to the top of Cerro Campanario. When you reach the Península Llao Llao (Km 25.5), bear right to Puerto Pañuelo, where boats embark on lake excursions to Isla Victoria, Puerto Blest, and the boat crossing to Chile. Across from the Puerto Pañuelo, the Llao Llao Hotel & Resort (See Hotels in Bariloche) sits on a lakeside knoll with a backdrop of sheer cliffs and snow-covered mountains. Continue following Ruta 77 to Bahía López; you'll approach through a forest of ghostly, leafless *lenga* trees. After Bahía Lopez, the road crosses Arroyo Lopez (Lopez Creek); stop to hike to the waterfall or continue on Ruta 77 to Punto Panorámico, one of the most scenic overlooks on the peninsula. Cross Moreno Bridge, then leave Ruta 77 for Ruta 237 back to Bariloche.

CIRCUITO GRANDE

Leaving Bariloche on Ruta 237 heading east, follow the Río Limay into the Valle Encantado (Enchanted Valley), with its magical red rocks. Before crossing the bridge at Confluencia (where the Río Traful joins the Limay), turn left onto Ruta 65 to Lago Traful. Five km (3 miles) beyond the turnoff, a dirt road to Cuyín Manzano leads to astounding sandstone formations. Return to Ruta 65 and follow Lago Traful's shore. When you see the sign indicating a mirador, stop and climb the wooden stairs to one of the loveliest views in the region. At the intersection with Ruta 237, turn left and follow the shore of Lago Correntoso to the paved road down to Villa La Angostura. The road skirts Lago Nahuel Huapi back into Bariloche.

(top right) "With flowers in full bloom it couldn't get much better." –Josh Roe
(bottom right) Península Llao Llao

NEED A BREAK?

Circuito Chico: Chiado (⌧ *Av. Bustillo [R237], Km 18* 2944/448–152 *Closed Wed.*) is a log house with a corrugated metal roof, a stone terrace, and colorful plants hanging out over the lake. Views are through the gnarly branches of a giant *coihué* tree to blue water and mountains. The brie sorrentinos in pear and port sauce are as good as the view.

Circuito Grande: If you visit Lago Traful in the morning, chances are you'll hit Villa Traful in time for lunch at Ñancú Lahuen (⌧ *Village center, opposite chapel* 294/447–9017), a casual spot in the middle of town with home cooking. If you've brought a picnic, continue on past the town to the beach, where the road leaves the lake for Ruta 234 and Villa La Angostura. In Villa La Angostura, head to La Casita de la Oma (⌧ *Cerro Inacayal 303* 2944/494–602), which serves homemade cakes, pies, and scones. Any dulce de leche item is a sure bet.

8

The Lake District CIRCUITO CHICO Y CIRCUITO GRANDE

The northern Lake District has become Patagonia's most popular tourist region. Spread over three states and encompassing more than a million hectares (2½ million acres) of nature preserves, it offers more than natural beauty. The hundreds of sapphire lakes here allow visitors to experience an array of outdoor activities. Lakes such as Lago Nahuel Huapi and Lago Puelo are the focal points of eponymous national parks; at both you can choose between fishing, boating (whether in a kayak, raft, or motor launch), and swimming from a pretty playa.

Back on dry land other recreational opportunities await. In the warmer months, horseback riding, mountain biking, and hiking are popular pastimes; climbing Volcán Lanín for a wraparound view of the sublime landscape is another memorable option. In winter, conversely, snow-sport enthusiasts head for the hills. Cerro Catedral (the continent's oldest ski area) is notable for its size, terrain, and superb setting, while smaller areas like Chapelco attract mostly vacationing Argentineans and Brazilians.

A broad range of accommodations—ranging from rustic refugios and classic ranches to luxe destination hotels—cater to these travelers year-round. Yet despite growing popularity and heightened accessibility from developed towns like San Martín de los Andes and Bariloche, first-time visitors are constantly amazed at how easy it is to lose yourself in a silent forest, on a rugged mountaintop, or by one of the district's beautiful namesake lakes.

Planning

When to Go

June through September the weather is typical of any ski region—blowing snowstorms, rain, and fog punctuated by days of brilliant sunshine. August and September are the best months for skiing, as the slopes are crowded with vacationers in July.

In December the weather can be cool, breezy, overcast, or rainy, but the rewards for bringing an extra sweater and raingear are great: an abundance of wildflowers and few tourists. January and February are the peak summer months, with days that are warm and long (the sun sets at 10 pm). March and April are good months to visit; the leaves of lenga and *ñire* trees brighten the rolling green forests with splashes of yellow and red, but rainy, cloudy days and cold nights can curtail some excursions.

Getting Here and Around

The most efficient way to get here is by air from Buenos Aires or Calafate. The most scenic way to arrive is from Puerto Montt, Chile, by boat through the lakes. Buses are the new trains—fast, inexpensive, with varying degrees of luxury, including beds, meals, and attendants. A car or bus is the best way to travel between cities in the Lake District, and once you've settled in a destination, you can use local tours, buses, taxis, or a *remis* (a hired car with driver).

AIR

Aerolíneas Argentinas flies from Buenos Aires to Bariloche, Esquel, San Martín de los Andes, and Neuquén; it also connects Bariloche and Calafate. JetSMART and Flybondi fly from Buenos Aires to Bariloche, while the former also offers flights to Neuquén.

BOAT

Traveling between Bariloche and Puerto Montt, Chile, by boat is one of the most popular excursions in Argentina. It requires three lake crossings and various buses, and can be done in a day or overnight. Travel agents and tour operators in Bariloche and Buenos Aires can arrange this trip.

BUS

Buses arrive in Bariloche from every corner of Argentina—from Jujuy in the north, Ushuaia in the south, and everywhere in between.

CAR

Driving to the Lake District from Buenos Aires is a long haul: the trip takes at least three days, and the route—extending for more than 1,500 km (930 miles)—has interminable stretches with few hotels, gas stations, or restaurants. In Bariloche, unless you're on a tour or a ski-only vacation, renting a car gives you the freedom to stop when and where you want. The Ruta de los Siete Lagos closes when weather is bad; for winter travel, rent a 4X4. Hiring a remis is another option.

Restaurants

Restaurant reservations are seldom needed except during school, Easter, and summer holidays (July, January, and February). Attire is informal, and tipping is the same as in the rest of the country (about 10%). Most menus will feature regional dishes such as *trucha,*the salmon-like trout commonly found in the lakes and rivers of the district, as well as *cordero* (lamb), *ciervo* (venison), and *jabalí* (wild boar).

Hotels

Idyllic lake-view lodges, cozy *cabañas* (cabins), vast *estancias* (ranches), and inexpensive *hospedajes* or *residenciales* (bed-and-breakfasts) are found in towns and in the countryside throughout northern Patagonia. Superluxurious hotels in Bariloche and Villa La Angostura attract outdoor enthusiasts from all over the world, as do small family-run hostels where backpackers squeeze five to a room. Fishing lodges in the San Martín de los Andes area and the Cholila Valley are not only for anglers; they make great headquarters for hiking, boating, or just getting away. Most of them include all meals. Guides are extra. "Apart-hotels" have small, furnished apartments with kitchenettes. Local tourist offices are helpful in finding anything from a room in a residence to a country inn or a downtown hotel. Advance reservations are highly recommended if you're traveling during peak times (December–March; July for the ski resorts). Note: lodging prices include tax (IVA—which is 21%) unless otherwise noted.

Hotel reviews have been shortened. For full information, visit Fodors.com. Restaurant prices are the average cost of a main course at dinner or, if dinner is not served, at lunch. Hotel prices are the lowest cost of a standard double room in high season.

What It Costs in Argentine Pesos

$	$$	$$$	$$$$
RESTAURANTS			
Under 1,200 pesos	1,200 pesos– 2,100 pesos	2,100 pesos– 3,100 pesos	over 3,100 pesos
HOTELS (IN US$)			
Under $116	$116–$200	$201–$300	over $300

Tours

El Claro Turismo
GUIDED TOURS | For 29 years, El Claro Turismo has been leading excursions to Cerro Chapelco and Parque Nacional Lanín. Visitors can choose a half- or full-day tour to nearby attractions like Villa Quila Quina, or opt for a week-long package that includes accommodations, airport transfers, and some meals. ⊠ *Colonel Diaz 751, San Martín de los Andes* ☎ *2972/428–876, 2972/425–876* ⊕ *www. elclaroturismo.com.ar.*

Siete Lagos Turismo
GUIDED TOURS | This outfit provides a comprehensive range of tourism services including guided excursions, vehicle rentals, airport transfers, plus bus and hotel reservations. Its rafting adventures are particularly popular. ⊠ *Villegas 313, San Martín de los Andes* ☎ *2972/427–877, 294/462–6026 For WhatsApp.*

Destino Andino
HORSEBACK RIDING | This tour agency organizes horse-riding excursions to Cerro Chapelco and the surrounding mountains. ⊠ *Av. San Martín 555, San Martín de los Andes* ☎ *2972/41–1300* ⊕ *www.destinoandino.tur.ar/san-martin-de-los-andes/actividades/Cabalgatas/1/* ⊠ *From 4,500 pesos.*

Visitor Information

The comprehensive InterPatagonia website, covering every city and region in Patagonia, is an excellent resource for travelers. Local tourist offices (Direcciónes de Turismo) are helpful, easy to find, and usually open late every day.

Bariloche

1,615 km (1,001 miles) southwest of Buenos Aires (2 hours by plane); 432 km (268 miles) south of Neuquén on R237; 1,639 km (1,016 miles) north of Río Gallegos; 876 km (543 miles) northwest of Trelew; 357 km (221 miles) east of Puerto Montt, Chile, via lake crossing.

Bariloche is the gateway to all the recreational and scenic splendors of the northern Lake District and the headquarters for Parque Nacional Nahuel Huapi. Although planes, boats, and buses arrive daily, you can escape on land or water—or just by looking out a window—into a dazzling wilderness of lakes, waterfalls, mountain glaciers, forests, and meadows.

Skiing in Bariloche offers the best views of the lakes.

The town of Bariloche hugs the south-eastern shore of Lago Nahuel Huapi, expanding rapidly east toward the airport and west along the lake toward Llao Llao, as Argentineans and foreigners buy and build without any apparent zoning plan. Being the most popular vacation destination in Patagonia has not been kind to the town once called the "Switzerland of the Andes." Traffic barely moves on streets and sidewalks during holidays and the busy months (January, February, March, July, and August).

Nevertheless, the Centro Cívico (Civic Center) has not lost its architectural integrity. Designed by Alejandro Bustillo (1889–1982), the landmark square is as handsome as ever; and the buildings around it—with their gray-green local stone, brightly varnished wood, and decorative gable ends—are prime examples of the region's signature alpine style. With its view of the lake and mountains, the Centro Cívico is a good place to begin exploring Bariloche.

GETTING HERE AND AROUND

Many travelers choose to come via the Chilean Lakes crossing. If you're flying from Buenos Aires, regular nonstop flights take about two hours; by contrast, long-distance sleeper buses from the capital can take up to 23 hours. The airport is 30 minutes from the Centro Cívico, the bus terminal is 15; in either case, you can take a public bus into town (rutas 72 and 10, respectively) or grab a cab.

For long excursions, such as the Ruta de los Siete Lagos, Circuito Grande, or Tronadór, sign up for a tour through your hotel or with a local tour agency. The *Guía Busch,* available at car-rental agencies, kiosks, and hotels, has listings of the latter along with good maps. Fishing, rafting, and biking trips typically include transportation from your hotel; skiers can reach the slopes by public bus, although many hotels also have private shuttles. If you prefer the independence of figuring out maps and driving yourself, rent a car.

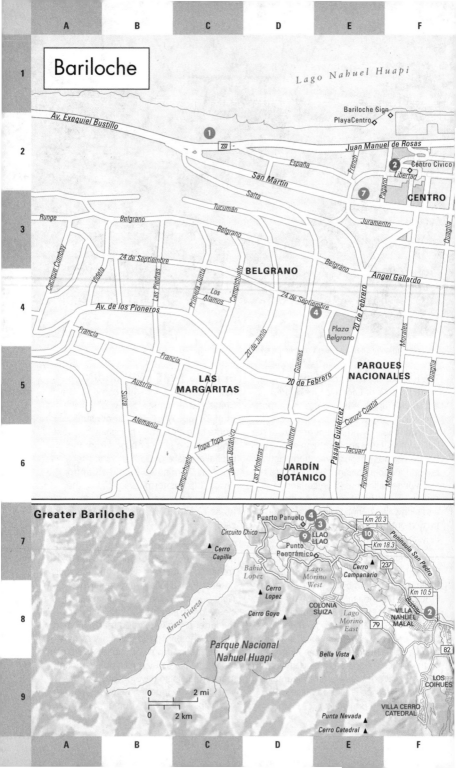

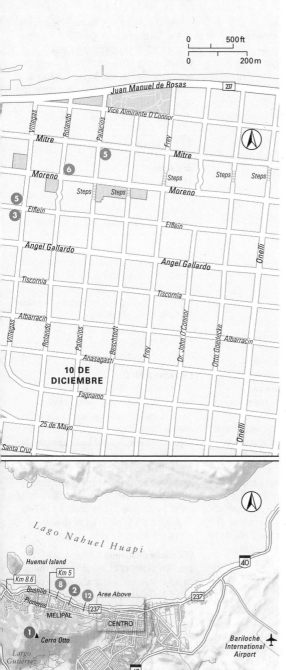

Driving in Bariloche requires total attention to blind corners, one-way streets, and stop signs where no one stops. Be wary of road construction as avenues such as Bustillo regularly undergo maintenance work. Don't leave anything in your car. Bariloche's challenging sidewalks are riddled with uneven steps, broken pavement, and unexpected holes—all potential ankle breakers.

ESSENTIALS

VISITOR AND TOUR INFORMATION

Oficina Municipal de Turismo. ✉ *Centro Cívico, across from clock tower, Bariloche* ☎ *2944/429–850* 🌐 *www.barilocheturismo.gob.ar.*

Sights

Cerro Otto

MOUNTAIN | For an aerial view of the area around Bariloche, ascend 1,405 meters (4,608 feet) to the top of Cerro Otto. A little red cable car owned by **Teleférico Cerro Otto** will carry you there in about 12 minutes, and all ticket proceeds go to local hospitals. **■ TIP→ A free shuttle bus leaves from the corner of Mitre and Villegas, and Perito Moreno and Independencia.** You can also hike or bike to the top, or drive up from Bariloche on a gravel road. In winter, cross-country skis and sleds are for rent at the cafeteria. In summer, hiking and mountain biking are the main activities. There is a revolving restaurant on the summit. For a real thrill, try soaring out over the lake in a paraplane. ✉ *Av. de los Pioneros, 5 km (3 miles) west of Bariloche, Bariloche* ☎ *2944/441–031, 2944/441–035 for information on schedules and equipment rental* 🌐 *www.telefericobariloche.com.ar* 🎫 *2,550 pesos* 🕒 *Cable car may close for a few wks in May for maintenance.*

Museo de la Patagonia

HISTORY MUSEUM | This small museum explains the social and geological history of northern Patagonia through displays of Indian and gaucho artifacts and exhibits on regional flora and fauna. The stories of the Mapuche and the Conquista del Desierto (Conquest of the Desert) are told in detail. ✉ *Centro Cívico, next to arch over Bartolomé Mitre, Bariloche* ☎ *2944/422–309* 🌐 *www.museodelapatagonia.nahuelhuapi.gov.ar* 🎫 *250 peso donation* 🕒 *Closed Sat. and Sun.*

Restaurants

★ Cassis

$$$$ | CONTEMPORARY | Chef Mariana Wolf combines the freshest seasonal ingredients, many from her own rural garden, in beautifully presented dishes that are both elegant and comforting. Savor standout dishes like prawns with rosehip relish, barley, and ginger while gazing at the tranquil shores of Lago Gutierrez. **Known for:** organic, homegrown ingredients; dazzling desserts; intimate service. [$] *Average main: US$45* ✉ *Ruta 82, Km 5.5, Lago Gutiérrez, Bariloche* ☎ *294/459-3650* 🕒 *Closed Sun.–Tues. and low season. No lunch.*

Cerveceria Blest

$$ | ARGENTINE | This lively spot claims that it was the first brewpub in Argentina, and its relaxed bustle hits the spot after a day on the slopes. You can come in just for an après-ski beer sampler or stay for pizzas, steak potpies, and other Anglophile dinner options. **Known for:** extensive range of artisan beer; cozy atmosphere; hearty goulash. [$] *Average main: pesos1500* ✉ *Av. Bustillo km 4, Bariloche* ☎ *294/451–8422* 🌐 *www.cervezablest.com.*

El Boliche de Alberto

$$$ | STEAKHOUSE | Leather place mats, calfskin menus, and the smell of beef all hint heavily at steak house. El Boliche has the best beef in Bariloche. **Known for:** rich, creamy pastas; family-size servings; succulent beef. [$] *Average main: pesos1800* ✉ *Elflein 158, Bariloche* ☎ *2944/401–040* 🌐 *www.elbolichedealberto.com.ar.*

Chilean Lakes Crossing

Cruce a Chile por Los Lagos (*Chile Lake Crossing*). This unique excursion by land and lakes can be done in one or two days in either direction. Travelers board the boat at Puerto Pañuelo, west of Bariloche, then travel by bus up to Laguna Frías, a cold glacial lake frozen in winter. After crossing that lake to Puerto Frías, you pass Argentine customs, then board another bus that climbs through lush rain forest over a pass before descending to Peulla. Clear Chilean customs just before a lodge by Lago Todos los Santos, where you stop for lunch. You may spend the night at the lodge (recommended) or head straight to Chile by catamaran from Peulla, with volcano views. An overnight stay is mandatory in winter. The boat trip ends at the port of Petrohué. Your final bus ride skirts Lago Llanquihue, stopping at the Petrohué waterfalls, and arriving at last in the the town of Puerto Varas. Guides usually speak English, but if you want to stay on the safe side, do this trip with a tour group. ⊠ *Mitre 219, Bariloche* ☎ *2944/426–228* ⊕ *www.cruceandino.com* ✉ *US$392 (not including lunch).*

If you're pressed for time, return to Bariloche by paved road via Osorno, crossing at Cardenal Samoré (aka Paso Puyehue) to Villa La Angostura, which is 125 km (78 miles) from the border to Bariloche on Ruta Nacional 231.

Other Crossings

Paso Hua Hum is the only crossing open year-round. It may be the shortest route—only 47 km (29 miles) from San Martín de los Andes on Ruta Provincial 48—as the condor flies, but it's the longest journey by road, after factoring in the 1½-hour ferry ride across Lake Pirehueico on the Chilean side. There are three ferries daily, and buses leave regularly from San Martín de los Andes. You can also make this crossing by raft on the river Hua Hum.

Farther north, and accessible via Junín de los Andes, are two passes that require a longer excursion. Mamuil Malal (aka Paso Tromen) is 67 km (42 miles) northwest of Junín de los Andes on Ruta Provincial 60. This dirt road crosses Parque Nacional Lanín and passes through a forest of ancient araucaria trees as it heads for the foot of Volcán Lanín. Just before the park office, a road leads to good picnic spots and campsites on Lago Tromen. If you continue on to Chile, you'll see the Villarrica and Quetupillán volcanoes to the south and Pucón to the north.

Paso Icalma is 132 km (82 miles) west of Zapala on Ruta Nacional 13. Villa Pehuenia, 10 km (6 miles) before the pass, is a small village on the shore of Lake Alluminé with modern accommodations and restaurants. Rafting, fishing, or horse, bike, and raft rentals might tempt you to stay awhile.

No fresh fruits, meats, dairy products, or vegetables are allowed across the border, so bring a snack for long stretches without food. Lake crossings are not fun in driving rain and high waves. Snow may close some passes in winter. If driving, double-check with your rental agent that you have all the necessary paperwork. It's also good to have some Chilean pesos with you; it can be expensive to change them at the border.

Did You Know?

Bariloche is located at the bottom of the Andes Mountains and is within the Nahuel Huapi National Park, Argentina's oldest national park.

Il Gabbiano

$$$$ | **ITALIAN** | Staff at this cozy but elegant candlelit house on the Circuito Chico near Llao Llao boast, "we don't serve lunch because preparing dinner takes all day." It's hard to argue with that after you sample the exquisite Italian menu, which changes weekly. Look for pumpkin ravioli or tortelloni stuffed with wild boar; they also have a way with fresh trout. **Known for:** charming bow-tie wearing waiters; melt-in-your-mouth osso buco; authentic, homemade pastas. [$] *Average main: pesos6500* ✉ *Av. Bustillo, Km 24.300, Bariloche* ☎ *2944/448–346, 294/428–4591 WhatsApp* 🌐 *www.facebook.com/ilgabbiano.bariloche/* 🕓 *Closed Mon.–Wed. No lunch.*

Jauja

$$$ | **ARGENTINE** | Locals come to this friendly restaurant for its outstanding pastas and variety of entrées: expect meats from Patagonia to the pampas, fish from both oceans, local game, and fresh vegetables. Hearty portions make this an ideal place to end a long day on the slopes. ■**TIP→ Empanadas and take-out items can be ordered at the entrance.** **Known for:** generous servings; regional dishes; delicious pastas. [$] *Average main: pesos2100* ✉ *Elflein 148, Bariloche* ☎ *2944/422–952* 🌐 *www.restaurantejauja.com.ar.*

Hotels

If you don't have a car, finding a place in town may be the most convenient option. That said, local buses run regularly and choosing a hotel or cabin en route to the Llao Llao Peninsula will give you better access to hiking trails and lake views. Many of the restaurants with the best views are also located away from the city center. Distances listed for out-of-town dining and lodging properties are measured in kilometers from the Bariloche Centro Cívico.

Cacique Inacayal

$$ | **HOTEL** | The waterside Cacique Inacayal has a spectacular spa and swimming pool with views overlooking Lake Nahuel Huapi. **Pros:** impressive views; central location; pianist in lobby. **Cons:** no air-conditioning; dated decor; rooms facing nearby disco can be noisy. [$] *Rooms from: US$180* ✉ *Juan Manuel de Rosas 625, Bariloche* ☎ *2944/433–888* 🌐 *www.hotelinacayal.com.ar* 🛏 *67 rooms* 🍴 *Free Breakfast.*

El Casco Art Hotel

$$$ | **HOTEL** | At this stunning modern hotel all public spaces—halls, wine bar, gourmet restaurant, even the downstairs gym, indoor-out pool, and large Jacuzzi—face the lake, and a private launch docked at the pier makes getting out on the water easy. **Pros:** art everywhere; activities galore; the area's most stylish option. **Cons:** next to highway; transport required to get to city center; dim lighting in rooms. [$] *Rooms from: US$240* ✉ *Av. Bustillo, Km 11.5, Bariloche* ☎ *2944/463–131* 🌐 *www.hotelelcasco.com* 🛏 *32 suites* 🍴 *Free Breakfast.*

Hostería Katy

$ | **B&B/INN** | **FAMILY** | This charming country cottage is surrounded by more than an acre of forest and offers simple rooms that are clean, quiet, and filled with natural light. **Pros:** stunning location surrounded by nature; car rental and airport transfers available; homemade bread and jams at breakfast. **Cons:** difficult to get to and from without a car; basic rooms and amenities; far from the center of Bariloche. [$] *Rooms from: US$107* ✉ *Bustillo km 24.300* ☎ *2944/448–023* 🌐 *www.hosteriakaty.com* 🛏 *7 rooms* 🍴 *Free Breakfast.*

Hosteria Las Marianas

$$ | **B&B/INN** | On a quiet street surrounded by well-tended gardens, this perfectly proportioned Tyrolean villa in Barrio Belgrano (Bariloche's nicest neighborhood) is only four blocks from the city center, but it feels a world away. **Pros:** sunny hillside

location; away from the crowds; friendly, multilingual staff. **Cons:** tiny bathrooms; echoey hallways; uphill haul from city center. $ *Rooms from: US$150* ⊠ *24 de Septiembre 218, Bariloche* ☎ *2944/439–876* ⊕ *www.lasmarianashotel.com* ⤴ *16 rooms* ⦿ *Free Breakfast.*

Hotel Cristal
$$$ | HOTEL | This basic businesslike hotel lies in the center of Bariloche and has a fully equipped health club—complete with pool and spa. **Pros:** central location on a popular downtown street; good value; generous breakfast. **Cons:** street-facing rooms can be noisy; frequented by tour groups; small bathrooms. $ *Rooms from: US$220* ⊠ *Mitre 355, Bariloche* ☎ *2944/422–442* ⊕ *www.hotel-cristal.com.ar* ⤴ *50 rooms* ⦿ *Free Breakfast.*

Hotel Nahuel Huapi
$ | HOTEL | This slick hotel on a busy downtown street in Bariloche has a spacious lobby with a wine bar in one corner and a sit-around fireplace in another; some rooms have a nice view into the neighboring garden. **Pros:** central location; good accessibility for people with disabilities; comfy bed. **Cons:** elevator does not reach top floor; scatty Wi-Fi; rooms overlooking street might be noisy. $ *Rooms from: US$110* ⊠ *Moreno 252, Bariloche* ☎ *2944/442–6146* ⊕ *www.hotelnahuelhuapi.com.ar* ⤴ *74 rooms* ⦿ *Free Breakfast.*

Hotel NH Edelweiss
$$$ | HOTEL | This medium-sized hotel is within walking distance of everything in town and its top-floor rooms have stunning lake views and bay windows. **Pros:** great location; spacious rooms; fancy fitness center. **Cons:** so-so streetside restaurant; decor needs a makeover; no air conditioning. $ *Rooms from: US$250* ⊠ *Av. San Martín 202, Bariloche* ☎ *2944/445–500* ⊕ *www.edelweiss.com.ar* ⤴ *99 rooms* ⦿ *Free Breakfast.*

Hotel Tronadór
$$ | HOTEL | This all-inclusive stone-and-log lodge on Lago Mascardi is the perfect springboard to explore the glaciers and waterfalls of Monte Tronadór, which lies only 25 km (16 miles) up the road. **Pros:** practically in the lap of the region's highest mountain glacier; amenities include a game room, private beach, and organic garden; peaceful location. **Cons:** activities not included in price; difficult to get to and from; the road here is one-way heading toward the hotel 10:30 am–2 pm, one-way heading away 4 pm–7:30 pm, and two-way 7:30 pm–9 am only. $ *Rooms from: US$160* ⊠ *RN40 west from Bariloche 66 km, past Villa Masacardi, turn right on dirt road to west end of Lago Mascardi, Bariloche* ☎ *2944/490–550* ⊕ *www.hoteltronador.com* ⊙ *Closed mid-Apr.–mid-Nov.* ⤴ *36 rooms* ⦿ *Free Breakfast.*

★ Llao Llao Hotel & Resort
$$$$ | RESORT | This masterpiece by architect Alejandro Bustillo, surrounded by three lakes and looking out to cliffs and snow-covered mountains, caters to all tastes; the historic main building has quirky rooms with locally crafted, one-of-a-kind furniture pieces, while those in the newer Lake Moreno wing incorporate a more modern aesthetic. **Pros:** gorgeous setting with dramatic lake views; helpful staff; lots of activities. **Cons:** 40 minutes from Bariloche center; rooms in historic wing a little dated; pricey. $ *Rooms from: US$417* ⊠ *Av. Bustillo, Km 25, 25 km (16 miles) west of Bariloche, Bariloche* ☎ *2944/448–530* ⊕ *www.llaollao.com* ⤴ *205 rooms* ⦿ *Free Breakfast.*

Península Petit Hotel
$$ | HOTEL | Combining the amenities of a hotel with the warmth of a home, this handsome lodge sitting at the edge of Lake Nahuel Huapi is a great getaway spot for couples. **Pros:** all suites have lake views; waterfront activities; homemade breakfast. **Cons:** 25 minutes from center; walls are a bit thin; limited

capacity. $ *Rooms from: US$140* ✉ *Av. Campanario 493, Bariloche* ☎ *9294/427–5555* ⊕ *www.peninsulapetithotel.com. ar* ⊘ *Closed May* ⇨ *11 rooms* ⦿ *Free Breakfast.*

Peuma Hue

$$$$ | **HOTEL** | **FAMILY** | Inside Peuma Hue, a sense of rustic luxury prevails (picture pine beams overhead, kilim rugs on wood floors, and guests gathered around the stone fireplace); outside, Lago Gutiérrez shimmers through the trees across the lawn. **Pros:** lovely grounds; massage, yoga, and wine tastings are just the tip of the activities iceberg; delicious organic meals. **Cons:** remote location; little to do when the weather is bad; charges for extra activities. $ *Rooms from: US$399* ✉ *R40, Km 2014, Enter dirt road, about 2 miles to Lago Gutiérrez, Bariloche* ☎ *294/450-1030* ⊕ *www.peuma-hue.com* ⇨ *16 rooms* ⦿ *Free Breakfast* ⌕ *30% deposit required.*

Villa Huinid

$$$ | **HOTEL** | This peaceful complex consists of a grand hotel and older two-story log-and-stucco cottages on the lawns below—the latter have stone chimneys, well-tended gardens, and wooden decks that give them the appearance of private homes. **Pros:** cabins have one-to-four bedrooms, combining privacy with hotel amenities; lake-view pool and spa; family and play areas on-site. **Cons:** 15–20 minute walk into town; can be busy with tour groups, particularly at breakfast; outdoor hike from cabins to breakfast in hotel. $ *Rooms from: US$250* ✉ *Av. Bustillo, Km 2.6, Bariloche* ☎ *2944/523–523* ⇨ *91 rooms* ⦿ *Free Breakfast.*

🛍 Shopping

Along Bariloche's main streets, Calles Mitre and Moreno, and the cross streets from Quaglia to Rolando, you can find shops selling sports equipment, leather goods, hand-knit sweaters, and gourmet food like homemade jams, dried meats, and chocolate.

Ahumadero Familia Weiss

FOOD | Come here to buy delicious pâtés, cheeses, smoked fish, and wild game. ✉ *Vice Almte. O'Connor 401, Bariloche* ☎ *294/412-3776* ⊕ *ahumadero-familia-weiss.business.site.*

Asociación Civil de Artesanos de Bariloche

(*Bariloche Artisan Civil Association*) **CRAFTS** | This not-for-profit organization sells work from Bariloche's local artisans including jewelry, ornaments, and ceramics. ✉ *Ada María Elflein 38, Bariloche* ☎ *294/452–9521* ⊕ *www.facebook.com/lacasadelosartesanosbariloche/* ⊘ *Closed Sun.*

Mamuschka

CHOCOLATE | Crowned by giant mamuschka dolls, this renowned chocolate store is famous for its range of high quality, if slightly more expensive, chocolate and pastry products. Ask for the house specialty (a chocolate mousse "Timbal") or simply admire the beautifully decorated *bombones* (chocolate balls). ✉ *Mitre 298, Bariloche* ☎ *294/442–3294* ⊕ *www.mamuschka.com.*

Rapa Nui

CHOCOLATE | A Willy Wonka land overflowing with chocolate, sweets, and ice cream, Rapa Nui has treats to delight adults and children alike. Established in 1939, it is one of the longest-running *chocolaterías.* ✉ *Mitre 202, Bariloche* ☎ *0294/442–3779* ⊕ *www.chocolatesrapanui.com.ar.*

Activities

FISHING

Fishing season runs November 15–April 15 (extended through May in certain areas), and guides are available by the day or the week. Nahuel Huapi, Gutiérrez, Mascardi, Correntoso, and Traful are the most accessible lakes in the Lake District. If you're seeking the perfect pool or secret stream for fly-fishing, you may have to do some hiking, particularly along the banks of the Chimehuín, Limay, Traful, and Correntoso rivers. Near Junín de los Andes the Malleo and Currihué rivers, and lakes Huechulafquen, Paimún, and Lácar are good fishing grounds. Note that catch-and-release is usually compulsory.

Baruzzi Deportes
FISHING | Oscar Baruzzi at Baruzzi Deportes is a good local fishing guide. ✉ *Urquiza 250, Bariloche* ☎ *02944/428–374* ⊕ *www.barilochefishing.com.*

Direcciones Provinciales de Pesca
FISHING | Fishing licenses allowing you to catch brown, rainbow, and brook trout as well as perch and *salar sebago* (landlocked salmon) are obtainable in Bariloche at the Direcciones Provinciales de Pesca. You can also get licenses at the Nahuel Huapi National Park office and at most tackle shops. Nonresident license fees are 2,400 pesos/day and 12,800 pesos/season. ✉ *Elfleín 10, Bariloche* ⊕ *www.permisosdepesca.com.ar/ofertas.php.*

Patagonia Anglers
FISHING | This shop carries fishing and hunting equipment. ✉ *Moreno 205, Bariloche* ☎ *291/571–7718* ⊕ *www.patagoniaanglers.com.ar.*

Patagonia Fly Shop
FISHING | Ricardo Almeijeiras, also a guide, owns the Patagonia Fly Shop. ✉ *Quinchahuala 200, Av. Bustillo, Km 6.7, Bariloche* ☎ *2944/441–944* ⊕ *www.richard-ameijeiras.com.*

HIKING

For day hikes along the shores of Nahuel Huapi Lake, try the trails of the Circuito Chico in Parque Municipal Llao Llao. For altitude and grand panoramas, take the ski lift to the top of Cerro Catedral and follow the ridge trail to Refugio Frey, returning down to the base of the ski area. West of Bariloche, turn right at Villa Mascardi onto the dirt road to Pampa Linda; from there you can take a day-long hike to the Otto Meiling Refuge or make shorter forays to the glacier and nearby waterfalls. A three-day trek will take you right past Tronadór and its glacier, along the Alerce River, and over the Paso de los Nubes (Cloud Pass) to Puerto Blest, returning to Bariloche by boat.

Paseo de los Duendes
HIKING & WALKING | Looking for a child-friendly excursion? The 1-km (½-mile) Paseo de los Duendes—or Walk of the Elves—in Villa Los Coihues leads to a small but pretty waterfall. You can also hike onward for a view of the nearby Lago Gutiérrez or follow the 7½-km (5-mile) trail to Playa Muñoz. Once a campground, this area is still regenerating, and while wide paths make it easy to navigate, it does not have the same impact as other hiking trails. ✉ *Perito Moreno, Villa Los Coihues, Bariloche.*

Parque Municipal Llao Llao
HIKING & WALKING | Llao Llao Municipal Park has two main trails, each approximately 3 km (2 miles) long. One takes you through the mixed forest of coihues and mountain cypresses to the top of Cerro Llao Llao for a stunning view of Lake Nahuel Huapi. The other continues on to the small coastal beaches of Villa Tacul (Tacul Village), where you can paddle in the lake or explore the ruins of what is thought to be an abandoned World War II bunker. Access the park by taking the Route 20 bus to the end of the line or driving along Avenida Ezequiel Bustillo until you reach the beginning of the Circuito Chico. ✉ *Av. Bustillo Km 27.5, Bariloche.*

HORSEBACK RIDING
Bastión del Manso
WHITE-WATER RAFTING | This outfitter combines riding and rafting over the border to Chile. ✉ *Mitre 442, 2B, Bariloche* ☎ *2944/53–7024* ⊕ *bastiontravel.com* 💵 *From 2100 pesos.*

The Llao Llao Municipal Park trails offer stunning views of Lake Nahuel Huapi.

Carol Jones

HORSEBACK RIDING | The granddaughter of an early pioneering family, Carol Jones's ranch north of town does day rides and overnights from the Patagonian steppes into the mountains. ✉ *Modesta Victoria 5600, Bariloche* ☎ *2944/426–508* 🌐 *www.caroljones.com.ar* 🎫 *From $35 (cash only).*

Tom Wesley

HORSEBACK RIDING | Located at the Club Hípico Bariloche, Tom Wesley offers rides lasting from one hour to several days. ✉ *Av. Bustillo, Km 15.5, Bariloche* ☎ *2944/448–193* 🌐 *www.cabalgatastomwesley.com* 🎫 *From 2,500 pesos* 🕙 *Closed May–Jun.*

SKIING

Cerro Catedral (*Mount Cathedral*)

SKIING & SNOWBOARDING | Named for its Gothic-looking spires, Cerro Catedral is the oldest ski area in South America, with 38 lifts, 1,820 hectares (4,500 acres) of mostly intermediate terrain, and a comfortable altitude of 2,050 meters (6,725 feet). The runs are long, varied, and scenic. One side of the mountain has a vertical drop of 914 meters (3,000 feet), mostly in the fall line. Near the top of the highest chairlift at 2,250 meters (7,385 feet) is Refugio Lynch, a small restaurant on the edge of an abyss with a stupendous 360-degree view of Nahuel Huapi Lake. To the southwest, Monte Tronadór, an extinct volcano straddling the border with Chile, towers above lesser peaks that surround the lake. Other on-site facilities include a terrain park and picturesque cross-country ski trails. August and September are the best months to hit the slopes: avoid the first three weeks of July (school vacation).

Villa Catedral, at the base of the mountain, has numerous equipment retail and rental shops, information and ticket sales, ski-school offices, restaurants, and even a disco. Frequent buses transport skiers from Bariloche to the ski area. For information and trail maps, contact **La Secretaría de Turismo de Río Negro** (✉ *12 de Octubre 2944/429–896*). **Club Andino Bariloche** (✉ *20 de Febrero 2944/422–266*)

also has information and trail maps.
✉ *46 km (29 miles) west of Bariloche on R237; turn left at Km 8.5 just past Playa Bonita, Bariloche ⚓ 46 km (29 miles) west of town on Av. Bustillo (R237); turn left at Km 8.5 just past Playa Bonita* ☎ *2944/409–000* ⊕ *www.catedralaltapatagonia.com* 🖾 *From 3,000 pesos (high season)*.

San Martín de los Andes and Nearby

San Martín de los Andes

260 km (161 miles) north of Bariloche on R237, R40, and R234 via Junín de los Andes (a 4-hour drive); 158 km (98 miles) north of Bariloche on R237 and R63 over the Córdoba Pass (less than half is unpaved); 90 km (56 miles) northeast of Villa La Angostura on R234 (Ruta de los Siete Lagos, partly unpaved and closed for much of winter).

Surrounded by lakes, dense forests, and mountains, San Martín de los Andes lies in a natural basin at the foot of Lago Lácar. It's a small, easygoing town, much like Bariloche was many decades ago, with hotels and houses reflecting the distinctive Andean alpine architecture of Bustillo. Wide, flat streets lined with rosebushes run from the town pier on the eastern shore of Lago Lácar to the main square, Plaza San Martín, where two parallel streets—San Martín and General Villegas—teem with block after block of ski and fishing shops, chocolatiers, souvenir stores, clothing boutiques, and cafés.

The Mapuche lived in the area long before immigrants of Chilean, French, Dutch, and Italian descent founded the town in 1898. Because all of the water from this area runs into the Pacific, the territory was disputed by Chile, which claimed it as its own until 1902, when it was legally declared Argentine.

After Parque Nacional Lanín was established in 1937 and the ski area at Chapelco developed in the 1970s, tourism replaced forestry as the main source of income. Today San Martín is the major tourist center in Neuquén Province—the midpoint in the Ruta de los Siete Lagos and the gateway for exploring the Parque Nacional Lanín.

GETTING HERE AND AROUND
Aerolíneas Argentina makes the two-hour flight from Buenos Aires up to three times a day, but most people arrive from Bariloche via Junín de los Andes or along the Ruta de los Siete Lagos. El Valle buses make frequent daily trips between Bariloche and San Martín; the first typically leaves at 6 am and the last at 6 pm. The picturesque journey takes four hours with a brief stopover in Villa La Angostura. The centrally located San Martín bus terminal is within walking distance of most hotels.

Being flat, the town is pleasant for pedestrians. To access nearby beaches, hiking trails, or the ski area in winter, you need to rent a car, join a tour, or be an energetic cyclist. Taxis are inexpensive, and remises can be arranged through your hotel.

ESSENTIALS
VISITOR AND TOUR INFORMATION
Dirección Municipal de Turismo. ✉ *J.M. Rosas 790, at Av. San Martín, San Martín de los Andes* ☎ *2972/427–315* ⊕ *www.sanmartindelosandes.gov.ar.*

Sights

Mirador de las Bandurrias (*Bandurrias Overlook*)
VIEWPOINT | From town you can hike, mountain bike, or drive 5 km (3 miles) up a steep hill through a dense forest of cypress and oak to the Mirador de las Bandurrias, where you'll be rewarded

with a view of San Martín and the lake. The chance to visit **Paraje Trompul**—a Mapuche community that's home to about 40 families—is an added bonus. After taking a snack break in the *quincho* (café) and perusing the weavings and wood carvings sold here, you can continue another 5 km (3 miles) to see **Playa La Islita,** a small, rocky island in the middle of Lácar Lake.

If you're walking, take Avenida San Martín to the lake, turn right, cross the bridge behind the waterworks plant over Puahullo Creek, and then head uphill on a path around the mountain. By car, leave town on RP48 and drive about 4 km (3 miles) to a turnoff (no sign) on your left. Take the turn and continue to Comunidad Mapuche Curruhuinca, where you pay a fee for the lookout. ⊠ *San Martín de los Andes* 🏷 *150 pesos.*

Museo Primeros Pobladores (*Pioneer Museum*)

HISTORY MUSEUM | Next to the tourist office, this museum occupies the tiny building that served as the original city council lodge. It is mainly dedicated to Mapuche ceramics and weavings; a collection of 13,000-year-old tools and fossils gives an idea of ancient life in the region. ⊠ *J.M. de Rosas 700, San Martín de los Andes* ☎ *2972/412–306* 🏷 *By donation.*

🏖 Beaches

Playa Catritre

BEACH | **FAMILY** | Easy access and a family-friendly atmosphere have made Playa Catritre one of the most popular beaches in San Martín. On the south side of Lago Lácar, 4 km (3 miles) from the town center, it's a great spot to enjoy a dip in the calm, clear lake waters, and admire the view of the Cerro Bandurrias. Oak trees provide shade for picnics, and water activities for children are available. A Mapuche-run campground is nearby. **Amenities:** food and drink; water sports. **Best for:** swimming; walking. ☒ *4 km (3 miles) from San Martín on R234, San Martín de los Andes.*

Playa Quila Quina

BEACH | Situated in a Mapuche village, this small lakeside beach is a tourist hotspot with ferries bringing visitors from San Martín five times a day. It's possible to arrive by car, but be prepared for a steep descent down to the rocky beach. Although busy, Playa Quila Quina is perfect for swimming and enjoying the panoramic views of Lake Lácar. Not far from the shore, a trail leads to a small waterfall (Arroyo Grande). To reach Playa Quila Quina, turn off R234 2 km (1 mile) before the road to Catrite and get on R108. **Amenities:** food and drink; parking; toilets. **Best for:** swimming; walking. ☒ *18 km (11 miles) from San Martín on R108, San Martín de los Andes.*

 Restaurants

Fondue Betty

$$$ | ARGENTINE | FAMILY | It wouldn't be a ski town without a fondue restaurant, and this one is particularly appealing. The cheese fondue is smooth and rich, while the meat version comes with cubes of Argentine beef in assorted cuts and up to 12 condiments. **Known for:** family-friendly service; fantastic wine list; abundant fondue. ⓢ *Average main: pesos3000* ☒ *Obeid 956, San Martín de los Andes* ☎ *2972/422–522* ⊙ *No lunch.*

Kú

$$ | ARGENTINE | Cozy dark-wood tables and booths, a friendly staff, a chalkboard listing tempting specials—these are good building blocks for a restaurant. Order the smoked-meat plate with venison, boar,

trout, salmon, and cheese as a starter; then try the Patagonian lamb *al asador* (on the open fire). **Known for:** extensive dessert menu; cozy atmosphere; succulent steaks. ⓢ *Average main: pesos1000* ☒ *Av. San Martín 1053, San Martín de los Andes* ☎ *2972/427–039* ⊕ *www. facebook.com/kudelosandes.*

La Tasca

$$$ | ARGENTINE | This is one of the traditional top-end choices in town for locals and tourists alike. With tables scattered about the black-stone floor, and wine barrels, shelves, and every other imaginable surface stacked with pickled vegetables, smoked meats, cheese rounds, dried herbs, olive oils, and wine bottles, you might think you're in a Patagonian deli. **Known for:** rustic charm; homemade pastas; local wild game dishes. ⓢ *Average main: pesos2200* ☒ *Moreno 886, San Martín de los Andes* ☎ *2972/428–663.*

Hotels

Apart del Sauco

$$ | APARTMENT | Accommodating up to eight guests, these clean, well-equipped apartments are a practical option for families and for any travelers considering longer stays. **Pros:** swimming pool; full kitchen; good base for exploring national parks. **Cons:** basic hotel services; 15-minute walk to center; bland decor. ⓢ *Rooms from: US$130* ☒ *Calderón 364, San Martín de los Andes* ☎ *2972/411–900* ⊕ *www.delsauco.com.ar* ⤶ *15 rooms* ⦿ *Free Breakfast.*

Patagonia Plaza Hotel

$$$ | HOTEL | Located around the corner from shops, tourist offices, and restaurants, this modern downtown hotel swaps genteel rusticity for state-of-the-art amenities and services. **Pros:** central location; big rooms with modern bathrooms with hydromassage baths; fitness center with swimming pool and sauna. **Cons:** no air-conditioning; street-facing rooms can be noisy; restaurant lacks atmosphere. $ Rooms from: pesos230 ⊠ Av. San Martín at Rivadavia, San Martín de los Andes ☎ 2972/422–280 ⊕ www. hotelpatagoniaplaza.com.ar ⊋ 87 rooms ♚ Free Breakfast.

 Activities

Tour agencies can arrange rafting trips on the Hua Hum or Aluminé rivers, guided mountain biking, horseback riding, and fishing tours, plus excursions to lakes in both Lanín and Nahuel Huapi national parks.

El Refugio
HIKING & WALKING | Active travelers can join this full service tour company and travel agency for rafting, trekking, mountain biking, fly-fishing, and skiing excursions. Overland road tours are available for the less intrepid. El Refugio can also book accommodations. ⊠ Villegas 698, San Martín de los Andes ☎ 2972/425–140 ⊕ www.elrefugioturismo.com.ar ⊲ From 3,000 pesos.

BOATING
Lacar and Nonthue
BOATING | You can rent small boats, canoes, and kayaks at the pier from Lacar and Nonthue. You can also rent a bicycle and take an all-day excursion to the other side of Lake Lácar, where there is a nice beach and woods to explore. Another option is the boat tour to Hua Hum at the western end of the lake, where the river of the same name runs to the Chilean border. ⊠ Av. Costanera 901, San Martín de los Andes ☎ 2972/427–380 ⊕ lagolacarynonthue.com.

FISHING
During the fishing season (November 15–April 15, extended to the end of May in certain areas), local guides will take you to their favorite spots on lagos Lácar, Lolog, Villarino, and Falkner and on the ríos Caleufu, Quiquihue, Malleo, and Hermoso, or farther afield to the Chimehuín River and Lakes Huechulafquen and Paimún.

Intendencia de Parque Nacional Lanin
FISHING | Permits for fishing are available at the Lanín National Park Office or any licensed fishing store along Avenida San Martín. Most stores and tour operators can suggest guides. ⊠ Eduardo Elordi 600, San Martín de los Andes ☎ 2972/420–664 ⊕ www.pnlanin.org.

Jorge Cardillo
FISHING | Since opening his small Fly Shop in 1994, this well-known local guide has gained a reputation for his friendly, familial fishing trips to nearby rivers like Meliquina, Filo Hua-Hum, and Caleufu. ⊠ Villegas 1061, behind casino, San Martín de los Andes ☎ 2972/428–372.

HORSEBACK RIDING
Destino Andino
HORSEBACK RIDING | This tour agency organizes horse-riding excursions to Cerro Chapelco and the surrounding mountains. ⊠ Av. San Martín 555, San Martín de los Andes ☎ 2972/41–1300 ⊕ www.destinoandino.tur.ar/san-martin-de-los-andes/actividades/Cabalgatas/1/ ⊲ From 4,500 pesos.

MOUNTAIN BIKING
HG Rodados
BIKING | San Martín itself is flat, but from there everything goes up. Dirt and paved roads and trails lead through forests to lakes and waterfalls. You can rent bikes in town at HG Rodados. ⊠ Av. San Martín 1061, San Martín de los Andes ☎ 2972/427–345 ⊕ www.facebook.com/hgrodadossma ⊲ From 2,000 pesos per day.

SKIING
Cerro Chapelco (Chapelco Ski Resort)
SKIING & SNOWBOARDING | The Chapelco Ski Resort is ideal for families and beginner-to-intermediate skiers. It has modern facilities and lifts, including a high-speed telecabina (gondola) from the base. On a clear day almost all the runs are visible from the top—a height of 1991 meters (6,534 feet)—and Lanín Volcano dominates the horizon. Lift tickets cost

Parque Nacional Lanín has over 30 mountain lakes.

from 4,500 pesos per day in low season to 6,400 pesos in high season. Equipment rental facilities are available at the base camp (2,700–3,380 pesos per day for skis, boots, and poles). On some days cars need chains to get up to the mountain, so call and check the latest conditions before driving up. Taxis can also take you up or down for about 500 pesos each way.

■ TIP→ **In summer, the Adventure Center has mountain biking for experts and classes for beginners, plus horseback rides, hiking, archery, a swimming pool, an alpine slide, and children's activities.** ⊠ *Information office:, San Martín at Elordi, 23 km (14 miles) southeast of San Martín de los Andes, San Martín de los Andes* ☎ *2972/427–845* ⊕ *www.chapelco.com* ☞ *5 km (3 miles) of road is unpaved.*

WHITE-WATER RAFTING
El Claro Turismo
WHITE-WATER RAFTING | Offering both short and long trips in the area, El Claro Turismo is a good rafting choice. ⊠ *Col. Díaz 751, San Martín de los Andes*

☎ *2972/428–876, 2972/425–876* ⊕ *www. elclaroturismo.com.ar* ✉ *From 550 pesos (discount for cash).*

Siete Lagos Turismo
WHITE-WATER RAFTING | An all-day rafting trip that crosses into Chile on either Río Aluminé or Río Hua Hum can be arranged by Siete Lagos Turismo. Owner Fernando Aguirre, a lifelong resident of the area, also offers two- to four-day camping trips with combinations of rafting, hiking, riding, biking, and kayaking. ⊠ *San Martín 384, San Martín de los Andes* ☎ *2972/427–877* ✉ *From 550 pesos.*

Parque Nacional Lanín

The dramatically beautiful Parque Nacional Lanín contains 35 mountain lakes, countless rivers, ancient forests, and the Volcán Lanín. Tucked into the folds of the Andes along the Chilean border, it stretches 150 km (93 miles) north to south, covering 4,120 square km (1,590 square miles). The area is home to the Mapuche, and you can learn about their

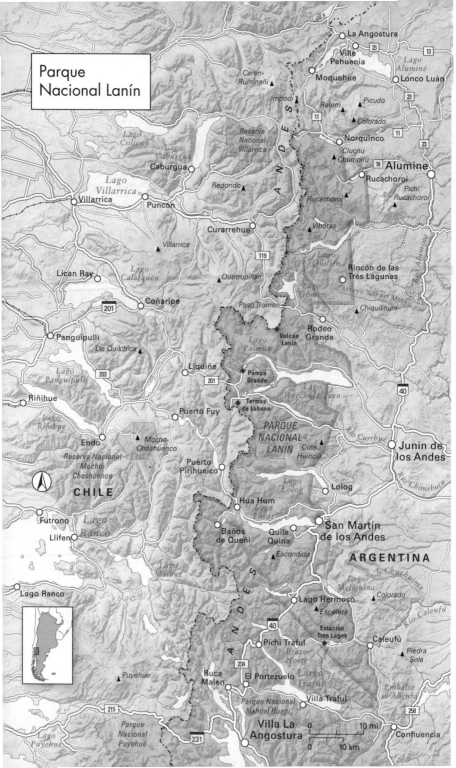

Parque Nacional Lanín

La Angostura
23
13
Lago
Aluminé
Ville
Pehuenia
Caren-
Rumiñañi
Moquehue
Lonco Luán
Impodi
23
Relem
Picudo
11
Colorado
Reserva
National
Villarrica
Norquinco
11
23
Clucnu
Chumpiru
18
Alumine
Lago
Colico
Lago
Caburgua
Caburgua
Rucachoroi
Pichi
Rucachoroi
Lago
Villarrica
Redondo
Rucachoroi
Villarrica
Puncón
Curarrehue
Viboras
Lago
Quillén
Rincón de las
Trés Lagunas
Villarrica
119
Lican Ray
Quetrupillan
Lago
Calafquén
Arroyo Nahuel Mapi
Chiquilihuin
Coñaripe
Lago
Tromen
201
Paso Tromen
Rodeo
Grande
Panguipulli
Volcán
Lanín
De Quilchica
Lago
Painin
Liquiñe
Pampa
Grande
Lago
Panguipulli
201
Lago
Huechulafquen
40
Lago
Riñihue
Puerto Fuy
Termas
de Lahuan
Riñihue
PARQUE
NACIONAL
LANÍN
Río Curruhué
Endo
Mocho-
Choshuenco
Colo
Huincul
Junin de
los Andes
Reserva Nacional
Mocho-
Choshuenco
Puerto
Pirihueico
Lago
Lolog
Lolog
Río Chimehuin
CHILE
Futrono
Hua Hum
San Martín
de los Andes
Lago
Ranco
Baños
de Queñi
Quila
Quina
ARGENTINA
Llifen
Escondido
A. Chuchuima
Lago
Maihue
Lago
Meliquina
Colorado
Lago Ranco
Lago Hermoso
Río Caleufú
Espeleta
Estación
Tres Lagos
Caleufú
40
Pichi Traful
Piedra
Sola
Puyehue
Brazo
Norte
Ruca
Malen
234
El Portezuelo
Largo
Traful
Embalse
Alicura
Villa Traful
Parque Nacional
Nahuel Huapi
258
215
Villa La
Angostura
0   10 mi
Parque
Nacional
Puyehué
231
0   10 km
Confluencia

history and buy their handicrafts in one of the 50 communities throughout the park.

GETTING HERE AND AROUND

Three towns have access to the park. The northernmost section is reached from Aluminé: 145 km (90 miles) west of Zapala on Ruta Provincial 46, it's a typical Andean community with no paved streets but an abundance of nearby lakes (including Aluminé, Quillén, and Mohquehue). Junín de los Andes, in the middle section, is at the end of the paved road from Bariloche. Another paved road leads 41 km (25 miles) to San Martín, the park's major town, in the southern section. Daily buses run from San Martín and Junín to Lago Huechulafquen and Volcán Lanín; however, service can be unreliable and timetables change depending on the season. In Aluminé, public transport is largely nonexistent, so cars or remises are the only option. Note that all three of these towns have roads leading to the border with Chile (See Chilean Lakes Crossing box).

ESSENTIALS

VISITOR INFORMATION Intendencia de Parques Nacionales. (*National Park Office*) ⊠ *Eduardo Elordi 600, San Martín de los Andes* ☎ *2972/420–664* ⊕ *www.pnlanin. org.*

Sights

Araucaria Araucana

FOREST | Found only in this part of the Andes, the ancient Araucaria Araucana tree grows to 30 meters (100 feet) and has long spiny branches. Cones the size of bowling balls are full of pinon nuts that provided nourishment to the Mapuche, who call these trees *pehuenes.* The northern portion of the park near Lago Huechulafquen and Aluminé is one of the best places to view these peculiar giants. ⊠ *Lago Huechulafquen.*

Volcán Lanín

VOLCANO | Rising 3,773 meters (12,378 feet) in solitary snow-clad splendor on the western horizon, Volcán Lanín towers over the area and is visible from every direction. It sits on the Chilean border, with Lanín National Park on one side and Chile's Villarica National Park on the other. The closest Argentine access is from Junín, but the northern route to Paso Tromen also offers endless photo ops through the tangled branches of the araucaria trees. You can climb Lanín in three to four days round-trip with a guide. ⊕ *www.pnlanin.org.*

Villa Traful

60 km (37 miles) north of Villa La Angostura on R231 and R65; 39 km (23 miles) from Confluencia on R65; 100 km (60 miles) northwest of Bariloche on R237 and R65.

If there were a prize for the most beautiful lake in the region, Lago Traful would win for its clarity, serenity, and wild surroundings. Small log houses peek through the cypress forest along the way to Villa Traful, a village of about 500 inhabitants.

The tiny community consists of log cabins, horse corrals, shops for picnic and fishing supplies, a school, a post office, and a park ranger's office. Well-maintained campgrounds border the lake, and ranches and private fishing lodges are hidden in the surrounding mountains. By day swimmers play on rocky beaches, kayakers cut the still blue water, and divers go below to explore the mysteries of a submerged forest. Night brings silence, stars, and the glow of lakeside campfires.

GETTING HERE AND AROUND

On the Ruta de los Siete Lagos, Villa Traful can be reached by bus from Bariloche, San Martín, and Villa la Angostura (the nearest town); bus operators include Via Bariloche. Otherwise you can come by car or with a tour group. The waterside hamlet is contained within a single

Snow-capped volcano Lanín is visible from almost every part of Parque Nacional Lanín.

circuit, and most stores are in walking distance of the pier.

ESSENTIALS

VISITOR INFORMATION Oficina Municipal de Turismo. ✉ *Across from municipal pier, Ruta provincial No. 65, Villa Traful* ☎ *9294/461–4571* 🌐 *www.villatraful.gob.ar/?q=atencion.*

Hotels

Cabañas Ruca Lico

$$$ | **B&B/INN** | Intimate Ruca Lico hits the sweet spot between ranch and resort; the quaint, rustic interiors are very cozy, and you can admire views of Lago Traful from a private balcony or hot tub. **Pros:** close to lake, trails, and town center; self-catering facilities; price includes airport transfers. **Cons:** small bathroom; challenging walk to lake; limited services. [$] *Rooms from: US$230* ✉ *RP65, Km 35, Villa Traful* ☎ *2944/479–004* 🌐 *www.rucalico.com* 🛏 *6 rooms* 🍴 *No Meals.*

Activities

HIKING

Arroyo Blanco and Arroyo Coa Có

HIKING & WALKING | Drive, walk, or pedal about 3 km (2 miles) up from the village to the trailhead at Pampa de los Alamos, a clearing where the trail to Arroyo Blanco descends into a forest of 1,000-year-old coihué trees with ghostly naked trunks, gigantic lenga (deciduous beech), and ñires that grow only at high altitudes. The trail leads to a wooden walkway along a steep cliff—the only way one could possibly view the waterfall tumbling 20 meters (66 feet) into a dark chasm. Follow the wooden trail along the cliff for increasingly amazing glimpses of this wild gorge, then return up the same route. Arroyo Coa Có is in the opposite direction, with a view of both the waterfall and Lago Traful. ✉ *Villa Traful.*

Casacada Co Lemú

HIKING & WALKING | At the end of an arduous trail, the Casacada Co Lemú thunders down 20 meters (67 feet) with a deafening roar. Drive 8 km (5 miles) west toward the Seven Lakes Route to the bridge over Arroyo Cataratas. Before you cross the stream, on your left, the trail—covering 19 km (12 miles), round-trip—climbs slowly at first, then straight up to the falls. ⊠ *Villa Traful.*

Cerro Negro

HIKING & WALKING | A strenuous seven-hour hike from the village to Cerro Negro climbs up through forests of cypress, coihué, lenga, and ñire, passing strange rock formations en route to the top. The summit—at 1,829 meters (6,000 feet)—promises a splendid view of Lago Traful and across the Andes all the way to Lanín. ⊠ *Villa Traful.*

Laguna Las Mellizas y Pinturas Rupestres

(*The Twins Lagoon and Cave paintings*)
HIKING & WALKING | A 15-minute boat trip across the lake from the wharf takes you to a sandy beach on the northern shore. A two-hour walk down a trail into a steep gully leads to the pools. Nearby caves with 600-year-old Tehuelche cave paintings are worth exploring. The area is protected and registration with national park officials is required. ⊠ *Villa Traful.*

SCUBA DIVING

Bosque Sumergido

SCUBA DIVING | In 1975, a violent earthquake caused half a mountain and its forest of cypress trees to slide to the bottom of the lake, creating the Bosque Sumergido. You can dive to 30 meters (98 feet) in crystalline water and explore this sunken forest. Boat trips can be arranged at **Cabañas Aiken** (☎ 9294/432–9045 *www.aiken.com.ar*). ⊠ *Villa Traful.*

Villa La Angostura

81 km (50 miles) northwest of Bariloche (an hour's drive on R231 around the east end of Lago Nahuel Huapi; also accessible by boat from Bariloche); 90 km (56 miles) southwest of San Martín de los Andes on R234 (the Ruta de los Siete Lagos, partly unpaved and closed for much of winter).

Sitting on a narrow *angostura* (isthmus) on the northern shore of Lake Nahuel Huapi, Villa La Angostura was once a mere hamlet. But, having benefited from thoughtful planning and strict adherence to business codes, it's now the second most popular tourist area in the Lake District. Its first hotel was built in 1923, 10 years before the town was founded, and today some of the most luxurious accommodations in Patagonia look out on the lake from discreet hiding places along its wooded shores.

Shops and restaurants line the Avenida Arrayanes, where you can stop for homemade ice cream or cakes while window-shopping in the three-block-long commercial zone. The tourist office and municipal buildings are at El Cruce (the Crossroads), where Ruta 231 from Bariloche to the Chilean border intersects with the road to the port and the Ruta de los Siete Lagos (Ruta 234) to San Martín de los Andes.

GETTING HERE AND AROUND

Fast and frequent El Valle buses make the two-hour trip from Bariloche at least six times a day; however, you'll want a car to get around the environs, which are creeping slowly from Lago Correntoso to Puerto Manzano.

ESSENTIALS

VISITOR AND TOUR INFORMATION Secretaría de Turismo y Cultura. ⊠ *Av. Arrayanes 9, Villa La Angostura* ☎ *2944/494–124* ⊕ *www.villalaangostura.gov.ar.*

Continued on page 340

FLY FISHING

Chile and Argentina are the final frontier of fly fishing. With so many unexplored rivers, lakes, and spring creeks—most of which are un-dammed and free flowing to the ocean—every type of fishing is available for all levels of experience. You'll find many species of fish, including rainbow trout, browns, sea-run browns, brooks, sea trout, and steelhead.

Above: Flyfishing in Torres del Paine National Park, Patagonia, Chile

The Southern Cone has endless—and endlessly evolving—rivers, streams, and lakes, which is why they're so good for fly fishing. These waterways formed millions of years ago, as volcanic eruptions and receding glaciers carved out the paths for riverbeds and lakes that feed into the Pacific or Atlantic Oceans. With more than 2,006 volcanoes in Chile alone (including South America's most active mountain, Volcano Llaima, outside of Temuco), the Lake Districts of both countries are still evolving, creating raw and pristine fishing grounds.

Why choose Chile or Argentina for your next fly fishing adventure? If you're only after huge fish, stick to California. What these two South American countries offer is a chance to combine fishing, culture, and food in a unique package during the northern hemisphere's off season. With the right guide, you just might find yourself two hours down a dirt road, fishing turquoise water in the shadow of a glacial peak, with not a soul in sight but the occasional gaucho or huaso. It's an experience you will find nowhere else.

WHAT TO EXPECT ON THE GROUND

Fishing, Chile

LOGISTICS
You'll probably fly into Bariloche, Argentina, or Puerto Montt, Chile. You won't need more than two weeks for a good trip, and hiring a guide can make a big difference in the quality of your experience. Since most rivers are un-dammed, you'll need the extra help managing your drift boat or locating foot access for wading that stream you've spotted around the bend.

GUIDES VS. LODGES
You can purchase your trip package through either an independent guide or a specific lodge property. In both cases, packages usually last one week to 10 days, and include breakfast, lunch, and dinner. If you opt to purchase through a lodge, you have the benefit of property-specific guides who know every nook and cranny of stream surrounding the lodge. On the other hand, hiring an independent guide will give you more power to customize your trip and go farther afield.

TIMING
Contact your guide or lodge in October or November, during the southern hemisphere's spring; the upcoming season's peak fishing times depend on snow melt. Plan on traveling in February or March.

CHOOSING YOUR GUIDE
What type of fishing suits you best? Do you like to fish from a boat, or do you prefer wading the river as it rushes by? Ask guides these questions to find the best one for you.

WHAT TO ASK A GUIDE
- How early do you start in the morning?
- Do you mainly spin cast or fly fish?
- How long have you been in business?
- Do you always catch and release?
- Will I fish with you or another guide?
- Can I see pictures of your raft or drift boat?
- Do you supply the flies?
- Where do you get your flies?
- Can we fish a river twice if we like it?
- Which rivers and lakes do you float?
- Can we set an itinerary before I arrive?

WHAT TO BRING

5 to 7 Weight Rod: at least 9 foot (consider bringing 9½ foot for larger rivers, windy days, lakes, and sink-tip streamer fishing).

Floating Lines: for dry fly fishing and nymphing.

Streamers: for use while wading to or from the drift boat.

Lines: 15 to 20 foot sink-tip lines with a sink rate of 5.5 to 8 inches per second. It's good to carry two to four different sink rate lines.

Intermediate sink lines: for lakes and shallow depth fishing.

Line Cleaner: because low-ozone areas (the hole in the ozone is close to Antarctica) will eat up lines if you don't treat and clean the lines daily.

Hook sharpener: most guides don't have this very important item.

Small gifts: for the people you meet. Gift-giving can help you gain access to private rivers and lakes. Chocolates, such as Hershey Kisses, or some unique fly pattern, such as a dragon fly, always go over well.

Good map: Turistel, in Chile, puts out the best maps and internal information for that country (⊕ *www.turistel.com*). Check Argentina Tourism (⊕ *www.turismo.gov.ar*) for help with that country.

Coffee: Chile has Nescafé instant coffee just about everywhere you go. So if you like a good cup of joe, bring a filter and your favorite coffee. That way all you need is a cup and hot water, and you're all set for your morning fishing.

FLIES

■ Ask your guide where he or she gets flies. Those bought at a discount in countries outside of the United States are often sub-par, so get good guidance on this.

■ If you can, get a list of flies for the time of year you're scheduled to arrive and buy them in the United States before you go. Pay particular attention to the size as well type of insect.

■ The big fish and the quality catches are fooled by the flies that are tied by the guides themselves, because the guides know the hatches and the times they occur.

■ Flies are divided up into similar categories in Chile and Argentina since South America has many of the same insects as we do in North America. Check and see what time each insect is hatching. Note their sizes and colors. **You'll need both dry and nymph versions of the following, in a variety of sizes, colors, and patterns:**

| Royal Wulff | Bead Head Pheasant Tail | Mudder Minnow |
| Living Damsel | Bitch Creek | Adams |

🍽 Restaurants

Australis

$$$ | ARGENTINE | Easily one of the best microbreweries in Patagonia, Australis boasts a hearty German-inspired menu, with standout dishes such as smoked trout-stuffed pretzels and goulash. **Known for:** snug atmosphere; live music some nights; flavorful artisan beer. $ *Average main: pesos2000* ⊠ *Ruta 231, Km 60, Av. Arrayanes 2490, Villa La Angostura* ☎ *2944/495–645* 🖃 *No credit cards* ⊘ *Closed May.*

La Casita de la Oma

$$$ | ARGENTINE | Between the bay and the main street, this teahouse, with its award-winning garden, serves home-made cakes, pies, and scones. Moist chocolate brownie cake with dulce de leche (sweet caramelized milk) is a winner, as is a pile of filo leaves with dulce de leche and meringue on top. Jars of jam line the shelves. **Known for:** fresh homemade jams; quaint tea-cozy charm; big desserts. $ *Average main: pesos2500* ⊠ *Cerro Inacayal 303, Villa La Angostura* ☎ *2944/494–602* ⊘ *Closed May and Oct.*

🛏 Hotels

Costa Serena

$$$$ | HOTEL | FAMILY | Every room at this complex in Puerto Manzano has a lake view; A-frame *cabañas* (cabins) with decks, kitchens, and outdoor barbecues sleep up to seven, while suites have huge wooden Jacuzzis with views to the water. **Pros:** stunning views; prime lakeside position; relaxing indoor-outdoor pool. **Cons:** limited restaurant services outside of high season; some rooms have low-running wooden beams; far from town and tourist attractions. $ *Rooms from: US$265* ⊠ *Los Pinos 435, Puerto Manzano, Villa La Angostura* ☎ *2944/475–203* ⊕ *www.costaserenavla.com.ar* 🛌 *11 rooms* ⦿ *Free Breakfast.*

★ Hotel Correntoso

$$$$ | HOTEL | Perched on a hill where the Correntoso River runs into Nahuel Huapi Lake, this landmark hotel is at once cozy and contemporary; from your bedroom window you can see the fish jumping. **Pros:** great location, food, and spa facilities; well-organized excursions; the bar often has live music. **Cons:** no air-conditioning; rooms are a little cramped; expensive. $ *Rooms from: US$470* ⊠ *RN231, Km 86, Puente Correntoso, Villa La Angostura* ☎ *2944/619–728, 11/4803–0030 in Buenos Aires* ⊕ *correntosolakeriverhotel.com-hotel.com/en* 🛌 *47 rooms* ⦿ *Free Breakfast.*

Puerto Sur

$$ | HOTEL | FAMILY | Stone and wood merge throughout the angular space of this hillside hotel in Puerto Manzano, which has views of the lake and mountains from enormous windows. **Pros:** quiet, secluded spot; incredible lake views; spa, pool, and private beach on-site. **Cons:** difficult to get to and from without a car; no restaurant; far from town and tourist activities. $ *Rooms from: US$160* ⊠ *Los Pinos 221, Puerto Manzano, Villa La Angostura* ☎ *2944/825–351* ⊕ *www.hosteriapuertosur.com.ar* ⊘ *Closed mid-May–Jun.* 🛌 *14 rooms* ⦿ *Free Breakfast.*

🛍 Shopping

En El Bosque Chocolate

CHOCOLATE | Follow your nose to En El Bosque, where the scent of delicious artisanal sweets wafts out onto the sidewalk. It ranks among the best of the many chocolate and ice cream shops here. ⊠ *Av. Arrayanes 218, Villa La Angostura* ☎ *2944/495–738* ⊕ *www.facebook.com/enelbosquechocolate/.*

Activities

Visitors will be delighted by the variety of activities offered by this small, lakeside town, which has totally recovered from the 2011 eruption of the Puyehue volcano; a trip to the Secretaría de Turismo y Cultura will give you a good overview of the many outdoor excursions available.

BOATING

Patagonia Infinita

KAYAKING | Full- and half-day kayaking tours of the Nahuel Huapi, Correntoso, and Espejo lakes are organized by Patagonia Infinita. Lunch is included in full-day trips, and snorkeling is available in summer. ⊠ *Arrayanes 204, Villa La Angostura* 🕾 *294/455–3954* ⊕ *www. patagoniainfinita.com* 🖭 *From US$50.*

HORSEBACK RIDING

Cabalgatas Montahue

HORSEBACK RIDING | Short- and long-distance riding adventures can be arranged through Cabalgatas Montahue. Opt for a two-hour trip to the Lake Correntoso lookout point or a four-day excursion to Inacayal Waterfall. ⊠ *Av. 7 Lagos 402, Villa La Angostura* 🕾 *9294/451–1345* ⊕ *facebook.com/cabalgatas.villalaangostura* 🖭 *From 5,000 pesos.*

MOUNTAIN BIKING

Alquiles Rental & Outdoors

BIKING | Mountain bikes can be rented by the day from Alquiles Rental. You can easily ride from the village to Laguna Verde, near the port, or off the Seven Lakes Route to Mirador Belvedere and on to the waterfalls at Inacayal. Kayaks and ski gear are also available. ⊠ *Cerro Bayo 69, Villa La Angostura* 🕾 *9294/430–8348, 2944/494–303* 🖭 *From 2,500 pesos.*

Parque Nacional Nahuel Huapi

Created in 1934, Parque Nacional Nahuel Huapi is the oldest national park in Argentina. It's also one of the largest, encompassing more than 7,050 square km (2,720 square miles) along the eastern side of the Andes in the provinces of Neuquén and Río Negro, on the frontier with Chile. Because much of the park is covered by lakes—Lago Nahuel Huapi being the most sizable one—some of your exploration will be by boat to islands, down narrow fjords, or to distant shores on organized excursions. Multiple hiking trails also wind through the park, leading visitors from the thick undergrowth to open lakeside beaches. Nearby destinations such as the Circuito Chico, Circuito Grande, Tronadór, or the ski area at Catedral can be done in a day.

GETTING AROUND

The easy way to get around is to rent a car, hire a remis, or sign on with a local tour operator. When planning all-day or overnight trips, remember that distances are long and unpaved roads slow you down.

ESSENTIALS

VISITOR INFORMATION Intendencia del Parque Nacional Nahuel Huapi. ⊠ *Av. San Martín 24, at Civic Center, Bariloche* 🕾 *2944/423–111* ⊕ *www.nahuelhuapi. gov.ar.*

Sights

Isla Victoria

ISLAND | The most popular excursion on Lago Nahuel Huapi is the 30-minute boat ride from Puerto Pañuelo on the Península Llao Llao to Isla Victoria, the largest island in the lake. A grove of redwoods transplanted from California thrives in

Did You Know?

Nahuel Huapi National Park offers many recreational activities, such as mountain biking, kite surfing, paragliding, and much more.

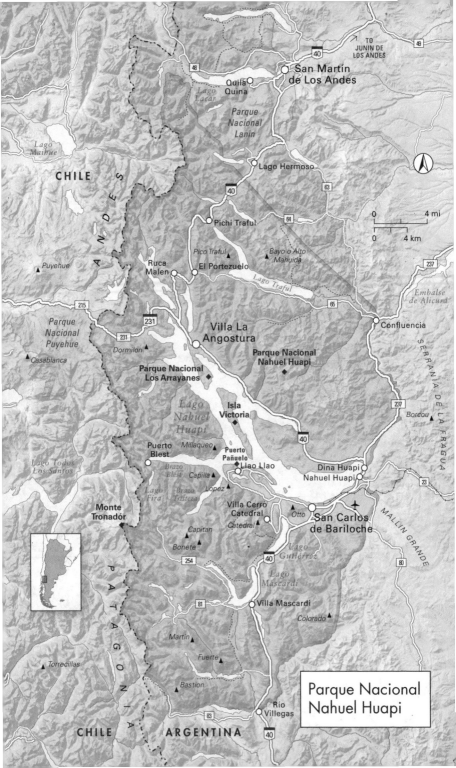

Parque Nacional
Nahuel Huapi

the middle of it. Walk on trails that lead to enchanting views of emerald bays and still lagoons; then board the boat to sail on to the Parque Nacional los Arrayanes. Boats go daily at 10 am and 2 pm (more frequently in high season). The earlier departure includes time for lunch on the island in a cafeteria-style restaurant. The later departure is a shorter trip. Vessels are run by **Cau Cau** (✉ Mitre 139, Bariloche ☎ 2944/431–372 ⊕ www.islavictoriayarrayanes.com) and **Turisur** (✉ Mitre 219, Bariloche ☎ 2944/426–109 ⊕ www.turisur.com.ar). ✉ *Nahuel Huapi National Park*

Monte Tronadór (*Thunder Mountain*)
MOUNTAIN | A visit to Monte Tronadór requires an all-day outing, covering 170 km (105 miles) round-trip from Bariloche. This 3,658-meter (12,000-foot) extinct volcano—the highest mountain in the northern Lake District—straddles the frontier with Chile, with one peak on either side. Take R258 south along the shores of Lago Gutiérrez and Lago Mascardi. Between the two lakes the road crosses from the Atlantic to the Pacific watershed. At Km 35, turn off onto a road marked "Tronadór" and "Pampa Linda" and continue along the shore of Lago Mascardi, passing a village of the same name. Just beyond the village the road forks, and you continue on a gravel road, R254. Near the bridge the road branches left to Lago Hess and Cascada Los Alerces—a detour you might want to take on your way out.

As you bear right after crossing Los Rápidos Bridge, the road narrows: note that it's one-way heading up 10 am–2 pm, one-way heading down 4 pm–6 pm, and two-way 7:30 pm–9 am only. The lake ends in a narrow arm (Brazo Tronadór) at the Hotel Tronadór, which has a dock for tours arriving by boat. The road then follows the Río Manso to **Pampa Linda,** which has a lodge, restaurant, park ranger's office, campsites, and the trailhead

for the climb up to the Refugio Otto Meiling at the snow line. Guided horseback rides are organized at the lodge. The road ends 7 km (5 miles) beyond Pampa Linda in a parking lot that was once at the tip of the receding **Glaciar Negro** (Black Glacier). As the glacier flows down from the mountain, the dirt and black sediment of its lateral moraines are ground up and cover the ice. At first glance it's hard to imagine the tons of ice that lie beneath its black cap.

Parque Nacional los Arrayanes
NATIONAL PARK | Lago Nahuel Huapi's entire Quetrihue Peninsula, with its unique forest of *arrayanes* (myrtle trees), is protected by the Parque Nacional los Arrayanes. These trees absorb so much water through their thin skins that all other vegetation around them dies, leaving a barren forest of peeling cinnamon-colored trunks. A stroll up and down wide wooden steps and walkways is a memorable experience, as light filters through the twisted naked trunks, reflecting a weird red glow. You can make this excursion from the pier at Bahía Brava in Villa La Angostura (or by boat from Bariloche via Isla Victoria). In summer, you can walk (three hours) or cycle, after registering at the *Guardaparque* office (ranger station) near the pier. ■**TIP→ Leave in the morning, as the park entrance closes at 2 pm (11am in winter). A nice combination is to go by boat and return by bike (it's all downhill that way). If returning by boat, buy your return ticket at the pier before you leave.** ✉ *12 km (8 miles) along trail from Península Quetrihué* ☎ *2944/423–111* ⊕ *www.argentina.gob.ar/parquesnacionales/losarrayanes* 🎫 *1,820 pesos.*

Parque Nacional Nahuel Huapi
NATIONAL PARK | This national park is notable for having the highest concentration of lakes in Argentina. The largest of them, Lago Nahuel Huapi, covers 897 square km (346 square miles) and has seven arms—the longest of which is 96

km (60 miles) long and 12 km (7 miles) wide—reaching deep into forests of coihue (a native beech), cypress, and lenga (deciduous beech) trees. Intensely blue across its vast expanse and aqua green in its shallow bays, the lake meanders into distant lagoons and misty inlets where the mountains, covered with vegetation at their base, rise straight up out of the water.

Inside the park, nearly every water sport invented can be arranged through local travel agencies, tour offices, or hotels. Boating is particularly popular, with options ranging from a placid Isla Victoria outing to challenging white-water-rafting adventures. Information offices throughout the park can also offer tips about tackling the miles of mountain and woodland trails. Small towns like Villa La Angostura and Villa Traful are excellent destinations for further explorations on foot or horseback. Since most of the park is at a low elevation (under 1,829 meters or 6,000 feet), getting around in winter is not difficult—just cold. Fall foliage, long, warm summer days, and spring flowers are the rewards of other seasons. ✉ *Av. San Martín 24, Bariloche* ☎ *2944/423–111, 2944/423–121* 🌐 *www.argentina.gob.ar/parquesnacionales/nahuelhuapi* 🎫 *1,820 pesos.*

Hotels

Isla Victoria Lodge

$$$$ | RESORT | Poised dramatically on a cliff overlooking the lake and forests, this classic stone-and-wood lodge enjoys one of the most beautiful settings on earth: the architecture harmonizes with the natural surroundings, and the tranquil interior—with white walls, pine trim, leather upholstery, and fine Mapuche woven rugs—conveys a sense of peace. **Pros:** facilities include a heated outdoor pool and hiking trails; rates cover meals; gourmet meals. **Cons:** isolated; pricey; no nightlife. [$] *Rooms from: US$375* ✉ *Isla Victoria CC 26, Nahuel Huapi National Park, Bariloche* ☎ *11/43-949-605* 🌐 *www.islavictoria.com* 🛏 *22 rooms* 🍴 *Free Breakfast.*

Río Mel Lodge

$$ | HOTEL | Taking "off the beaten track" to a whole new level, this homey lodge sits on the banks of the Meliquina River in the middle of Parque Nacional Lanín and is a favorite with both fly fishermen and families. **Pros:** beautiful setting overlooking river; spacious suites; great spot for fishing. **Cons:** noise from adjacent rooms; no cell phone reception; difficult to reach without a car. [$] *Rooms from: US$120* ✉ *Río Meliquina, 42 km (26 miles) south of San Martín de los Andes, San Martín de los Andes* ☎ *02972/427–199* 🌐 *www.riomellodge.com* 💳 *No credit cards* 🕒 *Closed May* 🛏 *4 rooms, 3 cabins.*

Activities

HIKING

Nahuel Huapi National Park has many forest trails near Bariloche, El Bolsón, and Villa La Angostura. Hiking guides can be recommended by local tour offices. For trail maps and information on all of the Lake District, look for the booklet (in Spanish) *Guía Sendas y Bosques* (*Guide to Trails and Forests*) sold at kiosks and bookstores.

Club Andino Bariloche

HIKING & WALKING | For ambitious treks, mountaineering, or information about mountain huts and climbing permits, contact Club Andino Bariloche. ✉ *20 de Febrero 30, Bariloche* ☎ *2944/422–266* 🌐 *www.clubandino.org/refugios-y-campings.*

MOUNTAIN BIKING

The entire park is ripe for all levels of mountain biking. Popular rides go from the parking lot at the Cerro Catedral ski area to Lago Gutiérrez and down from Cerro Otto. Local tour agencies can arrange guided tours by the hour or day and even international excursions to Chile. Rental agencies provide maps and suggestions and sometimes recommend guides.

Dirty Bikes

BIKING | Day trips all over the Lake District (including long-distance ones to Chile and back) are organized by Dirty Bikes. Options for many ages and ability levels are available. ⊠ *Bariloche* ☏ *2944/529–821* 🔗 *$45 per day.*

WHITE-WATER RAFTING

Thanks to all of its interconnected lakes and rivers, the national park offers rafters everything from a basic family float down the swift-flowing, scenic Río Limay to a wild and exciting ride down Río Manso (Class II), which carries you 16 km (10 miles) in three hours. If you're really adventurous, you can take the Manso all the way to Chile (Class IV).

Aguas Blancas

WHITE-WATER RAFTING | This outfit specializes in the Manso River and offers an overnight trip to Chile with asado and return by horseback. They also run guided inflatable kayak trips. ⊠ *Morales 564, Bariloche* ☏ *2944/432–799* ⊕ *aguas-blancas.com.ar* 🔗 *From 7,000 pesos* ⊘ *Closed May–Oct.*

Extremo Sur

WHITE-WATER RAFTING | Trips on the Ríos Limay and Manso are arranged by Extremo Sur. ⊠ *Pasaje Gutiérrez 828, Bariloche* ☏ *2944/427–301* ⊕ *www.extremosur.com* 🔗 *From 6,800 pesos for 4 hrs.*

Rio Manso Expediciones

WHITE-WATER RAFTING | This agency offers a range of expeditions, from child-friendly raft trips to class IV excursions to the Chilean border. ⊠ *Runge 870, Bariloche* ☏ *294/443–3260, 9294/466–2010 WhatsApp* ⊕ *www.riomansoexpediciones.com.*

El Bolsón and Nearby

El Bolsón

131 km (80 miles) south of Bariloche via R40.

El Bolsón ("the purse") lies in a valley enclosed on either side by the jagged peaks of two mountain ranges. You catch your first glimpse of the valley about 66 km (41 miles) from Bariloche, with the glaciers of Perito Moreno and Hielo Azul—both more than 1,980 meters (6,500 feet) high—on the horizon south and west.

The first in Argentina to declare their town a nonnuclear zone, El Bolsón's residents have preserved the purity of its air, water, and land. In spring (late November–December), the roads are lined with ribbons of lupine in every shade of pink and purple imaginable. Red berry fruits, which are exported in large quantities, thrive on hillsides and in backyard *chacras* (farms); and huge fields of green hops support the exploding Patagonian microbrew industry.

GETTING HERE AND AROUND

Most travelers come from Bariloche by car or bus; if you choose the latter, El Valle and Via Bariloche make the three-hour journey multiple times per day and deposit passengers downtown. The main street, San Martín, has shops, restaurants, and some lodgings within a two- to three-block area. A grassy plaza next to the tourist office is the center of activities; trails along the Río Azul or to nearby waterfalls and mountaintops are a short taxi or bike ride from it.

ESSENTIALS

VISITOR AND TOUR INFORMATION Sec-retaría de Turismo. ⊠ *Plaza Pagano at Av. San Martín, El Bolsón* ☏ *2944/492–604, 2944/455–336* ⊕ *www.turismoelbolson.gob.ar.*

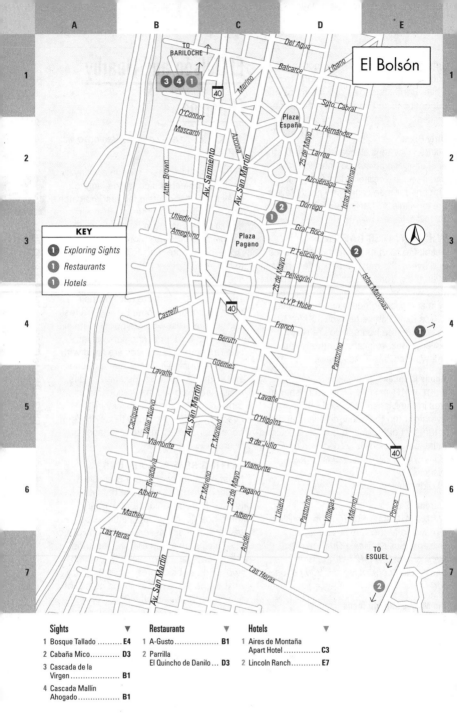

El Bolsón

KEY
- 1 Exploring Sights
- 1 Restaurants
- 1 Hotels

TO BARILOCHE

TO ESQUEL

Sights	▼	Restaurants	▼	Hotels	▼
1 Bosque Tallado **E4**		1 A-Gusto **B1**		1 Aires de Montaña	
2 Cabaña Mico............ **D3**		2 Parrilla		Apart Hotel **C3**	
3 Cascada de la		El Quincho de Danilo ... **D3**		2 Lincoln Ranch............ **E7**	
Virgen **B1**					
4 Cascada Mallín					
Ahogado **B1**					

Sights

Bolsón International Jazz Festival
PERFORMANCE VENUE | In February, the Bolsón International Jazz Festival brings music to streets and restaurants around town. The Fiesta Nacional de Lúpolo (National Hop Festival) is celebrated the same month. ✉ *El Bolsón.*

Bosque Tallado (*Carved Forest*)
FOREST | About 1 km (½ mile) from the base of Piltriquitrón, you'll find fire-damaged beech trees that have been carved over the years by 13 notable Argentine artists. Thirty-one monumental sculptures transform the dead forest into a living gallery. Tours can be arranged through Maputur. ✉ *El Bolsón* ☎ *2944/491–440 Maputur.*

Cabaña Mico
FARM/RANCH | Don't leave the El Bolsón area without a jar of jam! Cabaña Mico has a long table lined with little jam pots (and disposable sticks), so you can sample the 40 different flavors before making your purchase. ✉ *Islas Malvinas at Roca, El Bolsón* ☎ *2944/492–691* 🌐 *www.mico.com.ar* 🕒 *Closed Sun.*

Cascada de la Virgen (*Waterfall of the Virgin*)
WATERFALL | Venture 15 km (9 miles) north of El Bolsón to see the Cascada de la Virgen. It's most impressive in spring, when the runoff from the mountain falls in a series of three cascades visible from the road coming from Bariloche. ✉ *El Bolsón.*

Cascada Mallín Ahogado (*Drowned Meadow Waterfall*)
WATERFALL | Four km (3 miles) north of El Bolsón on R258, the Cascada Mallín Ahogado makes a great picnic spot. ✉ *El Bolsón.*

Restaurants

Parrilla El Quincho de Danilo
$$$ | **ARGENTINE** | About 10 minutes north of town, on the bank of the river Arroyo del Medio, Parrilla El Quincho is the primo place to try *cordero patagónico al asador* (lamb roasted slowly on a metal cross over a fire), along with sizzling platters of beef. Vegetarian options are also available. **Known for:** generous barbeque platters; coffee cooked on embers; lovely setting surrounded by trees. [$] *Average main: pesos2500* ✉ *Mallín Ahogado, El Bolsón* ☎ *2944/492–870* 🌐 *el-quincho-de-danilo.negocio.site* 💳 *No credit cards* 🕒 *Closed in winter.*

A-Gusto
$$$ | **ARGENTINE** | "With the nobility of fire" is how this lively steakhouse introduces itself, and for good reason—it offers a large menu of parrilla classics, in generous servings, as well as wood-fired pizzas. Fairy lights decorate the outdoor patio, while inside, the oak tables and low-lighting give the restaurant an intimate feel. **Known for:** elaborate desserts; creamy trout pastas; plentiful meat platters. [$] *Average main: pesos3000* ✉ *Dorrego 539, El Bolsón* ☎ *294/4720744* 🌐 *www.facebook.com/agustoelbolson/* 🕒 *No lunch weekdays.*

Hotels

The hotel selection in downtown El Bolsón is woefully inadequate. Numerous guesthouses take small groups, but the Hotel Amancay is the only full-service hotel worth recommending. You'll find more choices in **Villa Turismo,** a hillside community of cabins, bed-and-breakfasts, and small inns located about 2 km (1½ miles) south of town, off Avenida Belgrano. Lodges in the surrounding mountains open for fishing season in summer (November–April) and close in winter (May–October).

Beer Sampling

This region has long been the biggest producer of hops in Argentina, and with a local population dedicated to agricultural pursuits, it's logical that entrepreneurial *cervecerías artesanales* (artisanal breweries) would become a growing industry.

Cervezería El Bolsón. About 2 km (1 mile) north of town, Cervezería El Bolsón is the brewery that started the Patagonian "cerveza artesanal craze," and even if it is now the least artisanal of the bunch, it's still a local landmark. Every night from December through March, and Fridays and Saturdays for the rest of the year, the brewery's tasting room turns into a hopping bar and restaurant, where *picadas* (kind of like tapas), pizzas, sausages with sauerkraut, and a hearty goulash are listed on one side of the menu with suggested beers on the other. For instance, black beer is recommended with smoked meats; chocolate beer with dessert. There are 14 types of brew for you to taste, and descriptions of their ingredients are provided. A large campground is conveniently located by the river in back. ■ **TIP→ There is now a second location (Cervezeria El Bolsón Centro) in town at the corner of San Martin and Juez Fernandez.** ✉ *Ruta 258, Km 123.9, El Bolsón* ☎ *2944/492–595.*

Mystic Fog Beer & Co. Nestled beside the Cajon del Azul, at the confluence of Río Sur and Río Blanco, this brewery is famous both for its craft beer and spectacular location. It was founded by Shea Jordan in 2015, and since then, has become one of El Bolsón's most popular spots. Hikers stop by after a long day in the mountains to enjoy blends such as coconut stout, as well as the brewery's hearty cheddar and *bondiola* fries. There is even a hop plantation on site. Getting there is difficult—only four-wheel drives can access the road, but you can stop at the campsite Charca Wharton, and walk the rest of the way (2 km/1 mile) on foot. Be warned that the return journey is uphill. ✉ *La Confluencia, El Bolsón* ☎ *294/491–2831* 🌐 *www.facebook.com/mysticfogbeerco.*

Aires de Montaña Apart Hotel
$$ | **APARTMENT** | Located in the heart of downtown Bolsón, these neat and bright apartments serve as a good base to explore the surrounding sights. **Pros:** two blocks from central square; very attentive owners; spacious outdoor areas. **Cons:** no-frills decor; limited availability (only three cabins); two-day minimum reservation. [$] *Rooms from: US$200* ✉ *Perito Moreno 2851, El Bolsón* ☎ *9280/469–4442* 🌐 *www.xn–airesdemontaa-tkb.com.ar* 🛏 *Cabins for 5 people and 3 people, plus studio (with no kitchen).*

Lincoln Ranch
$ | **HOUSE** | Perched higher than all the other cabin complexes, these modern cottages have plenty of room and all the accoutrements of a vacation home. **Pros:** lots of space; easy walk up to Piltriquitrón; helpful staff. **Cons:** outdated decor; hard to get to without a car; far from restaurants and downtown shops. [$] *Rooms from: US$100* ✉ *Villa Turismo, Subida Los Maitenes, El Bolsón* ☎ *2944/492–073* 🌐 *www.facebook.com/lincolnranch* 🛏 *6 cabins* 🍴 *No Meals.*

El Bolsón sits between the Rio Negro and the Andes mountains.

🏃 Activities

HORSEBACK RIDING

Cabalgatas en Azul

HORSEBACK RIDING | Javier Eduardo offers guided horseback tours to the Azul Canyon, a gorge named for the river's deep blue waters. He also leads tours around Cascada Mallín Ahogado; more adventurous riders can opt to go all the way to the glaciers. ✉ *El Bolsón* ☎ *2944/483–590* ✉ *6,000 pesos for a full day.*

MOUNTAIN BIKING
SKIING

Cerro Perito Moreno

SKIING & SNOWBOARDING | Used mainly by local families, the ski area at Cerro Perito Moreno is owned and operated by Club Andino Piltriquitrón, which also runs a restaurant at the base where you can rent skis, snowboards, and sleds. Four short tows for beginners and one T-bar access the 750 meters (2,460 feet) of skiable terrain on east-facing slopes. Since storms approach from the west, snowfall can be minimal; it's best to call the tourist office or Club Andino before you go. ✉ *25 km (15 miles) northwest of El Bolsón, El Bolsón* ☎ *2944/498–490* 🌐 *laderas.com.ar* ✉ *Five-day passes from 13,100 pesos.*

Parque Nacional Lago Puelo

18 km (11 miles) south of El Bolsón on RN40 and RP16.

Parque Nacional Lago Puelo is one of the smallest national parks in the southern Andes and one of the warmest spots in the region. The oh-so-blue lake for which it's named (glacial sediment creates the distinctive color) offers a host of recreational opportunities. The land around it, meanwhile, is ideal for hiking and threaded with trails that lead all the way to the Chilean border.

GETTING HERE AND AROUND

To come by car, follow Ruta 16 to Villa Lago Puelo; from there, a 4-km (3-mile) gravel trail leads to the park entrance. If you don't have your own vehicle, your hotel will happily arrange transport with a local remis driver. You can get information on the park at the tourist office in El Bolsón; picnic and fishing supplies can be purchased in a roadside store at the turnoff to the trail.

Sights

Parque Nacional Lago Puelo

FOREST | Set more than 200 meters (656 feet) above sea level, this park's titular lake has warm water for swimmers, plentiful fish stocks for anglers, plus a selection of on-the-water excursions for boaters. Hiking options abound in the area as well—the most interesting of which are at the west end of the lake on the Chilean border. ⊠ *18 km (11 miles) south of El Bolsón on R16*

Activities

BOAT EXCURSIONS

Three launches, including Nautica Puelo, wait at the dock to take you out on Lago Puelo. The trip to El Turbio, an ancient settlement at the southern end of the lake on the Chilean border, is the longest. One side of the lake is inaccessible, as the Valdivian rain forest grows on steep rocky slopes right down into the water. Campgrounds are at the park entrance by the ranger's station, in a bay on the Brazo Occidental, and at the Turbio and Epuyén river outlets.

Chapter 9

PATAGONIA

Updated by
Jimmy Langman

👁 Sights	🍴 Restaurants	🛏 Hotels	🛍 Shopping	🍸 Nightlife
★★★★★	★★★★☆	★★★★★	★★★☆☆	★★★☆☆

WELCOME TO PATAGONIA

TOP REASONS TO GO

★ **Glaciers and Mountains:** Set yourself opposite an impossibly massive wall of ice and contemplate the blue-green-turquoise spectrum trapped within. Meanwhile, stark granite peaks planted like spears in the Cordillera beckon.

★ **Marine Life:** Península Valdés is home to breeding populations of sea lions, elephant seals, orcas, and the southern right whale. Punta Tombo is the world's largest Magellanic-penguin colony.

★ **Estancia Stay:** Visit an estancia, a working ranch where you can ride horses alongside tough-as-nails gauchos (cowboys) and dine on spit-roasted lamb under the stars.

★ **Earth, Sea, and Fire:** Patagonian cuisine has some of the most exquisite natural flavors in the world. Specialties include sumptuous king crab; flavorful Patagonian lamb; and indulgent Welsh teacakes.

★ **Brushing Up on Your Welsh:** In the largest Welsh colony outside Wales, the people of Gaiman have preserved their traditions and language.

Most of Patagonia is windswept desert steppe inhabited by rabbits, sheep, *guanacos* (a larger, woollier version of the llama), and a few hardy human beings. The population centers—and attractions—are either along the coast or in a narrow strip of land that runs along the base of the Andes mountain range, where massive glaciers spill into large turquoise lakes. In nearby Chile, Puerto Natales is the gateway town to Parque Nacional Torres del Paine. At the bottom end of the continent, separated by the Magellan Strait, lies Tierra del Fuego. The resort town of Ushuaia, Argentina, base camp for explorations of the Beagle Channel and the forested peaks of the Cordillera Darwin mountain range, is the leading tourist attraction of the region.

1 Puerto Madryn and Península Valdés. Puerto Madryn provides easy access to Península Valdés, one of the world's best places for marine wildlife viewing.

2 Trelew, Gaiman, and Punta Tombo. Gaiman and Trelew's teahouses and rose gardens date back to the original 19th-century Welsh settlers. Head south to Punta Tombo, the largest penguin rookery in South America.

3 Sarmiento. This small, friendly town is a green oasis. Nearby are stunning petrified forests and a paleontology "park" with life-size dinosaur replicas.

4 El Calafate, El Chaltén, and Parque Nacional los Glaciares. The wild Parque Nacional los Glaciares dramatically contrasts with nearby boomtown El Calafate. North is El Chaltén, base camp for hikes to Cerros Torre and Fitzroy.

5 Puerto Natales and Torres del Paine, Chile. Border town Puerto Natales is the last stop before one of the finest national parks in South America, Parque Nacional Torres del Paine.

6 Ushuaia and Tierra del Fuego. This rugged, windswept land straddles Chile and Argentina. Ushuaia, in Argentina, is the world's southernmost city.

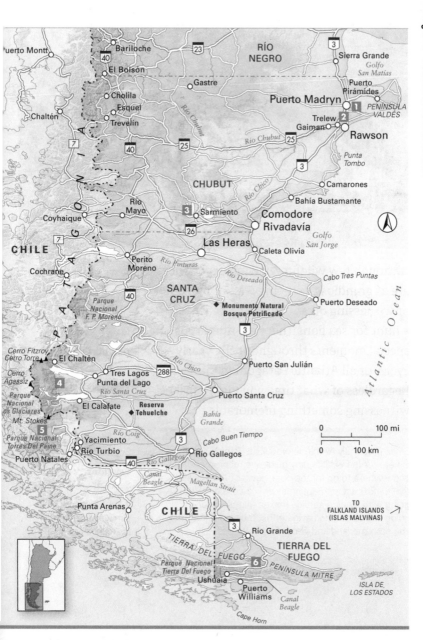

CALENDAR OF FAUNA ON PENÍNSULA VALDÉS

Elephant seals

Although few wildlife-viewing experiences are as grandiose as seeing whales breach or witnessing orcas charge the beaches in a hunt for sea lions, there are numerous special moments throughout the yearly cycles of all Atlantic Patagonian fauna. Regardless of what time you visit, you'll be witnessing something memorable.

Since practically everyone who visits Península Valdés is here for the wildlife, any guide we recommend will know where to go for the best views of the wildlife that's most active. Renting a car is a possibility, but going with a guide service makes things easier—your guide will be able to navigate the unpaved roads while you scan the land and water for creatures.

WHEN TO GO

Birds: June–December

Whales: May–December

Dolphins: December–March

Elephant Seals: year-round

Sea Lions: year-round

Orcas: September–April

Penguins: September–March

■ TIP→ Consider purchasing or renting binoculars or a scope.

LOOK TO THE WATER FOR...

Dolphin Gull

Southern Right Whales. The first southern right whales arrive in Golfo Nuevo at the end of April and can be observed from beaches in and along Puerto Madryn as well as the Península Valdés. Your best chance of seeing them will be from a whale-watching point at Puerto Pirámides. These whales are between 36 and 59 feet long, and have several endearing behaviors such as "sailing," where they hold their fins up in the air, and when a mother uses her flippers to teach calves how to swim.

Elephant Seals. Elephant seals are larger mammals than sea lions, and have a different way of moving—using their flippers to waddle along on land, whereas sea lions use both front and back flippers to thrust themselves forward. The biggest elephant-seal colonies are in Península Valdés, at Punta Cantor and Punta Delgada.

Sea Lions. In January and February sea lions begin to form "harems," with each dominant male taking up to a dozen females. The fights to maintain these harems can be violent, and it's possible to witness an invading male drag off one of the females from the harem with his teeth. Most of the year, however, sea-lion colonies appear peaceful: the animals sun themselves or swim, and the pups are curious and playful. They can be observed year-round all along the Atlantic Coast. From December through April sea lions and elephant seals are reproducing and raising pups.

Orcas. It's possible to see the black fins of orcas cutting through the water along the coastline, occasionally storming the beach in violent and spectacular chases. The best place to see orcas is at the extreme northern tip of Península Valdés, Punta Norte, in April.

Southern Right Whale off Puerto Pirámides

LOOK TO THE AIR AND LAND FOR...

Seabirds. Among the many seabirds found in Patagonia—including dolphin gulls, kelp geese, southern giant petrels, rock and blue-eyed cormorants, snowy sheathbills, blackish oystercatchers, and steamer ducks—one species, the arctic tern, has the longest migration—it flies over 21,750 miles annually from the Arctic to Antarctica and back.

Penguins. Along Atlantic Patagonia—most notably Punta Tombo—there are large rookeries of Magellanic penguins, with up to 500,000 of these flightless birds. The males arrive from the sea each August, followed by the females a month later when territorial battles begin. In October and into November the nesting pairs incubate the eggs. Once the chicks hatch in November, the parents make continual trips to the ocean for food. In January the chicks leave the nest, learning to swim in February. Their plumage matures throughout the fall, when the penguins begin migrating north to Brazil.

Patagonia is a wild and rugged land filled with breathtaking landscapes and eye-catching wildlife. There are few other places in the world where you can feel such a great isolation and vast emptiness and yet see waters teeming with wildlife; visit gauchos living on windswept estancias; and get so close to ancient glaciers that you can actually walk inside these ice cathedrals. Spanning over a million square kilometers Patagonia has many worlds to discover.

Atlantic Patagonia is where the low pampas meet the ocean. It's a land of immense panoramic horizons and a coastline of bays, inlets, and peninsulas abounding with birds and marine wildlife. The region is most famous for Península Valdés, a UNESCO Natural World Heritage Site with southern right whales, orcas, elephant seals, and sea lions. There are seemingly endless dirt roads where you won't see another person or vehicle for hours—only guanacos, rheas, and other animals running across the steppe.

Farther south and inland to the Andes, the towns of El Calafate and El Chaltén come alive in summer (December through March) with the influx of visitors to the Parque Nacional los Glaciares, and climbers headed for Cerro Torre and Cerro Fitzroy. Imagine sailing across a blue lake full of icebergs, or traversing an advancing glacier in the shadow of the Andes mountain range, watching a

valley being formed before your eyes. The Perito Moreno glacier attracts tourists continuously to this region.

Experiencing Patagonia, however, still means crossing vast deserts to reach isolated population centers, taking deep breaths of mountain air and draughts of pure stream water in the shadow of dramatic snowcapped peaks. Most of all, it means being embraced by independent, pioneering souls beginning to understand the importance of tourism as traditional industries—wool, livestock, fishing, and oil—are drying up.

Patagonia is a hybrid of the cultures of primarily European immigrants, who came here in the 19th century, and the cultures of the indigenous peoples, mainly the Tehuelche and Mapuche. The native Tehuelches fished and hunted the coast and pampas, and their spears and arrowheads are still found along river-beds and beaches, although sadly that is all that remains today after General Roca's four-year genocidal "Conquest of the Desert" campaign (1879–83).

The first Spanish explorer, Hernando Magallanes, arrived in Golfo Nuevo in 1516, and was followed by several other Spanish expeditions throughout the 17th and 18th centuries. Inland, a Welsh pioneer named Henry Jones explored the Chubut River valley in 1814; he was later followed by waves of Welsh immigrants that forged colonies in Gaiman, Trelew, Rawson, and Puerto Madryn. Beginning in the mid-19th century, the Argentine government courted settlers from all over Europe, including Italy, Spain, and Germany, as well as Boers from South Africa, offering land as a strategy for displacing indigenous populations and fortifying the young nation against neighboring Chile. These settlers adapted their agrarian traditions to the Patagonian terrain and continued their cultural traditions and cuisine, such as Welsh tea, still found throughout Patagonia today.

Planning

When to Go

Late September to March—spring and summer in the Southern Hemisphere—is high season in Patagonia. Reservations are advised, especially in September and October in Atlantic Patagonia and December through February in Southern Patagonia. Although the summer sun can be strong, the winds whistle year-round, so always bring extra layers and a windbreaker. In Atlantic Patagonia, many properties close in April and May to prepare for the first whale-watchers in June and July. While most of Southern Patagonia grinds almost to a halt from May to September, the ski season in Ushuaia is increasingly popular.

Getting Here and Around

AIR

Flying is the best way to reach Patagonia from Buenos Aires (through which flights from most other parts of the country also pass). Always allow some buffer time when traveling to Patagonia: bad weather, heavy fog, and strikes can cause common delays on either side of the journey.

Aerolíneas Argentinas and LATAM have regular, direct flights to Trelew, Comodoro Rivadavía, Río Gallegos, El Calafate, and Ushuaia from Buenos Aires.

LADE (Líneas Aéreas del Estado) connects Comodoro Rivadavía to Rio Gallegos and Rio Grande with weekly flights in the summer. Andes Líneas Aéreas has direct flights between Buenos Aires and Puerto Madryn every day in peak season.

BUS

Comfortable overnight sleeper buses connect Patagonia to Buenos Aires (and other major cities). However, as getting to even the closest city in Atlantic Patagonia, Puerto Madryn, takes 20 hours, most travelers feel it's worth the price to fly. All the same, buses are a major form of transportation between destinations up to about 600 km (370 miles) apart. Don Otto is a reliable carrier.

CAR

If you truly enjoy the call of the open road, there are few places that can rival the vast emptiness and jaw-dropping beauty of Patagonia. Be prepared for miles and miles of semidesert steppes with no gas stations, towns, or even restrooms. Always carry plenty of water, snacks, a jack, and tire-changing tools, with at least one spare. Take extra care when driving on *ripios* (gravel roads): it's easy to flip small cars at speeds over 80 kph (55 mph). Fill your tank at every opportunity. If you're not driving, consider simply paying for a *remis* (car with driver) for day excursions.

Restaurants

With so many miles of coastline, it's not surprising that Atlantic Patagonia is famous for its seafood, notably sole and salmon, *mejillones* (mussels), and *pulpo* (octopus). *Centolla* (king crab) is another specialty, especially south of Comodoro Rivadavía. Most restaurants are sit-down-and-take-your-time affairs that don't open for dinner until at least 8, and despite all the seafood on offer, steak still reigns supreme. The other carnivorous staple in the area is *cordero patagónico*, local lamb, usually served barbecued or stewed. Dining prices in most Patagonian cities rival those of upper-end Buenos Aires restaurants. Thankfully, so do the skills of local chefs, although expect more basic offerings of pizza, milanesas, and empanadas in smaller towns. Whenever possible, accompany your meal with a bottle of wine from one of the increasing number of Patagonian wineries.

Huge numbers of foreign visitors mean that vegetarian options are getting better, although vegan food is still scarce. Most cafés and bars serve quick bites known as *minutas*. The region is also famous for its stone fruits, which are used in various jams, preserves, sweets, and *alfajores* (a chocolate-covered sandwich of two cookies with jam in the middle). When in El Calafate, be sure to nibble on some calafate berries (or drink them in cocktails like the Calafate Sour)—legend has it if you eat them in El Calafate you are destined to return one day soon.

Hotels

There aren't many budget accommodations in Patagonia; the luxury market, on the other hand, is booming. Patagonia is a "once-in-a-lifetime" destination that most people are happy to splurge on, and the increasing cruise culture doesn't ease accommodation prices. In most cities and towns you'll find a mix of big, expensive hotels with comfortable resorts, local flavor estancias, and small B&B-style *hosterías*.

The terms *hospedaje* and *hostal* are used interchangeably in the region, so don't make assumptions based on the name. Many *hostals* are fine hotels—not youth hostels with multiple beds—just very small. By contrast, some *hospedajes* are little more than a spare room in someone's home. Campsites in the national parks often have shelter and can offer some of the best views in Patagonia.

Hotel reviews have been shortened. For full information, visit Fodors.com. Restaurant prices are the average cost of a main course at dinner or, if dinner is not served, at lunch. Hotel prices are the lowest cost of a standard double room in high season.

What It Costs in Argentine Pesos			
$	$$	$$$	$$$$
RESTAURANTS			
Under 300 pesos	300–500 pesos	501–750 pesos	over 750 pesos
HOTELS (IN USD)			
Under $116	$116–$200	$201–$300	over $300

Health and Safety

Most mountains are not high enough to induce altitude sickness, but the weather can turn nasty quickly. Sunglasses and sunscreen are essential. Although tap water is safe to drink throughout the region, most travelers still choose to drink bottled water. Do not approach or let your children approach sea lions, penguins, or any other animals, no matter how docile or curious they might seem.

Border Crossing

The border between Chile and Argentina is still strictly maintained, but crossing it doesn't present much difficulty beyond getting out your passport and waiting in a line to get the stamp. Most travelers end up crossing the border by bus, which means getting out of the vehicle for 30–45 minutes to go through the bureaucratic proceedings, then loading back in.

Crossing by car is also quite manageable (check with your car-rental company for restrictions on international travel). Chilean customs officers are extremely strict about bringing food into the country, especially compared with their Argentinean counterparts. Always declare food products (they are usually flexible once items are declared); otherwise, you face a hefty fine.

EMERGENCY SERVICES Coast Guard. ☎ *106.* **Fire.** ☎ *100.* **Forest Fire.** ☎ *103.* **Hospital.** ☎ *107.* **Police.** ☎ *101.*

Patagonia Cruise Planner

Cruising in Patagonia

Cruising is a leisurely and comfortable way to take in the rugged marvels of Patagonia and the southernmost region of the world. Sailing through remote channels and reaching islands virtually untouched by man, you'll witness fjords, snowcapped mountains and granite peaks, and glacial lakes. You'll get a close look at elephant seals, migrating whales, colonies of Magellanic penguins, and cormorants from the comfort of your vessel and during shore excursions taken in Zodiacs (small motorized boats) led by naturalist guides. Far from the beaten path, you'll visit small fishing villages accessible only by sea, explore fantastic temperate rain forests, and enjoy the freshest seafood and local wines.

Most short cruises depart from Ushuaia, Argentina, or Punta Arenas, Chile. Longer and more luxurious itineraries typically depart from either Buenos Aires or Santiago.

WHEN TO GO

In the Southern Hemisphere, where the seasons are reversed, November through March is considered high season. However, the weather in Patagonia is unpredictable: strong winds and sudden storms are common. Summertime (December through February) is the best time to visit. Shoulder months—October, November, March, and April—tend to have cooler temperatures but also less wind. In winter, cruise companies all but hibernate for the season.

September and October (spring). The whale watching season runs from early June to mid December, but this is the very best time to witness the whale migration as well as the immense colonies of elephant seals and sea lions in Península Valdés.

November (late spring). The natural nesting cycle of Magellanic penguins is November to February. Penguins arrive at the rookeries at the beginning of the month. Spring flowers are in full bloom. This is the best time to catch the bird nesting of finches, sparrows, condors, albatrosses, and other species.

December and January (high summer). The warmest months see penguin chicks hatch in Tierra del Fuego. Long daylight hours also mean great photography opportunities all over Patagonia.

February and March (late summer). Receding ice allows for easier exploration farther south. Whale-watching is at its best. Penguin colonies are very active, as the adults feed the chicks.

BOOKING YOUR CRUISE

The majority of cruisers plan their trips four to six months ahead of time. Book a year ahead if you're planning to sail on a small adventure vessel, as popular itineraries may be full six to eight months ahead.

Consider booking shore excursions when you book your cruise to avoid disappointment later. You can even book your spa services pre-cruise to have your pick of popular times, such as sea days.

Although most travel is booked over the Internet nowadays, for cruises, booking with a travel agent who specializes in Patagonia cruises is still your best bet. Agents have strong relationships with the lines and have a better chance of getting you the cabin you want, possibly even a free upgrade. Cruise Lines International Association (☎ 202/759–9370) lists recognized agents throughout the United States.

Puerto Madryn and Península Valdés

Visiting populations of whales, orcas, sea lions, elephant seals, and penguins all gather to breed or feed on or near the shores of this unique peninsula, which comprises one of the lowest points in South America. The wildlife isn't only water-based; wandering the Patagonian scrub are guanacos, gray foxes, *maras* (Patagonian hares), skunks, armadillos, and rheas, while myriad bird species fill the air. There are also three inland salt lakes, and the curving gulf at Puerto Pirámides is one of the few places in Argentina where the sun sets over the water, not the land. With nature putting on such a generous display, it's not surprising that the 3,625-square-km (1,400-square-mile) peninsula has been designated a UNESCO World Heritage Site and is the main reason visitors come to Atlantic Patagonia.

Puerto Madryn is where you'll head first for organized excursions onto the peninsula. While a major part of the town's identity is a staging ground for these trips, it's also well worth exploring and has an interesting history. The first economic boom came in 1886, when the Patagonian railroad was introduced, spurring port activities along with the salt and fishing industries. Although it isn't likely that the original Welsh settlers who arrived here in 1865 could have imagined just how much Puerto Madryn would evolve, a large part of the town's success is owed to their hardworking traditions, which continue with their descendants today. The anniversary of their arrival is celebrated every July 28 here and in other Chubut towns. Only a statue—the Tehuelche Indian Monument—serves as a reminder of the indigenous people who once lived here and who helped the Welsh survive.

Puerto Madryn

67 km (42 miles) north of Trelew; 104 km (64 miles) west of Puerto Pirámides.

Approaching from Ruta 3, it's hard to believe that the horizon line of buildings perched just beyond the windswept dunes and badlands is the most successful of all coastal Patagonia settlements. But once you get past the outskirts of town and onto the wide coastal road known as the Rambla, the picture begins to change. Ranged along the clear and tranquil Golfo Nuevo are restaurants,

Cruising the southern tip of South America reveals fjords, glaciers, lagoons, lakes, narrow channels, waterfalls, forested shorelines, fishing villages, and wildlife.

cafés, dive shops, and hotels, all busy—but not yet overcrowded—with tourists from around the world.

Puerto Madryn is more a base for visiting nearby wildlife-watching sites like Península Valdés and Punta Tombo than a destination in its own right. The town's architecture is unremarkable, and beyond a walk along the coast there isn't much to do. Indeed, even the few museums serve mainly to introduce you to the fauna you'll see elsewhere. The exception is the beginning of whale season (May through July), when the huge animals cavort right in the bay before heading north—you can even walk out alongside them on the pier. During these months it's worth the extra expense for a room with a sea view.

The many tour agencies and rental-car companies here make excursion planning easy. Aim to spend most of your time here on one- or two-day trips exploring the surroundings.

■ TIP➜ Note that competition is fierce between tourism operators in destinations such as Puerto Madryn and Puerto Pirámides on Península Valdés. Take information that tour operators and even the tourism office give you about these with a grain of salt: they often exaggerate Madryn's virtues and other areas' flaws.

GETTING HERE AND AROUND

Madryn is just small enough to walk around in, and many hotels are on or near the 3½-km-long (2-mile-long) Avenida Almirante Brown—often referred to as "La Rambla"—which runs alongside the bay and has a wide pedestrian walkway. Renting a bicycle is a great way to reach the EcoCentro and (if you're feeling fit) the Punta Loma nature reserve. Otherwise, to get to either of these, to El Doradillo beach north of town, and to Península Valdés and Punta Tombo, you'll need to either rent a vehicle, travel with a tour, or take a remis. Mar y Valle also runs two daily bus services between Puerto Madryn's bus terminal and Puerto Pirámides on the Península Valdés.

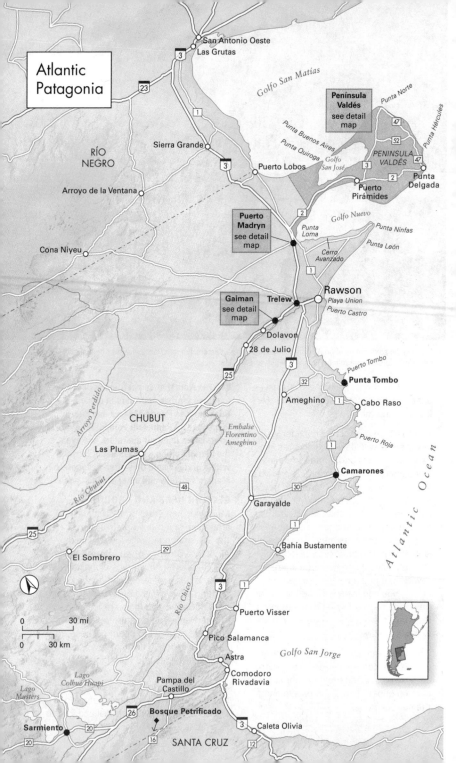

Atlantic Patagonia

San Antonio Oeste
Las Grutas
3
23
Golfo San Matías

Península
Valdés
see detail
map
Punta Norte
47
Punta Buenos Aires
Punta Quiroga
Golfo
San José
52
Punta Hércules
PENÍNSULA
VALDÉS
47

Sierra Grande
RÍO
NEGRO
3
1
Puerto Lobos
3
Puerto
Pirámides
2
Punta
Delgada

Arroyo de la Ventana
Puerto Madryn
see detail
map
2
Golfo Nuevo
Punta Ninfas
Punta León
Punta
Loma
Cona Niyeu
Cerro
Avanzado
1

Gaiman
see detail
map
Trelew
Rawson
Playa Union
Puerto Castro
Dolavon
28 de Julio
3
Puerto Tombo
Punta Tombo
Cabo Raso
1
32
Ameghino

CHUBUT
Arroyo Perdido
Embalse
Florentino
Ameghino
Puerto Roja
1

Las Plumas
Río Chubut
48
Camarones
30
25
Garayalde
1
El Sombrero
29
Atlantic Ocean
Bahía Bustamante
Río Chico
3
1
Puerto Visser

25
Pico Salamanca
Astra
Golfo San Jorge
Lago
Colhué Huapi
Pampa del
Castillo
Comodoro
Rivadavia
Lago
Musters
26
Bosque Petrificado
3
Caleta Olivia
Sarmiento
20
20
16
SANTA CRUZ
12

0   30 mi
0   30 km

For those flying in and out of Trelew, Transfer PMY operates a shuttle service direct to any hotel in Puerto Madryn (about US$15) or there are taxis available. There are services every half hour between Puerto Madryn and Trelew and Gaiman with the bus company 28 de Julio. Andesmar and Don Otto connect Puerto Madryn to Buenos Aires, Bariloche, Río Gallegos, and Puerto Montt in Chile. Numerous car rental agencies are along Avenida Roca.

ESSENTIALS
VISITOR INFORMATION Puerto Madryn.
✉ *Av. Roca 223, Puerto Madryn* ☎ *0280/445–3504* ⊕ *www.madryn.gob.ar/turismo.*

TOURS
Puerto Madryn is a useful base for exploring nearby wildlife sites such as Península Valdés and Punta Tombo. If time is tight, or you don't feel like driving the several hundred kilometers round-trip, consider taking an organized day tour. The regular services offered by the many agencies around town vary little in price and content. Try to book a couple of days ahead if you can, although midweek many companies accept bookings the night before the tour leaves.

Note that the English spoken by most guides can vary wildly, so read up on the area first. Drinks, snacks, and meals are rarely included: bring plenty of your own along, and be prepared to spend a long, long time on your minibus.

Standard tours to Península Valdés typically include a stop at the visitor center, a whale-watching boat trip (June through December), and a visit to two other wildlife spots on the peninsula. Time is often tight, and tours can feel more like working through a fauna checklist than getting close to nature. Companies can drop you off in Puerto Pirámides on the way back if you've decided to stay there overnight.

Day trips to Punta Tombo stop off at Rawson for dolphin-watching (not always included in the tour price), then continue south to the penguin reserve, where you get a scant hour or so. They usually return via Gaiman (with a visit to a Welsh teahouse) or Trelew (to see the dinosaur museum). Most companies are happy to drop you at the Trelew airport on the way back if you have an evening flight.

For more information, see the Getting Here and Around sections for Península Valdés and Punta Tombo.

Argentina Vision
ADVENTURE TOURS | With more than 35 years of experience, this tour company offers excursions including visiting Península Valdés, kayaking and diving with seals in Punta Loma, bird-watching boat tours, whale-spotting, and horseback riding. They also do a half-day 4X4 outing to Punta Loma. ✉ *Av. Roca 536, Puerto Madryn* ☎ *0280/445–5888* ⊕ *www.argentinavision.com* ⌨ *From 1,200 pesos.*

Bottazzi
ADVENTURE TOURS | One of the first whale-watching operators in Puerto Madryn, Bottazzi specializes in whale-watching from its own fleet of 20-, 50-, and 80-passenger boats from Puerto Pirámides. Guided trips last about an hour and a half. When it isn't whale season, they offer dolphin-watching trips at Puerto Rawson, where you can watch toninas, the world's smallest dolphins, at play. One of the most popular tours combines a full-day Punta Tombo excursion (which includes transport from Puerto Madryn) to see penguins with dolphin-watching. Bottazzi also offers other sightseeing tours and activities. ✉ *Av. Roca 31, Puerto Madryn* ☎ *0280/447–4110* ⊕ *www.bottazzi.com.ar* ⌨ *From 1,300 pesos.*

Causana Viajes
ADVENTURE TOURS | Custom-tour operator Causana Viajes will organize the tour or schedule you want with your own chauffeur and guide. The most requested tours are full-day excursions to Península Valdés with whale-watching, and full-day tours to Punta Tombo for penguins and dolphin-spotting. ⊠ *Rawson 1331, Puerto Madryn* ☎ *0280/447–5919* ⊕ *www.causanatour.com.ar* 🕿 *From 6,000 pesos.*

Miras del Mar
ADVENTURE TOURS | The most popular tour through this outfitter is the full-day Punta Tombo excursion, which includes a stopover for Welsh tea at Gaiman and Trelew's paleontology museum and includes transport from Puerto Madryn. ⊠ *Moreno 38, Puerto Madryn* ☎ *0280/447–4316* ⊕ *www.mirasdelmar.com* 🕿 *From 1,000 pesos.*

Nievemar
ADVENTURE TOURS | As well as full-day tours to Punta Tombo and Península Valdés, Nievemar offers private day tours to the Petrified Forest, half days visiting the tonina dolphins, and whale-spotting visits from Playa el Doradillo. You can book tours from their Puerto Madryn and Trelew offices. ⊠ *Av. Roca 493, Puerto Madryn* ☎ *0280/445–5544* ⊕ *www.nievemartours.com.ar* 🕿 *From 1,100 pesos.*

◉ Sights

★ El Doradillo
BEACH | FAMILY | Following the coastal road 14 km (9 miles) north from Puerto Madryn brings you to this whale-watching spot. The ocean floor drops away steeply from the beach, so between June and mid-December you can stand on the sand with a close up view of the southern right whales right from the shore, usually mothers teaching their young to swim. During the rest of the year, it's just a regular beach. It's a pleasant 1½ hours' bike ride from Puerto Madryn. Alternatively, taxis charge about

2,500 pesos for the round-trip including a 45-minute stay. Grab some food to go and make it a picnic spot. ⊠ *Puerto Madryn* 🕿 *Free.*

Museo Provincial del Hombre y el Mar (Ciencias Naturales y Oceanografía)
HISTORY MUSEUM | This whimsical collection of taxidermied animals, shells, skeletons, and engravings examines humankind's relationship with the sea. Housed in a restored 1915 building, the beautifully displayed exhibits evoke the marine myths of the Tehuelche (the area's indigenous people), imagined European sea monsters, the ideas of 19th-century naturalists, through to modern ecology. It's more about experience than explanation, so don't worry about the scarcity of English translations, although the excellent room on orca behavior is a welcome exception. Finish by looking out over the city and surrounding steppes from the tower. ⊠ *Domecq García at José Menéndez, Puerto Madryn* ☎ *0280/445–1139* 🕿 *Free* ◷ *Closed weekends.*

Punta Loma Sea Lion Reserve
NATURE PRESERVE | Some 600 South American sea lions lounge on the shore below a tall, crescent bluff at Punta Loma, 17 km (11 miles) southeast of the city. Aim to visit during low tide. You can reach the reserve by car (follow signs toward Punta Ninfas); by bicycle on a scenic but hilly road if the wind is not too strong; or by taxi—expect to pay about 3,000 pesos for the return trip, including a 45-minute stay. ⊠ *Punta Loma, Puerto Madryn* 🕿 *Free.*

🍴 Restaurants

★ Cantina El Náutico
$$$$ | INTERNATIONAL | Founded in 1963, photos of visiting Argentine celebrities mingle with the marine-themed doodads that cover the walls at this local favorite. The best bet in town, they are most known for their large portions of fish and seafood dishes but they also offer

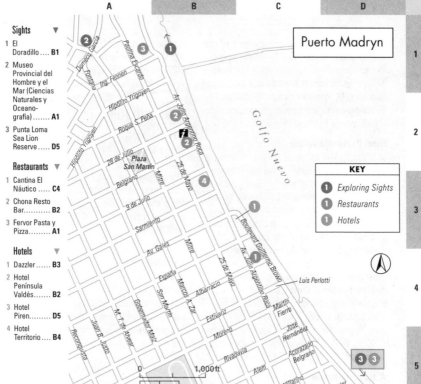

Sights ▼

1 El Doradillo **B1**

2 Museo Provincial del Hombre y el Mar (Ciencias Naturales y Oceanografía) **A1**

3 Punta Loma Sea Lion Reserve **D5**

Restaurants ▼

1 Cantina El Náutico **C4**

2 Chona Resto Bar........... **B2**

3 Fervor Pasta y Pizza......... **A1**

Hotels ▼

1 Dazzler...... **B3**

2 Hotel Península Valdés....... **B2**

3 Hotel Piren......... **D5**

4 Hotel Territorio.... **B4**

KEY

❶ Exploring Sights

❶ Restaurants

❶ Hotels

Golfo Nuevo

Luis Perlotti

traditional Argentine cuisine. **Known for:** good fish and seafood; homemade pasta; big portions. ⑤ *Average main: pesos900* ⊠ *Av. Roca 790, Puerto Madryn* ☎ *0280/447–1404* ⊕ *www.cantinaelnautico.com.*

Chona Resto Bar

$$$$ | **ARGENTINE** | An eclectic menu with a mix of seafood, international and Argentine classics, including all manner of beef options, this is a fine stop for a meal. They also have vegetarian and gluten free dishes. **Known for:** good service; vegetarian options; Argentine gourmet. ⑤ *Average main: pesos2100* ⊠ *Av. Julio Argentino Roca 249, Puerto Madryn* ☎ *280/420–1135.*

Fervor Pasta y Pizza

$$$ | **ITALIAN** | Sour dough pizzas that leave any pizza aficionado content, Fervor has high quality, homemade pastas and incredible pizzas. Dine in a warm atmosphere with good food that won't break your bank. **Known for:** sourdough pizza; reasonable prices; homemade pasta. ⑤ *Average main: pesos690* ⊠ *Av. Guillermo Rawson 153, Puerto Madryn* ☎ *280/477–7440* ⊕ *www.fervor.ar.*

 Hotels

Dazzler

$$ | **HOTEL** | Right on the beachfront in the city center, Dazzler's sea views will keep you eagerly hunting for whales, while the comfy beds and generous amenities will pull you away from the window for just a little while. **Pros:** central beachfront location; friendly staff; great views of the coast. **Cons:** no bathtubs; parking costs extra; centralized temperature control. [$] *Rooms from: US$182* ✉ *Bul. Almirante Brown 637, Puerto Madryn* ☎ *0280/447–5758* 🌐 *www.dazzlerpuertomadryn.com* 🛏 *95 rooms* 🍴 *Free Breakfast.*

Hotel Península Valdés

$$ | HOTEL | The minimal gray-and-taupe lobby and slick, wooden-walled breakfast bar are the result of the gradual renovation of this well-established hotel; some rooms are cramped and still outdated but the *panorámicos* have bigger beds and fabulous views of the bay, and the Peninsula Suite has an outdoor balcony and a Jacuzzi tub with a bay view. **Pros:** oceanfront location; good service; disabled access. **Cons:** gym is tiny; old fashioned decor; some rooms are cramped. [$] *Rooms from: US$150* ✉ *Av. Julio Argentino Roca 151, Puerto Madryn* ☎ *0280/447–1292* 🌐 *www.hotelpeninsula.com.ar* 🛏 *76 rooms* 🍴 *Free Breakfast.*

★ **Hotel Territorio**

$$ | HOTEL | This well-designed boutique hotel on the outskirts of town, on the beach, is a good find if you want peace and quiet and don't mind being away from the city center. **Pros:** all rooms have sea views; quiet, boutique hotel; attention to details. **Cons:** five-minute drive from city center; not enough parking spaces; limited options in restaurant. [$] *Rooms from: US$125* ✉ *Blvd. Almirante Brown 3251, Puerto Madryn* ☎ *11/5263–0628* 🌐 *www.hotelterritorio.com.ar* 🛏 *38 rooms* 🍴 *Free Breakfast.*

Hotel Piren

$$ | HOTEL | In the center of Puerto Madryn, this modern hotel towers over the beachfront and is near all the best restaurants and shops. **Pros:** modern, well-maintained hotel; attentive service; good breakfast. **Cons:** small parking garage; street noise; no air conditioning. [$] *Rooms from: US$120* ✉ *Av. Julio A. Roca 439, Puerto Madryn* ☎ *280/445–6276* 🌐 *www.hotelpiren.com.ar* 🛏 *98 rooms* 🍴 *Free Breakfast.*

Activities

BICYCLING

Napra Club

BIKING | Cycling is a great way to reach El Doradillo and Punta Loma. You can rent mountain bikes by the hour or the day from this windsurf school on the beach. ✉ *Av. Almte. Brown 860, Puerto Madryn* ☎ *0280/445–5633* 🌐 *www.napraclub.com.*

DIVING

★ **Lobo Larsen Buceo**

SCUBA DIVING | This is one of those once-in-a-lifetime excursions. Lobo Larson offers unforgettable experiences snorkeling up close with sea lions and their cubs as they play around you in the crystal clear waters. Their English-speaking dive masters also offer snorkeling and introductory dives and courses to non-divers, and wreck and reef outings to certified divers. Equipment and transport from Puerto Madryn is provided; special polar dry suits allow for winter diving. ✉ *Av. Roca 885, Puerto Madryn* ☎ *0280/451–6314* 🌐 *www.lobolarsen.com.*

KAYAKING AND WINDSURFING

Escuela Windsurf Napra Club

KAYAKING | FAMILY | This excellent outfit rents sea kayaks and windsurf equipment. They also run highly regarded nature-watching kayak tours to nearby bays. During their summer Sea School, local instructors teach children snorkeling, windsurfing, bait and lure fishing, and identification of local fauna. ✉ *Av. Almte. Brown 860, Puerto Madryn* ☎ *0280/445–5633* 🌐 *www.napraclub.com.*

Continued on page 378

INTO THE PATAGONIAN WILD

Patagonia will shatter your sense of scale. You will feel very small, surrounded by an epic expanse of mountains and plains, sea, and sky. Whether facing down an advancing wall of glacial ice, watching an ostrich-like rhea racing across the open steppe, or getting splashed by a breaching right whale off the Valdez Peninsula, prepare to gasp at the majesty of the Patagonian wild.

GLACIERS OF PATAGONIA

Cruise on Perito Moreno glacier (above). Glacier Grey, Torres del Paine National Park, Chile (right).

The Patagonia ice field covers much of the southern end of the Andean mountain range, straddling the Argentina–Chile border. The glaciers that spill off the high altitude ice field are basically rivers of slowly moving ice and snow that grind and push their way across the mountains, crushing soft rock and sculpting granite peaks.

Most of Patagonia's glaciers spill into lakes, rivers, or fjords. Chunks of ice calve off the face of the glacier into the water, a dramatic display of nature's power that you can view at several locations. The larger pieces of ice become icebergs that scud across the water surface like white sailboats blown by the wind.

TRAVEL SHRINKS

The link between high-impact activities—such as air travel—and climate change is clear, leading to a disturbing irony: the more people come to see the glaciers of Patagonia, the more carbon is released into the atmosphere, and the more the glaciers shrink.

WEATHER

Weather is unpredictable around glaciers: it's not uncommon to experience sunshine, rain, and snow squalls in a single afternoon.

ICE COLORS

Although clear days are best for panoramas, cloudy days bring out the translucent blue of the glacial ice, creating great opportunities for magical photographs. You'll also see black or gray streaks in the ice caused by sediment picked up by the glacier as it grinds down the mountain valley. When that sediment is deposited into lakes, it hangs suspended in the water, turning the lake a pale milky blue.

ENVIRONMENTAL CONCERN

There's no question that human-induced climate change is taking its toll on Patagonia's glaciers. Although the famous Perito Moreno glacier is still advancing, nearly all the others have shrunk in recent years, some dramatically. You can find out more about the effects of climate change and their impact on the glaciers at Calafate's Glaciarium museum.

GLACIERS TO SEE

- Perito Moreno Glacier, Santa Cruz, Argentina

- Upsala Glacier, Santa Cruz, Argentina

- Martial Glacier, Tierra del Fuego, Argentina

- Serrano Glacier, Tierra del Fuego, Chile

- O'Higgins Glacier, Southern Coast, Chile

FIRE AND ICE: MOUNTAINS OF PATAGONIA

A trekker takes in the view of Cerro Torre (left) and Fitz Roy in Los Glaciares National Park, Patagonia.

In Patagonia, mountains mean the Andes, a relatively young range but a precocious one that stretches for more than 4,000 miles. The Patagonian Andes are of special interest to geologists, who study how fire, water, and ice have shaped the mountains into their present form.

CREATION

Plate tectonics are the most fundamental factor in the formation of the southern Andes, with the oceanic Nazca plate slipping beneath the continental South American plate and forcing the peaks skyward. Volcanic activity is a symptom of this dynamic process, and there are several active volcanoes on the Chilean side of the range.

GLACIAL IMPRINT

Glacial activity has also played an important role in chiseling the most iconic Patagonian peaks. The spires that form the distinctive skylines of Torres del Paine and the Fitzroy range are solid columns that were created when rising glaciers ripped away weaker rock, leaving only hard granite skeletons that stand rigid at the edge of the ice fields.

MOUNTAIN HIGH BORDERS

Because the border between Chile and Argentina cuts through the most impenetrable reaches of the ice field, the actual border line is unclear in areas of the far south. Even in the more temperate north, border crossings are often located at mountain passes, and the officials who stamp visas seem more like mountain guides than bureaucrats.

MOUNTAINS OF THE SEA

Tierra del Fuego and the countless islands off the coast of southern Chile were once connected to the mainland. Over the years the sea swept into the valleys, isolated the peaks, and created an archipelago that, viewed on a map, looks as abstract as a Jackson Pollack painting. From the water these island mountains appear especially dramatic, misty pinnacles of rock and ice rising from the crashing sea.

Right: Mt. Fitzroy

**PROMINENT PEAKS
AND RANGES**

■ Mt. Fitzroy and Cerro
  Torre, Santa Cruz,
  Argentina

■ Cuernos of Torres del
  Paine, Chile

■ Beagle Channel
  Mountains, Tierra del
  Fuego, Chile/Argentina

■ Cerro Piltriqitron,
  El Bolson, Argentina

■ Osorno Volcano, Lake
  District, Chile

PENGUINS OF PATAGONIA

Magellanic Penguins

Everyone loves penguins. How could you not feel affection for such cute, curious, and loyal little creatures? On land, their awkward waddle is endearing, and you can get close enough to see the inquisitive gaze in their eyes as they turn their heads from side to side for a good look at you. In the water, penguins transform from goofballs into Olympic athletes, streaking through the waves and returning to the nest with mouthfuls of fish and squid for their chicks.

TYPES

Most of the penguins you'll see here are Magellanic penguins, black and white colored birds that gather in large breeding colonies on the beaches of Patagonia in the summer and retreat north to warmer climes during winter. Also keep an eye out for the red-beaked Gentoo penguins that nest among the Magellanics.

If your image of penguins is the large and colorful Emperor penguins of Antarctica that featured in the documentary March of the Penguins, you might be slightly underwhelmed by the little Magellanics. Adults stand about 30 inches tall and

weigh between 15 and 20 pounds. What they lack in glamour, Patagonia's penguins make up in vanity—and numbers. Many breeding sites are home to tens of thousands of individuals, all preening and strutting as if they were about to walk the red carpet at the Academy Awards.

PENGUIN RELATIONS

Male and female penguins form monogamous pairs and share the task of raising the chicks, which hatch in small burrows that the parents return to year after year. If you sit and observe a pair of penguins for a little while you'll notice how affectionate they appear, grooming each other with their beaks and huddling together on the nest.

HUMAN CONTACT

Although penguins are not shy of humans who keep a respectful distance (about 8 feet is a good rule of thumb), the history of penguin-human relations is not entirely one of peaceful curiosity. Early pioneers and stranded sailors would raid penguin nests for food, and in modern times, oil spills have devastated penguin colonies in Patagonia.

WHERE & WHEN

The best time to see penguins is from November through February, which coincides with the best weather in coastal Patagonia. Some of the most convenient and impressive colonies to visit are:

- Punta Tombo, Chubut, Argentina

- Cabo Virgenes, Santa Cruz, Argentina

- Isla Madalena, Chile

- Martillo Island, Tierra del Fuego, Argentina

- Puerto San Julian, Santa Cruz, Argentina

IN THE SEA

The Patagonian coast teems with marine life, including numerous "charismatic megafauna" such as whales, dolphins, sea lions, and seals.

❶ Seals and Sea Lions

In the springtime massive elephant seals and southern sea lions drag themselves onto Patagonian beaches for mating season—hopefully out of range of hungry orcas. These giant pinnipeds form two groups in the breeding colonies. Big, tough alpha bulls have their own harems of breeding females and their young, while so-called bachelor males hang out nearby like freshman boys at a fraternity party, hoping to entice a stray female away from the alpha bull's harem.

❷ Orcas

Orcas aren't as common as dolphins, but you can spot them off the Valdez Peninsula, Argentina, hunting seals and sea lions along the shore. Sometimes hungry orcas will chase their prey a few feet too far and beach themselves above the tide line, where they perish of dehydration.

❸ Whales

The Valdez Peninsula is also one of the best places to observe right whales, gentle giants of the ocean. Although the name right whale derives from whalers who designated it as the "right" whale to kill, the right whale is now protected by both national legislation and international agreements.

❹ Dolphins

Dolphins are easy to spot on tours, because they're curious and swim up to the boat, sometimes even surfing the bow wake. Commerson's dolphins are a common species in coastal Argentina and the Straights of Magellan. Among the world's tiniest dolphins, their white and black coloring has earned them the nickname "skunk dolphin" and prompted comparisons with their distant cousins, orcas.

IN THE AIR

Patagonia is a twitcher's paradise. Even non-bird-lovers marvel at the colorful species that squawk, flutter, and soar through Patagonia's skies.

5 Albatross

You can spot several species of albatross off the Patagonian coast, gliding on fixed wings above the waves. The albatross lives almost entirely at sea, touching down on land to breed and raise its young. Unless you're visiting Antarctica or the Falklands, your best bet for seeing an albatross is to take a cruise from Punta Arenas or Ushuaia.

6 Andean Condor

You probably won't see a condor up close. They nest on high-altitude rock ledges and spend their days soaring in circles on high thermals, scanning mountain slopes and plains for carrion. With a wing span of up to 10 feet, however, the king of the Andean skies is impressive even when viewed from a distance. Condors live longer than almost any other bird. Some could qualify for Social Security.

7 Magellanic Woodpecker

You can hear the distinctive rat-tat of this enormous woodpecker in nothofagus forests of Chilean Patagonia and parts of Argentina. Males have a bright red head and a black body, while females are almost entirely black.

8 Rhea (Nandu)

No, it's not an ostrich. The rhea is an extremely large flightless bird that roams the Patagonian steppe. Although they're not normally aggressive, males have been known to charge humans who get too close to their partner's nests.

9 Kelp Goose

As the name implies, kelp geese love kelp. In fact, kelp is the only thing they eat. The geese travel along the rocky shores of Tierra del Fuego in search of their favorite seaweed salad.

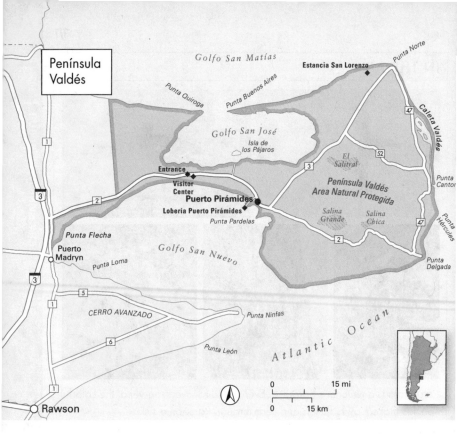

Península Valdés

104 km (64 miles) northeast of Puerto Madryn

The biggest attraction in Península Valdés is the *ballena franca* (southern right whale) population, which feeds, mates, and gives birth here. These protected mammals are the top attraction for the more than 340,000 visitors that come here every year, especially from June, when the whales first arrive, through December. During the peak season of September and October, people crowd into boats at Puerto Pirámides to observe at close range as the 30- to 35-ton whales breach and blast giant V-shape spouts of water from their blowholes.

Yet Península Valdés is a year-round destination for wildlife that includes much more than the magnificent whales. In addition to sea lions, elephant seals roam the shores of the peninsula year-round. Orcas, or killer whales, frequent the beaches from September to April. And the Magellanic penguins are spring and summer visitors; in fact, the seashore around Estancia San Lorenzo is now the continent's largest breeding site for this charismatic flightless bird.

GETTING HERE AND AROUND

About 60 km (37 miles) northeast along the coast on Ruta 2 from Puerto Madryn, the land narrows to form an isthmus. A ranger's station here marks the entrance to the Península Valdés Area Natural Protegida (Protected Natural Area), where you pay a park entry fee of about US$20. A further 22 km (14 miles) down the road is the remodeled Centro de Visitantes Istmo Ameghino (Ameghino Isthmus

Visitor Center). A series of rather dry displays provides a basic introduction to the marine, coastal, and continental flora and fauna ahead of you. More exciting are the complete skeleton of a southern right whale and the views over the isthmus from the lookout tower.

From the visitor center it's another 24 km (15 miles) to the junction leading to Puerto Pirámides, 2 km (3 miles) to the south. By following the road 5 km (3 miles) east, you reach the start of the circuit of the interconnected 32- to 64-km (20- to 40-mile) dirt roads around the peninsula.

There are different ways to explore the peninsula. If you prefer natural surroundings to cityscapes and really want to see all the area has to offer, plan on spending at least a night or two here rather than using Puerto Madryn as your base. The accommodations in Puerto Pirámides easily rival those in town, and when the tour parties leave, you get the rugged, windswept coastal landscape to yourself. Hearing whales splashing offshore at night is a particularly magical experience. By staying you also have time to do an additional whale-watching trip at sunset, and to go hiking, kayaking, or snorkeling with sea lions.

However, if your schedule is tight, consider one of the many organized day trips that operate out of Puerto Madryn. A minibus typically picks you up at your hotel around 8 am, stops briefly at the visitor center, then continues to Puerto Pirámides for whale-watching (June through December only) and lunch. During the afternoon, you visit two other spots on the peninsula before returning to Puerto Madryn by about 7 pm. These tours are reasonably priced (starting at 1,400 pesos per person) and pack a lot in. However, you spend most of the day crammed in the minibus, don't get to visit the entire peninsula, and have little time to linger at wildlife spots.

To visit the peninsula more extensively at your own pace, you need to rent a car and stay overnight. Having your own wheels also gives you the freedom to stay in the beautiful but remote lodgings at Punta Delgada and Punta Norte. Bear in mind, though, that you'll have to drive several hundred kilometers on dirt and gravel roads in varying states of repair. Stock your vehicle well with drinks, snacks, and gas (the only station is at Puerto Pirámides), and don't try to overtake the tour buses: cars are much lighter, and flipping is unfortunately a common accident here. Economy vehicle rental starts at about US$60 per day; the nearest place to rent from is Puerto Madryn—there are numerous car rentals along Avenida Roca.

If all you want to do is whale-watch, you can reach Puerto Pirámides on the daily public bus service from Puerto Madryn run by Mar y Valle (in high season they shuttle back and forth twice a day). Tickets cost $140 each way.

For the freedom of having your own car without the responsibility of driving, arrange for a remis. You can do this as a day trip from Puerto Madryn through most local tour operators (prices vary), or from Puerto Pirámides, if you're staying there, with El Gauchito. Expect to pay about 2,400 pesos for a full day (six hours) exploring the peninsula.

Finally, you can combine some of the above approaches and get an overview of the peninsula on a tour, but then get off at Puerto Pirámides on the way back and stay overnight, do other excursions, and then return on the public bus.

ESSENTIALS
BUS CONTACTS Mar y Valle. ⊠ *Terminal de Ómnibus, Puerto Madryn* ☎ *0280/445–0600.*

REMIS TOURS El Gauchito. ☎ *0280/449–5014.*

Did You Know?

Elephant seals that live on the Patagonian coast in Argentina are known to be able to hold their breath underwater for more than 100 minutes.

VISITOR INFORMATION Centro de Visitantes Istmo Ameghino (Ameghino Isthmus Visitor Center). ✉ *At entrance to Peninsula* ☎ *0280/445–0489.*

Sights

PUERTO PIRÁMIDES

The only settlement on Península Valdés is tiny Puerto Pirámides, which transforms into Argentina's whale-watching capital between June and December. The main street, Avenida de las Ballenas, runs parallel to the shore about 200 meters inland, and is lined with pretty tin-roofed buildings among dunes and scrubby flowers. Two streets run down from it to the sea; all the whale-watching operations are clustered around the first of these, known as La Primera Bajada.

For ecological reasons, only 565 people are allowed to live here permanently, but there is a good selection of hotels and restaurants.

■ TIP→ Bring plenty of money with you, as the one ATM may be out of cash.

In addition to whale-watching and lounging around with a beer while looking out on the pyramid-shape cliffs that gave the town its name, you can go scuba diving or snorkeling with sea lions, kayaking, sand boarding, paddle boarding, and mountain biking.

★ Lobería Puerto Pirámides

NATURE SIGHT | Some 4 km (3 miles) from Puerto Pirámides lies the Lobería Puerto Pirámides, a year-round sea-lion colony that is also a great bird-watching spot. A signposted turnoff from the main road into town leads here, or you can follow the coastal path on foot. ✉ *Puerto Pirámides.*

★ Estancia San Lorenzo

NATURE SIGHT | At the peninsula's northern tip is the world's largest Magellanic penguin colony at and around Estancia San Lorenzo, numbering some 600,000 penguins. San Lorenzo offers three guided tours (1 hour and 15 minutes) to the penguin colony every afternoon, always with a ranger. Also on site are a restaurant and visitors can tour a sheep ranch and the ruins of a former factory that once processed sea lion blubber and skin. ✉ *Puerto Pirámides* ☎ *280/436–9390* ✉ *pinguinerasanlorenzo@argentinavision.com* 🌐 *www.pinguinospuntanorte.com.ar* 🎟 *US$ 65 for adults* 🕓 *Closed Apr.–Sept. 6* ✍ *Contact by email or Whatsapp to reserve your guided tour.*

Restaurants

For quick sandwiches or burgers before a whale-watching trip, try one of the snack bars that are interspersed with the tour operators on the Primera Bajada. All close at about 7 pm. Aside from the food joints on the main drag, check out the hotel restaurants for good options, too.

La Covacha

$$$$ | **ARGENTINE** | A seaside feel and menu is what this sunny spot prides itself on, serving up pizzas, fried calamari, and chilled brews with a view to the ocean. **Known for:** afternoon beers on the seafront; pub grub; relaxed pace. [$] *Average main: pesos1800* ✉ *Osvaldo Bayern, Puerto Pirámides* ☎ *0280/496–9528.*

Bar La Estación

$$$$ | **ARGENTINE** | The coolest bar in Pirámides is also the town's best seafood restaurant where amid nets, nautical gear, and glam-rock posters the requisite fish and steak dishes are offered alongside pizzas and homemade pastas. **Known for:** comfort food; good beer range; cozy, unpretentious vibe. [$] *Average main: pesos800* ✉ *Av. de las Ballenas s/n, Puerto Pirámides* ☎ *0280/456–2855* 🕓 *Dinner every day; lunch only on weekends.*

Hotels

Del Nómade Eco Hotel

$$ | **HOTEL** | When you're staying in a wildlife reserve, taking care of Mother Nature seems only right; while this eco-friendly hotel uses solar panels, low-energy fittings, and recycles its water, they don't skimp on style or luxury. **Pros:** eco-awareness at no loss to comfort; book expeditions through informed staff; fabulous breakfasts. **Cons:** patchy Wi-Fi; some rooms have limited views; slightly removed from the restaurants on the main drag. [$] *Rooms from: US$165* ✉ *Av. de las Ballenas s/n, Puerto Pirámides* ☎ *0280/449–5044* 🌐 *www.ecohosteria.com.ar* ⏲ *Closed mid-Aug.–mid-Apr.* 🛏 *8 rooms* 🍴 *Free Breakfast.*

Las Restingas

$$$ | **HOTEL** | The powder-blue clapboard facade of this hotel stretches along the beachfront: squint and you can see whales from the huge picture windows in the front-facing rooms and lobby lounge. **Pros:** restaurant with deck overlooking the sea; sea (and whale) views from some rooms; large rooms. **Cons:** tiny bathrooms; inconsistent service; rooms are overpriced. [$] *Rooms from: US$229* ✉ *Primera Bajada at beach, Puerto Pirámides* ☎ *0280/449–5101* 🌐 *www.lasrestingas.com* ⏲ *Closed Apr.–May* 🛏 *12 rooms* 🍴 *Free Breakfast.*

★ Océano Patagonia

$$$ | **HOTEL** | These unique "eco residences" have an ideal location, steps away from the center of the tiny town yet tucked away on the oceanfront. **Pros:** eco-friendly architecture; kitchenettes; mesmerizing ocean views. **Cons:** trees block view from ground floor suites; parking costs extra; wifi is intermittent. [$] *Rooms from: US$220* ✉ *Accesso Ballanero, Puerto Pirámides* ☎ *911/6730–7300* 🌐 *www.oceanopatagonia.com* 🛏 *11 rooms* 🍴 *Free Breakfast.*

Activities

From June to December, the main attractions at Puerto Pirámides are whale-watching boat trips into the Golfo Nuevo to see southern right whales. Experienced captains pilot the boats between the huge mammals while bilingual guides tell you about their habits and habitats. Expect to use up lots of your camera memory as the graceful creatures dive, spout water, and salute you with their tails.

Most whale-watching companies operate several trips a day while the whales are in town, especially during the peak months of September and October. Standard daytime excursions last about 1¼ hours, and the price is set each year by the municipality. Trips in smaller boats and longer tours are usually more expensive. Although no boat is allowed closer than 15 meters to the whales (the animals themselves sometimes break the rules by diving under your boat), you certainly feel closer from smaller vessels. On clear days, the magical sunset tours are definitely worth paying extra for: you see the whales frolic as the sun sets over the water around them. It's best to call a day or two ahead to reserve, although many companies will fit you in if you show up on the day.

BOAT TOURS

★ Bottazzi

WILDLIFE-WATCHING | Bottazzi pioneered whale watching in Peninsula Valdes. Their excursions are longer than other companies' and have excellent English-speaking guides. The sunset trips are on very small boats, and include wine and cheese back at their office afterwards. Moreover, their trips are green certified, and with a percentage of the profits financing a companion foundation that works to protect wildlife on the peninsula. Highly recommended. ✉ *Primera Bajada, Puerto Pirámides* ☎ *0280/447–4110* 🌐 *www.bottazzi.com.ar.*

Hydrosport
BOATING | Hydrosport is a reliable, long-running operator with three different boat sizes, among them the biggest whale watching boat in South America holding up to 72 people. ✉ *Primera Bajada, Puerto Pirámides* ☎ *0280/449–5065.*

Southern Spirit
BOATING | This outfitter allows you not only to see but also to hear the whales, thanks to their underwater sound-detection system. They use large but fairly low boats and operate up to five 90-minute trips a day, including a sunset outing. ✉ *Av. de las Ballenas at Primera Bajada, Puerto Pirámides* ☎ *280/449–5094* ⊕ *www.southernspirit.com.ar.*

KAYAKING
Patagonia Explorers
KAYAKING | Kayaking in the Golfo Nuevo and the Golfo San José is offered by Patagonia Explorers, who also have English-speaking guides. ✉ *Av. de las Ballenas at Primera Bajada, Puerto Pirámides* ☎ *280/4340–619* ⊕ *www.patagoniaexplorers.com.*

Trelew, Gaiman, and Punta Tombo

When the Welsh settlers landed on the desert-like Patagonian coast in 1865, they realized they would need to move inland to find suitable land for farming. Some 25 km (15 miles) inland, in the fertile Chubut River valley, they founded Trelew and Gaiman. Both retain Welsh traditions to this day: Trelew holds an Eisteddfod (festival of Welsh poetry, song, and dance) each October, and Gaiman is the largest Welsh settlement outside of Wales.

With 108,000 inhabitants, Trelew is now a large city by Patagonian standards, and its airport is the gateway to Atlantic Patagonia. Beyond the excellent dinosaur museum, however, the dusty, windswept center is of little interest to tourists. With

its teahouses, rose gardens, and chapels, Gaiman retains a country-town feel. Indeed, farms and stone-fruit orchards still fill the countryside surrounding it.

On the coast 120 km (74 miles) south of Trelew lies the Punta Tombo penguin reserve, which you can easily visit on a day trip from Trelew, Gaiman, or Puerto Madryn.

Trelew

11 km (6 miles) east of Gaiman; 67 km (42 miles) south of Puerto Madryn.

Trelew (pronounced Tre- *leh*-ew) is a commercial, industrial, and service hub that contains the region's main airport. Its biggest attractions are its paleontology museum (with enormous dinosaur fossils on exhibit) and its proximity to the Punta Tombo reserve (though both can also be reached on day trips from Gaiman and Puerto Madryn). Otherwise, the city has little to recommend it: its mediocre hotels are notoriously overpriced, and aside from rental-car firms its tourism infrastructure is far less organized than at Puerto Madryn. If you come in the second half of October you can watch part of the Eisteddfod, a Welsh literary and music festival first held in Patagonia in 1875.

Trelew was founded in 1886 as a result of the construction of the now-defunct Chubut railway line, which connected the Chubut River valley with the Atlantic coast. The town is named after its Welsh founder, Lewis Jones (*Tre* means "town" in Welsh, and *Lew* stands for Lewis), who fought to establish this railroad.

GETTING HERE AND AROUND
If you're driving, from the Ruta Nacional 3, take Ruta Nacional 25 to Avenida Fontana. The long-distance bus terminal is at Urquiza and Lewis Jones, along the Plaza Centenario. Most of what you'll visit is found in the half-dozen blocks between Plaza Centenario and Plaza

Trelew's Museo Paleontológico Egidio Feruglio, or Paleontology Museum, is bursting with fossil treasures.

Independencia, which is also where you'll find the tourist office.

ESSENTIALS

BUS CONTACTS Andesmar. ✉ *Terminal de Ómnibus, Urquiza and Lewis Jones, Trelew* ☎ *0280/443–3535.* **Don Otto.** ✉ *Terminal de Ómnibus, Urquiza and Lewis Jones, Trelew* ☎ *0280/442–9496.* **TAC.** ✉ *Terminal de Ómnibus, Urquiza and Lewis Jones, Trelew* ☎ *0810/333–7575.*

CAR RENTAL Hertz. ✉ *Aeropuerto de Trelew, Trelew* ☎ *0280/442–4421* ⊕ *www.hertz.com.ar.*

VISITOR AND TOUR INFORMATION
Tourist Office. ✉ *Mitre 387, Trelew* ☎ *0280/442–0139* ⊕ *www.trelewpatagonia.gov.ar.*

 Sights

★ Museo Paleontológico Egidio Feruglio (MEF)

SCIENCE MUSEUM | FAMILY | Trelew's star attraction is the paleontology museum, where four hushed and darkened

galleries of fossils both real and replica take you back in time. You start among the South American megafauna (giant armadillos and the like) that may have cohabited with the first humans here, then plunge back to a time before the Andes existed. Back then Patagonia was a subtropical rain forest filled with dinosaurs, including one of the largest creatures ever to walk the earth: the 70-ton, 120-foot-long Argentinosaurus. Replicas of its massive leg bones are on display, along with countless other dino skeletons, including the latest discovery of the largest dinosaur in the world—a 130-foot-long herbivore. Other highlights include a 290-million-year-old spider fossil with a 3-foot leg span and the 70-million-year-old petrified eggs of a Carnotaurus. The visit ends with a peek into the workshop where paleontologists study and preserve newly unearthed fossils. Tours in English are available—they're a good idea, as only the introductions to each room are translated. ✉ *Av. Fontana 140, Trelew* ☎ *0280/443–2100* ⊕ *www.mef.org.ar* 🖃 *1,200 pesos.*

Museo Regional Pueblo de Luis (*Trelew Regional Museum*)

HISTORY MUSEUM | Across the street from MEF is Trelew's old train station, which now contains a small museum of the town's history. Photos, clothing, and objects from local houses, offices, and schools form the mishmash of fascinating displays on the European influence in the region, the indigenous populations of the area, and wildlife. ⊠ *Av. 9 de Julio at Av. Fontana, Trelew* ☎ *0280/442–4062* ⊠ *80 pesos.*

 Restaurants

Raices

$$$$ | **ITALIAN** | With its paneled walls, sleek black tables, and vintage photos, this retro Italo-Argentine diner is popular with locals and visitors alike for its pasta specialties. Try the stuffed gnocchi and the good prix-fixe menus. **Known for:** one of Trelew's liveliest restaurants; succulent roast meat; excellent pasta. ⓢ *Average main: pesos1200* ⊠ *Av. Fontana 246, Trelew* ☎ *0280/443–0403* ⊗ *Closed Sun.*

Touring Club

$$$$ | **CAFÉ** | Legend has it that Butch Cassidy and the Sundance Kid once stayed here—search long enough and you might find them among the old photos cluttering the walls. This cavernous old *confitería* (café) was founded in 1895, and became Chubut's first hotel in 1926. **Known for:** great bar; barely comfortable rooms; historic spot. ⓢ *Average main: pesos1000* ⊠ *Av. Fontana 240, Trelew* ☎ *0280/443–3997* ⊕ *www.touringpatagonia.com.ar.*

★ Sugar

$$$$ | **FUSION** | This central restaurant serves up every meal of the day and while the chocolate fondue has some fame in the town, it's really the fusion cuisine in the evening that keeps punters returning. There's a relaxed but professional bistro vibe to Sugar and the chef has an eye for smart presentation. **Known**

for: chocolate fondue; enviable plaza-side location; international flavors in Welsh Patagonia. ⓢ *Average main: pesos1350* ⊠ *25 de Mayo 247, Trelew* ☎ *0280/442–1210* ⊗ *Closed Sun.*

Hotels

Hotel Libertador

$ | **HOTEL** | This big hotel has definitely seen better days, and while rooms are clean (if worn around the edges), the faded bedcovers and scuffed furnishings of the standard rooms really aren't up to the price, although it still remains one of the best of the rather limited options in town. **Pros:** on-site parking; amenable staff; superior rooms are a bit more modern. **Cons:** simple breakfast; lacking amenities; outdated rooms. ⓢ *Rooms from: US$75* ⊠ *Av. Rivadavia 31, Trelew* ☎ *0280/442–0220* ⊕ *www.hotellibertador.com.ar* ⌂ *90 rooms* ⓞ| *Free Breakfast.*

Gaiman

17 km (11 miles) west of Trelew

The most Welsh of the Atlantic Patagonian settlements, sleepy Gaiman (pronounced *Guy*-mon) is far more charming than nearby Trelew and Rawson. A small museum lovingly preserves the history of the Welsh colony, and many residents still speak Welsh (although day-to-day communication is now in Spanish). A connection to Wales continues with teachers, preachers, and visitors going back and forth frequently (often with copies of family trees in hand). Even the younger generation maintains an interest in the culture and language.

Perhaps the town's greatest draws are its four Welsh teahouses (*casas de té*)—Ty Gwyn, Plas-y-Coed, Ty Cymraeg, and Ty Té Caerdydd. Each serves a similar set menu of tea and home-baked bread, scones, and a dazzling array of cakes made from family recipes, although the

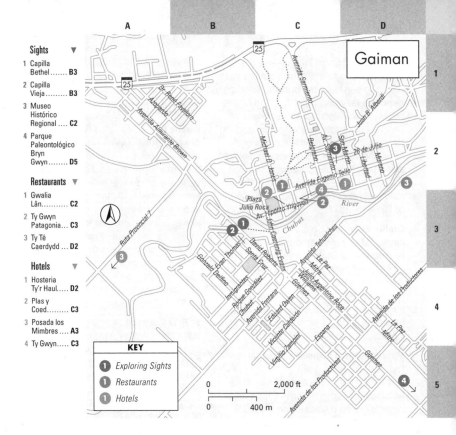

KEY

① Exploring Sights
① Restaurants
① Hotels

odd dulce de leche–filled concoction is testament to Argentine cultural imperatives. Most teahouses are open daily 3–8 and charge about US$15 per person for tea (the spreads are generous enough to replace lunch or dinner, and you can usually take away a doggy bag of any cake you don't finish). Each establishment has its own family history and atmosphere, and there's healthy competition between them as to which is the most authentically Welsh.

GETTING HERE AND AROUND

Gaiman is easily walkable: nearly all the teahouses and other attractions are within a five-block radius of the town square at Avenue Eugenio Tello and M.D. Jones. If you don't have a car, you can access the few sites outside of town—such as the Bryn Gwyn Paleontology Park—by taking an inexpensive remis from one of the *remiserías* on the square.

Although their English isn't great, the friendly young staff at the tourist office give enthusiastic advice on what to visit in Gaiman and hand out detailed maps of the town and its surroundings.

ESSENTIALS

VISITOR AND TOUR INFORMATION Tourist Office. ⊠ *Belgrano 574, at Rivadavia, Gaiman* ☎ *0280/449–1571.*

◉ Sights

Capilla Bethel

CHURCH | Throughout the Chubut Valley there are three dozen or so chapels where the Welsh settlers prayed, went to school, and held meetings, trials, and social events. Two of these simple brick chapels stand alongside each other just over the river from Gaiman—they're usually closed to the public, but are interesting to see from the outside. To reach the chapels, walk south from the square on J.C. Evans and cross the pedestrian bridge. Locals take a shortcut by ducking through the fencing where the bridge ends and walking 100 meters to the right along the riverside. Otherwise take the first right into Morgan and follow the dirt road around several bends. ⊠ *Gaiman* ☎ *280/449–1571.*

Capilla Vieja (*Old Chapel*)

CHURCH | The aptly named Capilla Vieja, next to Capilla Bethel, was built in 1880 and is used each year for the traditional Welsh Eisteddfod, when townspeople gather to celebrate—and compete with each other in—song, poetry, and dance under the chapel's wooden vaulted ceiling. ⊠ *Gaiman* ☎ *280/449–1571.*

Museo Histórico Regional (*Regional Historical Museum*)

HISTORY MUSEUM | Photographs and testimonies of Gaiman's original 160 Welsh settlers are on display in the Museo Histórico Regional, along with household objects they brought with them or made on arrival. The staff are passionate about their history and will happily show you round the tiny building, which used to be Gaiman's train station. ⊠ *28 de Julio 705, at Sarmiento, Gaiman* ☎ *0280/400–1263* ☉ *Closed Tues.*

Parque Paleontológico Bryn Gwyn (*Bryn Gwyn Paleontology Park*)

NATURE SIGHT | Just south of Gaiman the green river valley gives way to arid steppes where clearly visible strata reveal more than 40 million years of geological history. Some 600 acres of these badlands—many of them bursting with fossils—make up the Parque Paleontológico Bryn Gwyn, a branch of the Museo Paleontológico Egidio Feruglio in Trelew where a fossil trail and botanical gardens await. Confirm with the museum before going as the park can close periodically after heavy rain.

⊠ *8 km (5 miles) south of town, Gaiman* ☎ *0280/442–0012* 🖫 *250 pesos.*

Restaurants

Gwalia Lân

$$ | **ARGENTINE** | **FAMILY** | Homemade pastas are the specialty here, but locals also tuck into hearty grilled dishes of steak, pork, and chicken at this lively restaurant with exposed brick, low lighting, wooden booths, and a traditional pub-like atmosphere. Some come just for a beer while others come to dine. **Known for:** juicy steaks drizzled in creamy sauce; jovial atmosphere; large pasta dishes. $ *Average main: pesos410* ⊠ *M.D. Jones 418, at Tello on plaza, Gaiman* ☎ *280/436–5840* ☉ *Closed Mon. No dinner Fri.–Sun.*

★ Ty Té Caerdydd

$$$$ | **CAFÉ** | A short way out of town lies Gaiman's largest teahouse (where Lady Di famously took tea in the 1990s), surrounded by cypress trees, sculpted gardens, and a giant tea pot. It stands apart from its rivals culturally, too: it's run by descendants of a Spanish family, which shows in the sprawling colonial-style architecture. **Known for:** indulgent tea cakes; Lady Diana shrine; peaceful and picturesque location. $ *Average main: pesos900* ⊠ *Finca 202, Zona de Chacras, Gaiman* ☎ *0280/449–1510.*

Ty Gwyn Patagonia

$$$$ | **DESSERTS** | Founded in 1974, this traditional Welsh tea room caters to tourists with its delicious cakes, desserts, and homemade bread. Located in a warm house reminiscent of a chapel, every object has a story to tell: paintings and embroidery by local artists, tablecloths with recipes and words in Welsh, it is a veritable showroom for the family's antiques, including a wood-burning stove surrounded by utensils used by Welsh settlers to cook and heat the home. **Known for:** Welsh antiques; tasty tea; fantastic cakes and desserts. $ *Average*

main: pesos2200 ⊠ 9 de Julio 111,
Gaiman ☏ 280/449–1009 ⊘ Closed Tues.

🛏 Hotels

Plas y Coed

$ | **B&B/INN** | Gaiman's oldest teahouse
has also been a bed-and-breakfast since
1997, and a stay here is rather like visiting
with a favorite aunt: the rooms are
simple but immaculate, have polished
wooden floors and pastel bedspreads,
and there's a comfy lounge area for
relaxing in. **Pros:** family atmosphere;
great teahouse and cakes; comfortable
common room. **Cons:** simple amenities;
some rooms a bit tight; credit cards
not accepted. $ *Rooms from: US$75*
⊠ *Irigoyen 320, Gaiman* ☏ *0280/449–
1133* ▭ *No credit cards* ⤵ *5 rooms*
†◯† *Free Breakfast.*

Posada Los Mimbres

$$ | **B&B/INN** | Wandering the nature trail
alongside the Chubut River, picking fruit
from the orchard, and helping at milking
time are just some of the joys of staying
on this working century-old farm where
the family fills you with homemade treats
and you'll rest nicely on the comfy beds.
Pros: you don't need to go back into town
for meals; most ingredients are sourced
from the farm; rural setting and historic
farmhouse. **Cons:** poor Wi-Fi; simple
lodgings; isolated from town if you don't
have a vehicle. $ *Rooms from: US$120*
⊠ *Chacra 211, Gaiman* ☏ *0280/453–0773*
⊕ *www.posadalosmimbres.com.ar*
▭ *No credit cards* ⤵ *9 rooms, 1 cottage*
†◯† *Free Breakfast.*

Ty Gwyn

$ | **B&B/INN** | The soaring ceilings, wooden
rafters, and cobbled white walls of this
cavernous home double as a teahouse
and a B&B. **Pros:** rooms overlook the riv-
er; generous breakfasts include fruit and
eggs; well-kept lawn. **Cons:** behind a pop-
ular tea house; old fashioned ambience;
cruise-ship groups arrive regularly in high
season. $ *Rooms from: US$60* ⊠ *Av. 9*

de Julio 111, Gaiman ☏ 0280/449–1009
⊕ www.tygwyn.com.ar ⤵ 4 rooms
†◯† Free Breakfast.

Hosteria Ty'r Haul

$ | **B&B/INN** | This B&B personally run by
its owners is good for an inexpensive,
overnight stay. **Pros:** attractive building;
simple and clean rooms; good breakfast.
Cons: no frills; thin walls; no air condi-
tioning in summer months. $ *Rooms
from: US$35* ⊠ *Sarmiento 121, Gaiman*
☏ *280/402–6853* ⊕ *www.hosteriatyrhaul.
com.ar* ⤵ *4 rooms* †◯† *Free Breakfast.*

Punta Tombo

120 km (74 miles) south of Trelew

This protected area is home to one of the
world's biggest colonies of Magellanic
penguins; they come for the season to
lay eggs and feed their newly hatched
young. The park is also a great spot for
observing other seabirds along with
guanacos, seals, and hares.

👁 Sights

★ Area Natural Protegido Punta Tombo

(*Punta Tombo Protected Natural Area*)
NATURE PRESERVE | From the middle of
September through mid-April, almost
400,000 penguins live in the Area Natural
Protegido Punta Tombo, the world's
second-largest colony of Magellanic pen-
guins and one of the most varied seabird
rookeries. From the park entrance, a
series of trails, boardwalks, and bridges
lead you 3½ km (2 miles) through the
scrubby landscape where the penguins
nest to the sea. The quizzical creatures
seem unafraid of humans, and peer up
at you from under the bushes where,
between September and November,
both males and females incubate eggs,
often right beside the trail. Look for the
bald vertical strips on the penguins'
abdomens: they pluck out feathers so
the eggs can sit warm against their

You're not the only visitor to Punta Tombo: guanacos might join you as you scope out the Magellanic penguins.

skin. Come December, the ground is teeming with fluffy gray young, and the adult penguins waddle back and forth from the sea to feed them. They may move comically on land, but once you reach the rocky outcrops overlooking the water you'll see how graceful and powerful these creatures become when they enter the water. You may also spot guanacos, seals, and Patagonian hares in the reserve, as well as cormorants and a host of other seabirds.

The last 22 km (14 miles) of the road from Trelew is fairly bumpy gravel. If you're not driving, you can easily reach Punta Tombo on a day tour from Trelew, Gaiman, or Puerto Madryn, although note that these often give you a scant 1½ hours in the reserve. A small restaurant next to the carpark serves good lamb empanadas and also has burgers, coffee, cakes, and cold beverages. ✉ *Punta Tombo* ⊕ *www.puntatombo.com* 💳 *1,000 pesos*.

Sarmiento and the Bosque Petrificado

545 km (339 miles) southwest of Gaiman.

Built in a fertile valley formed by the Río Senguer and its two interconnected lakes, Lago Musters and Lago Colhué Huapi, the Sarmiento area is a green oasis in the middle of the hard Patagonian steppe. The town itself—home to about 13,000 people—is relatively unattractive, but a visit here gives you a taste of what is undeniably and unpretentiously the "real Patagonia." Relatively few foreign travelers come here, even though the lakes and river, petrified forest, and paleontology park are great attractions, and the rolling farmland outside of town is truly striking, with its tall windbreaks of Lombardy poplars twisting in the strong wind.

While you're in the area, stop at **Lago Musters,** 7 km (4 miles) from Sarmiento, and **Lago Colhué Huapi,** a little farther on. At Lago Musters you can swim, and there's fishing year-round.

GETTING HERE AND AROUND

There are several daily bus services between Sarmiento and Comodoro Rivadavía run by ETAP and Don Otto. The latter also has services to Esquel and Bariloche. Buses arrive at the bus station at 12 de Octubre and Avenida San Martín, which runs through the center of town.

Sarmiento is only 15 blocks long and 8 blocks wide, and can be walked easily, but if you get tired or would like to arrange a trip outside of town, there are various remiserías along Avenida San Martín.

ESSENTIALS

BUS CONTACTS Don Otto. ✉ *Terminal de Ómnibus, Sarmiento* ☎ *0810/333–7575* 🌐 *www.donotto.com.ar.* **ETAP.** ✉ *Terminal de Ómnibus, Sarmiento* ☎ *297/489–3058.*

VISITOR AND TOUR INFORMATION
Sarmiento. ✉ *Av. Regimiento de Infanteria 25 at Pietrobelli, Sarmiento* ☎ *297/489–2105* 🌐 *www.coloniasarmiento.gob.ar.*

Sights

Monumento Natural Bosque Petrificado Sarmiento (*Sarmiento Petrified Forest Natural Monument*)
NATURE SIGHT | An eerie and vast landscape scattered with hundreds of petrified trees takes you more than 75 million years back in time. The palm and conifer trees originally arrived here by river when the area was a tropical delta, although now the sun-bleached and striated badlands are anything but tropical. Dry, parched, and whipped by winds, this place requires a jacket any time of year. Entrance is free, but consider paying for a guide to help you understand exactly what you are looking at. The Monumento Natural Bosque Petrificado Sarmiento is about 30 km (19 miles) from Sarmiento following R26 until you reach the access road on the right. If you don't have your own vehicle, book a remis from Sarmiento: most will charge you for the return trip, including an hour's waiting time. ✉ *30 km (19 miles) from Sarmiento, Sarmiento* ☎ *297/489–8282* 🎫 *20 pesos.*

Parque Paleontológico Valle de los Gigantes (*Valley of the Giants Paleontology Park*)
OTHER ATTRACTION | **FAMILY** | Walk among life-size and scientifically accurate replicas of a dozen different dinosaurs whose fossils were discovered in the region. Guided visits in English leave directly from the tourist office every hour on the hour—arrive 10 minutes ahead to get your ticket. ✉ *200 meters from tourist office, Sarmiento* ☎ *297/489–2105* 🎫 *20 pesos.*

Hotels

Los Lagos
$ | **HOTEL** | The new section in this small, affordable hotel has updated carpets, furnishings, and bathrooms; the staff doesn't speak much English but they're friendly and helpful. **Pros:** affordable; free Wi-Fi; one of few options in Sarmiento. **Cons:** street noise; old part is considerably worse than new section; can get hot in summer. [$] *Rooms from: US$65* ✉ *Av. Roca at Alberdi, Sarmiento* ☎ *2974/893–046* 💳 *No credit cards* 🛏 *20 rooms* 🍴 *Free Breakfast.*

El Calafate, El Chaltén, and Parque Nacional los Glaciares

The Hielo Continental (Continental Ice Cap) spreads its icy mantle from the Pacific Ocean across Chile and the Andes into Argentina, covering an area of 21,700 square km (8,400 square miles). Approximately 1½ million acres of it are contained within the Parque Nacional los Glaciares (Glaciers National Park), a UNESCO World Heritage Site. The park extends along the Chilean border for 350 km (217 miles), and 40% of it is covered by ice fields that branch off into 47 glaciers feeding two enormous lakes—the 15,000-year-old **Lago Argentino** (Argentine Lake, the largest body of water in Argentina and the third largest in South America) at the park's southern end, and **Lago Viedma** (Lake Viedma) at the northern end near **Cerro Fitzroy,** which rises 11,138 feet.

Plan on a minimum of two to three days to see the glaciers and enjoy El Calafate—more if you plan to visit El Chaltén or any of the other lakes. Entrance to the southern section of the park, which includes Perito Moreno Glacier, costs 500 pesos for non-Argentineans.

El Calafate

320 km (225 miles) north of Río Gallegos via R5; 253 km (157 miles) east of Río Turbio on Chilean border via R40; 213 km (123 miles) south of El Chaltén via R40.

Founded in 1927 as a frontier town, El Calafate is the base for excursions to the Parque Nacional Los Glaciares, which was created in 1937 as a showcase for one of South America's most spectacular sights, the Glaciar Perito Moreno. Because it's on the southern shore of Lago Argentino, the town enjoys a

microclimate much milder than the rest of southern Patagonia.

To call El Calafate a boomtown would be a gross understatement. In the first decade of this millennium the town's population exploded from 4,000 to more than 25,000, and it shows no signs of slowing down; at every turn you'll see new construction, with many boutique hotels and new cafés cropping up. As a result, the downtown has a new sheen to it, although most buildings are constructed of wood and corrugated iron with a rustic aesthetic.

Now with a paved road between El Calafate and the glacier, the visitors continue to flock in to see the creaking ice sculptures. These visitors include luxury-package tourists bound for hand-some estancias in the park surroundings, backpackers over from Chile's Parque Nacional Torres del Paine, and *porteños* (from Buenes Aires) in town for a long weekend.

GETTING HERE AND AROUND

Daily flights from Buenos Aires, Ushuaia, and Río Gallegos, and direct flights from Bariloche transport tourists to El Cala-fate's 21st-century glass-and-steel airport with the promise of adventure and discovery in distant mountains and glaciers. El Calafate is so popular that the flights sell out weeks in advance, so don't plan on booking at the last minute.

If you can't get on a flight or are looking for a cheaper option, there are daily bus-es between El Calafate, El Chaltén, Río Gallegos, Ushuaia, and Puerto Natales in Chile—all of which can be booked at the bus terminal. El Calafate is also the start-ing (or finishing) point for the legendary Ruta 40 journey to Bariloche. If you can bear the bus travel for a few days, you'll pass some exceptional scenery, and most operators allow you to hop on and hop off at canyons, lakes, and the famous handprint-covered caves en route.

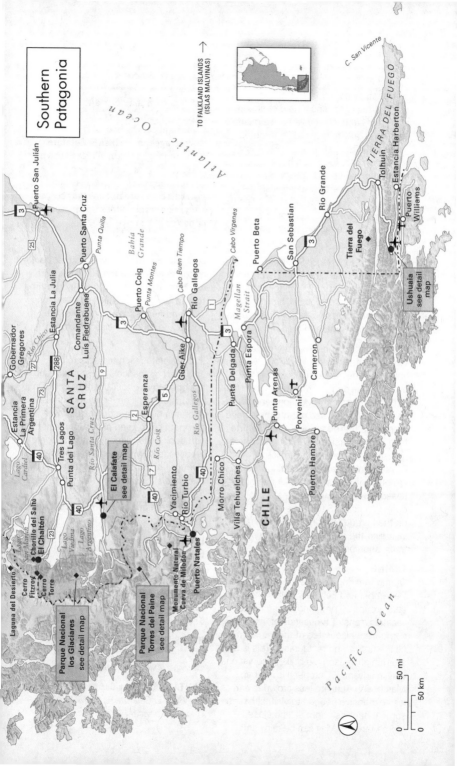

Southern Patagonia

Atlantic Ocean

Pacific Ocean

TO FALKLAND ISLANDS
(ISLAS MALVINAS)

C. San Vicente

TIERRA DEL FUEGO

Estancia Harberton
Ushuaia
see detail
map
Puerto Williams

Tolhuin

Río Grande

San Sebastián

Tierra del Fuego

Cameron

Porvenir

Puerto Hambre

CHILE

Puerto Beta

Cabo Vírgenes

Magellan Strait

Punta Delgada
Punta Espora

Punta Arenas

Río Gallegos

Cabo Buen Tiempo

Punta Montes

Puerto Coig

Punta Quilla

Bahía Grande

Puerto Santa Cruz

Puerto San Julián

Gobernador Gregores

Río Chico

Estancia La Julia

Comandante
Luis Piedrabuena

SANTA CRUZ

Estancia
La Primera
Argentina

Tres Lagos
Punta del Lago

Lago
Cardiel

Río Santa Cruz

Río Coig

Río Gallegos

Esperanza

Güer Aike

Villa Tehuelches

Morro Chico

Yacimiento
Río Turbio

El Calafate
see detail map

Punta del Lago

Lago
San Martín

Laguna del Desierto

Cerro
Fitzroy
Chorillo del Salto
El Chaltén
Cerro
Torre

Lago
Viedma

Lago
Argentino

Parque Nacional
los Glaciares
see detail map

Parque Nacional
Torres del Paine
see detail map

Monumento Natural
Cueva de Milodón

Puerto Natales

0   50 mi

0   50 km

Driving from Río Gallegos takes about four hours across desolate plains enlivened by occasional sightings of a gaucho, his dogs, and a herd of sheep, and ñandú (rheas), shy llama-like guanacos, silver-gray foxes, and fleet-footed hares the size of small deer. Esperanza is the only gas, food, and bathroom stop halfway between the two towns. Driving from Puerto Natales is similar, although snow-topped mountains line the distance; arriving by road from Ushuaia requires four border crossings and more than 18 hours.

Avenida del Libertador San Martín (known simply as Libertador) is El Calafate's main street, with tour offices, restaurants, and shops selling regional specialties, sportswear, camping and fishing equipment, and food.

A staircase ascends from the middle of Libertador to Avenida Julio Roca, where you'll find the bus terminal and a very busy Oficina de Turismo with a board listing available accommodations and campgrounds; you can also get brochures and maps, and there's a multilingual staff to help plan excursions. The tourism office has another location on the corner of Rosales and Libertador; both locations are open daily from 8 to 8 (during high season). The Oficina Parques Nacionales, open weekdays 8 to 4, has information on the Parque Nacional Los Glaciares, including the glaciers, area history, hiking trails, and flora and fauna.

TIMING

During the long summer days between December and February (when the sun sets around 10 pm), and during Easter vacation, tens of thousands of visitors come from all corners of the world and fill the hotels and restaurants. This is the area's high season, so make reservations well in advance. October, November, March, and April are less crowded and less expensive periods to visit, although some estancias might still be closed. March through May can be rainy and

Cash Woes

For a town that lives and dies on tourism, one of the most infuriating elements of the boom is the cash shortage that strikes El Calafate during high season. ATMs in town frequently run out of money, especially over the weekend, and credit cards are not always accepted in restaurants. Stock up on pesos before you arrive.

cool, but it's also less windy and often quite pleasant, and the autumn colors can be quite stunning. The only bad time to visit is winter, particularly May, June, July, and August, when many of the hotels and tour agencies are closed.

TOURS

In El Calafate, each tour has to be approved by the local government and is assigned to one tour operator only. On the upside you'll never fall foul of a shady operator, but on the downside there is no competition to keep prices low. Whether you book a tour directly with the operator who leads it, with another operator, or through your hotel or other tour agency, the price should remain the same. Take note that most tour prices do not include the park entrance fee, an extra 500 pesos for foreigners.

ESSENTIALS
BUS CONTACTS TAQSA. ⊠ Bus terminal, El Calafate ☎ 2902/491–843 ⊕ www. taqsa.com.ar. **Turismo Zaahj.** ⊠ Terminal de Omnibus, Calle Antoine De Saint-Exupéry 87, El Calafate ☎ 2902/491–631 ⊕ www.turismozaahj.co.cl.

REMIS Taxi Remis Calafate. ⊠ Av. Roca 1004, El Calafate ☎ 2902/484–111 ⊕ www.taxiremiscalafate.com.ar.

RENTAL CARS ServiCar. ⊠ Av. Libertador 695, El Calafate ☎ 2902/492–541 ⊕ www.servicar4x4.com.ar.

VISITOR AND TOUR INFORMATION Secretaría de Turismo El Calafate. ⊠ *Rosales at Libertador, El Calafate* ☎ *2902/491–090* ⊕ *www.elcalafate.gov.ar.* **Oficina Parques Nacionales.** ⊠ *Av. Libertador 1302, El Calafate* ☎ *2902/491–005* ⊕ *www.parquesnacionales.gob.ar.*

 Sights

Glaciarium

SCIENCE MUSEUM | About 10 km (6 miles) from town, this glacier museum gives you an educational walk through the formation and life of glaciers (particularly in Patagonia) and the effects of climate change, as well as temporary art exhibitions. A 3D film about the national park and plenty of brightly lit displays, along with the stark glacier-shape architecture, give it a modern appeal. Don't miss the Glaciobar—the first ice bar in Argentina—where you can don thermal suits, boots, and gloves, and where a whiskey on the rocks means 200-year-old glacier rocks from Perito Moreno. ⊠ *Ruta 11, Km 6, El Calafate* ⊹ *Arrive by taxi (200 pesos each way), 1 hr walking, or by free shuttle service from tourism office leaving every hr* ☎ *2902/497–912* ⊕ *www.glaciarium. com* 🖼 *1,400 pesos.*

★ **Glaciar Perito Moreno**

NATURE SIGHT | Eighty km (50 miles) away on R11, the road to the Glaciar Perito Moreno has now been entirely paved. From the park entrance the road winds through hills and forests of lenga and ñire trees, until all at once the glacier comes into full view. Descending like a long white tongue through distant mountains, it ends abruptly in a translucent azure wall 5 km (3 miles) wide and 240 feet high at the edge of frosty green Lago Argentino.

Although it's possible to rent a car and go on your own (which can give you the advantage of avoiding large tourist groups), virtually everyone visits the park on a day trip booked through one of the many travel agents in El Calafate. The most basic tours start at 4,000 pesos for the round-trip (excluding entrance) and take you to see the glacier from a viewing area composed of a series of platforms wrapped around the point of the Península de Magallanes. The platforms, which offer perhaps the most impressive view of the glacier, allow you to wander back and forth, looking across the Canal de los Tempanos (Iceberg Channel). Here you listen and wait for nature's number-one ice show—first, a cracking sound, followed by tons of ice breaking away and falling with a thunderous crash into the lake. As the glacier creeps across this narrow channel and meets the land on the other side, an ice dam sometimes builds up between the inlet of Brazo Rico on the left and the rest of the lake on the right. As the pressure on the dam increases, everyone waits for the day it will rupture again.

In recent years the surge in the number of visitors to Glaciar Perito Moreno has created a crowded scene that is not always conducive to reflective encounters with nature's majesty. Although the glacier remains spectacular, savvy travelers would do well to minimize time at the madhouse that the viewing area becomes at midday in high season, and instead encounter the glacier by boat or on a mini-trekking excursion. Better yet, rent a car and get an early start to beat the tour buses, or visit Perito Moreno in the off-season when a spectacular rupture is just as likely as in midsummer, and you won't have to crane over other people's heads to see it. ⊠ *El Calafate* 🖼 *500 pesos park entrance.*

Glaciar Upsala

NATURE SIGHT | The largest glacier in South America, Glaciar Upsala is 55 km (35 miles) long and 10 km (6 miles) wide, and accessible only by boat. Daily cruises depart from Puerto Banderas (40 km [25 miles] west of El Calafate via R11) for the 2½-hour trip. Dodging floating

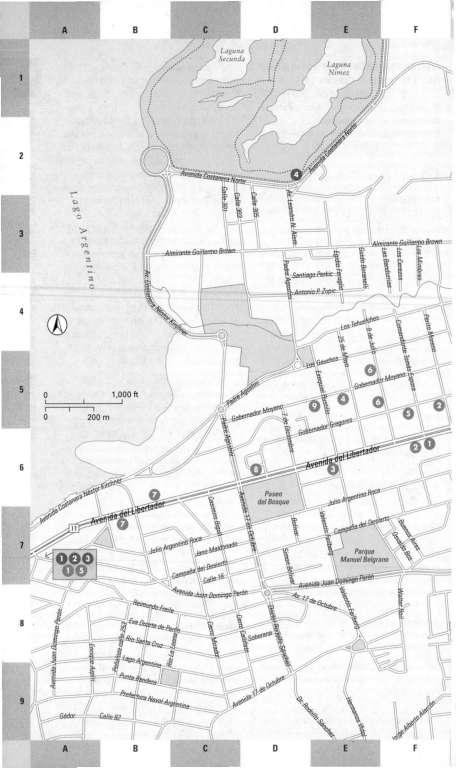

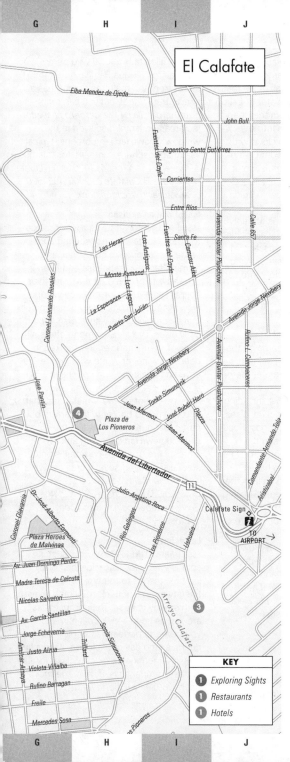

Sights ▼

1 Glaciar Perito Moreno **A7**
2 Glaciar Upsala **A7**
3 Glaciarium......................... **A7**
4 Laguna Nimez
  Reserva Natural **D2**

Restaurants ▼

1 Casimiro Biguá..................... **F6**
2 Isabel cocina al disco............. **F5**
3 La Lechuza **E6**
4 La Tablita......................... **H5**
5 La Zaina........................... **F5**
6 Olivia Coffee Shop................. **E5**
7 Pura Vida **B6**

Hotels ▼

1 Eolo............................... **A7**
2 Estancia Cristina.................. **F6**
3 Hotel Kau-Yatún.................... **I8**
4 Kosten Aike........................ **E5**
5 Los Ponchos Apart Boutique..... **A7**
6 Madre Tierra **E5**
7 Mirador del Lago **B7**
8 Nibepo Aike **D6**
9 Posada los Alamos................. **E5**

icebergs (*tempanos*), some as large as a small island, the boats maneuver as close as they dare to the wall of ice that rises from the aqua-green water of Lago Argentino. The seven glaciers that feed the lake deposit their debris into the runoff, causing the water to cloud with minerals ground to fine powder by the glacier's moraine (the accumulation of earth and stones left by the glacier). Condors and black-chested buzzard eagles build their nests in the rocky cliffs above the lake. When the boat stops for lunch at Onelli Bay, don't miss the walk behind the restaurant into a wild landscape of small glaciers and milky rivers carrying chunks of ice from four glaciers into Lago Onelli. Glaciar Upsala has diminished in size in recent years. ✉ *El Calafate* 🚢 *Cruises start from 13,500 pesos.*

Laguna Nimez Reserva Natural

NATURE PRESERVE | A marshy area on the shore of Lago Argentino just a short walk from downtown El Calafate, the Laguna Nimez Reserva Natural is home to many species of waterfowl, including black-necked swans, buff-necked ibises, southern lapwings, and flamingos. Road construction along its edge and the rapidly advancing town threaten to stifle this avian oasis, but it's still a haven for bird-watchers and a relaxing walk in the early morning or late afternoon. Strolling along footpaths among grazing horses and flocks of birds may not be as intense an experience as, say, trekking on a glacier, but a trip to the lagoon provides a good sense of the local landscape. Don't forget your binoculars and a telephoto lens. ✉ *1 km (½ mile) north of downtown, just off Av. Alem, El Calafate* 🕿 *2902/495–536* 🚢 *500 pesos.*

🍽 Restaurants

Casimiro Biguá

$$$$ | **ARGENTINE** | This restaurant and wine bar boasts a hipper-than-thou interior and modern menu serving such delights as Patagonian lamb with calafate sauce (calafate is a local wild berry). The Casimiro Biguá Parrilla, down the street from the main restaurant, has a similar trendy feel, but you can recognize the *parrilla* by the *cordero al asador* (spit-roasted lamb) displayed in the window. **Known for:** big portions; typical asado atmosphere; fantastic roast lamb. 💲 *Average main: pesos2000* ✉ *Av. Libertador 963, El Calafate* 🕿 *2902/492–590* ⊕ *www.casimirobigua.com.*

Isabel cocina al disco

$$$$ | **ARGENTINE** | It takes a lot of moxie to open a restaurant not serving *cordero,* barbecue, or pizza in Patagonia, and former "fancy" chefs José and Leandro show they have just that with their homey restaurant, which uses vintage plow wheels to cook a traditional and ultimately delicious stew-style dish known as *al disco.* The *al disco* menu offers all sorts of meats and veggies cooked in beer, red wine, or white wine; more creative and quasi-modern options like Bife al Napolitana; or you can create your own. And you've got to love a restaurant that tells you not to bother with starters but rather just dunk your bread in the disco sauce. **Known for:** charming and lively atmosphere; massive portions; signature stew dish cooked several creative ways. 💲 *Average main: pesos2500* ✉ *Perito Moreno 95, El Calafate* 🕿 *2902/489–000* ⊕ *www.isabelcocinaaldisco.com* 🕒 *Closed Wed.*

La Lechuza

$$$$ | **ARGENTINE** | **FAMILY** | This bustling spot is where locals go for their pizza joint fix, thanks to the typical Argentine-style pizza of thick crust, and layered with stringy cheese. Their empanadas are just as good—pick up a few and you have the perfect pastry pick-me-up during a long day of exploring. **Known for:** classic Argentine pizza; crowds of locals; fantastic empanadas. 💲 *Average main: pesos950* ✉ *Av. Libertador at 1 de Mayo, El Calafate* 🕿 *2902/491–610.*

La Tablita

$$$$ | **ARGENTINE** | It's a couple of extra blocks from downtown and across a little white bridge, but this *parrilla* is where the locals go for a special night out to watch their food as it's cooking; Patagonian lamb and beef ribs roast gaucho-style on frames hanging over a circular asador, and an enormous grill along the back wall is full of steaks, chorizos, and *morcilla* (blood sausage). The whole place is filled with a warm glow despite the lackluster decor. **Known for:** tasty empanadas; big crowds on weekends; great traditional parrilla. [$] *Average main: pesos800* ✉ *Coronel Rosales 28, El Calafate* ☎ *2902/491–065* 🌐 *www.la-tablita.com.*

★ La Zaina

$$$$ | **ARGENTINE** | This trendy bistro is filled with seductive cocktails, colorful plates, and fusion flavors. It might be located in a rural Patagonian town at the end of the world, but these dishes could easily come straight out of a trendy Buenos Aires restaurant—served with edible flowers, spirit infusions, and plenty of attitude. **Known for:** creative cuisine; trendy bar service; Instagram-worthy plates. [$] *Average main: pesos400* ✉ *Gobernador Gregores 1057, El Calafate* ☎ *2902/496–789.*

Olivia Coffee Shop

$$$$ | **CAFÉ** | For a chilled out cuppa and delicious sweet treats, this modern and calm café off the main strip offers a moment of peace with a caffeine boost. **Known for:** decent coffee; good playlist; scrumptious muffins. [$] *Average main: pesos200* ✉ *9 de Julio 131, El Calafate* ☎ *2902/488–038* 🕒 *Closed mornings in winter.*

Pura Vida

$$$$ | **ARGENTINE** | Bohemian music, homemade cooking, and colorful patchwork cushions set the tone for this unpretentious, friendly restaurant several blocks from downtown. You'll be surrounded by funky artwork, couples whispering under low-hung lights, and laid-back but efficient staff as you try to decide which big-enough-to-share dish you'll order while working your way through a great dome of steaming bread. **Known for:** great vegetarian options; fun and eclectic decor; lamb stew inside a pumpkin. [$] *Average main: pesos850* ✉ *Av. Libertador 1876, El Calafate* ☎ *2902/493–356* 🌐 *www.puravidaavlibertador1876.negocio.site/* 🕒 *Closed Wed. No lunch.*

Hotels

★ Eolo

$$$$ | **HOTEL** | A luxury lodge on the road to Perito Moreno, Eolo offers full-board stays in handsome accommodations where you can take in the beauty of Patagonia's vast, empty lands and see Lago Argentino in the distance. **Pros:** beautiful location; luxury service; endless acres of estate to explore. **Cons:** no drinks included in meal plans; far from town or any services; expensive. [$] *Rooms from: US$1265* ✉ *Ruta Provincial N 11, Km 23,000, El Calafate* ☎ *2902/492–042* 🌐 *www.eolo.com.ar* 🕒 *Closed May–Sept.* 🛏 *17 rooms.*

★ Estancia Cristina

$$$ | **HOTEL** | Arriving at Estancia Cristina by catamaran on Lago Argentina past fields of ice and imposing mountains is just the beginning of a remarkable Patagonian adventure: on arrival you'll be treated to cozy accommodations, delicious cuisine, and unbeatable excursions to little-explored corners of the park. **Pros:** fantastic excursions; excellent restaurant; incredible views from well-appointed rooms. **Cons:** expensive; no alcoholic drinks included in price; patchy Wi-Fi. [$] *Rooms from: US$750* ✉ *Punta Bandera, El Calafate* ☎ *2902/491–133* 🌐 *www.estanciacristina.com* 🕒 *Closed mid-Apr.–mid-Oct.* 🛏 *20 rooms* 🍴 *All-Inclusive.*

Hotel Kau-Yatún

$$ | **HOTEL** | This converted ranch is nestled in a quiet tree-lined valley by a

Did You Know?

Glacier Perito Moreno is one of three glaciers in the world that grows rather than becoming smaller. The large ruptures and loss of glacier mass creates an equal balance for the glacier, ensuring it stays basically the same size year-round.

stream yet lies just six blocks from the main street and offers a full schedule of mountain biking, horseback riding, and four-wheel-drive expeditions in the 42,000-acre Estancia 25 de Mayo that lies just behind the hotel. **Pros:** good value; nice details; central location. **Cons:** lost a bit of personality from chain takeover; Wi-Fi and modern amenities sparse; water pressure is only adequate. $ *Rooms from: US$124* ⊠ *25 de Mayo, El Calafate* ☎ *2902/491–059* ⊕ *www. kauyatun.com* ☉ *Closed Apr.–Sept.* ⇆ *44 rooms* ℐ⌷ *Free Breakfast.*

Kosten Aike

$$ | **HOTEL** | Lined with wooden balconies, high-beamed ceilings, and a slate floor, this hotel is a paragon of Andean Patagonian architecture, while a sunny rooftop spa, gym, and spacious Jacuzzi offer great views over town to Lago Argentino. **Pros:** large rooms and spa; central location; good value at this price point. **Cons:** rooms are simply furnished; some rooms get outside noise; dining room decor is uninspired. $ *Rooms from: US$145* ⊠ *G. Moyano 1243, at 25 de Mayo, El Calafate* ☎ *2902/492–424* ⊕ *www.kostenaike. com.ar* ☉ *Closed May–Sept.* ⇆ *80 rooms* ℐ⌷ *Free Breakfast.*

Los Ponchos Apart Boutique

$$$ | **B&B/INN** | Cozy and handsomely designed two-floor apartments in this boutique complex have beautiful views over Lago Argentina and offer some independence and privacy with a self-catering kitchen and homey, gaucho-chic decoration. **Pros:** warm service; cozy atmosphere; private. **Cons:** street dogs noisy at night; pricey compared to local competition; a long walk from town. $ *Rooms from: US$245* ⊠ *Los Alamos 3321, El Calafate* ☎ *2902/496–330* ⊕ *www. losponchosapart.com.ar* ☉ *Closed May–Sept.* ⇆ *11 units* ℐ⌷ *Free Breakfast.*

Madre Tierra

$$ | **B&B/INN** | **FAMILY** | The friendly welcome from the owners makes staying

at this B&B feel like visiting a friend's home (with great attention to detail in design and well-chosen furnishings). **Pros:** personalized and friendly service; central location; authentic. **Cons:** expensive; small rooms for price; walls are thin and noise travels. $ *Rooms from: US$185* ⊠ *9 de Julio 239, El Calafate* ☎ *2902/489–880* ⊕ *www.madretierrapatagonia.com* ⇆ *7 rooms* ℐ⌷ *Free Breakfast.*

Mirador del Lago

$$ | **HOTEL** | Great views across the lake are the main selling point of this smartly kept hotel, where each lakeside vista has a seated window or armchair so you can watch the beautiful sunset colors dance across the sky. **Pros:** good value; modern; open all year. **Cons:** impersonal service; lots of steps; a bit of a walk from town. $ *Rooms from: US$182* ⊠ *Av. del Libertador 2047, El Calafate* ☎ *2902/493–213* ⊕ *www.miradordellago.com.ar* ⇆ *68 rooms* ℐ⌷ *Free Breakfast.*

Nibepo Aike

$$$$ | **ALL-INCLUSIVE** | **FAMILY** | This lovely estancia is an hour and a half from El Calafate in a bucolic valley overlooking Lago Roca and backed by snow-capped mountain peaks; where sheep and horses graze, friendly gauchos give horse-racing and sheep-shearing demonstrations, and every evening a communal table is laid for a supper of spit-roasted locally reared lamb. **Pros:** spectacular scenery; classic estancia experience; friendly guides and excellent horseback riding. **Cons:** restaurant has limited offerings; patchy Wi-Fi; expensive for simple amenities. $ *Rooms from: US$375* ⊠ *Av. Libertador 1215, El Calafate* ☎ *2902/492–797* ⊕ *www.nibepoaike. com.ar* ☉ *Closed May–Sept.* ⇆ *10 rooms* ℐ⌷ *Free Breakfast.*

Posada los Alamos

$$ | **HOTEL** | **FAMILY** | Surrounded by tall, leafy alamo trees, this enormous complex incorporates a country manor

Kayak or hike through Patagonia to see the array of birds and rugged scenery.

house, half a dozen convention rooms, a spa, and an indoor swimming pool, but for what it has in amenities Los Alamos lacks in service and attention. **Pros:** spa and gym; beautiful gardens; long breakfast hours. **Cons:** small rooms; inattentive staff; tired furnishings and decor. [$] *Rooms from: US$175* ✉ *Guatti 1135, El Calafate* ☎ *2902/491–144* 🌐 *www.posadalosalamos.com* 🛏 *144 rooms* 🍴 *Free Breakfast.*

Activities

BOAT TOURS

Glaciares Gourmet

BOATING | If fine dining and sipping wine while admiring the glaciers is your style, this is the no-effort-required cruise for you. With a maximum of 28 passengers, the deluxe cruise liner visits Spegazzini and Upsala glaciers and stops for a short leg-stretching walk at beauty spot Puesto de las Vacas before the six-course gourmet lunch with wine. If a full day isn't enough, you can opt for the two-night cruise option. ✉ *Cruceros Marpatag, 9 de Julio (Local 4, Galleria de los Pajaros), El Calafate* ☎ *2902/492–118* 🌐 *www.crucerosmarpatag.com* 🎫 *From 15,000 pesos.*

Safari Náutico

BOATING | Boats depart from a small port 7 km (4 miles) from Perito Moreno glacier and take tourists on an hour-long cruise around the glacier's south face for a closer inspection of the advancing glacier and floating icebergs. On a good day, you can stand on the deck for the best up-close photo opportunities. Tours happen all year and can be reserved at the port or in advance in the downtown office or other tour agencies. ✉ *Hielo y Aventura, Av. Libertador 935, El Calafate* ☎ *2902/492–205* 🌐 *www.hieloyaventura.com* 🎫 *From 3,000 pesos.*

Solo Patagonia

BOATING | With two different full-day boat excursions, Solo Patagonia has been navigating the milky waters for years. Their fleet of large cruisers offers access to some of the best views of the Perito Moreno, Upsala, and Spegazzini glaciers from October to March. ✉ *Av. Libertador 1265, El Calafate* ☎ *2902/491–155* ⊕ *www.solopatagonia.com* ✉ *From 13,500 pesos.*

HORSEBACK RIDING AND ESTANCIAS

Estancia El Galpón del Glaciar

HORSEBACK RIDING | This estancia welcomes guests overnight or for the day—for a horseback ride, bird-watching, or an afternoon program that includes a demonstration of sheep dogs working, a walk to the lake with a naturalist, sheep-shearing, and dinner in the former sheep-shearing barn served right off the asador by knife-wielding gauchos. ✉ *Ruta 11, Km 22, El Calafate* ☎ *11/5217–6720* ⊕ *www.elgalpondelglaciar.com.ar.*

Nibepo Aike

HORSEBACK RIDING | This pretty estancia an hour and a half from El Calafate offers a range of horseback experiences from hour-long excursions to full-day, nine-hour rides to view glaciers in the distance. It's possible to visit Nibepo Aike by booking a day trip at the office in downtown El Calafate, or you can stay overnight at the estancia. ✉ *53 km (31 miles) from El Calafate near Lago Roca on Ruta 15, El Calafate* ☎ *2902/492–797* ⊕ *www.nibepoaike.com.ar.*

ICE TREKKING

Hielo y Aventura

HIKING & WALKING | For the most up-close-and-personal experience with Perito Moreno glacier, book yourself onto an ice trekking day where you'll don crampons and walk over the glacier studying crevasses and ice lakes before finishing with a whiskey on the rocks using ice from the glacier. The full day Mini Trekking excursion includes a 90-minute ice trek, a short trek in the forest, a 20-minute boat ride, and a transfer to the park from your hotel. You'll have to pay your own park entrance,

bring a packed lunch, and wear the right clothing (crampons are provided), but you also get over an hour to enjoy the view of Perito Moreno Glacier from the park. For a more in-depth and challenging ice day, opt for the Big Ice trek, which includes more time on the ice and ducking through bright-blue ice tunnels. ✉ *Av. Libertador 935, El Calafate* ☎ *2902/492–205* ⊕ *www.hieloyaventura.com* ✉ *From 22,500 pesos.*

KAYAKING

Mil Outdoor

KAYAKING | Those brave enough to get in the milky ice waters can get dropped off by a boat on the glacier's edge and take a two-hour guided kayaking excursion with this outfitter, weather permitting (not available in June and July). ✉ *Av. Libertador 1037, El Calafate* ☎ *2902/491–446* ⊕ *www.miloutdoor.com.ar* ✉ *From 15,900 pesos.*

LAND ROVER EXCURSIONS

Mil Outdoor

FOUR-WHEELING | If pedaling uphill sounds like too much work, check out the Land Rover expeditions offered by Mil Outdoor October to April. These trips use large tour trucks to follow dirt tracks into the hills above town for stunning views of Lago Argentino. On a clear day, you can even see the peaks of Cerro Torre and Cerro Fitzroy on the horizon. During the winter, the same company (also known as Calafate Mountain Park) runs a children's snow park with sledding and snowmobiling. ✉ *Av. Libertador 1037, El Calafate* ☎ *2902/491–446* ⊕ *www.miloutdoor.com.ar* ✉ *From 4,800 pesos.*

MOUNTAIN BIKING

Bike Rental

BIKING | Mountain biking is popular along the dirt roads and mountain paths that lead to the lakes, glaciers, and ranches. There are several places to rent bikes in town; two options are **HLS Travesías** (Perito Moreno 95) and **E-Bike Calafate** (Av. Libertador 932). ✉ *El Calafate.*

El Chaltén

222 km (138 miles) north of El Calafate (35 km [22 miles] east on R11 to R40, then north on R40 to R23 north).

Founded in 1985, El Chaltén is Argentina's newest town, and it's growing at an astounding rate. Originally just a few shacks and lodges near the entrance to Parque Nacional Los Glaciares, the town is starting to fill a steep-walled valley in front of Cerro Torre and Cerro Fitzroy, two of the most impressive peaks in Argentina.

Famous for the exploits of rock climbers who started their pilgrimage to climb some of the most difficult rock walls in the world in the 1950s, the range is now drawing hikers whose more earthbound ambitions run to dazzling mountain scenery and unscripted encounters with wildlife including condors, Patagonian parrots, red-crested woodpeckers, and the *huemul,* an endangered deer species.

GETTING HERE AND AROUND
The three-hour car or bus trip to El Chaltén from El Calafate makes staying at least one night here a good idea. The only gas, food, and restroom facilities en route are at La Leona, a historically significant ranch 110 km (68 miles) from El Calafate where Butch Cassidy and the Sundance Kid once hid from the long arm of the law.

Before you cross the bridge into town over Río Fitzroy, stop at the Parque Nacional office. It's extremely well organized and staffed by bilingual rangers who can help you plan your mountain treks and point you to accommodations and restaurants in town. It's an essential stop; orientation talks are given in coordination with arriving buses, which automatically stop here before continuing on to the bus depot.

There's only one ATM in town (it's in the bus station), and it's in high demand; because of servicing schedules, on the weekend El Chaltén runs into the same cash availability problems that El Calafate does, though on a smaller scale.

■ TIP→ **During the week, stockpile the cash you'll need for the weekend, or bring it with you if you're arriving between midday Friday and midday Monday.**

ESSENTIALS
VISITOR INFORMATION Parque Nacional Office. ⊠ *Av. M.M. de Güemes 21, El Chaltén* ☎ *2962/493–004.*

Sights

Cerro Torre and Cerro Fitzroy
TRAIL | You don't need a guide to do the classic treks to Cerro Torre and Cerro Fitzroy, each about six to eight hours round-trip out of El Chaltén. If your legs feel up to it the day you do the Fitzroy walk, tack on an hour of steep switchbacks to Mirador Tres Lagos, the lookout with the best views of Mt. Fitzroy and its glacial lakes. Both routes, plus the Mirador and various side trails, can be combined in a two- or three-day trip. ⊠ *El Chaltén.*

Chorillo del Salta (*Trickling Falls*)
WATERFALL | Just 4 km (2.5 miles) north of town on the road to Lago del Desierto, the Chorillo del Salta waterfall is no Iguazú, but the area is extremely pleasant and sheltered from the wind. A short hike uphill leads to secluded river pools and sun-splashed rocks where locals enjoy picnics on their days off. If you don't feel up to a more ambitious hike, the short stroll to the falls is an excellent way to spend the better part of an afternoon. Pack a bottle of wine and a sandwich and enjoy the solitude. ⊠ *El Chaltén.*

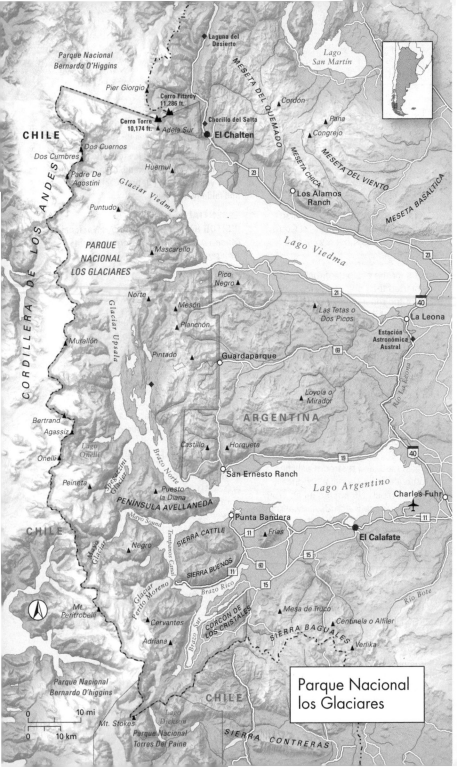

Laguna del Desierto (*Lake of the Desert*)
BODY OF WATER | A lovely lake surrounded by lush forest, complete with orchids and mossy trees, the Laguna del Desierto is 37 km (23 miles) north of El Chaltén on R23, a dirt road. Hotels in El Chaltén can arrange a trip for about $50 for the day. Locals recommend visiting Lago del Desierto on a rainy day, when more ambitious hikes are not an option and the dripping green misty forest is extra mysterious. ⊠ *El Chaltén.*

 Restaurants

Aonikenk
$$$$ | **ARGENTINE** | **FAMILY** | In a dark wooden dining hall you'll share hearty steaks, warming soups, and wine poured from penguin-shaped ceramic jugs in a family restaurant that includes a hostel upstairs. It's rustic, and the food is not spectacular, but you can't beat the friendly atmosphere in what is easily El Chaltén's largest and most popular restaurant.
Known for: standard Argentine cuisine; open hours even in the off-season; family-friendly atmosphere. $ *Average main: pesos950* ⊠ *Av. M.M. de Güemes 23, El Chaltén* ☎ *2962/493–070* ▭ *No credit cards.*

★ **La Cervecería Chaltén**
$$$$ | **ARGENTINE** | This successful microbrewery is famous in the region for its brews and comfort food. Of course, it's not just the hops bringing in the crowds; they also cook up delicious soups, snacks, empanadas, and a great *locro* (hearty traditional northern Argentine stew). **Known for:** hearty comfort food; welcoming atmosphere; impressive craft beer. $ *Average main: pesos550* ⊠ *San Martín 320, El Chaltén* ☎ *2962/493–109* ⊙ *Closed June–Oct.*

 Hotels

Aguas Arriba Lodge
$$$$ | **HOTEL** | Accessible only by boat or a three-hour trek, Aguas Arriba has a privileged location right on the Lago del Desierto, with a glimmer of Mt. Fitzroy in the distance. **Pros:** fantastic location; attended by owners; excellent excursions. **Cons:** private shuttle to lake required in addition to walk/boat; no phone signal; noise travels between rooms. $ *Rooms from: US$957* ⊠ *Lago del Desierto, El Chaltén* ☎ *11/4152–5697 Buenos Aires* ⊕ *www.aguasarribalodge. com* ⊙ *Closed mid-Apr.–Sept.* ⇨ *6 rooms* ⦿⊙ *Free Breakfast.*

Nothofagus
$ | **B&B/INN** | A simple B&B off the main road, Nothofagus is named after the southern beech tree, and the lodge has a rough-hewn, woodsy feel with exposed beams and leaves stamped into the lampshades. **Pros:** great views; bright and sunny breakfast room; good value. **Cons:** spartan rooms and bathrooms, some of which are shared; simple breakfast; staff energy too low for some. $ *Rooms from: US$75* ⊠ *Hensen, at Riquelme, El Chaltén* ☎ *2962/493–087* ⊕ *www. nothofagusbb.com.ar* ▭ *No credit cards* ⊙ *Closed May–Sept.* ⇨ *9 rooms* ⦿⊙ *Free Breakfast.*

Posada Lunajuim
$ | **HOTEL** | A traditional A-frame roof keeps the lid on a funky, modern lodge filled with contemporary artwork, exposed brick masonry, and a spacious lounge and dining room complete with a roaring fireplace and a library stacked with an intriguing mix of travel books. **Pros:** great lounge area; friendly staff; awesome food and wine list. **Cons:** baths are quite small; slow Wi-Fi; not all rooms have views. $ *Rooms from: US$115* ⊠ *Trevisan 45, El Chaltén* ☎ *2962/493–047* ⊕ *www.lunajuim.com* ⇨ *26 rooms* ⦿⊙ *Free Breakfast.*

A guide is required if you want to enter the ice field or trek on any of the glaciers in Los Glaciares National Park, so be sure to check tour guide options before your trip.

🏃 Activities

El Chaltén owes its existence to those who wanted a base for trekking into this corner of Los Glaciares National Park, specifically Cerro Torre and Cerro Fitzroy. It's no surprise that nearly everyone who comes here considers hiking up to those two mountains to be the main event—though the locro and microbrews at the end of the day are a plus.

MOUNTAIN CLIMBING
Casa de Guias
MOUNTAIN CLIMBING | A guide is required if you want to enter the ice field or trek on any of the glaciers in Los Glaciares National Park. Casa de Guias is a group of professional, multilingual guides who offer fully equipped multiday treks covering all the classic routes in the national park, and longer trips exploring the ice field. They even offer a taste of big-wall climbing on one of the spires in the Fitzroy range. ✉ *Av. San Martín 310, El Chaltén* ☎ *2962/493–118* ⊕ *www. casadeguias.com.ar.*

El Chaltén Mountain Guides
MOUNTAIN CLIMBING | Five mountain guides offer expeditions in and around El Chaltén, as well as many other destinations in Argentina. One-day and multiday treks and ascents to rock and ice-climbing expeditions are available. In the winter they also offer backcountry skiing tours. ✉ *Rio de las Vueltas 212, El Chaltén* ☎ *2962/493–329* ⊕ *www.ecmg. com.ar.*

Puerto Natales and Torres del Paine, Chile

Serious hikers often come to this area and use Puerto Natales as their base for hiking the classic "W" or circuit treks in **Torres del Paine,** which take between four days and a week to complete. Others choose to spend a couple of nights in one of the park's luxury hotels and take in the sights during day hikes.

If you have less time, however, it's possible to spend just one day touring the park, as many people do, with Puerto Natales as your starting point. In that case, rather than drive, you'll want to book a one-day Torres del Paine tour with one of the many tour operators here. Most tours pick you up at your hotel between 8 and 9 am and follow the same route, visiting several lakes and mountain vistas, seeing Lago Grey and its glacier, and stopping for lunch in Hostería Lago Grey or one of the other hotels inside the park. These tours return around sunset. A budget option is the daily bus tour (year-round) from the bus station with Transportes María José, which also offers hop-on, hop-off options for hikers and campers.

While visiting Torres del Paine remains the most popular excursion, nearby Parque Bernardo O'Higgins is also ripe for exploration with popular boat tours to glaciers with companies Turismo 21 de Mayo (year-round) and Agunsa (September through April).

Argentina's magnificent **Glaciar Perito Moreno,** near El Calafate, can be visited on a popular (but extremely long) one-day tour, leaving at the crack of dawn and returning late at night—don't forget your passport. It's a four-hour-plus trip in each direction; some tours sensibly include overnights in El Calafate.

Please note, if calling outside of Chile, you will require the international dialing code (+56). From within Chile you need to add 0 before dialing any local code.

Prices for restaurants and hotels in Puerto Natales and Torres del Paine are given in Chilean pesos. As of this writing, the exchange rate was US$1 to 595 Chilean pesos.

Puerto Natales, Chile

242 km (150 miles) northwest of Punta Arenas.

Puerto Natales has become the main base for exploring a number of southern Patagonia's top attractions, including Parque Nacional Torres del Paine and Parque Nacional Bernardo O'Higgins. The medium-sized fishing town offers picturesque views of the Seno Última Esperanza (Last Hope Sound) channel, which was named so by Spanish navigator Juan Ladrillero in the 16th century as it was his last hope to reach the Strait of Magellan.

As a launching point for many touristic sites, Puerto Natales has recently seen a large increase in tourism and development with a new surge of luxury accommodation offering all-inclusive stays with excursions. The town has added a string of hip eateries, cafés, and boutique hotels recently, and is starting to challenge the more staid larger city of Punto Arenas as a hub for exploring the entire region.

GETTING HERE AND AROUND
The trip to Puerto Natales from El Calafate is a beautiful journey through color-washed Patagonian landscapes with white peaked mountains in the distance and picturesque estancias and cattle ranches dotted along the way.

Puerto Natales centers on the Plaza de Armas, a lovely, well-landscaped sanctuary. A few blocks west of the plaza on Avenida Bulnes you'll find the small Museo Histórico Municipal. On a clear day, an early morning walk along Avenida Pedro Montt, which follows the shoreline of the Seno Última Esperanza (or Canal Señoret, as it's called on some maps), can be a soul-cleansing experience. The rising sun gradually casts a glow on the mountain peaks to the west.

ESSENTIALS
BUS CONTACTS Buses Fernández.
✉ *Eleuterio Ramirez 399, Puerto Natales* ☎ *9/9438–5125* ⊕ *www.busesfernandez. com.* **Transportes María José.** ✉ *Av. España 1455, Puerto Natales* ☎ *9/9321–1378, 61/241–0951* ⊕ *www.busesmariajose. com.*

RENTAL CARS Avis (Emsa). ✉ *Barros Arana 118, Puerto Natales* ☎ *61/261–4388* ⊕ *www.emsarentacar.com.*

Sights

Iglesia Parroquial
CHURCH | Across from the Plaza de Armas is the squat, little Iglesia Parroquial. The ornate altarpiece in this church depicts the town's founders, Indigenous peoples, and the Virgin Mary all in front of the Torres del Paine. ✉ *Arturo Prat and Eberhard, Puerto Natales.*

Museo Histórico Municipal
HISTORY MUSEUM | A highlight in the small but interesting Museo Historico Municipal is a room filled with antique prints of Aonikenk and Kawéskar peoples. Another room is devoted to the exploits of Hermann Eberhard, a German explorer considered the region's first settler. Check out his celebrated collapsible boat. In an adjacent room you will find some vestiges of the old Bories sheep plant, which processed the meat and wool of more than 300,000 sheep a year. ✉ *Av. Bulnes 285, Puerto Natales* ☎ *61/220–9534* 🖾 *1,000 pesos* ☉ *Closed Sun.*

Monumento Natural Cueva de Milodón
CAVE | In 1896, Hermann Eberhard stumbled upon a gaping cave that extended 200 meters (650 feet) into the earth. Venturing inside, he discovered the bones and dried pieces of hide (with deep red fur) of an animal he could not identify. It was later determined that what Eberhard had discovered were the extraordinarily well-preserved remains of a prehistoric

herbivorous mammal, *mylodon darwini,* about twice the height of a man, which they called a *milodón.* The discovery of a stone wall in the cave, and of neatly cut grass stalks in the animal's feces led researchers to conclude that 15,000 years ago the extinct beast inhabited this place and that an ancient tribe of Tehuelches likely captured the animal there. The cave at the Monumento Natural Cueva de Milodón is an impressive, cathedral-size space carved out of a solid rock wall by rising waters. It makes for an interesting stop for anyone fascinated by paleontology, or for fans of Bruce Chatwin's legendary travel book, *In Patagonia,* which centers in part on Chatwin's quest to find the origins of the remnant of mylodon skin he saw in his grandmother's home as a boy that she had told him came from a "brontosaurus." ✉ *Ruta Y-290, km 8, Puerto Natales* ⊹ *5 km (3 miles) off Ruta 9 signpost, 28 km (17 miles) northwest of Puerto Natales* ☎ *61/236–0485, 61/241–1438* ⊕ *www. cuevadelmilodon.cl* 🖾 *8400 pesos.*

Plaza de Armas
PLAZA/SQUARE | A few blocks east of the waterfront overlooking Seno Última Esperanza is the Plaza de Armas. This well-manicured, open square with gardens and a fountain is one of the town's pride and joys. An old church and several shops and restaurants surround the plaza, making it a pleasant spot to spend some time. ✉ *Arturo Prat at Eberhard, Puerto Natales.*

🍴 Restaurants

Asador Patagónico
$$$ | CHILEAN | This restaurant is zealous about meat; so zealous, in fact, that there's no seafood on the menu. Great care is taken with the excellent *lomo* and other grilled steaks, and the room is filled with the smell of roasting meat. **Known for:** mouthwatering meats; cozy open fire; hard to get a table. 🛅 *Average main:*

pesos13000 ⊠ Prat 158, Puerto Natales 🕾 61/241–3553 ⊘ Closed June.

Cangrejo Rojo

$$ | **SEAFOOD** | A bit off-the-beaten path, but only about a 10-minute walk from the center of town, this is an excellent nautical-chic café. The tasty, feel-good food prepared lovingly by the marine biologist owners, Francisco and Nuriys, is well worth the effort to get there. **Known for:** homemade waffles; organic wine menu; excellent king crab. $ Average main: pesos8500 ⊠ Santiago Bueras Av. 782, Puerto Natales 🕾 61/241–2436 ⊘ Closed Sun.

The Coffee Maker

$$ | **CAFÉ** | This coffee bar is the best spot for a steaming cup of joe in Puerto Natales, thanks to its well-sourced beans, expert baristas, and some of the best views in town. The Coffee Maker also sells sandwiches, salads, vegetarian options, delicious cakes, and has a daily set menu. **Known for:** unique pisco sours; great views; the best coffee in town. $ Average main: pesos8000 ⊠ Kau, Pedro Montt 161, Puerto Natales 🕾 61/241–4611.

Espacio Ñandu

$$ | **CHILEAN** | **FAMILY** | Right on the corner of the plaza, this superb souvenir and bookshop doubles as a restaurant, bar, café, post office, and the best Wi-Fi spot in town, where you can surf on your own computer or rent one of theirs. With empanadas, tacos, seafood, and salads, you've got all bases covered for breakfast, lunch, dinner, or just coffee and a snack. **Known for:** souvenir shopping over lunch; local beers; quick bites. $ Average main: pesos7500 ⊠ Eberhard and Arturo Prat, Puerto Natales 🕾 61/241–5660.

Kosten

$$$ | **CONTEMPORARY** | You'll watch the wind whip the Seno Última Esperanza from a comfortable lounge in front of the fireplace at this modern bar and café in the hotel NOI Indigo Patagonia. It is a nice spot for a Calafate sour, and when you're ready, just amble downstairs to the small restaurant where they have an excellent menu with a little bit of everything, including organic salads made with veggies from their very own huerto (garden). **Known for:** fun cocktail list; organic salads; good views. $ Average main: pesos11900 ⊠ NOI Indigo Hotel, Ladrilleros 105, Puerto Natales 🕾 61/261–3450 ⊕ www.noihotels.com.

Restaurant Última Esperanza

$$$ | **CHILEAN** | Named for the strait on which Puerto Natales is located, Restaurant Última Esperanza is perhaps your last chance to try Patagonian seafood classics in a town being overrun by hip eateries. This traditional restaurant is well known for attentive, if formal, service, and top-quality, typical dishes. **Known for:** poached conger eel in shellfish sauce; old-school service; classic king crab stew. $ Average main: pesos10000 ⊠ Av. Eberhard 354, Puerto Natales 🕾 61/241–1391 ⊕ www.restaurantultimaesperanza.com ⊘ Closed July.

Hotels

Hostal Francis Drake

$$ | **B&B/INN** | Toss a coin in the wishing well out front before you enter this half-timbered house near the center of town; inside, the proprietor is a delightful European who dotes on her guests and carefully maintains cleanliness. **Pros:** among the better of Natales's budget options; clean and well cared for; central location. **Cons:** all the wind off the lake, but no views; basic rooms; the beds are not the most comfortable. $ Rooms from: pesos52000 ⊠ Philippi 383, Puerto Natales 🕾 61/241–1553 ⊕ www.hostalfrancisdrake.com ⤳ 12 rooms ⋈ Free Breakfast.

Hotel Lady Florence Dixie

$$ | **B&B/INN** | Named after an aristocratic English immigrant and tireless traveler, this long-established hotel with an

alpine-inspired facade is on the town's main street; its bright, spacious upstairs lounge is a good people-watching perch. **Pros:** convenient location; relaxed atmosphere; good value. **Cons:** dowdy rooms; basic breakfast; simple amenities. [$] *Rooms from: pesos81000* ✉ *Av. Bulnes 655, Puerto Natales* ☎ *61/241–1158* 🌐 *www.hotelflorencedixie.cl* 🛏 *19 rooms* 🍴 *Free Breakfast.*

Hotel CostAustralis

$$$ | **HOTEL** | This old grande dame of Puerto Natales has been somewhat superseded by more modern, eye-catching hotels, but its peaked, turreted roof and distinctive architecture still dominate the waterfront. **Pros:** great views from bay-facing rooms; courteous and professional staff; startlingly low off-season rates. **Cons:** endless corridors a little impersonal; wind and street noise; rooms are somewhat bland. [$] *Rooms from: pesos113000* ✉ *Av. Pedro Montt 262, at Av. Bulnes, Puerto Natales* ☎ *61/271–5037* 🌐 *www.hotelcostaustralis.com* 🛏 *110 rooms* 🍴 *Free Breakfast.*

Hotel Martín Gusinde

$$$$ | **HOTEL** | Don't let the dowdy exterior put you off—inside is a modern hotel with a good downtown location and simple but well-equipped rooms. **Pros:** urbane atmosphere; comfortable beds; central location. **Cons:** simple breakfast; noise travels; weak Wi-Fi. [$] *Rooms from: pesos123000* ✉ *Carlos Bories 278, Puerto Natales* ☎ *61/271–2100* 🌐 *www.martingusinde.com* 🛏 *28 rooms* 🍴 *Free Breakfast.*

NOI Indigo Patagonia

$$$$ | **HOTEL** | Chilean architect Sebastian Irarrazabel was given free rein to redesign this building along a nautical theme; inside, a maze of gangplanks, ramps, and staircases shoot out across cavernous open spaces, minimalist wood panels line walls and ceilings, and water burbles down a waterfall that borders the central walkway. **Pros:** some rooms have great views of the fjord; nice on-site restaurant; good location. **Cons:** standard rooms are smallish; no parking; restaurant open only for dinner. [$] *Rooms from: pesos164000* ✉ *Ladrilleros 105, Puerto Natales* ☎ *61/274–0670* 🌐 *www.noihotels.com* 🛏 *41 rooms* 🍴 *Free Breakfast.*

Kau Lodge

$$$ | **B&B/INN** | This waterfront B&B comes with excellent views of the fjord, comfy and large beds draped in wool throws, and insider touring tips from the mountain-guide owner. **Pros:** cozy rooms; good location; fantastic coffee. **Cons:** basic breakfast; small showers; wind can be noisy on windows. [$] *Rooms from: pesos88500* ✉ *Pedro Montt 161, Puerto Natales* ☎ *61/241–4611* 🌐 *www.kau-lodge.com* 🛏 *9 rooms* 🍴 *Free Breakfast.*

OUTSIDE PUERTO NATALES

Several lodges have been constructed on a bluff overlooking the Seno Ultima Esperanza, about a mile outside of town. The views at these hotels are spectacular, with broad panoramas and unforgettable sunsets. While some might complain about the 10- to 30-minute trek into town, it is an easy walk along the seafront. A taxi will set you back around 2,000–2,500 Chilean pesos.

Altiplánico Sur

$$$$ | **HOTEL** | This is the Patagonian representative of the Altiplánico line of thoughtfully designed eco-hotels, and nature takes center stage: the hotel blends so seamlessly with its surroundings, it's almost subterranean. **Pros:** eco-friendly; stellar views; quiet location. **Cons:** few technological amenities, including television; patchy Wi-Fi; slow service. [$] *Rooms from: pesos149000* ✉ *Ruta 9 Norte, Km 1.5, Huerto 282, Puerto Natales* ☎ *61/241–2525* 🌐 *www.altiplanico.cl* 🕒 *Closed May–Sept.* 🛏 *22 rooms* 🍴 *Free Breakfast.*

★ **Remota**

$$$$ | **HOTEL** | The eye-catching architecture of Remota competes with stunning views over the Última Esperanza for your

attention, especially at night when the soft orange lighting beckons. **Pros:** great spa area; restaurant menu of delicious, native ingredients; inspiring design. **Cons:** unstable Wi-Fi in rooms; expensive; wind noises can be wild in the common areas. [$] *Rooms from: pesos218000* ✉ *Ruta 9 Norte, Km 1.5, Huerto 279, Puerto Natales* ☎ *61/241-4040* 🌐 *www.remota-hotel.com* 🛏 *72 rooms.*

★ The Singular Patagonia

$$$$ | **HOTEL** | Inhabiting the former Bories Cold-Storage Plant, which used to process and export more than 250,000 sheep a year and practically built Puerto Natales as a town, the Singular may well be Puerto Natales's most luxurious and tasteful hotel. **Pros:** one-of-a-kind historic setting; expeditions and tours for all levels of fitness; fantastic restaurant. **Cons:** super pricey; breakfast can get busy; taxi ride from town. [$] *Rooms from: pesos300000* ✉ *Y-300 Rd., toward Torres del Paine National Park, Puerto Bories* ☎ *61/272–2030* 🌐 *www.thesingular.com* 🛏 *57 rooms.*

Weskar Patagonian Lodge

$$$$ | **HOTEL** | Weskar stands for "hill" in the language of the Kawéskar, to whom owner Juan José Pantoja, a marine biologist, pays homage in creating and maintaining this cozy lodge, which is high on a ridge overlooking the Última Esperanza fjord. **Pros:** great views from your room; cozy log-cabin decor; rustic and cozy design. **Cons:** Wi-Fi and TV only in common areas; poor temperature regulation; less luxurious than neighbors. [$] *Rooms from: pesos128000* ✉ *Ruta 9 Norte, Km 1/Puerto Natales, Puerto Natales* ☎ *61/241–4168, 61/224–0494* 🌐 *www.weskar.cl* 🛏 *31 rooms* 🍴 *Free Breakfast.*

Parque Nacional Torres del Paine, Chile

80 km (50 miles) northwest of Puerto Natales.

A top global destination for hikers and nature spotters, Torres del Paine National Park is, quite simply, outstanding. With breathtaking mountains, glaciers, and lakes, along with wildlife like guanacos, rheas, and pumas, the Park offers plenty of picture-perfect moments. Frequently changeable Patagonian weather is the only blemish in this UNESCO World Heritage Site, which attracts more than 150,000 visitors a year.

ESSENTIALS

VISITOR INFORMATION CONAF. ✉ *CONAF station in southern section of the park past Hotel Explora* ☎ *61/269–1931* 🌐 *www.conaf.cl.*

Sights

★ Parque Nacional Torres del Paine

NATIONAL PARK | About 12 million years ago, lava flows pushed up through the thick sedimentary crust that covered the southwestern coast of South America, cooling to form a granite mass. Glaciers then swept through the region, grinding away all but the twisted ash-gray spire, the "towers" of Paine (pronounced "pie-nay"; it's the old Tehuelche word for "blue"), which rise over the landscape to create one of the world's most beautiful natural phenomena, now the Parque Nacional Torres del Paine. The park was established in 1959. Rock formations, windswept trees, and waterfalls dazzle at every turn of road, and the sunset views are spectacular. The 2,420-square-km (934-square-mile) park's most astonishing attractions are its lakes of turquoise, aquamarine, and emerald waters; its magnificent Grey Glacier; and the Cuernos del Paine ("Paine Horns"), the

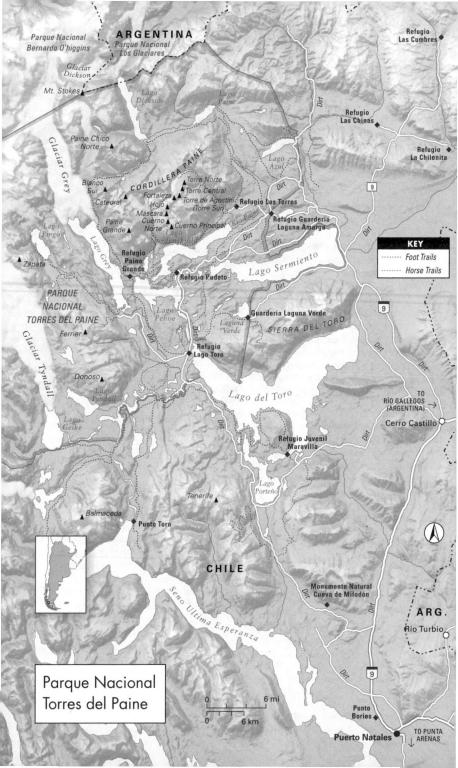

geological showpiece of the immense granite massif.

Another draw is the park's wildlife; creatures like the guanaco and the ñandú abound. They are acclimated to visitors and don't seem to be bothered by approaching cars and people with cameras. Predators like the gray fox make less frequent appearances. You may also spot the dramatic aerobatics of falcons and the graceful soaring of endangered condors. The beautiful puma, the apex predator of the ecosystem here, is an especially elusive cat, but sightings have grown more common.

The vast majority of visitors come during the summer months of January and February, which means the trails can get congested. Early spring, when wildflowers add flashes of color to the meadows, can be an ideal time to visit because the crowds have not yet arrived. In summer, the winds can be incredibly fierce, but the days are also incredibly longer (in December, there's light for almost 20 hours). During the wintertime of June to September, the days are sunnier yet colder (averaging around freezing) and shorter, but the winds all but disappear and wildlife sightings become more frequent. The park is open all year, but some trails are not accessible in winter. Storms can hit without warning, so be prepared for sudden rain at any time of year. The sight of the Paine peaks in clear weather is stunning; if you have any flexibility in your itinerary, visit the park on the first clear day. ⊕ conaf.cl/parques/parque-nacional-torres-del-paine 21,000 pesos.

EXPLORING THE PARK
There are three entrances to the park: Laguna Amarga (all bus arrivals), Lago Sarmiento, and Laguna Azul. You are required to sign in when you arrive, and pay your entrance fee (around US$35 in high season). Guardaparques (park rangers) staff six stations around the reserve, and can provide a map and up-to-the-day information about the state of various

trails. A regular minivan service connects Laguna Amarga with the Hostería Las Torres, 7 km (4½ miles) to the west. Alternatively, you can walk approximately two hours before reaching the starting point of the hiking circuits.

Although considerable walking is necessary to take full advantage of Parque Nacional Torres del Paine, you need not be a hard-core trekker. Many people choose to hike the "W" route, which takes four days, but others prefer to stay in one of the comfortable lodges and hit the trails in the morning or afternoon. Glaciar Grey, with its fragmented icebergs, makes a rewarding and easy hike; equally rewarding is the spectacular boat or kayak ride across the lake, past icebergs, and up to the glacier, which leaves from Hostería Lago Grey. Another great excursion is the 900-meter (3,000-foot) ascent to the sensational views from Mirador Las Torres, four hours one way from Las Torres Patagonia. Even if you're not staying at the Hostería, you can arrange a morning drop-off there, and a late-afternoon pickup, so that you can see the Mirador while still keeping your base in Puerto Natales or elsewhere in the park; alternatively, you can drive to the Hostería and park there for the day.

If you do the "W," you'll begin (or end, if you reverse the route) at Laguna Amarga and continue to Mirador Las Torres and Los Cuernos, then continue along a breathtaking path up Valle Frances to its awe-inspiring and fiendishly windy lookout (hold on to your hat!) and finally Lago Grey. The W runs for 100 kilometers (62 miles), but always follows clearly marked paths, with gradual climbs and descents at relatively low altitude. The challenge comes from the weather. Winds whip up to 90 mph, and a clear sky can suddenly darken with storm clouds, producing rain, hail, or snow in a matter of minutes. An even more ambitious route is the "Circuito," which essentially leads around the entire park and takes from a week

Did You Know?

The sight of the Paine peaks in clear weather is stunning; if you have any flexibility in your itinerary, visit Parque Nacional Torres del Paine on the first clear day.

to 10 days. Along the way some people sleep at the dozen or so humble *refugios* (shelters) evenly spaced along the trail, and many others bring their own tents.

Driving is an easy way to enjoy the park: a new road cuts the distance to Puerto Natales from a meandering 140 km (87 miles) to a more direct 80 km (50 miles). Inside the national park more than 100 km (62 miles) of roads leading to the most popular sights are safe and well maintained, though unpaved.

■TIP→ **If you stick to the road, you won't need four-wheel drive.**

You can also hire horses from the Hostería Las Torres and trek to the Torres, the Cuernos, or along the shore of Lago Nordenskjold (which offers the finest views in the park, as the lake's waters reflect the chiseled massif). Alternatively, many Puerto Natales–based operators offer multiday horseback tours. Water transport is also available, with numerous tour operators offering sailboat, kayak, and inflatable Zodiac speedboat options along the Río Serrano toward the Paine massif and the southern ice field. Additionally, the Hostería Lago Grey operates the *Grey II,* a large catamaran making a three-hour return trip to Glaciar Grey four times daily as well as dinghy runs down the Pingo and Grey rivers. Another boat runs between Refugio Pudeto and Refugio Lago Pehoé.

Erratic Rock

HOTEL | For anyone seriously contemplating trekking the W or the full Circuit around Torres del Paine, the Erratic Rock hostel in Puerto Natales offers a free seminar on how best to make the journey. Rustyn Mesdag, the hostel's Oregonian co-owner, is a rambunctious, opinionated guide who gives the not-to-be-missed "Three O'Clock Talk" describing all the routes, tips, and tricks you need to complete one of South America's most challenging treks. His hour-long

presentation to a room full of eager hikers starts promptly at 3 pm every day of the high season, and is full of advice on camping, equipment, food, and provisions, including the latest reports on weather and trail conditions inside the park. It's a great introduction to possible trekking partners, as CONAF doesn't allow you to complete the walk on your own. The irrepressible Mr. Mesdag also publishes the ubiquitous Black Sheep newspaper in English. ✉ *Baquedano 719, Puerto Natales* ☏ *61/414–317* ⊕ *www. erraticrock.com.*

 Hotels

Hotel Lago Grey

$$$$ | **HOTEL** | The panoramic view from the restaurant and bar, past the lake dappled with floating icebergs to the glacier beyond, is worth the somewhat difficult journey here. **Pros:** great views in communal areas; excellent location; heated bathroom floors. **Cons:** Wi-Fi is weak; standard rooms are basic; gravel road to hotel is a rocky ride. Ⓢ *Rooms from: pesos160000* ✉ *Lago Grey* ☏ *61/271– 2100* ⊕ *www.lagogrey.com* ⊅ *60 rooms* ⦿ *Free Breakfast.*

★ Hotel Explora

$$$$ | **HOTEL** | There's no better location in the park than Hotel Explora: on top of a gently babbling waterfall on the southeast corner of Lago Pehoé with a shimmering lake offset by tiny rocky islets and a perfect view of Torres del Paine. **Pros:** the grande dame of Patagonian hospitality; heart-stopping views from the center of the national park; adventurous park excursions. **Cons:** poor Wi-Fi and no TV in rooms; 4-night minimum; a bank breaker. Ⓢ *Rooms from: pesos2610000* ✉ *Lago Pehoé, Parque Nacional Torres Del Paine* ☏ *2/2395–2800 in Santiago* ⊕ *www. explora.com* ⊅ *49 rooms* ⦿ *All-Inclusive.*

★ Hotel Río Serrano

$$$$ | HOTEL | A good value option among the pricey in-park lodgings, this grand hotel has great service and magnificent views of the entire Torres del Paine mountain range, with the Serrano River and windswept forest in the foreground. **Pros:** stunning location and all-encompassing views; comfortable rooms; great indoor pool and spa. **Cons:** Wi-Fi is unstable; no TV in standard rooms; limited menu for lunch and dinner. $ *Rooms from: pesos268000* ✉ *Lago Toro, Torres del Paine* ☎ *9/3255–3915* ⊕ *www.rios-errano.com* ⊘ *Closed May–Oct.* ⇱ *106 rooms* ⦿ *Free Breakfast.*

Las Torres Patagonia

$$$$ | HOTEL | Owned by one of the earliest families to settle in what eventually became the park, Las Torres has a long history and is the closest hotel to the main trails into the heart of the Torres del Paine itself. **Pros:** friendly and efficient; homey atmosphere; close access to top trail in the park. **Cons:** poor Wi-Fi; noisy bar; not cheap and prices keep rising. $ *Rooms from: pesos300000* ✉ *Lago Amarga* ☎ *2/2898–6043, 9/5358–0026* ⊕ *www.lastorres.com* ⊘ *Closed May to Sept.* ⇱ *74 rooms* ⦿ *Free Breakfast.*

Ushuaia and Tierra del Fuego

Tierra del Fuego, a more or less triangular island separated from the southernmost tip of the South American mainland by the twists and bends of the Estrecho de Magallanes, is indeed a world unto itself. The vast plains on its northern reaches are dotted with trees bent low by the savage winds that frequently lash the coast. The mountains that rise in the south are equally forbidding, traversed by huge glaciers slowly making their way to the sea.

The first European to set foot on this island was Spanish explorer Hernando de Magallanes, who sailed here in 1520. The smoke that he saw coming from the fires lighted by the native peoples prompted him to call it Tierra del Humo (Land of Smoke). King Charles V of Spain, disliking that name, rechristened it Tierra del Fuego, or Land of Fire.

Tierra del Fuego is split in half. The island's northernmost tip, well within Chilean territory, is its closest point to the continent. The only town of any size here is Porvenir. Its southern extremity, part of Argentina, points out into the Atlantic toward the Falkland Islands. Here you'll find Ushuaia, the main destination, on the shores of the Canal Beagle. Farther south is Cape Horn, the southernmost point of land before Antarctica (still a good 500 miles across the brutal Drake Passage).

Ushuaia

230 km (143 miles) south of Río Grande; 596 km (370 miles) south of Río Gallegos; 914 km (567 miles) south of El Calafate; 3,580 km (2,212 miles) south of Buenos Aires.

At 55 degrees latitude south, Ushuaia (pronounced oo-swy-ah) is closer to the South Pole than to Argentina's northern border with Bolivia. It is the capital and tourism base for Tierra del Fuego, the island at the southernmost tip of Argentina.

The city rightly (if perhaps too loudly) promotes itself as the southernmost city in the world (Puerto Williams, a few miles south on the Chilean side of the Beagle Channel, is a small town). You can make your way to the tourism office to get your clichéd, but oh-so-necessary, "Southernmost City in the World" passport stamp. Ushuaia feels like a frontier boomtown, at heart still a rugged, weather-beaten fishing village, but exhibiting the frayed edges of a city that quadrupled in size in the '70s and '80s and just keeps growing. Unpaved portions of Ruta 3, the last stretch of the Pan-American Highway, which connects Alaska to Tierra del Fuego, are finally being paved. The summer months (December through March) draw more than 120,000 visitors, and dozens of cruise ships. The city is trying to extend those visits with events like March's Marathon at the End of the World and by increasing the gamut of winter activities buoyed by the excellent snow conditions.

A terrific trail winds through the town up to the Martial Glacier, where a ski lift can help cut down a steep kilometer of your journey. The chaotic and contradictory urban landscape includes a handful of luxury hotels amid the concrete of public housing projects. Scores of "sled hous-es" (wooden shacks) sit precariously on upright piers, ready for speedy displace-ment to a different site. But there are also many small, picturesque homes with tiny, carefully tended gardens. Many of the newer homes are built in a Swiss-chalet style, reinforcing the idea that this is a town into which tourism has breathed new life. At the same time, the weather-worn pastel colors that dominate the town's landscape remind you that Ushuaia was once just a tiny fishing village, snuggled at the end of the Earth.

As you stand on the banks of the Canal Beagle (Beagle Channel) near Ushuaia, the spirit of the farthest corner of the world takes hold. What stands out is the light: at sundown the landscape is cast in a subdued, sensual tone; everything feels closer, softer, and more human in dimen-sion despite the vastness of the setting. The snowcapped mountains reflect the setting sun back onto a stream rolling into the channel, as nearby peaks echo their image—on a windless day—in the still waters.

Above the city rise the last mountains of the Andean Cordillera, and just south and west of Ushuaia they finally vanish into the often-stormy sea. Snow whitens the peaks well into summer. Nature is the principal attraction here, with trek-king, fishing, horseback riding, wildlife spotting, and sailing among the most rewarding activities, especially in the Parque Nacional Tierra del Fuego (Tierra del Fuego National Park).

GETTING HERE AND AROUND

Arriving by air is the preferred option. Ushuaia's Aeropuerto Internacional Malvinas Argentinas (Peninsula de Ushuaia ☎ 2901/431–232) is 5 km (3 miles) from town and is served daily by flights to and from Buenos Aires, Río Gallegos, El Calafate, Trelew, and Como-doro Rivadavía. There are also flights to Santiago via Punta Arenas in Chile. A taxi into town costs about US$8.

Arriving by road on the Ruta Nacional 3 involves Argentine and Chilean immigra-tions/customs, a ferry crossing, and a lot of time. Buses to and from Punta Arenas make the trip five days a week in sum-mer, four in winter. Daily buses to Río Gallegos leave in the predawn hours, and multiple border crossings mean an all-day journey. Check prices on the 55-minute flight, which can be a much better value. There is no central bus terminal, just individual company locations.

There is no regular passenger transport (besides cruises) by sea.

CRUISE TRAVEL TO USHUAIA

As you sail into Ushuaia, the captain almost always takes you around the picturesque lighthouse at the "end of the world": a beacon for the southernmost city perched on the edge of the Canal Beagle. The port is just two blocks from the main street, leaving you in a central location once you disembark.

Before undertaking the five-minute walk into town, stop at the Tourism Office (right in front of the port), where you can gather information and take advantage of the free Wi-Fi. Most city attractions can be reached on foot, although if you're spending the night here, you may need to take a taxi to your hotel. If you're in Ushuaia only for the day, lace on some good shoes, as the city is built on a hill and requires calves of steel.

ESSENTIALS

BUS SERVICES Tecni-Austral. ✉ *Juana Genoveva Fadul 40, Ushuaia* ☎ *2901/608–088* ⊕ *www.tecniaustral. com.*

VISITOR INFORMATION Ushuaia Tourist Office. ✉ *Prefectura Naval 470, Ushuaia* ☎ *2901/437–666, 2901/432–001* ⊕ *www. turismoushuaia.com.*

 Sights

Antigua Casa Beban (*Old Beban House*) **HISTORIC HOME** | One of Ushuaia's original houses, the Antigua Casa Beban long served as the city's social center. Built between 1911 and 1913 by Fortunato Beban, it's said he ordered the house through a Swiss catalog. In the 1980s the Beban family donated the house to the city to avoid demolition. It was moved to its current location along the coast and restored, and is now a cultural center with art exhibits. ✉ *Maipú at Pluschow, Ushuaia* ☎ *2901/431–386* 🎟 *Free* ⊗ *Closed weekends.*

★ **Canal Beagle**
BODY OF WATER | Several tour operators run trips along the Canal Beagle, on which you can get a startling close-up view of sea mammals and birds on **Isla de los Lobos, Isla de los Pájaros,** and near **Les Eclaireurs Lighthouse**. Catamarans, motorboats, and sailboats usually leave from the tourist pier at 9:30, 10, 3, and 3:30 (trips depend on weather; few trips go in winter). Some trips include hikes on the islands. Check with the tourist office for the latest details; you can also book

through any of the local travel agencies or scope out the offers yourself by walking around the kiosks on the tourist pier. ✉ *Ushuaia* 🎟 *From 6,200 pesos.*

Canal Fun
SCENIC DRIVE | This unconventional tour goes to Monte Olivia, the tallest mountain along the Canal Beagle, rising 1,358 meters (4,455 feet) above sea level. You also pass the Five Brothers Mountains and go through the Garibaldi Pass, which begins at the Rancho Hambre, climbs into the mountain range, and ends with a spectacular view of Lago Escondido. From here you continue on to Lago Fagnano through the countryside past sawmills and lumber yards. To do this tour in a four-wheel-drive truck with an excellent bilingual guide, contact Canal Fun; you'll drive *through* Lago Fagnano (about 3 feet of water at this point) to a secluded cabin on the shore and have a delicious asado, complete with wine and dessert. In winter they can also organize tailor-made dogsledding and cross-country-skiing trips. ✉ *Roca 136, Ushuaia* ☎ *2901/435–777* ⊕ *www.canalfun.com.*

Estancia Harberton (*Harberton Ranch*)
FARM/RANCH | This property—50,000 acres of coastal marshland and wooded hillsides—was a late-19th-century gift from the Argentine government to Reverend Thomas Bridges, who authored a Yamana–English dictionary and is considered the patriarch of Tierra del Fuego. His son Lucas wrote *The Uttermost Part of the Earth,* a memoir about his frontier childhood. Today the ranch is managed by Bridges's great-grandson, Thomas Goodall, and his American wife, Natalie, a scientist and author who has cooperated with the National Geographic Society on conservation projects and operates the impressive marine mammal museum, Museo Acatushun. Most people visit as part of organized tours, but you'll be welcome if you arrive alone. They serve up a tasty tea in their house, the oldest

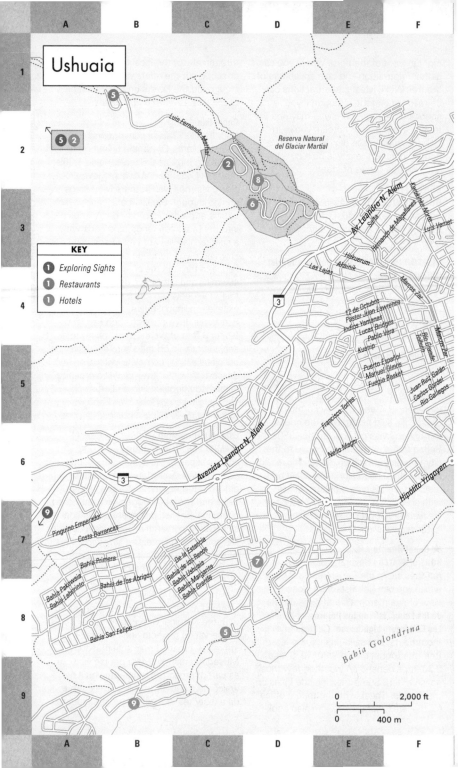

Ushuaia

KEY
- **1** Exploring Sights
- **1** Restaurants
- **1** Hotels

Reserva Natural
del Glaciar Martial

Luis Fernando Martial

Av. Leandro N. Alem
Salta
Hernando de Magallanes
Kerülruhen Norte
Luis Vernet

Las Lajas
Hakuerum
Atainik

12 de Octubre
Pastor Juan Lawrence
Indios Yamanas
Lucas Bridges
Pablo Vera
Kuanip
Puerto Español
Manuel Olmos
Fuegia Basket

Marcos Zar

Río Grande
Ushuaia
Juan Ruíz Galán
Carlos Gardel
Río Gallegos

Marcos Zar

Francisco Torres

Nello Magni

Avenida Leandro N. Alem

Hipólito Yrigoyen

Pingüino Emperador
Costa Barrancas

Bahía Primera
De la Estancia
Bahía de los Reués
Bahía Ushuaia
Bahía Paksuaia
Bahía Laberinto
Bahía de los Abrigos
Bahía Margarita
Bahía Grande

Bahía San Felipe

Bahía Golondrina

| 0 | | 2,000 ft |
| 0 | | 400 m |

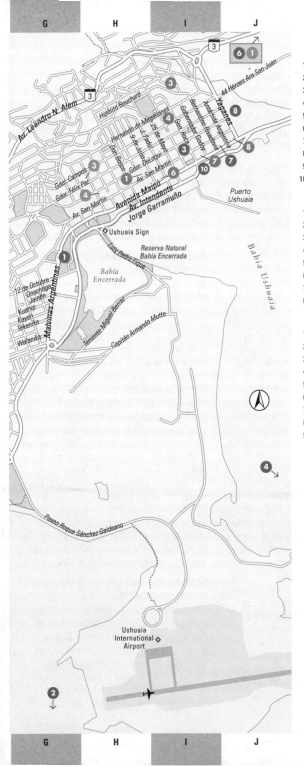

Sights ▼

1 Antigua Casa Beban **G3**
2 Canal Beagle **G9**
3 Canal Fun **I2**
4 Estancia Harberton **J6**
5 Glaciar Martial **A2**
6 Lago Escondido **J1**
7 Museo del Fin del Mundo **I2**
8 Museo Marítimo **J2**
9 Tren del Fin del Mundo **A7**
10 Tres Marias Excursiones **I2**

Restaurants ▼

1 Bodegón Fueguino **H2**
2 Chez Manu **C2**
3 Kalma Resto **I1**
4 Kaupé **I2**
5 La Cabaña Casa de Te **B1**
6 Ramos Generales **I2**
7 Tia Elvira **I2**
8 Volver **J2**

Hotels ▼

1 Arakur **J1**
2 Cumbres del Martial **A2**
3 Hosteria Patagonia Jarké **H2**
4 Hotel Fueguino **H3**
5 Hotel Los Yámanas **C8**
6 Hotel y Resort Las Hayas **D3**
7 La Tierra de Leyendas **D7**
8 Los Acebos **D2**
9 Los Cauquenes
   Resort and Spa **B9**

building on the island. For safety reasons, exploration of the ranch can be done only on guided tours (45–90 minutes). Lodging is available, either in the Old Shepherd's House or the Old Cook's House. Additionally, you can eat a three-course lunch at their Acawaia restaurant. Most tours reach the estancia by boat, offering a rare opportunity to explore the Isla Martillo penguin colony and a sea-lion refuge on Isla de los Lobos (Seal Island) along the way. ✉ *85 km (53 miles) east of Ushuaia, Ushuaia* ✎ *info@estanciaharberton.com* ⊕ *www.estanciaharberton.com* ▦ *2,500 pesos* ⊘ *Closed Tues.*

★ Glaciar Martial

NATURE SIGHT | It might pale in comparison to the glaciers in El Calafate, but a visit to the shrinking Glaciar Martial in the mountain range just above Ushuaia offers a nice walk. Named after Frenchman Luís F. Martial, a 19th-century scientist who wandered this way aboard the warship *Romanche* to observe the passing of the planet Venus, the glacier is reached via a panoramic *aerosilla* (ski lift) or by foot. Take the Camino al Glaciar (Glacier Road) 7 km (4.5 miles) out of town until it ends (this route is also served by the local tour companies). Stop off at one of the teahouses en route (at the foot of the ski lift, when it is functioning) because this is a steep, strenuous 90-minute hike to the top. You can cool your heels in one of the many gurgling, icy rivulets that cascade down water-worn shale shoots or enjoy a picnic while you wait for sunset (you can walk all the way down if you want to linger until after the aerosilla closes). When the sun drops behind the glacier's jagged crown of peaks, brilliant rays beam over the mountain's crest, spilling a halo of gold-flecked light on the glacier, valley, and channel below. Moments like these are why this land is so magical. Note that temperatures drop dramatically after sunset, so come prepared with warm clothing. ✉ *Glaciar Martial, Ushuaia.*

Lago Escondido (*Hidden Lake*)

BODY OF WATER | One good excursion in the area is to Lago Escondido and Lago Fagnano (Fagnano Lake). The Pan-American Highway out of Ushuaia goes through deciduous beech forests and past beavers' dams, peat bogs, and glaciers. The lakes have campsites and fishing and are good spots for a picnic or a hike. This can be done on your own or as a seven-hour trip, including lunch, booked through the local travel agencies (around 9,500 pesos with lunch and 4X4 transportation). ✉ *Ushuaia.*

Museo del Fin del Mundo (*End of the World Museum*)

HISTORY MUSEUM | Here you can see a large taxidermied condor and other native birds, indigenous artifacts, maritime instruments, a reconstruction of an old Patagonian general store, and such seafaring-related objects as an impressive mermaid figurehead taken from the bowsprit of a galleon. There are also photographs and histories of El Presidio's original inmates, such as Simon Radowitzky, a Russian immigrant anarchist who received a life sentence for killing an Argentine police colonel. The museum is split across two buildings—the first, and original, is in the 1905 residence of a Fuegonian governor at Maipú 173. The newer museum building is farther down the road at Maipú 465, where you can see extended exhibitions of the same style. ✉ *Maipú 173, at Rivadavía, Ushuaia* ☎ *2901/421–863* ⊕ *www.mfm.tierradelfuego.gob.ar* ▦ *500 pesos* ⊘ *Closed Sun.*

★ Museo Marítimo (*Maritime Museum*)

HISTORY MUSEUM | Part of the original penal colony, the Presidio building was built to hold political prisoners, murderous estancia owners, street orphans, and a variety of Buenos Aires' most violent criminals. Some even claim that singer Carlos Gardel landed in one of the cells for the petty crimes of his misspent youth. In its day it held 600 inmates in 380 cells. Today it's on the grounds of Ushuaia's naval base and holds the Museo Marítimo, which starts with exhibits on the canoe-making skills of the region's indigenous peoples, tracks the navigational history of Tierra del Fuego and Cape Horn and the Antarctic, and even has a display on other great jails of the world. You can enter cell blocks and read about the grisly crimes of the prisoners who lived in them and measure yourself against their eerie life-size plaster effigies. Of the five wings spreading out from the main guard house, one has been transformed into an art gallery and another has been kept untouched—and unheated. Bone-chattering cold and bleak, bare walls powerfully evoke the desolation of a long sentence at the tip of the continent. Well-presented tours (in Spanish only) are conducted at 11:30 am, 4:30 pm, and 6:30 pm daily. ⊠ Gobernador Paz at Yaganes, Ushuaia ☎ 2901/437–481 ⊕ www.museomaritimo.com ☎ 3,400 pesos (valid for 2 days).

Tren del Fin del Mundo (End of the World Train)
TRAIN/TRAIN STATION | Heavily promoted but a bit of a letdown, the Tren del Fin del Mundo purports to take you inside the Parque Nacional Tierra del Fuego, 12 km (8 miles) away from town, but you have to drive to get there, and it leaves visitors a long way short of the most spectacular scenery in the national park. The touristy 40-minute train ride's gimmick is a simulation of the trip El Presidio prisoners were forced to take into the forest to chop wood; but unlike them, you'll also get a good presentation of Ushuaia's history (in Spanish and English). The train departs daily at 9:30, noon, and 3 (only 10 and 3 in low season). One common way to do the trip is to hire a remís (taxi) that will drop you at the station for a one-way train ride and pick you up at the other end, then drive you around the Parque Nacional for two or three hours of sightseeing (which is far more scenic

than the train ride itself). ⊠ Ruta 3, Km 3042, Ushuaia ☎ 2901/431–600 ⊕ www.trendelfindelmundo.com.ar ☎ From 4,900 pesos.

Tres Marias Excursions
NAUTICAL SIGHT | Although there are a number of boat tours through the Canal Beagle or around the bays to Tierra del Fuego National Park, one offers an experience that will put you in the shoes of the earliest explorers to visit the far south. The operators of Tres Marias Excursions offer a half-day sailing trip to Island H, an outcrop in the middle of the channel, with cormorant colonies, families of snow geese, seaweed stands, and a weather station that records the howling winds blowing in from the misnamed Pacific Ocean. The guides are skillful sailors and storytellers. On a gusty day you'll marvel at the hardiness of the Yamana people, who survived frigid winters wearing little or no clothing by setting fires behind natural and man-made windbreaks. You'll find the same plant and moss species that grow in the high Andes; they thrive here at sea level because the conditions kill off less hardy, temperate species. On the way back you visit a sea lion colony, but won't soon forget arriving in Ushuaia under full sail as the late sun hits the mountains. It's only a little more expensive, and a lot more adventurous, than the motorized alternatives trawling for business at the dock. Tours only October to March. ⊠ Port, Ushuaia ☎ 2901/582–060 ☍ tresmarias-mail@gmail.com ☎ 5,600 pesos.

 **Restaurants**

Bodegón Fueguino
$$$$ | **ARGENTINE** | A mustard-yellow pioneer house that lights up the main street, this traditional eatery is driven by its ebullient owner Sergio Otero, a constant presence bustling around the bench seating, making suggestions, and revving up his staff. Sample the picada plate (king

Tierra del Fuego was the last land mass in the world to be inhabited—it was not until 9,000 BC that the ancestors of those native coastal inhabitants, the Yamana, arrived.

crab rolls, Roma-style calamari, marinated rabbit) over an artisanal Beagle Beer—the dark version is the perfect balm on a cold windy day. **Known for:** famous Patagonian lamb; no reservations but a quick wait; large and hearty portions. [$] *Average main: pesos900* ⊠ *San Martín 859, Ushuaia* ☎ *2901/431–972* ⊕ *www. tierradehumos.com* ⊗ *Closed Mon.*

★ Chez Manu

$$$$ | SEAFOOD | *Herbes de provence* in the greeting room, a tank of lively king crabs in the dining room: French chef Manu Herbin gives local seafood a French touch and creates some of Ushuaia's most memorable meals with views to match. The first-rate wine list includes Patagonian selections, while all dishes are created entirely with ingredients from Tierra del Fuego. **Known for:** excellent king crab gratin and other fresh seafood; fantastic wine list; amazing views of Beagle Channel. [$] *Average main: pesos1800* ⊠ *Camino Luís Martial 2135, Ushuaia* ☎ *2901/432–253* ⊕ *www.chezmanu.com* ⊗ *Closed Mon.*

Kalma Resto

$$$$ | ARGENTINE | Beautiful dishes and a contemporary twist on traditional Patagonian flavors meet at this funky little restaurant at the end of the world. Owner and chef Jorge says that recipes are inspired by his grandma's classics, but there is also a hint of Peruvian and Mediterranean with signature dishes like octopus ceviche, centolla, Beagle Channel mussels, and paella. **Known for:** fantastic tasting menu; sophisticated service; creative cuisine with wines to match. [$] *Average main: pesos1440* ⊠ *Gobernador Valdez 293, Ushuaia* ☎ *2901/425–786* ⊕ *www.kalmaresto. com.ar* ⊗ *Closed Sun.*

Kaupé

$$$$ | ARGENTINE | The white picket fence, manicured lawns, and planter boxes play up the fact that this out-of-the-way restaurant used to be a family home. Inside, the star ingredient is centolla, best presented as chowder with a hint of mustard. **Known for:** sunset views over the city; hard-to-find location; seafood

served with elegance and sophistication. $ *Average main: pesos3200* ⊠ *Roca 470, Ushuaia* ☎ *2901/422–704* ⊕ *www.kaupe. com.ar* ⊗ *Closed Sun.*

La Cabaña Casa de Té

$$$$ | ARGENTINE | This impeccably maintained riverside cottage is nestled in a verdant stand of lenga trees and overlooks the Beagle Channel and provides a warm, cozy spot for delicious loose-leaf tea or comforting snacks before or after a hike to the Martial Glacier (conveniently located at the end of the Martial road that leads up from Ushuaia). An afternoon tea with all the trimmings will satiate any peckish trekker, fondues are served at lunchtime, and at 8 pm in summer the menu shifts to pricier dinner fare with dishes like salmon in wine sauce (mainly for the guests at the adjoining cabin accommodation). **Known for:** traditional afternoon tea menu; lunchtime fondue; countryside setting and views. $ *Average main: pesos1000* ⊠ *Camino Luís Martial 3560, Ushuaia* ☎ *2901/424–779* ⊕ *www.lacabania.com.ar* ⊗ *Closed Apr. and May.*

Ramos Generales

$$$$ | ARGENTINE | Entering this café on the waterfront puts you in mind of a general store from the earliest frontier years of Ushuaia, which is why locals call it the *viejo almacén* (old grocery store). Burgers and picada platters are uninspiring; choose fresh-baked bread or scrumptious lemon croissants instead, and try the *submarino*—a mug of hot milk in which you plunge a bar of dark chocolate (goes well with a panini). **Known for:** sweet treats like lemon croissants; good hot chocolate; old-school frontier vibe. $ *Average main: pesos1200* ⊠ *Maipú 749, Ushuaia* ☎ *2901/424–317* ⊗ *Closed 3 wks in May.*

Tia Elvira

$$$$ | ARGENTINE | On the street that runs right along the Beagle Channel, Tia Elvira is a good place to sample the local catch. Garlicky shellfish appetizers and centolla

are delicious; even more memorable is the tender *merluza negra* (black sea bass). **Known for:** attentive service; kitschy decor; good local seafood. $ *Average main: pesos1150* ⊠ *Maipú 349, Ushuaia* ☎ *2901/424–725* ⊗ *Closed Sun.*

Volver

$$$$ | ARGENTINE | A giant king crab sign beckons you into this red-tin-walled restaurant, where the maritime bric-a-brac hanging from the ceiling can be a little distracting. The name means "return," and it succeeds in getting repeat visits on the strength of its seafood; the culinary highlight is the centolla, which comes served with a choice of five different sauces. **Known for:** waterfront views; cozy maritime atmosphere; great place to try signature dish of Tierra del Fuego, centolla. $ *Average main: pesos1550* ⊠ *Maipú 37, Ushuaia* ☎ *2901/423–977* ⊗ *No lunch Sun. Closed Mon.*

Hotels

Choosing a place to stay depends in part on whether you want to spend the night in town, several miles west toward the national park, or uphill in the hotels above town. The hotels with the best views all require a taxi ride or the various complimentary shuttle services to reach Ushuaia.

Arakur

$$$$ | RESORT | You can see this luxury hotel towering in the distance in front of Monte Olivia; it's one of the most extensive spa-and-resort complexes in Ushuaia and overlooks the entire bay and town from its own nature reserve out of town on the road to Cerro Castor. **Pros:** modern design with luxury fittings; sweeping views; nature reserve at doorstep. **Cons:** sterile atmosphere; far from town; expensive. $ *Rooms from: US$445* ⊠ *Cerro Alarken, Access via Av. Héroes de Malvinas 2617, Ushuaia* ☎ *2901/442–900* ⊕ *www.arakur.com* ⤳ *131 rooms* ⧖ *Free Breakfast.*

Cumbres de Martial

$$$ | **B&B/INN** | This charming complex of cabins and bungalows, painted a deep berry purple, is high above Ushuaia in the woods at the base of the ski lift to the Martial Glacier; each spacious room has an extremely comfortable bed and a small wooden deck with terrific views down to the Beagle Channel. **Pros:** easy access to the glacier and nature trails; romantic cabins; lovely spa. **Cons:** few restaurant options or services within walking distance; slow service; you need to cab it to and from town. [$] *Rooms from: US$290* ✉ *Camino Luís Martial 3560, Ushuaia* ☎ *2901/424–779* 🌐 *www.cumbresdelmartial.com.ar* ⏲ *Closed Apr. and May* 🛏 *10 units* 🍴 *Free Breakfast.*

Hostería Patagonia Jarké

$ | **B&B/INN** | Jarké means "spark" in a local native language, and this B&B is a bright, electric addition to Ushuaia; the three-story lodge cantilevers down a hillside on a dead-end street in the heart of town. **Pros:** warm, welcoming rooms with decent views; good price for Patagonia; friendly staff. **Cons:** can't compete with the views from the larger hotels farther uphill; noise travels through walls; steep walk home. [$] *Rooms from: US$88* ✉ *Gobernador Paz 1305, Ushuaia* ☎ *11/6385–4226* 🌐 *www.patagoniajarke.com.ar* 🛏 *15 rooms* 🍴 *Free Breakfast.*

Hotel Fueguino

$$$ | **HOTEL** | In downtown Ushuaia, the Fueguino boasts all the modern amenities: a conference center; a gym; a spa; shuttle service; outgoing, professional, multilingual staff; and one of the better Wi-Fi signals in town. **Pros:** blackout blinds; central location; on-site restaurant. **Cons:** small rooms; mattresses may be too firm for some; some street noise. [$] *Rooms from: US$208* ✉ *Gobernador Deloqui 1282, Ushuaia* ☎ *2901/424–894* 🌐 *www.fueguinohotel.com.ar* 🛏 *53 rooms* 🍴 *Free Breakfast.*

Hotel Los Yámanas

$$ | **HOTEL** | This cozy hotel 4 km (2.5 miles) from the center of town is named after the local tribe and offers a rustic mountain aesthetic. **Pros:** some stunning views from rooms; peaceful location; sauna is very nice. **Cons:** questionable taste in decoration; Wi-Fi not strong in rooms; far from town. [$] *Rooms from: US$173* ✉ *Costa de los Yámanas 2850, Km 4, Ushuaia* ☎ *2901/446–809* 🌐 *www.hotelyamanas.com.ar* ⏲ *Closed May* 🛏 *41 rooms* 🍴 *Free Breakfast.*

Hotel y Resort Las Hayas

$$$$ | **HOTEL** | In the wooded foothills of the Andes, Las Hayas is slightly dated in its facilities, but the views overlooking the town and channel below still make it worth the trip. **Pros:** great views; delicious restaurant; relaxing spa. **Cons:** facilities dated; rooms could use some revamping; decor doesn't suit everyone. [$] *Rooms from: US$315* ✉ *Camino Luís Martial 1650, Km 3, Ushuaia* ☎ *2901/442–000* 🌐 *www.lashayashotel.com* 🛏 *88 rooms* 🍴 *Free Breakfast.*

La Tierra de Leyendas

$$$ | **B&B/INN** | This adorable B&B is a honeymooners' delight, thanks to the multiple personal touches, from home-cooked cuisine to family photos on the walls. **Pros:** tasty food in restaurant; enthusiastic, personal, and attentive service; all seven rooms have views. **Cons:** immediate surroundings are a bit barren; closed during winter; the street name is no joke—it's insanely windy. [$] *Rooms from: US$280* ✉ *Tierra de Vientos 2448, Ushuaia* ☎ *2901/446–565* 🌐 *www.tierradeleyendas.com.ar* ⏲ *Closed mid-Apr.–mid-July* 🛏 *7 rooms* 🍴 *Free Breakfast.*

Los Acebos

$$ | **HOTEL** | **FAMILY** | From the owners of Las Hayas (just around the corner on the winding mountain road), Los Acebos is a modern hotel on a forested ridge with a commanding view over the Beagle Channel; spacious and superclean rooms feature the same iconoclastic decor

as Las Hayas, including the trademark fabric-padded walls, only this time with a '60s-style color scheme. **Pros:** spacious rooms; expansive views of the channel; friendly staff. **Cons:** no spa; simple breakfast; out of town. [$] *Rooms from: US$195* ✉ *Luis F. Martial 1911, Ushuaia* ☎ *2901/442–200* 🌐 *www.losacebos.com.ar* 🛏 *60 rooms.*

★ **Los Cauquenes Resort and Spa**
$$$ | **HOTEL** | Right on the shore of the Beagle Channel about 8 km (5 miles) west of town, this resort is in a private community with privileged beach access and a nature hike that starts right outside your room. **Pros:** luxurious spa offers comprehensive range of treatments and massages; free transfer into city; private boat excursions offered. **Cons:** thin walls can make for noisy nights; outside of town; rooms can get uncomfortably hot. [$] *Rooms from: US$290* ✉ *De la Ermita 3462, Barrio Bahía Cauquén, Ushuaia* ☎ *2901/441–300* 🌐 *www.loscauquenes.com* 🛏 *54 rooms* 🍴 *Free Breakfast.*

Nightlife

Ushuaia has lively nightlife in summer, with its casino, discos, and intimate cafés all close to each other.

Bar Ideal
BARS | This cozy and historic bar and café opens from 12:30 pm onward. ✉ *San Martín 393, at Roca, Ushuaia* ☎ *2901/437–860.*

El Náutico
DANCE CLUBS | The biggest and most popular pub in town, El Náutico attracts a young crowd with disco and techno music. ✉ *Belgrano 21, Ushuaia* ☎ *2901/61–8284.*

Tante Sara
BARS | This popular café-bar in the heart of town has a casual, old-world feel. Locals kick back with a book or a beer; they pour the local artisanal brews, too. During the day it's one of the few eateries to defy the 3–6 pm siesta and stays open late. Their other branch, at San Martín 175, closes at 8:30 pm. ✉ *San Martín 701, Ushuaia* ☎ *2901/432–308* 🌐 *www.tantesara.com.*

Shopping

Boutique del Libro–Antartida y Patagonia
BOOKS | Part of a bookstore chain, this branch specializes in Patagonian and polar exploration. Along with dozens of maps and picture books, postcards, and posters, it offers adventure classics detailing every Southern expedition from Darwin's *Voyage of the Beagle* to Ernest Shackleton's incredible journeys of Antarctic survival. While books in English are hard to come by in the rest of Argentina, here you're spoiled for choice, and the Antarctica trip logbooks on sale at the counter might inspire you to extend your travel farther south. ✉ *San Martín 1120, Ushuaia* ☎ *2901/4245–750* 🕓 *Closed Sun.*

Laguna Negra
CHOCOLATE | If you can't get to South America's chocolate capital Bariloche, pop into this chocolate boutique for planks of homemade chocolate and a selection of artisanal beers, chutneys, and spices. In the small coffee shop at the back, drop a glorious slab of dark chocolate into a mug of piping hot milk—one of the best *submarinos* in town. ✉ *San Martín 513, Ushuaia* ☎ *2901/41–7597* 🌐 *www.lagunanegra.com.ar.*

Parque Nacional Tierra del Fuego

21 km (13 miles) west of Ushuaia.

This park is one of the main reasons that travelers make a trip to the tip of Argentina. Its deep forests, glistening lakes, and wind-whipped trees will not disappoint. An easy day trip from Ushuaia, this

60,000-hectare park offers varied outdoor experiences and many wildlife-spotting opportunities.

 Sights

★ **Parque Nacional Tierra del Fuego**
NATIONAL PARK | The pristine park offers a chance to wander through peat bogs, stumble upon hidden lakes, trek through native *canelo, lenga,* and wild cherry forests, and experience the wonders of wind-whipped Tierra del Fuego's rich flora and fauna. Everywhere, lichens line the trunks of the ubiquitous lenga trees, and "Chinese lantern" parasites hang from the branches.

Another thing you'll see everywhere are the results of government folly, in the form of *castoreros* (beaver dams) and lodges. Fifty beaver couples were first brought here from Canada in 1948 so that they would breed and create a fur industry. In the years since, without any predators, the beaver population has exploded to plague proportions (more than 100,000) and now represents a major threat to the forests, as the dams flood the roots of the trees; you can see their effects on parched dead trees on the lake's edge. Believe it or not, the government used to pay hunters a bounty for each beaver they killed (they had to show a tail and head as proof). To make matters worse, the government, after creating the beaver problem, introduced weasels to kill the beavers, but the weasels killed birds instead; they then introduced foxes to kill the beavers and weasels, but they also killed the birds. With eradication efforts failing, some tour operators have accepted them as a permanent presence and now offer beaver-viewing trips.

Visits to the park, which is tucked up against the Chilean border, are commonly arranged through tour companies. Trips range from bus tours to horseback riding

to more adventurous excursions, such as canoe trips across Lapataia Bay. Entrance to the park is 2,100 pesos.

Several private bus companies travel through the park making numerous stops; you can get off the bus, explore the park, and then wait for the next bus to come by or trek to the next stop (the service operates only in summer; check providers with the tourism office). Another option is to drive to the park on R3 (take it until it ends and you see the famous sign indicating the end of the Pan-American Highway, which starts 17,848 km [11,065 miles] away in Alaska, and ends here). If you don't have a car, you can hire a private *remís* (taxi) to spend a few hours driving through the park, including the Pan-American terminus, and perhaps combining the excursion with the Tren del Fin del Mundo. Trail and camping information is available at the park-entrance ranger station or at the Ushuaia tourist office. At the park entrance is a gleaming restaurant and teahouse set amid the hills, Patagonia Mia (⊕ *www.patagoniamia.com*); it's a great place to stop for tea or coffee, or a full meal of roast lamb or Fuegian seafood. A nice excursion in the park is by boat from lovely Bahía Ensenada to Isla Redonda, a wildlife refuge where you can follow a footpath to the western side and see a wonderful view of the Canal Beagle. This is included on some of the day tours; it's harder to arrange on your own, but you can contact the tourist office to try. While on Isla Redonda you can send a postcard and get your passport stamped at the world's southernmost post office. You can also see the Ensenada bay and island (from afar) from a point on the shore that is reachable by car.

Other highlights of the park include the spectacular mountain-ringed lake, Lago Roca, as well as Laguna Verde, a lagoon whose green color comes from algae at its bottom. Much of the park is closed

Stumble upon hidden lakes, trek through native canelo, lenga, and wild cherry forests, and experience the wonders of wind-whipped Tierra del Fuego's rich flora and fauna.

from roughly June through September, when the descent to Bahía Ensenada is blocked by up to 6 feet of snow. Even in May and October, chains for your car are a good idea. No hotels are within the park—the only one burned down in the 1980s, and you can see its carcass as you drive by—but there are three simple camping areas around Lago Roca. ☎ 2901/577-931 ⊕ www.parquesnacionales.gob.ar ⛬ 2,100 pesos.

 Activities

FISHING
The rivers of Tierra del Fuego are home to trophy-size freshwater trout—including browns, rainbows, and brooks. Both fly- and spin-casting are available. The fishing season runs November through April; license fees range from 1,000 pesos per week to 1,200 pesos per season for nonresidents. Fishing expeditions are organized by the various local companies.

Asociación de Caza y Pesca
FISHING | Founded in 1959, the Asociación de Caza y Pesca is the principal hunting and fishing organization in the city. ⊠ Av. Maipú 822, Ushuaia ☎ 2901/423–168.

Rumbo Sur
FISHING | The city's oldest travel agency can assist in setting up fishing trips. ⊠ Av. San Martín 350 ☎ 2901/421–139 ⊕ www.rumbosur.com.ar.

Wind Fly
FISHING | In summer this outfitter is dedicated exclusively to fishing, and offers classes and arranges trips. ⊠ Av. los Nires 2466, Ushuaia ☎ 2901/515-158 ⊕ www.windflyushuaia.com.ar.

MOUNTAIN BIKING
A mountain bike is an excellent mode of transport in Ushuaia, giving you the freedom to roam without the rental-car price tag. Good mountain bikes normally cost about US$10 for a half day or US$15 for a full day. Guided tours are about the same price.

All Patagonia

BIKING | Guided bicycle tours (including rides through the national park) are organized by All Patagonia. ⊠ *Juana Fadul 58, Ushuaia* ☎ *2901/401–603* ⊕ *www.allpatagonia.com.*

Rumbo Sur

BIKING | One of the city's biggest travel agencies, Rumbo Sur can arrange cycling trips. ⊠ *San Martín 350, Ushuaia* ☎ *2901/421–139* ⊕ *www.rumbosur.com.ar.*

Ushuaia Extreme

BIKING | You can rent bikes or do a tour with Ushuaia Extreme. ⊠ *San Martín 830, Ushuaia* ☎ *2901/434–373* ⊕ *www.ushuaiaextremo.com.*

SCENIC FLIGHTS

The gorgeous scenery and island topography of the area is readily appreciated on a Cessna tour.

Aeroclub Ushuaia

SKYDIVING | Half-hour- and hour-long trips are available through Aeroclub Ushuaia. The half-hour flight ($95 per passenger with a group; $125 for single passengers) with a local pilot takes you over Ushuaia, Tierra del Fuego National Park, and the Beagle Channel with views of area glaciers, waterfalls, and snowcapped islands south to Cape Horn. A 60-minute flight ($155 per passenger with a group; $205 for single passengers) crosses the Andes to Escondida and Fagnano lakes. ⊠ *Antiguo Aeropuerto, Luis Pedro Fique 151, Ushuaia* ☎ *2901/421–717* ⊕ *www.aeroclubushuaia.org.ar.*

Heli-Ushuaia

SKYDIVING | All sorts of helicopter trips are available from Heli-Ushuaia, beginning with a seven-minute spin at $99 per person. There are plenty of longer trips and excursions if you have money to burn. ⊠ *Luis Pedro Fique 119, Ushuaia* ☎ *2901/444–444* ⊕ *www.heliushuaia.com.ar.*

SKIING

Canopy Ushuaia

SNOW SPORTS | Located at the Martial Glaciar, Canopy Ushuaia offers skiing in winter and canopy lines in summer. ⊠ *Cerro Martial, Luis Fernando Martial 3551, Ushuaia* ☎ *2901/1550–3767* ⊕ *www.canopyushuaia.com.ar.*

★ Cerro Castor

SKIING & SNOWBOARDING | With off-piste and alpine skiing and almost guaranteed snow, this has become a popular ski haunt for European Olympic teams looking for summer snow. Pistes range from beginners to black-diamond runs with more than 33 trails and five high-speed lifts, with a vertical descent of 772 meters (2,533 feet). You can rent skis and snowboards and take ski lessons at this resort 26 km (17 miles) northeast of Ushuaia on R3. Day passes are 2,265 pesos in high season, and there are restaurants, bars, and a ski lodge on-site. This well-run, family-owned resort is open June to October, with guaranteed snow (they have artificial snow to make up for any deficit). It's worth coming here for the views alone; they're some of the best in South America. ⊠ *Ruta 3, Km 26, Ushuaia* ☎ *2901/499–301* ⊕ *www.cerrocastor.com.*

Club Andino

SKIING & SNOWBOARDING | Ushuaia is the cross-country skiing (*esqui de fondo* in Spanish) center of South America, thanks to enthusiastic Club Andino members who took to the sport in the 1980s and made the forested hills of a high valley about 20 minutes from town a favorite destination for skiers. It's a magnet for international ski teams who come from Europe to train in the northern summer. ⊠ *Alem 2873, Ushuaia* ☎ *2901/440–732* ⊕ *www.clubandinoushuaia.com.ar.*

Index

439

Photo Credits

Front Cover: David R. Frazier Photolibrary, Inc. / Alamy Stock Photo [Description: Colorful buildings in the La Boca area of Buenos Aires, Argentina]. **Back cover, from left to right:** Ivotheeditors/iStockphoto, Diegograndi/iStockphoto, Galyna Andrushko/Shutterstock. **Spine:** Kamchatka/Dreamstime. **Interior, from left to right:** Danilovieira1/Shutterstock (1). Birdiegal/ Shutterstock (2). Klaus Balzano/Shutterstock (5). **Chapter 1: Experience Argentina:** Sharptoyou/Shutterstock (6-7). Ivo de Rooij/iStockphoto (8-9). Alexis Fioramonti/iStockphoto (9). @travelBuenosAires (9). Dmitryp/Dreamstime (10). Dani Figueiredo/Shutterstock (10). @travelBuenosAires (10). BaskaraRecords/Shutterstock (10). High fliers/Shutterstock (11). T photography/Shutterstock (11). Kylie Nicholson/Shutterstock (12). @travelBuenosAires (12). Matias Callejo (12). Matrix Reloaded/iStockphoto (12). Jiann Ho/iStockphoto (13). Tsuguliev/ Dreamstime (14). Eefje Varossieau/Shutterstock (14). Spectral-Design/Shutterstock (14). Fast Speeds Imagery/Shutterstock (14). Tiagofernandezphotography/Dreamstime (15). Kamchatka/Dreamstime (15). Aneta_Gu/Shutterstock (18). Carlanichiata/Dreamstime (18). AleTanevitch/Shutterstock (18). Plateresca/Shutterstock (18). Visit Argentina (19). Mfrade/ Dreamstime (20). Afagundes/Dreamstime (20). Algimantas Barzdzius/Shutterstock (20). Andrew Hagen/Shutterstock (20). Pstedrak/Dreamstime (21). Aleksandr Vorobev/iStockphoto (22). Martin Corr/Shutterstock (23). Sergey-73/Shutterstock (24). Saiko3p/Shutterstock (25). Fusionstudio/Shutterstock (26). Watch_Media_House/Shutterstock (27). Sunsinger/Shutterstock (28). Kseniya Ragozina/iStockphoto (28). Cerro De Los Siete Colores/iStockphoto (28). Rndmst/Dreamstime (28). Hitmans/Dreamstime (29). Coatchristophe/Dreamstime (33). traveler1116 (33). Rodrigolab/Dreamstime (34). Hendrick Ottsen, [CC BY-SA 2.0]/Wikimedia Commons (34). Mytravellessons/Dreamstime (34). Julio Roca, [CC BY-SA 2.0]/ Wikimedia Commons (35). Apeiron-Photo/ Alamy (35). Keystone Press / Alamy Stock Photo (36). Everett Collection Inc / Alamy Stock Photo (36). Pictorial Press Ltd / Alamy (36). Archivo Gráfico de Clarín (Argentina)[CC BY-SA 2.0]/Wikimedia Commons (37). Reuters/ Alamy Stock Photo (37). Griffiths911[CC BY-SA 2.0]/Wikimedia Commons (37). Christopher Pillitz / Alamy (38). Nikada/iStockphoto (38). Roberto Fiadone,[CC BY-SA 2.0]/Wikimedia Commons (39). Hospital Rawson, [CC BY-SA 2.0]/Wikimedia Commons (39). **Chapter 3: Buenos Aires:** Joel Miranda/Shutterstock (67). San Hoyano/Shutterstock (74). LouieLea/Shutterstock (80). T photography/Shutterstock (82). Anton_Ivanov/Shutterstock (84-85). Saiko3p/Shutterstock (89). Gvictoria/Shutterstock (92). Hecke61/Shutterstock (97). Diego Grandi/Shutterstock (98). Jess Kraft/Shutterstock (102). SC Image/Shutterstock (104). Cacio Murilo/Shutterstock (109). El Greco 1973/Shutterstock (111). Khyim/Dreamstime (117). flickr.com (118). Eyalos.com/ Shutterstock (119). Picture Contact / Alamy (120). Christina wilson / Alamy (120). Alexander Zabara (120). Archivo General de la Nación/wikipedia.org (121). Danita Delimont / Alamy (121). **Chapter 4: Side Trips from Buenos Aires:** Kavram/Shutterstock (125). Diego Grandi/ Shutterstock (132). Jeremy Hoare/ Alamy Stock Photo (136-137). South American Pictures/ Chris Sharp. PabloDFlores, [CC BY-SA 2.0]/Wikimedia Commons (139). Jeremy Hoare / Alamy (140). Jeremy Hoare/ Alamy Stock Photo (141). Kseniya Ragozina/Shutterstock (142). Johannes Odland/Shutterstock (142). **Chapter 5: Side Trips to Uruguay:** Ivo Antonie de Rooij/Shutterstock (159). Ivo Antonie de Rooij/Shutterstock (167). DFLC Prints/Shutterstock (173). Don Mammoser/Shutterstock (178-179). Lux Blue/Shutterstock (185). Stefano Ember/ Shutterstock (190). **Chapter 6: The Northwest:** Danilovieira1/Shutterstock (195). Buchpetzer/ Shutterstock (207). Fotystory/Shutterstock (208). Ignafarina/Shutterstock (211). Eric Kolly/Shutterstock (215). Jose a/Shutterstock (216-217). Flormdk/Dreamstime (218). Jon Arnold Images Ltd / Alamy Stock Photo (219). borderlys (219). Klaus Balzano/Shutterstock (220-221). Clive Ellston (222). Joris Van Ostaeyen/iStockphoto (222). Lee Torrens/Shutterstock (222). Humawaka,[CC BY-SA 2.0]/Creative Commons (223). Anibaltrejo/Dreamstime.com (224). Karil Nunes Soar/Shutterstock (226). JopsStock/Shutterstock (233). Sunsinger/Shutterstock (236). Sunsinger/Shutterstock (240-241). Natalia Di Marco/Shutterstock (244-245). **Chapter 7: Mendoza and the Wine Regions:** Milosz Maslanka/Shutterstock (249). DFLC Prints/ Shutterstock (252). José Carlos Pires Pereira/iStockphoto (253). Fainmen/Flickr (253). Everton Lourenco/Shutterstock (259). Ksenia Ragozina/Shutterstock (270-271). .Luc._Flickr (275). Dizzy / Alamy (278). Jam Travels/Shutterstock (278-279). Alberto Loyo/Shutterstock (280). Jose Luis Stephens/Shutterstock (280). Brastock/Shutterstock (280). Jakub Kyncl/Shutterstock (280). Pablo Abuliak (281). John and Brenda Davenport (281). Pablo Abuliak (281). matetic.com (281). Pablo Abuliak (283). Casa Del Visitante Familia Zuccardi, Mendoza (283). Mark Surman (283). Alexandr Vorobev/Shutterstock (284). Guaxinim/Shutterstock (297). Andre Charland/Flickr (298). **Chapter 8: The Lake District:** Jonas Tufvesson/Shutterstock (305).Erik_nm/Shutterstock (308). Greg Cooper/iStockphoto (309). Przemyslaw Skibinski/Shutterstock (309). HappyTrvlr (310). Josh Roe (311). ArielMartin/Shutterstock (311). Everton Lourenco/ Shutterstock. (315). Dudarev Mikhail/Shutterstock (320-321). Christina Fink/Shutterstock (326). Erik_nm/Shutterstock (331). Phil O'nector/Shutterstock (334). Design Pics Inc / Alamy Stock Photo (336-337). Flyfishingnation/Dreamstime (338). Tetyana Dotsenko/Shutterstock (342-343). Erlantz P.R/Shutterstock (351). **Chapter 9: Patagonia:** Oleg Senkov/Shutterstock (353). Foto 4440/Shutterstock (356). Eduardo Rivero/Shutterstock (357). Pablo Caridad/Shutterstock (357). Sunsinger/Shutterstock (363). Galyna Andrushko/Shutterstock (369). Meunierd/Shutterstock (370). SCStock/Shutterstock (371). Seumas Christie-Johnston/Shutterstock (372). Kavram/ Shutterstock (373). A35mmporhora/Shutterstock (374). Visit Argentina (375). Laura Hart/Shutterstock (376). Cosmopol/Dreamstime (376). jan.kneschke,[CC BY 2.0]/Flickr (376). Foto4440/Dreamstime (376). Tarpan/Shutterstock (377). Agami Photo Agency/Shutterstock (377). Derek Dammann/iStockphoto (377). Magellanic Woodpecker/ iStockphoto (377). RudiErnst/Shutterstock (377). Migel/Shutterstock (380-381). BearFotos/Shutterstock (385). Pav-Pro Photography Ltd/Shutterstock (390). Allen.G/Shutterstock (400-401). MSMondadori/Shutterstock (403). Galyna Andrushko/Shutterstock (408). David Ionut/Shutterstock (416-417). Saiko3p/Shutterstock (426). Oleg Senkov/Shutterstock (431). **About Our Writers:** All photos are courtesy of the writers.

*Every effort has been made to trace the copyright holders, and we apologize in advance for any accidental errors. We would be happy to apply the corrections in the following edition of this publication.

Notes

Notes

Notes

Notes

Notes

Notes

Notes

Fodor's ESSENTIAL ARGENTINA

Publisher: Stephen Horowitz, *General Manager*

Editorial: Douglas Stallings, *Editorial Director;* Jill Fergus, Amanda Sadlowski, *Senior Editors;* Kayla Becker, Brian Eschrich, Alexis Kelly, *Editors;* Angelique Kennedy-Chavannes, *Assistant Editor*

Design: Tina Malaney, *Director of Design and Production;* Jessica Gonzalez, *Graphic Designer;* Erin Caceres, *Graphic Design Associate*

Production: Jennifer DePrima, *Editorial Production Manager;* Elyse Rozelle, *Senior Production Editor;* Monica White, *Production Editor*

Maps: Rebecca Baer, *Senior Map Editor;* Mark Stroud (Moon Street Cartography) and David Lindroth, *Cartographers*

Photography: Viviane Teles, *Senior Photo Editor;* Namrata Aggarwal, Neha Gupta, Payal Gupta, Ashok Kumar, *Photo Editors;* Eddie Aldrete, *Photo Production Intern;* Kadeem McPherson, *Photo Production Associate Intern*

Business and Operations: Chuck Hoover, *Chief Marketing Officer;* Robert Ames, *Group General Manager;* Devin Duckworth, *Director of Print Publishing*

Public Relations and Marketing: Joe Ewaskiw, *Senior Director of Communications and Public Relations*

Fodors.com: Jeremy Tarr, *Editorial Director;* Rachael Levitt, *Managing Editor*

Technology: Jon Atkinson, *Director of Technology;* Rudresh Teotia, *Lead Developer*

Writers: Allan Kelin, Melissa Kitson, Jimmy Langman, Sorrel Moseley-Williams

Editor: Angelique Kennedy-Chavannes

Production Editor: Jennifer DePrima

2nd Edition

ISBN 978-1-64097-414-2

ISSN 2576-9316

SPECIAL SALES

This book is available at special discounts for bulk purchases for sales promotions or premiums. For more information, e-mail SpecialMarkets@fodors.com.

PRINTED IN CANADA

10 9 8 7 6 5 4 3 2 1

About Our Writers

 After much of a lifetime in New York City, **Allan Kelin** lived in Italy for a long while before making Buenos Aires his home for the last dozen years. He worked as the copy editor for the Buenos Aires Herald before starting a busy freelance career as a translator of food, wine and art books, as well as translating for a few of Argentina's wonderful wineries.

Melissa Kitson is an Australian writer who began her love affair with Latin America in Mexico, first as a journalist for the *Guadalajara Reporter,* then as a translator for the Pan American Games. She has lived in Buenos Aires and in Quito, and is now based in Madrid where she is the deputy editor of the English section of *EL PAÍS*. For this edition, Melissa refreshed her love for the natural beauty of Argentina as she updated the Lake District chapter.

 Jimmy Langman lives in southern Chile, where he is executive editor of Patagon Journal, a magazine about nature, the environment, culture, travel and outdoor sports in Argentine and Chilean Patagonia and the world's last wild places. He has also worked as a foreign correspondent for publications such as Newsweek, San Francisco Chronicle, The Guardian, and Toronto Globe and Mail and started his career out working at environmental groups. Jimmy updated the Patagonia chapter.

Sorrel Moseley-Williams is a freelance journalist and sommelier based in Argentina since 2006. She focuses on Latin American food, travel, and wine, and can be found on the pages of *Wine Enthusiast, Monocle, Condé Nast Traveler, Travel + Leisure, Decanter,* and *Lugares* among other publications. While her heart is in Buenos Aires, Sorrel has a major crush on Lima's food scene, equally adores Mendoza wine country, and runs a pop-up wine bar, Come Wine With Us. On Instagram: @sorrelita